Seventh Edition

Small Group Communication

- -

Theory & Practice

Robert S. Cathcart

Queens College of the City University of New York, Emeritus

Larry A. Samovar

San Diego State University

Linda D. Henman

Webster University

Brown & Benchmark
PUBLISHERS

Madison   Dubuque, IA   Guilford, CT   Chicago   Toronto   London
Caracas   Mexico City   Buenos Aires   Madrid   Bogota   Sydney

Book Team

Executive Publisher *Edgar J. Laube*
Acquisitions Editor *Eric Ziegler*
Developmental Editor *Mary Rossa*
Publishing Services Coordinator *Peggy Selle*
Proofreading Coordinator *Carrie Barker*
Permissions Coordinator *Gail I. Wheatley*
Production Manager *Beth Kundert*
Production/Costing Manager *Sherry Padden*
Visuals/Design Freelance Specialist *Mary L. Christianson*
Marketing Manager *Katie Rose*
Copywriter *M. J. Kelly*

Basal Text *10/12 Times Roman*
Display Type *Helvetica Bold*
Typesetting System *Mac/QuarkXPress*
Paper Stock *50# Solutions*
Production Services *Shepherd's Inc.*

President and Chief Executive Officer *Thomas E. Doran*
Vice President of Production and Business Development *Vickie Putman*
Vice President of Sales and Marketing *Bob McLaughlin*
Director of Marketing *John Finn*

 A Times Mirror Company

Cover design by Kay Fulton Design

Copyedited by Shepherd's Inc.; Proofread by Nancy Phan

Library of Congress Catalog Card Number: 95–75004

ISBN 0–697–20437–5

Printed in the United States of America by Times Mirror Higher Education Group, Inc.,
2460 Kerper Boulevard, Dubuque, IA 52001

10 9 8 7 6 5 4 3 2 1

Contents

Preface

The seventh edition of *Small Group Communication* brings a significant change in organization and use from that of the six earlier editions. We have moved in the direction of making this volume a combination introductory textbook and reader. A new author has been added, Professor Linda Henman. Linda brings to this work a strong background in business communication derived from her long experience with workshops and training sessions for people in business and industry as well as her university and community college teaching. With her assistance, we have produced a mini-textbook on small group communication that introduces students to the basic principles and concepts in this field. We have done this by providing a lengthy introductory essay for each of the seven chapters that presents the pertinent concepts and explains the readings that follow. The introductory essays lead students to a basic understanding of the elements of small group communication as set forth in each of the seven chapters: Understanding Small Groups, How Groups are Organized, What Groups Do, Taking Part in Groups, Communicating in Groups, Diversity in Groups, and Leading Groups. In addition, we have made another important change in this edition for the benefit of both students and teachers by providing a list of individual and classroom activities at the end of each chapter. These activities help students understand the concepts covered in the chapter readings and enable class groups to test their knowledge of the readings and improve their small group performance.

The changes we have made in this edition are significant; however, we have not abandoned our long-standing goal of bringing students the most up-to-date theories and constructs developed by the most renowned researchers and practitioners in the field of small group communication. As in the past, with the selected readings, we have endeavored to strike a balance between what represents the core of the field and what is new and innovative. Because the composition and makeup of the people who engage in small group activity has changed, we have included selections that reflect this variance. Many of the established areas of small group performance have been reexamined, and in our efforts to stay abreast of these developments, we have added new readings covering the topics of stress, emotion, and humor. In the spirit of the emerging "global village," we have added a whole new chapter on cultural diversity and how it impacts small group interaction.

In keeping with our desire to offer students and teachers a mini-textbook on small group communication, we have reduced the number of readings from forty-six in the sixth edition to twenty-nine in the seventh edition. We believe that by providing students with extensive introductory material with an understanding of the basics of the small group process they will be in a position to better understand and apply the principles and concepts set forth in the readings.

Approach and Philosophy

In this edition, as in all the others, our philosophy has remained the same. We believe that communication, be it in a small group or on the public platform, is a *social activity*. It is something we do with other people that has a consequence. Since it is a behavior, we maintain that the study of communication must emphasize the link between what we **do** and the **results** of that action. Therefore, we have put into this book information and advice that we believe are **usable**. Once again we selected readings that stress individual skills necessary for effective performance in small groups. In short, our approach continues to affirm the notion that any book on communication must convert ideas into practice.

A vivid example of our desire to fuse theory with practice is seen in the large number of essays that ask the reader to engage in some exercise or activity. For instance, there are projects aimed at evaluating and measuring conversation within the group, self-disclosure, communication apprehension, group participation, and leadership.

Organization and Content

The seventh edition presents a reorganized format. The seven chapters each begin with an extensive introduction covering the principles developed in the chapter. These introductions, written by the editors, are designed to give students an overall view of the content of each area covered along with enough explanation to enable students to comprehend and apply the materials to be found in the selected readings for that chapter. Much like a textbook, these introductions prepare the student, new to the study of small group communication, with basic information that will guide further reading and classroom performance. Also, at the end of the introductory material, students are provided with a description of what is to be found in each of the essays in that chapter. Each of the seven chapters is concluded with a set of exercises and activities designed to help the individual student and the classroom groups to put into practice the principles and concepts described and analyzed in each chapter.

Chapter 1, *Understanding Small Groups*, presents four essays introducing students to definitions and characteristics of small groups. Chapter 2, *How Groups are Organized*, provides four essays explaining the different types of groups one will find in business and community life and how these groups are structured externally and internally in order to accomplish their desired ends. Chapter 3, *What Groups Do*, contains five essays describing and analyzing how groups go about making decisions, what are the most useful ways of decision making, what are the obstacles groups must confront, and what are the dangers groups face when they become so wrapped up in themselves they fall into the trap of "groupthink." Chapter 4, *Taking Part in Groups*, contains four articles examining how groupness affects individuals and how individuals influence the group. The material presented ranges over conformity, stress, emotion, and humor. Chapter 5, *Communicating in Groups*, includes four essays that investigate the nature of the communication process as it is exhibited in small groups. Specifically, the chapter focuses on how the messages people send and receive alter the course and flow of discussion. Chapter 6, *Diversity in Groups*, provides four essays that prepare students for the challenge of working closely with members of the opposite sex and with those from differing ethnic backgrounds. Readers are alerted to the difficulties that can arise in small groups when members fail to understand and appreciate differences and at the same time are encouraged to overcome these obstacles. Chapter 7, *Leading Groups*, contains five articles that are concerned with both the theoretical and practical aspects of group leadership. The selections concentrate on understanding types of leaders, principles of leadership, and the various communication skills that can improve leadership in small groups. Many of the essays include extensive references that may be used to guide students to other works that amplify the ideas developed in the chapter.

Use

This edition offers an introduction to the field of small group communication through the seven introductory essays written by the editors. Students, reading these, will gain a basic knowledge of the principles of small group process and an awareness of the skills necessary to successful performance of small group communication. As in the earlier editions, we again offer a collection of readings designed to provide students with an awareness of the latest theoretical and practical advances in the field, as well as an understanding of how this discipline has evolved. We give the students and teacher an overview of the field and, at the same time, present recently developed processes and techniques for training in small group communication.

This book makes available in one volume representative articles and essays from psychology, sociology, business and industrial management, and speech communication, all arranged to give readers easy access to the basic principles of small group communication. As in the past, we intend this anthology for the general reader. We have therefore leaned toward materials that are broadly based, comprehensive, and suitable for both undergraduate and graduate students. We have also avoided advocating any one particular approach to small group processes, preferring instead to give readers a sampling of the diverse philosophies and concepts that constitute this fascinating and practical area of study. By bringing together theoreticians and practitioners, we have been able to offer knowledge related to both the research and practices of small group communication.

The eclectic bent of this volume enables it to fit the needs of a number of different classes. First, this book is designed to serve as a *basic text* for courses whose primary purpose is the study of small group communication. Second, this collection of readings may be used as *supplementary text* in courses that deal with group discussion, interpersonal communication, and basic skills. Third, the book can provide *resource material* for courses in communication theory, organizational and business communication, social welfare, education, human relations, and health care. The long list of potential uses only serves to underscore the pervasiveness of small group communication in the 1990s.

As is the case with any collection of readings, the level of difficulty often varies from article to article, yet none goes beyond the level found in most textbooks aimed at the college and university student.

Acknowledgements

In a culture that values change, we would not have been able to persevere for over twenty years if we had not been fortunate enough to have so many scholars willing to contribute original essays for each of the seven volumes. Here, in this seventh edition, we want to acknowledge the original work of Ann Margaret Trautlein, Larry A. Samovar, Linda D. Henman, and Stephen W. King, Linda L. Putnam, Marshall Scott Poole, Randy Y. Hirokawa, Dennis S. Gouran, Bolanie A. Olaniran, Patricia Hayes Andrews, Sally M. Vogl-Bauer, Carolyn C. Clark and Richard W. Sline, W. Jack Duncan, Larry R. Smeltzer, and Terry L. Leap, Judy K. Burgoon, Beth Haslett and John R. Olgilvie, Larry A. Erbert, Kittie W. Watson, Richard E. Porter and Larry A. Samovar, Myron W. Lustig and Laura L. Cassotta, Susan B. Shimanoff and Mercilee M. Jenkins, Robert S. Cathcart, Sandra M. Ketrow and Beatrice Schultz.

We would also like to thank our reviewers: Stephen A. March, Grand Canyon University; Michael Nicolai, University of Wisconsin, Stout; and Thomas E. Ruddick, Edison State Community College.

Robert S. Cathcart
Larry A. Samovar
Linda D. Henman

1
Understanding Small Groups

Humans are communicators. Every second that we are alive, we are communicating. Some of this communication happens intrapersonally, within the individual; some of it is dyadic, between two people; but much of it occurs in small groups. We are social creatures who associate in groups in every aspect of our lives. We learn to communicate through our membership in the social framework of the family, our first group affiliation. But before long we are engaging in peer, educational, and religious groups too. As we grow up we realize that groups are a part of our personal and professional lives.

Group Concepts

What is a small group? A small group is a gathering of people interacting and communicating interpersonally over time in order to reach a goal. There are five basic elements of a group that distinguish it from any general collection of individuals: numbers, purpose, belongingness, interfacing, and expectations.

First, the **number of people** is significant. Most definitions of small groups set the minimum number of people at three and the maximum number at somewhere between twelve and fifteen. Five to seven seems to be the ideal size for problem-solving groups.

Second, groups have a **mutually interdependent purpose**. The success of the entire group is at least partially dependent upon the success of each member. Task-oriented groups share a desire to achieve a commonly agreed upon goal, while maintenance-oriented, or friendship groups rely on their members to give support to one another and to satisfy our need for inclusion. In either situation, the success of the group depends on the contributions of the individuals.

The third element that distinguishes a small group from an aggregate of people is a **sense of belonging or membership**. Group members should be able to identify themselves as a member of a group because of the shared characteristics that help participants define themselves through membership in a particular group. For example, people will even introduce themselves by saying, "I'm a Teamster, Alpha Gamma Delta, Marine, Elk, Catholic, or Republican." And while these are not all small groups, the tendency for people to describe themselves through group association becomes apparent. People want to align themselves with others in a group because they find the experience rewarding for whatever reason.

William Shutz has identified three basic needs that motivate people to join groups: inclusion, control, and affinity. **Inclusion** is the basic human need to belong—to feel connected to other humans. Recognition from the group further helps to satisfy this need or involvement.

Control, or a perception that we are able to manage our destiny, is a need that group membership addresses. Sensing that we can, to some degree, direct others as well as maintain self-control gives us a feeling of power.

Affinity involves our need for relationships. We want affection from and trust of others. Affection can take the form of friendship, attachment, or concern, depending on the nature of the group. Group involvement is not the only way to gratify inclusion, control, and affinity needs, but it does furnish an arena that provides opportunities.

The fourth component of a small group has traditionally been defined as **face-to-face interaction**. With only rare exceptions, group members are expected to speak to one another in the group and to respond to nonverbal signals. The immediacy of feedback in a face-to-face encounter allows members to react and respond to each other. Seeing each other during an oral exchange of ideas affords participants the opportunity to adjust, control, and correct as the need arises.

The advent of electronic interactions, however, challenges the necessity of the face-to-face element of small group process. Some would expand the definition of groups to include a cluster of people who interact via computer networks over a period of time to achieve a goal. The nonverbal signals would be denied these people, but the other factors that define group interaction would be present. The debate continues.

The fifth aspect of a group concerns the members' behavior. The behaviors and actions of group members can be classified by determining whether the behavior increases or decreases the group's effectiveness, whether it is functional or dysfunctional.

Functional behavior is behavior that increases the productivity of the group. When individuals encourage or try to encourage participation on the part of more quiet members, clarify messages they are working toward, and create an open, supportive climate, they are exhibiting functional behavior. This atmosphere then allows participants to clearly define the goals of the group and to concentrate on task realization.

Conversely, **dysfunctional behavior** is behavior that tends to decrease the advancement of the group. Generally, it is unproductive and disruptive behavior that leads to defensiveness or a feeling among group members that they are not accepted, liked, or included by the other members. When a group member feels defensive or threatened in some way, the group no longer functions in a productive way. Excessive criticism of another individual, preventing ideas and feelings from being expressed, verbal attacks, and excessive joking are examples of conduct that limits a group's progress.

Functional and dysfunctional are general classifications of behavior, but each group defines for itself its norms for procedures and decorum, the expectations for inclusion in the group.

Explicit or implicit, these rules govern the conduct and interlocking roles of the participants. A group's success depends on the individuals accepting and applying these norms and fulfilling the role expectations associated with them.

Roles are present in all groups. They are a set of expected behaviors that are associated with a specific position within the group. There are two broad categories for defining roles: Task roles and maintenance roles.

Task roles are the roles or behaviors that are oriented toward goal completion. Persons who perform task roles exhibit behavior that shows a concern for achieving the group's purpose and for doing it well. This causes the group to stay focused.

Maintenance or socioemotional roles, on the other hand, are behaviors that display a primary concern for people and the relationships that exist among group members. Persons performing maintenance roles are interested in how people are getting along with each other. They look to see if members like or dislike each other, or if they feel included or hostile.

Categorizing behaviors as either task or maintenance does not imply that people are either one or the other. On the contrary, **mixed roles** often occur when members display a combination of part task and maintenance behaviors. Roles, whether task oriented, maintenance oriented, or mixed, develop differently in different groups, and more than one group member may perform similar roles. Balancing a concern for the goal with an interest in the people creates an ideal group environment.

Kinds of Groups

Groups form for a variety of reasons and can be classified according to their most common forms in the everyday world: families, teams, conferences, subcommittees, therapy groups, etc. Often groups have a specific, well-defined function, such as completion of a task, but frequently groups form to address the psychological needs of the participants. There are two general divisions into which each of the aforementioned groups would fall: obligatory and voluntary groups.

Obligatory groups are groups, such as work groups, that an individual feels compelled to join. In a professional setting, group membership can be mandated by a supervisor, and often leadership is designated by someone outside the group. Work responsibilities, union requirements, and corporate culture are overt factors that may push a person to join a group. Pressure to join a certain group can be more subtle, however, and can occur in religious, civic, and social environments as well.

Voluntary groups are groups, such as therapy groups or social groups, that an individual joins because of a desire for membership. Belonging to the group meets the person's individual needs. Sometimes there is a need to solve a problem or achieve a goal, and other times people just need to feel a part of something. These groups can be highly structured, like a softball team, or extremely unstructured, like a group of friends going out to dinner.

Whether obligatory or voluntary, an analysis of the classification of groups can be more specific by examining the purpose of the group. Problem-solving groups, such as committees, have been assigned or have freely taken on the task of solving an existing problem. **Problem-solving groups** must generate their own solutions to the problem and decide the best course of action. At this point the purpose may change to decision making.

Decision-making groups are groups that have been assigned or have freely assumed the task of making a decision based on a fixed or set number of choices. Often decision making happens after problem solving has occurred; however, this is not always the case. Commonly groups skip problem solving and try to make a decision without going through a step-by-step process.

Group Process

Group process differs from group *content*. Content refers to what is being discussed or *what* is being done by the group. Group process, however, refers to *how* the entire group is interacting—factors include the time, place, mood of group members, seating arrangement, underlying conflicts, style of leadership, and its effectiveness and norms. Every factor that influences how the group members interact is an element of group process.

Synergy is a phenomenon of group process that causes groups to inspire better decisions than individuals working alone could make. Synergy is the concept that 1 + 1 = *3* rather than *2*. In other words, the combination of talents and knowledge is greater than the sum of the individual contributions.

For example, groups are generally more efficient than individuals at recalling information because the ideas of one person often trigger a response from another person that neither would have thought of individually. Taking these cues from each other usually causes groups to make more correct, reasonable decisions. The errors in judgment or accuracy that might escape an individual working alone will often be noticed by another group member.

Synergy is one of the conditions that energizes groups to experience **change**. The characteristic of process that makes groups most effective is their ability to provoke change. Change can be produced in two basic ways: (1) change in group members, and (2) change in issues or events.

Change in group members occurs because members of small groups are both **targets** and **agents** for change. Members are targets for change in that groups influence or alter, to some degree, the behavior of the members. Subtle or overt pressure from the whole causes the individual to act a certain way within that group, and, often, outside the group.

While groups are influencing the individual, each individual impacts the group. Members are agents for change in that a group member can exert pressure on others in the group to alter their behaviors. Each group, then, is different because of the unique blend of personalities. Whether a person is acting as a target for or an agent of change, the changes may be slight or drastic, permanent or temporary, deliberate or unconscious.

Change in issues or events occur because groups have a greater capacity to move circumstances from the status quo to a different, more extreme, or more ideal state. Large groups, such as unions, can exert power that individuals working alone could not hope to realize. Throughout history, groups, rather than individuals, have accounted for most of the dramatic social changes.

The changes that groups engender, the inevitability of group membership, and the personal identity that each person derives from group membership make understanding group process a major concern of business, government, the military, and society. Understanding group dynamics is significant because the effectiveness of the group is related to the quality of life of the individual members.

Introduction to Readings

Chapter 1 focuses on some of the current thought concerning what constitutes a group, what its characteristics are, and how we should go about examining groups. We raise the question, "What is a small group and how is it defined?" The answers given in the following essays point out there is no agreed upon scientific definition of the small group. Instead of searching for "the" definition, the authors here suggest we are better served by developing operational definitions based on where, how, and under what circumstances individuals meet and interact with others in small group settings.

Small groups play an important role in all our lives. Often we have no choice about the groups we are born into or socially assigned to, and we must adjust to the demands of the group. This often leads to the belief that groups are organizations that somehow transcend and supersede the individuals within the group. This notion of group as a single entity implies that individualism is diminished once we are affiliated with a group. Although we would agree that each group does take on a certain identity and impose group norms on the individual, we believe that members of a group, no matter what its origin, continue to function as individuals and to make personal choices. We must, therefore, understand what effects the group has on the individual and how the individuals in a group continue to influence the form and function of the group. The essays in this chapter take the position that if we are to understand what constitutes a small group, we must focus on the interactions of the individuals within the group as well as the group's response to its surroundings.

We begin Chapter 1 with an essay written expressly for this edition by Larry Samovar, Linda Henman, and Stephen King. Entitled, "Small Group Process," it gives us an overview of the kinds of groups we do or will participate in. The authors then present a workable definition of small group discussion with emphasis on the critical function of communication within the group setting. This is followed by a description of each component of the small group process. They conclude with consideration of the differences between the way group discussion actually operates and the ideal of group discussion. How groups are perceived and notions of group that people carry with them decidedly influence how individuals react to group involvement.

Our next selection from a well-known textbook, *Group Discussion: A Practical Guide to Participation and Leadership,* by Julia T. Wood, Gerald M. Phillips, and Douglas J. Pedersen, is entitled "Understanding the Group as a System." It provides us with a way of thinking about groups based on *general systems theory.* The authors contend that thinking of the small group as an "open system" is a most useful way of understanding group process. Using the open system model—that is groups are sets of interrelated and interacting parts continually involved in maintaining balance within their particular environments—they set forth and explain four premises to guide our thinking about small groups.

"Five Kinds of Small Social Groups," by Michael Argyle, our next selection, demonstrates the diversity of group experience. Argyle concentrates on what he considers to be "real-life" groups; the family, the work group, groups of friends, committees, and therapy groups. He defines each type of group, analyzes their similarities and differences, and considers some of the research findings pertinent to each type of group. This essay helps us differentiate among groups and better understand their purposes.

The final essay in this chapter, "The Rock, Egg, and Chicken: Metaphorical Perspectives on the Concept of a Group," by Ann Margaret Trautlein, provides us with a personal and witty tour through the many attempts to come up with "the" definition of a small group. She then devises her own system of defining groups based upon a metaphorical perspective. She argues that her rock, egg, and chicken metaphors are useful for separating collections of individuals to whom the label *group* can apply, but who are nonetheless distinctly different types of entities.

Small Group Process

Larry A. Samovar, Linda D. Henman, and Stephen W. King

You are sitting in the third meeting of a group assigned the task of finding ways your club can raise money for charity. You are bored! "Why do I get myself into these things?" After some reflection you conclude that avoiding groups is a virtual impossibility; in fact, you participate in groups quite often. How frequently do you participate in groups? While answers to this question vary considerably, one conclusion is clear: a significant portion of communication activity occurs in a group setting.

When you interact in groups, you are both a target of and an agent for change. Groups to which you belong influence your behavior, and you, in turn, impact to some degree the behavior of others in the group. This change may be limited to group members, or it can be more widespread, affecting people outside the group. Defining groups, explaining their processes, and examining *how* and *why* they cause change can increase our understanding of the importance of groups in our society.

Why We Participate in Groups

You may find yourself in voluntary or obligatory professional and personal groups identifiable in at least three ways: social groups, self-oriented groups, and problem-solving groups. Our first groups, our families and early peer groups, initiate us into *social groups* by teaching us how to behave, and the acceptable and unacceptable ways to interact. Social groups, which exist for the purpose of giving support or maintenance to its members, are probably the most common type of group. The members show concern for the relationships that exist among them, and their primary reason for existing is to meet the universal needs that each person has for inclusion and affection. People will continue to be a member of such groups as long as the experience remains rewarding.

Some of the groups in which you participate are *self-oriented* groups, the purpose of which is to aid the development within each individual person. Study groups, consciousness-raising groups, therapy groups, and support groups are examples of this type of group. The change within the individual is influenced and supported by the interaction among the group members who share a common need to grow or change.

A third type of group experience is the *problem-solving* group. Problem-solving groups are created when several people share a common task and communicate with each other in order to resolve the task or problem. Problem-solving groups face a task that usually requires a decision; accordingly, such groups are often called "problem-solving groups," "task groups," or "decision-making groups." A parents' committee charged with deciding which playground equipment to purchase and a corporate board of directors are examples of the various kinds of problem-solving groups.

This essay was rewritten for the 7th edition. All rights reserved. Permission to reprint must be obtained from the publisher and the authors. Larry A. Samovar is affiliated with the Department of Speech Communication, San Diego State University; Linda D. Henman is affiliated with the Human Resource Development Graduate School, Webster University; and Stephen W. King is Dean of the School of Communication, California State University at Chico.

Problem-solving groups are ubiquitous; everywhere you turn you find decision-making groups at work. Education, religion, government, and business all rely on group decision making. The success or failure of the group affects each individual's success or failure. For example, if a person is a member of a small group in an advertising firm charged with designing an advertising campaign to win a large contract and the group's proposal fails, the group's failure would likely affect the professional future of all of the group members. It should be noted, however, that problem-solving groups can affect our lives whether or not we are a member of the group. The decisions of a few often impact many.

The need for group decision making increases as the complexity of the problems and the diversity of participants' skills and knowledge required for their solutions both increase. Simply, the utility of and need for effective problem-solving discussion increases as our lives and the issues we face become more complicated. Individuals often do not have the wherewithal to make these challenging decisions. Clearly for personal, professional, and societal reasons, we need an understanding of group discussion.

Small Group Communication

Small group discussion is both a particular type of communication setting and a specific type of communication activity. Both the setting and the activity are suggested by the following definition of small group discussion:

> Small group discussion is communication among a limited number of people in a single place directed toward the achievement of a common goal.

Let's examine the crucial parts of this definition individually.

Communication. The definition of small group discussion just offered characterizes the activity as communication in a particular setting among a limited number of people for the purpose of achieving a common objective, primarily directed toward the resolution of a common problem. Communication can be defined as "a process whereby symbols generated by people are received and responded to by other people." This definition suggests several significant attributes about communication that will be important in the study and practice of small group discussion.

First, communication is a transactional process, the continuous and simultaneous interaction of persons, not simply a one-way sequence of events involving an active source and a passive receiver. This ongoing series of exchanges results in something different from the original occurrence. Therefore, group members are mutually interdependent. That is, the success of the entire group is at least partially dependent upon the communication competence of each participant.

Second, the observation that communication is symbolic requires consideration of all forms of symbolic behavior, both verbal and nonverbal, and the problems involved with symbol generation, perception, encoding, and symbol reception decoding. Realizing that *meaning* is created in the individual person rather than inherent in the symbol helps to avoid communication breakdown. If two people assign a word or gesture different meanings, communication will fail.

Third, communication is said to have occurred only when symbols have been received and responded to; that is, communication is a receiver phenomenon. As such, the *intention* of the sender whose symbols cause meaning to be derived by a receiver is only a small part of the process. The *decoding* of the symbol is the most significant part of the transaction. Characterized in this way, the study of communication in the group setting clearly involves the complex, unrepeatable interaction of people applying and interpreting symbols, verbal or nonverbal, intentional or unintentional.

Small Group Definition. How small is a small group? The answer to this question usually reflects the respondent's biases more than the facts of the matter. Our bias is that the minimum size for a "group" to exist is three persons, while the maximum number for a "group" is nine or ten. Our bias is based on the belief that a three-person group is the minimum size for certain important group properties to emerge, such as communication networks, leadership, coalitions, and majorities.

At the other end of the spectrum, groups larger than nine or ten often develop subgroups with their own goals, diminish the participation of each individual member, and are less likely to sustain commonly perceived relationships among the members of the group. Between these two extremes, groups of five or seven seem to be the optimum size for effective decision making, the odd number of members precluding deadlocks.

Same Place. The traditional definitional requirement that small group discussion take place among persons in the same place is based on two observations. First, by communicating face-to-face small group participants can take maximum advantage of both verbal and nonverbal communication cues. With all possible communication channels open and the maximum number of communication cues available, communication can be optimally effective in the resolution of the task the group faces.

Second, when all group members are in the same place, every member shares the impact of the communication setting. If a number of people conversed on a conference call or communicated on a computer network, each person would not have access to many nonverbal communication cues and could, unknown to the others, be subject to different communication environments. Maximum communication cue availability and common impact of communication setting both contribute to effective communication in the small group discussion setting.

Common Goal. The shared commitment to a common purpose is the factor that distinguishes a group from a collection of individuals and small group discussion from random, unstructured conversation. Whether the issue before the group is a problem to be solved, a task to be accomplished, a decision to be made, or support to be provided, the distinguishing feature of a group is that the individual group members share a perception of their common objective. Aggregations of persons who do not share a goal, such as a collection of people waiting in line for a movie or the occupants of a dentist's waiting room, are merely collections of individuals, not groups. Some may argue that the individuals in these examples *do* share common goals: to get into a movie or to see a dentist. There is one major distinguishing factor, however. The people in line or in the waiting room may have the same objective, but they do not rely on each other to complete the task.

Similarly, group discussions are distinguishable from casual conversation by the apparent *purpose* or *function* of the communication. Casual conversation among a number of people is relatively unsystematic and capricious, as it need not contribute to any outcome other than the establishment of a pleasant social atmosphere. Group discussion, on the other hand, is communication directed toward the achievement of the group goal and, therefore, is nonrandom and is somewhat structured or constrained by the task the group faces. Group members typically engage in exchanges that are task and/or maintenance oriented that contribute to goal accomplishment and support respectively.

This shared commitment is one of the reasons that groups develop norms or standards of behavior. These explicit or implied expectations are often unique to a given group and serve to unite the group members or to cause rejection when one of the members violates a group rule.

The Ideal of Small Group Discussion

There is a pervasive ideal of small group discussion existent in Western democratic societies. While we are not prepared to declare the ideal a "myth," we feel it is important to articulate the ideal carefully and compare the ideal with reality. The substance of the ideal of small group discussion is that small group discussion occurs when:

1. A task brings together people who share an interest or concern with the achievement of the task.
2. Members pool their resources toward that end.
3. They have sufficient time and freedom for a full and rational consideration of the issue.
4. There is faith that "truth" will be discovered if all the information is available and all members contribute.
5. Each person is an effective communicator who possesses attitudes conducive to cooperative idea development.

In fact, small group discussion is often an experience far different from that characterized in the preceding ideal. Taking each component of the ideal in turn:

1. Discussion groups are often formed by people who are not particularly interested in the ostensible group task. An individual may simply not be concerned with the task or its solution, as could be the case for a person assigned to the group. Or an individual may have personal purposes—hidden agendas he or she wants the group to serve, such as finish before a 4 o'clock tennis date or other personal objectives that are at cross purposes with the group's goal. As Haiman noted,

    The individuals in any group vary in the degree to which they are really part of the organization and committed to achievement of the group's goals. Some are on the fringes—they are peripherally involved. Some devote the major part of their lives and thoughts to the group—they are centrally involved. The others range in between.

2. Resources are often not pooled in group discussion. The failure to pool resources may be due to a variety of factors; for example, the information or ability of an individual is intentionally or accidentally withheld, the value of a particular member is ignored, the resolution of the task may not require pooling talents, or the strained relationships among group members may preclude free contributions.

3. Groups frequently do not have sufficient time or freedom to adequately consider their task. Real or perceived time constraints exist for virtually all decision-making groups. Furthermore, real or imagined external constraints and pressures often affect group operation.
4. Groups seldom have the time or ability for full consideration of the issues before them. "Rational" decision making is unlikely as small group decision making involves emotional people. Even at their "rational" best, people in groups are influenced by emotion when making decisions, solving problems, and accomplishing tasks; the outcome often seems irrational.
5. The single "truth" or "best decision" to other than the most trivial of issues seldom exists. Most alternatives involve pros and cons that complicate the discovery of the superlative.
6. Communication is a dynamic, complex process that produces limitless chances for failure. Each person in a group brings different language and communication skills and different predispositions to communicate. This can cause perceptual difference, conflict, and a general breakdown in communication.
7. Each person in a group brings different attitudes and a unique personality. Accordingly, although some members may be predisposed to exhibit functional, cooperative, and selfless behaviors, others are likely to be dysfunctional, competitive and self-serving. Conditions that stimulate and invigorate some may retard and trouble others.

Obviously there are substantial differences between the way group discussion actually operates and the ideal of group discussion. We did not, however, introduce this issue merely to demonstrate the difference between theory and practice.

Defining groups and examining the *reality* of their processes provides a starting point by delineating the weaknesses that need to be overcome. Describing the *ideal* for group discussion clarifies the objective for examining group interaction and provides a standard for measuring progress. Perfectly functioning groups will never exist; however, improving group effectiveness will help to make professional and personal group membership a more meaningful and profitable experience for the participants, the organization, and society.

References

Fraser, Douglas (May 26, 1980). "Labor's Voice on the Board," *Newsweek* 13.

Haiman, Franklyn S. (1951). *Group Leadership and Democratic Action* 82. New York: Houghton Mifflin.

King, Stephen W. (1979). "The Nature of Communication." In Robert S. Cathcart and Larry A. Samovar (eds.), *Small Group Communication: A Reader,* 3rd ed., 273, Dubuque, Iowa: Wm. C. Brown.

Understanding the Group as a System

Julia T. Wood, Gerald M. Phillips, and Douglas J. Pedersen

During your lifetime you've probably taken part in a number of group discussions. The meetings of the school spirit committee, planning sessions for the senior prom, organizing ticket sales for the school play, and the group assignments you worked out in class all qualify as formal problem-solving discussions. If you're like most people, you've been pleased with your participation in some cases and less satisfied in others, yet you might find it difficult to explain why some discussions seemed more productive and comfortable than others. It is easy to feel frustrated and confused in group situations and even to conclude that groups are so chaotic they defy understanding by sane people.

Groups are not really as chaotic as they sometimes appear. They are, however, very complex, since a variety of influences operates within them. Because groups are so complex, understanding them requires a theoretical perspective sufficiently powerful to explain the many forces that work simultaneously within them. . . . Once you recognize key aspects of group interaction and appreciate the ways they tend to influence individual and collective behavior, you'll have a basis for making sound choices regarding your own actions in group situations.

You may select your behaviors based on awareness of the dynamics of participation and on reasoned predictions of how alternative choices on your part are likely to affect what others do and what the group achieves. Toward this goal, this chapter explains the *systems* perspective that provides our theoretical basis. . . .

The Systems Perspective

Of the many theories about human social behavior from which we could choose, *general systems theory* seems especially appropriate to the study of the small group. General systems theory originated with Ludwig Von Bertelanffy, a theoretical biologist, as a way to think about and study the constant, dynamic adjustments of living phenomena. His ideas have subsequently been adopted by many social scientists and humanists who seek to understand complicated interpersonal interaction. Many who study group discussion regard general systems theory as the most useful approach to teaching and research in small-group behavior.[1]

According to the theory, an open system such as a group is defined as an *organized set of interrelated and interacting parts that attempts to maintain its own balance amid the influences from its surrounding environment*. Think, for example, about your college or university. It can be analyzed in a great many ways. We could consider students, faculty, maintenance personnel, administration, alumni, and so on as components made

Selected excerpts from *Group Discussion: A Practical Guide to Participation and Leadership, Second Edition* by Julia T. Wood, et al. © 1986 by Harper & Row Publishers, Inc. Reprinted by permission of HarperCollins Publishers, Inc. Julia T. Wood is affiliated with the Department of Speech Communication at The University of North Carolina, Chapel Hill. Gerald M. Phillips and Douglas J. Pedersen are affiliated with the Department of Speech.

up of people. We could also consider teaching/learning, research/publishing, maintaining/ caretaking, fund-raising, and so on as activities carried on in the university. However we choose to divide it up, our metaphor would be to a living organism—a plant, for example. A plant is made up of roots, leaves, stem, flowers, all of which contribute to the nature of the organism. What happens to the roots affects leaves, stem, and flowers. Any outside force that affects the plant affects all components of the plant. Turning back to your school, an outside force affecting the institution as a whole (like the amount of money given by the legislature or the trustees) affects each component of the system. If faculty salaries go up, the faculty changes accordingly. A change in the faculty changes the influence on the students, which in turn might alter administration, and so on. From this model of an *open system,* we can derive four premises to guide how we think about group discussion.

Any Part of a System Can Be Understood Only Within the Context of the Entire System. We cannot understand one part of a group in isolation. To take it out of the group context produces distortion. For instance, we cannot account for how one member acts without considering group norms, the power structure, leadership, and so on. Similarly, to explain a group's decisions we need to analyze member goals, leadership style, resources available to the group, and a host of other factors. (Consider, for example, how the faculty at your school makes decisions about teaching based on the nature of the students; how the nature of the students depends on the tuition, how the tuition depends on the funding, and conversely, how funding affects the morale of the faculty, which in turn affects how they deal with the students, who in turn respond to teaching, and so on.) As you participate in discussions, try to avoid analyzing parts of your group out of context. Remember that any components can be understood only in light of the whole system.

A System Is More Than the Sum of Its Parts. At first glance, this premise seems odd. However, it is central to a systems view of groups. The premise suggests that we cannot understand a group simply by adding up all its separate parts. If we add members, physical setting, communication patterns, and decision reached, we will not have an accurate picture. What is missing is the interactions; how physical setting affected members' communication patterns and how the result affects the outcome.

Within a group, the parts interact dynamically to create new features not present at the outset. For example, Smith may be naturally quiet outside the group, but the presence of Jones gets him excited. Smith and Jones develop a relationship unique to a particular group. The group is confronted with more than the behavior of Smith plus the behavior of Jones. They are confronted with a Smith/Jones dyad. Other members will relate both to the individuals and to their relationship. The total pattern of relationships forms the group norms against which the behavior of individuals is judged. The behavior of individuals, however, forms the norms. Norms are not present when the members first sit down; they result from interaction. Over time, the relationships take on new qualities in response to the pattern of responses. The process reflects the dynamic interactions characteristic of living (open) systems. Once formed, a system engages in an ongoing process of defining and redefining itself, constantly changing as it attempts to sustain itself against events inside and outside. (For example, we may be enjoying a party, nibbling away on the food, which gives us heartburn, which makes us irritable, which interferes with the conversation we are having, which has been interrupted several times by other people, which . . . . And if someone asks how was the party, would it be possible to single out just one feature?)

All Parts of a System Interact Dynamically and Constantly. This premise extends the previous ones. The parts of a group are intricately interconnected; each part affects all others. Many systems theorists point out that a change in any part of a system creates change in all other parts. This is because the parts are so interrelated that any change reverberates throughout the whole system. When one element alters, all others must adjust to accommodate it if the system is to survive in a healthy state.

Some changes have obvious and immediate effects. For example, when participation is stifled, member satisfaction declines. There is a direct relationship between participation and satisfaction. (What would be the effect on a group if the boss dropped in to hear a discussion on problems with his latest policy proposal?)

At other times, the influence is indirect. For instance, inhibiting participation reduces members' satisfaction (direct impact), which in turn reduces their commitment to the group, which in turn materially decreases the probability that the group will achieve a top quality outcome. In both cases, stifling participation is the action that influences other events in the group system, but some of the responses are easier to discern than others.

If we pursued this example even further, we'd need to ask why the participation was stifled. To answer this, we'd need to analyze the entire group system. Why did the boss come in to listen? Was she dissatisfied with what she heard was going on? Who might have directed information outside the system? Notice that events inside the system can have an effect outside the system, which in turn can influence the system itself. Each time we ask why something happened, we are pushed to further appreciation of the complex interrelationships among parts of a group system, along with the pressures and influences from outside the system that affect the system as a whole and individual elements as well. To think systematically is to think in very complex fashion. It is inappropriate to think in terms of specific causes of events in a system.

An Open System Interacts with Its Environment in Mutually Influential Ways. Just as we cannot consider parts of a group in isolation, neither can we consider the group apart from its context. Any group is embedded in many other systems, such as organizations, companies, communities, and cultures. Because they are parts of their larger environments, groups influence these environments and are influenced by them. There is, for example, a constant exchange of resources so that a committee produces policies for the institution it serves. The institution provides the meeting place and the salaries for the members. It also shapes member attitudes toward the institution, which are reflected in opinions expressed inside the group, which have an impact on the policies the group lays down, which affect the institution in ways that affect the members, and so on. Furthermore, members come and go. Each new member brings a new cargo of influence from outside. Each departing member changes the shape of the interactions inside the group.

Because groups interact with other parts of their environment, there is always the potential for conflicts arising from incompatible demands of multiple systems. Individuals may lack the time and energy to participate effectively in work groups,

Table 1
Small-Group System and Surrounding Environment

Surrounding Environment		
Initial Elements	*Process Elements*	*Outcomes*
Members Group Size	Verbal Communication Nonverbal Behavior	Satisfaction Decision Effectiveness
Group Record Group Charge	Norms Power Distribution Decision-Making Style Group Autonomy Cohesion	Change in Environment

social action groups, and interpersonal systems. Tension arises, stress increases. Either individuals sacrifice membership in some of their systems, reduce investment in some, or suffer the consequences of burnout. In addition, people sometimes experience conflict of interest between the values of two or more systems. It may, for example, be to the interest of an employee's family to keep salaries high; it may be to the interest of the company to keep salaries low. High salaries may put the company out of business, but low salaries may make it difficult to live. How will any given employee respond? Consider how a person who worked for a nuclear power plant and belonged to the Sierra Club would feel. The two systems have clashing values. Furthermore, the values, expectations, and rules of the social milieu constrain and shape the ideas a problem-solving group may prudently recommend. To understand any group, we must recognize its place in the broader environment.

The four premises we've just discussed summarize the systems approach to small-group problem solving. We can now build on this orientation by examining some of the components of group systems. We may have to focus on one part at a time in order to explain it clearly. Keep the system perspective in mind as we go on to remind yourself that each component interacts with *all* the others. We start with a discussion of the importance of a group's environment on its problem-solving activity. Then we consider four initial elements of groups: members, group size, group record, and group purpose. In Chapter 3 (Woods, Phillips, Pedersen text) we will consider seven process elements that arise out of the initial elements. We will also discuss three possible outcomes from group systems. Throughout, the systems model will guide our discussion.

The Environment Surrounding a Group

Our fourth premise about systems stated that groups interact with their environments in mutually influential ways. We want to explain how this idea applies to problem-solving groups. Any group is influenced and sometimes pressured by the institution to which it belongs, as well as by other groups within that institution. For example, a task force (committee) charged to plan a sales campaign is primarily responsible to the company that sets it up and pays its members. In addition, the task force must coordinate its efforts with the group that plans production, as well as the sales staff. In order to operate effectively, groups must work within the general guidelines and policies established by the company and administered by its executives. They must also stay within the limits of their setting. Thus, the task force must take into account the limitations of production and the capabilities of the sales force in its planning. It cannot, for example, cut prices despite the fact that doing so would bring more sales, if doing so would compel production to reduce quality, counter to company policy. Furthermore, the sales campaign planners cannot anticipate a campaign that would require sales personnel to cover more territory than is reasonable. They cannot add to the sales force if the size of the sales force is limited by policy. They can recommend changes in company policy, but if they do, both production and sales personnel will be affected by the changes. Thus, the external environment limits the behavior of the group. If, on the other hand, the group succeeds in changing the external environment, other groups will be affected, which in turn will affect the group that initiated the change.

A group also functions within a community. Each social layer exerts influence to the extent that the group is part of it. A public group attempting to establish group homes for retarded citizens will be constrained by the politics of the community regarding zoning and taxation, as well as the perceived interests of householders in the neighborhood where the group home is to be located. Church and civic groups will have attitudes on the question. So will real estate agents and merchants. Moral values of those who want to "do right" by the retarded citizens may clash with economic values of householders who believe the group home will reduce property values. Even students in college discussion classes must fit within the community, including the university, the town, the state, and society in general. Their conduct during discussion sessions, the topics they choose to discuss, and the manner in which they conduct the discussions will be affected by rules of conduct applying to classes, goals and objectives of the instructor, potential to interact with the community, obligations of members to other courses and activities in both university and community, and space available in which to conduct business.

Constituency is very important for problem-solving groups. A company's product must be desired by someone, otherwise there is no point in making it. The best designed "kadody" will not sell if no one knows what it is for and no one wants to pay money for it. Educational policy in universities may be controlled by faculty committees, but academic institutions will collapse if they alienate students, trustees, or contribution-giving alumni. The faculty committee may decide it is desirable that all students take Sanskrit, but if the students do not see the point, they may go elsewhere. If enrollment drops, contributions may dwindle. If both happen, faculty members may be terminated. Thus, any decision-making or problem-solving body must take into account the impact of decisions on *all* those who will be affected. Furthermore, they must consider how those constituents, once affected, may behave in ways that affect the decision makers or problem solvers. The faculty committee must be sensitive to the various constituencies as a matter of simple survival.

Prevailing public standards or norms affect the manner in which groups do business. Prior to widespread concern about fuel supplies, for example, car manufacturers produced powerful engines and sleek designs. Public demand for economical fuel consumption, a direct result of dwindling fuel supplies and growing environmental awareness, pressured companies into producing cars that consumed less fuel, which required changes in design, which affected costs, which affected the rate at which the public bought cars. If a pulp mill believes it can reduce costs by reducing the expense of waste disposal, it must take into account the effects of its action on both a national and local level.

Thus, to ensure survival, group members must be sensitive to the values of their communities. Some of those values are brought into the group by members who represent outside constituencies. A group member does not sacrifice other loyalties when she or he comes into the group. On the contrary, it is important that the member adequately represent those concerns. On the other hand, group members must consider the principle of equity in dealing with people who represent other interests so there is fairness in the exchange between the group and the community.

It is important for groups that lack official status to secure constituencies. Student task groups, for example, generally have no formal titles or recognized status. They may be regarded as upstarts not only by the faculty, but by other students. To win support from the external community may mean securing representation from the community, opening dialogue with it, or anticipating its needs and interests and taking them into account. A student group which advocated a textbook exchange on campus might find objection from bookstore owners, from faculty who believe books for low enrollment courses might be more difficult to obtain, and from others whose ability to move about might be affected by a change in traffic flow brought about by the book exchange. The students must find a way to enlist existing agencies in their campaign. Faculty might be invited to participate. Merchants could be solicited for information about their needs. Existing organizations could be canvassed to secure secretarial assistance, computer accounts, or funds for a survey. It is, after all, very easy to make decisions about other people so long as the other people don't know you are doing so and so long as the decisions will have no effect. If a group expects to be influential, members must be sensitive to their context.

Groups are materially influenced by adjacent groups. Recurrent problems arise from competition between groups.[2] Group morale and cohesiveness increase in a group that perceives itself in competition with another group, often to the point of antagonism toward both the other group and individuals in it. Members of both groups may unrealistically evaluate their work. They may overevaluate their own work and underestimate the work of their competitors. This may lead to a decline in self-criticism and to the care taken with decisions. Competition may lead to overconfidence and groupthink. The result is usually sloppy and ineffective recommendations. In the final analysis, it is not the competing group whose positive evaluation is necessary, it is the rest of the environment's. Groups contending for research funds, for example, need not solicit the approval of other competing groups. Their effort should be focused on their proposal and the demonstration of how it will serve the environment in general.

Finally, every group exists within the context of an overall culture that influences both individual members and the group as a whole. Most of us take for granted a broad array of values, expectations, and codes of conduct that we have learned over the years. Our table manners, the way we greet acquaintances, our small talk, the way we dress are all features of our culture. They are so familiar to us we do not even realize we're operating from internalized cultural assumptions. Yet to understand much of what happens in a group, we must raise our cultural assumptions to a conscious level.

The sense of how a group should operate is culturally influenced. For instance, most groups in America adopt a more or less democratic style of leadership (or at least claim to). Group members rarely discuss matters of style, yet most seem to find the democratic process quite familiar. It is a culturally conditioned belief. Similarly, some groups typically expect a male to act as leader and a female as recorder. Regardless of qualifications for the position, most of us succumb to sex stereotypes that influence expectations of who should do what.

The influence of cultural assumptions is clearly reflected in the contrast between Japanese and American styles of decision making. Typically the Japanese devote extensive time to defining and analyzing problems, but move with great speed in making final decisions. Americans follow an opposite path in which minimum time is devoted to analysis, while making the final decision consumes substantial time. No wonder international negotiations are often so frustrating for all parties.[3] We all reflect the culture in which we have been socialized through our participation in discussion. We are so tightly bound to our culture that sometimes Americans of different ethnic origin or from different parts of the country have to work at synthesizing differences in the way things are done.

Thus, it is a good idea to reflect on the influence exerted by the surrounding environment. By consciously identifying major influences, members find it easier to discover common ground in the way they talk to one another. Furthermore, they are sensitive to differing needs and values and take them into account in problem solving.

Initial Elements in Group Systems

At the outset, there are four main features in a work-oriented (problem-solving or decision-making) discussion group: individual members, size of the group, group purpose, and group record.

Individual Members

Groups are made up of individuals. Each member has a unique personality, personal needs, abilities, and self-esteem. In addition, the nature of membership is often affected by entrance requirements—that is, their specialties or the fact that they represent an outside reference group.

The work of Murray[4] and Edwards[5] is especially helpful in understanding how personality styles and needs influence group interaction. Between them, Murray and Edwards identified fifteen personality needs we each have:

Achievement	Deference	Order	Exhibition	Autonomy
Affiliation	Intraception	Succorance	Dominance	Abasement
Heterosexuality	Nurturance	Endurance	Aggression	Change

We don't offer this list for you to memorize but to illustrate the complexity of individual needs that come into play as people interact in discussion. Personality needs clearly influence individual styles of participation, as well as goals for membership in groups. Consider the personality profile of a student in one of the author's discussion classes:

> I think my highest need is for achievement, followed closely by needs for order and endurance (sticking with the task). I have pretty low needs for deference, affiliation, and nurturance. I like to concentrate on getting a job done as quickly and well as possible, and I don't need a lot of recognition for doing it.

As you may have inferred, this student was a workaholic, a perfectionistic, highly task-oriented person, and he seized leadership of his group and proceeded to run it as a one-man show. Would you consider this effective? Actually, it's impossible to judge his effectiveness solely on the basis of what we know about him as an individual. We must consider his personality in relation to others in his group. He would be effective with members who had high needs for deference, order, and abasement. On the other hand, he would clash with individuals who had high needs for dominance, change, and aggression, or with those who required a lot of nurturance and affiliation to motivate them. There is no ideal discussant personality; what matters is that the members' personalities fit together to form a workable system.

Gender was once considered an important personality influence on group interaction. Research dating back to the 1920s identified differences in the content and style of male and female participants. One major finding was that men tended to talk about task issues, while women dealt with interpersonal issues and matters of climate.[6] More recent studies, however, failed to confirm these early findings.[7] Rosenfeld and Christie summarized five years of research with the report that men and women do not differ appreciably in their participation styles.[8] In a later study, Rosenfeld and Fowler found men and women did not differ in the way they exercised leadership either.[9] Although sex stereotypes still exist in many people's minds, there is compelling evidence that there are no important differences between men and women as leaders or members of discussion groups. Despite this evidence, however, biases persist and seem to influence how men and women judge each other.[10] In a problem-solving model, these judgments often get in the way of consensus and sometimes deprive the group of important contributions from highly competent members.

In addition to personality, each member brings particular abilities to the problem-solving scene. Some are meticulous researchers, others may be skilled interviewers. Some may have the ability to write and edit; others may be able to ferret out important facts and subtle details. Some abilities are not so welcome. Some members may be more skillful at argument than others. They may be able to use sarcasm and ridicule, or display the ability to criticize others severely. Nobody is talented in all dimensions. The real problem for the group is to find and utilize member strengths, while discouraging the display of skills that might subvert the work of the group.

Each member has some image of self. Self-esteem has impact on participation. Those who have high regard for themselves are willing to take risks in offering ideas, can take criticism, assume their share of blame, and take credit graciously. By contrast, people with low self-esteem tend to be hypercritical of themselves and others, defensive about their worth and efforts, pessimistic about what the group can achieve, and in constant need of assurance of their merit (although often they are unable to accept compliments).[11] Members can affect the self-esteem of colleagues by rewarding constructive contributions and diverting counterproductive activity.

In addition to personality-related variables, groups can be affected by formal or informal membership requirements. Almost all groups limit membership at least to the extent that membership in the larger setting is restricted. The potential membership of any student group is affected by the entrance requirements of the college. Memberships in community action groups are limited by residence, interest in the issue, and economic and social factors that prevail in the community. In addition, there are informal requirements, such as visibility in context. People who are asked to serve on committees, for example, are those the person appointing the committee can remember.

Membership is sometimes limited by self-screening. People decide what groups they want to join. They may favor a cause supported by one group, or share a hobby with members of another. When individuals seek to join an established group, they do so on the basis of some "advertisement." They believe the group stands for something and membership might be profitable because it is compatible with what they think represents the group's norms. We can assume they are committed and motivated.

But a drawback of voluntary groups is there may be little sense of responsibility. If the group doesn't live up to what the new member imagined, he or she drops out. If there are no standards for membership, newcomers often make little commitment to the group. Others, however, may have a deep commitment. But the rule of voluntary organizations is that those who volunteer in can volunteer out. Hard workers can burn out, become discouraged, or be distracted by rewards promised by other groups. Those who are lukewarm can remain on the group rolls for a long time, but never contribute anything. Furthermore, volunteers often want to do things their way and resist leadership. They may be uncritical and argumentative in problem solving, seeking mainly to persuade others to support their pet biases. And if everyone in the group has exactly the same beliefs and goals, there is little that can be done besides mutual reinforcement. Consensus may be too easy and consequently unproductive.

Membership qualifications may be set by the group itself. Some groups are open to all, others maintain a numerical quota, and still others use elaborate screening procedures. The way members are picked affects group morale. In one of the author's colleges, for example, there is a hierarchy of committees. Professors struggle to get on what they regard as major committees, appointment to which is a sign of the dean's favor. There is a group of committees newcomers start with, and if they behave properly, they may work up the ladder until they are appointed to the Promotion and Tenure Committee, which gives them considerable power over their colleagues. There is a striking similarity between this process and the process of rushing and pledging fraternities, securing new members in lodges and fraternal organizations, or admitting people to membership in learned societies and professional associations.

A now-classic experiment conducted in 1959 demonstrated the impact of entrance requirements on member attitudes toward groups.[12] In response to a membership appeal, a number of college women applied to join a club that would spend its time discussing sex (something not openly done in 1959). The applicants were told by the experimenters that they had to be screened, so those who were excessively embarrassed by talking about sexual topics could be excluded.

For one-third of the women, the screening procedure consisted of reading to the male experimenter twelve obscene words and two sexually explicit passages from novels. This was considered an extreme initiation. For another third, the procedure consisted of reading aloud five words related to sex, but not obscene. This was mild initiation. The final third, the control group, was simply asked whether sexual discussions would cause embarrassment. All the women were then informed they had been admitted to the club.

The women were then taken into another room, where they were told to listen to a discussion already in progress by members of the club they had just joined so they could get an idea of what the group was like and be ready to participate at the next meeting. What the women really heard was a tape recording the experimenters had designed to be as uninteresting and unprovocative as possible. After hearing the recording, the women were asked to evaluate the overall worth of the discussion and the quality of the club members.

When the responses were analyzed, the experimenters found that the women who had had the mild initiation and those in the control group had about the same evaluations of the discussion and the club members. Those who had undergone the severe initiation, however, rated the worth of the discussion as much higher than the other two groups. They also judged the quality of club members to be higher. From these results, the researchers concluded that when it is costly to enter a group, the investment leads the new member to place a higher value on the group.

This kind of experiment could not take place today because researchers are now bound by government guidelines for treatment of human subjects. (Researchers too are constrained by the rules of their contexts!) Throughout this chapter we will report experiments in which subjects' rights were not adequately taken into account. However, the findings are very useful. In this case, the investigator discovered that the personal value assigned to membership in a group shapes the value the person assigns to the group. Even in your classroom groups, members will become intensely involved depending on their commitment to the task, to learning in general, and to a grade. It is important to consider individual commitments, for the interaction of personal commitments will have a great deal to do with the norms of newly formed groups.

Group Size

The size of a group is a second initial feature that influences the process and outcomes of problem solving. There seem to be limits to the size of a problem-oriented group beyond which efficiency drops. Based on the early work of Robert Bales, most authorities believe five or seven is the ideal size for a problem-solving group.[13] With less than five, a group lacks the diversity of opinion necessary for a broad perspective and consideration of various solutions. Furthermore, members are reluctant to disagree in groups of four or less. They fear alienating their colleagues. The sense of closeness that develops impedes critical, reflective analysis of issues.

Equally serious problems affect groups with more than seven members. As the group grows in size, there is a tendency for hierarchies to develop. Once status is assigned, higher-status members affect participation of lower-status members. The stronger members dominate and feel good about participation, while the weaker members suffer a drop in self-esteem and are dissatisfied with their participation.[14] Subgroups also tend to develop in larger discussion groups. When this happens, discussion becomes an exercise in politics, rather than a deliberation about issues. Power plays may disrupt group cohesion, which in turn leads to dissatisfied members, some of whom may decide to leave the group.[15]

Often you do not have control over how many members there are in the group. The information we have just presented should alert you to potential problems so you can do your best to minimize their effect. At other times you may be able to suggest breaking an oversized group into subcommittees to encourage more intense participation. If your group is too small or has lost membership over time, you can encourage increasing the size by appointing replacements or by recruiting new members. It is worthwhile to try to get groups to optimum size in order to facilitate effective participation and quality output.

Group Charge

Groups do not come into being by accident. They are formed for reasons that provide a collective goal which should unify members. In the early days of group discussion instruction, students were often put into groups and told to find a topic to discuss. This is unrealistic. It does not happen in commerce or government, where groups are created to respond to conditions in the larger organization. A group's charge or purpose may be as explicit as designing a new method of parceling out dormitory rooms on campus or very vague, like trying to improve student morale. The purpose may be imposed from the outside, as in the case of a committee created and charged to submit recommendations to meet some emergency condition, like adjust the college budget to accommodate to reduced appropriations. It may be generated from the inside, like a faculty committee to find ways to distribute limited funds.

If your classroom group is assigned to find a topic for discussion, it is important to agree on something that interests all the members—a real topic on which the group might exert real influence. Your group must seek a topic feasible to discuss, where information is readily available. A group interested in the general topic of campus safety, for example, might narrow its focus to consideration of the services provided by campus police. It may narrow down even further to find ways and means to inform other students about services provided by campus police. From any general topic different charges may be generated, but groups can pursue only one at a time. Effective groups narrow the scope of their topics to a manageable size.

Understanding the purpose is crucial to success. It is not possible for a group to be effective unless all members understand precisely what the task is and what the final outcome is to be. For this reason, groups that are charged from the outside often need to ask for clarification of purpose. Charging authorities are not always clear in explaining why the group was formed and what is wanted as a final output. A group without clear purpose or in which members disagree about the goal tends to falter. Members become disillusioned as the group becomes paralyzed with the apathy of confusion. Clarification of purpose is the first active step toward success.

Group Record

The final influence in the initial group system is the history of past work by the group. This feature is relevant only in groups that have a history. However, a newly formed group begins writing its history from the moment its members sit down at the first meeting. Each event affects those that follow.

Standing committees and other groups that have existed for a long time can be viewed as products of their own evolution. Studies of developing groups suggest strongly that members increase their commitment to groups that achieve their goals; the more successful the group, the more interested the members.[16] Initial success leads members to have confidence in the group's capacity to meet future challenges.

When a group fails, however, members tend to be disappointed and frustrated. They may seek a target for blame. Once blaming starts, the group can factionalize, or resentments can fester below the surface. Members will set low goals for future work because they have lost confidence in each other as well as the group. Some groups do not turn inward after suffering failure, however. They may blame someone or something outside the group. Members find it comforting to believe that "the system was rigged against us from the start," or "rejecting our proposal was a typical muddle-headed bureaucratic decision." Excuses are easy to find, and sometimes they are legitimate.

In either case, it is important to recognize the consequences of scapegoating. Finding the person who caused the failure is not as productive as seeking a way to be successful the next time. Furthermore, groups can become very cohesive on the issue of blaming. They may pull together under the stress of threat and engage in groupthink, setting excessively high goals for themselves and deluding themselves about the quality of their work. Supergroup, after all, can do anything, even jump mile-high administration buildings in a single bound.

You may not be able to guarantee that your group will succeed (although skillful participation surely increases the odds that it will), but you can use what you know about how groups operate to help guide you toward behavior that facilitates success.

We have examined the elements that form the initial system of problem-solving groups and considered the environment in which groups operate. At the outset, groups consist of individuals with diverse personalities, abilities, and degrees of self-esteem. They have different sizes, charges, and histories. These elements interact with one another and the environment to influence both the process and the outcome of group discussion.

Notes

1. Ludwig Von Bertelanffy, *General Systems Theory* (New York: George Braziller, 1968); John K. Brilhart, *Effective Group Discussion,* 4th ed. (Dubuque, IA: Wm. C. Brown, 1982), 23–24; Stewart Tubbs, *A Systems Approach to Small Group Interaction* (Reading, MA: Addison-Wesley, 1981).
2. Muzafer Sherif and Carolyn W. Sherif, *Social Psychology* (New York: Harper & Row, 1969), 221–266.
3. William Ouchi, *Theory Z: How American Business Can Meet the Japanese Challenge* (Reading, MA: Addison-Wesley, 1981).
4. Henry Murray, *Explorations in Personality* (New York: Oxford University Press, 1938).

5.   Allen Edwards, *The Edwards Personal Preference Schedule* (New York: Psychological Corporation, 1953).

6.   Steven M. Alderton and William E. Jurma, "Genderless/Gender Related Task Leader Communication and Group Satisfaction: A Test of Two Hypotheses," *Southern Journal of Speech Communication* 46 (Fall 1980), 48–60.

7.   Steven M. Alderton, William E. Jurma, and John E. Baird, "Sex Differences in Group Communication: A Review of Relevant Research," *Quarterly Journal of Speech* 62 (1976), 179–192.

8.   L.B. Rosenfeld and V. Christie, "Sex and Personality Revisited," *Western Journal of Speech Communication* 38 (1974), 244–253.

9.   L.B. Rosenfeld and G.D. Fowler, "Personality, Sex, and Leadership Style," *Communication Monographs* 43 (1976), 320–324; G.D. Fowler and L.B. Rosenfeld, "Sex Differences and Democratic Leader Behavior," *Southern Journal of Speech Communication* 45 (Fall 1979), 69–78.

10. E.G. Bormann, J. Pratt, and L. Putnam, "Power, Authority, and Sex: Male Response to Female Leadership," *Communication Monographs* 45 (June 1978), 119–155.

11. G.E. Meyers and M.T. Meyers, *The Dynamics of Human Communication* (New York: McGraw-Hill, 1973), 109–110.

12. E. Aronson and J. Mills, "The Effect of Severity of Initiation on Liking for a Group," *Journal of Abnormal and Social Psychology* 50 (1959), 177–181.

13. R.F. Bales and E.F. Borgatta, "Size of a Group as a Factor in the Interaction Profile." In A.P. Hare, E.F. Borgatta, and R.F. Bales (eds.), *Small Groups: Studies in Social Interaction* (New York: Knopf, 1955), 396–413.

14. P.E. Slater, "Contrasting Correlates of Group Size," *Sociometry* 21 (1958), 129–139.

15. B. Indik, "Organization Size and Member Participation: Some Empirical Tests of Alternative Explanations," *Human Relations* 8 (1965), 339–350.

16. H.P. Shelley, "Level of Aspiration Phenomena in Small Groups," *Journal of Abnormal and Social Psychology* 40 (1954), 149–164.

Five Kinds of Small Social Groups

Michael Argyle

The concentration of research on laboratory groups has diverted attention away from the varied kinds of interaction taking place in real life groups. We shall describe interaction in the three most important types of group—the family, work groups, and groups of friends (we shall concentrate on adolescent friendship groups). In addition an account will be given of some other kinds of groups which have been extensively studied—committees, T-groups, and therapy groups. . . .

The Family as a Small Group

There is something like a family in all species of mammals: the mother has to care for the young, and the father often provides food and protection during this period. Only in humans does the father become an enduring member of the family, and only in humans is there a life-long link between children and parents. What is probably the most important kind of small group in human society is often overlooked by small group researchers—and consequently there are important features of the family group which have never been embodied in small group experiments or theorizing.

The nuclear family consists of two parents, sons and daughters, and can thus be regarded as a four-role system, divided by generation and sex (Parsons and Bales 1955). There are also characteristic relations between older and younger brothers, and between older and younger sisters, so that it may be better to see the family as potentially a six-role system, though not all the positions may be filled (Murdock 1949). The basic features of the relationship between each pair of positions are much the same in all human societies. For example between older and younger brothers there is a "relationship of playmates, developing into that of comrades; economic cooperation under leadership of elder; moderate responsibility of elder for instruction and discipline of younger" (Murdock, op. cit.). The family has some of the features of a formal organization—a set of positions, each associated with a role, including patterns of interaction with occupants of other positions. . . .

Unlike groups of friends, family members have tasks to perform. In primitive societies these are mainly the growing and preparation of food, the rearing and education of children, and maintenance of the house. In modern society some of these activities are performed by outside agencies, but there are still the domestic jobs connected with eating, sleeping, and the care of young children. In addition there are leisure activities such as TV, gardening, games, and family outings. Some of these are like activities of friends in that they are performed because of the interaction involved. Interaction in the family is closely connected with these joint activities—eating, watching, or playing together. Interaction is also brought about through the members pursuing their private goals under conditions of physical proximity, and where their joint activities have to be more or less closely coordinated—this is an extension of the necessity for meshing. The physical environment and technology have an important effect on family life. Overcrowding of other animals results in aggression, and the murder rate is greater in overcrowded areas (Henry and Short 1954). The family tasks include looking after one another, in particular caring for the bodily needs of members: in addition to close physical proximity there is also intimacy and interdependence. . . .

What goes on inside the family is private and not readily subject to external control. Models of how families should behave are, however, provided by magazines and TV, and by the previous families of the parents. The actual elements of interaction of which family life consists differ from all other groups, in that greater intimacy, aggression, affection, and emotional violence occurs. Family members see each other undressed, or naked, and there is almost no attempt at self-presentation; they know each other's weaknesses and understand each other extremely well; family life is very much "off-stage," in Goffman's terminology (1956). There is physical aggression, mainly of parents toward children, but also between children; there is aggression between parents, but it is mainly verbal. Affection is equally violent and often takes the form of bodily contact, between parents, and between parents and children until they "get too old for it." Members of laboratory groups do not usually take their clothes off, laugh uproariously, cry, attack or kiss each other, or crawl all over each other, as members of families commonly do. Interaction in the family is more complex and subtle than most other interaction because of the intense and complex relationships between members, and their long history of previous interaction. Spiegel (1956) describes cases of tense mother-daughter interaction, and suggests that various unconscious fantasies and projections are taking place in addition to what seems to be occurring. This is similar to the interpersonal behavior found in some neurotics. The subtler nonverbal communications may be very important—as in the possible effect of "double-bind" parents in making children schizophrenic. The dimensions of parent behavior which have the greatest effect on children, however, are probably warmth *v.* rejection, strictness *v.* permissiveness, and type of discipline (Sears, Maccoby, & Levin 1957). . . .

Adolescent Groups

Friendship groups are one of the basic forms of social grouping in animals and men; they are distinguished by the fact that members are brought together primarily through interpersonal motivations and attractions, not through concern with any task. Of all friendship groups, adolescent groups are the most interesting. During adolescence work and family attachments are weak and the strongest attachments are to friends. These groups are formed of young people between the ages of eleven and twelve up to twenty-one to twenty-three, when the members marry and settle down in jobs, and other kinds of groups become more important to them.

The motivations of members are partly to engage in various joint activities, but more important are interpersonal needs—sexual, affiliative, and the establishment of identity. It has been suggested that there are certain "developmental tasks" during this period of life to develop an identity independent of the family, and to establish a changed relation with adults (Erikson 1956; Muuss 1962). . . .

The activities of adolescent groups vary with the culture: in the USA groups of boys are concerned with cars, entertainment, sports, and girls (Sherif and Sherif 1964). There is avoidance of the tasks of home and school. Many group activities are invented, whose chief point is the social interaction involved—such as dancing, listening to records, and drinking coffee. The forms of social interaction involved are rather different from those in other groups—there is more bodily contact, joking, aggressive horseplay, and just being together, less problem-centered discussion. Schmuck and Lohman (1965) observe that "adolescents in a group often engage in infantile behaviour and pranks, while giggling and laughing hilariously: and are encouraged to feel silly together, and to withhold evaluation from such experiences" (27). They suggest that this behavioural abandon has a regressive element. There is an easy intimacy and social acceptance of those who wear the right uniform. Conversation is mainly about other adolescents, parents, interpersonal feelings, and social interaction. These are probably the only natural groups that discuss social interaction (T-groups do it too). Such topics are discussed because adolescents have problems to solve in this area—as well as working out an identity and establishing a changed relationship with adults, they have to acquire the social skills of dealing with the opposite sex, to come to terms with the difficulty of playing different roles on different occasions, and having relationships of different degrees of intimacy with different people (Fleming 1963).

Adolescent groups are of interest to us because a number of special processes can be seen, which are not present in laboratory groups. (1) There is no specific task, but joint activities are devised which entail the kinds of interaction which meet the needs of members. (2) One of these needs is the establishing of an ego-identity, independent of the family of origin (Erikson 1956). This explains the emphasis on clothes, the great self-consciousness, and the concern about acceptance by members of these groups. (3) Sexual motivation is a major factor in adolescent groups, and is partly responsible for the intensity of attraction to the groups, and for their pairing structure. (4) There is a group task of acquiring together the social skills of dealing with the opposite sex and dealing with adults.

Work Groups

In groups of animals the work of gathering food and building homes is often carried out by males. In ants it is a specialized and highly organized group activity. In primitive society this work may be carried out by males or females, and follows a seasonal cycle. In modern communities work outside the home has become a highly specialized activity, mainly performed by adult males, for financial reward, and is done in special social organizations. Work is performed in groups for several reasons—(1) One man alone may not be able to perform the task; in primitive societies this is the case with hunting and building; (2) there can be division of labor, so that different people can use or develop specialized skills; this is a central feature of work in modern communities; (3) people prefer to work together because of their social motivations; (4) another factor is social facilitation; the presence of others is arousing, so more work is done. Even ants work harder when there is more than one of them on the job (Zajonc 1963).

Work groups are at the opposite pole from adolescent groups in that their primary concern is with carrying out a task. They are the other main kind of group outside the family in which adults spend most of their time. They are not so well defined as the other two kinds, and often have no clear membership. It is sometimes difficult, in a factory for example, to decide which are the group—all that can be seen are a lot of people, some of whom collaborate over work or interact informally from time to time. Such groups can be defined in terms of the formal organization—having the same supervisor or being paid jointly, or in terms of informal group-formation—sociometric cliques, or people who think of themselves as a group. Much research in this area has been on groups of manual workers—gangs of men engaged in the maintenance of railway track, men on assembly lines. There has also been research on the more technically skilled men in charge of automated plants, and recently attention has turned to the work of engineers, accountants, scientists, and managers. In these latter cases much of the social interaction is between people two at a time, so there is a network rather than a group. They may also meet in committees and similar talking and decision-making groups, which will be discussed separately in the following section. In this section we are concerned with groups which have a definite task to do, and where the social interaction arises out of the task activity. . . .

What form does interaction take in work groups? In the first place the task performance may partly consist of interaction. If A passes a brick to B, this is both task behavior and interaction; if A likes B, more bricks will be passed (Van Zelst 1952). He will pass them with accompanying verbal and nonverbal signals, not strictly necessary for the task, but which sustain the social relationship. If A talks to B, where B is his supervisor or colleague, it is impossible to disentangle the task and the informal interaction elements of the conversation. Much work in fact consists almost entirely of social interaction—the work of supervisors, interviewers, teachers, and many others. In addition to interaction linked to the task, interaction may take place during coffee breaks, in the lunch hour, after hours, and during unauthorized pauses from work. Nonverbal communication, such as gestures, may occur during the work process. Social interaction of the usual kind is perhaps more limited in work groups than in groups of other kinds. The relationships established may only operate in the work situation—as when good working relations exist between members of different racial and social class groups. Only part of the personality is involved, but it is an important part, and work relations can be very important to people. Friendships are made at work, especially between people of equal status in the organization; many of the links joining family members to the outside world are made in the work situation. Relationships at work may also, on occasion, resemble the relaxed informality of the family. This is most common among young people, who know each other very well and have shared emotional experiences. Life in the services has something of this quality. There is often considerable intensity of feeling in work groups, because the economic position, the career, the self-image, and sometimes the safety of members is at stake. . . .

What special interaction processes are found in work groups? (1) Interaction arises out of cooperation and communication over task activity, and can be regarded as a secondary or informal system that sustains working relationships and satisfies interpersonal needs. (2) Social relationships at work differ from those in the family or in adolescent groups in that they are based on concern for the task, tend to be less permanent and less intimate, and often do not operate outside the work situation. (3) The boundaries of work groups are vague, and these groups may in fact consist of networks. (4) In addition to one or more informal leaders, there may be a leader of the opposition.

Committees, Problem-Solving, and Creative Groups

This kind of group does its work entirely by talking, and consequently is not found in any species apart from man. Committees are concerned with making decisions and solving problems; there are other kinds of working groups, for example groups of research workers, who are more concerned with the creative solution of problems. There is no sharp division between the two kinds of group.

Committees are small groups of a rather special kind; while their devotion to problem solving and their degree of formality make them different from other groups, these features are found to some extent in most other groups too. . . .

Interaction in committees is unlike interaction in most other groups. It is primarily verbal; furthermore it consists of a number of carefully delivered utterances, in the formal mode of speech. The twelve categories of the Bales system (Bales 1950) were devised to record interaction in groups of this kind. As well as pure task categories—asking for and giving opinions and suggestions, it includes socioemotional categories—agreeing and disagreeing, showing tension, showing antagonism, and solidarity. As with work groups, interpersonal relations are established and maintained during the execution of the task. There is considerable use of nonverbal signals. To speak it may be necessary to catch the chairman's eye, and the regulation of who speaks and for how long is achieved by eye-movements, headnods, and smiles. Comments on what A is saying may be indicated by B's facial and gestural signals; these may be directed to A, or to another listener C. When the nonverbal channel proves inadequate, written messages may be passed along the table. To be an effective committee member requires special skills. These include squaring other people before the meeting, studying the papers before the meeting, and the usual social skills of persuasion and handling groups. There also appear to be skills unique to committees: a member should not seem to be emotionally involved with an issue, but be concerned with what will be acceptable to the others. A chairman should do his or her best to come to solutions which are acceptable to all members, rather than coming to majority decisions.

The activities of a committee are problem solving and decision making. These terms refer to two different elements—arriving at new solutions to problems, and coming to agreements. These are rather different matters which are, however, closely bound up together in committee work. Coming to an agreement has . . . been considered in connection with conformity; each agenda item produces in miniature a norm-formation situation. The item will be more or less closely related to more general norms held by the group, and to issues on which subgroups have their own views. The problem-solving process can be divided into two stages—information exchange and the study of hypotheses. Thibaut and Kelley (1959) discuss the conditions under which information is offered and accepted in groups, and what happens when the information is complementary, conflicting, or simply heterogeneous. A number of experiments have been carried out in which the task of the group consists of putting together information related in these ways. In real committees this is certainly part of the story, but information exchange is usually followed by the study of suggestions and is affected by conformity processes. There is a great deal of experimental work in this area, of which one sample will be given. Freedman and Sears (1965), reviewing experiments by themselves and others, show that people do *not* just seek information that supports their existing views, as dissonance theory would seem to predict, but actually want to find out the facts. Thibaut and Kelley (op. cit.) argue that both individuals and groups start to engage in problem-solving activity when they think that they may be able to deal with the external world to better advantage. . . .

T-Groups and Therapy Groups

Finally we turn to a kind of group which did not exist until psychologists invented it. Just as physicists study particles created by special experimental techniques so it is of interest to study the forms social interaction *can* take under quite new conditions. In fact the processes of feedback and analysis of the group found in this setting also take place, although with less intensity, in other groups too. On the other hand these groups are very different from natural groups in a number of ways, so that the findings cannot simply be generalized to other kinds of group. There has been a certain shift of interest away from laboratory groups toward T-groups (cf. Mann et al. 1967), simply because the latter last longer and can be studied in greater detail. Apart from the limited generality of the findings it should be pointed out that most of these studies are essentially clinical investigations of a rather small number of groups (cf. Stock 1964).

In most T-groups, about twelve trainees meet with a trainer for a number of two-hour sessions; they may meet once a week, or more frequently for up to two weeks. The Harvard version has twenty to thirty members. The leader introduces himself, explains that he is there to help the members study the group, and then takes a passive role and leaves the group to get on with this task as best it can. From time to time he will intervene in various ways: (1) he shows how to make constructive and nonevaluative comments on the behavior of members; (2) he shows how to receive such comments non-defensively, and learn from them; (3) he makes interpretations, i.e., explains what he thinks is happening, interpersonally, in the group; (4) he discusses the relevance and application of the group experiences to behavior in real-life situations; (5) he tries to teach the members a more cooperative and less authoritarian attitude to people in authority. In addition to the T-group sessions proper there are sometimes lectures, role-playing, and other ancillary training experiences (cf. Bradford, Gibb, & Benne 1964).

Therapy groups consist of a psychiatrist and usually six to nine mental patients. The main differences from T-groups are that: (1) the members are emotionally disturbed and at a lower level of social competence, often suffering from real interpersonal difficulties; (2) the content of conversation is the actual symptoms or difficulties of group members; (3) the therapist creates an atmosphere of acceptance for sexual and aggressive material, but makes sure that the tension level does not get too high; (4) there is a greater gap between leader and group members—the former is not simply a more experienced member of the group; (5) the behavior of members in the group situation is used to diagnose basic personality disturbances, rather than indicating their level of social competence (Powdermaker & Frank 1953; Foulkes & Anthony 1957). . . .

The "task" of T-groups, like that of committees, consists of conversation, and is difficult to separate from "interaction." However, some kinds of conversation are regarded as more relevant to the task—conversation which is concerned with the interaction and relationships of members of the group, and about the symptoms of members of therapy groups. The goal to be attained is insight and understanding of group processes and emotional problems respectively. An important sub-goal is the formation of a sufficiently cohesive group for this understanding to develop in the group setting—for example, the internal and external goals are closely intertwined (Tuckman 1965). Unlike committees, however, these groups have no agenda, and proceed in a largely undirected and rambling manner, the leader taking whatever opportunities he can for explaining various phenomena. The content of the conversation is most unusual; language in the natural world is usually about external matters and other people, rather than about relations between speaker and hearer, or about embarrassing personal matters. This kind of task is emotionally arousing and awkward, and for these reasons is often avoided in periods of "flight" from the task—by making jokes, talking about other matters, and silence. . . .

The social interaction in T-groups can be thought of as including the task activity. Various classification schemes have been devised to deal with it, which between them provide some account of the forms interaction takes. . . . It should be added that the general atmosphere and flow of interaction are very different in these groups from those in the other groups which we have considered. While committees are formal, and groups of adolescents are relaxed and intimate, T-groups and therapy groups are tense and awkward. Both T-group and therapy group practitioners maintain that some degree of emotionality is necessary for any fundamental changes of behavior to occur. Interaction sequences are reported in these groups which may be unique to them, for example: (a) an intensification of the process of becoming aware of the self-image from the reactions of others—which are here unusually frank and uninhibited; (b) obtaining insight into oneself through the close observation and study of another person with similar attributes or problems; (c) the "condenser" phenomenon, in which interaction loosens group resistances, and common emotions, normally repressed, are suddenly released (Foulkes & Anthony 1957). . . .

References

Bales, R.F. (1950). *Interaction Process Analysis.* Cambridge, MA: Addison-Wesley.

Bradford, L.P., Gibb, J.R., and Benne, K.D. (1964). *T-Group Theory and Laboratory Method.* New York: Wiley.

Erikson, E.H. (1956). "The Problem of Ego-Identity." *American Journal of Psychoanalysis* 4, 56–121.

Fleming, C.M. (1963). *Adolescence.* London: Routledge & Kegan Paul.

Foulkes, S.H., and Anthony, E.J. (1957). *Group Psychotherapy: The Psychoanalytic Approach.* London: Penguin.

Freedman, J.L., and Sears, D.O. (1965). "Selective Exposure." In L. Berkowitz (ed.), *Advances in Experimental Social Psychology* 2. New York: Academic Press.

Goffman, E. (1956). *The Presentation of Self in Everyday Life.* Edinburgh: Edinburgh University Press.

Henry, A.F., and Short, J.F. (1954). *Suicide and Homicide.* Glencoe, IL: Free Press.

Mann, R.D., et al. (1967). *Interpersonal Styles and Group Development.* New York: Wiley.

Murdock, G.P. (1949). *Social Structure.* New York: Macmillan.

Muuss, R.E. (1962). *Theories of Adolescence.* New York: Random House.

Parsons, T., and Bales, R.F. (1955). *Family, Socialization, and Interaction Process*. Glencoe, IL: Free Press.

Powdermaker, F.B., and Frank, J.D. (1953). *Group Psychotherapy*. Cambridge, MA: Harvard University Press.

Schmuck, R., and Lohman, A. (1965). "Peer Relations and Personality Development." Institute for Social Research, University of Michigan, Ann Arbor, MI. Unpublished manuscript.

Sears, R.R., Maccoby, E.E., and Levin, H. (1957). *Patterns of Child Rearing*. Peterson, New York: Row.

Sherif, M., and Sherif, C.W. (1964). *Reference Groups*. New York: Harper.

Spiegel, J.P. (1956). "Interpersonal Influences Within the Family." In B. Schaffner (ed.), *Group Processes*. New York: Josiah Macy Foundation.

Stock, D. (1964). "A Survey of Research on T-Groups." In L.P. Bradford, J.R. Gibb, and K.D. Benne (eds.), *T-Group Theory and Laboratory Method*. New York: Wiley.

Thibaut, J.W., and Kelley, H.H. (1959). *The Social Psychology of Groups*. New York: Wiley.

Tuckman, B.W. (1965). "Developmental Sequence in Small Groups." *Psychological Bulletin* 63, 384–399.

Van Zelst, R.H. (1952). "Validation of a Sociometric Regrouping Procedure." *Journal of Abnormal and Social Psychology* 47, 299–301.

Zajonc, R.B. (1963). "Social Facilitation." *Science* 149, 269–274.

The Rock, Egg, and Chicken: Metaphorical Perspectives on the Concept of a Group

Ann Margaret Trautlein

Sociological, social psychological, and communication literature abounds with attempts to define the concept "group." There is no universal agreement on a definition of groups, however, nor will there likely ever be. Still, attempts to devise a single, general definition continue. The pursuit of this end has provided us with increasing insight into the elements, behaviors, structures, characteristics, and perceptions of groups, but the core concept remains unclear. If it were unimportant, the lack of an agreed upon definition would not be especially problematic. However, thought and research concerning groups have progressed, and, if anything, our concern with groups has grown greater.

This essay presents a brief overview of the complex and ever-changing views relating to the elements of a group, samples definitions of "group," and distinguishes among various social entities often designated by the single label of "group." On the basis of recently published literature, I also characterize the type of entity one usually has in mind when he or she refers to a "group."

When I first became concerned about the characteristics of groups, I thought to myself, "What problems have I encountered in existing definitions of a group that prompt me to offer a revision?" I felt uncomfortable with the concept, but was not sure what exactly contributed to that discomfort. To answer the question, I looked to an essay by Charles S. Palazzolo I had read recently, entitled "The Social Group: Definitions."

Palazzolo reviews several conceptions of groups that illustrate the difficulty in settling on a uniform view of what a "group" is. Homans identifies the need for communicating among a number of people as critical. Specifically, a group is "a number of persons who communicate often with one another over a span of time, and who are few enough so that each person is able to communicate with all the others, not at a second hand, through other people, but face to face" (1). This definition falls short of being universal because it requires face-to-face interaction. Modern technology has made this requirement obsolete with the advent of electronic conferencing (Johansen, Vallee, and Spangler, 151).

Another conception to which Palazzolo points portrays a group as a structured collectivity of individuals who enact reciprocal roles and pursue common goals on the basis of norms, interests, and values (6). This concept of role reciprocity is valuable because it replaces Homans's "face-to-face" requirement with the more crucial element of interaction in a group. However, the definition falls short of being universally applicable because it imposes pursuit of common goals as a necessary condition. We have each found in our own daily lives, however, that we can work with others as group members, experience deep satisfaction, and possibly not even be aware of one another's goals.

From A.M. Trautlein, "The Rock, Egg, and Chicken," in *The Pennsylvania Speech Communication Annual*, vol. XLVII, pp. 75–86, 1991. Reprinted by permission of the editor.

Some conceptions of groups view them as systems of interaction that range from "barely organized" to "highly organized" and vary in extensiveness of interests, duration, and direction of interaction (Palazzolo, 6). Representative of this point of view are McDavid and Harari, who define a group as an "organized system of two or more individuals who are interrelated so that the system performs some function . . ." (237). This seems closer to the essential nature of groups as people participate in them.

Sprott conceives of a group as a "plurality of persons interacting in a given context more than they do with any one else" (9). I found this definition to be unbearably empty, yet it produced the following questions: "Is this existence, then, perceived, and if so, when, and by whom?" Apparently, identification is not essential from this perspective.

Like Sprott, others have attempted to define groups in terms of a single distinguishing characteristic. Bass, for instance, defines a group as a "collection of individuals whose existence as a collection is rewarding to the individuals" (39). Mills, conceives of groups in terms of commonality of purpose. Specifically, groups are "units composed of two or more persons who come into contact for a purpose and who consider that contact meaningful." All such efforts to limit definitions suffer from the fact that we can identify collections of people who lack the essential defining characteristic, but whom we nevertheless regard as constituting a group.

As a final illustration, Shaw defines a group as consisting of "two or more persons who are interacting with one another in such a manner that each person influences and is influenced by each other person" (8). Often the most parsimonious definition is the best. Upon closer scrutiny, however, Shaw's definition is quite complex. It incorporates the concept of interaction as a living system when joining the notions of influencing and being influenced. It describes communication as the systematic process I believe it is and that sets "groups" in the most meaningful sense of the term apart from other collections of individuals.

After forming some opinions on the subject of groups and developing thoughts on what the concept meant to me, I reflected on a past discussion in which I had participated. The central question was: "What is a group?" Opinions swayed back and forth for quite some time. Eventually, all agreed that a committee was a "group," that a team was a "group," and that people at a dinner party were a "group." Then one member asked whether several people standing in line constituted a group. The answer that seemed to emerge was: "They are a group, but they aren't a *group*." That did not quite clear things up for most of us, and in applying various characteristics with which we were familiar, we discovered numerous inadequacies and became more perplexed by the difficulty of saying precisely what we meant by a "group."

Luckily, we went on to other topics, but the issue remained unresolved in my mind. It frustrated me that I, as a speech communication major, could not articulate what I seem to know in my heart. I was so sure of myself, yet the best clarification I could muster was that those standing in line were like a group, but they weren't a *group*. Why do we call them a group if they aren't? I share that basic human need to find order in disorder and organization where no organization seems present, and I failed to find a definitive answer to my exact question.

At first I hoped not to become so involved, but rather simply to come up with other names for collections of people and, thereby, to end the confusion. But that has already been done. There are items like clusters, lists, packets of, cartons of, packs of, closets full, decks of, racks of, communities, clubs, alliances, societies, organizations, constituencies, families, associations, teams, gangs, memberships, branches, sections, committees, forces, leagues, parties, clans, congregations, etc. As one can see, the list goes on and on and fails to satisfy the question of what is distinctive about a group. Therefore, I resolved to formulate my own concept.

My purpose was to pinpoint what I think is assumed, but has never been made explicit, thus leaving us without a clear conception of groups. The problem is that we use the same label to apply to distinctly different entities. The solution, however, is not to find different labels, but to understand the differences and to recognize that no single definition will adequately reflect them. In attempting to make this point, I have found a metaphorical perspective helpful.

The metaphors of "rock," "egg," and "chicken" are useful for understanding three types of social entities to which we commonly apply the label *group*. The "Rock Group" is a nominal collection of two or more of anything, including human beings. Its members share at least one characteristic. An identical, similar, interchangeable or equivalent feature, such as color, shape, composition, purpose, texture, size, or position, permits these objects to occupy the same category (Turner, 44). It can be observed by others, but cannot be perceived from within because the members, in and of themselves, either are not aware or capable of recognizing that they constitute an entity. Such perceptions are external to the members.

The constituents of such "groups" are merely classified as belonging together, but such a collection is static, and relationships among the members undergo no perceptible evolution. Examples of Rock Groups include inanimate objects like piles of rocks, jugs full of pennies, and packs of cigarettes. All of the above group types are predetermined, but not by any effort of their members. They are collections of objects only. Their conditions are set upon them.

Such collections can also consist of animate objects. People may constitute a group by virtue of some ascribed characteristic, such as race, gender, achievement, intelligence, and the like. When "grouped" in this way, they are no different from collections of inanimate objects. Membership is the only defining characteristic.

At this level, there is no element of cohesion in a group, for there is no necessary perception of one's relationship to the other members of the group in order for the person to be included. There is no degree of mutual interpersonal attraction binding these members together to result in even the slightest sense of cohesiveness or belongingness (Hogg, 91). The Rock Group has only a single element found in all groups. That one overriding characteristic, necessary for defining what a collection of individuals needs to be a Rock Group, is called "commonality" (Havelock & Sashkin, 359).

The second type of entity is what I call the "Egg Group." I call it such because this type of collection possesses all the necessary ingredients to evolve into a functioning social entity, but has not done so. This notion comes closer to what characterizes social groups. Like the chicken egg or the apple seed, the members of this group possess intrinsic properties that allow the group to change when external forces, or internal galvanized processes, are manifest. In other words, the Egg Group is a Chicken Group in the incipient stage.

Either the Egg Group has not had the inclination or opportunity to change and grow through external pressure or influence, or nothing within it has contributed to interpersonal attraction or the development of cohesion. The potential to become a chicken or a rooster lies within the genetic codes of the egg, but this does not assure that development will occur. Many temporary collections of individuals would seem to be in this position.

The Egg Group has the essential ingredient of the Rock Groups—commonality. The commonality may be reflected more in members' backgrounds, interests, circumstances, values, problems, or even needs, however (Havelock & Sashkin, 359). Examples of this type of group are people shopping in a grocery store, attending a movie, waiting for a bus, or sitting in a class listening to a lecture. The common elements allow for development. In the case of Rock Groups, they do not.

The Egg Group observes an established set of rules that indicate how something ought to be done or what is good and bad. These rules are formed to tell members what the group expects of them, if they are to remain in good standing, and are generally called "group norms" (Poole, 277). Norms are characteristically determined by what the collective society deems "common courtesies," such as forming lines in order of arrival at a certain position and waiting one's turn. When norms are violated, the violator is naturally seen as deviating by the other members, but, there is usually no consequence greater than a scowl or a dirty look.

This group has the potential to affect a deviant member in accordance with the law of effect. People tend to behave in ways that are reinforcing and avoid or withhold behaviors that are likely to be punished (Napier & Gershenfeld, 122). An individual might react specifically to the deviant, but the Egg Group's level of cohesiveness is either nonexistent, or so low that its members do not perceive it. The members do not think of themselves as a group: therefore, they do not take on behavior characteristic of groups whose members do. Nor are they likely to have the degree of interpersonal attraction and valuation of group membership that would prompt an effort to act as a unified entity. The obvious conclusion of these aforementioned assertions implies that a *group* is "a number of people who *think* they are a group and act like a group," which is the definition presented by Hearn (253). The generation of group behavior from this perspective "depends upon the affective dynamics of interpersonal attraction and the determinants of attraction thus become the antecedents of psychological group formation" (Hogg, 91).

The members of the Egg Group are not present because of any interpersonal attraction, nor do they have any real sense of cohesion. Cohesiveness is a product of forces acting on all the members to remain in the group (Festinger, 274). In this case, there are few such forces. Little cohesion exists because the individuals typically do not act in ways that contribute to group development, for example, discovering shared beliefs, attitudes, or values. The individuals are not aware of many commonalities that exist among them and do not seek out others like them. They are independent and pursue individual rather than collective goals. Even though several members may have the same goals, for instance, to withdraw cash, catch a bus to work, or to eat, in each case, the individual would be doing what he or she is whether others are present or not. The members merely happen to be engaged in the same activities for similar reasons at the same time.

"If the communicative behavior or even the mere presence of others makes a difference to you in some way, which leads to reciprocal behavior on your part which influences them, then in a rudimentary way you constitute a group" (Swogger, 65). This observation illustrates the notion that any behavioral action, coupled by a response from others present, can contribute to the creation of a group. The observation further implies that interaction among members is critical to the formation of a group. One could conclude, then, that if two or more people are consciously aware that their behavior is mutually influencing them, they begin to constitute a group, but only in the incipient stage.

Key elements of the Egg Group include the commonality found in the Rock Group and a mutuality of influence. One may even begin to notice the observance of emergent norms. These additional characteristics are a product of interaction. Swogger suggests that interaction exists when there is even the slightest degree of reciprocity, and when observed among individuals, it constitutes a degree of relatedness necessary for individuals to become a "real" group in one's sense of the term. Interaction is "the process in which an individual notices and responds to others who are noticing and responding to that individual" (Hearn, 263).

According to Poole, the very existence of a group depends on members' interactions. "If members stopped interacting (or never interacted) and broke off their relationships (or never initiated any) with one another, the group would cease to exist (or never form). It is a group in name only, and members do not identify with the group or feel accountable to each other" (277). As important as interaction is to the existence of the group, it alone is insufficient for understanding what a group is.

The third and final metaphorical perspective can be best illustrated by what I refer to as the "Chicken Group." The Egg Group has the intrinsic potential to transfigure itself into a unique entity. It harbors an "actualizing tendency, an inherent tendency of the organism to expand and develop itself' (Yacom, 57). The Egg Group, in contrast, has not utilized, employed, or required any dependency on other members of its group. When those constituting an Egg Group finally realize a collective need, then they may begin to evolve into what most people appear to have in mind when they refer to a group.

The Chicken Group possesses all aspects of the first two types. It possesses the element of commonality, it adopts and creates rules and norms, and its members interact with one another by some physical means, such as face-to-face communication, audio-visual technology, computer, fax machine, or even conventional mail. They may perform any number of different tasks as a result of common interests and needs among the members. Behavior of the members is characterized by collective action.

The Chicken Group has organization, which implies "a complex hierarchical structure with flexible functioning and a memory" (Hutten, 151). When an individual joins a group, he or she vastly enriches the information structure. The Chicken Group has "an evolutionary need for increased integration for improving its capabilities and capacities, thus bringing dynamic growth and development about" (Hutten, 156).

The collection of individuals who constitute the Chicken Group achieve a "wholeness" among very different "parts." Members are complementary. They value their "parts" in the "whole" because: (1) they like the other members; (2) the group can manage problems not reasonable without it; or (3) the group offers a means for satisfying members' personal needs (Napier & Gershenfeld, 80). Therefore, when we think of a group, we implicitly accept the Gestalt assumption with the "wholeness of the group, despite what may be very different 'parts,' reflects the interdependence of those 'parts'" (Hogg, 92).

"Groups of individuals become a system, and distinguish themselves from other groups, as they develop a shared pattern or relatedness and a set of norms" (Swogger, 65). The members who comprise the Chicken Group develop rules and patterns of communication that make certain modes of conduct and ways of thinking acceptable or unacceptable (Swogger, 67). As a result of these shared rules and concomitant patterns of communication, groups develop unique jargon, taboos, etc. (Swogger, 67). In fact, the group becomes a culture and thereby is distinguishable as a unique social entity.

From this perspective, a group is a continually evolving social system, in which members pool resources to satisfy needs they have in common (Havelock & Sashkin, 359). Their transformation is observable and can be described (Swogger, 65). Structuration of the system (group), or "the production and reproduction of the social systems through members' use of rules and resources in interaction" (Poole, 277), serves as a kind of "filtering mechanism" (Havelock & Sashkin, 360) that contributes to the ever-changing characteristics of groups and the relationships among their members.

The emergent structuration implies that: (1) interaction and relationships are primary constituents of the group system; (2) structures are the "tools" used to create and maintain the system; (3) these structures are produced and reproduced; and (4) a member's influence in the process of structuration is limited by external factors and the actions of other members (Poole, 277–279).

I hope that this essay has brought greater conceptual clarity to the ongoing discussion of what a group is. The Rock, Egg, and Chicken are metaphors for different facets of "groupness" and are useful for separating collections of individuals to whom the label *group* can apply, but who are nonetheless distinctly different types of entities. The Rock Group is defined by a simple overriding characteristic of commonality. An Egg Group also has the characteristic of commonality, but its members show signs of developing and altering norms, as well as possessing the ability and potential to transform themselves into a more complex entity. Finally, the Chicken Group encompasses all related aspects of the first two categories, but has a hierarchical structure that affects patterns of interaction among members and, thereby, their relationships, their attitudes, values, and beliefs, and the manner in which they collectively act. It is this dynamic interplay between structure and interaction that give a group its sense of self and distinctiveness and what causes most of us to think of the collection of individuals as a group.

The metaphorical perspectives may appear to be simplistic, but they serve the functions of categorizing and delineating the range of concepts that are often confused under the single heading of *group*. Using the Rock, Egg, and Chicken as metaphors, one can more readily decipher the level of groupness he or she is observing, or is a part of, and begin to think of different types of entities called groups in more meaningful and discriminating terms.

References

Bass, B.M. (1960). *Leadership, Psychology, and Organizational Behavior.* New York: Harper & Row.
Festinger, L. (1950). "Informal Social Communication." *Psychological Review* 57, 271–282.

Havelock, R.G., and Sashkin, M. (1983). "HELP SCORES: A Guide to Promoting Change in Groups and Organizations." In H.H. Blumberg, A.P. Hare, V. Kent, and M.F. Davies (eds.), *Small Groups and Social Interaction* 2, 357–369. New York: John Wiley & Sons.

Hearn, G. (1979). "Small Group Behavior and Development: A Selective Bibliography." In J.E. Jones and J.W. Pfeiffer (eds.), *The 1979 Annual Handbook for Group Facilitators,* 252–269. San Diego: University Associates Publishers.

Hogg, M.C. (1987). "Social Identity and Group Cohesiveness." In J.C. Turner (ed.), *Rediscovering the Social Group: A Self Categorization Theory,* 89–116. New York: Basil Blackwell, Ltd.

Homans, G.C. (1950). *The Human Group.* New York: Harcourt, Brace & World.

Hutten, E.H. "Meaning and Information in the Group Process." In M. Pines (ed.), *The Evolution of Group Analysis,* 151–166. Boston: Routledge & Kegan Paul.

Johansen, R., Vallee, J., and Spangler, K. (1988). "Teleconferencing: Electronic Group Meetings." In R.S. Cathcart and L.A. Samovar (eds.), *Small Group Communication: A Reader* 5th ed., 140–154, Dubuque, IA: Wm. C. Brown.

McDavid, J.W., and Harari, H. (1968). *Social Psychology: Individuals, Groups, and Societies.* New York: Harper & Row.

Mills, T. (1967). *The Sociology of Small Groups.* Englewood Cliffs, NJ: Prentice-Hall.

Napier, R.W., and Gershenfeld, M.K. (1985). *Groups: Theory and Experience* 3rd ed., Boston: Houghton Mifflin Company.

Palazzolo, C.S. (1988). "The Social Group: Definitions." In R.S. Cathcart and L.A. Samovar (eds.), *Small Group Communication: A Reader* 5th ed., 6–19, Dubuque, IA: Wm. C. Brown.

Poole, M.S. (1988). "Group Communication and the Structuring Process." In R.S. Cathcart and L.A. Samovar (eds.), *Small Group Communication: A Reader* 5th ed., 275–287, Dubuque, IA: Wm. C. Brown.

Shaw, M.E. (1981). *Group Dynamics: The Psychology of Small Group Behavior* 3rd ed. New York: McGraw-Hill.

Sprott, W.J.H. (1958). *Human Groups.* Baltimore, MD: Penguin Books.

Swogger, Jr., G. (1981). "Human Communication and Group Experience." In J.E. Durkin (ed.), *Living Groups: Group Psychotherapy and General System Theory,* 63–78. N.Y.: Brunner/Mazel.

Turner, J.C. (1987). *Rediscovering the Social Group: A Self Categorization Theory.* N.Y.: Basil Blackwell, Inc.

Yacom, I.D. (1985). *The Theory and Practice of Group Psychotherapy.* N.Y.: Basic Books, Inc.

ACTIVITIES

Activity 1

Purpose: The purpose of this assignment is to introduce the idea of supportive and nonsupportive behaviors within a small group.

Procedure: In small groups develop a list of supportive behaviors and another list of nonsupportive behaviors.

SUPPORTIVE BEHAVIORS: (Example: Head nodding)

1.

2.

3.

4.

5.

6.

7.

8.

NONSUPPORTIVE BEHAVIORS: (Example: Saying "That is a dumb idea.")

1.

2.

3.

4.

5.

6.

7.

8.

Activity 2

Purpose: The purpose of this exercise is to allow students to examine the preconceived ideas that they have about small group process.

Procedure: The class is divided into groups of three to five. Each individual writes "D" (disagree) or "A" (agree) beside each statement. After the individuals react to each statement, the group tries to come to a consensus. Reaching a consensus implies that decisions are made by agreement, not by vote.

1. There are times when a group member should be "fired."

2. Group decision making is superior to other decision-making processes.

3. A strong leader will cause individuals to feel that they can express themselves more openly than they would in a leaderless group.

4. Sometimes an individual's withdrawal from the group will help the group process.

5. There are times in groups when democratic methods must be abandoned in order to solve practical problems.

6. Sometimes it is necessary to try to change people, even when they object.

7. There are occasions when an individual who is part of a decision-making group should do what he or she thinks is right, regardless of what the group decides.

8. Each person in a group should try to contribute to the group task, even if he or she feels the contributions are not important.

9. As long as the group task is accomplished, it matters little how the group members feel about how well they work together.

10. When a group member knows how to solve the group's problem, the individual should "take over" the group.

Activity 3

Purpose: The purpose of this activity is to highlight positive communication behaviors that can influence group interaction.

Procedure: In small groups, make up an "ideal" culture. Concentrate on the following two categories: (1) the values of the "ideal" culture; and (2) the communication patterns of the "ideal" culture.

VALUES: (Example: Cooperation)

1.

2.

3.

4.

5.

6.

COMMUNICATION PATTERNS: (Example: Accurate feedback)

1.

2.

3.

4.

5.

6.

Activity 4

Purpose: The purpose of this activity is to help people in the class identify their individual communication style when they are a member of a group.

Procedure: Each member of the class will answer the following questions and give the responses (in writing) to the instructor.

When I am a member of a group:

1. Do I give people my full attention?

2. Do I seem at ease or tense?

3. Do I often change the subject without taking the other person into consideration?

4. Do I deprecate the statements of others?

5. Do I smile often?

6. Do I interrupt repeatedly?

7. Do I show sympathy when someone has a problem?

8. Do my actions tend to lower the other person's self-esteem?

9. Do I sit in a manner that demonstrates interest in the person and topic?

Activity 5

Purpose: The purpose of this activity is to imagine how other members of the class might perceive you when you are a member of a small group.

Procedure: Each person should prepare two lists. The first list should contain *ten cultural characteristics* that you believe others would use to describe you. The second should list *ten individual characteristics* that you believe others would use to describe you.

CULTURAL CHARACTERISTICS

1.
2.
3.
4.
5.
6.
7.
8.
9.
10.

INDIVIDUAL CHARACTERISTICS

1.
2.
3.
4.
5.
6.
7.
8.
9.
10.

After the preparation of the two lists, members of the class should share their findings.

2
How Groups Are Organized

Examining how and why groups organize focuses attention on a simple premise: Communication *does not* take place in a vacuum. The individual and the setting combine to create the communication event. The various environments that place us in the company of others underscore the inseparable link that exists between people and places. Most of us have learned that small groups are often the most effective means of accomplishing a wide range of professional and personal tasks, goals, and needs. Most professions, organizations, and institutions utilize small groups to help achieve objectives, solve problems, work out rules, create agreements, build rapport, and establish policy. The personalities, climate, and purpose will vary with each group, but the principle remains consistent: individuals are motivated to join others who have similar concerns.

Individuals in Groups

Why is an understanding of the individual's behavior significant to an examination of group process? The study of the individual in relation to group life has developed at an ever-increasing pace since early in this century when John Dewey, an American philosopher and educator, recognized that the child cannot be truly educated apart from the groups that form the immediate world and when psychologist Floyd Allport found that an individual's behavior is always influenced by the groups to which the subject belongs. Discovering how the individual personalities of the group members impact the group's structure, work, and cohesion offers some insight into how and why groups form the way they do.

The social psychologists of this century brought people into the laboratory and developed the techniques of scientific research and statistical measurement, which eventually led to the experimental study of human groups. Some of these investigations dealt generally with different personalities in group situations. Realizing the significance of recognizing personality differences, and the influence that this mixture can have on group climate and structure, helps to understand why groups vary in their effectiveness.

Administering personality tests such as the Myers-Briggs Type Indicator (MBTI), the DISC Personal Profile System, and the Team Management Index (TMI) has become a popular way of predicting what is likely to occur when different types of people come together. The MGTI is an instrument that can be used to determine whether people tend to be extroverted or introverted, sensing or intuitive, feeling or thinking, perceiving or judging. Each of these characteristics can be beneficial to a group's productivity; therefore, ideal groups are comprised of individuals who, to some degree, collectively exhibit each of these eight traits. However, some combinations of traits can detract from group effectiveness when they cause clashes and conflict among the individuals.

The DISC measures dominance, influence, steadiness, and conscientiousness. The purpose of this instrument is to help individuals understand their own personal work styles and to increase appreciation of other work styles. Knowledge of different styles, therefore, can help to identify and minimize potential conflicts with others.

Another tool, TMI, focuses more directly on behaviors that are likely to be related to professional groups: relationships issues, information gathering, decision making, and organizational techniques. These specific work-related behaviors can be grouped under more general orientations than the MBTI identifies. Tests such as the MBTI, the DISC, and the TMI may not provide infallible data for predicting group performance, but they do, at least, provide an awareness that different combinations of traits will alter interaction patterns, and the information gleaned from them can help leaders make more informed decisions about group composition.

Group Climate

Although members of a group continue to function as individuals, the process of group formation and structuring causes the collection of individuals to form a new entity with a new, unique identity. Groups do not consist of mindless individuals all conforming to some preordained path to group consensus. Rather, individuals in groups are continually structuring their groups through their communication behaviors. All groups, no matter how stable they appear, are continually being produced and reproduced by members' communication interactions, a process that is shaped by both internal and external factors.

The **type** of group that is formed will affect group climate and interaction. We can be members of many groups simultaneously. Our family and friends make up our **personal groups,** and the associations that we form at work are usually classified as **professional groups.** The most basic way to identify **professional groups** is to distinguish between **formal** and **informal** groups in the organization. Organizations often create **formal groups** to direct members toward some important goal. These groups may be voluntary or obligatory. Usually these work groups will be influenced by a **chain of command**—an organization's rules regarding who reports to whom. The command structure that forms in this kind of formal group is significant to problem solving, use of power, and protocol. The formality of the group and its organization can differ significantly, but generally speaking, a clearly defined command structure will help to facilitate **task** accomplishment.

Informal groups, on the other hand, lack the well-defined, systematic approach of formal groups. Informal groups form when people establish friendships and social networks. Often, the same cluster of individuals will choose to eat lunch together, share break time, or meet for happy hour; through these social interactions an informal group will develop.

The Group's Purpose

The group's task, or its **goal** will play a role in how the group forms, and the group that forms, in turn, will impact goal accomplishment. Individual members sometimes create their own personal goals or **hidden agendas** that are at cross-purposes with the group's goal, but not without the group's effectiveness suffering. For example, participants may decide to draw attention to themselves by monopolizing discussion or by attempting to address personal concerns rather than the group's concerns. A member might even want the group to fail and try to sabotage the group's efforts.

On the other hand, when members agree to direct their attention to a mutually accepted course of action, achievement of the goal becomes more likely. The group's goal is its purpose or guide for action; it is the motivation for individuals to cooperate to accomplish their objective. Groups function best when each person understands the task, finds it desirable and challenging, and agrees on the importance and probability of its completion. Clear, concrete, and specific language helps group members to concentrate their efforts.

Organizations often have special **task groups** when individuals with a specific interest or expertise, regardless of their rank or position, form a group to accomplish a certain goal. Standing committees, quality circles, ad hoc committees, and work teams are examples of the kinds of task groups that can exist in a work setting.

Standing committees are permanent groups that deal with ongoing problems or tasks. Boards and commissions are two examples of standing committees. Members may be elected or appointed to serve for a period of time, and they are typically responsible for taking into account the interests of those who appointed them.

The **quality circle** is one example of a standing committee. These groups usually consist of six to eight volunteers who meet regularly to discuss work-related problems; as the name implies, they are generally concerned with improving quality within the organization. To accomplish this goal, they typically analyze the causes of the problem, recommend solutions, plan the implementation of the solutions, and monitor the results. The activities of these groups vary, depending on how the organization chooses to use them and on the power and autonomy that they are given. While the uses of quality circles vary, one thing is clear: corporations are actively soliciting and utilizing the ideas of employee groups at nearly all levels.

In contrast to the standing committee, the **ad hoc committee** is a temporary group that is formed for the express purpose of dealing with an immediate problem that cannot be adequately handled within the existing organizational framework. These groups are not part of a formal structure and have a limited life. This type of task force will dissolve once the task has been realized.

Work teams can be either standing or ad hoc groups that are allowed to function with a large degree of autonomy. They are responsible for the quality of their work and are generally successful and productive. In past decades one person could construct and run a business single-handedly. Today's corporate environment, however, is more complex. Success often depends on the achievements of a work team rather than on the efforts of a single person. In turn, the success of the work team depends on the participants experiencing ups and downs in the process of developing into a cohesive unit.

In contrast to the formal group, the informal group frequently develops naturally without direction from management. Usually informal groups are not influenced by company policies, and they seldom have formal agendas or procedures. Nevertheless, exceptions do occur. For example, written or unwritten policy may discourage management from socializing with labor; or in a military environment, regulations prohibit officers from fraternizing with enlisted personnel.

Busy schedules and frequent relocation can cause people to look for friendship and social affiliations within the professional arena. The informal groups that form are neither inherently positive nor negative. Rather, the impact on the organization will be determined by the types of groups that emerge. If the positive aspects of group life—cohesion and affection—transfer from the informal groups to the larger group, the result will be advantageous. If, however, the reverse takes place and the conflict and discord of failed relationships bleeds into the workplace, problems will occur. In either case, there is very little that can be done to prevent or to force this informal group affiliation.

In both formal and informal groups, members will assume **roles,** specialized behaviors that cause the group to function in a given pattern. The emergence of different roles in formal or informal groups is a natural and inevitable process; however, the particular role a person plays will often vary from group to group. People assume roles based on their interests and abilities and on the needs of the group. The process of role development can be subtle and extensive and usually results from other group members encouraging the role. Often an individual will not be aware of the group's attempts to reinforce or extinguish a role behavior or even of the group's expectations for a role. The division of labor that occurs causes a unique structure in each group. However, roles can be generally categorized as relationship-oriented, self-oriented, and task-oriented.

Relationship-oriented roles address the people aspects of the group and the interpersonal relationships of the individuals. Members who assume these roles try to build unity in the group by reducing tension, often mediating conflicts and attempting to reconcile differences. They create group harmony by praising and encouraging others and by showing acceptance and tolerance. Frequently relationship-oriented participants encourage less talkative members and suggest ways the group might operate more smoothly.

In both professional and personal situations, dysfunctional behavior will interfere with the group's process. **Self-oriented** or self-centered members, frequently because of hidden agendas, detract from overall group effectiveness by drawing attention to themselves and their personal accomplishments. They can be stubborn, resistant, manipulative, and distant. They sometimes deflate the status of the other group members either by attacking the contributions of others or by self-aggrandizing. Neither the lack of interest of self-oriented members nor their opposite tendency to monopolize group time contributes to the group's overall functioning.

Task-oriented behaviors deal with goal completion. A person who is concerned with task realization will try to keep the group focused on the goal by defining the group's objective, guiding discussion, prodding people to participate, and sharing personal opinions. Energizing the group into action whenever interest drops and coordinating and clarifying ideas also help the task-oriented member to keep the group directed.

Not all groups are task groups, however. Each group has a purpose, but the purpose may be to support the other members. **Personal groups,** or maintenance groups, are present in our private lives, and occasionally in our professional lives, to address our need for association. Because humans have the need to belong, they form long-term groups that consist of **significant others.** These people—families, friends, neighbors and social group members—give affection and support to each other. Association with these significant others, particularly family members, has a significant impact on our attitudes and values. Usually personal groups are informal and unstructured, but sometimes, when special needs arise, we seek the help of more structured groups.

Self-help groups are support systems that exist to address the concerns of the membership. These groups can focus on problems, self-fulfillment, personal growth, consciousness raising, or social change. A true self-help group has shared leadership or direction from a facilitator who shares the problem or concern. While professional advice is often incorporated into a meeting, the membership assumes complete control.

Therapy groups are similar to self-help groups in that their purpose is to give support and help to their members; however, they differ in structure. Encounter groups and therapy groups provide treatment under the leadership of a trained professional who may not have ever experienced a given problem first hand. The degree to which the psychologist, psychiatrist, or social worker is involved will vary with the needs and desires of the group. Usually the professionals direct the discussion, apply research as needed, and respond to the individuals' needs.

Groups exist for a variety of reasons having to do with the unique personalities of the participants, the functions of the group, and each person's intentions; however, one consistency prevails: individuals improve through group involvement, and groups improve through individual growth. Groups help the individual explore self-image and develop sensitivity to others. In this way, the study of group process has come full circle. An understanding of group process helps the group function more effectively as a contributor to our sociopolitical system; the group, in turn, serves as a resource and a means of enhancing the life of the individual.

Introduction to Readings

Small groups, even the most casual, must have some organization and structure if they are to achieve an objective and produce member satisfaction. The essays in this chapter describe how groups are organized, where they fit into organizational patterns, how they are structured internally, and what patterns are most suited to group problem solving. In this chapter, we have gathered a series of articles that are intended to introduce you to some of the uses people and institutions make of small groups. While each group's structure and goals might seem different, they all follow certain patterns and employ problem-solving methods.

We begin this chapter with a selection that reminds us of the link among organizations, communication, and group behavior. All organizations, regardless of scope, size, or purpose, use small groups to get things accomplished. However, because organizational groups are actually subsets of much larger groups, they have attributes that mark them as somewhat unique. In her essay, "Rethinking the Nature of Groups in Organizations," Linda L. Putnam explores three of these special characteristics: connectivity, hierarchical structure, and multiple-group membership. She explains how these characteristics are ever present, and discusses the ways in which they determine the success of and satisfaction within small groups that are part of larger organizations. She also stresses the importance of communication within organizations and among groups.

Our second essay, "Understanding Groups at Work," by Seth Allcorn, deals with the kinds of groups that exist in the workplace. Allcorn, an administrator of a large medical institution, emphasizes the importance of understanding the psychological aspects of organizational life. He examines three group cultures that produce psychological defensiveness against the anxieties that arise from group participation. He then goes on to describe a fourth type of group, the **intentional group,** that encourages nondefensive participation by protecting individuals' security and self-esteem. He provides a number of charts and diagrams detailing the actions that will maintain an intentional group culture.

In past decades one person could construct and run a business or organization single-handedly. As Dick McCann and Charles Margerison point out, however, "Today's business environment is so complex and in such a continual state of change that success often depends on the outputs of teams or work groups rather than the efforts of a single person." Teams and work groups have traditionally occupied central roles as problem solvers within large organizations, and now, according to the authors, a new form has appeared. They call it "high-performance teams." These are teams within an organization that come together to deal with a common and immediate concern. The question that interests McCann and Margerison is why some teams work together and develop synergy while other teams fail. They indicate that some of the reasons follow from the manner in which team members approach the task. After interviewing many teams from industry, finance, consulting, marketing, planning, and engineering, they were able to identify nine key functions that mark the successful team. As a way of making your performance in groups more productive and rewarding, McCann and Margerison offer a discussion of those functions. More importantly, they list the general traits of those individual team members that helped the group the most. To illustrate the value of those traits the authors offer three cases that move their suggestions from theory to practice. By learning the characteristics of successful team members, you may be able to refine your own performance as a team member.

In the final essay of this chapter, Marshall Scott Poole reminds us that groups do not consist of mindless individuals all conforming to some preordained path to group consensus. In his essay, "Group Communication and the Structuring Process," he sets forth a theory of **structuration;** a theory concerned with how people structure their groups by making active uses of social rules and resources. He suggests that the process by which members structure groups is ongoing and continuous, and he explains the internal and external factors that shape this structuring process in small groups. Poole explains how individuals in groups are continually restructuring their groups through their communication interactions.

Rethinking the Nature of Groups in Organizations

Linda L. Putnam

The advent of quality circles, self-regulated work teams, design groups, and strategic management teams has led to a resurgence of interest in organizational groups (Ancona 1990). Groups are performing a wide array of organizational functions. To increase productivity and fight competition with foreign markets, management and labor have joined forces on product improvement teams. To adapt to rapidly changing markets, organizations employ focus groups and evaluation teams that link internal departments to customers, suppliers, and competitors (Ancona 1990). The proliferation of groups as units of organizational activity extends beyond decision making into such arenas as planning, policy implementation, innovation, and conflict management. Even though groups exhibit a number of pathologies that inhibit their overall effectiveness, they bring together individuals with diverse resources to promote rapid communication in a complex structure.

Organizational groups, while similar in some respects to groups in other settings, differ from them in important ways. Organizations offer more than just a "place" for groups to meet. They constitute a complex structure of groups embedded in other groups. Hence, a project team exists within a research and development group which, in turn, resides within the engineering department. This overlay of groups nested within other groups poses unique problems, ones that affect communication within and between groups. This chapter explores three unique characteristics of organizational groups: connectivity, embeddedness, and membership in multiple groups. More specifically, it examines the way communication between and within groups shapes and is shaped by a group's interdependence with its immediate context and its permeability of boundaries (Putnam & Stohl, in press).

Connectivity: Communication as Tight and Loose Connections

Even though organizational groups exist in a web of interrelated units, linkages between groups vary in degrees from loosely connected threads to tightly coupled bonds. Tight couplings between groups evolve from overlapping tasks, shared goals, a high frequency of communication, and mutual fate control. Tightly coupled or **interdependent** groups share a mutual dependency; both groups rely on one another to accomplish their respective goals. Because they are tightly connected, changes in one group alter activities in the other unit. For instance, the manufacturing group depends on the supply unit for its resources and the supply group relies on the manufacturing department to determine what materials need to be ordered. If manufacturing changes the parts in its blueprint, supply must adapt with similar changes in acquisition of

Permission to reprint must be obtained from the author. Linda L. Putnam is Professor and Head, Department of Speech Communication, Texas A&M University, College Station, TX.

materials. In like manner, if the marketplace reveals a shortage of certain raw materials, the manufacturing group must change its design of the product to adapt to this problem. Both groups, then, depend on one another for their respective needs.

Loosely coupled or **autonomous** groups share some activities, but they conduct their work independent of the other group. The two groups may be linked together through loosely connected exchanges, but they accomplish their task independent of the other group. Departments in a university setting are prime examples of autonomous groups. Even though the English and the Speech Communication departments may share the same building, the two groups function as semi-autonomous units. Each department runs its own governance system and policies independent of the operations of the other. Occasionally they interact to negotiate space, to exchange students, or to settle disputes over academic turf, but for the most part, they function independently. This tradition of operating as autonomous units makes it difficult for members of academic departments to build interdisciplinary programs.

Even though connectivity stems from task function and work-flow interdependence, loosely and tightly connected relationships are ultimately defined through communication. That is, interdependence varies in degrees; it is not a rigid characteristic of a group's relationships (Weick 1979). Overlapping tasks may entwine the supply and the assembly departments, but the way they accomplish their work is a communicative problem. The frequency, type, and pattern of interaction between them ultimately defines the nature of their relationship and the extent of their dependence on one another. It is possible, then, for autonomous groups to become interdependent if they interact frequently and if they control one another's fate.

In particular, research and development groups often perform their tasks independent of other groups. They conduct market research, analyze the competition, and create a new product to enhance the company's productivity. If this process is conducted without any input from the engineering manager, the R & D group functions autonomously. At some point, however, the company has to implement the new product and R & D must work closely with engineering and manufacturing groups. These interactions shape relationships between the groups and lead to changes in group process and in R & D's product design. Through communication, then, groups redefine autonomous relationships into interdependent ones.

Moreover, if the engineering group sees R & D's autonomy as a power play, they may be resentful and cautious in redefining their relationship. They might contend that major coordination problems would not have occurred if R & D had kept them informed. In essence, connectivity between groups is an ever-changing process, not a static event. It is derived, in part, from the way communication molds intergroup relationships.

External Context as a Resource

The degree of interdependence between two groups also hinges on what gets imported or exported across group boundaries and on how members actively shape their internal and external environments (Putnam & Stohl, in press). For instance, some groups actively influence the tasks and deadlines imposed by external groups while other units work religiously within the constraints set by external agents. Other groups, however, may question the authority or jurisdiction of outside individuals and ignore the constraints they set. Three functions, then, appear to characterize the reciprocal relationship between groups and their context. First, group members import and export information from their external context through scouting, scanning, negotiating, and serving as ambassadors. Secondly, members respond to external initiatives through monitoring the import of information and through guarding the group's turf. Finally, members determine who is included and who is excluded in their groups through immigrating across boundaries (Ancona & Caldwell 1988).

Task effectiveness may hinge on a group's ability to maintain frequent and influential communication with its external environment (Ancona 1990; Thornton 1978). In fact, organizational groups that operate in complete isolation for most tasks may experience failure in accomplishing their ultimate goals (Putnam & Stohl, in press).

Effective communication outside the group also impinges on the internal dynamics of the unit. In particular, members may experience a radical shift in stages of group development as a result of outside intervention that limits their choices, moves them forward, or energizes them (Gersick 1988, 1989). Moreover, in the early stages of a group's development, tight coupling with the external environment may lead to low cohesiveness and less satisfaction with the group (Ancona 1990; Stohl 1986).

This discussion indicates the need for trade-offs between internal and external communication. At various stages of a group's development, members may devote more time to communication outside the group and less attention to interaction with team members. Other contingencies such as urgency and complexity of the task and changing environmental conditions urge members to concentrate on the internal dynamics of their group and to reduce contacts with external groups (Tushman 1978).

Individuals as Linkages Between Groups

Group members who bridge intergroup boundaries through message exchange across organizational units are known as key communicators. They typically assume structural roles and linkage functions defined by their communication patterns (Putnam 1989). A **gatekeeper** serves as a member of one group who filters incoming and outgoing information. Secretaries often regulate communication traffic and filter information to management groups. A **liaison** bridges communication between two groups but does not belong to either group. A staff member in personnel may facilitate hiring between the engineering department and the sales group, but this liaison individual is not a member of either group. A **linking pin** belongs to two or more groups and coordinates activities between them. Supervisors typically assume linking-pin roles since they belong to work groups and managerial teams. Members of project teams frequently serve as representatives of their departments as well as participants on a task force. Finally, **boundary spanners** are individuals who link departments and the organization to other organizations. Employees in marketing, public relations, advertising, and supply frequently serve as boundary spanners to connect their departments to the community at large. Boundary spanners, unlike linking pins, translate and interpret equivocal information from external sources; hence, they have strong linkages within the group, within the organization, and outside the organization.

Communication within and outside the group influences the emergence of linkage roles and the frequency of their contacts with external units. High-performing teams have more frequent contacts with other groups than do low-performing units. Research teams rely on several members to perform gatekeeping and boundary-spanning functions while design groups channel their communication through primarily one member (Tushman & Katz 1980). In most cases, this member is the team's supervisor, particularly for the liaison activities of the group. Boundary-role spanners, however, are frequently professional employees who have a particular technical competence (MacDonald 1976; Tushman & Scanlan 1981). Liaisons tend to perform administrative functions while boundary spanners specialize in information gathering and decision making. Over 40 percent of the employees who are key communicators in their own groups also serve as linkages to other groups, to other departments, and to sources outside the organization (Tushman & Scanlan 1981).

These specialized roles shape communication within and outside the work group. Blau (1954) notes in his study of law enforcement agents that individuals who receive the greatest number of external messages during the day participate more frequently in group discussions, clarify problems, and take initiatives in meetings. Moreover, groups with clearly developed internal roles and centralized decision making engage in more external communication than do groups with role instability and decentralized decision making.

Individuals who perform boundary functions for groups, however, often lack formal authority, frequently feel trapped between conflicting demands, and can become scapegoats for organizational ills. They experience considerable role conflict and are rarely rewarded for their contributions as integrators (Organ 1971). No doubt some individuals cope with this conflict better than others do.

Our problems in understanding how employees cope with this conflict may stem from research problems in this area. Too much research on linkages between groups concentrates on the amount and direction of communication between individuals and ignores the content, meaning, and quality of messages. Perhaps researchers as well as practitioners should heed Barnard's (1938) advice that groups and organizations are formed not by an assemblage of persons, but by their interactions and their coordinated activities.

Embeddedness: Groups as a Reflection of Organizational Structures

Groups are shaped by and in turn shape an organization's structures. Groups are embedded in an organization's vertical and horizontal levels. Vertical levels signify layers of managerial authority while horizontal levels differentiate departments or functional units. Both levels are represented in an organization's formal chart. Even though the formal structure undergoes frequent changes, its existence often impacts on the composition, function, and communicative patterns of organizational groups (Bormann 1975). Groups also shape organizational structures through integrating tasks and personnel across vertical and horizontal levels. For example, in some organizations, production teams report to several managers, cross multiple departments, and include individuals from different vertical and horizontal levels. The existence of such teams may lead to redesigning production, restructuring levels, and reconfiguring the organizational chart. Other organizations employ group structures that resemble clans, federations, and matrix arrangements in which the vertical structure has only a few levels of management and the horizontal structure consists of a complex array of overlapping but loosely connected groups.

The type of group meeting in addition to the levels of the organization also influence the degree of embeddedness. Formal meetings, ones that are officially sanctioned and scheduled by management, differ from spontaneous and informal conferences. Meetings that cross vertical levels of the hierarchy reduce the number of informal sessions between boss and subordinates. In contrast, formal meetings that cross horizontal levels increase the need for informal contacts to coordinate across departments.

Group Functions and Types

Organizational structure also impinges on and is shaped by the types and functions of groups. One way to classify organizational groups is to distinguish between **ongoing** and **temporary** units. Ongoing groups continue to meet even though membership and task function varies. One type of ongoing group, a **standing committee,** meets on a regular basis to perform vital maintenance functions. Executive committees and middle management groups serve these functions at the apex of the vertical hierarchy. Executive committees make policies and coordinate information generated from middle management, while middle managers execute the decisions made by upper management. Since middle management often feels trapped between the policy makers and the technology of the organization, their communication patterns parallel those of top management and make it difficult for them to function as policy executors rather than policy formulators (Fry, Rubin & Plovnick 1981).

Work groups or **production teams** constitute ongoing groups at the lower levels of the hierarchy. Production teams have primary responsibility for a task. Work groups typically have assigned goals and membership with a designated leader. In many organizations, these groups assemble products with minimal interaction among their members. However, semi-autonomous and socio-technical work groups meet on a regular basis to determine such issues as how to adapt production to technology or how to reorganize the work schedule. These groups rotate their members, handle a myriad of problems on an ongoing basis, and work with less direct supervision than regular production groups. **Quality circles,** another type of production group, are teams that meet regularly to discuss ways of improving the quality of goods and services. Some quality circles also monitor the planning and implementation of their suggestions for improving the product (Baird 1982; Stohl & Jennings 1988). These teams are comprised of individuals from the work units who actually assemble the product under discussion.

Temporary groups consist of **ad hoc committees** and **task forces.** After these groups complete their task, they disband. An **ad hoc group** comes together to solve a particular problem. For example, a personnel department might form an ad hoc group to study the problem of loop holes in the benefits program. In a university setting, an ongoing curriculum committee might form an ad hoc group to study the feasibility of introducing a separate advertising major for the communication department. Ad hoc committees function at the discretion of an individual, departmental unit, or ongoing group. Hence, these groups typically recommend courses of action to other units rather than make the final decision on their own.

In a similar manner, a **task force** consists of representatives from different departments who are subcontracted to work on a highly skilled technical project. Since members of these groups also belong to other units, coordination of the project may become a problem. Projects that are low in priority tend to drag on indefinitely, but high-priority tasks produce action-oriented meetings and increased communication with external sources (Pearson & Gunz 1981). In addition to completing the assigned project, task force members must clarify the nature of their task, keep members motivated, and reach agreement on the group's jurisdiction.

In addition to formal groups that perform organizational tasks and meet during company time, **informal groups** come together in organizations to provide social activities, recreational events, informal networking, political alliances, and personal support (Goodall 1990; Ross 1989). Brown-bag-lunch groups, bridge groups, coffee clubs, bowling teams, and social support groups are types of informal groups that meet either regularly or occasionally. These groups, however, often exert control over organizational policies, deliberations in formal groups, and interpretations of company events. Informal groups, then, are intertwined with formal ones in a complex web of interrelationships.

Organizational Roles and Group Embeddedness

Organizational level not only impacts on the functions of groups at work, but it also affects relationships among group members. Individuals bring their organizational titles, prestige, and status into the group setting. The presence of a vice president or dean, as Janis's seminal work on "groupthink" demonstrates, often inhibits discussion of diverse viewpoints, a process that can lead to ineffective policy decisions (Janis 1982). Since executives frequently run group meetings, they represent the interests and values of the organization as a whole; thus they transmit to members, either implicitly or explicitly, their criteria for effective decisions. Open confrontation about these values or even differences of opinion on decision criteria can result in adverse consequences to an "outspoken" employee.

Farris (1981) describes an incident that occurs during the board meeting of a subsidiary of a large multinational corporation. The president of the company chairs the eleven-person management committee, which is comprised of the executive vice president, other vice presidents, and heads of the major departments. The group is considering whether to renew a current contract or to adopt a new pricing policy. Their decision will be sent to executives of the parent company for final approval. After thirty minutes of discussion, it becomes obvious that the president and the executive vice president differ in their opinions of the new pricing policy. During the meeting a senior vice president speaks out; otherwise group members avoid taking sides with either of the two highest ranking officials of the company.

Since no consensus is reached during the first meeting, a second one is scheduled. Prior to this session, four of the committee members informally contact executives of the parent company. Once they learn that the parent company intends to reject the new pricing proposal, group members remain silent and let the president and executive vice president fight it out without input from the committee. As Farris (1981, 99) observes, "The small benefits from active participation are strongly outweighed by the high costs of alienating either the president or the executive vice president."

The informal group system coupled with status differentials between members forms a political alliance. A political model of group interaction diametrically opposes our logical, rational notions about organizations. It suggests that power relationships between individuals lead to coalition formation, pressures to conform, and bureaucratic wheeling and dealing. Group interaction, then, parallels negotiation whereby representatives from various departments persuade, cajole, and compromise to reach decisions. When the group faces a critical decision, communication between members may consist of defining and affirming power relationships and using subtle maneuvers to entice key individuals to adopt pet viewpoints.

An example of this political process occurs when faculty members in a department complete interviews with job applicants and must decide which one will receive the final offer. Several members who favor a particular candidate may form a coalition with other key faculty. These individuals plot strategies to "overwhelm" the opposition and form a power block to gain a competitive edge for their candidate. In a similar manner, a student senate committee comprised of representatives from Greek and non-Greek organizations may barter and politic to reach decisions on homecoming activities. The Greeks may form power blocks to override suggestions of the non-Greeks; the non-Greeks may ask for more than their share in hopes that their interests will not be compromised. As these examples suggest, decision making within the political model relies on negotiation rather than on group consensus. Trivial issues and routine matters may occupy formal meeting time while critical policy issues are settled in backroom corridors behind closed doors.

Politics are a fact of organizational life, even though they have a dark and devious side. Researchers have studied this phenomenon in the military, university settings, and the British Broadcasting Company (Beard 1976; Burns 1977). They conclude that it is less than ideal as a model for effective intergroup relations. There are ways to reduce the ill effects of political wheeling and dealing. Pfeffer and Salancik (1974) report that political decision making is more commonplace when groups are loosely connected. Since autonomous groups have fewer opportunities to develop effective intergroup relations, they rely on expediency when confronted with coordination problems. Increasing interdependence among subunits, then, may reduce excessive influences of political alliances.

The political model, however, urges us to be cautious in accepting group communication at face value. In some cases, organizational groups are primarily symbolic entities, political means of delaying actions on controversial issues. Killing a good proposal by sending it to a committee rings true in a number of organizations. Moreover, certain leadership styles thrive on the "appearance" of participatory decision making. Employees spend endless hours meeting and preparing committee reports, only to find that their manager conveniently ignores their efforts. Political models, then, often provide us with insights about the symbolic meaning of organizational groups.

Multiple-Group Membership:
Communication as a Reflection of Divided Loyalties

Differentiation into formal and informal groups suggests that individuals function as members of multiple groups. An engineer may serve on a production team, a quality circle group, a task force on employee grievances, and an informal company softball team. Managers, especially linking pins, conduct their own staff meetings while serving as members of upper-level executive groups. In the university setting, a faculty member's time may be divided into service on an interdisciplinary research team, an ad hoc committee on faculty governance, a standing committee on curriculum matters, and an ongoing group on women's studies. Belonging to several groups integrates levels of the organization, but also it can lead to divided loyalties and dispersed commitments. In effect, we are only "partially included" in any group. If we have only a limited number of work hours per day, the critical test of commitment surfaces when mutiple membership creates time pressures, value conflicts, and opposing commitments.

Members bring to their group settings divergent interests, disparate values, and specialized jargon that reflects occupational and departmental differences. They sometimes hold stereotypic beliefs about other departments, e.g., "accountants are picky," "computer jocks are antisocial." Members of "warring factions" may take their intergroup conflicts into task forces and ad hoc committees (Putnam & Poole 1987). Thus, temporary groups may face challenges in building common norms and procedures, maintaining commitment to the group and the task, and getting participants to allay departmental biases for the activities of the group.

In some cases, members serve as representatives of their "home" groups; hence they are reluctant to adopt the norms, procedures, and goals of another group. For example, a strong allegiance to a representative role leads a supervisor to feel she must fight for her department's position on an issue rather than search for the optimal solution to a problem. Group members also carry "implicit" representativeness of their organizational and community roles across situations. A black engineer in an ad hoc committee on personnel policies may monitor his interactions in the presence of the company's only black manager, even though race is irrelevant to the group's task.

Service on a college-wide promotion and tenure committee provides an example of both explicit and implicit representativeness. Members from respective departments meet to establish promotion and tenure standards and to agree upon the avenues for enforcing these standards. The department chairs and full professors who serve on this committee hold their primary allegiances to their respective departments, especially to the administrative, teaching, and research needs within their departments. Moreover, they possess the particular knowledge and skills necessary for evaluating their own faculty members.

Yet, they are faced with the realization that crucial decisions about their department's future lie in the hands of a group of faculty who are only loosely coupled and who are frequently in pursuit of diverse ends. Even though the committee may continue to function as a loose collection of individuals with weak ties internally and strong ones externally, they must strive to build interdependence by developing common means and by establishing shared goals. Weick (1979, 90–91) argues convincingly that groups coalesce around common *means* for conducting their business; common *ends* evolve after members develop shared means. This practice requires a de-emphasis on technical expertise of members and an emphasis on their interpersonal communication skills—especially conflict management. Group members never abandon their diverse ends; they simply subjugate them for the sake of the group.

Overlapping membership among formal and informal groups means that members may interact with each other in the future (Putnam & Stohl, in press). For example, a female manager in an all-male management team knows that another woman in her lunch group is planning to file a sexual harassment charge against a male member of this management team. Since the female manager also chairs a separate affirmative action grievance committee, she knows she may encounter her male colleague in a very different group context in the future. Awareness of this potential for future interaction serves as a barometer for gauging present interactions. In a similar example, a new member of a standing committee who is upset with the group's past actions may decide to withhold his objections when he sees that two of the members belong to a country club that he wants to join. In addition, informal friendships among team members outside the group may influence political alliances, stances on controversial proposals, and open confrontation during and outside of the group.

In summary, since organizations consist of overlapping and interconnected groups, we need to examine the influence of communication between units as well as within groups. This embeddedness urges us to be cautious about generalizing from research on self-contained groups to organizational settings. We need to incorporate assumptions of connectivity, embeddedness, and membership in multiple groups into our conceptual schemes of small-group communication.

In a practical vein, attention to the dynamics of both internal and external group communication may help us uncover disputes about work standards between groups, accusations of blame and irresponsibility, and accounts for why groups "get stuck" in certain phases of development. Triads and small groups are "eminently sensible as places to understand the major workings of organizations" (Weick 1979, 236). Organizations that are loosely connected between groups and tightly coupled within subunits tend to persist as stable collectives.

References

Ancona, D.G. (1990). "Outward Bound: Strategies for Team Survival in an Organization," *Academy of Management Journal* 33, 334–365.

Ancona, D.G., and Caldwell, D.F. (1988). "Beyond Task and Maintenance: Defining External Functions in Groups," *Group and Organizational Studies* 13, 468–494.

Baird, J.E., Jr. (1982). *Quality Circles.* Prospect Heights, IL: Waveland Press.

Barnard, C.I. (1938). *The Functions of the Executive.* Cambridge, MA: Harvard University Press.

Beard, E. (1976). *Developing the ICBM: A Study in Bureaucratic Politics.* New York: Columbia University Press.

Blau, P.M. (1954). "Patterns of Interaction Among a Group of Officials in a Government Agency," *Human Relations* 7, 337–348.

Bormann, E.G. (1975). *Discussion and Group Methods: Theory and Practice.* New York: Harper & Row.

Burns, T. (1977). *The BBC: Public Institution and Private World.* New York: Macmillan.

Farris, G.F. (1981). "Groups and the Informal Organization," in R. Payne and C. L. Cooper (eds.), *Groups at Work,* 95–117. New York: John Wiley & Sons.

Fry, R., Rubin, I., and Plovnick, M. (1981). "Dynamics of Groups that Execute or Manage Policy," in R. Payne and C.L. Cooper (eds.), *Groups at Work,* 41–58. New York: John Wiley & Sons.

Gersick, C.J.G. (1988). "Time and Transition in Work Teams: Toward a New Model of Group Development," *Academy of Management Journal* 31, 9–41.

Gersick, C.J.G. (1989). "Marking Time: Predictable Transitions in Task Groups," *Academy of Management Journal* 32, 274–309.

Goodall, H.L., Jr. (1990). *Small Group Communication in Organizations* 2d ed. Dubuque, IA: Wm. C. Brown.

Janis, I.L. (1982). *Groupthink.* Boston: Houghton Mifflin.

MacDonald, D. (1976). "Communication Roles and Communication Networks in a Formal Organization," *Human Communication Research* 2, 365–375.

Organ, D.W. (1971). "Linking Pins Between Organizations and Environment," *Business Horizons* 14, 73–80.

Pearson, A.W., and Gunz, H.P. (1981). "Project Groups," in R. Payne and C.L. Cooper (eds.), *Groups at Work,* 139–164. New York: John Wiley & Sons.

Pfeffer, J., and Salancik, G.R. (1974). "Organizational Decision Making as a Political Process: The Case of a University Budget," *Administrative Science Quarterly* 19, 135–151.

Putnam, L.L. (1989). "Perspectives for Research on Group Embeddedness in Organizations," in S.S. King (ed.), *Human Communication as a Field of Study,* 153–181. New York: State University of New York Press.

Putnam, L.L., and Poole, M.S. (1987). "Conflict and Negotiation," in F.M. Jablin, L.L. Putnam, K.H. Roberts, and L.W. Porter (eds.), *Handbook of Organizational Communication: An Interdisciplinary Perspective,* 549–599. Newbury Park, CA: Sage

Putnam, L.L., and Stohl, C. (in press). "Bona Fide Groups: A Reconceptualization of Groups in Context," *Communication Studies.*

Ross, R.S. (1989). *Small Groups in Organizational Settings.* Englewood Cliffs, NJ: Prentice Hall.

Stohl, C. (1986). "Quality Circles and Changing Patterns of Communication," in M.L. McLaughlin (ed.), *Communication Yearbook* 9, 511–531. Newbury Park, CA: Sage.

Stohl, C., and Jennings, K. (1988). "Volunteerism and Voice in Quality Circles," *Western Journal of Speech Communication* 52, 238–251.

Thornton, B.C. (1978). "Health Care Teams and Multimethodological Research," in B.D. Ruben (ed.), *Communication Yearbook* 2, 539–553. New Brunswick, NJ: Transaction Books.

Tushman, M.L. (1978). "Technical Communication in R & D Laboratories: The Impact of Project Work Characteristics." *Academy of Management Journal* 21, 624–645.

Tushman, M.L., and Katz, R. (1980). "External Communication and Project Performance: An Investigation into the Role of Gatekeepers," *Managerial Science* 26, 1071–1085.

Tushman, M.L., and Scanlan, T.J. (1981). "Boundary Spanning Individuals: Their Role in Information Transfer and Their Antecedents," *Academy of Management Journal* 24, 289–305.

Weick, K.E. (1979). *The Social Psychology of Organizing* 2d ed. Reading, MA: Addison-Wesley.

Understanding Groups at Work

Seth Allcorn

A key to understanding how the organization works—or doesn't work—lies in understanding the *kinds of groups that exist at work* and how their dynamics influence behavior. After all, every organization consists of groups of people—work units, task forces, departments, divisions, etc. . . .

The Psychology of the Workplace

Managing individual and group behavior in organizations requires an understanding of the psychological aspects of organizational life. HR and other managers—as well as their employees—need conceptual frames of reference by which to understand complex interpersonal and group dynamics.

One particularly useful framework is derived from individual and group psychoanalytic theories, which form the basis for a model that explains the psychodynamics of large organizations. The model assumes that even though group behavior arises from a core of individual psychological processes, it can be understood when viewed as a whole. We will look at three group cultures that offer group members collective and individual psychological defenses against any anxiety they may feel as a result of their group membership. A fourth work group—the type of group that is desirable in the workplace—will then be discussed.

Work Group Typologies

The first three groups are what is called "defensive" in psychological terms. These are the *homogenized* group, the *institutionalized* group, and the *autocratic* group. Each offers its members a different solution to the same problem: anxiety arising from group membership. By contrast, the fourth group, which is the *intentional* group, deals with group participation in a nondefensive way. All four groups are dynamic. Change is driven by the members' individual needs for security and self-esteem and by threats to the group's existence that come from the operating environment. Below is an analysis of each of the four groups. A summary of the differences is presented in Tables 1 and 2.

The Homogenized Group

The homogenized group is the most primitive of the three defensive groups. Members behave as though the group lacks effective leadership and a clear agenda or task, even though these may be present to some degree. Members are uncertain as to what to do and how to act, and they feel isolated from their work and from one another.

Table 1
The Cultures of the Four Workplace Groups

Homogenized Group	Institutionalized Group	Autocratic Group	Intentional Group
All members have equal **status,** with no clear individual **roles.**	Each member is assigned a particular **role** and **status,** and given guidelines for changing the role and status.	All members are assigned **roles** with **status,** but no clear guidelines are provided for self-advancement.	All members assume and accept **roles** and **status** based on the needs of the group and the leader.
No **leader** is acknowledged to exist or permitted to arise.	**Leadership** is designated by the group's operating structure.	The **leader** is viewed as omnipotent and is clearly in control of the group.	A permanent **leader** may be found among the members or **leadership** may be passed among members based on each person's unique ability to lead the group at the time.
Autonomous behavior such as the offering of ideas is either attacked or not supported by others.	**Autonomous behavior** such as the offering of ideas is controlled by procedures.	**Autonomous behavior** such as the offering of ideas may be rewarded or punished by the leader, who may offer no reasons for his or her decision.	**Autonomous behavior** is acknowledged as valuable as long as it contributes to the group's purpose.
Members are unable to find a **direction for the group.**	The **direction of the group** is limited by the organization structure.	All skills for **directing the group** are held by the leader.	Members actively participate in offering **direction** to the group.
The group acts as though time and the environment had been temporarily suspended, and as if there were nothing more than the group's experience.	**The group acts as though** the organization were in control of events and the process, and as if work were to be accomplished as planned.	**The group acts as though** the leader will take care of everything if he or she is permitted to do so.	**The group acts as though** all members were responsible for the group's work and leadership.

Table 1—*Continued*

Homogenized Group	Institutionalized Group	Autocratic Group	Intentional Group
Some group members may be **singled out and stigmatized** for their willingness to express their feelings and thoughts. They may be coaxed into increasing emotionalism until they are rendered incompetent and discarded.	Some group members may be **singled out and praised** for participating in the group as expected, or they may be **publicly punished** for deviating.	Some members may be **singled out for rewards** for actions the leader finds supportive, or **punished for deviations** from the leader's expectations.	Contributions of members are **acknowledged by the group** as a whole.
Little **work on the group's task** is accomplished and no plans are made to do any work.	**Work on the group's task** is accomplished as specified by the organizational work process.	**Work on the group's task** as specified by the leader is accomplished according to the leader's instructions.	**Work on the group's task** becomes the responsibility of all the members with no one individual (including the leader) assuming complete responsibility for the work.

Participation in the group is unrewarding, since individuals feel neither secure nor good about the group and themselves. The group culture discourages members from offering direction or asserting leadership. Members may become hostile toward others, the group, and those who assigned them to the group, although hostility is often suppressed by other group members, and rarely expressed (see Figure 1).

Homogenization, in psychological terms, is what occurs when the individual fails to satisfy his or her need to feel valued by others. This failure produces fear for one's safety and, consequently, feelings of anxiety. Group members lack a feeling of connectedness with the others on the team, and they fear for their own well-being. They react by psychologically and, sometimes physically withdrawing. Paradoxically, the greater their desire for interpersonal connections, the greater the likelihood that they will feel isolated. This isolation results when they try to protect themselves from being used by others who are similarly seeking to fulfill their needs to feel connected to and valued by others.

Under these conditions the group accomplishes little work, since each member's unacknowledged but primary task is psychological survival. Few opportunities exist for group members to gain interpersonal support—just when such support is badly needed. Members feel that they are neither in nor out of the group. They are unable to commit

Table 2
Membership Experience in the Four Workplace Groups

Homogenized Group	Institutionalized Group	Autocratic Group	Intentional Group
Members fear the consequences of speaking out and taking action.	**Members fear the consequences of speaking out** in other than the prescribed manner, and of taking independent action without prior approval.	**Members fear the consequences of speaking out** without some idea of the leader's likely response, and of taking independent action without the leader's consent.	**Members are eager to offer their points of view** regarding the group's work.
Helplessness is experienced, as others are attacked by group members.	**Helplessness** is experienced as those who deviate are attacked.	**Helplessness** is experienced because little can be done to change the leader's mind or to influence events.	**Helplessness** is not an element of group membership experience.
Members feel **security** in being unnoticed.	Members feel that **safety** lies in following the rules.	Members feel **unsafe** and **insecure** because the leader may become dissatisfied with them unexpectedly.	The group offers a sense of **safety and security** to its members.
Members feel that they and the group have lost their **purpose.**	Members feel that they have lost their individual **purpose** in the face of the predominance of the group's goals.	Individuals lose their sense of personal **purpose** in the face of the all-powerful leader.	Members experience a sense of **purpose** because they and their contributions are acknowledged by the group.
Frustration is evident in that members feel as if nothing can be done to help the situation. No ideas are generated to improve the group's performance.	**Frustration** occurs, as members feel that nothing can be done to change the organization.	**Frustration** develops because group members cannot solve problems that stem from the leader's direction and style.	**Frustrations** over the group's progress and direction are openly discussed.

Group Culture

Alternate Group Process

Homogenized groups control anxiety and the threat of violence within the group by denying individual needs and differences: If everyone is the same, there is nothing to fight over.

The Homogenized Problem

The outcome of the homogenized group process is fear or self- and group annihilation if control within the group is lost. The anxiety promotes further individual and group regression and increased reliance upon psychological defenses. These actions produce either greater reliance upon homogenization and repression or a fight-flight response that signals a readiness to follow a leader in a process of change.

Group Action

As the group acts to deny and repress individual differences, the hope that anxiety will be controlled emerges. Individuals no longer feel responsible for their actions or the group's behavior. No one is willing to risk self-differentiation for fear of attracting the group's hostility. As a result, no one tries to assume leadership, and no one follows a leader who steps up.

Group Consequences

The homogenized group process results in aimless activity, the loss of self boundaries, distressing feelings of obliteration and alienation, fear of group annihilation by the external environment, renewed anxiety because of unmet interpersonal needs, competition, and violence.

Figure 1. The homogenized group.

themselves to group participation, yet they are also unable to separate themselves from the group because of internal and/or external pressure. Group members may behave in an aimless manner or they may joke in order to relieve anxiety. Group behavior may even become combative. Ultimately the group may lose touch with important aspects of its work objectives.

Figure 1 illustrates the dynamic aspects of the homogenized group. It indicates that the group can continue its destructive patterns, or it can learn from its experience and change, becoming a more productive team. Two requirements for such a change are (1) the availability of suitable and willing leadership, and (2) the readiness of the group to follow that leader.

The Institutionalized Group

By contrast with the homogenized group, whose members and leader fail to participate effectively, institutionalized group members control their anxieties by creating an external defense system. The result is a hierarchical organization structure that (1) regulates interactions between members and (2) provides nonthreatening leadership by specifying the degree of power and authority a leader will have (see Figure 2). Instead of encouraging meaningful interpersonal relations, the institutionalized group controls its members' actions by creating rigid routines. These routines provide members with the comforting illusion that they are in a stable, predictable environment in which everyone is equal. The primary task of the group is to control members' feelings, beliefs, and actions. Productivity is of secondary importance, although unlike homogenized groups, institutionalized groups are able to accomplish work by following the rules.

Group Culture

Alternate Group Process

Institutionalized groups control anxiety and the threat of violence within the group by imposing rigorous rules, regulations, policies, procedures, and roles that regulate group members' actions. A structured leadership role is created.

The Institutionalized Problem

The outcome of the institutionalized group process is resentment of its oppressiveness. Should the organization be threatened by the task environment, group anxiety will increase. This results in further regression and dependence of psychological defenses. These actions produce either a greater reliance on institutionalization or a fight-flight response that signals a readiness to follow a new leader in a process of change.

Group Action

As the group acts to regulate the actions of individuals, the hope that anxiety can be controlled emerges. Organization and structured leadership provide clear individual and group boundaries and create a sense of uniformity, predictability, and justice. Work on the group task is accomplished (by the book) to sustain group life.

Group Consequences

The institutionalized group process produces structured activities and interpersonal relationships. Members find the organization and its rules to be oppressive and stifling. Because the organization is rigid, it is slow to learn and adapt to its task environment, which may threaten its existence.

Figure 2. The institutionalized group.

Rigid, hierarchical organizations have several drawbacks. Many people note that bureaucracies have difficulty learning from experience and adjusting to new circumstances, and that they encourage their members to be dependent on management. As illustrated in Figure 2, this group structure may fail over the long run. Feelings of oppression and alienation may emerge, threatening the group's security. This threat may lead to an even greater reliance on institutionalization. On the other hand, with the right leadership (and a willingness on the part of the members to follow this leader), the group may adopt a different structure and group process.

The Autocratic Group

The autocratic group addresses members' anxieties by identifying a powerful, charismatic leader who members believe will ensure their security (see Figure 3). The result is an organization that is dominated by its leader, who provides direction, rewards, and punishments, and who maintains as much control as possible in an effort to minimize members' anxiety. The leader may use this position to fulfill his or her own need to feel powerful and admired. He or she may locate admirers and supporters within the group and elevate them to important roles, and may find ways to avoid making tough decisions and dealing with enemies.

Inevitably the group members will discover that this charismatic leader does, in fact, have feet of clay—a realization that will cause them to fear that the leader will not protect them from the anxieties arising from group membership. Ultimately aggression from some of the more frustrated and anxious group members or, perhaps, from a higher-level manager may lead to the removal of the leader. As illustrated in Figure 3, a new leader may renew the cycle of autocratic structure or may lead the group to create an alternate structure and group process.

It is important to note that the autocratic group can be productive, and that it may even achieve great success. The group can rapidly move to take advantage of sudden opportunities; but it is also likely to follow a leader in any direction—even down a wrong path.

The Intentional Group

Unlike members of the first three groups, those of the intentional group are relatively free of the need to defend themselves from anxiety and from other members' aggression. They understand their feelings and behavior, and participate in the group's work. These individuals do not fall victim to the defensive tendencies of the other groups because they are able to deal openly with group fantasies, unconscious motivations, personal needs, and defensive behavior. Conflicts are acknowledged; members have little reason to flee from participation or resort to psychological defenses. Figure 4 illustrates how the intentional group may fail to sustain its intentionality and may become one of the three defensive groups.

Model Dynamics

The situations depicted in Figures 1 through 4 are dynamic. Each group culture elicits behavior that is consistent with the group's underlying tendencies. Members of

Group Culture

The autocratic group controls anxiety and the threat of violence within the group by appointing a powerful and authoritative leader to regulate behavior. The leader imposes order by providing purpose, direction, and individual and group boundaries while managing and, at times, manipulating the feelings of group members to meet his or her personal needs and to accomplish work.

Alternate Group Process

The Autocratic Problem

The outcome of the autocratic group process is that members become envious and suspicious of those who are close to the leader, and they come to fear that the leader will be arbitrary in his or her use of power. These feelings (perhaps reinforced by the leader's behavior) serve to heighten anxiety and individual and group regression. The need to control the leader, favored group members, and the group process (so that the leader's needs do not take priority over the group's work) grows. Should the group be threatened, it may develop an even greater dependence upon the leader or a fight-flight response that signals a readiness to follow a new leader in a process of change.

Group Action

As the group acts to ensure that individual behavior is regulated by the leader, the hope that anxiety can be controlled emerges. The group may idealize the leader and expect near-perfect performance. The leader is expected to control the group's perverse tendencies, to protect members from each other, and to protect the group from its task environment. To accomplish the last expectation, the leader is expected to direct the group in its work.

Group Consequences

The autocratic group process results in stability which is subject only to change by the leader. However, the power of the leader to impose change may increase anxiety and feelings of alienation and powerlessness in group members. The presence of the leader may also provoke competition for his or her favor. Favored members may provoke feelings of envy and suspicion on the part of others. Members may also fear that the leader will abuse his or her power and authority.

Figure 3. The autocratic group.

Group Culture

Alternate Group Process

The intentional group encourages group members to work on their task by facilitating open discussions of individual needs, anxieties, fears, and envious feelings. Individuals are encouraged to learn about themselves and how they are contributing to the work of the group. The group does not suppress feelings and individual differences, but seeks to capitalize on them. Leadership and organization are provided only as needed. They are not used to control members' actions or feelings.

The Problem of Regression

The outcome of the intentional group process is often self-actualizing work by members, combined with considerable learning and self-discipline. However, stress provided by regressive tendencies may result in a threat to the intentionality. Individual and group behavior may gradually become threatening, as members withdraw from participation. As a result, the group may either reassert its intentional tendencies or develop a fight-flight response that signals a readiness to follow a new leader in a process of change.

Group Action

As the group works on its tasks, positive feelings develop from group membership. Pleasure is taken in working together. There is no need to hope that things will get better in the future. Issues created by self-differentiation, and feelings like fear and envy are open to discussion. This permits members to appreciate the problems others are having working in the group.

Group Consequences

The intentional group process results in an atmosphere that is open to interpersonal interactions. Group members remain responsible for regulating their own actions and for participating. From time to time members may find that they are not able to maintain the level of self-reflection and learning that is necessary to sustain intentionality. Should group members lose intentionality, individual and group regression will occur as membership in the group comes to be experienced as threatening.

Figure 4. The intentional group.

the first three groups may realize that the group has a problem and that they need to decide how to solve it. If the pain of group life is sufficient, change will occur. The critical requirements for change are: (1) the availability of a group member to lead the group in a change effort and (2) the readiness of group members to follow a leader who promises to make things better. As the figures indicate, the direction any change will take is unknown. An organization needs to find ways to encourage groups to change in the direction of intentionality.

Encouraging Group Change

The discussion that follows provides members and leaders of a group with a basis for analyzing group structure and process. When the structure and process lead to competition, in-fighting, the creation of coalitions, delays, confusion, indifference, withdrawal, and ritualistic inactivity, the group is encouraged to see this group behavior as a system of psychological defenses that protect group members from the loss of security, individuality, autonomy, and self-esteem. In many cases membership in a group can be unrewarding and threatening. Being a member, then, becomes undesirable—but exiting the group may not be permitted or may be frowned upon. The only resort for many people is to develop defensive coping responses involving themselves (they may deny failure, for example) or the group (they may advocate more or less control by the leader or a change in leadership.)

When enough members come to share the same defenses, the group has developed its own culture. The culture may change spontaneously, or a group-process intervention may help it to change. It is not easy to change any of the three defensive groups into an intentional one, because many intentional behaviors and group-process interventions are threatening to defensive-group members. These people, by assuming a psychologically defensive posture, attempt to flee from personal responsibility. A successful intervention strategy will include many of the characteristics proposed below.

Keep in mind that the group member who seeks to use group-process intervention will be differentiating himself or herself from the other group members, which may threaten some if not many of them. This group member or manager must have the courage to set himself or herself apart, the skills to understand the group's culture, and a conceptual model of group process that helps him or her to understand and interpret the actions of others in the group. The following discussion presumes that an intervention may be made by the group leader or by any group member.

Making a Summary

An intervention will be most likely to succeed if it is used when the group is beginning to develop a culture. Once the culture is formed, group members must know—even though they may not admit it—that the group is in trouble before they will be receptive to an intervention. In either case, the manager or group member should begin the intervention by providing the group with a summary of its work to date. The summary should not sound like a judgment or an evaluation of the group's performance. If the group does not agree with the summary, then an intervention should not be attempted, since under these circumstances group members are not likely to agree that a change is needed.

If the summary is generally accepted, however, the manager or group member should temporarily assume leadership of the group. He or she can then ask for an assessment of the current situation: For example, "As we seem to accept that we have fallen behind schedule, I am wondering what role our group structure and process have played in this outcome." He or she can add one of three points: "In particular, we seem to have (1) "failed to establish any type of effective leadership" (in the case of a homogenized group), (2) "developed too much bureaucracy and red tape to get anything done" (in the case of an institutionalized group), or (3) "unloaded the entire responsibility for the group's performance on one of our members" (in the case of an autocratic group).

He or she can then ask, "Does this seem to be the case to the rest of you?" It is important for the manager or group member to compare his or her perceptions and understanding in this way with the views of other group members, who may offer responses like, "You know, I agree with you; we have completely bogged ourselves down in red tape." Dissenting comments are also likely to be offered. All comments should be considered carefully; a supportive comment, although certainly welcome, may signal a member's need to retain a dependent role; a dissenting comment may signal a member's desire to take over the leadership position or may offer a fresh insight into the group's process. Comments that are off the subject may signal that a member is uncomfortable with the subject or wants to undermine the intervention.

Virtually all comments can be incorporated into the intervention. In particular, the leader should ask members if they agree or disagree with each comment. This discussion can result in another opportunity to assess and summarize the group's status. Eventually, a thoughtful and properly timed summary of the group's perceptions should be accepted by the members. The completion of this summary will signal that it is time to take the next step. At this point, the leader can suggest that since members seem to agree that they have a problem, a shift away from the current group culture is needed. Members are asked to examine the group's structure and process, and the leader's role. This step can be threatening to group members: Their acknowledgment that the group is in trouble because of its structure and process may not necessarily lead them to the next logical step—change. Many unconscious individual and group forces will militate against change, even though members know that change is needed to prevent failure.

Resistance to Change

The person who leads the intervention needs to be sensitive to these forces. He or she can acknowledge that contemplating change makes everyone anxious, and that anxiety can block change efforts. The group members should be encouraged to discuss change in general, and the problems of implementing it, as a way of diffusing anxiety.

The leader of the intervention may also bring up the nature of the change. At this point the group should be close to assuming many of the attributes of the intentional group. Members should be encouraged to make an intentional decision as to how the group should function in the future.

Regressive tendencies, which will threaten to derail the intervention and return the group to its defensive status, may develop during the course of the change process. The leader should be cautious but persistent in challenging these tendencies. He or she may say, for example, "It seems to me that if we decide in favor of this proposal, we will be creating some new red tape, which I thought we had agreed we wanted to avoid." At any point the group may bolt from the intervention process and return to the defensive status. The leader should initially resist this development; however, if the pressure is irresistible, he or she should abandon the intervention that is causing the anxiety. As long as the intervention leader has not alienated group members by being too resistant, he or she may try a new intervention in the future. In many cases, however, a well-respected leader can say he or she does not accept what is happening, and can refuse to go along with it. The group may realize that a defensive group process will not relieve the anxiety that is caused by the intervention leader's rejection of the group's direction and may return to the intervention process.

Maintaining Change

Toward the end of a successful intervention, the leader should make sure that the group understands what actions are associated with the intentional group so that the basis for maintenance of the intentional culture is well established. Thereafter, the intervention leader can continue to point out regressive trends that conflict with the group's progress toward intentionality.

Our discussion indicates that interventions are more difficult for group leaders and members to implement than for outsiders with group-process skills, who can act as consultants. This is so for two reasons. First, most managers and employees have not had extensive training in interpersonal and group dynamics; a successful intervention requires considerable skill and insight on the part of the leader. Second, a group member who attempts an intervention will inevitably be seen as a threatening figure. It is difficult and frequently unrewarding to be a process interventionist. Despite these problems, however, successful interventions by group members are possible; human resources managers should encourage groups to rely on themselves rather than to depend on external authorities.

Skills Training

Educators, trainers, and consultants should contribute further to the development of group-process skills. Regrettably, few business curricula include courses that lead to the development of these skills; corporate trainers tend to provide training that is limited and often superficial; and organization-development staffs and internal and external group-process consultants tend to create dependency by providing process consultations rather than a learning experience.

Individual and group behavior is highly complex, difficult to understand, and even more difficult to manage. Managers need conceptual maps that can help them to understand and appreciate the psychodynamics of human behavior in groups. The theoretical model provided here provides one such map.

High-Performance Teams

Dick McCann and Charles Margerison

Through seven years of research, we have been intrigued as to why some teams are highly successful while others fail, even when the abilities of team members in both the winning and losing teams seem about the same. What is it that allows the members of some teams to work together and develop synergy, whereas other teams collapse or even tear themselves apart?

We have become convinced that the answer lies in determining individual work-style preferences. Managers and leaders of teams can only be successful if they fully understand differences among their team members. Team members often have a different approach to work—a different way of doing things—than team leaders. Only by understanding and managing those differences can teams work through their conflicts and link themselves together in coherent wholes.

Work Functions

The starting point for our research was to identify the key work elements that need to be addressed if a team is to be successful. We interviewed countless teams from different business sectors—industry, finance, consulting, marketing, planning, and engineering. We developed a "Types of Work" model, which identifies nine key work functions that are common to all teams, regardless of their work content (see Figure 1). The work functions are described below.

Advising. Advising work is associated with gathering information and disseminating it to others. People engaged in this type of work typically will gather data from reports or from contacts with others and will put them in report form to use in decision making. Some people may spend up to 70 percent of their time in advising activities and collecting data and passing them on for action to others in the team. Corporate planners and information officers often fit into the advising category.

Innovating. After an organization has gathered information about "the state of the art," or has found out what its competitors are doing, the work activity may then move into the innovating phase. Here, people will think up new products or services or ways to improve existing ones. The goal is to create some fundamental idea that could put the organization ahead of its competitors. People working in a research and development function may spend much of their time innovating.

Promoting. Merely thinking up ideas is no good unless the ideas can be "sold" to the organization. Essentially, that process is the promoting function—an important component of the work of any team. Many good ideas are lost simply because they are

Figure 1. Types of work.

poorly promoted to others. Poor promotion is often a weakness in the work of teams. During our research, several chief executives mentioned their disappointment in many of their managers because of the managers' inability to "sell" really good ideas to others.

Developing. After an idea has been sold, the work activity often moves into the developing phase. Making the idea work often requires further development. There may be two or three different ways of implementing the idea or certain practical constraints imposed by the nature of the organization. Developing may involve prototype testing or assessing alternative versions of the idea before implementation.

Organizing. Now the idea is ready for implementation. Plans have to be made, budgets approved, and schedules established so that the product or service can be implemented according to deadlines and bottom-line outputs. Those activities are part of the organizing activity for many line managers. Project managers, in particular, may spend more than 50 percent of their work activity organizing.

Producing. Once the plans and schedules are in place, teams can start producing the product or service on a regular basis, according to standards of effectiveness and efficiency. This is the repetitive work of the organization and the activity that contributes most directly to the bottom line. Production managers typically spend much of their time in the "producing" work function.

Inspecting. Inspecting activities are important in all organizations to ensure that quality is maintained and controls over finances are established. Many teams we have worked with fail because of weaknesses in inspecting. People working in finance and accounting, as well as quality-control engineers, often spend much of their time in this work function.

Maintaining. All teams and organizations need to provide a solid infrastructure so that all other work activities can proceed in the most efficient manner. Administrative personnel often provide maintaining activities through their corporate support functions. Regardless of who provides it, maintaining is an important function of all work teams.

Linking. Finally, linking is the central function that coordinates and integrates all other work functions. Linking is often one of a team leader's major responsibilities, although in mature teams every team member spends some time working on linking activities.

Work Preferences

In speaking with people engaged in any of the nine work functions, we found that those who really enjoyed their work showed common behavioral characteristics. "Promoting" people, for example, were quite creative, whereas "producing" people tended to be more practical. That observation prompted us to explore other relationships between the Types of Work model and personal characteristics.

We experimented with the Myers-Briggs Type Indicator (MBTI) as a way of characterizing people, but were disappointed in the reliability of results we obtained, probably because the MBTI attempts to assess a personality type across both work and nonwork situations. We now know from our own work and that of others that "work" and "nonwork" are often two distinct compartments in a person's life and that behaviors in each compartment can be totally different. For example, someone who is extroverted at work may act introverted in a nonwork situation, so as to "recharge the batteries" for the next day.

We believe that Carl Jung's original work in the 1920s on psychological types is a powerful way to characterize people's differences. We therefore decided to go back to Jung and redefine his constructs for the workplace. In doing so, we developed and validated a new instrument known as the "Team Management Index" (TMI).

The TMI identifies four key issues that are at the heart of managerial differences and decision-making preferences in the workplace:

> how people prefer to relate with others;
> how people prefer to gather and use information;
> how people prefer to make decisions;
> how people prefer to organize themselves and others.

Each day at work, managers have to relate to other people to get the work of the organization done. Some managers do it in an extroverted way, meeting frequently with others, talking through ideas, and enjoying a variety of tasks and activities. Other managers are more introverted, preferring to think through ideas on their own before speaking, and generally not having a high need to interact with others.

In the process of relating to others, managers gather and use various types of information, often in either a practical manner or a creative manner. Practical people usually prefer to work with tested ideas and pay attention to facts and details. Creative people, who are future-oriented, enjoy ambiguous situations and are always looking at the possibilities and implications.

Once the information has been gathered, it is necessary to make decisions. Some managers go about that in an analytical way, setting up objective decision criteria and choosing solutions that maximize the payoff. Others tend to make decisions according to their beliefs, personal principles, and values.

When implementing decisions within an organizational framework, managers exhibit two distinct preferences. Some like structured environments in which things are neat and tidy and action is taken quickly to resolve issues. Others prefer to be more flexible and to make sure they have gathered all possible information before making decisions. They prefer to spend their time diagnosing situations and will tend to put off "concluding" or "resolving" them until all the information is in.

The Team Management Wheel

To relate the Team Management Index data to the Types of Work model, we developed and conducted a study in 1988, which has since been published by the National Consulting and Training Institute (New Berlin, Wisconsin). In the study, we asked managers to describe their work preferences in terms of the nine different work functions, while we simultaneously tested them with the TMI.

The result was a mapping of the Jungian constructs, as defined by the TMI, onto the Types of Work model. For example, people with a preference for extroverted relationships, creative information gathering, analytical decision making, and flexible organization (for which we used the acronym ECAF) correlated strongly with the "promoting" role on the wheel. So too did people with an ECBS preference (extroversion, creative information gathering, belief-oriented decision making, and structured organization). Those with a preference for introversion, practical information gathering, analytical decision making, and flexible organization (IPAFs) correlated strongly with the "inspecting" role, as did IPBS people, who differed from IPAFs in their decision making and organizational preferences.

The final result of our work was a teamwork tool called The Team Management Wheel (see Figure 2), on which a person's score from the TMI can be mapped. We have subsequently used the wheel in studies of more than 5,000 managers worldwide. The wheel has eight outer sectors labeled with "double-barreled" words, such as explorer-promoter and assessor-developer. The first word in each label, such as "explorer," indicates the behavior exhibited by a person mapping into that sector; the second word derives from the work content in the Types of Work model.

The TMI scoring indicates one sector as a person's major preference and two additional sectors as related or back-up roles. Thus someone might show a preference as a creator-innovator with related roles of thruster-organizer and concluder-producer, or as a controller-inspector with related roles of concluder-producer and upholder-maintainer.

The output from the TMI processing is a 4,000-word report describing preferences in terms of decision making, interpersonal skills, team building, leadership, and the like. Here are some general characteristics of each sector:

Creator-Innovators

These people are future-oriented and enjoy thinking up new ideas and new ways of doing things. Usually they are independent and will pursue their ideas regardless of

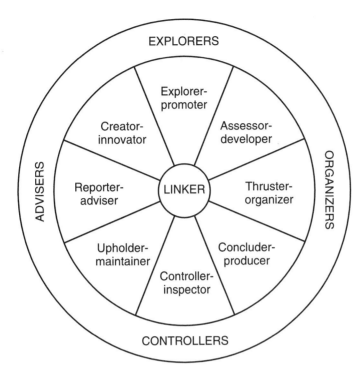

Figure 2. The team management wheel.

present systems and methods. They need to be managed in such a way that their ideas can be developed without too many organizational constraints. Some organizations set up research and development units (often separated from the production units) to allow such people to experiment with ideas.

Creator-innovators are sometimes accused (usually by opposites on the wheel) of having their "heads in the clouds," but usually that is because they are looking to tomorrow rather than worrying about today. They often are not structured in the way they go about things and may appear disorganized or absent-minded. Some creator-innovators are more introverted, preferring to stay in the "back room," working on projects on their own or in small groups. Others can be outgoing, even zealous, in the way they put forward ideas they really believe in.

Explorer-Promoters

Explorer-promoters are excellent at taking ideas and promoting them to others, both inside and outside the organization. They enjoy being with people and often have a network of people that they use when gathering information and testing out opportunities. They often are advocates of change and are highly energized, active people who tend to have several activities going on at once. They enjoy being "out and about" and are good at bringing back contacts and resources that can help the organization move forward.

Explorer-promoters are entrepreneurial risk takers who can be very persuasive. They are often influential and can talk easily, even on subjects about which they are not experts. They are excellent at seeing "the big picture" and at generating enthusiasm for an innovation among other people. However, they are not always interested in "controlling" or "organizing" and do not always pay sufficient attention to details. In that regard they can benefit from having a concluder-producer or a controller-inspector to work with, although they may sometimes have difficulties interacting with those people.

Explorer-promoters enjoy "off-the-cuff" conversations and need to interact with others to be at their productive best. They do not thrive on sitting in a back room, working alone on their problems—they need people to stimulate them. In that regard they can be energy-draining, almost sucking energy from people around them.

Many explorer-promoters have "elastic egos." They are quick to see opportunities and seize them before they disappear. Sooner or later in their careers they get their fingers burned, but it doesn't seem to worry them—they rebound, looking for the next opportunity. That characteristic, of course, is essential for a successful entrepreneur.

Assessor-Developers

On the wheel, assessor-developers are located midway between explorer-promoters and thruster-organizers, and exhibit both of those types of characteristics. They may not always think up good ideas for themselves but they are excellent at making someone else's ideas work in practice. They are usually sociable, outgoing people who enjoy looking for new markets or opportunities. They can take an idea and match it to the opportunity, always mindful of the organization's bottom-line constraints. They often make good product-development managers or assessors of new ventures.

Assessor-developers usually display a strong analytical approach and are at their best when they have several possibilities to analyze and develop before making a decision. They like organizing new activities and respond well to new challenges where they can push forward an idea into a workable scheme. Once the activity has been set up and shown to work, however, they tend to lose interest, preferring to move on to the next project rather than engage in the production and control of the output.

Thruster-Organizers

These are people who enjoy making things happen. They are analytical decision makers, always doing what is best for the task, even if their actions sometimes upset others. Their great ability is to get things done on time and to budget; for that reason they are often found working in project-management positions. They will thrust forward toward a goal, meeting conflict head-on if necessary.

Usually thruster-organizers prefer to work according to an established plan and in a structured manner so that objectives are clearly set out and everyone in the team knows what has to be achieved and by when. They excel at organizing people and systems so that deadlines are met. They will set objectives, establish plans, work out who should do what, and then press for action. They tend to be task-oriented and, in their pursuit of goals, may sometimes ignore people's feelings. That more than anything can get them into difficulties with their subordinates and colleagues.

Concluder-Producers

Concluder-producers are strong, practical people who can be counted on to carry things through to the end. Their strength is in setting up plans and standard systems so that output can be achieved on a regular basis in a controlled and orderly fashion. They usually do not like rapid change, as it interferes with the efficient systems they have established for doing the work. Their efficient manner may sometimes cause them difficulties with creator-innovators and explorer-promoters, who continually try to change the way of doing things.

For concluder-producers the challenge lies not in dreaming up new ideas but in "a job well done." They are often more patient with others with routine work, and as a result, are sought after as managers for their ability to work in a quick, reliable, dependable, and stable manner and for their ability to deliver results. Our studies have shown that concluder-producers are in demand as managers: of a worldwide sample of middle and senior managers, 27 percent showed the concluder-producer characteristic as their major preference.

Controller-Inspectors

These are quiet, reflective people who enjoy the detailed side of work and like working with facts and figures. Controller-inspectors usually are careful and meticulous and can spend long periods of time on a particular task, working quietly on their own. That ability to work alone stands in direct contrast to explorer-promoters, who need a wide variety of tasks to engage their attention, and people with whom they can interact.

Controller-inspectors are comfortable working within rules and regulations that others have established. They probably would argue that the rules have been made to ensure that the organization works in the most efficient manner and that therefore everyone should obey them. For that reason, they enjoy working in situations where their output is guided by organizational or governmental regulations. We have found many of them working in finance, accounting, and quality-control positions, where their "inspecting" preferences are important assets in the work they do.

Upholder-Maintainers

Upholder-maintainers are people with strong personal values and principles, which are of prime importance in their decision making. Usually they have high concern for people and will be strongly supportive of those who share the same ideals and values as they do.

They prefer to work in a control-oriented, supportive environment, where they can make sure things are done according to their standards. In addition, they prefer to take an advisory role in the background rather than a leading executive role. Because of their strong principles, however, they will "dig their heels in" when confronting issues that oppose their beliefs. They will not react in an extroverted, quick-tempered way but in a more resilient, obstinate manner, which can be irritating to thruster-organizers. In fact, a meeting between a thruster-organizer and an upholder-maintainer can be like an irresistible force meeting an immovable object!

Reporter-Advisers

Reporter-advisers represent the classic advisory role on the Team Management Wheel. They are excellent at gathering information and putting it together in a readily understandable way. If they are introverted, they probably will rely on written formats for their information; if they are extroverted, they likely will be good communicators and may rely on a network of colleagues and acquaintances for their data.

Reporter-advisers are patient people who prefer to make sure they have all the information before they take action. That often causes others, particularly thruster-organizers, to accuse them of procrastination, but reporter-advisers typically will respond with "How can I take action until I have all the information?" Thruster-organizers, who often take action with only 20 percent of the information, sometimes find such caution hard to understand.

Reporter-advisers do not enjoy conflict and have "antennae" out that can detect a potential conflict well before it happens. Usually they will move to defuse the conflict or position themselves well away from any direct effects.

Team Role Distributions

In a sample population of 3,783 managers from the United States, the United Kingdom, Canada, Australia, New Zealand, and Southeast Asia, 71 percent fell on the right-hand side of the wheel in the three sectors of concluder-producer, thruster-organizer, and assessor-developer (see Table 1). Those sectors have in common a preference for organizing. On the basis of this sample, it would seem that most mature organizations look for managers who have organizational preferences.

Some organizations in the sample show a different distribution, with an emphasis on the explorer-promoter and creator-innovator preferences. For example, at Hewlett-Packard Laboratories in Palo Alto, California, 22 percent of managers are in the creator-innovator sector—quite appropriate for an organization with short product life cycles and where innovation is part of the company culture.

Table 1
Distribution of Team Roles

Team Role	Proportion
Concluder-producer	26.7
Thruster-organizer	26.5
Assessor-developer	17.5
Creator-innovator	9.2
Explorer-promoter	8.7
Controller-inspector	7.5
Reporter-adviser	2.1
Upholder-maintainer	1.9

Balanced Teams

In working with management teams all over the world, two prerequisites for success appear time and again:

> high-performing management teams are well-balanced with respect to the team roles of the various team members;
> the teams have excellent "linking" skills.

When people's job functions match their work preferences, they are more likely to be highly energized and better performers. Therefore, in setting up project teams, leaders should aim to balance the team roles as much as possible.

The best football teams are those that have offense experts as well as defense experts, because many players who excel at offense are weaker at defense. So it is with management teams. Explorer-promoters can be excellent at pushing forward with new opportunities but weak when it comes to details. Controller-inspectors are great at "defense" but often find exploratory or "offense" roles stressful.

Managers who want to put together teams with high-performance potential should understand their own preferences and then build around them teams that complement their team roles. A manager with a creator-innovator preference, for example, will benefit greatly from having thruster-organizers on his or her team, while a concluder-producer manager may need an explorer-promoter on the team to identify opportunities and promote the team's capability to others in the organization.

Unfortunately, many managers hire clones of themselves. Concluder-producers, for example, usually like other concluder-producers because they see the world similarly and have common frames of reference. But teams that are vulnerable to "groupthink" can quickly become unbalanced.

Balanced teams encourage multiple descriptions of the same event; they will solicit and consider diverse views before making decisions. We have shown in many management-development programs that balanced teams outperform teams with people whose personalities cluster around one particular part of the wheel.

Our "favorite" team in years of running management-team games has been a team of nothing but thruster-organizers. Every time we have run a team game, the team of thruster-organizers has finished last. Of course, one or two thruster-organizers on a team is great, but too many cause the team to rupture and fall apart. Each thruster-organizer usually ends up "thrusting" in a different direction, and there is no teamwork.

Although balance is necessary for high performance, it is not enough. In a balanced team, different "models of reality" are constantly interacting and presenting different descriptions of the same situation. Some conflict will always be present in a balanced team. A certain amount of conflict is healthy as it prevents "groupthink," but the team—particularly the team leader—needs to work hard to develop the skills of linking so that the contributions of the team members become synergistic.

Linking

We call the hub of the Team Management Wheel the "linker," and that is often the main role of the team leader. The linker role is different from the outer-sector roles, as it is skills-based rather than preference-based. The outer sectors are based on the Jungian constructs; people take years to develop the characteristics of those roles. The linking role, however, is based on skills that every manager can learn relatively quickly. Thus all managers should aim to occupy the central hub of the model as well as their outer-sector preferences.

In general, linking has three major aspects—external linking, internal linking, and informal linking.

> **External linking.** Managers who are good external linkers are in many ways good "foreign ambassadors." They represent their team well in high-level negotiations and ensure that adequate resources are on hand to do the job. They often open communication channels with other groups working at the same level and will defend their teams against external criticism. They usually have identified any external links that need to be strengthened and ways to do it beforehand. A person described as an "organizational politician" is often a good external linker.
>
> **Internal linking.** People who are effective at internal linking will be good at integrating and producing working arrangements between people. They will ensure that the team members are updated on important issues and that there is a high degree of team cohesiveness and cooperation. They are excellent at allocating work and will set high-quality standards and examples for others to follow. They are readily available when problems arise and will act to ensure that resolutions are reached effectively and efficiently.
>
> **Informal linking.** Informal linking involves people who actually facilitate interactions between employees and across departments to ensure that work is done effectively. Many people who are good at informal linking do not have a formal role as manager or leader, but "link" naturally as part of their jobs. For example, many secretaries have developed excellent linking skills by acting as coordinating points for members working in teams, particularly where the leader has concentrated on external linking at the expense of internal linking.

In our experience, we have not found a team that has been successful without one or more people acting in a linking role. Indeed, in teams where linking skills were low, we have also found poor performances. Therefore, it seems unlikely that a team can succeed unless it has one or more people acting strongly in linking roles. That means that beyond their normal contributions to specific technical areas, those people must give time to the more general role of bringing the team together and establishing effective teamwork practices. In new teams the leader usually takes on the role of the informal linker, but in mature teams the highest performance usually results when every team member contributes something to the central linking role.

During our research on high-performing teams, we interviewed successful and unsuccessful teams and asked them about linking practices. Many common traits appeared among the teams, and we have grouped those data into ten skills of linking:

> listen before deciding;
> keep team members up-to-date on a regular basis;
> be available and responsive to people's problems;
> develop balanced teams;

allocate work to people based on their capabilities;
encourage respect and understanding among team members;
delegate work that is not essential for them to do;
set a high-quality example for the team;
coordinate and represent team members;
involve team members in solving key problems.

Team Development at Work

To illustrate how we have used the Team Management Wheel successfully, we offer three examples from our casebook.

Rearranging Work Preferences

Jack was a person who was keen on developing his team but was not sure how to go about it. He knew he had a lot of intelligent and motivated people in his group, but they didn't seem to work well together.

We decided to present a one-day, team-development workshop using the Team Management Wheel. During the workshop, we gave all members a chance to read their team profiles and suggested that everyone share their profiles and read the comments about each other. That led to an interesting and open discussion about people's strengths and weaknesses.

Next, Jack asked the team members how they thought they should develop in order to tackle the tasks before them. They generally agreed that they needed more cooperation. He asked the team how that could be achieved. Several people suggested that perhaps the team should consider reallocating some of the work so that it matched people's preferences more closely. A discussion ensued, and a number of specific ideas were put forward for improving teamwork. The team split into subgroups, and each subgroup was charged with bringing specific proposals to the next meeting.

At the next meeting, the team reported considerable progress. Jack said that some duties were being rearranged so that people's strengths would be used more effectively. In particular, some "exploring" work currently done by a concluder-producer had been exchanged for some detailed work currently done by an explorer-promoter. Both parties said they were pleased with the changes and felt "rejuvenated." Other team members said their various meetings has been "tremendous" and that the team was now using everyone's skills more effectively and in a complementary way.

Incorporating New Views

Two years ago, in working with a factory team, we had the members map their work preferences on the Team Management Wheel. The members agreed that their team was adequate in the thruster-organizer, concluder-producer, and controller-inspector roles, but deficient in the areas of exploring and advising.

After a long discussion on what to do about it, the team members decided to take off two days from their usual work and to spend that time operating in the creator-innovator sector of the wheel. To get into the "creating-innovating" mode, they hired a creative consultant to introduce new perspectives into their views of work and the workplace.

The two days were enlightening. As a result of the process and the support of an experienced facilitator skilled in running creative meetings, two developments emerged that helped the team balance itself on the Team Management Wheel:

> The members felt encouraged to "journey" into the creator-innovator sector of the wheel—an area previously foreign to their mapped preferences. The consultant introduced to them some fundamental new perspectives and showed them how to harness the innate creativity within the team.

> They decided to repeat the exercise annually and to make more use of consultants, who invariably could bring in fresh perspectives from the advising and exploring part of the wheel. The members agreed that the team could certainly benefit from regular interaction with consultants, who could help them "balance up the team," even though the thruster-organizers, concluder-producers, and controller-inspectors probably would not want them around permanently.

Balancing the Team

Another team within a large organization comprised a sales manager and several regional sales representatives. All of them mapped into the explorer-promoter, assessor-developer, and thruster-organizer sectors of the Team Management Wheel. Upon discussing the results, the members seemed pleased that they were all in that upper quadrant.

When we pointed out that there were no "controllers" in the team, the members said they didn't need that function on their team because the central-administration department took care of those activities. When asked how often they met with central administration, the members simultaneously answered, "never."

We pointed out that their team should include representatives from the control side of the organization. After much discussion the sales team agreed and arranged to invite the administration manager to the next sales meeting. It was the start of a new era of cooperation between two parts of an organization that traditionally had taken an "us-them" view of the workplace.

Understanding Team Dynamics

Too often, managers "manage" without understanding why teams work together effectively at times and ineffectively at other times. In team management workshops, much time is spent explaining to managers some of the reasons for high performance.

During discussions of the major functions of teamwork in terms of the Team Management Wheel, managers can see, often for the first time, that their teams are not well balanced. The question we ask them then is "What can you do about that imbalance?"

Some teams will be able to correct an imbalance by moving people elsewhere in the organization and bringing in people to "plug" the gaps. That is not always possible. Some groups are put together on an ad hoc basis, with no choice of team members, and may be heavily weighted on one side of the wheel. In those cases, it is important to realize the potential weaknesses of the group and to take corrective action if possible. The Team Management Wheel makes possible such analyses of team management and development problems and provides insight into long-term solutions.

Group Communication and the Structuring Process

Marshall Scott Poole

Most social scientific research paints a picture of group members as passive, reactive creatures. Members' behavior is said to be determined by communication networks, group norms, status structures, peer pressure, feedback, and numerous other forces. Members are pictured as though all they do is react to these factors. They are pawns, moved about by forces beyond their control. And the picture of the group as a whole is no less passive. Its effectiveness is explained in terms of the influences of groupthink and other social fallacies, by its level of cohesiveness, its collective motivations, by "necessary" stages of problem solving, and many other factors. If all an alien from another planet knew about people was what he or she read in the social scientific journals, he or she would be highly likely to conclude that they are robots, driven by external and internal forces and with no minds of their own.

We all know that this is not a true picture. Certainly, we are subject to forces beyond our control. Certainly, dynamics like groupthink can take over as though they had a life of their own and lead a group into remarkably bad decisions. But we do have freedom to act as we wish, to make choices that shape our lives. If the group has a norm that we do not agree with, we can choose to break the norm, and we may persist even in the face of severe pressure from other members. If we understand how groupthink works, we can try to prevent it from occurring and, when it does occur, we can inform our group and take measures to counteract its effect. In short, we can control our actions and the actions our groups take. Any social scientific research must take this into account, or it will produce an inaccurate explanation of human behavior.

Now this is not to say that people have total control over their behavior or over how their interactions with others will go. We live in a world not of our own making. Outside forces intrude and shape how we can act. A small architectural firm may suddenly hear that it is in danger of running behind on a project and, therefore, may lose its biggest customer. Group members must drop whatever they are doing and work until this threat to group survival is conquered. Practices and traditions internal to our groups constrain what we can do. If a committee has a ten-year tradition of electing a new chair every six months, a new member, no matter how motivated or well-intentioned, is unlikely to be able to convince the group to change the term to two years. The member is better advised to accept the tradition until the group accepts him or her. Then there is a chance of changing it (unless the new member has come to believe that a six-month term really is the best for this group!). We cannot exert absolute control over other group members, and we are affected by their activities. If a

Permission to reprint must be obtained from the author. Marshall Scott Poole is affiliated with the Department of Speech Communication, Texas A&M University, College Station, Texas. I would like to acknowledge the contributions of Robert D. McPhee and David R. Seibold to this research. All of us worked together to develop these ideas. I would like to thank Lydia Ford, Lisa O'Dell, and Kimberly Poole for their comments and help in preparing the manuscript.

member starts to cry for no apparent reason at all, we might feel constrained to disregard other business for a while and comfort him or her. Interaction is a give and take that no one, no matter how forceful and determined, can control.

So, people can actively control their behavior, but they do so within constraints of external forces, internal group structures, and other members' behavior.

For instance, in a very cohesive secretarial group, which is normally pretty productive, members may decide to take the afternoon off and go on an extended lunch. In this case high cohesiveness does not cause high productivity; it actually works against it. And whether cohesiveness increases or decreases productivity depends on what the group members choose to do. This does not mean that there are no causal forces acting on groups. Productivity will in general be facilitated by higher levels of cohesiveness. But because level of productivity depends on how the members choose to respond to the task, there will be cases where this relationship does not hold.

It is hard to describe and explain the influence of free will on behavior, because there are so many possible ways in which the group could go. Simple cause-effect patterns are no longer possible. To be realistic in our thinking about group behavior forces us to adopt much more complex and less definite explanations. The advantage of this is that our theories of group behavior will be based on much more realistic assumptions than are simple cause-effect theories.

A Theory of Structuration

What would this type of theory be like? It would have to recognize that people in groups actively control their behavior. It would also have to recognize that behavior is shaped and constrained by forces not totally under the control of the members. The influence of these forces is channeled by members' choices about how to react to them.

One theory of social behavior that accepts this challenge is the *theory of structuration*. This theory is concerned with how people structure their groups by making active use of social rules and resources. As the word structuration suggests, the process in which members structure groups is ongoing and continuous. It happens throughout the life of the group and is never finished. According to this theory, members are always structuring their groups. They do so with every act. If the structure of the group changes, it is because members have done something that has changed it. If the structure of the group stays the same, it is because members are acting in such a way that the same structure is created and maintained with every act. According to this theory, nothing is ever completely accomplished. The group is never finished or static. Instead, groups are always in the process of creation and re-creation. Nothing ever stops. Even if the group looks very stable and conservative, it is because members are acting in such a way to create the same group structure over and over, creating an appearance of sameness and stability. However, underlying this is a constant process of change.

Definitions

So far we have not defined several terms—structure, rules, and resources. First we will do that and explain a few of the basic assumptions of the theory of structuration.

Then we will give an example of structuration in groups. After that we will discuss the theory in more detail.

One of the basic distinctions in the theory of structuration is the distinction between system and structure. A *system* is an observable pattern of relationships among people. A *structure* is a set of rules and resources used to generate the system. These rules and resources are unobservable and must be deduced from how the system operates. Often people are aware of rules and resources that they use. *Rules* are propositions that indicate how something ought to be done or what is good or bad. For example, a norm is a rule that tells members what the group expects of them if they are to remain in good standing. Another example is the communication rules that define the meanings of terms and what various behaviors mean. *Resources* are materials, possessions, or attributes that can be used to influence or control the actions of the group or its members. Examples of resources include money, special knowledge in an area important to the group, status outside the group, and a formal leadership position.

The final important term structuration has a very complex definition, but one that can be understood, if we take it apart. *Structuration* can be defined as the *production and reproduction of the social systems through members' use of rules and resources in interaction.* This is a very complex statement that contains a number of ideas.

First, the notion of structuration implies that the primary constituents of the group system are interaction and relationships among members. The very existence of a group depends on members' interactions. If members stopped interacting and broke off their relationships with one another, the group would cease to exist. This is true even of formal groups, such as organizational work groups, where members are assigned and expected to show up. If members decide to work individually and never meet or interact as a group, there really is no group. It is a group in name only, and members do not identify with the group or feel accountable to each other.

Second, the definition implies that rules and resources (structures) are the "tools" members use to interact. Hence rules and resources are the "tools" that create and maintain the group system. As we noted above, a group system is composed of patterns of relationships and interaction among members. These patterns are created and maintained by members' use of rules and resources. For example, if one norm (rule) is that members of the group must all be good friends, then members will try to get to know each other. They guide their interaction by the rule. In following this rule, members employ various resources—such as their social skills and their status outside the group—to get others to like them. If they are successful at getting to know one another, their interaction will create and maintain a dense communication network. This in turn will make the group more cohesive. The two properties of the group—high cohesiveness and a dense network—are direct results of members using rules and resources. The properties will exist only as long as group members continue to apply the rules and resources just mentioned. If members choose not to follow the norm or if they decide to use resources like social skills to control each other rather than to build friendships, the group system will change. The group will have a different character.

So far we have emphasized rules and resources as tools for action. However, they are equally important as tools for interpreting what is occurring in group interaction. For example, consider the group system in the previous paragraph. If a member teases another member for always being late for meetings, the teasing will probably be interpreted as friendly chiding. However, in another group in which there has been considerable tension and in which there is a strong norm favoring punctuality, the same teasing may be construed as a rather "catty" personal attack. Rules are tools for interpreting others' behavior. We think about their behavior in light of related rules. The same is true of resources. If members regularly use their special expert knowledge to influence the group, then making a suggestion is likely to be interpreted as an attempt to be seen as an expert.

A third point is one that makes structurational theory quite different from many other points of view: Structures—rules and resources—are produced and reproduced along with the system. As Anthony Giddens wrote: "Structures are both the medium and the outcome of action." To illustrate what this means, think about rules and resources in groups you have been in. In every group there are somewhat different rules. Even for very common rules, groups develop their own versions and special interpretations. For example, majority voting is often used to make decisions—but this rule differs in different groups. In some groups "majority" really means "the two most important members," while in others it is actually "more than half the members." In some groups a majority vote is interpreted as an expression of democracy; in other groups it is viewed as a power move by which the majority can force the minority to do what it does not want to do. Resources, too, vary from group to group. A college degree is a source of influence in a group of teachers. In a group of steel workers it may actually be a disadvantage.

So each group has, in effect, its own rules and resources. The group's particular structure of rules and resources is created and maintained by members' interaction. For example, a few members might become friends and decide this helped their work. They would then encourage others to build friendships, creating a norm favoring close relationships among group members. As this norm continues to be followed, it becomes a permanent, prominent feature of the group. At some point, however, members may begin to believe that maintaining close friendships saps their energy and prevents the group from functioning as well as it could. If they begin to place less emphasis on building relationships, the norm will become less important. At the extreme, members may stop using the norm altogether, and it will no longer be part of the group's structure. And so it is with every group. The group copies its own versions of some rules and resources and develops others on its own. And, knowingly or unconsciously, it may change or eliminate rules and resources.

Rules and resources do not exist independent of an interaction system. They only continue to exist in a group if members use them. So systems and structures have a reciprocal relationship. Members use rules and resources to create the group system, but rules and resources can only exist by virtue of being used in the system. In producing and reproducing the group system, people are producing and reproducing rules and resources.

As we have noted, a group can change, reinterpret, and even eliminate rules and resources. Sometimes this is done by conscious choices of members. A member might, for example, argue that majority voting procedures are unfair to the minority and convince the group to adopt motions only if all members favor them. More often, structural change comes about without planning or awareness. Members may just gradually drop or reinterpret a norm, without realizing they are doing so. A major interest of research into structuration is how members initiate, maintain, and change rules and resources. We will discuss this in more detail below.

A fourth and final point is needed to qualify what has been said up to here: Members do not totally control the process of structuration. Members' activities are influenced by external forces that limit what they can do. For example, if the group is assigned a very difficult task, members cannot organize their work in any way they please. To be successful, they must structure their work so it is appropriate for the task. The task places limits on their choices. External factors, including the nature of group tasks or goals, the group's general environment (including the larger organization the group is part of), and members' level of competence are limits. Members' actions can "restructure" these external forces. For example, the group may break the difficult task into smaller, easier subtasks. This redefinition changes the task to some extent. Yet the task still exerts a powerful defining force on group interaction.

Another limitation on members' control over structuration processes is the actions of other members. Interaction, by definition, is beyond the control of any single actor. Members' actions often blend together so that interaction unfolds in unexpected directions. For example, in a conflict one member might make an attempt at reconciliation. If another member attacks the response, it may make the first counterattack, resulting in an escalating conflict no one wanted in the first place. External forces and uncontrollable interaction dynamics can result in *unanticipated consequences* of structuration.

So, according to the theory of structuration, the groups that appear so "real" and stable to us are actually continuously in flux. They are continuously being produced and reproduced by members' interactions. It is the job of researchers to explain how this process of production and reproduction leads to stability or change in groups. An example of structuration processes will serve to illustrate many of the points we have just made.

A Case

The group in question was dedicated to teaching newly-graduated methods of diagnosing psychological ailments. It was composed of three psychiatrists who had M.D. degrees, a psychologist, and two social workers. The group's leader, Jerry, was a "take-charge" person who fully intended to create a democratically run group, but ended up as the head of a small clique, which made decisions in an authoritarian manner.

All of the members of the group were very competent in their areas. When the medical school created the group, the deans handpicked strong, competent people who had shown exceptional teaching ability. The deans told the group it was free to develop the program as it saw best, provided members could get grants from public and private agencies to support their operations. Jerry had numerous contacts and was able to get a very large grant to support the project for its first two years.

When the group first met to plan the program, it was decided that all decisions would be made "rationally." That is, a decision would be accepted only if *all* members were satisfied it was sound. Jerry was appointed "leader" of the group, but there was an understanding that he would encourage participation and equalize influence over the decision. And Jerry made an active effort to do this. He strongly believed that the best decisions were those with the most member input. He read books on group communication, and did everything he could to facilitate group interaction.

However, there were forces working against democratic control of the group. All members had worked extensively in medical settings and had great respect for people with M.D. degrees. This gave the three members of the group with M.D. degrees more clout than those without them. Further, members knew that continuation of their program depended on garnering funds. This gave Jerry something of an advantage, because he was the primary source of funds for the project.

As a result of these two forces, the psychologist and social workers (the non-M.D.'s) tended to give in to the psychiatrists (the M.D.'s). The non-M.D.'s did not speak as often or as long as the M.D.'s. They were also more tentative than the M.D.'s and let their ideas "die" or be swept aside more easily than did the M.D.'s. These were not large effects, but they did result in a less democratic group than was originally envisioned. And the non-M.D.'s felt they had less influence than the M.D.'s. They were frustrated, and often talked with one another about their lack of influence. In meetings they exchanged meaningful glances that implied "here we go again!" when M.D.'s expressed their opinions.

Jerry noticed that non-M.D.'s contributed less than M.D.'s. He also spoke with one of the social workers, and she expressed her dissatisfaction. He attempted to involve the non-M.D.'s by calling on them, and setting aside special periods for "brainstorming." But this undermined democracy still further because Jerry was, in effect, directing members to contribute. The non-M.D.'s came to depend on Jerry as an advocate. Ironically, this contributed to his power in the group.

Jerry's manner of running meetings also contributed to the development of a pecking order in the group. He was a rather forceful participant, and talked more than other members. The more a member talks, the more influence he or she has. Jerry also attempted to "help" the group by rephrasing and redefining ideas in order to improve them. Despite his good intentions, Jerry rephrased other members' contributions in line with his own thinking. Without realizing it, he influenced decision making. And members (especially non-M.D.'s) came to value and count on his rephrasings, reinforcing Jerry's influence. The M.D.'s began to change non-M.D. ideas, to talk longer and more confidently, and to interrupt non-M.D.'s more frequently.

The end result was movement toward a more authoritarian leadership style. The group developed a "pecking order," in which M.D.'s were accorded higher status than non-M.D.'s. The non-M.D.'s lost the confidence necessary for maintaining equal democratic participation. Non-M.D.'s were dissatisfied with the group. Conflict increased and was not handled well, resulting in a tense climate. An outside observer would see a divided group, with clear differentiations in status and power. In spite of its members' best intentions, this group structured an authoritarian climate.

In the psychological training group the following elements can be discerned: The *system* is the pattern of interaction among members, specifically the "pecking order" and communication network. The *structures* in this case are (a) *rules* related to "rational" decision making, the communication and phrasing of proposals and ideas, and contributions of "superior" members, and (b) *resources*, including medical degrees, access to funding, and Jerry's interaction skills. *External forces* that influenced group interaction include the task set for the group by the deans and the need to garner funds to keep the project going.

Structuration processes reinforced and reproduced the rules and resources related to authoritarian group structures. Rules relating to preference for contributions of "superior" members and resources such as medical degrees were supported and validated in the group. At the same time other rules and resources that would support democratic decision making were not emphasized or reproduced. So, norms like those favoring equal time for each member to talk did not evolve and resources such as the amount of energy and commitment members have were not valued as much as those favoring evolution of status orders.

Structuration led to a group quite different from what members hoped for. Their interaction "got away" from them, producing unintended consequences. In part this was due to the pressure of external forces, particularly the need to get funds to continue the project. This pressure encouraged members to turn to Jerry who could, they thought, "get the job done." The structure also "got away" from members because changes happened very gradually. The shift from a democratic to an authoritarian group did not occur all at once. It emerged slowly, as rules and resources favoring authoritarian operations were used more and more (and therefore reproduced), while rules favoring democracy were used less. And when democratic structures were employed, they were often justified on the grounds that proposals had to be put in "rational" format so that all proposals would be given equal weight. A democratic veneer was put on an autocratic move. The effects of structuration often "sneak up" on groups, because they are so gradual.

Structure Development

Where do structures come from and why do groups choose the structures they do? Occasionally groups create their own rules and resources. For example, some groups develop unique code words for sensitive topics. One group developed a code word for its higher level supervisor. Group members called her "Waldo" when outsiders were present, so the outsiders wouldn't know members were talking about her.

But these instances are relatively rare. Usually, groups borrow or adopt rules and resources from other groups or social institutions. Members draw on their own experiences and on what they have learned. They try to do things as they have seen them done in other groups. As a result, we encounter different versions of the same rules and resources in many groups. For example, various interpretations and adaptations of majority voting are found in many groups. The same is true of education as a resource. It is a widely respected source of influence, although it is interpreted differently and has different weight in various groups. When rules and resources are widely accepted and used, they become *institutions* in their own right. Majority rule, for example, is often equated with democracy.

So an important part of structuration is the groups' *appropriation* of social institutions for its own uses. Groups fashion themselves after other groups and after their members' ideas about institutions. In doing this the group creates its own version of these institutions. The strength of a social institution—determined by how widespread it is and how much a part of the culture it is—has an important influence on how likely it is to be reproduced. A structure drawn from an institution has a clear reference point, and will be relatively long-lived, even if it is seldom used. Structures created uniquely by the group must be used quite often or they will die out. The more "institutionalized" the structure is, the less it must be used if it is to survive in the group.

But what are institutions anyway? Although the majority-rule procedure is very common, there is no such thing as a "general" or "abstract" majority-rule principle. Majority rule only exists in the groups that use it. The reason majority rule seems to be an abstraction is that it is widely used and that it is taught and talked about in the abstract. However, this is only an illusion. The majority rule procedure exists only insofar as it is used in our society. And survival of majority rule and other institutions depends on their structuration by groups. If groups (and other social organizations) stopped using majority rule altogether, it would pass out of existence. So groups reproduce social institutions as they produce and reproduce themselves.

Why do groups choose the particular structures they do? There are at least three reasons. In some cases rules and resources are used because the group gives members negative reinforcement if they "deviate." For example, in a group that employed majority rule, a member who attempted to seize control would likely meet with disapproval from the group, and perhaps would be asked to leave. Another reason members use rules and resources is that they are traditions in the group. Often we follow traditions without thinking. They are second nature, used by habit. For example, if a group has always taken a vote to confirm important decisions, members will often continue to do so without really thinking. A final, and probably the most important reason members use rules and resources is because they are useful—they enable members to achieve their goals and build the group. Resources like status, a leadership position, or special knowledge are also useful for members, and so they form an important part of the group system.

Influences on Structuration

What factors influence structuration? Three types of influences on structuration can be identified:

(1) *Member characteristics and orientations.* Members' motivations in the group influence which structures they use and how they use them. Members who are primarily concerned with the group and with getting the job done, will use structures in very different ways than will members whose goal is to realize their own individual interests or to control the group. Group-oriented members will generally use structures in "the spirit" of the rule or resource. Members concerned primarily with themselves or with controlling the group often turn structures in very different directions, as Jerry did in the psychological diagnostic group.

Members' characteristic interaction styles also influence structuration. An autocratic leader will use majority voting procedures very differently than will a democratic leader. Other stylistic differences, such as differences in group conflict-management styles, will also influence how structures are used.

Members' degree of knowledge and experience with structures also affect structuration. For example, groups that have had a lot of training in decision-making procedures will incorporate techniques like nominal group procedure into their structures with more success than will less knowledgeable groups.

(2) *External factors.* As mentioned above, forces beyond members' control also influence structuration. Factors such as the nature of group task, the effects of larger organizations on the group, and the talents of personnel assigned to the group limit what the group can do.

(3) *Structural dynamics.* A third influence on structuration are the relationships between different rules and resources. Two main types of relationships can be discerned:

   (a) *Mediation* occurs when one structure influences the operation or interpretation of another. In effect, the first structure controls the second. For example, because business is such an important part of American culture, it is common for groups to use an economic cost return metaphor to guide their behavior. Alternatives are rated with respect to gains or losses they promise, and decisions are made with formal or informal calculations. This even affects how value-related decisions are made. Often groups faced with value choices do not debate ethics or higher ends. Instead they decide which values are important, rate each alternative on the values, and calculate a "utility" score for the alternatives. That alternative with the highest score is chosen. This converts an ethical choice into a "rational" calculation. Economic thinking mediates and controls ethical thinking.

   (b) *Contradiction* occurs when two structures, each of which is important to the operation of the group, work against each other. Contradictions in structures create conflicts and dilemmas in groups. Sometimes these take some time to show up, but when they do, they can disrupt the group and often stimulate change. There was a contradiction in the psychological diagnosis group discussed above. Democratic principles were very important to members, and they used these to justify their actions and as behavioral ideals. However, the group operated according to an autocratic structure. The contradiction between democratic values and autocratic operations set up tensions in the group. The members who were left out of decisions resented it, and over time this developed into a major split in the group. Eventually there was a prolonged conflict and the two social workers quit. Contradictions fueled change in the group.

Member characteristics, external forces, and structural dynamics combine to influence how groups structure themselves. To explain structuration it is necessary to account for the influence of these forces on members' actions.

Studying Structuration

Why is it useful to study structuration? There are three reasons to study structuration. First, it gives a more accurate picture of group processes than traditional social scientific theories. The theory of structuration accepts the fact that group members actively control their behavior but it also recognizes limitations and constraints on members' activities. The theory attempts to show how action influences the operation of "deterministic" forces and how external forces constrain action. This can produce important insights into group behavior, as the case of the psychological diagnosis group shows. Many of the points raised there could only have been uncovered through analysis of structuration.

A second advantage of the structurational model is its recognition of the importance of gradual change and unintended consequences of members' behavior. Because of its emphasis on the continuous production and reproduction of social systems and structures, the theory of structuration makes us aware of how small, incremental changes can mount up to a major change in the system. It is well-equipped to study these gradual developments. In addition, the theory explains how structuring processes can lead to outcomes completely different from those intended by the members. These surprises often mark turning points in group development.

Third, and perhaps most important, the theory of structuration suggests ways for members—especially those with little power—to change their groups. The theory points out how members can effect change by altering their behavior in what appear to be small ways. If persistent, these small changes can alter the group's directions. This strategy is often particularly effective (for members with little or no power) because small moves are less noticeable to powerful members who might squelch attempts at change. In the psychological diagnosis group, the group was temporarily turned in a more democratic direction with this strategy. One of the social workers decided that she would stop allowing Jerry to rephrase her ideas. She insisted that they be stated as she said them. This made Jerry more conscientious of preserving other members' ideas, and for a while the group operated in a more democratic fashion. Eventually, however, a crisis arose and members (without meaning to) again fell back into their old habits. Jerry was a key figure in handling the crisis, and members continued to turn to him for help after it had passed. As a result, the social worker was unable to sustain her initiative. If changes such as this could have been reproduced, the group could have changed. However, forces operating in the autocratic direction were stronger.

Decision-making methods like Nominal Group Technique, brainstorming, and Reflective Thinking are often employed to structure group interaction and change how groups make decisions. However, their effectiveness depends on how these structures are produced and reproduced in the group. If used as designed, these techniques can equalize power and contribute to more rational decision making. However, they can also be used to control the group. On one occasion Jerry decided to use brainstorming in the psychological diagnosis group. However, since he ran the session himself, non-M.D.'s were hesitant to contribute and censored their ideas. Although the group believed it was increasing participation by using brainstorming, the end result was a reproduction of the same autocratic patterns.

The theory of structuration has the potential to help members understand and control the forces that influence group interaction. Its goal is to make people aware of the part they play in the creation and maintenance of structures they would otherwise take for granted.

Bibliography

Folger, Joseph P., and Poole, Marshall Scott (1983). *Working Through Conflict.* Glenview, IL: Scott, Foresman.

Giddens, Anthony (1976). *New Rules of Sociological Method.* New York: Basic Books.

Giddens, Anthony (1979). *Central Problems in Social Theory.* Berkeley, CA: University of California Press.

Poole, Marshall Scott, Seibold, David R., and McPhee, Robert D. (1985). "Group Decision-Making as a Structurational Process," *Quarterly Journal of Speech* 71, 74–102.

Poole, Marshall Scott, Seibold, David R., and McPhee, Robert D. (1986). "A Structurational Approach to Theory Building in Decision-Making Research," in R.Y. Hirokawa and M.S. Poole (eds.), *Communication and Group Decision-Making.* Beverly Hills: Sage.

ACTIVITIES

Activity 1

Purpose: The purpose of this activity is to encourage students to discover how and why groups are formed.

Procedure: In small groups the students list the groups that they have joined during their lives. As each group is mentioned, the student states what caused her or him to join that group, what change in self took place, and what change in the group took place as a result of that person being a member of it. As a large group, the class then lists the different groups and discusses the similar and varied reasons that people have for joining groups.

Activity 2

Purpose: The purpose of this exercise is to determine how and why professional groups differ from personal groups, and to prioritize the most significant strengths and weaknesses of each type of group.

Procedure: Divide the class into groups of 3–5 people. Each group chooses five positive and five negative characteristics of a professional group from the list below. Then, the group does the same for personal groups. After 20–30 minutes the class reconvenes and the individual groups "defend" their choices.

aggressive	formal
autocratic	goal-oriented
calm	heterogeneous
cohesive	homogeneous
collaborative	humorous
competitive	independent
compromising	informal
controversial	interdependent
creative	involved
democratic	stable
dynamic	structured
effective	warm
efficient	

Activity 3

Purpose: The purpose of this exercise is to examine the perceptions students have about teams.

Procedure: In small groups the class decides what words will make up the "TEAMBUILDING" acronym. The groups think of one word associated with teams and team building that can stand for each letter in the word. The small groups then share their ideas with the large group, and the class decides on the best acronym.

T

E

A

M

B

U

I

L

D

I

N

G

Activity 4

Purpose: The objective of this activity is to show that groups require members to assume certain roles.

Procedure: The class remains in the same groups that it had for the other activities in this chapter. Working independently, members assign themselves and others the roles listed below. The members then discuss why members are sometimes seen differently by themselves than they are by others; and why different members of the group sometimes react differently to an individual.

TASK-ORIENTED ROLES	YOUR ROLES	OTHERS
Initiator, contributor		
Information seeker		
Opinion giver		
Energizer		
Information giver		
Coordinator		

RELATIONSHIP-ORIENTED ROLES

Harmonizer

Compromiser

Encourager

Gatekeeper

Expediter

SELF-ORIENTED ROLES

Blocker

Recognition seeker

Dominator

Avoider

Aggressor

3
What Groups Do

Sayings like "two heads are better than one" express a folk wisdom that reflects accumulated knowledge about human behavior in groups. When individuals join each other to solve problems and reach decisions, synergy occurs; knowledge, resources and experiences are shared; and usually, better decisions result. Effective decisions involve a systematic evaluation of alternatives and realistic actions that will move the group toward the goal it wishes to achieve. Much depends, however, on the members understanding decision-making dynamics, including the elements that contribute to and detract from group decision-making effectiveness.

A systematic approach to problem solving is the first step to effective decision making. In 1910, John Dewey introduced the "Steps of Reflective Thinking," which provide a kind of "map" of the problem. This sequence involves **defining or identifying** the problem, **analyzing** the problem and setting criteria for possible solutions, **suggesting** possible solutions, **evaluating** possible solutions, and **selecting** the best solution. The group can then plan implementation of the best solution.

This approach has been modified and questioned through the years, but one principle remains clear: a structured approach to problem solving will increase the chances that the group will meet its objective.

Principles of Group Decision Making

The quality of the decisions will depend on the interaction patterns among the members and the information exchange that they experience. Listening to each participant and encouraging every person to contribute will help to coordinate knowledge, thereby correcting errors or blind spots. This process usually results in the group recognizing and rejecting incorrect solutions.

Expressing different perspectives, or opinions, allows members to consider many different points of view. These interactions contribute to increased comprehension, acceptance of differing attitudes, accurate assessment of the situation, in-depth analysis, and retention of information. Sharing a variety of perspectives also allows the group to have less fixation on one course of action and to consider more extreme courses of action than an individual working alone would consider. This discussion of different positions enhances members' involvement with the issues, a situation that becomes more significant when the group is considering a radical decision.

Individual vs. Group Decision Making

Individuals can make decisions more quickly than groups can, but the quality of a group's decision will usually be higher. When group members use time and resources wisely, they are able to pool knowledge to solve problems, and ultimately, reach a better-thought-out conclusion. While there are few certifiably "correct" decisions, group members working together can usually produce a higher-quality resolution that can be fully implemented. Groups can typically outperform, or match, the efforts of the individual.

Should groups make all decisions? Although there are no absolute rules, generally circumstances will determine when an individual working alone should make a decision and when a group should be involved.

Groups should make decisions when the following conditions exist.

1. Usually one person working alone is too cautious to take pronounced risks because of the blame or responsibility that occurs if an extreme course of action fails. In groups, both the culpability and the glory are dispersed among the members.
2. Frequently there are many parts or steps to the problem, or a great deal of expertise, credibility, or creativity is required to reach a conclusion. A single person will not usually have the resources that a group can provide.
3. If the individuals involved are likely to be affected by or responsible for the consequences of the decision, especially when their understanding, cooperation, and commitment will be necessary, soliciting their input will increase the likelihood that they will be committed to carrying out the decision.
4. Asking groups to solve problems helps to build democracy and confidence and allows the leader to hear feedback from the members.
5. When implementing the decision demands the coordination of resources, a division of labor, or interdependence, the group members will be able to determine the role that each member must play.
6. When attitudes concerning the problem are likely to be diverse, or when individual members are likely to resist a solution, asking them to reach their own conclusions often engenders cooperation.

On the other hand, circumstances sometimes indicate that an individual, rather than a group, should make a decision. Individuals should make decisions in the following situations.

1. If time is short and/or if all the data is available to make the decision, a person working alone will be able to make the decision more quickly than a group could.
2. Often when the outcome is relatively unimportant to the group or when the outcome does not affect participants directly, especially if the members feel that they attend too many meetings already, they will resist working toward solving a problem.
3. Sometimes one or two group members tend to dominate discussions and cause social pressure within the group to conform—circumstances that can reduce the

discussion to a debate or an intimidating situation. When leaders perceive this kind of situation occurring, making the decision alone or assigning an individual the task of deciding can help to prevent the pessimism and destructive conflict that might occur during a group meeting.

4. If group members are not qualified to make a decision, the individual who is capable of finding a solution should do so.
5. If the information needed to make an informed decision is confidential, only the person who needs to know the data should be involved in the decision-making process.

Situations will determine when group decision making is advisable, but generally, assigning a group the task of reaching a decision will result in a better decision for several reasons. First, **motivation** to make high-quality decisions is often higher for group members than for individuals. Usually people working in groups perform more effectively than individuals who are working alone because social interaction plays a role in their wanting to "measure up." Also, group affiliation allows members to emulate more motivated and skilled individuals and, by doing so, allows them to compare contributions and to raise the standard. The support and encouragement that individuals receive from others in the group contribute to effective decisions which members can then reevaluate and rethink.

Methods of Decision Making

There are several alternatives available to groups when selecting an approach to decision making. Often the nature of the decision or circumstances will play a role in determining the process that will be most effective.

Consensus after discussion involves all members agreeing to support a decision. This method requires the highest degree of input and can take the greatest amount of time, but it has the strongest chance for successful implementation since members feel a certain amount of ownership of the decision.

Negotiation or compromise involves more of a settling or compromising situation than consensus does. Group members give in on some points in order to achieve their important goals. This settlement can result in partial satisfaction and, therefore, only questionable commitment to the outcome.

Voting is one of the fastest methods for decision making, but this method is not without its problems. Voting does not guarantee that the group will choose the best or most appropriate alternative. Even **majority vote**, which involves over 50 percent of the participants agreeing to a course of action, can create difficulties if the decision requires the commitment of each person, even the dissenting ones.

A worse problem, **minority rule**, occurs when less than 50 percent of the members support a decision, a situation that is likely when there are three or more alternatives. This division of support can cause the final outcome to be without substantial advocacy. Sometimes, when a noncritical issue is being considered, a committee or subgroup can make a decision without using and perhaps wasting, the entire group's time. However, when important decisions are involved, more group involvement is advisable.

Both majority and minority rule can cause problems for the group since, in either situation, a significant number of group members may not be motivated to implement the decision.

Sometimes an **authority** or **expert** in the group, after hearing discussion of the alternatives, will make the final decision. If the members recognize the expertise of the person and feel that their contributions have been considered, they will support the decision. However, if the reverse is true, the group's acceptance of the conclusion will be tenuous.

Barriers to Effective Decision Making

When group members make effective decisions, they are able to do so because they have used time and resources well, resulting in correct, or at least well-thought-out conclusions that can be easily carried out. There are, however, problems that will interfere with this process.

Lack of group maturity, that is, not enough time together as a group or inexperience with the task, can cause the group to select an inappropriate course of action. Insufficient time to complete the task, inappropriate group size, and ineffective leadership will further reduce the likelihood of reaching an effective decision.

Pessimism causes the group members to perceive a "no-win" situation that causes them to procrastinate or stall. Dismal hope about reaching an objective can also cause the members to shift responsibility, or to "pass the buck," because each individual fears blame.

Self-centeredness and conflicting goals can cause participants to fail to use information, knowledge, or resources. This desire of some individuals to shine or stand out often results in the group being impaired.

Agreement seeking will often occur when the group lacks heterogeneity, or differences. The homogeneity or sameness of the group is particularly problematic when there is a dominant leader of a powerful subgroup, because the already cohesive group is particularly vulnerable to these strong influences. Groupthink is likely.

Groupthink is a decision-making process first identified by Irving Janis, a social psychologist, in which proposals are accepted without scrutiny, in which suppression of opposing thoughts takes place, and in which members decide to limit analysis or disagreement. Janis blames groupthink for such historical fiascoes as Pearl Harbor, the Bay of Pigs Invasion, the Vietnam War, and the Watergate break-in.

Groupthink, which is often a result of too much cohesion, causes the group to make an incomplete examination of the data and the available options. This can lead the participants to a simplistic solution to a complex problem.

Causes of Groupthink

High cohesion, a positive group dynamic in many instances, can create problems if the group experiences an excessive amount of it. When groups become too unified, the members, especially the insecure or weak ones, allow loyalty to the group to cloud their ability to make effective determinations. Often these weak participants engage in self-censorship because they perceive that "the group knows better." This, coupled with their fear of rejection and the stronger members exerting direct pressure to conform, discourages the voicing of dissenting ideas.

Mind guarding will routinely take place in these highly cohesive groups. Through subtle or overt pressure, powerful members create an atmosphere in which dissonance is not tolerated and in which dissenters are prevented from raising objections. Lack of encouragement to critically evaluate options can even cause members to shut down their own analysis of solutions. The absence of obvious dissent leads members to conclude that the others concur; they assume that there is agreement. There is an *illusion of unanimity*. Mind guarding and high cohesion can further lead to *collective rationalization*. Members invent justification for their actions, causing a feeling that they are acting in the best interest of the group.

This rationalization process can then lead to an *unquestioning belief in the morality of the group*. Ethical consequences are ignored and a Machiavellian attitude develops when the group believes that the "end justifies the means" if they are addressing a "bigger good." This chauvinistic approach causes the group to *stereotype* competitors or critics. By categorizing their opponents as incompetent, nonthreatening, or ignorant, the group can dismiss dissenters as undeserving of consideration. The group can begin to feel cut off and invincible.

This *illusion of invulnerability* occurs when group members feel that they are isolated or insulated from outsiders or qualified associates and imagine that they are not accountable to anyone. This "safety in numbers" mentality and perception of unaccountability can cause excessive risk taking.

Inadequate search and evaluation procedures occur when time constraints and pressures cause the group to look for a "quick fix." Inadequate appraisal can cause a group to settle for the first decent alternative, a situation that becomes more likely if the members are pessimistic about finding a better solution than the obvious one.

When a group limits its discussion to a few solutions without considering all available information, its members fail to discern the subtleties of their preferred choice and of the rejected alternatives. The obvious determines the decision. Under these circumstances the group often fails to work out contingency plans that would contribute to the success. By refusing to consider drawbacks and potential setbacks, the group can inadvertently sabotage its own efforts.

Authoritative leaders, or directive leaders, who express opinions freely may very well be putting the group in a position to develop groupthink. Nonpowerful members may try to win favor by kowtowing to authority. The more obvious the leader's position, the less likely it is that the group will challenge the decision.

Preventing Groupthink

High-quality decision making depends on groups preventing groupthink by structuring a systematic approach for evaluating alternatives.

An impartial leader can refrain from expressing a point of view. If a leader does indicate a preference for a solution, the referent and legitimate power and charisma of the person can sometimes cause the group to support a choice that does not represent an exhaustive appraisal of the available options. By limiting comments to unbiased descriptions and by avoiding the tendency to advocate a specific proposal, the leader will encourage the group to evaluate thoroughly all available information.

The leader can further enhance the evaluation process by assigning one of the members the role of *devil's advocate*. This person is responsible for challenging positions and questioning options. The group is then forced to exercise critical-thinking skills, allowing individuals to remain separate from ideas. Often a specific individual will be assigned the role of devil's advocate, but the leader should encourage every member to be a *critical evaluator*. Inviting outside experts to examine information can also contribute to productivity. By welcoming criticism of their own ideas and by demonstrating that they are willing to be influenced by logic and evidence, leaders can show that critical evaluation and an open climate for discussion are more important than harmony or deference.

The chance to rethink a decision occurs if a *second-chance meeting* is an option. The group can avoid feeling "under the gun" by agreeing that no final decision will be made during the first meeting. Time and distance from the decision will allow group members to avoid impulsiveness and quick-fix methodology.

Groups do not provide the perfect arena for solving all problems or for making all decisions. Working in groups is not without its difficulties; however, when challenges are managed and the talents and resources of each member are used, groups have tremendous potential. When participants understand decision-making dynamics and the pitfalls that accompany them, the group can more effectually reach a conclusion.

Introduction to Readings

All our social institutions, as well as businesses and industries, are permeated with task groups in which individuals join together to solve problems. Every organization is made up of one or more small groups, each with assigned tasks. All governmental and academic institutions are dependent on departmental groups and committees to make decisions and formulate policies. In short, we all spend a great deal of time in groups making decisions. It behooves us, therefore, to study the group decision-making process if we are to better understand the dynamics of small-group communication.

Group decision making is still one of the primary areas of research in small-group study, and we have drawn upon the writings of some of the leading researchers for this chapter. In the first essay, Randy Y. Hirokawa describes some of the early theories concerning the role of communication in decision making, and finds them lacking in useful application because they treat communication as a passive or neutral factor in the process. In his essay, "Communication and Group Decision-Making Efficacy," he points out that the quality of communication may well be the single most important determinant of success or failure in the decision-making group. He proceeds to discuss the latest research findings, which have led him to a "Functional Communication Theory." This theory specifies the factors that contribute to high- or low-quality group decisions such as understanding the problem, formulating a data base for analyzing the problem and assessing the solution, and recognizing available choices. Hirokawa explains how all of these factors are influenced by the quality of communication in the group.

In this chapter's second essay, Dennis S. Gouran turns the coin and examines the forces, which he calls counteractive influences, that hinder effective group decision making. His essay, "Principles of Counteractive Influence in Decision-Making and Problem-Solving Groups," argues that it is not enough to know the steps and procedures that lead to good decisions, but that groups can avoid serious breakdowns and frustrations if the members are aware of the ever-present influences that stand in the way of good problem solving. He offers advice concerning how individuals can confront the counteractive influences of authority relations, pressures for uniformity, status struggles, disruptive behavior, and incompatible goals. When group members are aware of these influences they are in a better position to confront them and prevent them from causing decision-making breakdowns.

Today's global corporations, with their dependence on advanced technology, require decision-making processes that are equal to the demands of this fast-paced world. Bolanle A. Olaniran offers us a glimpse into the world of electronic meetings in his essay, "Group Satisfaction and Decision Quality in Computer-Mediated Communication." He sets out to examine how computer-mediated communication helps fulfill the needs of modern organizations where personnel are spread over the globe, and where face-to-face interactions are difficult and costly to arrange. He proceeds to compare and contrast the computer-mediated group with the more traditional face-to-face group. He examines such important elements as group outcomes, relationship development, consensus, feedback, and group-decision quality. He finds that computer-mediated meetings increase group satisfaction and decision quality by masking the status of group members, not overlooking contributions, reducing negative responses, producing more inputs and ideas, and bringing out more opinions. Olaniran does not propose that computer-mediated groups replace face-to-face communication, but rather that individuals learn how to participate in electronic meetings as another useful type of group process in appropriate settings.

Joseph C. Chilberg, in our next essay, points out that most methods and practices designed to aid group problem solving deal with the total group process. His intent in "Group Process Designs for Facilitating Communication in Problem-Solving Groups," is to describe and apply the practice of *facilitative* behavior to the problem-solving situation. By facilitative behavior he means the communicative activity that helps make an activity or outcome easier to perform or achieve. He sets out to identify the procedural role functions and requisite types of message behaviors relevant to facilitating group problem solving. He calls this "group process design" (GPD) and describes the three aspects of this design, which facilitates problem solving: role specialization, procedures and rules, and technologies. He supplies ample data, examples, and diagrams to provide a clear idea of how facilitative behavior can aid in group decision making.

Our final essay in Chapter 3 reexamines the groupthink hypothesis identified by Irving Janis. Groupthink results when members of a group are so involved in maintaining a cohesive in-group mentality that they fail to engage in realistic evaluations that might disturb the group's equilibrium, leading to faulty decision making. Gregory Moorhead, Richard Ference, and Chris P. Neck in their essay, "Space Shuttle *Challenger* and a Groupthink Framework," report the results of their detailed analysis of the decision-making process that led to the worst disaster in space flight history— the explosion of the space shuttle *Challenger*. They identify the antecedent conditions, the groupthink symptoms, and the decision-making defects that produced the deadly decisions. Through their descriptions and analysis they provide a new framework for recognizing the occurrence of groupthink, and they conclude with suggestions for added means of preventing groupthink.

Communication and Group Decision-Making Efficacy

Randy Y. Hirokawa

Benjamin Franklin once wrote that "in this world nothing is certain but death and taxes." If Franklin were alive today, he would probably revise his statement to include group decision participation.

Surely few would deny the important role that decision-making groups play in our society. Many private and public organizations rely on groups to solve organizational problems and make important planning decisions. A recent survey of *Fortune* "500" companies, for example, found that over 90 percent reported using groups in their daily operations (Lawler & Mohrman 1985). Our democratic government would similarly come to a grinding halt without the aid of groups. To be sure, the work of commissions, boards, and committees of various kinds makes it possible for government leaders to properly administer public programs and attend to the myriad of problems associated with them. Likewise, our educational system could not function effectively without the aid of decision-making groups. Faculty committees, parent-teacher groups, and professional associations all play a prominent role in the daily operation of our schools and universities. One recent survey, in fact, found that the average tenured university professor served on six committees simultaneously and spent eleven hours per week in meetings of various kinds (Brilhart & Galanes 1989, 7).

Our growing dependency on groups to deal with important problems and decisions is unfortunately not an occasion for optimism. Humorous folklore sayings like, "A camel is a horse designed by a committee," or "A committee is a group that keeps minutes and wastes hours," attests to the fact that groups frequently do not work as they should. Indeed some of the most foolhardy and disastrous decisions made by our government have been made by well-informed groups (Janis 1982).

Why Groups Succeed or Fail

The fact that groups often fail to perform as they should has prompted many small group researchers to investigate the question of what contributes to effective group decision-making performance. The results of these studies have identified several different factors that contribute to a group's ability to reach a high-quality decision. One important factor is the *amount and accuracy of information* available to the group. In general, researchers have found that the better informed a group is about the problem it is required to solve, as well as the positive and negative qualities of optional choices available to it, the better able it is to reach a high-quality decision. In fact, numerous authors have indicated that the ability of a group to gather and retain a wide range of information is the single most important determinant of high-quality decision making (Kelley & Thibaut 1969).

A second factor that appears to make a difference in group decision-making efficacy is the *amount of effort* group members put forth in trying to reach a decision. More

Permission to reprint must be obtained from the author. Randy Y. Hirokawa is affiliated with the Department of Communication Studies, University of Iowa.

precisely, researchers have discovered that groups are more likely to reach a high-quality decision when they engage in "vigilant decision making" (Janis & Mann 1977). Vigilant decision making occurs when group members carefully and painstakingly examine and reexamine the information upon which a consequential decision is based. According to Janis (1982), it is this kind of perseverant effort that helps a group overcome negative groupthink forces that can lead it to a remarkably bad decision.

A third factor that appears to affect group performance is the *quality of thinking* that occurs among group members as they attempt to reach a collective decision. In particular, studies have discovered that the ability of a group to reach a high-quality decision is dependent on its members' ability to draw correct or warranted inferences from information bearing on the decision (Gouran 1986). In other words, a group is more likely to reach a high-quality decision when its members are able to draw appropriate conclusions from decision-relevant data available to them.

Importance of Group Communication

While it is clear that group decision-making performance is greatly affected by the amount of information a group possesses, the amount and quality of effort it puts forth during its deliberation, and the quality of thinking it displays in reaching a final decision; it is vitally important to also recognize the role that group communication plays in group decision-making effectiveness. Indeed several authors have suggested that the quality of communication that occurs as a group attempts to reach a decision may well be the single, most important determinant of the decision-making success or failure of that group (Hackman & Morris 1975).

How does a group's communication affect the quality of its decision making? Early theorists speculated that group communication served as a medium or channel through which the true determinants of group decision performance were able to exert their influence. Specifically, it was suggested that group discussion affects the quality of group performance in three general ways.

First, *discussion allows group members to distribute and pool available informational resources necessary for effective decision making and problem solving.* Barnlund (1959), for example, maintained that open discussion is especially important for successful group decision making when the group is characterized by the unequal distribution of vital information. Here the opportunity for group discussion enables informed individuals to disseminate information that is needed by the group, in general, to reach a high-quality choice. A similar point is made by Leavitt (1951), who argued that group discussion facilitates effective group performance when it results in the effective centralization of information in the hands of people who need it to help the group arrive at a high-quality decision. Here the true determinant of group performance is assumed to be the presence of relevant information, and group communication provides the medium through which this information is distributed among group members and subsequently brought to bear on the decision task.

A second view holds that *discussion allows group members to catch and remedy errors of individual judgment.* According to Taylor and Faust (1952), the principal reason why groups generally outperform individual decision makers is because the discussion of ideas, suggestions, and rationales for preferred choices tends to expose informational, judgmental, and reasoning deficiencies within individual members that might go undetected if those individuals were making decisions on their own. Moreover, group discussion provides the opportunity for members to point out and correct these problems before they can contribute to a regrettable final decision. In this case, the true determinant of group decision-making effectiveness is the occurrence of judgment errors by group members, and group interaction provides a medium for detecting and correcting these errors before they can adversely affect group performance.

A third perspective views *discussion as a means for intra-group persuasion.* Riecken (1958) suggested that group discussion affects group decision performance by serving as a medium for persuasion among group members. He notes that group discussion provides members with the opportunity to present and support their decisional preferences and, in so doing, convince others to go along with those alternatives. According to Riecken, the overall quality of a group's decision will often depend on the decision preference of the group's most persuasive member(s). A similar notion is provided by Shaw and Penrod (1962). They suggest that group discussion provides members with the opportunity to convince others to accept and utilize available information in arriving at a collective choice. Their research indicated that the presence of knowledgeable group members does not necessarily lead to high levels of group performance unless those individuals are able to persuade others to accept and utilize the information they possess in arriving at a group decision. According to this view, then, the actual determinants of group performance are the amount and quality of information group members possess, the quality of the alternatives they favor, and their ability to persuade others to accept their information and/or decisional preferences. Group communication thus represents a convenient opportunity for those individuals to display their persuasive skills in convincing others to accept their informational or decisional preferences.

Communication as an Active Medium

In contrast to earlier theorists who viewed the group discussion process as a more or less passive medium that allows the actual factors that affect group decision performance to exert their influence on the group, recent theorists have advocated the more *active* role that communication plays in effective group decision making. This perspective assumes that group communication is more than a convenient channel that group members use to distribute information or make their preferences known to others in the group. Rather, it is a social instrument (or tool) that group members use to create (or constitute) group decisions. As a social tool, however, communication in a group can exert its own distorting and biasing effects on group decisions (Poole & Hirokawa 1986).

One of the most recent theories of group decision-making effectiveness that adopts an active view of the group communication process is the *Functional Communication Theory.* Briefly, this theory is based on two general assumptions: First, all decision-making tasks are characterized by certain requirements that have to be fulfilled in order for a group to reach a high-quality decision; and second, group communication represents the means by which group members attempt to fulfill the critical requirements of their task. In short, the Functional Communication Theory adopts an instrumental view of group communication and sees it as the primary "means by which group members attempt to meet the requisites for successful group decision making" (Gouran & Hirokawa 1983).

Functional Communication Theory

The Functional Communication Theory begins with a general description of the process used by groups to make decisions. According to the theory, a group's decision is usually the end result of a series of prior conclusions reached by the members of that group in regard to three general issues: (1) Is there something about the present state of affairs that requires improvement or change? (2) What do we want to achieve or accomplish in deciding what to do about the problem? and (3) What are the choices available to us, and what are the positive and negative aspects of those choices?

Groups usually attend to these issues in a more or less organized manner. This process represents the operation of the group's informal *decision logic*; that is, the system of critical thinking or reasoning that it employs in arriving at a collective group decision. Although the specific order in which these issues are addressed by a group can, and often does, vary from group to group, the general process can be described as follows.

Groups usually begin by attempting to *understand the problematic situation* presented to them. The amount of time a group spends discussing its problem will depend on the complexity of the problem, as well as the amount of knowledge each member has about it. In general, however, the group will attempt to identify and assess the specific aspects of the current situation that make it an undesirable state of affairs. This discussion is likely to focus on such questions as: What happened? Who was involved? Why did it happen? What harms resulted from the event(s)? Who was hurt?

Once the group is satisfied with its understanding of the problematic situation and, moreover, is convinced that action is needed to deal with the problem, it generally proceeds in one of two directions. In some cases, the group will *consider the alternative courses of action available to it*. Here the group will either examine choices that have been presented to it, or generate its own set of options if none already exist. Alternatively, the group may *discuss what they want to accomplish* in selecting a course of action for dealing with the current situation. Here the group will attempt to reach an agreement regarding the goal(s) or objective(s) that they seek to attain through their choice making. In some cases, this goal may simply be to minimize the amount of work that the group has to engage in. However, many groups will seek to accomplish multiple goals (e.g., save money, conserve resources, maintain equity and fairness) in arriving at a final decision.

Upon reaching an ostensible agreement regarding the goal(s) that it seeks to achieve with this choice making, as well as the choices available to it, the group will usually turn its attention to the positive and negative qualities of available choices. This discussion will usually involve two interrelated facets: first, the group will seek to identify the positive and/or negative qualities of optional choices, and second, it will compare those positive and negative qualities to determine which option, or combination of options, offers the best or most acceptable "package" of positive and negative outcomes. This determination will usually lead to the group's final choice. In evaluating alternative choices, it is important to recognize that a group will usually not examine exhaustively the positive and negative qualities associated with available options. Rather, it will tend to focus on the most salient or obvious positive and negative attributes of given choices.

Throughout all phases of the group's decision-making process, its members will rely on information available to it. Some of this information is provided by knowledgeable group members, while other data may be obtained from sources outside the group. Still, more information will take the form of assumptions and inferences that group members draw from existing facts or opinions. Regardless of the origin of the information, however, a group will actively attend to its *information base.* That is, throughout the decision-making process, group members will often examine, and occasionally, challenge the validity and relevancy of available information, as well as assess how that information should be used to formulate a final decision. Figure 1 summarizes the general model of group decision making that we have been describing.

By conceptualizing the group decision-making process as the operation of an informal reasoning system characterized by a number of interrelated subdecisions that leads to a final group decision, the Functional Communication Theory is able to specify the factors that contribute to high- or low-quality group decisions. Specifically, the theory proposes that the quality of a group's decision is largely determined by the influence of group interaction on four facets of the reasoning system employed by a group in arriving at a collective decision. These include: (1) the analysis of the problematic

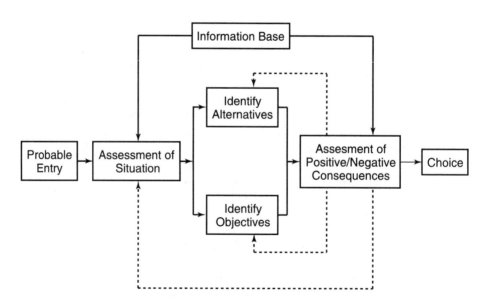

Figure 1. General model of group decision making. (From Hirokawa, R. Y., and D. R. Scheerhorn, 1986. "Communication in Faulty Group Decision Making." In R. Y. Hirokawa and M. S. Poole (eds.), *Communication and Group Decision Making*, 63–80. Beverly Hills, CA: Sage. Reprinted by permission of Sage Publishers.)

situation; (2) the establishment of goals and objectives; (3) the evaluation of positive and negative qualities of available choices; and (4) the formulation and utilization of available information.

Analysis of the Problematic Situation

The quality of a group's final decision is partially affected by its efforts to understand the problematic situation that serves as the stimulus for choice making. Since this analysis tends to occur fairly early in the group's decision-making process, errors occurring at this stage of the reasoning process are likely to carry over, and adversely affect other phases of the process as well. One such error is the group's failure to recognize the existence of a problematic (or potentially problematic) situation. If this happens, the group will most likely terminate the decision-making process prematurely and subsequently neglect to take appropriate action to alleviate the existing problem. Another type of error is the group's failure to properly identify the cause(s) of the existing problem. When a group is unable to identify, or somehow misidentifies, the reason(s) for the existence of the problematic situation, it is unlikely to focus on alternative courses of action that will function to remedy or eliminate the factor(s) that are responsible for the existence of the problem. In short, it is vital for a group to properly understand the problem it is dealing with in order to effectively proceed through subsequent phases of the decision-making process, and ultimately arrive at a high-quality decision.

The tragic crash of the space shuttle *Challenger* provides an unfortunate example of what can happen when a decision-making group fails to properly assess the problem presented to it. Immediately following the disaster, President Reagan appointed a special investigation committee to determine the cause of the accident. The committee determined that the primary cause of the fatal accident was a mechanical failure in one of the joints of the right solid rocket booster. Had this malfunction never occurred in the past, the committee would probably have concluded that the accident was the result of an anomaly that no one could have reasonably anticipated or prevented. However, the investigating body discovered that mechanical failure in the rocket joints had been an ongoing problem for several years prior to the disaster. In fact, engineers with Morton Thiokol, the manufacturer of the rocket booster, had designated the O-ring seals as a "Criticality 1" component—that is, "a failure point—without backup—that could cause a loss of life or vehicle if the component fails" (Report 1986, 84). Despite the presence of the "Criticality 1" designation, the available data indicates that during the decision-making process involving the *Challenger* launch, key decision makers with both Morton Thiokol and NASA believed that a problem with the O-ring seals *did not* exist. Specifically, they were convinced that the seals were functioning properly, and moreover, the system had sufficient safeguards to prevent the occurrence of any disastrous consequences should the O-ring seals actually fail (Hirokawa, Gouran & Martz 1988, 416–419). In short, the launch decision team decided to proceed with the launch because its members did not perceive the existence of a problematic situation. Had the group properly perceived the problem, it is unlikely that it would have approved the launch.

Establishment of Goals and Objectives

Group decision-making efficacy is also affected by the goal(s) or objective(s) that the group seeks to achieve through its choice making. In general, a group is more likely to make a high-quality choice when it strives to attain objective(s) that, if achieved, will substantially improve or remedy the current problematic situation. On the other hand, group decision-making effectiveness can be severely hampered if one (or both) of the following problems arise: (1) the group neglects to seek objective(s) that need to be achieved in order to substantially improve or correct the problematic situation; and (2) the group aspires to attain goals that, even if achieved, will not substantially improve or remedy the problematic situation. Simply put, when the goals that a group seeks to attain through its choice making are somehow inappropriate, the final decision that it reaches is also likely to be inappropriate because a group's goals usually serve as the basis for the selection and defense of an available alternative.

Once again, the space shuttle *Challenger* case provides a clear illustration of how improper goals and objectives can adversely affect group decision making. Traditionally, NASA decisions involving the launch of manned space vehicles were governed by a very conservative rule which dictated that a launch should be canceled if there is any doubt of its safety. Thus, NASA's primary objective in deciding to launch a vehicle was the success of the mission and the safety of the crew. In the case of the *Challenger*, however, available evidence indicates that some very different objectives may have been operating during the decision-making process. Several participants in the decision-making process subsequently indicated feeling pressure to maintain the ambitious schedule that NASA had established for the shuttle program. This pressure was further exacerbated by the tremendous media attention that had been focused on the upcoming launch because it involved civilian personnel and symbolized the insep-arability of space exploration and the future of education (Gouran, Hirokawa & Martz 1986). In short, it appears that the decision makers involved in the *Challenger* launch, while still concerned with safety, were heavily influenced by a desire to maintain their launch schedule. In fact, there is evidence that this objective overrode the long-standing objective of safety that NASA had always pursued and may have contributed to the ill-advised decision to launch the *Challenger* (Hirokawa et al. 1988).

Evaluation of Positive and Negative Qualities

The group's evaluation of the positive and negative qualities of available choices is a third factor that affects group decision efficacy. Since a group usually relies on its assessment of the positive and/or negative aspects of available alternatives in making a final decision, breakdowns at this stage of the group deliberation process can directly affect a group's ability to arrive at a high-quality choice. Specifically, there are four types of errors that can adversely affect a group's efforts to make a high-quality choice: (1) failure to recognize the positive qualities of available choices; (2) failure to recognize the negative qualities of available choices; (3) overestimation of the positive qualities of available choices; and (4) overestimation of the negative qualities of available choices.

A group's ability to make a high-quality choice is enhanced by its recognition of the positive features of available choices. At the same time, a failure to properly recognize the positive qualities of a given alternative can cause the group to bypass that alternative in favor of a less desirable one. To illustrate this point, consider the hypothetical case of the Dreadful Freds, the perennial doormat of the Iowa City Fantasy Football League. Fred Antczak, owner of the Freds, is a firm believer in group decision making. Tired of always finishing in last place, he calls a meeting of his top executives to discuss the team's consistently woeful performance. After discussing various reasons why the team always finishes in last place, the group reaches the conclusion that the team's poor performance is due to the absence of an outstanding quarterback. The group thus decides to obtain a topnotch quarterback in the upcoming player draft. Before examining available choices, the group agrees that it wants to attain two objectives in making its choice: (1) increase the number of rushing and passing yards the team gains next year; and (2) increase the number of touchdowns the team scores next year. The group then proceeds to assess the positive and negative qualities of quarterbacks available in the upcoming player draft. This evaluation leads the group to believe that the best choice is John E. United. If the group's evaluation is thorough and accurate, it is likely that they will have made a good choice. However, if the group somehow fails to recognize certain positive qualities of one of the available candidates (for example, the group fails to recognize the running and passing ability of Terry Broadstraw, or overlooks the leadership skills of Roger Starbuck), the group can easily bypass a better candidate in favor of a lesser quality one.

Similarly, the group's efforts to make a high-quality choice can also be thwarted by its failure to recognize the negative qualities of available choices. Here the group's inability to acknowledge the negative qualities of available alternatives can cause it to select a less-favorable alternative over other more favorable ones. Returning to the deliberation of the Dreadful Freds executive committee, suppose it fails to recognize that John E. United's contract with his former team entitles him to certain long-term benefits and options that the Freds are unable to provide. Had the group known about these hidden benefits, it would not have selected United. Unfortunately, in failing to recognize this important negative quality, the group ended up making a highly regrettable decision.

Clearly a group's failure to recognize the positive or negative qualities of available choices can directly contribute to faulty choice making. Equally problematic, however, are the related evaluation errors associated with the overestimation of the positive or negative qualities of available choices. Clearly, a group can make a faulty decision if it overestimates the positive qualities of available choices. By believing that a particular choice has more desirable features than it actually possesses, a group can select a choice that turns out to be less desirable than other available options. For example, if our committee of football executives somehow overestimates the positive qualities of one of its candidates—say, it believes that Terry Broadstraw is a better runner and passer than he is—and relies on that inflated judgment in making its decision, the group can easily make a choice that it later regrets.

Similarly, a group can make a poor choice if it somehow overestimates the negative qualities of available choices. In this case, by believing that a given alternative has more negative features than it actually possesses, the group can risk bypassing a high-quality choice in favor of a less desirable one. For instance, if our group of football executives mistakenly believes that Roger Starbuck's bad knees make him less mobile than he really is, the group can easily overlook an outstanding quarterback.

Formulation and Utilization of Information

A fourth factor that can contribute to the quality of a group's decision making concerns the information that a group possesses, as well as the manner in which it utilizes that information in arriving at a collective decision. According to our decision-making model, the information available to a group plays an important role in all phases of the critical-reasoning process. As such, errors associated with the establishment and utilization of available information can adversely affect all phases of the decision-making process, and consequently, contribute to faulty decisions.

Errors in the establishment of a group's information base can occur in several ways. One way is for a group to accept invalid or false information. In his book, *Victims of Groupthink*, Janis (1982) notes that our government's ill-advised decision to invade the Bay of Pigs in Cuba was heavily influenced by faulty information that was provided by the Central Intelligence Agency regarding the presence of Soviet military personnel in that part of Cuba. According to Janis, this false information caused the Kennedy administration to perceive a threat to U.S. security that was not warranted at the time. This misperception of the problem subsequently prompted the Cabinet to decide on an inappropriate course of action that resulted in public embarrassment for the U.S. government and the Kennedy administration.

A second type of information error concerns the group's rejection of valid or factual information. In this case, the group fails to take into account information that might prove helpful in understanding the problem or assessing the positive or negative qualities of alternative choices. In some cases, valid information may be rejected because it does not support a preferred course of action. At other times, it is rejected because it does not conform to the experiences of the group. Whatever the reason, rejection of valid information can prove problematic in effective group decision making. For example, Janis (1982) maintains that the ill-advised decision to keep the Pacific Fleet in Pearl Harbor prior to the Japanese surprise attack on December 7, 1941, was precipitated by the Pacific Fleet commanders' rejection of accurate military intelligence data indicating that the Japanese planned to launch a major attack on a U.S. naval base. In fact, the group of naval officers in charge of Pearl Harbor had received information that a major armada had left Japan in the direction of Hawaii. While the information provided was not specific in regards to the precise target of the attack, the most likely possibilities were limited to Hawaii and the Philippines. According to Janis, had the Pacific Fleet commanders taken these intelligence data seriously and acted on them by better protecting the ships in Pearl Harbor, the Japanese attack might neither have been a surprise nor a success. Sadly, the group chose to ignore the data and left the ships completely vulnerable to the enemy.

A third type of informational error concerns the group's utilization of available information. In this instance, although the information may be essentially correct, the manner in which the group interprets and employs that information in analyzing the problem or evaluating alternative choices is flawed. As a result, the group can make a choice that it later regrets. The previously discussed *Challenger* case can again be used to illustrate this point. The investigation of the accident revealed that NASA officials were provided with sufficient information to warrant the postponement of the scheduled launch. For example, weather information indicated extremely cold temperature and corresponding ice buildup on the shuttle, its main fuel tank, and the launch platform prior to the scheduled launch. In fact, officials with Rockwell, designer and builder of the shuttle, expressed concern that the icing might damage the shuttle or its fuel tank if the launch were to take place before the ice had a chance to melt off. Additionally, engineers with Morton Thiokol, designer and builder of the solid rocket motors, expressed concern that the subfreezing temperature would further diminish the already questionable performance of the O-ring seals.

A crucial question raised during the investigation of the accident was why NASA officials did not postpone the launch on the basis of the information available to them? On the surface, it appears that they simply ignored the information. Upon closer inspection, however, the problem had to do with the conclusions that were drawn from that information. The clearest example of this faulty reasoning was displayed by George Hardy, Deputy Director of Science and Engineering with NASA. Hardy stated that his interpretation of the engineering data indicating prior O-ring malfunctions led him to the conclusion that the launch *should* proceed. When the investigation committee pointed out that NASA had been informed that the malfunction could have catastrophic consequences, Hardy replied that such a possibility was "true of every other flight we had" (Report 1986). His reasoning was that since past risk taking had not produced catastrophic consequences, it was unlikely to occur in the case of the *Challenger*. The obvious flaw in Hardy's reasoning is akin to the famous "gambler's fallacy." That is, when dealing with independent events, the probability of an event occurring in the future has nothing to do with whether it had occurred in the past. In short, just because previous O-ring malfunctions had not affected the success of previous shuttle missions, Hardy was not justified in concluding that future missions would also be successful, since each flight would be an independent event.

Summary and Conclusions

It should be clear at this point that effective group decision making usually does not happen by accident. In most cases, a group is able to make a high-quality choice because the system of reasoning that it employed in arriving at a final choice was characterized by (1) proper understanding of the problematic situation; (2) appropriate choice-making objectives; (3) accurate evaluation of the positive and negative qualities of available choices; and (4) warranted utilization of high-quality information in arriving at a final decision.

We have argued that it is very easy for errors to occur in various phases of the group's reasoning process. In fact, we have suggested that errors occurring in one phase can facilitate additional errors in subsequent phases. The important question that remains to be answered at this point is *why* these errors occur. Throughout this essay, we have intimated that group communication plays a crucial role in the facilitation *and* prevention of reasoning errors. That is to say, the communicative actions of group members can both cause an error to occur, as well as keep it from occurring. What we don't quite understand, however, is why group communication produces reasoning errors in some cases but not in others.

One possible explanation focuses on the persuasive skills of group members. We have long known that the performance of a group can be predicted on the basis of the knowledge and skills of its individual members. In other words, groups with talented members are likely to out-perform groups with less talented members. Recently, however, we have discovered that the relationship between individual member ability and group performance outcomes is dependent on the persuasive skills of group members. For example, a group may possess members who are very knowledgeable about the problem, but unless those members are skillful at communicating this knowledge to the rest of the group, it is unlikely that the group's understanding of the problem will match that of its knowledgeable members. Typically this communication involves the use of arguments and other persuasive tactics to convince less knowledgeable members to accept the views of the more knowledgeable members. If this persuasive communication is unsuccessful, or the less knowledgeable members prove to be more influential, errors of reasoning can easily occur.

A second possible explanation concerns the influence of interpersonal relationships among group members. Group communication theorists have long recognized that group members seek to achieve multiple objectives through their communicative actions. That is to say, a group member, in making a contribution to the discussion, may attempt to both (1) advance the thought line of the group, and (2) support the previous contribution of a friend in the group. In short, group members often strive to satisfy both *task* and *social* goals in their communication with others. In many instances, these task and social goals are compatible—that is, an individual can accomplish multiple goals through his or her communicative actions. Occasionally, however, task and social goals may be in conflict with each other. For example, a group member may clearly recognize a problem with the suggestion of a fellow member, but because that individual is a close friend (or superior), the group member will refrain from saying anything negative about the idea. Here the task goal (accurate evaluation) is superseded by the conflicting social goal (maintaining positive relationship), thereby resulting in a breakdown in reasoning. Similarly, a group member may choose to argue against a good idea simply because it was produced by a fellow member whom she or he dislikes. Once again the task goal is superseded by the social goal. In short, it is possible that errors in group reasoning occur because of the displacement of task goals in favor of social ones during group interaction.

Clearly there is still much we need to understand about the role that group communication plays in the effective performance of the group. Fortunately, the theoretical perspective discussed in this essay provides us with a useful framework for better understanding this role. As we discover more about how communicative forces positively and negatively influence the reasoning system employed by a group in arriving at a decision, we will be in a much better position to offer warranted prescriptions for improving the quality of group interaction and performance. For the moment, however, it may be sufficient for groups to simply recognize the reasoning process they are employing to arrive at a decision, and to be aware of breakdowns that can occur in that process. Such self-conscious deliberation can pay big dividends in insuring effective group decision making.

References

Barnlund, D.C. (1959). "A Comparative Study of Individual, Majority, and Group Judgment." *Journal of Abnormal and Social Psychology* 58, 55–60.

Brilhart, J.K., and Galanes, G.J. (1989). *Effective Group Discussion* 6th ed. Dubuque, IA: Wm. C. Brown.

Gouran, D.S. (1982). *Making Decisions in Groups: Choices and Consequences.* Glenview, IL: Scott Foresman.

Gouran, D.S., and Hirokawa, R.Y. (1983). "The Role of Communication in Decision-Making Groups: A Functional Perspective." In M.S. Mander (ed.), *Communications in Transition,* 168–185. New York: Praeger.

Gouran, D.S., Hirokawa, R.Y., and Martz, A.E. (1986). "A Critical Analysis of Factors Related to Decisional Processes Involved in the *Challenger* Disaster." *Central States Speech Journal* 37, 119–135.

Hackman, J.R., and Morris, C.G. (1975). "Group Tasks, Group Interaction Process, and Group Performance Effectiveness: A Review and Proposed Integration." In L. Berkowitz (ed.), *Advances in Experimental Social Psychology* 8, 45–99. New York: Academic Press.

Hirokawa, R.Y., Gouran, D.S., and Martz, A.E. (1988). "Understanding the Sources of Faulty Group Decision Making: A Lesson From the *Challenger* Disaster." *Small Group Behavior* 19, 411–433.

Hirokawa, R.Y., and Scheerhorn, D.R. (1986). "Communication in Faulty Group Decision Making." In R.Y. Hirokawa and M.S. Poole (eds.), *Communication and Group Decision Making,* 63–80. Beverly Hills, CA: Sage.

Janis, I.L. (1982). *Victims of Groupthink* 2d ed. Boston: Houghton Mifflin.

Janis, I.L., and Mann, L. (1977). *Decision Making.* New York: Free Press.

Kelley, H.H., and Thibaut, J.W. (1969). "Group Problem Solving." In G. Lindzey and E. Aronson (eds.), *Handbook of Social Psychology,* 1–101. Cambridge, MA: Addison-Wesley.

Lawler, E., and Mohrman, S. (1985, January–February). "Quality Circles After the Fad." *Harvard Business Review,* 65–71.

Leavitt, H.J. (1951). "Some Effects of Certain Communication Patterns on Group Performance." *Journal of Abnormal and Social Psychology* 46, 38–50.

Poole, M.S., and Hirokawa, R.Y. (1986). "Communication and Group Decision Making: A Critical Assessment." In R.Y. Hirokawa and M.S. Poole (eds.), *Communication and Group Decision Making,* 15–31. Beverly Hills, CA: Sage.

Report of the Presidential Commission on the Space Shuttle Challenger Disaster. (1986). Washington D.C.: Alderson Reporting.

Riecken, H.W. (1958). "The Effects of Talkativeness on Ability to Influence Group Solutions to Problems." *Sociometry* 21, 309–321.

Shaw, M.E., and Penrod, W.T. (1962). "Does More Information Available to a Group Always Improve Group Performance? *Sociometry* 25, 377–390.

Taylor, D.W., and Faust, W.L. (1952). "Twenty Questions: Efficiency in Problem Solving as a Function of Size of Group. *Journal of Experimental Psychology* 44, 360–368.

Principles of Counteractive Influence in Decision-Making and Problem-Solving Groups

Dennis S. Gouran

In a 1978 article entitled "Humans Would Do Better Without Groups," Christian J. Buys expresses a sentiment that undoubtedly has been shared at one time or another by virtually everyone who has some experience participating in decision-making and problem-solving groups.[1] Although such a reaction to one's involvement with groups is more likely to be the exception than the rule, in moments of frustration atypical occurrences are the things that tend to stand out. Because they are more memorable, particularly dissatisfying group experiences are the ones to which an individual is likely to refer when envisioning the consequences of future participation.[2]

Despite his seeming exaggeration of the negative qualities of group life, Buys nevertheless has touched on a matter to which nearly all of us can relate. Participation in groups (for purposes of this essay, decision-making and problem-solving groups especially) is frequently a dissatisfying and unproductive experience. Even those who are well schooled in the principles of effective group interaction often feel powerless to contend with problem group discussions that appear to be going nowhere—or at least, not where they are supposed to be going.

Unfortunately, pedagogically oriented literature and formal instruction in the dynamics of group process have inadequately addressed the full range of issues and behavioral competencies of which a practitioner needs to be aware. As a result of this deficiency, most of us are not prepared to contribute to decision-making and problem-solving discussions in ways that maximize the chances for achieving desired group objectives. In the present case, these objectives entail finding the most appropriate answer to a controversial question or the most effective resolution of a problem. However, before we can fully appreciate the basis for the preceding criticism, we need to have an understanding of the general classes of influence that determine how well or poorly groups perform.

Sources of Influence in the Performance of Decision-Making and Problem-Solving Groups

Let us begin with a discussion of a metaphor commonly applied to the performance of groups. This metaphor likens groups to vehicles moving along a pathway from a starting point toward some predetermined destination. This likeness is particularly apt in the case of decision-making and problem-solving groups. In the context of the metaphor, movement along the goal-path is controlled by a series of forces or, perhaps more appropriately, influences.[3] The interaction among these influences determines whether or not a group will arrive at its intended destination.

Although there are many ways in which one can classify the influences that affect direction of movement, three designations that appear to be particularly useful are:

Permission to reprint must be obtained from the author. Dennis S. Gouran is affiliated with the Speech Communication Department, the Pennsylvania State University.

(1) proactive influences, (2) inertial influences, and (3) counteractive influences. Following is a brief examination of the essential properties of each type.

Proactive Influences

Proactive influences represent classes of behavior that, in an obstacle-free environment, would enable the members of a group to move directly toward their goal. The behavior in question is suggested by the nature of the task the group is performing and the inherently logical sequence in which necessary functions ought to be performed, for instance, defining the nature of a problem, determining its causes, establishing the criteria that a solution ideally would meet, identifying possible solutions, assessing alternatives in relation to each criterion, and selecting the solution that best satisfies the agreed upon criteria. Few, if any, task environments are obstacle-free. In most groups, therefore, at some point movement will either be halted or diverted from the goal-path. Whether or not a group successfully resumes movement or returns to the goal-path is a function of the relative strength of the other two categories of influence.

Inertial Influences

In physics, inertia refers to the tendency for an object at rest to remain at rest and for an object in motion to remain in motion. Applied in the context of group life, the concept can refer to either behavior contributing to an inability to progress along the path to a goal, or behavior which sustains movement in whatever direction a group is heading.

Inertial forces, it should be clear, may have both facilitative and inhibitory consequences. To the extent that they contribute to movement in a desired direction, they are facilitative. If they help forestall movement or sustain it in a direction away from a group's goal, they are inhibitory.

Counteractive Influences

When a group's inertia is inhibiting movement, counteractive influences may come into play. Broadly defined, there are behaviors directed toward restoration of movement along a group's goal-path.[4] If the amount of counteractive force generated in an influence attempt is insufficient to overcome the group's inertia, movement will either remain in an arrested state or continue in the wrong direction.

An Extended Example

Since the preceding discussion is somewhat abstract, an extended concrete illustration may serve to clarify the concepts just introduced. Consider a group discussing the question, "What should be done to deal with the problem of alcohol abuse among college students?" Preceding any consideration of alternative policy options, logically, would be an effort to determine whether there is a serious enough problem to warrant some kind of action. A first step in this determination might be for the members of the group to achieve agreement on what they mean by alcohol abuse.

Suppose that a participant recognizing the definitional requirement observes, "I think that we need to specify what constitutes alcohol abuse." Another responds that she thinks "alcohol abuse exists whenever a consumer reaches the point that he or she loses self-control." "Could you be more specific?", requests a third party. To this point, the group is under the control of proactive influences. In other words, it is trying to deal with a primary requisite of the discussion task, a definition has been offered, and one member is attempting to elicit a clearer conception of the crucial term in the question being considered.

Now further suppose that someone in the group complains, "We'll never be able to define alcohol abuse. It's all a matter of personal opinion." The first obstacle has been erected in the goal-path. The line of communication initiated by this act, moreover, conceivably could begin to turn the group in a direction other than the one in which the members had intended to move. That is, they might begin quibbling over whether or not terms like *alcohol abuse* are amenable to definition. Were this to happen and were the inertia in that direction to build, the possibility of finding an appropriate answer to the discussion question could well be subverted.

In the situation just described, a member sensitive to the group's departure from its goal-path might try to avert an unnecessary squabble by reframing the issue. For example, "No definition of something as elusive as alcohol abuse, of course, will be completely satisfactory, but surely we can say what we mean by the term in ways to which all of us are able to relate. I believe that most people would agree that the individual who exceeds the legal limit of alcohol consumption and drives an automobile is guilty of abuse; but that is just one type of abuse. Why don't we try to list all of the situations involving the excessive use of alcohol which gave rise to the question in the first place?" An observation of this sort could do much to counteract the digression created by the dissident group member and, thereby, rechannel the participants' interaction toward their original objective. How likely the chance of such a comment having the desired effect would depend on how far the group's inertia had carried it from the goal-path.

Deficiencies in Discussion Training

Having examined the influences that affect the achievement of group goals in decision-making and problem-solving discussions, I can more fully develop my earlier criticism of pedagogically oriented literature and instruction. Most discussion training and the materials on which it draws focus are what I have been calling proactive influences. That is, its aim is to acquaint the practitioner with principles of performance which, in an environment free of major obstacles, would be sufficient to assure the achievement of a group's goal(s). Such instruction often derives from rational models of problem solving and decisional choice. Typically, these models specify (1) the sequence of requirements involved in finding a correct solution to a problem or in making an informed decision, and (2) the activities that seemingly best fulfill these requirements.[5]

The crux of my concern is not that the emphasis in discussion instruction is misplaced, but that it does not go far enough. Training based on rational considerations alone does not adequately prepare one to respond intelligently to certain realities of group life that can and do seriously limit the possibilities of achieving desired outcomes. This is not to suggest that those of us involved in offering instruction in decision-making and problem-solving discussions ignore the various and sundry obstacles to effective performance. If our pedagogical practices have been deficient, the problem lies not in a failure to call attention to inhibitory influences. Rather, the difficulty is that we do not provide sufficient bases for knowing how to respond when such influences are operative. In short, we have too little to say about the *art of counteractive influence.*

Exercising Counteractive Influence: Some Behavioral Principles

Since most of the research which examines obstacles to effective performance in small groups has concentrated on their impact rather than the means of overcoming them, the previously mentioned weaknesses in instruction are quite understandable. As a counterpoint to this argument, one might feel that if we know what negatively influences the performance of decision-making and problem-solving groups, then by implication, we should know how to deal with them. The issue is not that simple, however. Knowing, for example, that an autocratic style of leadership inhibits the objective examination of alternative policy options provides no necessary indications of how one might go about managing the problem.

In spite of the need for considerably more research on the role of counteractive influence and the behavioral principles that enable one to exercise it successfully, present knowledge in a few select areas does allow for the formulation of general guidelines. In the remainder of this essay, therefore, I offer advice concerning how one might counteract the inertial tendencies that come into play when a group specifically confronts obstacles posed by (1) authority relations, (2) pressure for uniformity, (3) status differentiation, (4) disruptive behavior, and (5) incompatibility between individual and collective goals. The problems arising in these five categories by no means exhaust the complete range. Nevertheless, they represent a familiar and recurrent set of difficulties with which participants in decision-making and problem-solving groups often feel ill-prepared to contend.

Overcoming Obstacles Posed by Authority Relations

Among other things, the study of authority relations has revealed how easily people in positions of power can ordinarily elicit compliant responses to their influence attempts. Milgram's controversial research on obedience to authority, for example, rather dramatically underscores this observation.[6] Other research, moreover, has established that because of the relative ease with which authority figures induce compliance, groups may be led to foolish, inappropriate, or otherwise costly decisions.[7]

Apparently, in some circumstances in which authority figures effectively exercise an unhealthy influence, a kind of "pluralistic ignorance" sets in. Although most, if not all, of the other members of the group privately oppose the direction in which the authority figure wishes to move, they remain silent because of the erroneous perception that others are favorably disposed to what the authority figure is doing.[8] In most instances, however, the success of authority influence stems from the perception by less powerful group members that the authority has the right to determine the group's direction or that he or she possesses the resources with which to punish noncompliance.[9]

Not all influence attempts by authority figures have negative consequences, of course. When they do, however, the question that arises from the point of view of the person who recognizes that the authority figure is moving the group away from its goal, is how best to respond. What types of communicative strategies can be employed to redirect the members toward the goal-path? Does one apply some tactic of ingratiation? Will reasoning with the authority figure create a receptivity to redirection? Is a head-on confrontation likely to work?

Many people would follow their intuitive hunches in coping with the sort of situation described above. The danger, however, is that one might do more harm than good. The individual who recognizes the need to counteract the influence of an authority figure requires something more than intuition to guide his or her judgment about how to treat the problem. The question is, can we frame a general principle that will better inform such judgments? I believe that we can.

The knowledge that the power of authority figures is determined by the target of influence suggests that his or her influence can be successfully counteracted.[10] In addition, we know that resistance to an authority figure's influence attempts increases the probability of others' displaying resistance.[11] Finally, we know that reinforcement of one's authority will often result in favorable responses to the source of reinforcement.[12] Guided by these bits of knowledge, we have the basis of a general behavioral principle for dealing with the inhibitory constraints on effective decision making and problem solving that authority figures sometimes impose. That principle can be stated in the following manner: *When an authority figure's influence is interfering with a group's progress toward its goal, if possible, try to establish resistance in a way that does not threaten his or her authority.*

To visualize how one might apply the principle of resistance implicit in the work of French, Adams and Romney, and Milgram, consider the following hypothetical situation. A hiring committee in a large business establishment has narrowed its list of job applicants for a position to three and is trying to decide the one to whom the job should be offered. The committee consists of a top level executive, a representative from the middle management level, and a recently appointed junior executive. The objective of the committee members is to select the best-qualified applicant; however, in the course of discussion, it soon becomes apparent that the upper level executive, who also happens to be chairing the committee, prefers the least well-qualified candidate. The chairperson further makes it clear that concurrence is expected.

One approach that the other committee members might take in dealing with the obstacle created by the chairperson's expressed preference would be simply to voice their disagreement and to make their own preference clear. However, this type of ganging-up tactic might only serve to intensify the chair's determination to have his or her way even if it required exercising autocratic rule.[13]

Under the circumstances, the interests of effective decision making would probably be better served were one of the subordinate committee members to ask the chairperson to show how the qualifications of the preferred candidate better satisfy the group's selection criteria than those of the other two choices. The remaining member, then, could reinforce the request. This more subtle form of counteractive influence attempt would redirect the group's attention to substantive concerns. Rather than simply voicing a preference, the chairperson would be obliged to provide the bases for his or her judgment.

From the perspective of theories of social power, the latter approach would be preferable because it would reinforce the superior's authority while simultaneously requiring that he or she focus on the point at issue in a more objective manner. Whether the influence attempt would be successful, of course, is a matter about which one could have no assurance. Still, it represents an intelligent way of avoiding the extremes of acquiescence or of antagonism to the authority figure. In addition, by inducing the authority figure to analyze his or her own judgment, there is a greater likelihood of a change in position. With authority figures, self-reflection tends to be a better stimulus for change than are attempts to impose externally generated influence.

Overcoming Obstacles Posed by Pressure for Uniformity

Pressure for uniformity is a second aspect of group life that sometimes requires the exercise of counteractive influence if a decision-making or problem-solving group is to progress along its goal-path. Deviation from a majority position frequently induces pressure for uniformity, particularly in cohesive groups.[14] Schacter has demonstrated that persistence in one's opposition can lead to rejection.[15] Since one loses all possibility of influencing a group's actions when he or she has been rejected, it is essential to avoid this outcome. Hence, many individuals will respond to pressure by conforming to the majority position.

Although pressure for uniformity and the conformity that it promotes are not intrinsically undesirable, on many occasions they contribute to the ineffective execution of a group's task. When a majority position is in error or is otherwise indefensible, pressure for uniformity constitutes a serious obstacle to those trying to keep the group headed toward its destination. The alternatives of either acquiescing or being rejected, moreover, can leave one with a sense of helplessness. For such individuals a knowledge of communicative strategies that will free them from this dilemma is most desirable.

As in the case of authority relations, previous scholarship has provided some useful leads in devising means of counteracting the inhibitory influence of pressure for uniformity. In a situation very much like the one studied by Schacter, Harnack found that by remaining reasonable and refraining from responding in kind to abusive remarks, not only did opinion deviates continue to be accepted by the majority they opposed, but they actually induced movement toward their own positions.[16] Valentine and Fisher also discovered that different types of deviance have different consequences for a group's performance.[17] The variety of deviant behavior they refer to as "innovative" appears to have constructive effects as opposed to "noninnovative" or simple opposition. The latter forms tend to be personally oriented and conflict producing. Finally, Bradley, Hamon, and Harris uncovered evidence showing that by being well informed, individuals playing a deviant role in decision-making groups were able to maintain their opposition quite effectively in the face of majority pressure. In fact, those who drew upon external sources of information to support their opinions on issues often influenced the thinking of majority group members, many of whom even adopted the deviates' positions as their own in subsequent discussions.[18]

None of these studies is conclusive, but collectively they indicate that one's response to pressure for uniformity need not be reduced to a choice between conformity and rejection. As important, they indicate that one may often be able to devise communicative strategies with which to alter the direction in which a majority is moving.

A common, but understandable, mistake in reacting to group pressure in decision-making and problem-solving discussions is for the target to become defensive.[19] Say, for instance, that the majority in a group, feeling that it has identified the appropriate option to endorse and eager to bring the discussion to a close, is pressuring an individual who is genuinely concerned that the best option has not been put forward. It would not be surprising if the holdout were to become angry and to express that anger. Such defensive communication, however, seldom has any salutary consequences.[20]

Rather than becoming defensive in the face of pressure and hence taking the risk of rejection, the individual in the preceding example would probably be well advised to respond initially with some remark like, "I know that everyone wants to wrap this up. So do I." Continuing, he or she could then point out the reasons for the reluctance to join in the apparent consensus. He or she might even go so far as to acknowledge the appeal of the preferred alternative before explaining the concerns that have led to the expressed opposition. If one wishes his or her ideas to have impact on others, it is necessary that they be in a receptive frame of mind.

The principle that follows from the analysis above and the research on which it is based is that: *When pressure for uniformity is inhibiting the ability of a group to pursue desired objectives, if possible, avoid responding defensively and instead concentrate on developing the substantive bases for opposing the majority position.*

Overcoming Obstacles Posed by Status Differentiation

The differences in status that separate the members of a group into roles of varying importance can lead to a high-ranking participant's having influence that is not commensurate with the worth of his or her contributions.[21] When this occurs, the group may be unknowingly led away from its task objective. For this reason, status differentiation is an especially important aspect of group performance, and most of us are not as well prepared to contend with its undesirable consequences.

The greater influence potential of high-status group members is usually attributable to others' perceptions that such individuals are more valuable to the group. As a result, those of comparatively lesser rank tend to be deferential in their interactions with persons of high status, to provide inaccurate feedback to them, to devalue their own opinions and judgments, and to be uncritical of the ideas expressed by the more valued members.[22] Even when the members of a group find a person of high status unattractive, they may overlook the offensive aspects of his or her behavior because of that individual's perceived value.[23]

That these aspects of status differentiation can adversely affect a group's ability to pursue its objectives dispassionately has been demonstrated by Torrance. In a study of problem-solving groups, he found that lower-status members having a correct solution were prone to endorse the one proposed by the highest ranking member even when it was incorrect.[24]

The privilege that high status affords its possessors to influence the judgment and performance of others is difficult to overcome. As Homans has pointed out, individuals having high status are viewed as controlling scarce psychological and/or material resources. Compliance with their influence attempts is motivated by a desire to share in the benefits these resources may provide.[25] Whether one, in fact, has control of such resources does not matter. In this case, it is the perception that counts. Because of the peculiar nature of high/low status relationships, questioning or challenging the judgment of a high-status group member is not likely to be taken graciously by that individual or others who see compliance as beneficial.

In the circumstances mentioned, how should one react when he or she believes that the influence of a high-status member is leading a group in the wrong direction or otherwise inhibiting its movement along the goal-path? Although this question has yet to be answered in any conclusive way, two facts about the maintenance of status offer some potentially valuable insights. First, the status that initial impressions and external factors allow one to have is not permanently assured. In addition, an individual possessing high status, although permitted a certain degree of freedom to violate the norms of a group, cannot engage in such behavior indefinitely. Persistent deviation will eventually result in a loss of status.[26]

The fluidity of status rankings within groups may hold the key to devising strategies for counteracting the influence of high-status participants when that influence is functioning in ways inimical to the achievement of desired objectives. It appears that the essential consideration is whether or not one can demonstrate that a high-status member's behavior constitutes a serious enough violation of accepted standards of performance to activate change.

By behaving in an ingratiating manner, participants in groups will often try to overcome obstacles created by status differentiation and the relatively greater influence potential of higher-status members. Sometimes this approach works, but more likely it will only serve to strengthen the influence of those having high status. To the extent that such individuals are interfering with a group's progress toward its goal, feeding their egos may only serve to exacerbate the problem. In addition, as Jones and Wortman suggest, ingratiation often backfires when the motives underlying its uses are transparent.[27]

Tactically more sound than ingratiation are applications of the principle that *in responding to the inhibitory influence of a high-status group member, if possible,* one should *make salient the norm(s) which that individual's behavior violates.* Since those possessing high status usually desire to protect it, awareness of the discrepancy can create an internal pressure to begin observing the violated norm(s).

One must be careful in devising strategies based on the principle of calling attention to a high status group member's failure to observe valued performance norms. Often a gentle nudge, such as, "Our usual practice in this situation is to . . . ," or, "Ordinarily, we would . . . ," is sufficient to create an awareness of the problem. More blatant tactics could damage interpersonal relationships and thereby pose additional obstacles with which the group would have to contend.

Overcoming Obstacles Posed by Disruptive Behavior

Disruptive behavior is perhaps the one occurrence with which the average participant in a decision-making or problem-solving group feels least equipped to cope. People are ill at ease when interpersonal flare-ups arise, when a group member becomes deliberately obstructive, or when a participant is being highly defensive about the value of his or her own ideas but completely nonreceptive to those of others. Such disruptions can be generally subsumed under the heading of "affective conflict." This species of conflict, we know from both experience and research, usually has more negative than positive consequences.[28]

Within the last quarter century a rather substantial literature on interpersonal relations has accumulated; it deals with the avoidance of breakdowns in interpersonal communication.[29] The thrust of this scholarship, however, is aimed at self-improvement through expanded awareness of the sources of behavior, the cultivation of sensitivity toward the needs and values of others, and the management of one's own personal problems. To the extent that a knowledge of what contributes to good interpersonal relationships minimizes the likelihood of one's behaving in a disruptive manner, the literature is valuable.

Unfortunately, the information that has to do with becoming more interpersonally competent does not adequately prepare one for responding to disruptive behavior in groups. The literature provides few insights on which one can draw in dealing with the exigencies created by disruptive acts in small groups. Counteracting the inhibiting influence of disruptiveness requires that one be able to make conflict work in a positive or constructive manner.

A potentially promising principle for responding to disruptive behavior is suggested by the differences between two major classifications of conflict in their impact on the performance of groups. Guetzkow and Gyr discovered that "substantive conflict," that is, disagreements deriving from the issues in a group's agenda, promotes effective interaction and contributes to consensus. "Affective," or personally oriented conflict, on the other hand, militates against consensus and leads to general dissatisfaction among group members.[30] Studies focused on efforts to convert affective conflict into substantive conflict hold some answers to the question of how best to counteract the unwanted influence of disruptive behavior. Several experiments have revealed that such a conversion is possible.[31]

If we take as our general principle the statement that, *"In responding to a disruptive act, if possible, try immediately to convert it to a constructive contribution,"* we can conceive of a variety of specific applications. To illustrate the principle in use, assume that someone in a discussion has reacted to another participant's comment by saying, "That is the most ridiculous thing I have ever heard!" Outbursts such as this usually and understandably induce antagonistic replies. Rather than giving in to the impulse to lash out at the offensive participant, however, the injured party in the example could just as easily inquire, "Why do you say that?" This response would place the offender in the position of being invited to become constructive. Accepting the invitation, of course, would entail giving reasons for the previously unflattering characterization of a fellow discussant's ideas. Under these conditions, the atmosphere would begin to calm, and the conflict could move from a personal to a substantive level. As Bell's research has indicated, moreover, substantive comments in a discussion increase the likelihood that similarly oriented contributions will follow.[32] The implication of this finding is that once the disruptive participant began to contribute constructively, the prospects of his or her and others continuing to do so would be enhanced.

The ability to defuse a potentially explosive interpersonal situation created by disruptive acts sometimes requires a very "thick skin," but the outcome can be worth it. If one is unwilling to tolerate some degree of personally antagonistic remarks, he or she may succeed only in contributing to the inertial forces that are moving a group progressively away from its goal. In our illustration, the failure to acknowledge that there could be some substance behind the disruptive group member's abusive comment would preclude the possibility of its being added to the exploration of issues related to the discussion question.

Overcoming Obstacles Posed by Incompatibility between Individual and Collective Goals

The final source of obstacles which this essay treats is the incompatibility between individual and collective goals that all too commonly exists in decision-making and problem-solving groups. When, for whatever reasons, the participants in such groups adopt a competitive orientation, they tend to perform less well than when they share an ostensibly collective goal. This is true even in so-called "mixed-motive" groups in which the interactant's objective is to gain at others' expense.[33]

Morton Deutsch identified the consequences of the compatibility and incompatibility of individual and collective goals early in the history of small group research; such positive and negative consequences have since been rather consistently demonstrated in investigations involving both laboratory and natural groups.[34] The effects of compatibility tend to be positive, whereas those deriving from incompatibility are largely negative.

Incompatibility produces a competitive orientation, at least among some members of a group. This orientation, when it surfaces in the interaction of decision-making and problem-solving groups, has implications for both the task and social dimensions of performance; for instance, productivity is reduced, morale tends to be low, and participants are more likely to attribute responsibility for failure to other group members. Not only is the possibility of achieving a group goal limited when the parties involved interact competitively, but individual goals are infrequently achieved.[35] In other words, everyone may be a loser.

Most situations involving decision-making and problem-solving groups call for a cooperative orientation and coordination of effort; competition, therefore, is the unnatural state of affairs. When individuals perceive their personal interests to be at odds with the goal of a group, however, it can be very difficult to prevent the emergence of a competitive climate. Trying to establish an acceptable degree of congruency between individual and group goals appears to be the best remedy to the problem.[36]

Converting a competitively oriented climate into a more cooperatively oriented one is a real test of one's skill in exercising counteractive influence. Direct appeals to become cooperative and to place the interests of the group above those of the individual have little chance of working. Possibly the best way to approach the problem is to break the pattern of communication characteristic of competitively oriented groups. In such groups, this pattern is one of alternation between extolling the virtues of one's own input and pointing to the deficiencies in the input of others. As the pattern in this kind of one-upmanship intensifies, there is a corresponding reduction in the level of objectivity displayed. When this falls below the minimum necessary for exercising sound judgment, finding workable solutions to problems and making intelligent choices become unlikely.

To break the cycle of competition, the operative principle should be to *look for opportunities, if possible, to express honest agreement with other group members even though it may appear that they are unwilling to do the same.* Agreement is reinforcing and increases the probability that the person to whom it is directed will on later occasions reciprocate.[37] Of course, I am not recommending that one agree with others just for the sake of agreeing. The point is that when there are grounds for agreement, one should exploit the opportunity to create a more cooperative group environment. As antagonists begin to point to areas of merit in one another's contributions, they are better able to develop a climate of mutual trust in which the focus of competition shifts from the producers of ideas to the ideas themselves.[38]

Some Final Thoughts

The most neglected aspect of preparing people for participation in decision-making and problem-solving groups has been guidance in how to deal with unforeseen obstacles. I have attempted to address that deficiency by outlining a set of principles on which we can draw in trying to counteract undesirable influences set in motion by authority relations, pressure for uniformity, status differentiation, disruptive behavior, and incompatibility between individual and collective goals.

The principles identified are intentionally general and allow for a variety of specific adaptations. Although a knowledge of these principles does not equip someone to deal effectively with every contingency, their application can do much to combat major sources of ineffectiveness in decision-making and problem-solving discussions.[39] To that end, I am hopeful that the ideas I have introduced contribute to the discussion participants feeling more confident of their ability to function constructively in overcoming the perpetual frustrations of group interaction. If enough people become adept in the exercise of counteractive influence, then, who knows, some day we may find an article entitled, "Humans Do Better Because of Groups."

Postscript—1988

Although little has occurred since 1984 to alter the views I expressed in this essay, two books with which I have since become familiar have reinforced the importance of two attributes that underlie much of the advice offered—specifically, the effort to control emotionally damaging responses to others' behavior and the effort to contribute to the development and maintenance of a cooperative climate for group interaction.

Carole Tavris (*Anger: The Misunderstood Emotion.* New York: Simon and Schuster 1982) reviewed a considerable body of research and theory dealing with anger in human relationships and found that the expression of anger tends not to solve problems, but more often than not either serves to intensify them or to create still others. Members of groups frequently behave in ways that provoke anger, but in most instances, looking for constructive ways of responding will have a much more salutary effect than releasing one's anger. In states of anger, we tend to say unfortunate things that not only impair relationships but result in the emotion, rather than the concern arousing it, becoming a group's object of attention. In the long run, such a condition will have little positive impact on the members' performance.

More recently, Alfie Kohn examined research on the relative merits of cooperation and competition. In a book entitled *No Contest: The Case Against Competition* (Boston: Houghton Mifflin 1986), he examines the destructive potential of competition in a broad range of human relationships and finds little to commend competitive forms of behavior. A cooperative climate in groups is difficult both to establish and to maintain because ideas are so often in competition and because we have been socialized to believe that competition is desirable. Competition among ideas can and does, therefore, promote competition among people. When this occurs, judgment will suffer, and the likelihood of a group choosing wisely will be substantially reduced. Consequently, it is all the more important that counteractive influence be exercised under conditions in which differences in the merits of ideas lead to participants becoming more concerned with having their views prevail than with making choices that are warranted.

Notes

1. *Personality and Social Psychology Bulletin* 4 (1978), 123–25.
2. For a carefully constructed analysis of the psychological influences that contribute to the sorts of perceptions discussed here, see Richard Nisbett and Lee Ross, *Human Inference: Strategies and Shortcomings of Social Judgment* (Englewood Cliffs, New Jersey: Prentice-Hall, l980).
3. In the terminology of Kurt Lewin's group dynamics, a force is "that which causes change." For a more thorough discussion of this concept, see Marvin E. Shaw and Philip R. Costanzo, *Theories of Social Psychology* 2d ed. (New York: McGraw-Hill, 1982), 121–26. I prefer the term *influence* even though, as Wheeler notes, the concept does not represent "a logical area that can be adequately defined" (p. vii). Rather, it is a product of implied agreements among scholars that certain processes of interest are its constituents. See Ladd Wheeler, *Interpersonal Influence* (Boston: Allyn and Bacon, 1970).
4. I have discussed the notion of counteractive influence in more detail elsewhere. See Dennis S. Gouran, *Making Decisions in Groups: Choices and Consequences* (Glenview, Illinois: Scott, Foresman, 1982), 149–52.
5. See, for instance, variations of John Dewey's model of reflective thinking in Gouran, *Making Decisions in Groups*; Irving L. Janis, *Groupthink* 2d ed. (Boston: Houghton Mifflin, 1982); Irving L. Janis and Leon Mann, *Decision Making* (New York: Free Press, 1977); Gerald M. Phillips, Douglas J. Pederson, and Julia T. Wood, *Group Discussion: A Practical Guide to Participation and Leadership* (Boston: Houghton Mifflin, 1979); and Thomas M. Scheidel and Laura Crowell, *Discussing and Deciding* (New York: Macmillan, 1979).
6. See Stanley Milgram, *Obedience to Authority* (New York: Harper Colophon Books, 1969).
7. See, for example, Janis's discussion of the Bay of Pigs invasion in *Groupthink*, 14 –47. See also Dennis S. Gouran, "The Watergate Coverup: Its Dynamics and Its Implications," *Communication Monographs* 43 (1976), 176–86.
8. This phenomenon has been discussed in Robert L. Schanck, "A Study of a Community and Its Groups and Institutions Conceived of as Behaviors of Individuals," *Psychological Monographs* 43 (1932), No. 195. Also see Jerry B. Harvey, "The Abilene Paradox: The Management of Agreement," *Organizational Dynamics* 3 (1974), 63–80.
9. See, for example, Homans' discussion of the reasons for compliance with authority figures in George C. Homans, *Social Behavior: Its Elementary Forms* 2d ed (New York: Harcourt Brace Jovanovich, 1974), 193–224. The concept of behavior control further accounts for compliant behavior. See John W. Thibaut and Harold H. Kelley, *The Social Psychology of Groups* (New York: Wiley, 1959), 100–125; and Harold H. Kelley and John W. Thibaut, *Interpersonal Relations* (New York: Wiley, 1978), 111–207.
10. See John R.P. French, Jr., "A Formal Theory of Social Power," *Psychological Review* 63 (1956), 181–94; and J. Stacy Adams and Antone K. Romney, "The Determinants of Authority Interactions," in *Decisions, Values, and Groups*, ed. Norman F. Washburn II (New York: Pergamon Press, 1962), 227–56.
11. Milgram, 113–22.
12. Adams and Romney.

13. Such stiffening of resistance is probable if an authority figure perceives opposition to his or her judgment as a threat to his or her freedom to exercise authority. This type of "boomerang" effect is sometimes referred to as "psychological reactance." For a more complete understanding of the dynamics involved, see Jack W. Brehm, *A Theory of Psychological Reactance* (New York: Academic Press, 1966).

14. See Stanley Schacter, "Deviation, Rejection, and Communication." *Journal of Abnormal and Social Psychology* 46 (1951), 190–207. See also Janis, *Groupthink*, 2–9.

15. Schacter.

16. R. Victor Harnack, "A Study of the Effect of an Organized Minority Upon a Discussion Group," *Journal of Communication* 13 (1963), 12–24.

17. Kristin B. Valentine and B. Aubrey Fisher, "An Interaction Analysis of Verbal Innovative Deviance in Small Groups," *Speech Monographs* 41 (1974), 413–20.

18. Patricia H. Bradley, C. Mac Hamon, and Alan M. Harris, "Dissent in Small Groups," *Journal of Communication* 26 (Autumn, 1976), 155–59.

19. This type of response is more likely among individuals who judge the appropriateness of their own views on moral grounds. At the other extreme are those who determine how to respond purely on the basis of anticipated costs and rewards associated with compliance and noncompliance. Neither sort of person does much to help overcome obstacles in a group's goal-path. For a more extensive treatment of the styles of conflict management typical of the types of individuals described, one should read Neal Gross, Ward S. Mason, and Alexander W. McEachern, *Explorations in Role Analysis: Studies of the School Superintendency Role* (New York: Wiley, 1957). More likely to be effective is the type of individual Willis and Hollander call "independent." These individuals tend to be above average in intelligence and knowledge and, hence, are better able than others to articulate the basis of their opposition when they choose to do so. See Richard H. Willis and Edwin P. Hollander, "An Experimental Study of Three Response Modes in Social Influence Situations," *Journal of Abnormal and Social Psychology* 69 (1964), 150–56.

20. The basis for this assertion may be found in Jack R. Gibb, "Defensive Communications," *ETC.: A Review of General Semantics* 22 (1965), 221–22.

21. See Paul V. Crosbie, "Status Structure," *Interaction in Small Groups.* Paul V. Crosbie (ed.) (New York: Macmillan, 1975), 177–85.

22. Evidence of such characteristics has been reported in the following studies: Harold H. Kelley, "Communication in Experimentally Created Hierarchies," *Human Relations* 4 (1951), 39–56; William H. Read, "Upward Communication in Industrial Hierarchies," *Human Relations* 15 (1962), 3–15; Fred L. Strodtbeck, Rita M. James, and Charles Hawkins, "Social Status in Jury Deliberations," *American Sociological Review* 22 (1957), 713–19; E. Paul Torrance, "Some Consequences of Power Differences on Decision Making in Permanent and Temporary Three-Man Groups," *Research Studies, Washington State College* 22 (1954), 130–40; J. C. Moore, Jr., "Status and Influence in Small Group Interactions," *Sociometry* 31 (1968), 47–63.

23. See Alvin Zander, "The Psychology of Removing Group Members and Recruiting New Ones," *Human Relations* 29 (1976), 969–87.

24. Torrance. See also a study of overestimation of high-status group members' performance: Muzafer Sherif, B. Jack White, and O.J. Harvey. "Status in Experimentally Produced Groups," *American Journal of Sociology* 60 (1955), 370–79.

25. Homans, 223.

26. See Crosbie, 182–83; and Eugene Burnstein and Robert B. Zajonc, "Individual Task Performance in a Changing Social Structure," *Sociometry* 28 (1965), 349–62. Hollander's notions concerning "idiosyncratic credit" are also supportive of this conclusion. See Edwin P. Hollander, "Conformity, Status, and Idiosyncratic Credit," *Psychological Review* 65 (1958), 117–27.

27. Edward E. Jones and Camille Wortman, *Ingratiation: An Attributional Approach* (Morristown, New Jersey: General Learning Press, 1973).

28. See Harold Guetzkow and John R. Gyr, "An Analysis of Conflict in Decision-Making Groups," *Human Relations* 7 (1954), 367–82; Dale G. Leathers, "The Process of Trust Destroying Behavior in the Small Group," *Speech Monographs* 37 (1970), 180–87; Thomas J. Knutson, "An Experimental Study of the Effects of Orientation Behavior on Small Group Consensus," *Speech Monographs* 39 (1972),159–65; Timothy A. Hill, "An Experimental Study of the Relationship between Opinionated Leadership and Small Group Consensus," *Communication Monographs* 43 (1976), 246–57.

29. See, for example, Leland P. Bradford, Jack R. Gibb, and Kenneth D. Benne (eds.), *T-Group Theory and Laboratory Method* (New York: Wiley, 1964); Gerard Egan, *Encounter: Group Processes for Interpersonal Growth* (Belmont, California: Brooks/Cole, 1970); Gerald R. Miller and Mark Steinberg, *Between People* (Chicago: Science Research Associates, 1975).

30. Guetzkow and Gyr.

31. See Dennis S. Gouran, "Variables Related to Consensus in Group Discussions of Questions of Policy," *Speech Monographs* 36 (1969), 387–91; Knutson, "An Experimental Study . . ."; John A. Kline, "Orientation and Group Consensus," *Central States Speech Journal* 23 (1972), 44–47; Thomas J. Knutson and Albert C. Kowitz, "Effects of Information Type and Levels of Orientation on Consensus Achievement in Substantive and Affective Small Group Conflict," *Central States Speech Journal* 28 (1977), 54–63.

32. Mae Arnold Bell, "The Effects of Substantive and Affective Conflict in Problem-Solving Discussions," *Speech Monographs* 41 (1974), 19–23.

33. Walton and McKersie, for instance, discuss the value of "integrative" bargaining in labor-management contract settlements. This type of bargaining entails emphasizing the gains both parties to a dispute can achieve from an agreement that is less attractive to either side than would ideally be hoped for. See Richard E. Walton and Robert B. McKersie, *A Behavioral Theory of Labor Negotiations* (New York: McGraw-Hill, 1965).

34. Morton Deutsch, "An Experimental Study of the Effects of Cooperation and Competition Upon Group Process," *Human Relations* 2 (1949), 199–231. For a review of other research, both on laboratory and natural groups, see Marvin E. Shaw, *Group Dynamics: The Psychology of Small Group Behavior* 3d ed. (New York: McGraw-Hill, 1980), 378–83.

35. For a convincing demonstration of this sort of outcome, one should read Morton Deutsch and Robert M. Krauss, "The Effect of Threat Upon Interpersonal Bargaining," *Journal of Abnormal and Social Psychology* 61 (1960), 181–89.

36. This idea is developed in considerable detail in Muzafer Sherif and Carolyn W. Sherif, *Groups in Harmony and Tension* (New York: Harper and Row, 1953).

37. The basis for this assertion has been established in the following sources: Thibaut and Kelley, *The Social Psychology of Groups*; Gay Lumsden, "An Experimental Study of the Effects of Verbal Agreement on Leadership Maintenance in Problem-Solving Discussions," *Central States Speech Journal* 25 (1974), 270–76; Jon M. Huegli, "An Investigation of Trustworthy Group Representatives' Communication Behavior" (diss. Indiana University, 1971).

38. An excellent discussion of trust-building statements may be found in Leathers.

39. The fact that strategies based on the principles covered will not always prove effective and the fact that those I have tried to discourage sometimes work should not dissuade one from believing that there is a process at work in group interaction. The more attuned one is to the dynamics of that process, the better he or she will be able to function within it.

Group Process Satisfaction and Decision Quality in Computer-Mediated Communication: An Examination of Contingent Relations

Bolanle A. Olaniran

Modern technology has created flexibility in the way meetings and group discussions are held. Meetings are no longer restricted to traditional face-to-face (FTF) interactions where all group members have to be physically present. These modern forms of meeting are generally categorized under the umbrella term, electronic meeting systems (EMS). EMS consists of communication media that allow individuals to electronically participate in the meeting process (Dennis, George, Jessup, Nunamaker, & Vogel 1988). Varieties of EMS are classified according to the medium and function that they perform: teleconferencing, video conferencing, group decision support system (GDSS), and computer-mediated communication (CMC). The major emphasis here will be on CMC.

Computers pervade our society; their prevalence can be compared to that of the videocassette recorder, which exists in a great majority of households in the United States. We use computers in many aspects of our daily existence, such as word processing and household maintenance (e.g., balancing the checkbook and chore arrangement and organization). More importantly, computers provide a gateway to information such as the Sears' network, "Prodigy," which accesses on-line information (home shopping, advertising, etc.).

While computers are helpful to individuals, their role in today's organizations, especially communication needs, are even more substantial. It is in this capacity that CMC will be examined to show how it helps fulfill the communication needs in organizations. For now, CMC can be defined as *communication taking place between people through the computer.* A more detailed definition will be provided later.

The role of communication in organizations is exemplified in the coordinating functions of organizational activities, including the need for improved communication with field workers and others in remote locations; reduction in waiting time for commencing a meeting; greater speed in responding to an inquiry; reduction of time spent in decision making; and the tendency to capitalize on distributed expertise across organizations. Consequently, these needs and functions are a few of the reasons that CMC is thriving and gaining wide recognition.

Perhaps no area of CMC application in organizations is receiving more attention than the group process, given the systemic interdependency assumption underlying organizational performance. That is, all components (e.g., members and departments) must work together to accomplish organizational goals. The assumption suggests that an effective organization is one capable of coordinating and co-orienting the activities of its members across functional units in the organization to accomplish goals (Kreps

This essay was written expressly for this 7th edition. Permission to reprint must be obtained from the author. Bolanle A. Olaniran is affiliated with the Department of Communication Studies, Texas Tech University.

1990). This argument suggests the appropriateness of groups in organizations. It is for this reason that CMC has come of age as a group-meeting aid.[1]

An important thing to bear in mind with CMC is that it is a new form of media that is different from FTF. Therefore, the most profitable way to view CMC is to realize the differences and accept them. Such an attitude is essential if one is to realize any potential benefits that CMC medium has to offer. More broadly, CMC can be defined as an electronically mediated communication system, that is, a computer that facilitates communication interaction through electronic mail (e-mail) messages between two or more persons who are not physically present at the same time. From this definition, it is clear that CMC allows communication between people who are not available for FTF interaction due to geographical separation. For instance, with CMC it is possible for someone in America to engage in communication process with people from Asia, Europe, and Africa, usually in a language common to all participants. However, some computer applications, such as Cyrillic font, allow senders to compose messages in their native language and have the message translated into a receiver's language. The ability of communication to transcend geographical boundaries through CMC provides quicker access to necessary information and resources. Therefore, people can coordinate their efforts on a particular goal or task without having to travel to a central location as is required for FTF interactions and meetings. Thus, we will demonstrate how the CMC process differs from the traditional FTF process so that their characteristics can be used to identify new communication potentials that could be derived from correctly using CMC.

General Characteristics of CMC

Types of Messages

The nature of messages in CMC differs from traditional FTF messages. The messages in CMC are textual rather than oral or spoken messages such as those found in FTF conversations. Given the textual nature of messages in CMC, messages or thoughts have to be input into the computer by typing and transmitting them to the intended recipient via electronic impulses. Because each communicator has to type messages into the computer terminal, there is a delay in the transmission process between thoughts and message completion. Therefore, CMC makes the communication process relatively slower than FTF process, where little time is wasted with oral transmission (Olaniran 1994).

Group Size

CMC allows for inclusion of more participants than FTF permits. That is, size is no barrier in CMC, whereas, large numbers of participants hinder the communication process in FTF. CMC has the capacity to eradicate some of the problems that characterize FTF interaction in terms of group size. For instance, in FTF interaction, the larger the numbers of people, the longer an individual may have to wait for a speaking turn. In fact, an individual may not get to speak at all; too many participants may also prevent a smooth communication flow. All of these factors make the communication process difficult to control, structure, or organize in a meaningful way. On the other hand, CMC allows for communication "concurrency"—the capacity for all participants to "talk" or exchange messages simultaneously without interfering with each other's messages (Valacich, Paranka, George, & Nunamaker 1993; Sproull, & Kiesler 1986). In other words, people do not need to take speaking turns since CMC fosters the opportunity for equal participation among group participants.

Record Keeping

CMC systems provide a record-tracking feature because its record-tracking device allows communication proceedings to be saved for later use. The text-based nature of messages in CMC makes the record keeping possible. The preservation of a permanent record of communication messages in CMC provides some advantages, such as provision of a record of achievement, a safeguard against costly forgetfulness, and protection against intentional memory modification for personal gains (i.e., selective amnesia), or general memory loss that is likely to occur when records are not available. Record keeping is usually unavailable in FTF, and when it is available, it is usually based on someone's accounts and summaries of what the individual views as important, unless another medium is used to record the communication process. As a result, CMC eliminates the potential for problems that result from lack of, or incomplete, record keeping. Permanent records of group interactions in CMC also allow group members the opportunity to go back at a later time and reflect on certain issues. Consequently, participants can change and reformulate arguments and make adjustments on previous arguments (i.e., self-reflection). The records can also help with the group structure as groups are able to separate resolved and unresolved issues, which provides the direction for proceeding on further deliberations. This structure helps groups avoid unnecessary delays and time-consuming controversies that plague FTF group processes. In order to understand some values of CMC in groups, it is essential to understand how CMC fits into the stages of decision making.

Decision Stages and CMC

All groups undergo some unique processes, or what is commonly referred to as "paths," in an attempt to reach a decision on a specified task. Research in group-decision support systems identifies the importance of group paths and suggests that decisional paths differ from group to group (Poole & DeSanctis 1992). In other words, no particular order or plan dominates all groups. Despite the differences in group decisional paths, there are two major decisional stages within which group decision-making processes may be categorized, regardless of the decisional paths or the order that a group chooses to follow.

The two stages consist of idea generation and evaluation stages. The idea-generation stage involves the group's attempt to analyze the problem, determine goals, and generate possible solutions for the task (e.g., a brainstorming process equivalent). The evaluation stage involves the group's effort to discuss implications of possible decisions and the solution for the given task. These stages provide some important functions in CMC groups (Olaniran, Friedrich, & VanGundy 1992; Olaniran 1994), such as providing some structure, or offering direction to a group on how it ought to proceed in the decision process. Alternately, the stages and activities in these stages influence the group outcomes.

Group Outcomes in CMC

Research in CMC has been confusing and sometimes inconsistent regarding satisfaction in CMC groups. The confusion, in part, may be due to different dimensions of satisfaction and different correlates of satisfaction. Group process satisfaction (GPS) is one of the many dimensions of satisfaction in groups. GPS describes the positive feelings that individuals experience with the procedure or group structuring of the decision-making process. It is fair to say that since groups involve different individuals working together as one, there are instances where members will feel more or less satisfied with the group process. Implied in our definition is that GPS focuses on the aggregate individual feelings that include both positive and negative experiences.

Two dimensions of communication behavior are essential to a successful and satisfying group process: the *"task"* and *"social"* dimensions of communication. The task dimension of communication behaviors focuses on the accomplishment of group goals, while the social dimension focuses on development and maintenance of interpersonal relationships in groups (Fisher & Ellis 1990). However, the accomplishment of either task or social dimensions of communication differs by communication media and groups.

Both task and social dimensions of group communication are directed toward certain factors that influence group process satisfaction, including participation, consensus, relationship development, and motivation. Each one of these factors is brought about in CMC group meetings.

Participation

Participation is the extent to which individuals are able to contribute their opinions in the group discussion. As stated earlier, one of the CMC system's features is the ability to offer communication concurrency. That is, opportunities exist for several participants to engage in the discussion process at the same time without having to wait for turns as they might when using other traditional media such as FTF and telephone. Therefore, the opportunity for equalized member participation increases within CMC groups. This greater freedom to participate in the decision process and the uninhibited communication in CMC have both been attributed to the lack of social context cues (Hiltz & Turoff 1978; Rice & Love 1987; Siegel, Dubrovsky, Kiesler, & McGuire 1986). This claim has some merit in the sense that the idea of group members working independently in their workstations without interference could allow group members more freedom and greater boldness in sharing their views during the discussion. It could also provide group members with the impression that their ideas are not going to be cut down or belittled in front of other members. Even when members' ideas are criticized in CMC, such criticism may not have the same negative social consequences as FTF (Olaniran 1994).

In addition, CMC offers the benefit of anonymity. That is, the systems allow users a chance to mask their identities when they do not want other members to know who they are or have their comments used against them. This anonymity provision helps create a disinhibitive effect that prevents the lack of willingness to participate, especially when one's opinions may be chastised. This anonymity mediates the problem characterizing groups whose members are in superior-subordinate relationships by equalizing the status. Thus, CMC has the potential to neutralize status effects, which would in turn equalize participation and prevent attempts by certain members to exert their dominance on the group toward selfish goals. One other advantage is that CMC could ultimately prevent good ideas from being recklessly discarded as insignificant, thereby eradicating the perception that certain ideas are not worth mentioning to the rest of the group. Furthermore, the anonymity offered by CMC may consequently encourage people who would otherwise not participate in FTF interaction (e.g., communication-apprehensive and reticent people). Thus, CMC offers the capacity to prevent "productivity loss" due to the lack of opportunity to participate. Consequently, potential for increased participation by CMC enhances member participation in both idea generation by allowing opportunity for a greater number of ideas, and in the evaluation stages by offering critical opinions and suggestions that do not jeopardize or emotionally threaten other members' positions. If CMC offers the potential for increased participation and greater latitude in getting one's ideas across in groups, then it should increase the potential for satisfaction with the group process.

Relationship Development

Through participation, CMC helps groups focus on both task and social goals. However, some people believe that CMC is much too task oriented, arguing that CMC media lack nonverbal and social-presence cues that facilitate interpersonal relationship development (Hiltz & Turoff 1978; Short, Williams, & Christie 1976). Since both task and social dimensions are necessary for group process satisfaction, the implicit assumption of the claim is that satisfaction will be low among CMC participants. The alternate argument is that CMC, because of transmission delays and typing, requires more time to get the same amount of work done as in an FTF interaction. Thus, CMC is no less rich in socioemotional messages than FTF. Furthermore, Walther (1992a; 1992b) stresses that the studies upon which declaration of task-orientation conclusions of CMC are based fail to take into account the very nonverbal aspect of FTF interaction, omitting any negative effects that the nonverbal cues may have on relationship development. As a result, there is the possibility for overstressing the positive effects of nonverbal messages in FTF interaction. Nonverbal communication, like verbal, can be either positive or negative. Until both negative and positive effects of nonverbal cues are taken into consideration, it is presumptuous to assume that all nonverbal and social context cues facilitate positive interpersonal relationship development and satisfaction with the group process.

Similarly, the fact that CMC messages are text based does not necessarily imply that the messages are always task oriented. Users with time find ways of conveying socioemotional expressions to their communication partners. The use of icons in CMC

Table 1
Sample Socioemotional Icons (Smiley-Faces)

:-)	= smile (happy mood)
:-(	= frowning
:-I	= indifferent
:->	= sarcasm (usually accompanies acrimonious remarks)
;-)	= flirtatious remark
(-:	= user is left handed
:-x	= lips are sealed
:d	= user is laughing at another user
:-}	= me too (i.e., ditto)
[ ]	= hugs
:-*	= kisses
[:-)	= user is wearing a headset
:-/	= skepticism
:-?	= user is smoking a pipe

Note: These are some of the icons commonly used in e-mail all over the world.

("smiley faces") help convey users' socioemotional states like happiness, sadness, and other emotions (see Table 1 for sample relational icons).

Even when users are not familiar with the icon message symbols, their feelings can still be expressed by elaborating parenthetically about what they mean. The following message is an example: "Are you guys naugts [sic]? How can you even think of such idea? It sounds stupid! (Just teasing, I just thought I should push your buttons a little.)" Here is a message that may initially indicate an angry group member, but with the parenthetical note, the recipient of the message would know that no harm was intended. Such a process reinforces the position of the relational communication approach, which posits that relationships develop in stages, moving from formal to less formal (i.e., intimacy). Therefore, the need for more time for CMC interaction and the learning effect become more pressing with CMC media. In other words, for intimate social interaction to occur in CMC, users must be allowed the necessary time to get to know their communication partners and to develop an affinity for using the new communication medium.

Consensus

Consensus means a group's ability to come to an agreement. Important to the group decision process, consensus is considered problematic in CMC groups. Hiltz, Johnson, and Turoff (1986) found that CMC groups reach consensus in group decisions less frequently than FTF groups. The reason often offered for this conclusion is that either the increased participation level of members results in large quantities of ideas, which means more decision alternatives to consider, or that participants maintain their opinions more rigidly and are less willing to yield to competing opinions.

While both arguments have merit, again the assumptions may have failed to take into account the "time" factor; evidence suggests that CMC groups are able to reach consensus on decisions when they are allowed enough time to interact (Weisband 1992). Olaniran (1994) found in a study that CMC groups take longer to reach consensus on a group decision than FTF groups. However, consensus is essential to GPS in several ways. It helps the group members to reflect on their decision, it allows group members to enjoy the comfort that their task accomplishment brings joy because members work together for the good of the group, and it helps foster the development and reinforcement of interpersonal relationships among group members.

Obviously, consensus can be achieved in both communication media. However, it seems that CMC groups may enjoy a slight advantage relative to FTF groups in terms of consensus development. Since CMC offers participants the opportunity for greater freedom and bolder participation in the decision process, there is an increased opportunity for a true consensus, rather than a false consensus where group members may feel pressured into conforming to the dominant view in the group in order to avoid conflict or confrontation. In other words, CMC may offer each group participant the opportunity to maintain an argumentative position more strongly until the position is dismissed because of an alternative believed to be superior. The key to this argument is that while similar procedures occur in FTF groups, there is a greater tendency to be overly concerned about any deviation perceived as a lack of loyalty that may hurt interpersonal relationships in the group. For instance, coercive consensus development statements such as "It's high time we come to a decision," and "The rest of us have reached an agreement, you're the only one we're waiting on," are present in both media. However, these statements can more easily be ignored without leaving any bad feelings among group members in CMC than they can in FTF. By ignoring these types of coercive attempts, groups may also be able to reach true consensus. Similarly, the disinhibitive effect created in CMC may mediate the potential negative consequences of an unreasoned emphasis on members' relationships. That is, an idea has the potential of being viewed on its potential contribution to the group process rather than from whom an idea originates. The implication is that it would be difficult for group members to experience high satisfaction with the group process when they know that they have been forced to compromise a uniquely viable position within the group. Therefore, GPS would seem to be higher in a group that is able to work together and reach a true consensus (i.e., CMC).

Feedback

Feedback consists of both positive and negative messages that acknowledge members' contributions and give direction for achieving a goal. Feedback messages are essential to the GPS in that they provide the measurement for groups regarding how well the group is progressing with its task. Hence, it is imperative that groups engage in effective feedback messages. One major characteristic of effective feedback is the "timeliness" of the message. As a result, feedback effectiveness is often measured in terms of the simultaneity of the message. Smith and Vanecek (1990) argue that the message simultaneity affects satisfaction, and indicate that the lack of opportunity in CMC meetings for instant feedback and issue clarification reduces groups' shared perceptions of progress toward group goals, thus resulting in reduced satisfaction. While the feedback process is slower in CMC given the slower message transmission rate,

FTF group participants have instantaneous access to requests, but there is a waiting period between requests in CMC. Furthermore, because CMC participants have control over how they choose to interact with other members (e.g., whether to read and ignore or respond to messages), the potential for questions to go unanswered is higher. The induced stress from slow or missing feedback in CMC could reduce members' satisfaction. Yet lack of feedback is not unique to CMC, although it may be more apparent in CMC, especially to new users. Accordingly, when GPS is compared with respect to feedback messages, CMC may be at a disadvantage.

Motivation

Motivation is the desire to remain a member in a group, and has a direct positive effect on GPS. The desire to remain in a group as a member indicates a desire to be actively involved in the group goals by contributing to the success of the group through effort, time, and money (Marston & Hecht 1988). Motivation could be described as perhaps the most significant variable to GPS since a member who has no motivation or desire to be part of a group is not going to demonstrate willingness to participate, help bring the group towards consensus, develop interpersonal relationships with other members, and facilitate the feedback process. While this is true for any group regardless of the communication medium, the implication is greater for new communication media like CMC. That is, regardless of the medium characteristics, CMC has to be used and used appropriately (just as much as the FTF has to be used) to bring about the desired effects, sometimes referred to as appropriation of structure (Poole & DeSanctis 1992).

Poole and DeSanctis indicate that communication technologies are social technologies where interaction processes are as important as the operations that the technologies require. The design of CMC does not "automatically determine how groups interact; they must be worked into the discussion to have impact" (p. 9). Such a stance suggests the need for users to be trained in the use of the CMC concerning the rules, structure, and other characteristics provided by this communication technology. However, for the training to be successful, users have to demonstrate the motivation to use the media, or the training will accomplish nothing. A similar argument involves the need for the users to be motivated to be a part of the CMC group, or they will be nothing more than passive participants (i.e., "lurkers"), there to observe but never take an active role in contributing to the group process. Thus, the level of motivation by CMC group participants will affect their satisfaction with the group process and the group members.

In summary, the CMC system characteristics have potential effects on different factors (i.e., participation, consensus, relation development, feedback, and motivation) when each factor is taken individually, which will consequently influence the GPS. However, the group experiences which ultimately determine members' GPS are based on the aggregate effects of all these factors, suggesting the need to examine the group interaction as a whole. Furthermore, accomplishing the goal for each GPS factor in a CMC group is dependent upon both individual and other members' performances. For instance, the CMC system may allow an individual to increase his or her level of participation and motivation in a group, but if the other members do not share a similar motivation or reciprocate the participation, that individual will end up being disappointed and experience low GPS. Consequently, the group interaction process plays a key role in the level of GPS experienced in a group, more so than individual characteristics of the CMC medium. Therefore, whether a CMC group surpasses or lags behind FTF groups in GPS, it is contingent on how the medium and its features are applied. The conclusion that may be drawn, then, is that CMC would better FTF on GPS only when used appropriately under the right condition and would do more poorly than FTF when used inappropriately. The caveat here is that by appropriate usage we mean group usage of the medium as a whole. Some members may use the medium the right way, while other members may not. Such situations will neither characterize appropriate usage nor effective interaction.

In addition to the factors described above, it is useful to identify other conditions where GPS may thrive in CMC. Easy access to the medium would reduce the inconveniences and other problems of participation. Adequate training and sufficient time are essential to ease potential CMC users into the system's capability and to explore the use of different features. Incentive provision is an identified reward (intrinsic or extrinsic) attractive to justify the use of the medium. This provision would also enhance the motivation to use the medium and to use it in a prudent manner. The reward need not be anything out of the ordinary. For instance, the reward may tie users' duties to their normal task performances such that the CMC focuses on the ease with which a goal could be accomplished or on time efficiency. Other rewards could stress the skill development that CMC usage would bring.

Group Decision Quality and CMC

Another major group outcome on which CMC is measured is the group effectiveness. Group effectiveness is measured in terms of the quality of the decision where interaction is essential to group decision quality. Similar to the argument on GPS, CMC features would not increase or decrease decision quality, unless its features are explored by the users. Therefore, the emphasis will be on examining how CMC attributes facilitate vigilant interaction process and, thus, enhance the group decision quality.

The Role of Idea Quantity

Group literature demonstrates the FTF communication results in productivity loss (Diehl & Stroebe 1991; Olaniran et al. 1992). This productivity loss is attributable to inhibitions resulting from the physical presence of other members and cues discerned from the group environment. Contrary to FTF interaction, research shows that CMC reduces productivity loss by masking the identity of the group members. Furthermore, the lack of social context cues in CMC facilitates greater disinhibitive communication messages that reflect status equalization, greater quality of participation, and less dominance by few group members (Connolly, Jessup, & Valacich 1988; Hiltz & Turoff 1978; Siegel et al. 1986; Sproull & Kiesler 1986). Therefore, anonymity and the disinhibitive effect offered by CMC would seem to result in greater reduction in productivity loss than would FTF interaction. The implication for the productivity loss can be addressed in two stages of the decision-making process. At the idea-generation stage,

CMC will be able to generate more ideas than in FTF groups. At the evaluation stage, discussion has the potential of not overlooking the group members' comments. These two goals are possible because members do not have to wait turn to input their ideas, and they do not have to dread negative evaluations of other members as in the FTF interaction.

Communication Media and the Vigilant Interaction

CMC, when utilized properly, facilitates vigilant interaction process, and in turn, fosters high decision quality. How does CMC medium facilitate vigilant interaction in groups? The position that large numbers of ideas facilitate decision quality is revisited because when large numbers of ideas are generated in a group, there is the tendency that critical issues and viewpoints will not be ignored. Thus, by generating large number of ideas at the idea generation stage, a group can move toward the vigilant-interaction process in the evaluation stage. At the evaluation stage, it seems that the CMC ability to encourage equitable participation would allow critical thinking and encourage members to express their opinions more candidly and willingly. When such interaction occurs, CMC groups would be able to thoroughly analyze both the pros and cons of each idea or decision choice and prevent the group from engaging in faulty interaction process. Consequently, the group would be able to accomplish the goal of vigilant interaction.

However, group decision is dependent on the group's ability to reach a consensus. Therefore, decision quality is contingent on the group's consensus. As presented earlier, consensus formation in CMC takes time, since CMC and FTF operate at different time rates. Therefore, generating large numbers of ideas in CMC would result in additional time being needed to reach consensus. However, when CMC groups are not under time constraints, they will be able to reach consensus and make accurate decisions. The rationale behind this thinking can be explored in terms of the contributions made by the medium from the two group stages that accommodate the vigilant interaction process. Therefore, it would seem that the possible advantage of CMC over FTF (large idea quantity) during the idea-generation stage would be the group decision quality. Accordingly, when the number of unique ideas is high, the group is given sufficient time to deliberate on a decision, and the freedom to express individual opinions by separation of issues from people (as in CMC), CMC should facilitate equal or better decision quality than FTF groups.

Other Factors

While logical, the argument that CMC groups may be superior to FTF groups in decision quality may not be that clear-cut. There are other situational factors that complicate interaction processes in groups regardless of the communication media. The factors could preempt the assertion that one medium (CMC in this case) could better the other. These factors include task clarity, level of task expertise, comfort with the medium (Olaniran et al. 1992), and anticipation of future interaction. Of these factors, emphasis would be given to anticipation of future interaction with group members. The reason is that other variables (e.g., task clarity and expertise, and comfort with the medium) are easily controllable through group assignment and training. Anticipation of future interaction, on the other hand, is more difficult to control, especially in organizational settings since group members are apt to continue to interact with one another beyond the completion of a group task. On this note, Walther (1994) argues that the effect of "anticipation of future interaction" is constant in FTF groups while the effect varies in CMC media. CMC participants either expect or do not expect future interactions with their group members. For example, in organizations the use of CMC does not prevent the members from future interaction through other communication media (e.g., FTF, memos, telephone). The anticipation of future contacts with group members could reduce the degree to which anonymity offered by CMC facilitates disinhibitive communication in the decision-making process. In other words, when group members are aware that future interaction is inevitable and their messages or comments are identifiable, they could become conscious of their actions (e.g., choice of message or interaction). Thus, the achievement of vigilant interaction process is affected in groups[2] and consequently, CMC will not automatically increase group decision quality.

Implications and Caveats

It has been shown that CMC provides an alternative to FTF group meetings. However, CMC should not be viewed as a replacement to FTF interaction since both media must be recognized for their different capabilities. Thus, the different media should be explored to determine how they might complement one another and to discover the most effective way to utilize these media in group processes. Given the different capabilities of the two media, one thing is clear: CMC must be applied in situations where group participants are allowed sufficient time to reach decision since CMC and FTF operate at different time spans. Thus, when time is of essence to a group, other communication media should be used. Furthermore, for effective use of CMC media, users must be given sufficient time to familiarize themselves with the new media so that users would know the best way to utilize the media to accomplish desired group goals and communication outcomes.

The direct implication for correct appropriation of CMC lies in the training, which should stress the differences between FTF and CMC to trainees. This is essential, because most of us are familiar with FTF interaction, which represents the yardstick by which we judge other communication media (McGrath 1990). However, this strategy is not the best way to warm up to CMC or new communication media in general. As stated earlier, it is necessary to realize that CMC and other new media are different from FTF, and to accept the differences. When someone is able to recognize the differences and accept them, he or she might be able to stop comparing CMC with FTF and see the system for what it is, working with it from that standpoint.

The role of interaction is critical in determining the benefits of any communication medium. Therefore, instead of looking at CMC in terms of its characteristics, people should use the medium appropriately to reach their desired goals. CMC should be seen as a tool for facilitating the communication process or for bringing about a desired group outcome, be it GPS or group decision quality. A CMC medium by itself will not automatically result in a bad or good communication outcome. Like all tools it must be used properly.

Notes

1. P. Archer (1990) presents a brief review of studies on computer-mediated conferences as a group inter-action and decision-making support tool. Business application of computer-mediated conferences has also been explored (Caswell, 1988; Kiesler, 1986; Rice, 1987).
2. B.A. Olaniran (1994) explored how anticipation of future interaction influences group performances in both idea generation and evaluation stages.

References

Archer, P. (1990). "A Comparison of Computer Conferences with Face-to-Face Meetings for Small Group Business Decisions." *Behaviour and Information Technology* 9, 307–317.

Caswell, S.A. (1988). *E-Mail.* Agincourt, Ontario: Gage Publishing.

Connolly, T., Jessup, L.M., and Valacich, J.S. (1988). "Idea Generation in a GDSS: Effects of Anonymity and Evaluative Tone." Unpublished manuscript, University of Arizona, Tucson, Arizona.

Dennis, A.R., George, J.F., Jessup, L.M., Nunamaker, Jr., J.F., and Vogel, D.R. (1988). "Information Technology to Support Electronic Meetings." *MIS Quarterly* 12, 591–619.

Diehl, M., and Stroebe, W. (1991). "Productivity Loss in Idea Generating Groups: Tracking Down the Blocking Effect." *Journal of Personality and Social Psychology* 61, 392–403.

Fisher, B.A., and Ellis, D.G. (1990). *Small Group Decision Making: Communication and the Group Process,* 3d ed. New York: McGraw-Hill.

Hiltz, S.R., and Turoff, M. (1978). *The Network Nation.* Reading, MA: Addison-Wesley.

Hiltz, S.R., Johnson, K., and Turoff, M. (1986). "Experiment in Group Decision Making Communication Process and Outcome in Face-to-Face Versus Computerized Conference." *Human Communication Research* 13, 225–252.

Kiesler, S. (1986). "The Messages in Computer Networks." *Harvard Business Review* 64, 46–60.

Kreps, G.L. (1990). *Organizational Communication,* 2d ed. New York, NY: Longman.

McGrath, J.E. (1990). "Time Matters in Groups." In J. Gallegher, R. Kraut, and C. Egido (eds.), *Intellectual Teamwork: Social and Technological Foundations of Cooperative Work.* Hillsdale, NJ: Lawrence Erlbaum Associates, Publishers.

Marston, P.J., and Hecht, M. (1988). "Group Satisfaction." In R.S. Cathcart and L.A. Samovar (eds.), *Small Group Communication: A Reader,* 236–246. Dubuque, Iowa: Wm. C. Brown Publishers.

Olaniran, B.A. (1994). "Group Performance and Computer-Mediated Communication." *Management Communication Quarterly.*

Olaniran, B.A., Friedrich, G.W., and VanGundy, A.B. (1992). "Computer-Mediated Communication in Small Group Decisional Phases." Paper presented at the International Communication Association. Miami, FL.

Poole, M.S., and DeSanctis, G. (1992). "Microlevel Structuration in Computer-Supported Group Decision Making." *Human Communication Research* 19, 5–49.

Rice, R.E. (1987). "Computer-Mediated Communication and Organizational Innovation." *Journal of Communication* 37, 157–187.

Rice, R.E., and Love, G. (1987). "Electronic Emotion: Socioemotional Content in a Computer-Mediated Network." *Communication Research* 14, 85–108.

Short, J., Williams, E., and Christie, B. (1976). *The Social Psychology of Telecommunications.* London: John Wiley & Sons.

Siegel, J., Dubrovsky, V., Kiesler, S., and McGuire, T.W. (1986). "Group Processes in Computer-Mediated Communication." *Organizational Behavior and Human Processes* 37, 157–187.

Smith, J.Y., and Vanecek, M.T. (1990). "Dispersed Group Decision Making Using Nonsimultaneous Computer Conferencing: A Report of Research." *Journal of Management Information System* 7, 71–92.

Sproull, L., and Kiesler, S. (1986). "Reducing Social Context Cues: Electronic Mail in Organizational Communication." *Management Science* 32, 1492–1512.

Valacich, J.S., Paranka, D., George, J.F., and Nunamaker, J.F., Jr., (1993). "Communication Concurrency and the New Media: A New Dimension for Media Richness." *Communication Research* 20, 249–276.

Walther, J.B. (1992a). "A Longitudinal Experiment on Computer-Mediated and Face-to-Face Interaction." *Proceedings of the Twenty-Fifth Hawaii International Conference on System Sciences* 4, 220–231. Los Alamitos, CA: IEEE Computer Society Press.

Walther, J.B. (1992b). "Interpersonal Effects in Computer-Mediated Communication: A Relational Perspective." *Communication Research* 19, 52–90. Beverly Hills: Sage.

Walther, J.B. (1994). "Anticipated Ongoing Interaction Versus Channel Effects on Relational Communication in Computer-Mediated Interaction." *Human Communication Research* 20, 473–501. Thousand Oaks, CA: Sage.

Weisband, S.P. (1992). "Group Discussion and First Advocacy, and Computer-Mediated and Face-to-Face Decision Making Groups." *Organizational Behaviour and Human Decisional Processes* 53, 352–380. San Diego: Academic Press, Inc.

A Review of Group Process Designs for Facilitating Communication in Problem-Solving Groups

Joseph C. Chilberg

During the past 30 years numerous methods, techniques, and practices have been developed and implemented in group problem solving (McPherson 1967; Moore 1987; Ulschak, Nathanson, & Gillan 1981; Van Gundy 1984). Many of these methods govern the total group process and designate a *facilitator role* to implement them (Broome & Keever 1986; Doyle & Straus 1976; Kepner & Tregoe 1981; Prince 1970). In effect, these methods are designs for facilitating the group problem-solving communication process.

The essential characteristic of facilitation is to help make an activity or outcome easier to perform or achieve. Facilitative behavior may be practiced in a number of settings including therapeutic, social, and learning groups. This essay, however, will focus on the facilitation of *task groups* concerned with decision making and problem solving. "Designed"[1] facilitation processes will be reviewed in an effort to (a) understand the role of communication in group facilitation and (b) identify practices relevant to group communication facilitation.

Facilitation in problem-solving groups occurs through both formal and informal practices. In *informal* facilitation a group leader or facilitator makes content or procedural suggestions, but does not establish or adopt a formal procedural agenda.

A *formal* group process design (GPD) is typically "complete and closed," scripting the steps and techniques of the problem-solving process. Group members are responsible for content (though in some cases the facilitator may be permitted to make content suggestions) and for implementing the formal design initiated and then monitored by the facilitator.

Alternatively, a formal design can be "partial or open," in which case certain rules and procedures are prescribed, while others are left to the group's discretion.

Functions of Procedural Group Communication

Benne and Sheats's (1948) classic study identified task, maintenance (relationship), and self-serving group role behaviors, and has guided the direction and elaboration of group communication research. However, Benne and Sheats did not articulate distinct procedural role functions. That is, they did not emphasize the "how" of task and maintenance functions. Of twelve task function behaviors, only two directly address procedure (e.g., initiator-contributor and coordinator). Only one role-maintenance function directly addresses procedure (e.g., gatekeeper/expediter). Consideration of the specific range of procedural role behaviors that contribute to fulfilling task and maintenance functions was largely overshadowed by a focus on task and maintenance message behavior per se.[2] Procedural role functions were treated as

From Joseph C. Chilberg, *Management Communication Quarterly*, Volume 3, Number 1, August 1989, pp. 51–70, copyright © 1989 by Sage Publications, Inc. Reprinted by permission of Sage Publications, Inc.

task and maintenance functions. This conceptualization relegated procedural role functions to a subordinate position and left the procedural communication function unexplained.

This article will identify the procedural role functions and requisite type of message behaviors relevant to facilitating group problem-solving communication. It will also identify the focus of procedural communication and its relationship to task and maintenance communication functions.

GPDs establish a distinct procedural role function by designating a facilitator. An examination of this role provides a basis for establishing the types of procedural message functions relevant to problem-solving groups. There are two general procedural role functions: selection and implementation. Selection involves the introduction and instruction of a procedure. This involves message behaviors characterized by initiating, justifying, and describing a procedure for use. For example. suggesting the use of brainstorming could involve a rationale for its use, instructional steps and rules of procedure. The implementation function facilitates the group's use of selected procedures. Implementation message behaviors are characterized by guiding, monitoring, and intervention. Once a procedure is selected there are message behaviors that get it started, maintain it, acknowledge broken rules, and reinstate or change procedure.

Procedural messages may focus on communication behavior in general or procedures in particular. That is, a procedural message can address the effectiveness of message behaviors per se (i.e., language use, paraphrasing, defensive statements. etc.) or it can address the communication practices of a procedure (i.e., establishing and maintaining the communication rules of an idea-generating technique). Procedural messages, regardless of focus, serve task and/or maintenance functions. They initiate, guide, and maintain effective task and relationship message behaviors. This is clearly the case in brainstorming (Osborn 1957) where idea generating serves the task function and the free form generation of ideas and postponed evaluation serve the maintenance function. In short, procedures and procedural messages affect both the task and maintenance functions of group problem solving.

GPDs are designed procedures and procedural role behaviors that maximize efficient and effective task and maintenance outcomes. An examination of GPDs suggests that they accomplish this at several levels of the group problem-solving process.

Levels of GPD Operation

Group problem solving operates at four distinct yet simultaneous levels. The macro or "event level" involves gathering a meeting of participants with a more or less common purpose. This level involves the group's purpose, goal, and situation (i.e., task complexity, communication climate, etc.). At event level, a group must match a GPD with the group problem-solving event.

The "episode level" involves the phases of a problem-solving meeting, such as analysis, order of topics, and idea generating. These steps typically order and guide the functional treatment of problem-solving content (e.g., problem identification, problem background, problem analysis) during the meeting.

At the "activity level," one or more distinct activities establish specific techniques for conducting a particular episode. For example, the idea-generating step of problem solving may involve several distinct activities: listing ideas, clarification, ranking, and so on. The activity level directs types of content behavior (e.g., fact sharing, evaluation) and message forms (e.g., written, oral, graphic). It also establishes the communication mode (e.g., intrapersonal, group) and interaction pattern (e g., circular, serial, parallel). At this level GPD task and maintenance practices are designed.

Specific message behaviors that constitute and operationalize an activity occur at the "act level"—a level typically dictated by the activity (i.e., solution evaluation leads to evaluative message behaviors). However, some activities may establish a specific manner for communicating an activity function. For example, synectics requires that negative solution evaluations be stated in a proactive form. Furthermore, some pre- scribed communication acts may not be associated with a given activity. Instead, they operate as general communication rules throughout the meeting (e.g., evaluate ideas, not people; or intervening when discussion is off focus). Acts are the facilitator's pri- mary means of instruction, of monitoring compliance, and of maintaining an activity and ultimately the GPD.

Although a GPD is developed to guide the task function of group problem solving it can directly and indirectly support maintenance functions. The procedural function of the GPD serves both task and maintenance functions through orienting and estab- lishing communication practices in group problem solving. Many activity procedures inherently serve maintenance functions by providing opportunities for involvement and reducing defensive behaviors. In some cases act rules are used to establish desired rela- tional behaviors (e.g., no personal attacks). All levels of a GPD can, to varying degrees, facilitate task and maintenance functions (see Table 1).

Table 1
GPD Levels and Communication Functions

Levels	Task	Maintenance
Event (Meeting)	Matching GPD with problem-solving situation (type of problem, group size, climate, etc.)	Establish group-centered problem solving by establishing shared goal and meeting norms
Episode (Steps)	Problem identification, analy-sis, solution generation and evaluation, and implementation	Common procedural outline for problem solving to reduce uncertainty
Activity (Techniques)	Techniques and practices to fulfill episode content objectives	Practices to maximize partici-pation and enhance supportive communication climate
Act (Behaviors)	Specific communication behaviors to fulfill activity objectives	Specific communication behaviors to enhance clarity and minimize defensiveness

Common Features of a GPD

GPDs share the following features: (1) role specialization, (2) procedures and rules, and (3) technologies. They separate the procedural and decision-making functions by designating procedural responsibility to the facilitator and decision-making responsibility to group members. Some designs provide further decision-making specialization such as idea generation, recording, and information management. This is largely determined by the GPD's purpose and practices suggested by research literature and field testing.

All GPDs provide procedures and rules for conducting activities that directly shape communication behaviors. Most rules are role- and activity-specific That is, an activity requires specific rules to be followed by the individuals occupying each role of the process design. Some rules may be designed to operate throughout the meeting process. For example, a "no attack rule," enforced by the facilitator and/or members at all times, may be established to reduce interpersonal conflicts and promote tack effectiveness.

Within a GPD, technology aids in recording, processing, and managing meeting information. Both relatively simple tools (easels, large note pads, markers, and tape) and more sophisticated technologies (overhead projectors, computers, and software, computer projectors, copying machines), and specially designed meeting rooms are used, depending on the group's goal(s) and task demands. Complex, unstructured problems in large group settings require the use of methods that can manage a large volume of information and perform complex information processes rapidly.

In summary, the essential features of a GPD are made up of its episodes, activities, and acts, which are operationalized through roles, rules, and technologies. The success of a GPD is largely dependent upon the appropriate match between the design, and the problem situation, the users' instruction in and acceptance of the design, and the design's fulfillment by the facilitator and members.

A Review of Selected Group Process Designs

Three GPDs used to facilitate problem-solving meetings were selected for review based partially on the author's personal experience with each of them as a facilitator, observer, and participant. All three approaches were designed with particular attention to task and maintenance considerations. In addition, they illustrate three distinct purposes and sets of procedures for conducting group problem-solving meetings (see Table 2). Finally, they illustrate the difference between partial/open and complete/closed designs.

Synectics

Description. Synectics is a highly specialized GPD that uses a small group in an atypical manner. The version of synectics reviewed here was developed by George Prince (1970) in order to tackle difficult problems creatively. Synectics applies creative problem-solving practices to problems unsolved by expert knowledge and analytic approaches. In this respect, synectics is a solution-centered approach: It emphasizes

Table 2
GPDs by Design Level

Level	Synectics	Interactive Management	Interaction Method
Event	Creative group problem solving	Group complex problem solving	Effective task group meetings

Episodes	Activities*	Activities*	Activities
Problem Identification	Client problem in how-to form	Facilitator and group broker(s) establish problem or goal	[Consensually decide on focus (e.g., problem) and method for addressing it (e.g., Reflective Thinking using selected appropriate techniques for each problem-solving episode)]
Problem Analysis	Client reviews problem as given for participants	Nominal Group Technique and/or Delphi, ISM	
Solution Generation	Participants Ideawrite metaphorical how-to's and ideas for solutions	Nominal Group Technique and/or Delphi, Options Field Method, Options Profile Method	
Solution Evaluation	Client uses Spectrum Policy to evaluate +/–	Trade Off Analysis	
Solution Implementation	Client develops plan for possible solution	Follow preferred alternatives developed in solution evaluation episode	

*Does not reflect the actual order or interrelationship of the activities.

activities to find solutions rather than to perform problem analysis (Gray, 1982). The design requires that participants use metaphors to create unfamiliar and unusual perspectives in an effort to find new and creative solutions. It is most applicable for open-ended problems that have no right solution. It works best on "thing problems" (e.g., how to make a light, compact frame for a portable solar mirror) although it can be used on "people problems" (e.g., how to reduce work force without reducing morale; McPherson 1967). Synectics is particularly useful on invention, research, and innovation problems. Numerous client organizations, among them IBM, GE, Ford, and Union Carbide, have reported successful use of synectics (McPherson 1967).

Synectics involves three specialized roles for conducting process episodes and activities: the facilitator, the participants, and the client. The client is most typically the individual who has the problem. This person is usually an expert in the problem area (i.e., an engineer with an invention problem or a manager with an operational problem), and therefore is responsible for defining the problem, providing background, and evaluating solutions.

The facilitator ensures group adherence to prescribed episodes, activities, and acts and sees that ideas are displayed. Most critically, a facilitator must instruct, guide, and monitor the client and group participants. Thus the facilitator must know what is going on during the session at all times in order to keep members in role and to conduct the procedures appropriately. This is the critical challenge for the facilitator of all GPDs.

Participants are strictly idea generators who use prescribed activities and acts designed for their role. Ideally neither the participants nor the facilitator have any particular expertise or connection to the client's problem. When group members are not versed in the problem domain or when they have a subordinate relationship to the client, creative idea generation is enhanced (Prince 1970).

The process begins with a meeting between the facilitator and client to review the synectics process and the "problem as given" (PAG), that is, background and desired outcome. During the synectics session in a review of the PAG is stated by the client in a "how-to" form (e.g., how to make a light, simple frame for a portable solar mirror). An analysis episode follows in which the client is asked: How is the PAG a problem for you? What has been tried to solve it? What have you thought of? What is desired from the group? (Prince 1970; Ulschak et al. 1981). Participants listen intently for implied wishes and goals and for any questions they may have while the client is presenting the analysis. While they are listening they are ideawriting "how-to" statements based on their perceptions of the client's explicit and implied problems, desires, and goals. The how-to's are highly metaphorical, solution-seeking statements (how to use a sky hook, enclose a mirror, use a umbrella) used to escape the routine associations of the problem field and to reframe and trigger new functional associations (Gray, Vanderven, Chilberg, Sullivan, & Zimmerman 1976; Prince 1970).

The facilitator moves the group into the next episode by listing selected how-to statements on newsprint before the client. The client is then asked to select a favored how-to statement and to generate any ideas for making it into a solution. If the client is unable to offer a solution, the participants are asked for their ideas on solving the PAG. This activity requires a participant to start with an idea that draws from the metaphorical context of the how-to statement. Other participants are permitted to build on the idea but not to shift the direction. Typically two or three builds are permitted before the facilitator asks the client to paraphrase the idea. The client is then asked to employ the Spectrum Policy (Prince 1970), which requires him to identify those things he likes about the idea and then to point out any perceived obstacles in a proactive form (e.g., would like to see . . .). While this is taking place participants listen and write down how-to's. The same cycle is then repeated in an effort to find solutions to the obstacles.

When a solution-development episode reaches an acceptable solution the client is asked to review steps for implementing the idea. Identifying these steps creates a "possible solution" and the client can then continue the solution-seeking effort by selecting another how-to statement.

Synectics exemplifies a complete and closed GPD in that it is totally prescribed. There are no deviations permitted in this process with the exception of introducing techniques (e.g., excursion: an imaginary vacation) to overcome blocks in generating highly metaphorical how-to statements and to help energize the group. A succinct outline of the synectics process is available in Ulschak et. al.'s book on small-group problem solving.

Analysis. Synectics was designed to use a group in order to solve clients' problems creatively. The group is not responsible for the problem itself. Rather, it is responsible for using the synectics process to serve the client. Commitment to the solution is required only by the client; commitment to the process is required of all group members. This arrangement is reflected in the task role specialization in which participants emphasize idea-generating activities, the client is responsible for problem identification and solution evaluation, and the facilitator maintains designated procedures.

Synectics's design reflects its solution-centered, creative problem-solving emphasis. This is apparent in the design's use of metaphors to generate new directions for solutions, in its development of one solution at a time, and in its use of the Spectrum Policy to conduct solution evaluation and development. A closer examination of these procedures will show how synectics addresses task and maintenance functions.

Participants' generation of metaphorical how-to statements clearly serves the task function of communication. However, the emphasis on metaphors within a solution-oriented phrase (i.e., how-to) reinforces not only the creative search for solutions but the solution emphasis of the process. Further, an emphasis on solution is reflected in the preceding analysis activity in which the client provides the problem's background.

The client's selection of a metaphoric how-to statement provides a direction for solution generation. Whoever starts the first concrete solution suggestion sets the focus for a solution development episode. The facilitator makes sure that the participants or client contribute additional ideas that expand or build upon this initial idea. No more than three ideas are typically permitted at a time. This requirement maintains a single task focus and manages solution complexity. It helps the client follow solution suggestions by "chunking" the solution's development into units of up to three builds for evaluation. The use of the "build rule" also serves maintenance functions. Working on a single solution idea at a time avoids the problem of disconfirming communication behaviors that result from ignoring or passing over a member's contribution. The build rule also enhances supportive communication practices by requiring other members to add to the previous idea, reinforcing the contributions of previous contributors, and shaping a solution composed of members' contributions. The build rule promotes task effectiveness, individual satisfaction, and participant cohesion.

The Spectrum Policy is the simplest yet most powerful procedure of synectics. It structures the client's relationally sensitive activity of evaluating the participants' solutions. The policy's main job is to evaluate participants' ideas in a proactive manner. This is important because the evaluation of others' contributions can lead to negative feelings that could stimulate reactions ranging from apathy to hostility. The Spectrum Policy requires the client to identify the positive attributes of the participants' solution followed by any concerns. The concerns, proactively stated, are phrased in terms of desired or needed solution attributes, not in terms of what is wrong or problematic. From a task perspective, this establishes solution attributes useful to the client, though the solution itself may not be completely satisfactory. Furthermore, identifying concerns with the solution provides a focus for another consideration of the initial solution idea. This cybernetic aspect of the Spectrum Policy provides a systematic approach to solution development.

The maintenance payoffs of the Spectrum Policy are also noteworthy. The requirement that the positive attributes of a solution idea be identified first, followed by the negative attributes stated in a proactive form, softens the harshness of evaluation. The proactive form of the solution critique not only provides a specific focus for solution development, but does so in a supportive manner by identifying what is needed instead of what is wrong.

Synectics is a specialized, highly structured, and rule-governed GPD. These characteristics are likely to appear quite alien and restrictive to the uninitiated user. However, a skilled facilitator can prepare participants and clients to use the process in a relatively short time, especially if they are open to trying a new approach to group problem solving. Once synectics is in place the procedures reinforce constructive task and maintenance communication practices and productive outcomes.

Interactive Management

Description. The Interactive Management (IM) approach was designed for group complex problem solving (e.g., policy development, organizational redesign, strategic planning) requiring the involvement of relevant stakeholders (Warfield 1976, 1982). It provides a mechanism for *an intact or ad hoc group's in-depth examination of a superordinate goal, and establishes a shared comprehensive understanding of the problems and possible solutions*. IM is most valuable for its thorough exploration of the problem and solution domain. It establishes a comprehensive picture of problem and solution relationships, arriving at strategic solution priorities based on the participants' knowledge and experience.

IM is an elaborate and incisive GPD that provides a sequence of steps and consensus methodologies (Broome & Christakis 1988; Broome & Keever 1986; Christakis, Krause, & Prabhu 1988; Warfield 1976, 1982) involving one or more activities. The process requires a facilitator, participants, support staff, and selected technologies. The facilitator works with the client group broker(s) to establish the session's superordinate goal and helps identify the appropriate participants. During IM sessions the facilitator orients the participants to the meeting goal and instructs them on the rules governing each consensus methodology as they occur in sequence. The facilitator also records ideas during information-generating activities of various methodologies. The support staff perform computation, reproduction, display, and set-up functions using simple (easels, diagrams, magnetic cards) and sophisticated technologies (computers, copiers, and projectors).

The consensus methodologies establish discrete episodes spanning several group sessions. The methodologies structure the sequence of activities and guide the manner and focus of participant involvement (see Table 3). Each methodology maximizes task and maintenance functions through activities that require input, joint decision making, and supportive styles of communication behavior.

The information-management demands of the complete IM process require a dedicated room designed to maximize participants' comfort, information manipulation, and access to displayed information.

IM is a complete and largely closed GPD. The specific sequence and types of episodes and activities can be modified to serve specific client constraints, usually determined by time limitations, the nature of the problem, or unanticipated information needs. In this respect, the overall GPD can address the client group's specific needs and circumstances.

IM is a sophisticated GPD for collaborative and complex group problem solving. It provides a means of identifying, managing, and conceptualizing large volumes of information for use in designing critical and comprehensive solution strategies. It has been used successfully by numerous client groups and has been installed in various organizations (e.g., U.S. Forest Service, George Mason University, City University of London, National Marine & Fisheries Service, Department of Defense, Americans for Indian Opportunity).

Analysis. IM is designed to help groups develop solutions to highly complex and unstructured problems in a manner that involves relevant stakeholders. In this respect, the problem-solving design emphasizes member involvement throughout the task episodes and activities. Unlike synectics, members perform several task function roles across the various activities (i.e., idea generation, information sharing, evaluation, etc.). However, these role functions are determined by the activity procedures of each episode. The performance of these roles by each member establishes joint problem and solution ownership, which can reinforce commitment to the group's superordinate goal and decisions.

IM design task functions emphasize information management, analysis, and decision making. The consensus methodology of each process episode involves methodic and varied information management practices, some form of analysis, and one or more decision activities. IM is more complex than other GPDs because it was designed to help groups make critical decisions on goals involving large volumes of information.

The information generated by the group is consistently made available to the members through several forms of visual display (e.g., easel, computer projection, handouts). Information involving complex computation (e.g., pairwise comparisons) is provided rapidly for the next activity. Providing data within a given meeting session ensures task efficiency by keeping the group on task. The facilitator and word-processing staff are required to use members' own language when displaying or transcribing contributions. This ensures the members' ownership of the information and the

Table 3
Interactive Management Consensus Methodologies

Methodologies*	Activities	Functions
Nominal Group Technique	Individual idea generation, round robin for master list, clarification, and ranking of items	Information sharing and idea generating
Interpretive Structural Modeling (ISM)	Pairwise comparison of selected items, voting on preference, computer computation and display	Analysis of interrelationship among items using one of six transitive relationships
Delphi**	At distance idea generation by participants/experts using trigger question followed by tabulation and distribution of results	Information gathering or idea generating by sources outside of meeting
Options Field Method†	Pairwise comparison of solution options, clarification, vote on preference, computer computation and display, label option clusters, pairwise comparison of clusters, clarification, vote on preference, computer computation and display	Construction of solution field
Options Profile Method†	Small groups select solution options within and across option categories and report to group	Construction of one or more solution profiles
Trade Off Analysis†	Review and analyze developed option profile(s) for implementation feasibility, adjust priorities if needed	Selection of preferred solution profile

* All methodology activities require group member participation.
** Delphi is used to obtain task-specific information relevant to continuing the decision-making process. It can involve nonparticipant information experts.
† An inherent function of these methodologies is to reveal and identify embedded issues, constraints, or needed information relevant to critical decision making.

task and avoids indirect contributions from or role conflicts with the facilitator. Thus information management practices also support maintenance functions by reinforcing the integrity of the individual member, displaying the contributions of all members, and avoiding cause for conflict with the facilitator or staff.

IM design emphasizes the analysis function. Virtually all the consensus methodologies require one or more analytic procedures (e.g., pairwise comparisons, labeling option clusters, option profiles; see Table 3). This emphasis on analysis provides a critical understanding of the problem/goal domain. It is accomplished through activities that require members to identify issues and conceptualize their relationships. Analytic tasks help the group manage the information load as well as reveal the critical issues embedded in a complex problem.

Task efficiency and productivity are achieved through decision-making practices at various junctures in idea-generating or analysis activities. Information sharing and idea generating are largely conducted through ideawriting (e.g., Nominal Group Technique), the round robin, and open question and answer periods for clarification purposes. Evaluation of others' contributions is not permitted. Decisions are established through ranking, voting, and consensus practices. Exercises such as silent idea generation, individual ranking, the round robin, and voting indicate IM's emphasis on individual contributions and interaction control. This emphasis maximizes member involvement and reduces the occurrence of dysfunctional communication behaviors (e.g., unconstructive criticism, inappropriate discussion tangents).

The Interaction Method

Description. The Interaction Method (Doyle & Straus 1976) is designed to address four pervasive meeting problems: (1) the wandering discussion focus, (2) inappropriate discussion focus management, (3) lack of decision-making participation, and (4) verbal aggression by group members. Its main purpose is to provide rules and roles for conducting productive task groups meetings. Although it does prescribe consensual decision making it does not require any particular design for problem solving. The Interaction Method is a GPD for enhancing effective group meetings in general.

The Interaction Method is made up of four roles: the facilitator, recorder, member, and manager/member. The facilitator's job is to ensure that meeting participants identify and maintain a single discussion focus and a procedure for managing that focus. In addition, the facilitator makes sure all members have an opportunity to contribute to the discussion and that decisions regarding focus, procedure, and decision issues are made consensually. The facilitator must also protect members from aggressive behaviors.

Members are responsible for following procedural rules as well as having sole responsibility for content. Thus they must reach agreement on their focus and on a method for maintaining it. In addition, they must ensure that the facilitator and recorder maintain their roles and do not become involved with meeting content (except when seeking permission to step out of role to contribute an idea). Even though the facilitator may suggest a practice for managing a selected focus, the members must consensually decide on the choice.

The recorder's sole function is to provide a legible public display ("Group Memory") of the meeting's progress, allowing the facilitator to manage the process and permitting members to concentrate on the meeting. The recorder must maintain content neutrality, accurately record members' ideas, and keep pace with the meeting.

The manager/member may establish the group's problem or goal and define substantive guidelines and constraints for decision making and problem solving. Otherwise, the manager is treated like any other member and subject to the same rules. The manager's role is to reduce the negative impact of power in the group decision-making process (i.e., reduced member input, process decisions guided by personal agendas, domination of discussion, etc.).

Like the previous GPDs, the Interaction Method utilizes roe specialization. Unlike them, however, it is partial and open. It does not prescribe episodes or activities other than the rules for conducting the meeting. Specific meeting foci can be identified and designed before the meeting or, owing to unexpected tasks or needs, while the meeting is in progress. Members are responsible for establishing the meeting foci and the procedures for managing them or for accepting the suggestions of the facilitator. The consummate facilitator should have a comprehensive knowledge of methods and interventions to help the group approach different types of agenda items and various group dynamics problems (e.g., troublesome members, conflict management, lack of participation). The facilitator must be an advocate and instructor of effective meeting practices.

Analysis. The Interaction Method was designed to improve meeting practices by providing two types of prescriptive rules communication and procedural. Communication rules require members to retrain from attacking other members or their ideas and to make decisions consensually. Procedural rules are meta-rules. They do not establish the task or provide the specific activity for conducting it, yet they require group members to identify what they are going to do and how they are going to do it. Because the Interaction Method does not prescribe episodes and activities, it is a partial GPD. Complete GPDs outline procedural guidelines, allowing members to focus their attention on substantive matters. However, the Interaction Method does provide several task and maintenance functions through its rules and role specialization.

Task functions are largely promoted through the "focus rule" and "tool rule" (selecting procedure or practices for conducting the selected focus). The facilitator makes sure these rules are used and that the group maintains the focus and the selected activity for conducting it. These two rules can increase task efficiency and effectiveness by requiring the group to establish and maintain a task and procedure. The facilitator may suggest an appropriate procedure for consideration by the group, but is not permitted to contribute substantive content. The group's responsibility for procedural and substantive decisions maintains its ownership of the meeting and of the decisions.

The recorder role provides a useful task-centered role function. The recorder tracks the meeting's progress by providing a visual display of group decisions. This establishes a common record and focuses the group's attention, which tends to encourage task activity. It also frees a member from having to perform recording duties.

The maintenance function is directly supported through the use of communication rules and the manager/member role. The "no attack rule" reduces the occurrence of defensive behaviors, and the consensus rule increases member involvement in all group decisions. Again, the facilitator ensures that these rules are practiced and even solicits input from less vocal members. The manager/member role relegates the formal group leader to member status during the meeting. This can encourage an open communication climate and promote group-centered communication.

Additional task and maintenance functions can occur based on selected procedures for conducting various meeting task foci. This is largely determined by the knowledge, appropriate selection, and implementation of practices to fit the task and the maintenance needs of the situation. Therefore, the Interaction Method ideally requires a facilitator who knows a variety of practices and techniques for conducting the various types of tasks and circumstances encountered in group decision making.

Although the Interaction Method does not provide a complete GPD, it does establish practices that require critical and systematic consideration of task activities, reduce dysfunctional meeting practices, and heighten awareness of relationship behaviors.

Conclusion

The three GPDs reviewed here are considered "second-generation" designs in that they go beyond substantive considerations. Second-generation methods emphasize group participation and cooperative action, and require unlearning competitive behaviors (Olsen 1982). They address the maintenance, as well as task functions, of group communication. The particular value of a GPD prescription is that it provides a process designed for a particular group situation and goal. It avoids the difficulty of having to identify appropriate processes for implementation. Steiner (1972) points out that members ordinarily are unfamiliar with the many prescribed practices available, thus they may use practices that do not maximize group success.

Group problem-solving design maximizes efficient and effective group communication. Although there is no conclusive evidence regarding the quality of decisions derived from the use of the reviewed GPDs, personal experience and testimonial outcomes are satisfactory if not exceptional. The few experiences I have had when the use of GPDs was not successful appeared to be the result of an unclear or misunderstood problem, lack of a shared problem goal, personal or hidden agenda, insufficient instruction, or a lack of commitment to the adopted procedures. These situations are harmful to the success of any group problem-solving effort.

The payoffs of a GPD are not without cost. There are monetary costs associated with obtaining a third-party facilitator or with installing the GPD in an organization. Installation of a GPD will likely require a commitment of personnel to serve as facilitators and may require the use of support staff.

The more difficult and demanding costs are those associated with the human factors. Managers will often have to act as group members and may not have the freedom to do what they want, when they want. They will be faced with sharing decision making and authority. Many managers may not be comfortable with group ownership and third-party interventions. Group members may be reluctant to assume responsibility for decision making, especially if there is an atmosphere of distrust, a closed-communication climate, or lack of confidence.

GPD's organized, rational, and systematic practices may not suit some members' decision-making styles or may interfere with personal meeting goals. Such conditions can lead to uncooperative behaviors and efforts to undermine the GPD process. Even though the facilitator must rectify such situations, they still threaten group effectiveness.

The use of GPDs is by no means widespread in view of the number of groups operating in public and private organizations. This is, in part, due to lack of information on the available GPDs and their purposes. Cultural values may contribute to adoption resistance, especially since our culture emphasizes individualism, competitive interpersonal styles, and hierarchical relationships, all of which are antithetical to the collaborative values inherent to the reviewed GPDs. Resistance may simply be the result of a lack of familiarity or adherence to tradition.

GPDs may receive more attention if Drucker's (1988) projection that the organization of the future will require the development of professionalism through the use of task forces is realized. A larger dependence on task groups will create a need for approaches to conduct problem-solving meetings effectively. GPDs will become the basic tools available for tackling the variety of problems and decisions faced by task forces. Professionalism will be enhanced through effective group problem solving and meeting communication.

Meanwhile, there is a strong need for more public education regarding the various GPDs available for group problem solving and for research identifying the efficacy of group process designs. Research is needed to determine the role of design features in fulfilling task and maintenance communication functions as well as their contribution to the quality of group decision making so we may better understand their value, limitations, and appropriate applications.

Notes

1. The term *designed* refers to a formal plan that establishes practices, rules, and roles for conducting the group problem-solving meeting.
2. This classic study was based on observations of natural groups. This may reflect the limited knowledge or considerations of procedural options in such groups. Thus the occurrence of procedural message behaviors would not reflect the range of possible procedural message behaviors.

References

Benne, K., and Sheats, P. (1948). "Functional Roles of Group Members." *Journal of Social Issues* 4, 41–49.

Broome, B.J., and Christakis, A.N. (1988). A culturally sensitive approach to tribal government issue management. *International Journal of Intercultural Relations* 12, 107–123.

Broome, B.J., and Keever, D.B. (1986). "Facilitating Group Communication: The Interactive Management Approach." Paper presented at the annual convention of the Speech Communication Association. Chicago.

Christakis, A.N., Krause, L.K., and Prabhu. Y. (1988). "Synthesis in a New Age: A Role for Systems Scientists in the Age of Design." *Systems Research* 5(2), 107–113.

Doyle, M., and Straus, D. (1976). *How to Make Meetings Work.* New York: Wyden.

Drucker, P.F. (1988, January–February). "The Coming of the New Organization." *Harvard Business Review,* 45–53.

Gray, B. (1982). "Synectics: A Solution Centered Approach to Problem Solving." Unpublished doctoral dissertation. Ohio University, Athens.

Gray, B., Vanderven, G., Chilberg, J., Sullivan, H., and Zimmerman, K. (1976). "A Synectics-Like Process for Problem Solving: An Explanation and Demonstration." Paper presented at the 8th Annual Communication Week. Ohio University, Athens.

Kepner, C., and Tregoe, B. (1981). *The New Rational Manager.* Princeton, NJ: Princeton Research Press.

McPherson, J.H. (1967). *The People, the Problems, and the Problem-Solving Methods.* Midland, MI: Pendell.

Moore, C.M. (1987). *Group Techniques for Idea Building.* Newbury Part, CA: Sage.

Olsen, S.A. (1982). "Background and State of the Art." In S. A. Olsen (ed.), *Group Planning and Problem-Solving Methods an Engineering Management.* New York: John Wiley.

Osborn, A.F. (1957). *Applied Imagination.* New York: Scribners.

Prince, G.M. (1970). *The Practice of Creativity.* New York: Harper & Row.

Steiner, I.D. (1972). *Group Process and Productivity.* New York: Academic Press.

Ulschak, Nathanson, and Gillian (1981).

Van Gundy (1984).

Warfield (1976).

Warfield (1982).

Group Decision Fiascoes Continue: Space Shuttle *Challenger* and a Groupthink Framework

Gregory Moorhead, Richard Ference, and Chris P. Neck

Introduction

In 1972 a new dimension was added to our understanding of group decision making with the proposal of the groupthink hypothesis by Janis (1972). Janis coined the term "groupthink" to refer to "a mode of thinking that people engage in when they are deeply involved in a cohesive in-group, when the members' striving for unanimity override their motivation to realistically appraise alternative courses of action" (Janis 1972, 8) The hypothesis was supported by his hindsight analysis of several political-military fiascoes and successes that are differentiated by the occurrence or nonoccurrence of antecedent conditions, groupthink symptoms, and decision-making defects.

In a subsequent volume, Janis further explicates the theory and adds an analysis of the Watergate transcripts and various published memoirs and accounts of principals involved, concluding that the Watergate cover-up decision also was a result of groupthink (Janis 1983). Both volumes propose prescriptions for preventing the occurrence of groupthink, many of which have appeared in popular press, in books on executive decision making, and in management textbooks. Multiple advocacy decision-making procedures have been adopted at the executive levels in many organizations, including the executive branch of the government. One would think that by 1986, thirteen years after the publication of a popular book, that its prescriptions might be well ingrained in our management and decision-making styles. Unfortunately, it has not happened.

On January 28, 1986 the space shuttle *Challenger* was launched from Kennedy Space Center. The temperature that morning was in the mid-20s, well below the previous low temperatures at which the shuttle engines had been tested. Seventy-three seconds after launch, the *Challenger* exploded, killing all seven astronauts aboard, and becoming the worst disaster in space flight history. The catastrophe shocked the nation, crippled the American space program, and is destined to be remembered as the most tragic national event since the assassination of John F. Kennedy in 1963.

The Presidential Commission that investigated the accident pointed to a flawed decision-making process as a primary contributory cause. The decision was made the night before the launch in the Level I Flight Readiness Review Meeting. Due to the work of the Presidential Commission, information concerning that meeting is available for analysis as a group decision possibly susceptible to groupthink.

In this paper, we report the results of our analysis of the Level I Flight Readiness Review Meeting as a decision-making situation that displays evidence of groupthink. We review the antecedent conditions, the groupthink symptoms, and the possible

From "Group Decision Fiascos Continue: Space Shuttle Challenger and a Groupthink Framework" by Moorhead, Ference, and Neck, pp. 539–550 in *Human Relations*, Volume 44, Number 6, 1991. Reprinted by permission of Plenum Publishing Corporation.

decision-making defects, as suggested by Janis (1983). In addition, we take the next and more important step of going beyond the development of another example of groupthink to make recommendations for renewed inquiry into group decision-making processes.

Theory and Evidence

The groupthink hypothesis has been presented in detail in numerous publications other than Janis's books (Flowers 1977; Courtright 1978; Leana 1985; Moorhead 1982; Moorhead & Montanari 1986) and will not be repeated here. The major categories will be used as a framework for organizing the evidence from the meeting. Within each category the key elements will be presented along with meeting details that pertain to each.

The meetings took place throughout the day and evening from 12:36 P.M. (EST), January 27, 1986 following the decision not to launch the *Challenger* due to high crosswinds at the launch site. Discussions continued through about 12:00 midnight (EST) via teleconferencing and Telefax systems connecting the Kennedy Space Center in Florida, Morton Thiokol (MTI) in Utah, Johnson Space Center in Houston, and the Marshall Space Flight Center. The Level I Flight Readiness Review is the highest level of review prior to launch. It comprises the highest level of management at the three space centers and at MTI, the private supplier of the solid rocket booster engines.

To briefly state the situation, the MTI engineers recommended not to launch if temperatures of the O-ring seals on the rocket were below 53 degrees Fahrenheit, which was the lowest temperature of any previous flight. Laurence B. Mulloy, manager of the Solid Rocket Booster Project at Marshall Space Flight Center, states:

> . . . The bottom line of that, though, initially was that Thiokol engineering, Bob Lund, who is the vice president and director of engineering, who is here today, recommended that 51-L [the *Challenger*] not be launched if the O-ring temperatures predicted at launch time would be lower than any previous launch, and that was 53 degrees . . . (*Report of the Presidential Commission on the Space Shuttle Accident,* 1986, p. 91–92).

This recommendation was made at 8:45 P.M., January 27, 1986 (*Report of the Presidential Commission on the Space Shuttle Accident,* 1986). Through the ensuing discussions the decision to launch was made.

Antecedent Conditions

The three primary antecedent conditions for the development of groupthink are: a highly cohesive group, leader preference for a certain decision, and insulation of the group from qualified outside opinions. These conditions existed in this situation.

Cohesive Group. The people who made the decision to launch had worked together for many years. They were familiar with each other and had grown through the ranks of the space program. A high degree of *esprit de corps* existed between the members.

Leader Preference. Two top level managers actively promoted their pro-launch opinions in the face of opposition. The commission report states that several managers at space centers and MTI pushed for launch, regardless of the low temperatures.

Insulation from Experts. MTI engineers made their recommendations relatively early in the evening. The top level decision-making group knew of their objections but did not meet with them directly to review their data and concerns. As Roger Boisjoly, a Thiokol engineer, states in his remarks to the Presidential Commission:

> . . . and the bottom line was that the engineering people would not recommend a launch below 53 degrees Fahrenheit . . . From this point on, management formulated the points to base their decision on. There was never one comment in favor, as I have said, of launching by any engineer or other nonmanagement person. . . . I was not even asked to participate in giving any input to the final decision charts (*Report of the Presidential Commission on the Space Shuttle Accident,* 1986, p. 91–92).

This testimonial indicates that the top decision-making team was insulated from the engineers who possessed the expertise regarding the functioning of the equipment.

Groupthink Symptoms

Janis identified eight symptoms of groupthink. They are presented here along with evidence from the *Report of the Presidential Commission on the Space Shuttle Accident* (1986).

Invulnerability. When groupthink occurs, most or all of the members of the decision-making group have an illusion of invulnerability that reassures them in the face of obvious dangers. This illusion leads the group to become overly optimistic and willing to take extraordinary risks. It may also cause them to ignore clear warnings of danger.

The solid rocket joint problem that destroyed *Challenger* was discussed often at flight readiness review meetings prior to flight. However, commission member Richard Feynman concluded from the testimony that a mentality of overconfidence existed due to the extraordinary record of success of space flights. Every time we send one up it is successful. Involved members may seem to think that on the next one we can lower our standards or take more risks because it always works (*Time* 1986).

The invulnerability illusion may have built up over time as a result of NASA's own spectacular history. NASA had not lost an astronaut since 1967 when a flash fire in the capsule of Apollo 1 killed three. Since that time NASA had a string of fifty-five successful missions. They had put a man on the moon, built and launched Skylab and the shuttle, and retrieved defective satellites from orbit. In the minds of most Americans and apparently their own, they could do no wrong.

Rationalization. Victims of groupthink collectively construct rationalizations that discount warnings and other forms of negative feedback. If these signals were taken seriously when presented, the group members would be forced to reconsider their assumptions each time they re-commit themselves to their past decisions.

In the Level I flight readiness meeting when the *Challenger* was given final launch approval, MTI engineers presented evidence that the joint would fail. Their argument was based on the fact that in the coldest previous launch (air temperature 30 degrees) the joint in question experienced serious erosion and that no data existed as to how the joint would perform at colder temperatures. Flight center officials put forth numerous technical rationalizations faulting MTI's analysis. One of these rationalizations was that the engineer's data were inconclusive. As Mr. Boisjoly emphasized to the commission:

> ... I was asked, yes, at that point in time I was asked to quantify my concerns, and I said I couldn't. I couldn't quantify it. I had no data to quantify it, but I did say I knew that it was away from goodness in the current data base. Someone on the net commented that we had soot blow-by on SRM-22 [Flight 61-A, October, 1985] which was launched at 75 degrees. I don't remember who made the comment, but that is where the first comment came in about the disparity between my conclusion and the observed data because SRM-22 [Flight 61-A, October 1985] had blow-by at essentially a room temperature launch. I then said that SRM-15 [Flight 51-C, January, 1985] had much more blow-by indication and that it was indeed telling us that lower temperature was a factor. I was asked again for data to support my claim, and I said I have none other than what is being presented (*Report of the Presidential Commission on the Space Shuttle Accident,* 1986, p. 89).

Discussions became twisted (compared to previous meetings) and no one detected it. Under normal conditions, MTI would have to prove the shuttle boosters' readiness for launch, instead they found themselves being forced to prove that the boosters were unsafe. Boisjoly's testimony supports this description of the discussion:

> ... This was a meeting where the determination was to launch, and it was up to us to prove beyond a shadow of a doubt that it was not safe to do so. This is in total reverse to what the position usually is in a preflight conversation or a flight readiness review. It is usually exactly opposite of that . . . (*Report of the Presidential Commission on the Space Shuttle Accident,* 1986, p. 93).

Morality. Group members often believe, without question, in the inherent morality of their position. They tend to ignore the ethical or moral consequences of their decision.

In the *Challenger* case, this point was raised by a very high level MTI manager, Allan J. McDonald, who tried to stop the launch and said that he would not want to have to defend the decision to launch. He stated to the commission:

> ... I made the statement that if we're wrong and something goes wrong on this flight, I wouldn't want to have to be the person to stand up in front of board in inquiry and say that I went ahead and told them to go ahead and fly this thing outside what the motor was qualified to . . . (*Report of the Presidential Commission on the Space Shuttle Accident,* 1986, p. 95).

Some members did not hear this statement because it occurred during a break. Three top officials who did hear it ignored it.

Stereotyped Views of Others. Victims of groupthink often have a stereotyped view of the opposition of anyone with a competing opinion. They feel that the opposition is too stupid or too weak to understand or deal effectively with the problem.

Two of the top three NASA officials responsible for the launch displayed this attitude. They felt that they completely understood the nature of the joint problem and never seriously considered the objections raised by the MTI engineers. In fact they denigrated and badgered the opposition and their information and opinions.

Pressure on Dissent. Group members often apply direct pressure to anyone who questions the validity of the arguments supporting a decision or position favored by the majority. These same two officials pressured MTI to change its position after MTI originally recommended that the launch not take place. These two officials pressured MTI personnel to prove that it was not safe to launch, rather than to prove the opposite. As mentioned earlier, this was a total reversal of normal preflight procedures. It was this pressure that top MTI management was responding to when they overruled their engineering staff and recommended launch. As the Commission report states:

> . . . At approximately 11 P.M. Eastern Standard Time, the Thiokol/NASA teleconference resumed, the Thiokol management stating that they had reassessed the problem, that the temperature effects were a concern, but that the data was admittedly inconclusive . . . (p. 96).

This seems to indicate that NASA's pressure on these Thiokol officials forced them to change their recommendation from delay to execution of the launch.

Self-Censorship. Group members tend to censor themselves when they have opinions or ideas that deviate from the apparent group consensus. Janis feels that this reflects each member's inclination to minimize to himself or herself the importance of his or her own doubts and counterarguments.

The most obvious evidence of self-censorship occurred when a vice president of MTI, who had previously presented information against launch, bowed to pressure from NASA and accepted their rationalizations for launch. He then wrote these up and presented them to NASA as the reasons that MTI had changed its recommendation to launch.

Illusion of Unanimity. Group members falling victim to groupthink share an illusion of unanimity concerning judgments made by members speaking in favor of the majority view. This symptom is caused in part by the preceding one and is aided by the false assumption that any participant who remains silent is in agreement with the majority opinion. The group leader and other members support each other by playing up points of convergence in their thinking at the expense of fully exploring points of divergence that might reveal unsettling problems.

No participant from NASA ever openly agreed with or even took sides with MTI in the discussion. The silence from NASA was probably amplified by the fact that the meeting was a teleconference linking the participants at three different locations. Obviously, body language which might have been evidenced by dissenters was not visible to others who might also have held a dissenting opinion. Thus, silence meant agreement.

Mindguarding. Certain group members assume the role of guarding the minds of others in the group. They attempt to shield the group from adverse information that might destroy the majority view of the facts regarding the appropriateness of the decision.

The top management at Marshall knew that the rocket casings had been ordered redesigned to correct a flaw five months previous to this launch. This information and other technical details concerning the history of the joint problem was withheld at the meeting.

Decision-Making Defects

The result of the antecedent conditions and the symptoms of groupthink is a defective decision-making process. Janis discusses several defects in decision making that can result.

Few Alternatives. The group considers only a few alternatives, often only two. No initial survey of all possible alternatives occurs. The Flight Readiness Review team had a launch/no-launch decision to make. These were the only two alternatives considered. Other possible alternatives might have been to delay the launch for further testing, or to delay until the temperatures reached an appropriate level.

No Re-Examination of Alternatives. The group fails to re-examine alternatives that may have been initially discarded based on early unfavorable information. Top NASA officials spent time and effort defending and strengthening their position, rather than examining the MTI position.

Rejecting Expert Opinions. Members make little or no attempt to seek outside experts opinions. NASA did not seek out other experts who might have some expertise in this area. They assumed that they had all the information.

Rejecting Negative Information. Members tend to focus on supportive information and ignore any data or information that might cast a negative light on their preferred alternative. MTI representatives repeatedly tried to point out errors in the rationale the NASA officials were using to justify the launch. Even after the decision was made, the argument continued until a NASA official told the MTI representative that it was no longer his concern.

No Contingency Plans. Members spend little time discussing the possible consequences of the decision and, therefore, fail to develop contingency plans. There is no documented evidence in the Rogers Commission Report of any discussion of the possible consequences of an incorrect decision.

Summary of the Evidence

The major categories and key elements of the groupthink hypothesis have been presented (albeit somewhat briefly) along with evidence from the discussions prior to the launching of the *Challenger*, as reported in the President's Commission to investigate the accident. The antecedent conditions were present in the decision-making group, even though the group was in several physical locations. The leaders had a preferred solution and engaged in behaviors designed to promote it rather than critically appraise alternatives. These behaviors were evidence of most of the symptoms leading to a defective decision-making process.

Discussion

This situation provides another example of decision making in which the group fell victim to the groupthink syndrome, as have so many previous groups. It illustrates the situation characteristics, the symptoms of groupthink, and decision-making defects as described by Janis. This situation, however, also illustrates several other aspects of situations that are critical to the development of groupthink that need to be included in a revised formulation of the groupthink model. First, the element of time in influencing the development of groupthink has not received adequate attention. In the decision to launch the space shuttle *Challenger*, time was a crucial part of the decision-making process. The launch had been delayed once, and the window for another launch was fast closing. The leaders of the decision team were concerned about public and congressional perceptions of the entire space shuttle program and its continued funding and may have felt that further delays of the launch could seriously impact future funding. With the space window fast closing, the decision team was faced with a launch now or seriously damage the program decision. One top level manager's response to Thiokol's initial recommendation to postpone the launch indicates the presence of time pressure:

> With this LCC (Launch Commit Criteria), i.e., do not launch with a temperature greater [sic] than 53 degrees, we may not be able to launch until next April. We need to consider this carefully before we jump to any conclusions . . . (*Report of the Presidential Commission on the Space Shuttle Accident,* 1986, p. 96).

Time pressure could have played a role in the group choosing to agree and to self-censor their comments. Therefore, time is a critical variable that needs to be highlighted in a revised groupthink framework. We propose that time is an important moderator between group characteristics and the development of the groupthink symptoms. That is, in certain situations when there is pressure to make a decision quickly, the elements may combine to foster the development of groupthink.

The second revision needs to be in the role of the leadership of the decision-making group. In the space shuttle *Challenger* incident, the leadership of the group varied from a shared type of leadership to a very clear leader in the situation. This may indicate that the leadership role needs to be clearly defined and a style that demands open disclosure of information, points of opposition, complaints, and dissension. Inclusion of leadership in a more powerful role in the groupthink framework needs to be more explicit than in the Janis formulation in which leadership is one of several group characteristics that can lead to the development of the groupthink symptoms. We propose the leadership style is a crucial variable that moderates the relationship between the group characteristics and the development of the symptoms. Janis (1983) is a primary form of evidence to support the inclusion of leadership style in the enhanced model. His account of why the *same* group succumbed to groupthink in one decision (Bay of Pigs) and not in another (Cuban

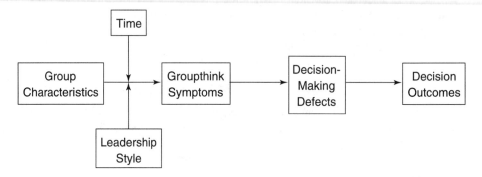

Figure 1. Revised groupthink framework.

Missile Crisis) supports the depiction of leadership style as a moderator variable. In these decisions, the only condition that changed was the leadership style of the president. In other words, the element that seemed to distinguish why groupthink occurred in the Bay of Pigs decision and not in the Cuban Missile Crisis situation is the president's change in his behavior.

These two variables, time and leadership style, are proposed as moderators of the impact of the group characteristics on groupthink symptoms. This relationship is portrayed graphically in Figure 1. In effect, we propose that the groupthink symptoms result from the group characteristics, as proposed by Janis, but only in the presence of the moderator variables of time and certain leadership styles.

Time, as an important element in the model, is relatively straightforward. When a decision must be made within a very short time frame, pressure on members to agree, to avoid time-consuming arguments and reports from outside experts, and to self-censor themselves may increase. These pressures inevitably cause group members to seek agreement. In Janis's original model, time was included indirectly as a function of the antecedent condition, group cohesion. Janis (1983) argued that time pressures can adversely affect decision quality in two ways. First, it affects the decision makers' mental efficiency and judgment, interfering with their ability to concentrate on complicated discussions, to absorb new information, and to use imagination to anticipate the future consequences of alternative courses of action. Second, time pressure is a source of stress that will have the effect of inducing a policy-making group to become more cohesive and more likely to engage in groupthink.

Leadership style is shown to be a moderator because of the importance it plays in either promoting or avoiding the development of the symptoms of the groupthink. The leader, even though she or he may not promote a preferred solution, may allow or even assist the group seeking agreement by not forcing the group to critically appraise all alternative courses of action. The focus of this leadership variable is on the degree to which the leader allows or promotes discussion and evaluation of alternatives. It is not a matter of simply not making known a preferred solution; the issue is one of stimulation of critical thinking among the group.

Impact on Prescriptions for Prevention

The revised model suggests that more specific prescriptions for prevention of groupthink can be made. First, group members need to be aware of the impact that a short decision time frame has on decision processes. When a decision must be made quickly, there will be more pressure to agree, i.e., discouragement of dissent, self-censorship, avoidance of expert opinion, and assumptions about unanimity. The type of leadership suggested here is not one that sits back and simply does not make known her or his preferred solution. This type of leader must be one that requires all members to speak up with concerns, questions, and new information. The leader must know what some of these concerns are and which members are likely to have serious doubts so that the people with concerns can be called upon to voice them. This type of group leadership does not simply assign the role of devil's advocate and step out of the way. This leader actually plays the role or makes sure that others do. A leader with the required style to avoid groupthink is not a laissez-faire leader or noninvolved participative leader. This leader is active in directing the activities of the group but does not make known a preferred solution. The group still must develop and evaluate alternative courses of action, but under the direct influence of a strong, demanding leader who forces critical appraisal of all alternatives.

Finally, a combination of the two variables suggests that the leader needs to help members to avoid the problems created by the time element. For example, the leader may be able to alter an externally imposed time frame for the decision by negotiating an extension or even paying late fees, if necessary. If an extension is not possible, the leader may need to help the group eliminate the effects of time on the decision processes. This can be done by forcing attention to issues rather than time, encouraging dissension and confrontation, and scheduling special sessions to hear reports from outside experts that challenge prevailing views within the group.

Janis presents, in both editions of his book, several recommendations for preventing the occurrence of groupthink. These recommendations focus on the inclusion of outside experts in the decision-making process, all members taking the role of devil's advocate and critically appraising all alternative courses of action, and the leader not expressing a preferred solution. The revised groupthink framework suggests several new prescriptions that may be helpful in preventing further decision fiascoes similar to the decision to launch the space shuttle *Challenger*.

Much additional research is necessary to test the revised framework. First, laboratory research is needed to refine details of how time affects the development of groupthink. Second, the impact of various types of leadership style that may be appropriate for group decision-making situations needs to be investigated. Finally, research which tests the revised framework with real decision-making groups will be needed to refine new prescriptions for preventing groupthink.

Conclusion

This paper has reviewed the basic tenets of groupthink and examined the decision to launch the space shuttle *Challenger* in January 1986. The report of the Presidential Commission provided enough evidence of the antecedent conditions, the symptoms, and the decision-making defects to support a conclusion that the decision to launch can be classified as a groupthink situation. We have proposed, in addition, that other conditions may play important roles in the development of groupthink. These two variables, time and leadership style, are proposed as moderators of the relationship between group characteristics and groupthink symptoms. These two moderators lead to new prescriptions for the prevention of groupthink. Much additional research is needed to test the degree to which the revised framework can be used to guide prescriptions for prevention.

References

Courtright, J.A. (1978). "A Laboratory Investigation of Groupthink." *Communications Monographs* 45, 229–246.

Time. (June 9, 1986). "Fixing NASA."

Flowers, M.L. (1977). "A Laboratory Test of Some Implications of Janis's Groupthink Hypothesis." *Journal of Personality and Social Psychology* 35, 888–896.

Janis, I.L. (1972). *Victims of Groupthink.* Boston: Houghton Mifflin.

Janis, I.L. (1983). *Groupthink* 2d ed., revised. Boston: Houghton Mifflin.

Leana, C.R. (1985). "A Partial Test of Janis's Groupthink Model: Effects of Group Cohesiveness and Leader Behavior on Defective Decision Making." *Journal of Management* 11, 5–17.

Moorhead, G. (1982). "Groupthink: Hypothesis in Need of Testing." *Group and Organization Studies* 7, 429–444.

Moorhead, G., and Montanari, J.R. (1986). "Empirical Analysis of the Groupthink Phenomenon." *Human Relations* 39, 399–410.

Report of the Presidential Commission on the Space Shuttle Accident. (July 1986). Washington, D.C.

ACTIVITIES

Activity 1

Purpose: The purpose of this case study is to illustrate the significance of groupthink.

Procedure: The students read the case study individually. In groups of three to five people they then discuss the questions at the end of the reading. After 20–30 minutes, the large group discusses its reactions.

Bay of Pigs Case Study

After examining the transcripts of meetings and conversations, Irving Janis, a sociologist, has concluded that *groupthink* contributed to the infamous Bay of Pigs Invasion. Because presidential advisors were hesitant to voice their doubts, the Kennedy Administration's decision to attack Cuba created an embarrassing and dangerous situation for the United States.

The invasion of Cuba was conceived during the 1960s, toward the end of the Eisenhower administration. The purpose of this invasion was to touch off a nationwide uprising against Castro. By financing and directing 1,500 anti-Castro Cuban exiles, the CIA hoped to overthrow Castro; however, the coup failed miserably. When Kennedy took office he abolished Eisenhower's Planning Board and Operations Coordinating Board, thereby abolishing the checks and balances inherent in Eisenhower's council.

On April 17, 1961, the landing of the 1,453 Cuban exiles on the southwestern coast of Cuba, within seventy-two hours, turned into a complete disaster, resulting in the capture of 1,179 invaders and the death of the remaining 274.

Not only did the invasion fail, but it also aggravated already hostile relations between the United States and Cuba, intensified international cold war tensions, and inspired the Soviet Union to install missiles with nuclear warheads in Cuba the following year.

Most experts agree that the participants who planned the invasion made some fundamental errors in judgment:

1. The decision to invade was made on the *theory* that the invasion would start a large-scale uprising, a miscalculation that later proved to be erroneous and costly.
2. Although secrecy was mandated, the plans were apparently known by Cubans living in Florida, American newsreporters, and presumably, the Cuban government. Consequently, the invasion force was unequal to the strength of Castro's troops, especially since the element of surprise had been eliminated.
3. Members of the People's Revolutionary Movement, considered the most capable of the anti-Castro forces, were not included in the invasion force, a decision that reduced the overall effectiveness.
4. The United States was not aggressive enough in its support. Specifically, Kennedy refused the U.S. air support needed to protect the exiles. The United States created an impression of irresolution that was crucial to the development of the Cuban

Missile Crisis of October 1962. The supposedly ineffective Cuban Air Force shot down half of the B-26s.

5. The original CIA plans called for an open invasion that would produce the shock effect needed to cause the Cuban uprisings. Although the CIA believed these uprisings to be essential to the success of the invasion, they went along with the "quiet landing" in order to have any invasion at all.

6. The quiet landing was intended to reduce the likelihood that the United States would be implicated in the invasion. Those involved naively failed to realize that the United States would be blamed regardless.

The following transcript is an amalgamation of events and conversations that preceded the Bay of Pigs Invasion. While this meeting did not take place exactly as represented here, the dialogue is based on historical accounts and is intended to represent the facts.

On March 11, 1961, President Kennedy held a meeting with the following:

—Allen Dulles, CIA director and member of Kennedy's "Yale good-old-boy network."
—Richard Bissell, Director of CIA covert operations. He aspired to the position of CIA director upon Dulles's retirement.
—McGeorge Bundy, national security adviser
—Dean Rusk, secretary of state (opposed operation but never said so)
—Admiral Burke, chief of naval operation
—General Lemnitzer, chairman, joint chiefs of staff
—Thomas Mann, representing the State Department
—Colonel "Jack" Hawkins, CIA military commander
—Robert McNamara, defense secretary

Meeting:

President Kennedy: I'm receiving conflicting reports about the advisability of continuing with the Cuban invasion at this time.

Bissell: Mr. President, we have to move now. Our intelligence indicates that we are facing the impending arrival of Soviet Mig fighters *and* Czech-trained Cuban pilots. You can't mañana this thing. [It would be months before the Cuban pilots could finish training in Czechoslovakia]. Besides, if we make this work, there will be no necessity for overt American intervention.

Dulles: "Don't forget we have a disposal problem too. We have all those anti-Castro forces waiting for action in Guatemala. If we have to take these men out of Guatemala, we will have to transfer them to the United States, and we can't have them wandering around the country telling everyone what they have been doing. Demobilization in Guatemala would be worse. The Cubans might resist being disarmed and spread word all over Latin America that the United States turned tail. This could trigger Communist takeovers elsewhere. No, Mr. President, Bissell is right. The time for action is now.

Colonel Hawkins:	I don't see Castro giving us much of a fight. His sketchy air force can be removed with an attack by six to eight Cuban-labeled B-26s.
Bundy:	We'll hit his Achilles' heel. It'll be the only noisy part of the enterprise.
Dulles:	With that kind of air support, we can do this thing. Besides, our intelligence says at least one-fourth of the Cuban population will support this thing on the ground. [Actually, only one-fourth opposed Castro. That does not guarantee support of an invasion.]
President Kennedy:	No, that's too spectacular. This is too much like a World War II invasion. I want a quiet landing, preferably at night, with no basis for American military intervention.
Mann:	I agree. We want to avoid anti-American reaction in the United Nations. Besides, the idea to use Trinidad won't work. Trinidad can't handle the B-26s. We wouldn't be able to get away with pretending that they were operating from Cuban bases.
Colonel Hawkins:	As I see it, we have three alternatives. Preston to the north, the southern coast of Las Villas, and the Bay of Pigs.
General Lemnitzer:	Well, of the three, the Bay of Pigs is the most feasible because its airstrip can handle those B-26s.
Rusk:	And don't forget our base at Guantánamo.
Bissell:	Yeah, Bay of Pigs could work. It has few access roads, so Castro's forces can't rush in. Besides, he has no communication networks in this area [there were two microwave radio shacks on the beach].
Admiral Burke:	[Relieved that Rusk's suggestion for use of the Navy's precious base at Guantánamo had been abandoned]. Well, I still like Trinidad, but Bay of Pigs may work.
Dulles:	Bay of Pigs is a good beach for an amphibian operation [it turned out to have razor-sharp reefs]. Let's forget the guerrilla operation and make this a full-fledged beach assault instead.
President Kennedy:	No, let's reduce the noise level here. In fact, make sure that all the ships are unloaded at night.
Bundy:	Sure! Besides if the brigade is defeated, the survivors can just disappear into Zapata swamps.
McNamara:	Yeah! If there's no civilian uprising, as we expect, we have the guerrilla option. There's a group of a hundred guerrillas operating in this area already. [No guerrillas have operated in the Zapata during the twentieth century.]
General Lemnitzer:	Well, you guys have obviously done your homework. It seems like the best alternative.
Bundy:	I agree. A substantial portion of the force would almost certainly be able to survive for a long period in guerrilla operation, but I'm having second thoughts.
Colonel Hawkins:	Me too. I'm a little worried about this thing getting too big. Besides, let's remember that those B-26s might be a little slow and short ranged for our needs.

Bissell:	Jack, let's not wash out more than a year of work on "what ifs." Quitting now isn't the answer. Where's your sense of loyalty?
Dulles:	No opposition is expected for the Airborne strike, and it'll take Castro's forces two to four days to appear. Besides, they lack training in offensive warfare, which will allow the brigade to make a strong hold.
President Kennedy:	I reserve the right to cancel this thing any time.
Bissell:	Absolutely, Mr. President. In fact, you can cancel at the last minute. The operation could be diverted to Vieques in Puerto Rico with little notice.
Dulles:	Now, let's make it work. We have to protect the shaky morale of the invading brigade. Let's not let anything depressing leak. The rest is history.

Discussion Questions

1. What antecedent conditions existed that allowed groupthink to occur?

2. What symptoms of groupthink were apparent at the meeting?

3. How was decision making compromised as a result of groupthink?

4. How could groupthink have been prevented?

Activity 2

Purpose: The purpose of this exercise is to point out the importance of setting concrete criteria when trying to solve a problem.

Procedure: In small groups the class sets criteria for each of the following problems. No solutions should be mentioned. The entire focus of the group should be on **criteria** or boundaries that an effective solution would have. As a large group the class then discusses how and why criteria setting can enhance problem solving.

For example, if your group were to set the criteria for one of the members who is about to buy a house, after consulting with the individual about his or her needs, you might determine the following:

It must cost no more than $75,000.
It must be on a quiet street because of the baby.
It must be in a neighborhood that has children living in it.
It must be no more than 30 minutes from work and school.
It must be no more than 45 minutes from the grandparents.
It must have public transportation available.

Write criteria for solving the following:

1. A person in your group is going to buy a car.

2. A person in the group is trying to decide where to vacation.

3. Your sister is trying to decide where to attend college.

Activity 3

Purpose: The purpose of this activity is to have the student experience a systematic problem-solving sequence.

Procedure: In small groups the class discusses the problem of homelessness in the United States. The groups should address each of these questions in order and then reconvene as a large group to discuss their reactions to the process. This activity can be repeated with different problems as the focus.

1. State the problem in the form of a question that is limited in scope, unbiased, and clear.

2. Establish criteria that a solution would have to meet. Consider legal, moral, ethical, social, and economic factors when setting criteria.

3. Suggest possible solutions. Brainstorm but don't evaluate. Write down all possible solutions.

4. Evaluate the solutions. What are the advantages and disadvantages of each?

5. Select the best solution and establish a time frame for testing this solution.

Activity 4

Purpose: The purpose of this exercise is to introduce the students to the different kinds of decision-making processes.

Procedure: The instructor brings a jar of pre-counted M&Ms to class. In small groups the class then competes to determine which group will share the candy. Each small group will be assigned a decision-making technique. After the winners are determined, the large group then discusses its reaction to the different types of decision-making processes. How did the participants feel in the different situations?

Group 1, Consensus: After discussion all members agree to a number. The discussion must continue until all members are convinced that this is the best answer.

Group 2, Majority Rule: When over 50 percent of the participants agree to a number, that answer will stand. The group can determine the number by voting, averaging numbers, or discussion, but when over half of the participants agree to an answer, it stands.

Group 3, Decision by Authority: The instructor will determine which group member is the best qualified to make this decision. This person alone will make the decision without consulting the other members. Math majors, engineers, and finance majors might be considered. (As is often the case, the *perception* of expertise is significant. Often authorities don't truly have the expertise to make a decision any more than a math major would have taken a course in candy counting.)

4
Taking Part in Groups

There is a crucial link existing between small-group behavior and communication. These two activities work in tandem, each influencing the other. In fact, it would be impossible to determine which is the cause and which is the consequence, which is the voice and which is the echo. Therefore, to understand both of these processes, group behavior and communication, we must be aware of their interdependence, cognizant of how these two activities influence each other, and in turn, the way we act when we are members of a group. Understanding how individuals behave in groups—the positive and negative behaviors that each brings to the group—allows a mindfulness of the factors that lead to personal and group success.

Cohesion

When people form a social or professional group, **cohesion** and often even a desire for **conformity**, are natural outcomes. These tendencies are neither good nor bad, just predictable. The outcome, however, as we discussed in Chapter 3, can be negative if groupthink or undue pressures to conform prevail.

In the absence of excess, however, the desire to be identified with others is often perceived as positive. People frequently join groups that mirror their values and preferences, and the members enjoy the link that exists between them and the group. Cohesion is the "glue" that causes the members to remain in the group even when there are pressures or influences to leave it. Sometimes the personal attraction among the participants contributes to cohesion, but often it is the satisfaction in achieving a goal that could not have been attained otherwise that causes the cohesion to develop.

Cohesive groups usually enjoy low turnover and high participation because members desire continuation of the group and its commitment to goal accomplishment. When trust, support, and affection exist among the participants, there is room for personal growth, even if that means an occasional expression of hostility, dissatisfaction, or frustration.

Groups that openly express their expectations for acceptable and unacceptable behavior clarify the rewards and consequences of behaving in certain ways, and in so doing, build unity. Cohesion enhances group norms, and norms contribute to cohesion. The two are intricately intertwined.

Norms

When individuals join others and identify with them, there is usually a conscious or unconscious effort to define parameters within which members are expected to operate. Invariably, social and professional groups develop **norms** that help to define appropriate behaviors for the group's members. These prescribed modes of conduct define the group's common beliefs and help to maintain behavioral consistency. They serve as guides to suitable conduct by reducing ambiguity, uncertainty, and insecurity. This, of course, applies only to explicit norms or commonly acknowledged rules. Occasionally, implicit norms *cause* uncertainty when members have difficulty determining what the others expect and want. The fear of disappointing other group members or of being rejected can produce rather than reduce stress within the group.

Not all norms apply to all members, and norms vary greatly from group to group. For this reason, the fear of violating implied norms can be intimidating since rejection from the group is often the consequence. Different or unclear expectations can frequently lead to stress, anger, and ultimately, conflict.

Stress

Members can experience stress from a variety of sources, but within the group setting itself, the causes of stress usually can be traced to either task accomplishment or interpersonal relationships. Stress related to goal completion can be linked to concerns about setting priorities, managing time, coordinating efforts, and distributing work. When goals are unclear or vague, or when members can't agree on the goal, stress is the inevitable outcome. Setting concrete, specific, measurable goals not only contributes to task completion, but also helps to circumvent one of the main causes of stress in groups.

Not all stress in groups is related to goal accomplishment, however. Often groups experience problems with interpersonal relationships. We are drawn to groups because of our needs for affection, control, and inclusion; when these needs are not met or when they are threatened, stress is the probable outcome. Agonizing about completing the task or worrying about personal rejection can both be sources of stress.

On the other hand, groups provide an area for relieving stress. Distributing responsibilities and talking with others who share our concerns can relieve tension and reduce stress. Feeling the freedom to express both positive and negative emotions can cause the participants to experience camaraderie that is unavailable except in group settings. Emotions, whether positive or negative, expressed or unexpressed, will impact the group's effectiveness.

Anger, like stress, is usually seen as something negative, an emotion to be avoided. When it is managed, though, anger can provide the energy that helps the group move toward action. Healthy group relationships depend on the ability of the participants to give accurate feedback to each other, even when this feedback is negative. Anger helps to do that.

Anger is the emotion that prompts us to act, but it is not usually the first emotion that we feel. Typically, something causes the anger; we tend to ignore the first emotion, however, and report the anger that follows. For instance, if the group is distracted, not focusing on the task, and generally just wasting time, a member might become frustrated or impatient. Instead of reporting these emotions to the group, he or she often waits until anger has taken over before saying anything. Ideally, members would spontaneously report emotions as they felt them, but most people are not good at or comfortable with this type of expression. Furthermore, most people view conflict as negative, so in trying to avoid controversy, they will put off reporting negative feelings until anger forces the issue. At this point, the group is motivated to resolve the problem, but only if the group members have effectively addressed their emotions. Misdirected anger has a way of sabotaging a group's efforts.

Conflict and Controversy

Conflict can occur any time desires, intentions, values, or opinions are in opposition to those of another group member. Conflicts are not "bad," but we avoid them because we fear the adverse conditions that may result if the controversy is not managed constructively. Resolving disagreements in groups can be more complicated than individuals resolving disputes because there is an audience involved. Face-saving, embarrassment, pride, and divided loyalties play a role when several people are affected by the struggle. When conflicts do occur within groups, they should be settled as soon as possible. If conflict is not negotiated to a conclusion, it will shadow all phases of the discussion process and will interfere with the group reaching its goal. This distraction can be particularly troublesome when the group is trying to operate under time constraints.

When clashes occur in groups, the members, as a rule, react in one of five ways. One undesirable way to deal with difficulties is to **withdraw** from the group by denying that a problem exists. Ignoring the situation causes the issues to grow rather than diminish.

Suppressing or smoothing over differences is similar to denial. Members may recognize that problems exist but refuse to take action to resolve them. Surface harmony exists because of the reluctance to deal with opposition. Evading the concerns of the members can lead to defensiveness and may sabotage the group's efforts.

The abuse of power or **dominance** by one or several members can cause disruptions if the other participants have no way to express their needs and desires. If individuals are frustrated because they see no way to win or even be considered, they will frequently be pessimistic and less productive.

Compromise or negotiation, considered positive by many, is certainly better than the previous three methods of addressing adversity. However, when each person gives up something in order to meet the others halfway, the result is only partial satisfaction for all concerned. Commitment to solutions will be questionable.

Collaboration or problem solving is the recommended course of action. When groups take the time to dig deeply into issues to find underlying concerns, a win/win result becomes more likely. Fully exploring alternatives and attempting to find solutions that satisfy all concerned create an environment in which talents and expertise are recognized and utilized. Collaboration that leads to consensus is ideal, but the process is time consuming, a factor that causes many groups to opt for a quicker fix.

While conflict resolution in groups differs somewhat from individuals resolving a disagreement, there are similarities between the two processes. The principles that apply to effective conflict resolution apply whether two or several people are involved in the negotiations.

Conflict can be either constructive or destructive. Much will be determined by how the disagreement is managed and by how the participants regard each other. If it is managed effectively and if participants view each other with respect, resolving differences can actually help the group function more efficiently; discussing problems increases awareness, encourages change, and increases motivation. If we don't know something is broken, we can't fix it. Often groups, like individuals, amble along until they are forced to reevaluate what has been causing the problem; then, members usually want to improve the situation.

Conflict can also serve to reduce small tensions within the group. We are inclined to allow problems to escalate to the boiling point before we are motivated to deal with them. Clearing the air before the explosion occurs helps us to maintain good relationships. In fact, conflict resolution can enrich relationships when each person realizes that the relationship can withstand stress. Many times we are intimidated by conflict because we are afraid that it will cause a major breakdown in rapport. Once we learn that this isn't true, we become more confident about the stability of the alliances and about resolving future disagreements.

There are no guarantees when human behavior is involved, but generally speaking, approaching the controversy in a non-defense-building, fair way will increase the likelihood that the dispute will be resolved favorably. Attacking the problem rather than the individuals, defining and narrowing the problem, and offering empathy, nonevaluative statements, and openness will all contribute to the overall value of the group's interaction.

Conflict within a group comes from a host of different directions—some interpersonal and some cultural. Regardless of the source of it, when left unchecked, conflict hampers the group's progress and damages interpersonal relationships.

Understanding group process means understanding how individual members' characteristics and personalities unite to form the unique culture of a given group. Satisfaction, performance, productivity, effectiveness, and turnover depend to a large degree on the socioemotional make-up of the group. When we understand some of the factors that contribute to successful interaction, we can adapt and adjust our communication behavior to the group situation and make choices that will benefit both the group and the individual.

Introduction to Readings

Your personal experiences have made you aware that being a member of a group is not an easy assignment. It often involves playing a variety of different roles. For example, being an effective participant asks you to strike a balance between individualism and collectivism. Put in slightly different terms, how do you maintain your individuality while still conforming to group norms? This question is the subject of our first essay by Patricia Hayes Andrews. Andrews begins by reminding us that pressure for uniformity and conformity in small groups is a simple fact of group life. She describes and analyzes past theories that have been used to account for group conformity and also cites her own research on this topic. She stresses the idea that effective group participation requires that each person understand the forces within that make them more or less vulnerable to group influences.

Our second selection, much like our first, looks at yet another common characteristic found in most groups—stress. In an article titled "Examining Stress in Small Groups," Sally Vogl-Bauer warns us about the hazards of this human characteristic. Her interest in the topic is predicated on two interrelated assumptions. First, cooperation and cohesion play an integral part in group success. Second, stress can erode the integration and bonding process that contributes to group cohesion. The author proposes that the sources of stress are numerous, can take a variety of forms, and while varying from person to person, usually grow out of a perception that we are in a situation that we cannot control. What is important to keep in mind is the idea that stress can be felt by both the **group** and the **individual**. To reduce many of the problems associated with stress, Vogl-Bauer suggests that group members (1) should plan and prepare in advance, (2) attempt to complete the project, (3) develop teamwork, (4) locate a comfortable and neutral environment, (5) use humor, (6) seek similarities, (7) become sensitive to the other members, and (8) engage in nontask self-disclosure.

Our next selection, by Carolyn Clark and Richard Sline, reminds us that the use of small groups, specifically teamwork groups, is spreading among American organizations. A logical outgrowth of these tight-knit groups (teams) is a high level of emotionality. To help us appreciate and understand the role of emotion in groups, Clark and Sline look at (1) various situations—both positive and negative—that trigger emotions within a group, and (2) how these emotions are expressed. They conclude their analysis by offering sound advice about emotions and communication. In short, they believe that emotional expression is a natural component of the human experience and that groups should not fear emotion when it appears. Rather, group members should welcome this increased intensity and establish individual norms for handling emotional expression.

It seems that conflict, in one form or another, emerges whenever people come together. As you would suspect, the small-group setting is not immune to periodic bouts of conflict. This topic of conflict is the main focus of our final selection. In his essay, Larry A. Erbert examines conflict from a number of perspectives. He begins with a brief discussion of management styles, strategies, and tactics that are normally employed when people are confronted with a situation that contains elements of conflict. He then looks at how conflicts are classified, how personality characteristics influence conflict, how relational interactions are affected by conflict, the role of social networks and systems in conflict, and communication factors that relate to conflict. Finally, Erbert raises some research issues centering on conflict. He believes that in the future we must know (1) whether conflict education improves conflict management, (2) whether proactive positions improve or hinder communication, (3) the place of humor in conflict management, (4) whether third-party intervention is a useful tool, and (5) whether conflict varies across cultures.

Group Conformity

Patricia Hayes Andrews

The January, 1986, *Challenger* tragedy provided a striking reminder of how groups of intelligent people can make flawed, disastrously poor decisions even when equipped with abundant information and sophisticated scientific technology. Historically, other groups of high-status, supposedly knowledgeable individuals have made similarly poor decisions resulting in the loss of billions of dollars, important battles, presidential elections, and hundreds of human lives. Although many scholars and theorists have attempted to explain this phenomenon, no one has done it better or more persuasively than psychologist Irving Janis whose treatise on "groupthink" provides a compelling explanation for such decision-making fiascoes as the Bay of Pigs invasion, the Watergate break-in and attempted cover-up, and the *Challenger* tragedy.[1]

Groupthink, however, cannot be applied to every group. Janis is largely concerned with decision making by groups that are quite cohesive, have worked together for some time, are deeply embedded in complex organizational structures, and are insulated from the views of others.[2] Undoubtedly, groups fitting this profile are prospective victims of groupthink, defined by Janis as "a deterioration of mental efficiency, reality testing, and moral judgment that results from in-group pressures."[3] However, other groups not meeting the criteria specified above are also capable of making poor decisions.

When groups make bad judgments, select ineffective solutions to problems, or choose seemingly stupid or unethical courses of action, they may do so for a variety of reasons. Sometimes they simply do not have or take the time to perform effectively. They may not have the assembled expertise needed to do the job well. They may have been assigned the task by a manager who has just learned that participative decision making is a good thing, but does not know how to prepare the group for its newly acquired responsibilities. Perhaps the group is hindered by personality conflict or by ineffectual leadership; possibly most important to the point being made here, the group may not understand the need for exploring diverse points of view before making a final decision. Yet, most scholars agree that any group's ability to openly examine the diverse, often conflicting, ideas advanced by individual group members is a crucial attribute—one that surely contributes to effective decision making. At the same time, scholars bewail the group's rather pronounced tendency to disregard constructive and critical thinking.

Whenever groups begin to act as if every group member should be and think alike, they typically exert pressure for uniformity. How this occurs, why it occurs, and how individuals respond to it have been widely studied. Of particular interest are the factors that help predict the likelihood that a given individual will conform to the expectations, or norms, of the group.

Permission to reprint must be obtained from the author. Patricia Hayes Andrews is affiliated with the Speech Communication Department, Indiana University, Bloomington.

Basic Definitions

Basic to the notion of any group or organization is the idea that individuals alone are often unable to fulfill all of their needs. As groups of men and women coordinate their efforts toward common goals, they may also find that they can accomplish more with relative effectiveness than any one of them could alone. Moreover, contemporary managers have grown to believe that their employees feel better and thus perform better when given the opportunity to participate in making decisions that affect their professional lives. In most cases, they are right. As a result, most of us find ourselves involved in a great deal of group activity, often involving problem solving and decision making.

As we interact in groups, we develop norms. Norms are sets of expectations held by group members concerning what kinds of behavior or opinion are acceptable or unacceptable, good or bad, right or wrong, appropriate or inappropriate. As new group members, we soon learn about what political views are popular, what competitors are respected or feared, and what procedures are considered appropriate for making decisions. We may discover, for instance, that when a certain hour arrives, no one should say anything to prolong the meeting, or we may learn that this particular group regularly socializes immediately following its Friday meeting.

An individual's compliance with a norm is readily measured by his or her public behavior. Do we join the group for pizza, or do we have other commitments? Do we stifle our criticisms or comments so that the meeting can be dismissed on time? If we do, we are conforming to the group's norms. Most of the time, an individual's act of conformity is assumed to extend to his or her private feelings or beliefs. We go for pizza because we want to go. However, common personal experience teaches us that this assumption is often false, that we may—some of us often—do things that others want us to do even though we do not want to do them. In the specific context of decision-making groups, we say things that we don't completely believe, or we simply refuse to voice our dissent. In these instances, we have complied with group norms publicly, but privately, we continue to feel differently. Thus, an important distinction must be made between public compliance and private acceptance. The needs to be liked, to seem congenial, and to fit in with the others can be powerful and can cause us to say things we don't believe and act in ways that we later regret. The inability or unwillingness to deviate from group expectations can affect anyone—teenagers, businesspeople, members of the president's cabinet, or distinguished scientists.

Whether or not an individual complies with a group's norms may depend, in part, on whether he or she is aware of them. Some norms are *explicit*, that is, they are formally stated. They may even be written and passed around. Explicit norms are easily understood because they are overtly expressed. *Implicit* norms, on the other hand, are generally not openly articulated. The new group member may not understand immediately that no one disagrees with the boss or that expressing a preference for Bach over Bon Jovi is a kiss of death. In fact, one of the little games that some groups play is trying to see how quickly a particular individual will figure out the implicit rules of the game.

Most writers discuss conformity in a negative light. It is important to recognize, however, that pressure for uniformity, and the conformity that often follows, is frequently a simple fact of group life. The act of conforming to the prevailing group sentiment is neither good nor bad; rather, conformity can only be evaluated as a group outcome by examining the process through which it occurs. If a group insists that every group member question group standards and takes the time to listen to those who present different points of view, excellent decisions may result. If, however, an individual complies with the group for fear of being ignored, ridiculed, or even rejected, then that brand of conformity will likely contribute to loss of self-esteem for the individual and a poor decision for the group.

Understanding Why Groups Exert Pressure

Many explanations have been offered for why groups exert pressure for uniformity. Leon Festinger's *group locomotion hypothesis,* for example, posits that groups have goals and typically attempt to function in ways designed to allow them to achieve these goals.[4] Some goals may even be viewed as instrumental to group survival. A quality-control group that cannot improve product quality seems self-defeating. A fund-raising group that cannot generate money will not exist for long. Many groups assume that they can only accomplish their goals if each of their members complies with group norms. Based on this belief, the group is motivated to pressure would-be deviates into conformity. This explanation for pressure for uniformity applies most readily to situations involving key norms, or norms directly associated with goal achievement. A top saleswoman may be permitted to wear a trendy hairstyle, but if she stops putting in long hours, thus causing the sales team to lose important sales, she will probably be forced to toe the line. Her hairstyle "deviation" is not perceived by the group as impeding its goal accomplishment and so is tolerated. Her slack work habits, however, are a different matter.

Another perspective for considering group pressure also comes from Festinger. According to this scholar's *social comparison theory,* most people do not need to consult the views of others to validate their perceptions of physical reality.[5] A stove is hot; an elephant is huge; a car is red. With matters of opinion and belief, however, an individual often finds comfort in knowing that others share his or her views. Is the new tax plan good or bad? Should this organization devest in South Africa? Should this curriculum committee add another year of foreign language to students' graduation requirements? These issues are not merely questions of fact. They are all complex, involving attitudes, opinions, and judgment. We can never be certain that our views on these kinds of issues are "right," but in trying to assure ourselves that they are valid, we often seek to affiliate with those whose views are similar to our own. As we join together in groups, share our ideas, and discover that we agree among ourselves, we create a kind of social reality. Social reality is not the same as factual reality, but it does allow us to validate our ideas, and thus, gives us the illusion of having discovered truth. The social validation process works best when group members are uniform in their beliefs. The opinion deviate, then, is pressured into uniformity so that the group's social reality can seem more plausible.

Finally, a number of theorists have advanced *balance theories,* some of which are relevant to understanding the group pressure phenomenon.[6] According to this perspective, any group prefers to exist in a balanced state. Consider the following example where imbalance or inconsistency has become a problem. A group of executives meets regularly to discuss quality problems and to make policy decisions. The group is close-knit, and there is a feeling of friendship. Suppose further that member A strongly opposes the other four members on an important policy issue. What are the options available to the members of the majority? They may (1) avoid discussing the issue, (2) decide that the issue is not as important as they had originally believed, (3) decide that member A must not understand the policy or has been misinformed, or (4) decide that member A is not as likable as they had once believed. The latter two options are particularly pertinent to this discussion of pressure for uniformity. If the third option is pursued and the assumption made that member A needs more information or is misguided, the majority should spend considerable time attempting to inform, elaborate, and persuade. If this approach were to fail, then the fourth option might restore balance or harmony within the group by making possible the rejection of the deviate. Research has shown that both of these options are pursued on occasion, particularly among highly cohesive groups that are dealing with issues they view as important.[7]

Clearly, groups may exert pressure for a variety of reasons, allowing them to better achieve their goals, feel more justified and certain of their views, and exist in a state of harmony and cooperation. Of course, not all groups exert pressure for uniformity; those who do strive for uniformity may be more tolerant of deviation on the part of some group members than others. If, for example, the individual deviate possesses extraordinary knowledge, has led the group toward positive results in the past, or possesses high status or power, he or she may be granted certain liberties that would never be permitted the rank-and-file member.[8] Even so, most groups consistently demonstrate a greater concern for maintaining uniformity than for encouraging individuality. While publicly affirming the need for innovation, many decision-making groups, often those embedded in conservative corporate structures, continue to reward those who blend in with and reinforce the views of the majority, or those already in power.[9]

Understanding Why Individuals Conform to Group Pressure

Understanding why groups are motivated to exert pressure is only half of the story. Equally critical is gaining some understanding of why individuals so often conform. Two of the perspectives discussed above provide some explanatory insight. First, from the perspective of Festinger's *group locomotion hypothesis,* the individual who is committed to helping the group achieve its goals and who believes that his or her conformity will facilitate the group's goal achievement will be internally motivated to conform. Some groups demand a unanimous vote before moving forward with any new plan or policy. Under these circumstances, it is clear that one dissenting vote blocks the group's action. Rather than prevent the group from moving forward, the individual may shrug his or her shoulders and inwardly (or outwardly) say, "I don't want to be the one to hold up the rest of the group." Votes obtained in this manner are clear instances of public compliance.

Also useful in helping us understand the motivation to conform is *balance theory.* This perspective reasons that, like the group, the individual strives for balance or consistency throughout his or her life. If the individual believes that the group has worthy goals and is comprised of people with good intentions and values, he or she may find it painful to recognize that his or her views differ. Rather than reject the group or realign perceptions of the majority's wisdom, he or she may elect to go along with the others. In fact, the individual may try very hard to convince himself or herself that the majority is correct. If successful, this attempt at self-persuasion will restore the individual's personal sense of balance or consistency. If unsuccessful, the individual may conform, but still experience considerable inner tension, or imbalance.

Yet another approach to understanding conformity is Homans's *social exchange view*.[10] According to Homans, conformity is a kind of strategic social act that allows the individual to obtain things he or she values from the group. The group may provide a satisfying social environment, prestige, or a sense of worth for the individual. In exchange, he or she supports the majority, in some cases putting aside true beliefs. The individual's self-censorship contributes to the positive social climate, while giving him or her certain rights and opportunities that he or she would not otherwise possess. In a real sense, conformity from this perspective becomes a technique of ingratiation.[11]

Research on Conformity

Social influence, and conformity in particular, has been the subject of scholarly investigation for many years. One of the earliest and most extensive conformity studies was conducted by Solomon Asch in the 1950s.[12] Asch confronted naive subjects with the unanimous and clearly erroneous opinions of several of his trained confederates and discovered marked movement in the direction of the majority. The task confronting Asch's subjects was a simple line discrimination exercise in which they were asked to match one of three lines with a comparison line. The correct answers were obvious. Yet, when confronted with the unanimous views of the majority, many of Asch's subjects conformed, announcing responses that clearly contradicted what they saw. In fact, only one-fourth of these naive subjects remained completely independent. It is important to recognize that not only were the line discrimination tasks used in this study extremely easy, they were of no intrinsic importance to the subjects. Moreover, the "groups" in this setting were hardly groups in the traditional sense, and the majority made no overt attempts to influence the naive subject's expressed views!

One of Asch's most interesting findings was the striking contrast he found between those individuals who never yielded to the majority's view and those who did so much of the time. Some investigators became intrigued with distinguishing these two basic "types" of individuals and sought to discover the personality characteristics that might be associated with yielding behavior. Crutchfield's research was one of the earliest to unearth a kind of contrasting character profile.[13] According to Crutchfield, the independent person demonstrates great intellectual effectiveness, ego strength, leadership ability, and maturity in social relations. He/she seems to lack inferiority feelings, rigid and excessive self-control, and authoritarian attitudes. Moreover, the independent individual is free from a compulsion to follow rules and is adventurous, assertive, and high in self-esteem. By contrast, Crutchfield argued that the "overconformist" has less ego strength, less ability to tolerate ambiguity, less willingness to accept responsibility, less self-insight and originality, more prejudiced and authoritarian attitudes, and greater emphasis on external and socially approved values.[14]

The quest for personality characteristics that might predict conformity behavior has received less attention in recent years. Most researchers have taken the view that personal attributes are often modified by situational or contextual variables. According to this view, the same individual may be confident and self-assertive in one situation and reticent and uncertain in another.

What are the situational variables that appear most likely to produce conformity behavior? Previous research points to the importance of a unanimous majority.[15] Having even one person (besides the naive subject) disagree with the majority may reduce the conformity rate by as much as 30 percent.[16] Another important situational variable has to do with the task itself. If an individual initially disagrees with the group's judgment on an issue that is unclear, uncertain, ambiguous, or difficult to understand, he or she is more likely to come around to the majority's point of view than if the group is dealing with a straightforward, clear-cut issue. After all, the individual reasons, ambiguous matters are open to interpretation—and the group could well be correct.[17] Finally, the extent to which the group is cohesive may have a pronounced impact on the individual's ability to remain independent. Cohesive groups are typically quite close-knit, have been around for some time, and may have weathered crises together. Group members usually enjoy each other's company and value their group experience.[18] Highly cohesive groups generally demand, and usually get, great loyalty and conformity from their members.[19]

In spite of the attention that has been devoted to conformity in the past, most scholars and practitioners remain uncomfortable with their understanding of the factors influencing conformity behavior. Perplexing questions remain. Why do some conform in virtually every situation while others almost never yield, regardless of the severity of the pressure? Why are some capable of great independence in certain situations but of equally striking conformity in others?

A Contemporary Examination of Conformity

In an attempt to grapple with the questions raised above, I recently undertook a study of conformity behavior.[20] I chose to compare two theoretical perspectives that had not been used in previous research with the hope that they might illuminate the extent to which conformity might be a behavioral predisposition or trait as opposed to a variable response to the discussion of a particular issue in a particular group.

The first theoretical perspective I selected was Sherif and Sherif's *social judgment theory*.[21] To predict the likelihood that an individual will remain uninfluenced by group pressure, this theory contends that one must assess the extent of his or her ego-involvement with the issue or action being considered. The highly ego-involved individual is deeply committed, probably viewing the issue as central to his or her value system. By contrast, the less involved individual is not so committed, viewing the matter as much more peripheral to his or her value core.

The Sherifs' social judgment theory argues that any one of us is likely to demonstrate an entire range of conformity to the group's norms. We might even appear to be both yielding and resistant to group pressures while functioning within the same group. What determines the likelihood of conformity is our degree of ego-involvement as the group moves from one issue to another. If the matter being discussed is of no great consequence to us (e.g., whether to adopt WordStar or WordPerfect as word processing software for the office), we may go right along with the group's preference. If, however, the question before the group pertains to one of our deep and enduring commitments (e.g., whether to support Star Wars), we should be much less likely to conform to others' views. In fact, according to the Sherifs, the highly ego-involved person would virtually never permit himself or herself to be open to group influence, regardless of the intensity of the pressures brought to bear.[22]

This explanation of ego-involvement as the mediator of conformity is very different from that proposed by another researcher, Mark Snyder.[23] Rather than viewing individuals in terms of their commitments to specific issues, Snyder focuses on their sensitivity to social expectations. In particular, he refers to individuals as being either high or low in self-monitoring. Those who are high in self-monitoring are very aware of and concerned with others' expectations for their behavior. They know what others want from them, and if possible, they would like to deliver. What we might expect from an individual who is high in self-monitoring, then, is a good deal of behavioral inconsistency. He or she is likely to conform to the views of others, even though his or her expressed views or actions may vary with movement among different groups with varying norms. By contrast, the non-self-monitoring person is less concerned with the appropriateness of his or her social behavior. This individual should remain relatively autonomous, maintaining consistent positions, regardless of the context in which the discussion occurs.

For my investigation, I placed ninety-six college students into small groups and asked them to discuss a question of value concerning living together before marriage. Before the discussions, the students were carefully pretested so that I knew whether they were very high or very low in ego-involvement with this particular discussion issue and whether they were high or low in self-monitoring. Each group contained students with diverse points of view and with a variety of ego-involvement and self-monitoring levels. I was interested both in the way that these students communicated with each other, and especially in the extent to which they influenced each other.

The results of my investigation provided a good deal of support for social judgment theory. That is, those students who were strongly committed to their views changed their positions far less than those low in ego-involvement. In addition, their communication behavior was influenced considerably by their ego-involvement. Statements made by highly ego-involved students were rated by trained judges as being less reasonable, more dominant, and more emotional than those made by students who were low in ego-involvement.

Although ego-involvement played a critical role in affecting these students' susceptibility to others' arguments and the quality of their communication behavior, their self-monitoring tendencies also proved important. That is, while highly ego-involved discussants refused to alter their expressed views, regardless of their sensitivity to others' expectations and opinions, students who were far less committed (that is, low in ego-involvement) were more likely to change their expressed opinions if they were aware of others' reactions and expectations (i.e., were high in self-monitoring). Self-monitoring also affected the discussants' communication behavior. For instance, students high in self-monitoring typically responded to others' position statements by seeking to find areas of compromise and accommodation, rather than by asserting their own ideas. Moreover, while highly ego-involved students tended to communicate emotionally when advancing their views, those who were high in self-monitoring did so far more than those low in self-monitoring. Apparently, highly ego-involved individuals who are sensitive to social cues are placed in a difficult spot when confronted with a group filled with diversified, often conflicting, points of view. Although in this study highly ego-involved students did not actually yield, their communication was judged as far more emotional, perhaps suggesting the tension created by the simultaneous and inconsistent desire to stick by their commitments, but submit to the demands of the consensus-reaching task as well.

Concluding Remarks

More than two decades ago psychologist Marie Jahoda examined historical and empirical instances of conformity behavior in an attempt to discover why some individuals were susceptible to group influence whereas others remained unmoved. She was particularly concerned with inconsistencies in conformity behavior occurring within the same individual. She concluded her examination of conformity with the view that the critical determinant of independence behavior in social influence settings was the individual's "emotional and intellectual investment in the issue."[24] When Sherif and Sherif articulated their social judgment theory, they provided a theoretical framework for assessing Jahoda's argument through an empirical investigation. The results of this study provide support for a social judgment view of conformity.

As was posited early in this piece, individual conformity to group norms is a frequent and often perplexing outcome associated with interacting groups. In many instances, individual movement must occur if group consensus is to be achieved. Yet, that movement can best enhance the quality of the group's decision if it represents the individual's conscious and rational desire to compromise for the benefit of the group. Although "mindless conformity" rarely facilitates any group's goal achievement in the long run, conscious conformity may be helpful, or even essential. Before individual group members can make intelligent choices about maintaining positions of dissent, opening themselves to group influence, or going along for the sake of appearance or civility, they need to understand something of the forces within themselves that might make them more or less vulnerable to group influence. The study reported here represents a step toward gaining that understanding.

Notes

1. Irving Janis, *Groupthink* 2d ed. (Boston: Houghton Mifflin Co., 1982).
2. *Ibid.*, 2–13.
3. *Ibid.*, 9.
4. Leon Festinger, "Informal Social Communication," *Psychological Review* 57 (1950), 271–282.
5. Leon Festinger, "A Theory of Social Comparison Processes," *Human Relations* 7 (1954), 117–140.
6. See, for example, Fritz Heider, "Attitudes and Cognitive Organization," *Journal of Psychology* 21 (1946), 107–112; and Charles E. Osgood and Percy H. Tannenbaum, "The Principle of Congruity in the Prediction of Attitude Change," *Psychological Review* 62 (1955), 42–55.
7. Stanley Schachter, "Deviation, Rejection, and Communication," *Journal of Abnormal and Social Psychology* 46 (1951),190–207; and Janis.
8. Leonard Berkowitz and J. R. Macaulay, "Some Effects of Differences in Status Level and Status Stability," *Human Relations* 14 (1961), 135–148; and Edwin P. Hollander, "Some Effects of Perceived Status on Responses to Innovative Behavior," *Journal of Abnormal and Social Psychology* 63 (1961), 247–250.

9. J. Patrick Wright, *On a Clear Day You Can See General Motors* (New York: Avon, 1979).

10. George C. Homans, "Social Behavior as Exchange," *American Journal of Sociology* 63 (1958), 597–606.

11. Edward E. Jones, "Conformity as a Tactic of Ingratiation," *Science* 149 (1965), 144–150.

12. Solomon E. Asch, "Studies of Independence and Conformity: A Minority of One Against a Unanimous Majority," *Psychological Monographs* 70 (1956), 1–70.

13. Richard S. Crutchfield, "Conformity and Character," *The American Psychologist* 10 (1955), 191–198.

14. *Ibid.,* 196.

15. Asch.

16. *Ibid.*

17. Patricia Hayes Bradley, "Socialization in Groups and Organizations: Toward a Concept of Creative Conformity," in Steward Ferguson and Sherry Devereaux Ferguson (eds.), *Intercom: Readings in Organizational Communication* (Rochelle Park, New Jersey: Hayden Book Co., 1980), 388–402.

18. C. Shepherd, *Small Groups* (Scranton, PA: Chandler Co., 1964); and Janis.

19. *Ibid.*

20. Patricia Hayes Andrews, "Ego-Involvement, Self-Monitoring, and Conformity in Small Groups: A Communicative Analysis," *Central States Speech Journal* 36 (1985), 51–61.

21. Carolyn W. Sherif, Muzafer Sherif, and Roger E. Nebergall, *Attitude and Attitude Change: The Social Judgment-Involvement Approach* (Philadelphia: Saunders, 1965).

22. *Ibid.,* 4–22.

23. Mark Snyder, "Self-Monitoring of Expressive Behavior," *Journal of Personality and Social Psychology* 30 (1974), 526–537; and Mark Snyder and Thomas C. Monson, "Persons, Situations, and the Control of Social Behavior," *Journal of Personality and Social Psychology* 32 (1975), 637–644.

24. Marie Jahoda, "Conformity and Independence: A Psychological Analysis," *Human Relations* 12 (1959), 103.

Examining Stress in Small Groups

Sally M. Vogl-Bauer

Interestingly, most people do not like to participate in small groups (e.g., classroom, organization) (Di Salvo, Nikkel, & Monroe 1989). This point is of great importance because groups are used extensively throughout government agencies, corporations, and classrooms. Yet, if members perceive the group experience as punishment or penalty, group outcomes are bound to suffer (Di Salvo, Nikkel, & Monroe 1989). Groups serve many purposes (Putnam & Stohl 1990). Individuals are often members of primary, social, and work/educational groups; membership within each group satisfies different personal needs. For example, primary groups include family and friends, and provide the basic social framework for individuals. Social groups may include classmates or teammates that people interact with on a short-term or regular basis. Special clubs or learning organizations provide individuals with additional opportunities to participate in groups (e.g., Spanish club). Groups in the workplace may be determined simply by holding a similar job in the company (e.g., clerical group, engineering department). As you can see, it is important to study small-group interaction because most people are working with at least two other people at some point during the day.

At times, individuals have little or no input into a group in which they are required to participate (e.g., classroom settings, organizational meetings). Group membership is often predetermined and difficult to change (Rose 1989). For example, supervisors often select the type(s) of activities in which they want their subordinates to participate. Subordinates usually need strong arguments if they want their supervisor to change his/her mind about involvement in a particular group. Thus, individuals are often forced to work in groups regardless of whether or not they would have chosen to be part of the group.

Because groups play such a vital part in society, it is important to study how to increase group-member satisfaction with group processes. Groups will only be as effective as their weakest members. Thus, cooperation and cohesion play an important part in group success. When groups break down and/or fail to accomplish their desired tasks, individual differences tend to be highlighted. Cohesion in groups suggests a bonding or union among group members, as well as greater acceptance of group member differences (Pace 1990). Stress is one factor that can hinder or break down the bonding process. Thus, stress factors should not be overlooked when studying effective and ineffective group processes and membership satisfaction.

Sources of Stress

Although there are many definitions of stress (Furnham & Walsh 1991; Keeley-Dyreson, Burgoon, & Bailey 1991; Westman & Eden 1991), it is virtually agreed upon that stress entails conflict between people and their environment, and has the potential

Permission to reprint must be obtained from the author. Sally M. Vogl-Bauer is affiliated with the Department of Comunication, Cleveland State University.

to pose some form of threat to the individual. Folkman says, "a situation is considered stressful only if an individual perceives it as such" (1984, cited in McDonald & Korabik 1991, 186). Thus, what is considered stressful for one person, may not be considered stressful for someone else if that person is able to manage the condition (e.g., deadlines).

McDonald and Korabik (1991) found gender differences between male and female managers' responses to what creates stress, the reasons for the stress, and the way(s) to cope with stressful situations in the workplace. They discovered that conflicts between work and home produced the most stress for females on the job. Males reported problems in relationships with other employees, in particular unfair criticism from their supervisors or low levels of cooperation with fellow co-workers as being stressful. While the events generating stress for males and females differed, the stress factor itself came from a common event: when males and females felt as if they had exceeded their ability to cope with a situation, their personal well-being was affected (McDonald & Korabik 1991).

Unfortunately, group stress is more difficult to define than individual stress. Should group stress focus on what group members say to each other (e.g., telling a group member that he or she talks too much) or how individual behaviors impact the group (e.g., one member never shows up for group meetings)? Furthermore, it is naive to completely separate a person's behavior (e.g., missing group meetings) because it is unclear what causal link, if any, exists between stressful comments made between group members and stressful behaviors exhibited (e.g., Susan said Sharon didn't care about the group because she missed the group meeting *or* Sharon missed the group meeting because she heard Susan say that she didn't care about the group).

Friedland and Keinan (1991) believe that when someone experiences stress, he or she ultimately needs to identify the *cause* of the stress. People want to be able to understand what created the stress. Since there are more variables present within the group setting (e.g., the number of group members, deadlines for the group project, personal issues, the inability of the group to meet), this could make it even more difficult for individuals to identify another group member's action as a cause or effect of stress. As a result, mistakes could be made when trying to explain or understand a member's behavior.

Effects of Stress

Stress plays an interesting role in group processes. Individuals cannot control group outcomes by themselves. Group members are forced to rely on other members to help complete their task. This dependence or interdependence on other members can often produce stress. Driskell and Salas (1991) looked at how stress impacts group decision-making processes. They found that some members became more authoritative in order to accomplish the group's goals. However, **status** of the group member influenced potential authority; status refers to a person's level of importance. Overall, members with higher status determined how members communicated with each other. When stress was not a factor, high-status members dominated the decision-making process and low-status members had limited input in the discussion. However, under stressful conditions, high-status group members were more willing to listen to feedback from low-status members. As a result, we see that stress may influence the amount of communication between high- and low-status group members, as well as what is done with the information provided by group members.

Westman and Eden's work on implicit stress theory (1991) is one of the few studies that examines the relationship between stress factors in the workplace and at home to stress factors within small groups. Implicit stress theory is based on beliefs that individuals have about how stress, strain, and performance interact. Westman and Eden (1991) suggest that if group members perceive the small-group process as stressful, their perceptions could lead them into a self-fulfilling prophecy. Since stress has often been thought to lead to poor performance, it should follow that when people feel stress, they may not do a good job. This, in turn, could negatively impact the group process and group performance, completing the self-fulfilling prophecy.

Unfortunately, many studies (Driskell & Salas 1991; Furnham & Walsh 1991; Wiebe 1991) focus on the stress felt by *individuals* within groups, rather than the stress of the group *as a whole*. The variables studied examine individual outcomes rather than group outcomes in stressful situations. Mitchell and Silver (1990) attempted to bridge the gap between individual and group outcomes and found that people tend to behave differently when in a group environment. Stressful conditions should enhance the differences between the attainment of individual and group goals because members may have to decide whether to satisfy personal objectives or the goals of the group.

An interesting connection may exist between the emotional health of group members and the stress generated in the group. Rook, Dooley, and Catalano (1991) studied the impact of husbands' job stress on the emotional health of their wives. They found that the stress husbands experienced at work had a negative impact on the psychological health of their wives. Rook et al. (1991) concluded that the nature of the relationship (e.g., marriage) may explain the emotional involvement of the wives. The wives became worried and anxious due to the job difficulties of their mates. In short, there appears to be a "burden of care" between a husband and wife when one of them (the husband in this study) experiences stress at the workplace. Perhaps the burden of care derived within the small-group setting explains why some group members take personal responsibility for the group's outcome when other members fail or are unable to complete their portion of the group's task.

In summary, factors that generate stress and those that occur as a result of a stressful situation tend to vary among individuals. However, one common theme appears to be present: "stress undermines individuals' sense of control and . . . stressed individuals actively engage in attempts to maintain or regain control" (Friedland & Keinan 1991, 89). Individuals and groups want to be able to maintain their surroundings. Containing the stress felt by the group and its members is one way to regain command of these surroundings.

Analyzing Stress in Groups

When small-group members were asked to identify the sources of stress for their small groups within a classroom setting, ten categories surfaced: (1) nature of the task assigned, (2) evaluation measures, (3) performance of the task, (4) coordinating the task, (5) initial group interactions, (6) [lack of] teamwork, (7) work distribution,

(8) member dissention from the group, (9) control/power struggles between group members, and (10) member differences. These categories emphasize either task-related or interpersonal issues.

Task-Related Issues. The first five categories focused on task concerns.

1. *Nature of the task assigned* examined what the group is being asked to do, with particular emphasis placed on the task. In short, simply having to do a group project generated stress. "I got kind of stressed just knowing that I had to do a group project. They're not my favorite things to do."
2. *Evaluation measures* looked at how the group would be judged based on the criteria of the task. Instructors' expectations for the task were also included. "The fact that a grade was dependent on our presentation caused stress."
3. *Performance of the task* focused on the events during the actual presentation. "The presentation was stressful. The group meeting wasn't stressful, just unproductive, which caused a little stress when the grade was given." "I had to talk in front of the class."
4. *Coordinating the task* centered on scheduling issues, organizing meeting times, coordinating schedules between group members, and dealing with time constraints and/or deadlines surrounding the assigned task. "The only stress experienced was due to lack of time and deadlines." "The only problem we had was finding a time to meet." "Procrastination was an issue."
5. *Work distribution* involved the assignment of specific tasks to group members and/or the completion of specific tasks by group members. "There was more work expected of some members." "One of our group members didn't care about the grade, so I was worried about whether or not she would do her share of the work well."

Interpersonal Issues. Five stress-related categories centered on the interaction between group members.

1. *Initial group interactions* looked at the impressions generated or the overall uncertainty felt during or after the group's first meeting. "The first meeting that we had was extremely stressful since it was our first time getting together. Later, at our second meeting, we knew each other better and therefore the stress was reduced."
2. *Teamwork concerns/problems* is the lack of cooperation and social skills demonstrated between group members when working together. "Members don't work well together and therefore you worry about how the group will do as a whole."
3. *Member dissention from the group* explored the issue of when a group member goes against the groups' goals and focuses on his or her own individual concerns instead. "One member misses class and it appeared at one point that we were going to have to work without her since we didn't know how to reach her."
4. *Control/power struggles between group members* emphasized when a group member wants to dominate group interactions. "I felt like I had to take control of the group to get anything done. We had a lot of stress over one member who wanted to dominate our groups' activities. We didn't have much input in the activities."

5. *Member differences* pertained to personal differences present between group members. Also, a lack of inclusion because a member is different or doesn't share something in common with other group members. "Age differences caused some initial discomfort and anxiety." "Perhaps not knowing each other was the biggest factor. Once the group became aware of everyone's backgrounds, we talked more freely."

In summary, perceptions of stress in small groups were based on two criteria. The first is the task that the group has been given to accomplish. The second criterion emphasizes the ability of the group members to work together within a task-structured environment, as well as the strength of their interpersonal skills in general. When any of these areas test or exceed acceptable levels for the group, an increase in stress is believed to occur. Perceptions of stress may result from our inability to separate our perceptions from reality. For some individuals, this could be one and the same.

Reducing Stress in Groups

Eight categories centered on ways group members attempted to reduce stress in groups: (1) task preparation, (2) task completion, (3) teamwork, (4) neutral meeting environment, (5) humor, (6) member similarity, (7) member sensitivity, and (8) self-disclosure outside of task-related areas. These categories also focused on task-related and interpersonal issues.

Task Related Categories. The first four categories centered on task-related issues.

1. *Task preparation* entailed advanced planning and preparation of meetings/activities to get the group ready to present the assigned task. "The stress in my group was reduced when we met much earlier to prepare for the second presentation. We all came a little more prepared, too, which helped!" "We all knew that we were prepared to talk and present our discussion."
2. *Task completion* referred to finishing/ending the duties related to the assigned task. "When the class was over, we were finished." "We completed the project and knew it would be long enough."
3. *Teamwork* was the cooperative effort demonstrated between group members to accomplish the task. "Our group participated and worked together to generate ideas for the project." "Everyone put forth an equal amount of effort, which is of the utmost importance in group work."
4. *Neutral meeting environment* referred to a comfortable, neutral setting to facilitate work. "We met at my house, so I wasn't stressed by the environment or the people."

Interpersonal Factors. The final four categories identified interpersonal issues that helped to reduce stress.

1. *Humor* referred to laughter or jokes used to facilitate positive interaction(s) between group members. "Humor. We could all laugh at everything—including ourselves." "Good humor meant having fun with what we were doing."
2. *Member sensitivity* focused on care, concern, or implied considerate behaviors exchanged between group members. "We all realized that we were bound to get on each others' nerves. Because everyone realized this, it was no big deal."

3. *Member similarity* centered on personal factors openly shared between group members. "All of our ages are similar and we are all female. I think I was lucky."
4. *Self-disclosure outside of task-related areas* emphasized sharing aspects of members' personal lives with each other that are not necessary to completing the task. "We all seemed to feel comfortable talking about our families. This self-disclosure reduced stress." "We sat around and chatted in general before we started the real work, and while we were working, we were able to laugh at some of the things we had talked about."

In summary, many of the comments given by participants focused on practical task and interpersonal behaviors that group members can perform to reduce stress. Thus, greater attention to the group task or improved communication between fellow group members may be all that is needed to reduce group stress.

Discussion

Not surprising, group stress had two main components: (1) task-related factors, and (2) interpersonal issues. Groups tended to perceive, contribute to, and/or reduce stress in their groups by focusing on the task the group was assigned or by talking with fellow group members. Interestingly, when members defined group stress, they focused on a togetherness versus a separate/individualistic theme. Comments became very negative when individuals broke away from what the group was trying to accomplish. This result tends to support some of Mitchell and Silver's findings (1990), stating that people work differently in groups, and often have to decide whether the individual's or the group's goals are met. This finding reinforces the need to view group stress within group boundaries rather than individual limits.

Stress appears to impact a small group's ability to accomplish the group task and to communicate with fellow members. Yet, individuals seem to know when a member goes outside the acceptable limits of group behavior and generates stress. Many small-group members also know how to stabilize a group that is experiencing stress by either changing their approach to the task or by trying to improve relations within the group.

Understanding group stress may help to answer (1) why individuals are dissatisfied with the group experience, and (2) what adjustments need to be made when using groups in different settings. Group stress may be a critical yet neglected factor in solving these problems. Small groups play an important part in lives, whether for personal, academic, or professional reasons. Thus, it is critical to understand how to improve the group process for group members.

References

Di Salvo, V.S., Nikkel, E., and Monroe, C. (1989). "Theory and Practice: A Field Investigation and Identification of Group Members' Perceptions of Problems Facing Natural Work Groups." *Small Group Behavior* 20 (4), 551–567.

Driskell, J.E., and Salas, E. (1991). "Group Decision Making under Stress." *Journal of Applied Psychology* 76 (3), 473–478.

Friedland, N., and Keinan, G. (1991). "The Effects of Stress, Ambiguity Tolerance, and Trait Anxiety on the Formation of Causal Relationships." *Journal of Research in Personality* 25, 88–107.

Furnham, A., and Walsh, J. (1991). "Consequences of Person-Environment Incongruence: Absenteeism, Frustration, and Stress. *The Journal of Social Psychology* 131 (2), 187–204.

Keeley-Dyreson, M., Burgoon, J.K., and Bailey, W. (1991). "The Effects of Stress and Gender on Nonverbal Decoding Accuracy in Kinesic and Vocalic Channels." *Human Communication Research* 17 (4), 584–605.

McDonald, L.M., and Korabik, K. (1991). "Sources of Stress and Ways of Coping among Male and Female Managers." *Journal of Social Behavior and Personality* 6 (7), 185–198.

Mitchell, T.R., and Silver, W.S. (1990). "Individual and Group Goals When Workers are Interdependent: Effects on Task Strategies and Performance." *Journal of Applied Psychology* 75 (2), 185–193.

Pace, R.C. (1990). "Personalized and Depersonalized Conflict in Small Group Discussions: An Examination of Differentiation." *Small Group Research* 21 (1), 79–96.

Putnam, L.L., and Stohl, C. (1990). "Bona Fide Groups: A Reconceptualization of Groups in Context." *Communication Studies* 41 (3), 248–265.

Rose, S.R. (1989). "Members Leaving Groups: Theoretical and Practical Considerations." *Small Group Behavior* 20 (4), 524–535.

Rook, K., Dooley, D., and Catalano, R. (1991). "Stress Transmission: The Effects of Husbands' Job Stressors on the Emotional Health of Their Wives." *Journal of Marriage and the Family* 53, 165–177.

Westman, M., and Eden, D. (1991). "Implicit Stress Theory: The Spurious Effects of Stress on Performance Ratings." *Journal of Social Behavior and Personality* 6 (7), 127–140.

Wiebe, D.J. (1991). "Hardiness and Stress Moderation: A Test of Proposed Mechanisms." *Journal of Personality and Social Psychology* 60 (1), 89–99.

Teaming with Emotion: The Impact of Emotionality on Work-Team Collaboration

Carolyn C. Clark and Richard W. Sline

Scholars of group communication have paid little attention to the impact of emotional expression on team interaction, although recent developments demonstrate that this is a timely and vital issue. These developments include the rapid spread of permanent work teams in American businesses, and the recognition of emotional expression as a central aspect of team interaction. This chapter will describe these trends, trace recent scholarship addressing emotional expression in the workplace, and summarize a study that focuses on the role of emotionality in the communication processes of tightly coupled work teams.

Team Structures

The popularity of work teams in modern corporations stems in part from today's intense global competition and the increasing complexity of the business environment. This complexity has forced American industry to explore alternative production strategies based on flexibility and quick response time rather than standard mass production. Organizations facing high uncertainty in their environments tend to mimic innovations that have already been implemented by successful companies. Leading U.S. firms such as Xerox, Procter & Gamble, and General Motors, for example, have drawn on Japan's use of participative structures by instituting self-directed teams, and a multitude of U.S. firms have followed suit. In support of these changes, former Harvard economist and current U.S. Secretary of Labor Robert Reich (1983, 1987) has proclaimed that teamwork structures are the most effective means for corporations to respond to the complexities of global competition and high-speed information processing in today's global market.

Emotional Expression and Teamwork

Such structural revisions, of course, are never easy to execute. In fact, significant organizational changes almost always develop in roller-coaster fashion, involving setbacks as well as advances. For example, even though the adoption of team structures may confer on workers a greater sense of responsibility, teamwork has been no panacea. In fact, there are several aspects of team communication that tend to foster anxiety and emotional tension among team members. The interdependency involved in successful teamwork demands a great deal of emotional energy and can highlight dissension. You can imagine the irritations that might develop among team members who are working in close proximity with the same group of people, day after day, as they attempt to collaborate in performing tasks under the time pressures. Besides this, the

Permission to reprint must be obtained from the authors. Carolyn C. Clark is affiliated with the University of Utah. Richard W. Sline is affiliated with Weber State University.

responsibility of joint decision making intensifies every member's information load. Since fewer decisions are delegated to individuals, the amount of material to be kept track of can snowball as each member sifts through data in order to contribute intelligently to group decisions. Finally, the deemphasis of traditional upward-downward channels of communication and the incorporation of lateral communication among teammates can generate additional anxiety because employees must learn to adjust to new patterns of communication.[1] Thus interdependency, increased information load, and changed communication patterns heighten the strain experienced by team members and increase the potential for emotional outbreaks. If emotions are managed appropriately, however, these same strong feelings can actually forge solid interpersonal relationships among teammates. In this way, emotional expression can function as either a bonding mechanism or a deterrent to collaboration.

Prior Research on Emotionality in the Workplace

Emotion has been identified as a crucial communication construct, a driving force that plays a significant role in sculpting the beliefs, attitudes, and values through which meaning and relationships are created and maintained in organizations. Pace and Faules (1983, 193) have defined relationships as "emotional connection[s]" between interacting individuals. Weick (1979) contends that shared feelings contribute more to group cohesiveness than shared opinions do, and Collins (1981) has asserted that "emotional energy" plays a primary role in successful interaction. It has also been recognized that, given the shift from traditional hierarchies of command to participative structures, it is no longer feasible for employees to suppress and ignore emotions in work contexts.

In Western tradition, however, reason, cognition, and thinking (i.e., "rationality") have been theoretically set in opposition to passion, affect, and feeling (i.e., "emotionality"). Organizational life has historically acclaimed and encouraged rationality, while it has considered emotionality to be either irrational or illegitimate. Managers typically treat emotionality as either inappropriate demeanor or as a commodity that can be used to increase organizational productivity. Zaleznik (1989) refers to the first conception (i.e., emotional expression as inappropriate demeanor) as the prevailing corporate code. He explains that according to this code, emotions detract from effective decision making and should be suppressed on the job. Managers who subscribe to this code assume that people are capable of ignoring their emotions and can make decisions and perform tasks based purely on rational goals, such as the maximization of profits. Managers fear that in situations where emotions are expressed openly, employees might not take their tasks seriously, or tension among team members might escalate. In support of this view, scholars of small-group communication have also observed that strongly expressed emotion can act as a disruptive breakpoint in group communication, particularly if the expression violates procedural norms.

The second conception (i.e., emotions as commodities) has been referred to by Hochschild (1983) as "emotional labor." Emotional labor is illustrated in the jobs of flight attendants, whose performance is judged by their ability to paste on smiles and retain them, no matter how they are feeling inside. Van Maanen's (1991) description of the "feeling business" at Disneyland provides another example of emotional labor. At

Disneyland, employees (or "performers") are constantly monitored by supervisors to ensure that they never express any signs of insincerity, sleepiness, or boredom in view of the guests. These accounts serve as poignant reminders of the potential for abusing emotionality as a business commodity.

Organization scholars point out that emotions have been devalued by rational models of organizing, and urge the development of alternative conceptualizations that honor emotional expression at work. Recent inquiries in the field of communication have exposed this "myth of rationality" as a social construction and claim that the suppression of emotions can generate feelings of alienation and fragmentation. Mumby and Putnam (1992) argue that a healthier working environment would be one in which feelings are not viewed instrumentally. They advocate the endorsement of a "bounded emotionality,"[2] in which emotional expression at work, as long as it is kept within certain bounds, should be clearly permissible. Constraints on emotional expression should not be imposed by organizational mandate, but by each person's consideration for his or her co-workers. According to this perspective, emotionality is not viewed as a commodity, but as an important constituent of communication that can enhance creativity, interrelatedness, mutual respect, a sense of community, and an appreciation of diversity among team members.

Empirical studies grounded in this perspective of bounded emotionality confirm the profound benefits of emotional expression at work and recognize the potential for detrimental effects when emotional expression exceeds certain bounds. Trujillo (1983), for example, suggests that expressive communication increases the togetherness of workers because the sharing of playful episodes functions as a powerful social force. Such episodes help define workers' social reality and create an expectation of smoothness in organizational life. In situations where the expression of playful emotions has become the norm, disruptive sentiments such as hostility are less likely to occur. The constructive expression of emotion among group members has also been associated with increased participant involvement and satisfaction. In addition, Zaleznik (1989, 122) argues that emotions should be viewed as a source of valuable information; the expression of emotions, he contends, encourages communication and thinking, and leads to improved problem definition and potential resolution, whereas restricting the expression of emotions reduces cooperation and "constricts individuals in their ability to grow." On the other hand, Wellins, Byham, and Wilson (1991) maintain that a pivotal emotional event in a team's life can prompt the team to "catapult into a more advanced or regressed state" in its development as a group. Kanter (1989) concedes that if emotional bonds among particular team members become too strong (i.e., cliques, romances, etc.), openness, collaboration, and trust among the team as a whole will usually diminish. Bocialetti (1988) suggests that, although the withholding of emotions may result in worker stress, suppression of critical feedback, and lowered motivation, when emotional expression becomes too intense there may be unwanted repercussions such as disruption of task activities, intimidation, or an unbusinesslike atmosphere.

Research Questions

Because we agree with the view that emotional expression is not inappropriate in the workplace and that emotionality is an issue of critical importance to communication scholars as well as practitioners, we designed a study to explore the impact of emotional expression on collaboration in work teams. We drew our sample from an organization that arranges staffing to fill in on a temporary basis for physicians around the country who are taking leaves of absence. The organization is structured into permanent work teams. All of the teams conform to Weick's (1979) characterization of "tightly coupled teams." That is, members have overlapping tasks, shared goals, a high frequency of interaction, and mutual fate control.

We investigated the following issues:

1. The types of events team members reported as being "triggers" of emotional reactions.
2. Members' perceptions of how those triggering events influence subsequent team collaboration.
3. The types of emotions that team members perceive they are expressing.
4. Characteristics related to the expression of specific types of emotions.

Triggering Events

The purpose of our first research question was to construct a typology of events that team members reported as being triggers of emotional reactions. Typologies are valuable because they allow comparisons among the various categories of triggering events and other variables.

Our typology divides both negative and positive triggering events into two main categories (individual-directed and team-directed), depending on whose action it was that impelled the emotional episode, and therefore became the recipient of the emotional outburst. Each of these main categories is further divided into subcategories corresponding to Bales's (1950) distinction between task and socioemotional activities. Figures 1 and 2 provide lists of these categories, along with definitions and representative accounts from our respondents.

When we compared frequencies, we found that the negative emotional events reported by our respondents were typically associated with criticism for **socioemotional** behavior and that the majority of these were situations in which the team was threatened. (See Table 1.) Conversely, positive emotional episodes were usually associated with praise that was directed at individuals and was based on **task-related** performance. (See Table 2.)

There are several possible explanations for these findings. Poor team collaboration may have been cited more frequently as a source of negative emotions than criticism directed at individuals simply because personal criticism occurs less frequently. Common observation, however, does not support this hypothesis. A second potential explanation stems from the tendency of members of well-functioning teams to construct a strong sense of group identity, pride, and unified commitment. This climate may engender feelings of protectiveness toward the team as an entity so that events involving teammates seem more striking than those that only concern oneself.

On the other hand, the fact that praise directed at individuals was most frequently associated with positive emotions might be attributable to people's natural tendency to "feel good" when they can clearly take individual credit for the accomplishment; if

1. **Individual-directed**
    a. **Task criticism:** Team member receives task-related criticism in the presence of teammates.

    > "I received feedback that I was allowing details to slip through the cracks."
    >
    > "I was questioned as to what I was actually doing all day."

    b. **Socioemotional criticism:** Team member is personally criticized in the presence of teammates for attitudes, personality traits, or interpersonal behavior.

    > "I felt like I was free-falling forever from a large jet when I was chewed out for not being supportive enough of my team."
    >
    > "My feelings were hurt when I received written feedback from my teammates that they were reluctant to be open and direct with me because I would always overreact and cry."

2. **Team-directed**
    a. **Imperious behavior:** Individuals or subgroups of the team behave in ways that communicate superiority, arrogance, favoritism, or cliquishness to other team members.

    > "One teammate treated us as if we were beneath her, acting as if he was the master and I was the servant."
    >
    > "A small group of our teammates excluded the rest of us from a social activity that was intended for the entire team."

    b. **Noncollaborative behavior:** A team member's actions communicate attitudes (such as lack of cooperation, support, and trust) which detract from the team's ability to cooperate.

    > "One team member referred to the team's upcoming retreat as 'bullshit'."
    >
    > "One team member was unwilling to relocate her own work station, even though it would improve the team's functioning."

Figure 1. Negative triggering events.

others have been involved, the feelings of responsibility for the success may be attenuated. Another explanation may be that when an achievement comes from a shared effort in which no individual is clearly identifiable as the source of the success, leaders may perceive less reason for recognizing the accomplishment.

Fisher and Ury's (1981) popular work, *Getting to Yes*, may provide some clues in interpreting the finding that negative emotions were primarily reported as springing from relational triggering events, whereas positive emotions were most frequently initiated by recognition for task-related achievements. These authors contend that, during emotional situations, individuals frequently fail to "separate the people from the problem" (Fisher and Ury 1981, 11). That is, when an individual behaves in a way that is not pleasing to us, we may judge this to be a personal attack, draw hasty inferences regarding that person's intentions, conclude that the other places little value on our

1. **Individual-directed:**
   a. **Task recognition:** Team member receives recognition in front of teammates for a job well done.

   > "My teammates gave me a real shot in the arm when they congratulated me for pulling in some big contracts for the company."
   >
   > "I was selected to represent the company at an important industry meeting."

   b. **Socioemotional recognition:** Team member receives praise for personal traits and supportive behaviors.

   > "I was thanked by my superior for having had the courage to give her constructive, negative feedback."
   >
   > "My teammates decorated my work station and gave me roses in celebration of my tenth anniversary with the company."

2. **Team-directed:**
   a. **Team pride:** Team member feels good about the task accomplishments of teammates.

   > "The whole team was jumping around and patting each other on their backs when we finished a difficult assignment on very short notice."
   >
   > "The company CEO called our team together to tell us how impressed and amazed he was with our accomplishments."

   b. **Team spirit:** Team member feels positive about being part of the team.

   > "My teammates worked overtime to cover her responsibilities so she could take time off to care for a critically ill family member."
   >
   > "Our team's sense of understanding and trust really grew as a result of our openness at the planning retreat."

Figure 2. Positive triggering events.

relationship, and react by trying to defend our own egos. If we are focused on the task, however, we are less prone to react in a negatively emotional manner, and can evaluate the conflict more objectively.

An alternate but related intuitive explanation may be that when we are reproached by teammates for committing task errors, the mistakes may be viewed as one-time slips that can be corrected in the future. When personal traits are perceived as displeasing, however, this is seen as more threatening, more difficult to change, and perhaps even taboo to discuss.

A third possible explanation for this tendency is that organizational reward systems typically assign credit for task achievements rather than for relational competence; thus we become conditioned to associate success at work with task accomplishment. Knowledge- or skills-based pay programs, for example, are growing in popularity with organizations structured with teamwork designs. Performance-based incentive systems, which reward individual and/or team accomplishments, are equally popular. In fact, the organization in this study has an incentive program that rewards a

Table 1
Percentages of Negative Triggering Events

Target of Triggering Event	%	Kind of Behavior	%
Individual-directed	38%	Task-related	19%
Team-directed	60%	Socioemotional-related	79%
Other	2%	Other	2%

Table 2
Percentages of Positive Triggering Events

Target of Triggering Event	%	Kind of Behavior	%
Individual-directed	65%	Task-related	57%
Team-directed	30%	Socioemotional-related	39%
Other	5%	Other	4%

combination of individual, team, and company performance. Individual recognition for task accomplishment provides these workers with salient, positive emotional experiences, particularly when such recognition is made in the presence of the entire organization.

Influence on Team Collaboration

Our second question centers on how negative and positive triggering events influenced perceptions of subsequent team collaboration. Collaboration is a vital construct to explore in studies of team interaction because it is considered to be a foundation for success. We measured two aspects of collaboration—**relationships** and **communication**. We chose these two measures because the characteristics of successful team relationships and communication had been extensively discussed and analyzed in this company's ongoing training program for upgrading employees' team collaboration skills so all team members were likely to share similar meanings for these terms.

When we analyzed the data, we found that most members perceived that team relationships had improved after positive emotional events and had remained essentially unchanged after negative emotional events. Even more notably, most respondents reported that team communication had improved following emotional events, regardless of whether the events were positive or negative in nature.

This implies that, in contrast to Zaleznik's (1989) explanation of the corporate code, which advocates the suppression of emotions in the workplace, the expression of emotions, both positive and negative, may not have the debilitating effect on subsequent team collaboration that managers typically expect. In fact, our respondent's open-ended descriptions of these events suggest that emotional expression frequently has a cathartic effect of relieving pent-up tension, and functions to bring team members closer together.

Types of Emotions

Our third research question elicited the types of emotions experienced by participants. Several authors have used bipolar schemes (i.e., they have lumped all negative emotions into one category, and all positive emotions into another). However, bipolar classifications may be obscuring important distinctions such as possible dissimilarities between the implications of anger versus fear. To explore such possible disparities, we supplied respondents with Ekman's (1973) well-known typology of emotions and asked them to indicate the cluster that most closely represented their feelings during each emotional episode. (See Table 3.)

Sixty-seven percent of our team members selected anger as the emotional cluster that best described the way they felt during the negative episode, and 77 percent chose joy as the primary emotion they felt during the positive episode. These choices coincide with those identified by Waldron and Krone (1991) in their study of employees functioning in a nonteamwork design. (See Table 4.) At first glance, we interpreted the

Table 3
Emotional Clusters

Cluster	Examples of Constituent Emotions
Anger	Annoyance, grouchiness, frustration, bitterness, scorn, disgust, envy, torment
Sadness	Hurt, unhappiness, disappointment, regret, embarrassment, rejection, sympathy
Surprise	Amazement, astonishment
Fear	Panic, worry, nervousness, uneasiness
Joy	Happiness, satisfaction, enthusiasm, relief, contentment, pride, optimism, enthrallment
Love	Liking, compassion, longing, desire

Table 4
Percentages of Emotional Clusters Reported by Waldron & Krone
Compared to Those Reported by Clark & Sline

Emotion Cluster	Waldron & Krone		Clark & Sline	
	Negative	Positive	Negative	Positive
Anger	48%	0%	67%	0%
Sadness	39%	0%	18%	0%
Surprise	11%	3%	11%	18%
Fear	37%	0%	5%	0%
Joy	0%	83%	0%	77%
Love	0%	7%	0%	5%

Note: Waldron and Krone's respondents reported multiple emotions; therefore, the percentages do not sum to 100 percent.

prevalence of anger and joy in both studies as an indication that emotions experienced in the workplace might follow similar patterns, regardless of work design.

Characteristics of Anger

Because anger appeared to be such a commonly felt emotion, we then compared the characteristics of anger to those of other negative emotions. Upon analyzing the data in more depth, however, we noted that 78 percent of the team-directed negative events were associated with anger, while more than half (53 percent) of the individual-directed events were associated with other emotions. (See Table 5.) This led us to revise our previous notion that emotions might function similarly in all work settings; instead, we surmised that there might indeed be some deeper connection between anger and team-directed situations.

We also discovered that anger was suppressed more than other emotions. (See Table 6.) Goffman (1969) has proposed that employees' choices of when and how to express their emotions may function as "control moves." On the other hand, Sutton and Rafaeli (1989) have suggested that displays of emotion may be related to perceived relational consequences. Many people, for example, consider anger, like conflict, to be detrimental to relationships, and therefore attempt to subdue angry feelings. A related explanation may be that members of highly interdependent work teams have been socialized to place the team's needs above individual needs. Team members who suppress their anger may do so based on a belief that the need to maintain a collaborative climate on the team is more important than a personal need for expression.

We reasoned that suppression could also be a function of the intensity of the emotion. When we tested this hunch, we found that expressed anger was usually reported as being more intense than suppressed anger. (See Figure 3.) It seems that individuals are no longer capable of exercising choice and containing their anger when it surpasses a certain threshold of intensity.

Table 5
Comparison of Anger to Other Emotional Clusters

Target of Triggering Event	Anger	Other
Individual-directed	47%	53%
Team-directed	78%	22%

Table 6
Suppression of Anger During Negative Episodes

Target of Triggering Event	Suppressed	Expressed
Anger	84%	16%
Other emotions	54%	46%

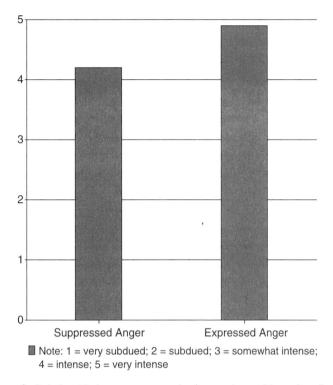

Figure 3. Relationship between suppression/expression and intensity of anger.

Conclusions

Because of the exploratory nature of this study, the specific results must be viewed tentatively. The findings do, however, suggest some general trends and reveal areas for future research.

This preliminary typology of triggering events suggests that important differences exist among individual-directed and team-directed emotional encounters, as well as between task and relational dimensions. Moreover, negative triggering events seem to exhibit characteristics that are qualitatively different than positive events. In addition, the role of anger in team interaction appears to be somewhat unique. Perhaps the most significant finding, however, is that negative emotional expression among our respondents did not generally have a negative influence on team collaboration. This discovery lends support to Mumby and Putnam's (1992) contention that organizations do not need to stifle emotional expression in fear of its consequences, but should acknowledge emotionality as a natural component of human interaction and allow team members to create their own norms for managing emotionality. Furthermore, this study suggests that additional examination of the role of anger in team interaction could be fruitful. Finally, these findings prompt us to advocate detailed research aimed at discerning the conditions under which emotional displays exceed the threshold of being beneficial and begin to push the envelope of bounded emotionality too far.

Notes

1. Barker, Melville, and Pacanowsky (1993) have argued that it is important to remember that a break-down of the communication hierarchy does not necessarily imply that the traditional roots of control in the organization have been altered; in the majority of cases it is merely the surface patterns of communication that have changed.
2. The phrase "bounded emotionality" parallels "bounded rationality," a term coined by Simon (1976) to portray the fact that human decision making cannot be truly rational. We are all bounded by our own perceptual biases and cognitive limitations, so that the choices we make are at best sufficient rather than optimal.

References

Bales, R.F. (1950). "A Set of Categories for the Analysis of Small Group Interaction." *American Sociological Review* 15, 257–263.

Barker, J.R., Melville, C.W., and Pacanowsky, M.E. (1993). "Self-Directed Teams at XEL: Changes in Communication Practices During a Program of Cultural Transformation." *Journal of Applied Communication Research* 21 (4), 297–312.

Bocialetti, G. (1988). "Teams and the Management of Emotion." In W. B. Reddy (ed.), *Team Building: Blueprints for Productivity and Satisfaction.* Alexandria, VA: NTL Institute.

Clark, C.L., and Sline, R.W. (1992). "Teaming with Emotion: The Impact of Emotionality on Team Collaboration." Paper presented at annual meeting of the Speech Communication Association, Chicago, IL.

Collins, R. (1981). "On the Microfoundations of Macrosociology." *American Journal of Sociology* 86, 984–1014.

Ekman, P. (1973). "Cross Culture Studies of Facial Expression." In P. Ekman (ed.), *Darwin and Facial Expression: A Century of Research in Review.* (169–222). NY: Academic Press.

Fisher, R., and Ury, W. (1981). *Getting to Yes: Negotiating Agreement without Giving in.* Boston: Houghton Mifflin.

Goffman, E. (1969). *Strategic Interaction.* Philadelphia: University of Pennsylvania Press.

Hochschild, A.R. (1983). *The Managed Heart.* Berkeley: University of California Press.

Kanter, R. (1989). *When Giants Learn to Dance.* New York: Simon and Schuster, Inc.

Mumby, D., and Putnam, L. (1992). "The Politics of Emotion: A Feminist Reading of Bounded Rationality." *The Academy of Management Review* 17, 465–486.

Pace, R.W., and Faules, D.F. (1983). *Organizational Communication* 2d ed. Englewood Cliffs, NJ: Prentice Hall.

Reich, R. (1983). "The Next American Frontier." *The Atlantic Monthly* 251 (3), 43–58.

Reich, R. (1987). "Entrepreneurship Reconsidered: The Team as Hero." *Harvard Business Review* 65 (3), 77–83.

Simon, H.A. (1976). *Administrative Behavior* 3d ed. New York: Free Press.

Sutton, R.I., and Rafaeli, A. (1988). "Untangling the Relationship between Displayed Emotions and Organizational Sales: The Case of Convenience Stores." *Academy of Management Journal* 31, 461–487.

Trujillo, N. (1983). "Performing Mintzberg's Roles: The Nature of Managerial Communication." In L.L. Putnam and M.E. Pacanowsky (eds.), *Communication and Organizations: An Interpretive Approach.* Newbury Park, CA: Sage.

Van Maanen, J. (1991). "The Smile Factory: Work at Disneyland." In P.J. Frost, L.F. Moore, M.R. Louis, C.C. Lundberg, and J. Martin (eds.), *Reframing Organizational Culture.* Newbury Park, CA: Sage.

Waldron, V.R., and Krone, K.J. (1991). "The Experience and Expression of Emotion in the Workplace: A Study of a Corrections Organization." *Management Communication Quarterly* 4, 287–309.

Weick, K.E. (1979). *The Social Psychology of Organizing* 2d ed. New York: Random House.

Wellins, R., Byham, W., and Wilson, J. (1991). *Empowered Teams: Creating Self-Directed Work Groups that Improve Quality, Productivity and Participation.* San Francisco: Jossey-Bass.

Zaleznik, A. (1989). *The Managerial Mystique: Restoring Leadership in Business.* New York: Harper & Row.

Conflict Management: Styles, Strategies, and Tactics

Larry A. Erbert

Relationships can be difficult, especially in the context of small-group interaction. When people find themselves in the midst of conflict in group interaction, the quality of interaction and satisfaction levels may be determined by the successful or unsuccessful management of that conflict. During conflict episodes, two basic choices exist: avoiding the conflict or handling the issue (Putnam & Folger 1988). A prevailing attitude in our culture toward conflict is that of avoidance; that is, conflict is not healthy or desirable and should therefore be avoided at all costs. However, since conflict plays a role in relational, small-group, and organizational environments, albeit to varying degrees, authorities agree that learning to productively manage conflict is an important skill (Deutsch 1973; Wall & Nolan 1987). In an analysis of conflict-management issues, this chapter will: (1) examine conflict-management styles, strategies, and tactics, and (2) explore conflict variables and alternate perspectives by which conflict may be conceptualized. By more fully understanding the complexities of managing conflict in small-group interaction, people may improve their chances for successful conflict outcomes.

Management Styles, Strategies, and Tactics

Once a decision to engage in conflict occurs, participants choose behaviors ranging from cooperation to competition (Deutsch 1973; Tjosvold 1989). A brief discussion of conflict styles, strategies, and tactics is therefore necessary for assessing how people may make changes to manage conflict more productively in small-group situations.

Conflict Styles

Generally speaking, **style** refers to the general predisposition or patterned way in which an individual responds to conflict (Folger, Poole, & Stutman 1993). This suggests that a person tends to behave in the same way when confronted with a variety of conflict situations. However, researchers may discuss style as referring to specific behaviors of conflict participants rather than predispositions to act in particular ways, which can result in confusion. Although no absolute line separates style from specific behaviors or strategies, clarifying the different types of styles may help people understand that styles are determined more by experience than by any innate quality of the person. Adopting different styles for different situations, therefore, may improve conflict outcomes.

Blake and Mouton (1964) developed a managerial grid to characterize five possible managerial styles based on two dimensions: concern for productivity and concern

This essay was written expressly for the 7th edition. Permission to reprint must be obtained from the author. Larry Erbert is associated with the University of Iowa.

for people. In conflict terms, the first dimension, cooperation, signifies a level of concern for an "opposition's" needs, wants, desires, and goals. The second dimension, competition, signifies a desire for the fulfillment of one's own needs and goals. The cooperation-competition dichotomy has been conceptualized as assertiveness and cooperativeness (Thomas 1976), concern for self and concern for others (Rahim & Bonoma 1979), productive and destructive (Deutsch 1973), and integrative and distributive (Psenicka & Rahim 1989). Conflict participants seek to resolve conflicts by engaging in at least one of three possible strategies: avoidance, cooperation, or competition. Although avoidance of conflict is not offered as a third dimension of resolution, since the use of avoidant tactics should result in either a cooperative or competitive position, it remains a viable option for participants in conflict situations.

Sillars (1980) and Zietlow and Sillars (1988), however, have suggested an active-passive strategy in place of avoidance. The difference between being passive and being avoidant is that avoidance implies an active move away from conflict, whereas passivity suggests nonresponsiveness. Explaining the management of conflict in terms of the cooperation-competition dichotomy is generally helpful, but does not describe the full range of choices or styles available to conflict participants.

Blake and Mouton (1964) elaborated on this two-dimensional perspective for the managerial grid; they outlined five specific behavioral positions (forcing, withdrawing, smoothing, compromising, and problem solving) that managers might adopt in working with employees in organizational settings. Remember, style is thought of as a general predisposition to act in certain ways, regardless of label given in the literature. Many researchers use the five styles of managerial behavior, with minor semantic variations, as the theoretical framework for styles of conflict management. For example, Hocker and Wilmot (1991), in utilizing the assertiveness-cooperation dimension, describe the five styles as avoidance, accommodation, competition, compromising, and collaboration. Canary and Cupach (1988) prefer a three-strategy approach consisting of avoidance, integrative (cooperative), and distributive (competitive). The latter framework, however, is often characterized as a strategy, rather than a style. Clearly, the line between strategy and style is not always clearly delineated as the above discussion indicates. What, then, is a strategy?

Conflict Strategies

Strategy and style are often used interchangeably in conflict literature. However, **strategy** can generally be defined as a conscious plan for dealing with conflict. The most widely accepted classification for conflict styles is the avoidant, integrative, and distributive framework.

The controversy about style versus strategy is that conflict participants do not readily distinguish compromising from collaboration, or accommodation from cooperation (Van de Vliert & Hordijk 1989). Conflict participants use only a three-style framework rather than a five-style framework. (See Van de Vliert and Prein [1989], and Van de Vliert and Hordijk [1989] for discussion.) However, Van de Vliert and Hordijk concluded that previous methodological findings of the strategy framework were based on observer responses to conflict scenarios rather than participants' actual responses to encounters. The authors examined conflict styles of Dutch construction workers using a self-report measure and determined that a clear distinction could be made concerning the differentiation of the five styles, even though compromise and cooperation were found to include greater amounts of assertiveness (fulfillment of personal needs and goals) than was previously suggested. Additionally, the five-style resolution grid was confirmed, but a distinction was made between actors' and observers' perceptions of stylistic differences. Thus, actor/observer differences illustrate that observers would be more likely to categorize behaviors in terms of avoidance, cooperation, and collaboration rather than the five-style typology. Thus, "individuals (actors) have a personalized cognitive map of subjective interrelations among the five types of conflict management" (Van de Vliert & Hordijk, 52).

To suggest that actors, however, have an accurate understanding of their own responses to conflict is not always accurate. In studies by Blake and Mouton (1978), pretest results revealed that 69.4 percent of managers believed their style of resolving conflicts fell into the problem-solving arena; yet posttest findings revealed only 24.6 percent of the managers actually used the problem-solving style of resolution. The majority of managers used competitive (34.9 percent) and compromising (34.5 percent) approaches, while accommodation (4.8 percent) and avoidance (1.2 percent) were used only sporadically. Cooper (1988) found that observers were better predictors of behavior than participants in conflict, in part because actors may be too preoccupied during conflict to carefully notice overt behavioral responses. Obviously, the importance of understanding the role of perceptual differences by both participants and observers is a significant variable for researchers and theorists to consider. When engaged in conflict, it may be helpful to realize that a person believes he or she is more cooperative than may be the case.

Regardless of the general proposed frameworks of management strategies, most researchers offer additional criteria for examining conflict interaction, usually in terms of specific behaviors referred to as tactics.

Conflict Tactics

Tactics can be defined as the specific choices made by participants in conflict interactions. Zietlow and Sillars (1988) describe behavioral choices as conflict codes rather than tactics, although both delineations refer more specifically to actions of conflict participants than either the style or strategy frameworks. Tactical choices fall into seven main clusters: (1) denial and equivocation, (2) topic avoidance, (3) noncommittal remarks, (4) irreverent remarks, (5) analytic remarks, (6) confrontative remarks, and (7) conciliatory remarks. While the list of codes described here is predominantly verbal in nature, Newton and Burgoon (1990) indicated that the incorporation of nonverbal signals must also be considered as an important variable during conflict interactions.

Regardless of the discrepancies of conflict-management approaches, it is evident that five conflict styles (avoidance, accommodation, competition, compromise, and collaboration), followed by three primary conflict strategies (avoidance, distributive, and integrative), and numerous conflict tactics provide the basic framework from which to study conflict interactions. The central difference between style and strategy seems to be the degree to which individuals are aware of their own thoughts and behaviors regarding relational conflict. Awareness of tactics, strategies, and styles may result in conscious changes in both the conceptualization of, and behaviors in dealing with, unproductive conflict. Working within a small group, a person must be cognizant not only of his or her own style, strategy, and behavior, but others' as well.

Management Factors and Issues

In this section, a number of conflict issues and frameworks will be examined that include both individual and group considerations. Thus, analysis of conflict situations requires consideration of personality issues, relational dimensions, social systems, and communication issues. The purpose of the following discussion is to provide the reader with a general overview of how conflict processes are being discussed in the field of conflict management and small-group interaction. By examining a number of alternative ways of conceptualizing the conflict process (some of which are not group related), I hope that the reader may become more aware of the complexities of conflict interaction.

While any behavior, action, situation, or life condition may be identified as a conflict component, the challenge for conflict scholars is to provide a framework that organizes the diversity of issues and findings. Rather than attempt to describe conflict processes per se, I will examine research that I have categorized into four distinct areas: personality dimensions, relational issues, social systems, and communication variables.

Personality Dimensions

Although groups might be characterized as possessing a single identity, each group is nonetheless composed of individual members. It is important, therefore, to ascertain what role personality characteristics might play in the management of conflicts.

In an organizational setting, Baron (1989) compared Type A behavior patterns and self-monitoring to the five conflict styles measured by the Thomas-Kilmann instrument. Self-monitoring refers to how much a person is aware of his or her behavior in interaction. It was hypothesized that actors who report Type A personalities and low self-monitoring would report a higher frequency of conflict and deal with conflict in noncooperative ways when compared to Type B and high self-monitoring personalities. Overall, it was discovered that Type A and low self-monitors experience a higher frequency of conflict and display noncooperative management tendencies. However, it was revealed that females high in self-monitoring also experience higher frequencies of conflict. In another organizational experiment, researchers studied psychosocial factors and work-related issues with climate, finding that the type of work (monotony, hectic pace, white collar status, etc.) may be indicative of increases in conflict at work (Appelberg, Romanov, Honkasalo, & Koskenvuo 1991).

In addition to personality measures, Papa and Natalle (1989) argued that gender differences exist. In trying to answer the question of style differences between men and women, researchers seem to be split on the issue. Based on Gilligan's (1982) assertion that men seek independence while women seek connection, it may be that men will resolve conflicts based on a need for independence, while women choose styles based on concern for the relationship.

From this perspective, men should use more competitive strategies and women more cooperative strategies. Miller (1991) explored the use of mental scripts and conflict styles among women and men in four stages of relational interactions using hypothetical scenarios. Results indicated that men tend to use more independent criteria whereas women use more interpersonal or interdependent standards; however, analysis was not based on actors' reports of conflict styles, but rather on the researcher's analysis of scripted material.

Support for differences between women and men was found in a study that examined both sex of subject *and* sex of target conflict management styles (Berryman-Fink & Brunner 1987). The Thomas-Kilmann Mode instrument was given to 147 undergraduate students from basic interpersonal courses and the reported differences revealed that men are more likely to use a competitive style and women a compromising style. However, the likelihood of using an accommodating style increases if the target of communication is a woman. Rosenthal and Hautaluoma (1988), using a revised version of the Thomas-Kilmann instrument, reported that women are likely to use an accommodating style while competition is preferred by men. Additionally, Fitzpatrick and Winke (1979) studied same-sex and opposite-sex friendship interactions to determine whether sex of participant had a bearing on resolution style choices. The authors found that in opposite-sex relationships, participants adopted emotional appeals, personal rejections, manipulation and non-negotiation as compliance-gaining strategies for management. (The higher the level of commitment, the greater the chance that participants would use emotional appeal and personal rejection.) No reported differences in gender were apparent in same-sex relationships.

Since many studies use self-report instruments or hypothetical scenarios, Papa and Natalle (1989) wanted to determine if reported style differences in gender would hold true for real-life settings. An actual conflict in an insurance company provided the backdrop for this study. Researchers wanted to determine whether conflict strategy use for men and women differed, and if the reported satisfaction levels of men and women would vary across three time periods (beginning, middle, and end of conflict encounter). Seven strategies were identified: reason, friendliness, coalition, bargaining, assertiveness, higher authority, and sanctions. Results with same-sex and opposite-sex dyads revealed that male-male dyads used high levels of assertiveness and reasoning for all time periods but did not use bargaining. In female-male dyads, high levels of reasoning and bargaining were noticed, with an increase in assertiveness in the second time period. Finally, in female-female dyads, high levels of assertiveness permeated the first two time periods and bargaining increased during the third. Although the conclusions indicated some gender differences in resolving conflict, issues of power, roles, personal needs, social constraints, and degree of liking may supercede gender considerations.

Chusmir and Mills (1989) hypothesized that men and women managers would report using similar conflict styles at work but different conflict styles at home. Results indicated that men and women managers did tend to use the same conflict strategies at work (competition more than accommodation) but also tended to use the same strategies at home. However, the authors noted one exception, low level women managers expressed a willingness to avoid or collaborate while low level men managers were more likely to compromise at home than at work.

Research on individual traits of group members has focused primarily on leadership qualities (see Fisher 1985; Barge & Hirokawa 1989; Cragan & Wright 1990; Ketrow 1991; Barge 1994). In terms of small group conflict, Schultz and Anderson (1984) argued that the trait of argumentativeness may be important for the successful management of conflict. That is, if a person is willing to be argumentative, he/she may be perceived as a leader who makes direct contributions to the group interaction by encouraging "the examination of many ideas, by discussing the advantages and disadvantages of a proposal, and by using conflict to delineate the appropriate choice or judgment" (337). From a broader perspective, engagement in conflict is generally seen as a positive quality.

One of the problems with seeing conflict-interaction style as a personality trait is that it may nurture the belief that a person cannot change the way he or she interacts with others. If this were true, people would have no control over the outcomes of conflict. While it is difficult to deny that people have a tendency to act consistently, the nature of each unique relationship can affect conflict interaction.

Relational Interaction Dimensions

How often do conflicts occur? What effect does level of intimacy, intensity, reciprocity, or commitment have on the perceptions and uses of resolution strategies? Hinde (1979) identified eight significant characteristics of relational interaction (diversity, frequency and patterning, content, quality, reciprocity and complementarity, intimacy, commitment, perception) that underpin this section of conflict dimensions. Although the eight characteristics identified by Hinde have not all been integrated into conflict research, many researchers, when investigating conflict issues, utilize one or two dimensions and recognize the importance of scrutinizing conflict from a relational perspective.

The way in which conflict is resolved is dependent on coorientational accuracy (CA), that is, knowing where the other conflict party stands on an issue, and what styles he or she is likely to use (Papa & Pood 1988). Accuracy in understanding another's position can be achieved through differentiation; however, Papa and Pood suggested that if differentiation occurs during conflict, the outcome may be destructive. Thus, preconflict differentiation should result in better coorientational accuracy. In comparing low CA dyads and high CA dyads, it was found that the development of CA requires partners to differentiate, and that compared to low CA dyads, high CA dyads spent less time differentiating during conflict and displayed more assertive-type management behaviors. In discussing limitations of the study, the authors suggested that intensity, relational history, and relational power may significantly affect coorientational accuracy and the development of differentiation.

In conflicts, relational partners may be likely to accuse their partners of being self-centered, or not accommodating enough. Rusbult, Verette, Whitney, Slovik, and Lipkus (1991) examined accommodation processes of distressed and nondistressed couples and found that: (1) self-centered partners tend to engage in more destructive conflict behavior, (2) relational importance, commitment, and happiness are associated with accommodation strategies, and (3) when partners engage in destructive behaviors, couple distress will increase.

As a relational issue, power has been examined extensively in interpersonal, organizational and international arenas (for a discussion of power and conflict, see Blalock 1989, Wortenberg 1990, and Hocker and Wilmot 1991). Power is presented as the product of relational interaction and not an attribute of the individual (Hocker & Wilmot 1985). The frequency, intensity and uses of power play an important role in the productive and/or destructive management of conflict. In tests of equal versus unequal power in conflict, Lawler, Ford, and Blegen (1988) tested bilateral deterrence and conflict spiral theories in conflict interactions. Bilateral deterrence theory predicts that the higher the power given to individuals, the less they will use punitive tactics. Conflict spiral theory suggests that when people with equal power in high level positions engage in conflict, the use of punitive tactics among participants will increase. Results supported the bilateral deterrence theory and not the conflict spiral theory, meaning that in situations where equal power exists between people, the use of punitive tactics will not increase.

In general, it could be argued that all conflicts take place within the confines of relational interactions, even in small groups. Why, then, the need for highlighting Hinde's eight dimensions of relationships? While it is true that many studies by conflict researchers include one or two elements of Hinde's dimensions, researchers have not fully integrated the primary elements of relational interaction. However, research to date provides a strong foundation for continuing to build a more comprehensive model of interaction characteristics. Part of the problem stems from the complexity of the nature of conflict as well as the diversity of conflict environments. Thus, exploring conflict characteristics in a social-systems context may shed some light on the problem.

Dimensions of Social Systems

Few conflict researchers have examined the interplay between social systems and conflict-management styles. However, there is an emerging trend in the study of small-group interaction to take into account the social or external conditions that affect group-decision interaction and outcomes (see Hirokawa and Johnston 1989, for discussion).

Social systems, as conceptualized here, refers to the influence of social structures, institutions, or networks on a group or person's beliefs, values, thoughts, and so forth. Druckman, Broome, and Korper (1988) compared conflict behaviors with personal interests and values to determine the "impact of conditions" and processes on conflict issues. Hypothetical scenarios of international conflicts were devised so that undergraduates could reach resolutions based on three approaches, (a) facilitation (values-first focus), (b) delinking (making a clear separation between values and issues), and (c) embedded (close link of values to positions). Results indicated that both the facilitation and delinking approaches produced more resolutions than the embedded approach. Additionally, both delinking and facilitation improved perceptions of opponent, climate, and compatibility of positions.

In a theoretical article, Haimes and Weiner (1986) constructed a conflict-resolution model based on hierarchical holography. The essence of the theory separates conflict into two types, soluble and insoluble. For soluble conflicts, "consensus will be achievable without requiring changes in images or trade-off" (Haimes & Weiner 1986, 200).

Insoluble conflict, however, is defined much more broadly as a range of issues, and is expressed in emotionally saturated and symbolic terms. In an insoluble conflict, it is vital for participants to learn about the complex issues such as face-saving or engaging in trade-offs that surround the conflict. Indeed, the authors discuss the need to comprehend the complexity of large-scale systems, and argue that no single system can represent all of the characteristic variables. Overlapping models or submodels may help clarify the complexity of conflict when analyzing conflict strategies on the personal and/or social level. In fact, Haimes and Weiner refer to the interdependence of one nation upon another as metassociation, and argued that with advances in global labor division and demand for scarce resources, interdependence is the result of an evolutionary process. Conceptually, the holographic modeling perspective is similar to Druckman, Broome, and Korper's proposed "new" directions, in which they describe the need to integrate both micro- and macroprocesses in conflict. In essence, Druckman, Broome, and Korper suggested that microprocesses (interpersonal relations, social learning, and communication) should be linked with macroprocesses (institutional structures and structures of regional systems, etc.), in order to more effectively understand the interdependent nature of conflict. For small-group members, this concept illustrates the necessity for understanding individual perceptions and perspectives as well as becoming more aware of the larger organizational and social factors that affect the small-group conflict.

How can researchers and laypersons determine what issues are relevant or interdependent in conflict situations? Interdependence and similarity of outcomes in conflict were examined by Surra and Longstreth (1990), and a method for studying interdependence in close relationships was devised. Partners' and actors' preferences for joint activities (interdependence) were hypothesized to be positively related with how much the partners engaged in joint activity. Thus, conflicts would increase with disagreements about what joint activity to share and decrease if the activity was equally desirable. Surprisingly, results indicated that participation in activities is better predicted by the partners' preferences than by the mutual liking for the activity. Additionally, it is the satisfaction with joint activities that determines satisfaction level of participants, with the exception of issues of relational maintenance, and food and errands. (See Surra and Longstreth 1990, 505 for a complete list of activity type measured.) At any rate, successful conflict management may be dependent on personal issues, relational interactions, and social networks; however, the process of communication is the central "linking" component of conflict behavior and management strategies.

Dimensions of Communication

"Communication is the central element of all interpersonal conflict" (Hocker & Wilmot 1991, 13). Conflict can be created, reflected, or managed in productive or destructive fashions, depending on the communication behaviors of conflict participants. The perceptions of individuals regarding degrees of communication competence, uses of styles or strategies, and overall communication satisfaction are reflected in communication behaviors and have a significant impact on conflict situations.

Sillars (1980) argued that decisions in communication and conflict are functions of social attribution elements such as intent, causality, and stability of conflict behaviors. Three issues—causal judgment (cause and effect), social inference (intentions and personality traits), and predictions of behaviors and outcomes—were studied in relation to passive-indirect strategies, and integrative and distributive strategies using college roommates. Results revealed that: (1) when cooperation was attributed to the other conflict party, integrative strategies were more likely used; (2) when individuals took responsibility for conflict, cooperative strategies were used; (3) if conflicts were perceived as less stable, cooperation strategies were employed more often; (4) responsibility for conflicts was attributed much more to roommates than actors; and (5) resolution and partner satisfaction would most likely occur when integrative strategies were utilized. Additionally, Sillars suggested that information exchange may not always solve the conflict; rather, exchange may increase conflict. If conflict is low in frequency and importance, integrative strategies predominate. Conversely, if frequency and importance of conflict are high, roommates will often use avoidance strategies. Even though attribution theory is supported, the importance of communication processes and communication competence should not be—but often is—underplayed in conflict research.

Specific and general appropriateness and effectiveness of communication was investigated by Canary and Spitzberg (1990) to determine attributional bias and communication competence. When distinguishing between actors' and partners' judgments of conflict messages, findings revealed that: (1) actors rate themselves as more appropriate and competent; (2) distributive tactics are more congruently perceived than integrative or avoidant tactics; (3) when assessing actor competence, effectiveness, and appropriateness, both partners and actors rely on integrative tactics; (4) when assessing specific appropriateness, both actors and partners rely on distributive behaviors; and (5) partners rely more on conflict tactics than actors do to assess actors' competence criteria. Thus, the findings generally support an attributional approach in explaining actor-partner judgments of communication competence.

One of the central concerns in small-group conflict is how communication affects group member satisfaction and the quality of the decision outcome. It is generally hypothesized that satisfaction with decision outcomes is related to the productive management of conflict and the quality of communication (Wall & Nolan 1987). Additionally, Wall, Galanes, and Love (1987) argued that conflict is harmful to small-group situations when the conflict destroys group cohesiveness, drains needed energy, or is reduced to individual concerns. Conversely, conflict is productive and satisfying if it "expands the available pool of ideas, opens up an issue, helps clarify it, alerts the system that corrective actions need to be taken, prevents a group from arriving at premature consensus, or increases the individual's involvement in the decision-making process" (Wall, Galanes, & Love 1987, 33). Reports of member satisfaction levels, however, may vary with the amount of conflict experienced. Wall and Nolan (1987) and Wall, Galanes, and Love (1987) found that satisfaction levels of group members decreased the more members experienced conflict, regardless of whether the conflict was person-centered or issue-centered.

In an effort to understand the relationship between communication, member satisfaction, and leadership in small-group conflict, Witteman (1991) attempted to distinguish the variables that could predict either productive or destructive conflict. In this study, productive conflict was characterized by a win/win or integrative approach, whereas destructive conflict was associated with a win/lose or distributive orientation. Witteman hypothesized that productive management of conflict would occur if group members: critically evaluated ideas, generated high levels of ideas, discussed group goals, displayed an integrative orientation, and demonstrated flexibility in perceptions and behaviors. In general, results revealed that the hypothesized relationship between productive conflict management and the aforementioned issues was confirmed. Nonetheless, Witteman suggested that further study be done to understand the relationship between conflict and persuasive message strategies. For the most part, one may conclude that communicative engagement in conflict issues is generally more helpful than non-engagement in successful management of conflict.

While this brief review of communication variables reinforces the importance of communicative practices in the management of conflict, in no way is it representative of the quantity or quality of research in this area. In fact, it is my hope that this cursory summary of the research will promote greater interest in the area so that people will better understand communication processes and how communication affects the nature of small-group conflict.

Conclusion

This chapter has provided an introduction to a number of key variables for understanding conflict interactions. Successful management of conflict requires at least some awareness of or reflection on the styles, strategies, and tactics used in conflicts. However, sensitivity to these concepts does not in any way guarantee conflict will be managed effectively. Conflicts result from the incompatible goals of at least two parties who have different needs and desires. The topics in this chapter represent a starting point for engaging in dialogue that focuses on mutual gain and successful interaction outcomes rather than relational destruction. Communicating the needs and goals of each conflict party will more likely result in a successful outcome. As members of groups, clarifying positions and attempting to use integrative approaches to conflict should enhance the quality of communication and satisfaction with decision outcomes.

References

Appelberg, K., Romanov, R., Honkasalo, M.L., and Koskenvuo, M. (1991). "Interpersonal Conflicts at Work and Psychosocial Characteristics of Employees." *Social Science Medicine* 32 (9), 1051–1056.

Barge, J.K. (1994). "Communication Skills and the Dialectics of Leadership." Paper presented at the annual meeting of the Central States Communication Association, Oklahoma City, Oklahoma.

Barge, J.K., and Hirokawa, R.Y. (1989). "Toward a Communication Competency Model of Group Leadership." *Small Group Behavior* 20 (2), 167–189.

Baron, R.A. (1989). "Personality and Organizational Conflict: Effects of the Type A Behavior Pattern and Self-Monitoring." *Organizational Behavior and Human Decision Processes* 44, 281–296.

Berryman-Fink, C., and Brunner, C.C. (1987). "The Effects of Source of Target on Interpersonal Conflict Management Styles." *The Southern Speech Communication Journal* 53, 38–48.

Blake, R.R., and Mouton, J.S. (1964). *The Managerial Grid.* Houston, TX: Gulf.

Blake, R.R., and Mouton, J.S. (1978). *Making Experience Work: The Grid Approach to Critique.* New York: McGraw-Hill.

Blalock, H.M. (1989). *Power and Conflict: Toward a General Theory.* London: Sage Publications.

Canary, D.J., and Cupach, W.R. (1988). "Relational and Episodic Characteristics Associated with Conflict Tactics." *Journal of Social and Personal Relationships* 5, 305–325.

Canary, D.J., and Spitzberg, B.H. (1990). "Attribution Biases and Associations between Conflict Strategies and Competence Outcomes." *Communication Monographs* 57, 139–151.

Chusmir, L.H., and Mills, J. (1989). "Gender Differences in Conflict Resolution Styles of Managers: At Home and at Work." *Sex Roles* 20 (3/4), 149–163.

Cooper, V.W. (1988). "The Measurement of Conflict Interaction Intensity: Observer and Participant Perceived Dimensions." *Human Relations* 41 (2), 171–178.

Cragan, J.F., and Wright, D.W. (1990). "Small Group Communication Research of the 1980's: A Synthesis and Critique." *Communication Studies* 41 (3), 212–236.

Deutsch, M. (1973). *The Resolution of Conflict: Constructive and Destructive Processes.* New Haven, CT: Yale University Press.

Druckman, D., Broome, B.J., and Korper, S.H. (1988). "Value Differences and Conflict Resolution." *Journal of Conflict Resolution* 32 (3), 489–510.

Fisher, B.A. (1985). "Leadership as Medium: Treating Complexity in Group Communication Research." *Small Group Behavior* 16 (2), 167–196.

Fitzpatrick, M.A., and Winke, J. (1979). "You Always Hurt the One You Love: Strategies and Tactics in Interpersonal Conflict." *Communication Quarterly* 27, 3–11.

Folger, J.P., and Poole, M.S., Stutman, R.K. (1993). *Working through Conflict: A Communication Perspective.* Glenview, IL: Scott Foresman.

Gilligan, C. (1982). *In a Different Voice: Psychological Theory and Women's Development.* Cambridge, MA: Harvard University Press.

Haimes, Y.Y., and Weiner, A. (1986). "Hierarchical Holographic Modeling for Conflict Resolution." *Philosophy of Science* 53, 200–222.

Hinde, R.A. (1979). *Towards Understanding Relationships.* New York: Academic Press.

Hirokawa, R.Y., and Johnston, D.D. (1989). "Toward a General Theory of Group Decision Making." *Small Group Behavior* 20 (4), 500–523.

Hocker, J.L., and Wilmot, W.W. (1985). *Interpersonal Conflict* 2d ed. Dubuque, IA: Wm. C. Brown Publishers.

Hocker, J.L., and Wilmot, W.W. (1991). *Interpersonal Conflict* 3d ed. Dubuque, IA: Wm. C. Brown Publishers.

Ketrow, S.M. (1991). "Communication Role Specializations and Perceptions of Leadership." *Small Group Research* 22(4), 492–514.

Lawler, E.J., Ford, R.S., and Blegen, M.A. (1988). "Coercive Capability in Conflict: A Test of Bilateral Deterrence versus Conflict Spiral Theory." *Social Psychological Quarterly* 51 (2), 93–107.

Miller, J.B. (1991). "Women's and Men's Scripts for Interpersonal Conflict." *Psychology of Women Quarterly* 15, 15–29.

Newton, D.A., and Burgoon, J.K. (1990). "Nonverbal Conflict Behaviors: Functions, Strategies, and Tactics." In D.D. Cahn (ed.), *Intimates in Conflict: A Communication Perspective* 77–104. Hillsdale, NJ: Lawrence Earlbaum Associates.

Papa, M.J., and Natalle, E.J. (1989). "Gender, Strategy Selection and Discussion Satisfaction in Interpersonal Conflict." *Western Journal of Speech Communication* 53, 260–272.

Papa, M.J., and Pood, E.A. (1988). "Coorientational Accuracy and Differentiation in the Management of Conflict." *Communication Research* 15 (4), 400–425.

Psenicka, C., and Rahim, A.M. (1989). "Integrative and Distributive Dimensions of Styles of Handling Interpersonal Conflict and Bargaining Outcome." In A.M. Rahim, (ed.), *Managing Conflict: An Interdisciplinary Approach* (33–40). New York: Praeger.

Putnam, L.J., and Folger, J.P. (1988). "Communication, Conflict and Dispute Resolution." *Communication Research* 15 (4), 349–359.

Rahim, M.A., and Bonoma, T.V. (1979). "Managing Organizational Conflict: A Model for Diagnosis and Intervention." *Psychological Reports* 44, 1323–1344.

Rosenthal, D.B., and Hautaluoma, J. (1988). "Effects of Importance of Issues, Gender, and Power of Contenders on Conflict Management Style." *The Journal of Social Psychology* 128 (5), 699–701.

Rusbult, C. E., Verette, J., Whitney, G. A., Slovik, L. F., and Lipkus, I. (1991). "Accommodation Processes in Close Relationships: Theory and Preliminary Empirical Evidence." *Journal of Personality and Social Psychology* 60 (1), 53–78.

Schultz, B., and Anderson, J. (1984). "Training in the Management of Co: A Communication Theory Perspective." *Small Group Behavior* 15 (3),

Sillars, A. L. (1980). "Attributions and Communication in Roommate C." *Communication Monographs* 47, 180–200.

Surra, C. A., and Longstreth, M. (1990). "Similarity of Outcomes, Interdependence, and Conflict in Dating Relationships." *Journal of Personality and Social Psychology* 59 (3), 501–516.

Thomas, K. (1976). Conflict and conflict management. In M. D. Dunnette (ed.), *Handbook of Industrial and Organizational Psychology*, 889–935. Chicago: Rand McNally.

Tjosvold, D. (1989). "Interdependence Approach to Conflict Management Organizations." In A. M. Rahim (ed.), *Managing Conflict: An Interdisciplinary Approach* (41–50). New York: Praeger.

Van de Vliert, E., and Hordijk, J. W. (1989). "A Theoretical Position Compromising among Other Styles of Conflict Management." *The Journal of Social Psychology* 129 (5), 681–690.

Van de Vliert, E., and Prein, H. C. M. (1989). "The Difference in the of Forcing in the Conflict Management of Actors and Observers." Rahim, M. A. (ed.), *Managing Conflict: An Interdisciplinary Approach* (New York: Praeger.

Wall, V. D., Galanes, G. J., and Love, S. B. (1987). "Small, Task-oriented Groups: Conflict, Conflict Management, Satisfaction, and Decision-Making." *Small Group Behavior* 18 (1), 31–55.

Wall, V. D., Nolan, L. L. (1987). "Small Group Conflict: A Look at Equity, Satisfaction, and Styles of Conflict Management." *Small Group Behavior* 18 (2), 188–211.

Witteman, H. (1991). "Group Member Satisfaction: A Conflict-Related Account." *Small Group Research* 22 (1), 24–58.

Wortenberg, T. E. (1990). *The Forms of Power.* Philadelphia: Temple University Press.

Zietlow, P. H., and Sillars, A. L. (1988). "Life-Stage Differences in Communication During Marital Conflicts." *Journal of Social and Personal Relationships* 5, 223–245.

ACTIVITIES

Activity 1

Purpose: The purpose of this activity is to demonstrate the difference between concrete, specific goals and vague goals.

Procedure: The class is divided into groups of three to five participants, and each group has one observer. The groups will compete against each other to determine which group can list the most answers in five minutes. The observers use the observation sheet to compare the group's behavior with the first and second tasks.

	FIRST TASK	SECOND TASK
1. Number of times a member repeated, read aloud, or tried to clarify the task.		
2. Number of times group members made comments not related to the goal.		
3. Number of times a participant looked around or sighed.		
4. Evidence of withdrawal or frustration (pushing back, crossing arms, etc.)		

First Goal: Develop a hypothetical list of parameters that could be used to maximize the cooperation and cohesive efforts of small groups engaged in formulating constructive team goals.

Second Goal: List all of the television programs that you can think of that have been broadcast in the last twenty years.

Activity 2

Purpose: The purpose of this activity is to encourage the class members to examine the ways that they deal with conflict and controversy.

Procedure: As a large group the class lists some rules of constructive controversy. These are the rules that they think would make resolving conflict in groups more productive and that they would like to see used in class. Rules like, "Attack ideas but not people," are appropriate. After the members of the class have agreed about the rules, the class is divided into smaller groups of three to five people. Each member of the small group then takes a turn to explain a strong personal opinion. This can be an opinion about anything, such as a social, political, religious, or legal issue. The group members then discuss each opinion for five minutes, taking care not to break any of the rules for constructive controversy. If a member does break one of the rules, the other group members should cease discussion about the original topic and address how they see a violation of the rules taking place.

Activity 3

Purpose: The purpose of this exercise is to have the students examine what behaviors they consider "clean" or "dirty" in group-conflict resolution.

Procedure: In small groups the class lists the behaviors that they would consider for fighting **clean,** that is, appropriate, constructive, or positive behaviors for resolving conflicts in a group setting. The rules for constructive controversy that were generated in the previous activity can provide ideas for this list. Then, the group lists the behaviors that they would consider for fighting **dirty,** that is, behaviors that they consider inappropriate, destructive, or negative in group-conflict situations. After fifteen to twenty minutes the groups share their conclusions with the rest of the class. The class can then create a master list of positive and negative behaviors.

Activity 4

Purpose: The purpose of this exercise is to have the students learn to identify unfamiliar and confusing behaviors that have their roots in cultural differences.

Procedure: In small groups, the students attempt to identify behaviors they have witnessed but have not understood when they have communicated with people of the other gender, another race, or religion, or a different cultural heritage. Each group creates two lists. The first list identifies the behavior that was confusing. The second list explains *why* the behavior was confusing and whether a misunderstanding led to conflict. Finally, each group should report its findings to the entire class.

Activity 5

Purpose: The purpose of this activity is to demonstrate the role of sexual stereotyping on perception and communication.

Procedure: In small groups identify the following list of traits as being either (a) male, (b) female, or (c) neutral.

TRAIT	MALE	FEMALE	NEUTRAL
leader			
ambitious			
secretive			
independent			
analytical			
complex			
passive			
controlled			
impulsive			
intuitive			
insensitive			
manipulative			
objective			
neurotic			
rational			
tough			
caring			

Each group should share its findings with the entire class.

Activity 6

Purpose: The purpose of this activity is to have the members of the class become acquainted with each other while learning about self-disclosure.

Procedure: Using the chart on this page, interview members of the class to find a person to correspond with each description. You may need to move from classmate to classmate to complete all of the items on the list.

NAME

ITEM

_____ I live over six hundred miles from campus.

_____ I can speak at least three languages.

_____ I like country western music.

_____ I am a complete vegetarian.

_____ I have two or more dogs.

_____ I have gone to school in a foreign country.

_____ I play two musical instruments.

_____ I have attended an opera.

_____ I have one brother and one sister.

_____ I have changed a diaper.

_____ I have ridden in a horse show.

_____ I ride a motorcycle.

_____ I have attended three plays by Shakespeare.

_____ I have visited five or more foreign countries.

_____ I have never received a speeding ticket.

_____ I can name ten movies I have seen in the last year.

Activity 7

Purpose: The purpose of this activity is to have the members of the class become acquainted with one another while expressing their views regarding small-group communication.

Procedure: First, ask the students, working alone, to answer the following questions:

1. Do you believe groups or individuals working alone reach better decisions?

2. What are your reservations about groups?

3. What do you expect from a group experience?

4. Do you trust group members whom you meet for the first time?

5. Do you like a strong leader in a group or shared leadership?

6. Would you rather be a leader of a group or a participant?

7. What are the characteristics of those groups with which you have enjoyed being affiliated?

8. What are the characteristics of those groups with which you have disliked being affiliated?

Second, have the class form small groups and discuss the results of their individual answers.

Third, have the entire class discuss some of the conclusions reached by each group.

5
Communicating in Groups

Human interaction is pervasive in our culture. We choose to be with other people some of the time, and other times we are forced into the company of others. Whenever these interactions take place, communication is occurring. It is through communication that we initiate, maintain, and perpetuate relationships; and many of these relationships take place in a group setting. Without communication we would have a difficult time fulfilling our needs and accomplishing our goals. Communication enables us to tell and to be told, to share our innermost feelings and ideas, to exercise some control over our environment, and to form the countless groups that offer us an opportunity to solve common problems. The link between group activity and communication is so strong that studying one without the other is virtually impossible. That is to say, to understand both of these processes—group behavior and communication—we must appreciate their interdependence. By viewing communication as an **activity**, something that we do that has consequences, we can learn to adjust our communication behavior to the group situation by making the right choices.

Recognizing the complexity of communication, especially communication in groups, helps us to make better choices. When we are mindful of all of the chances that communication has to fail when just two people are involved, we can appreciate how much more easily communication can break down when more people join together to form a group. Mixing several different people's perceptions, word choices, nonverbal symbols, and listening behaviors is bound to cause some confusion, especially if we take the communication process for granted.

Human communication is a two-way process, an ongoing series of interactions that results in something different from the original product or event. We use words and other symbols to convey meaning, but the meaning is in the people who send and receive those verbal and nonverbal symbols. The individual's perception or point of view forms the foundation of all communication.

Communication is the **dual process** of selecting and sending symbols in order to create a shared meaning and then receiving and interpreting these symbols. Therefore, it is a **dynamic**, transactional, and interactive process, rather than a stagnant one. Communication involves changes inside a person and between people because we affect each other during any situation by continually correcting and changing the verbal and nonverbal messages we are simultaneously sending and receiving.

Communication is complex but sometimes **unintentional.** We cannot *not* communicate. Because we are always communicating, others can inaccurately assign meaning to our words, actions, physical appearance, and group associations, often without our knowledge or intent.

Relationships with others create one of the significant aspects of what it means to be a human being. However, most communication problems occur because of the definition and the nature of the relationships rather than because of the content of the messages. In other words, the relationship between the communicators, rather than what is said, will cause the most problems.

In any group some relationships are **complementary or unequal,** some are **symmetrical or equal,** and some are a mixture. We might be equal in status but one person may be superior in skill or knowledge in a certain area. Under ideal circumstances interpersonal communication in a group is open, honest, and direct. However, ideals seldom prevail and barriers block effective interactions.

Barriers include anything that blocks or interferes with accurate communication. Internal (psychological or physiological) or external (physical) noise can cause communication to break down.

Perceptual differences are probably the most common causes of communication barriers because people react to situations differently. For instance, the inappropriate or careless choice of words or nonverbal symbols can cause defensive reactions and misunderstandings. Communication overload (too much information) can cause the listener to become overwhelmed and to give up or to tune out. Communication underload (not enough information) can cause people to react to vague or misleading information.

Principles of Perception

Perception is the foundation of all communication and makes communication possible. It is the process of influencing selectively, subjectively, creatively, and uniquely what we sense.

Selection is the first step in the perceptual process. We admit some stimuli and omit others based on whether the data are agreeable with attitudes, needs, interests, and expectations. We cannot process all available information because there is too much, especially when several people in the group are talking and interacting simultaneously.

We tend to expose ourselves only to circumstances or situations that we think we will need or that we expect will be agreeable with our current beliefs. We tend to avoid situations that we anticipate will expose us to perceptions that are unnecessary or that are in conflict with our beliefs or values. Given a choice, we tend to choose groups that we think we will enjoy or that we think will do us some good.

We pay attention to **immediately available stimuli** on a discriminating basis. The subjective decision, whether conscious or unconscious, to pay attention to some things and to ignore others usually distorts our perceptions to some degree. Since processing all available stimuli is impossible, we rely on our needs or motives to help us to choose which information to take in. However, this selection often simplifies or omits important data, which compromises perceptual accuracy. We see what we need to see or what we assume to be agreeable with our current beliefs. Individuals in a small-group setting represent a plethora of needs, motives, and agendas that can further endanger communication effectiveness.

Organization is the second step of the perceptual process during which we identify relationships that exist among current and past perceptions. We then put that information into categories.

Interpretation is the third step of the perceptual process during which we assign value to received stimuli. The perceiver makes evaluations and draws conclusions based on prior experience, knowledge, assumptions about human behavior, prior programming, and cultural norms. These judgments tell us what is good or bad, pretty or ugly, funny or not funny.

Our perceptions are **subjective** rather than **objective**. If they were objective, they would be tangible, concrete, and measurable, but that is not the case. Subjectivity is internalized, biased, personalized, and unique for each individual. We make a common mistake when we believe that perceptions are impartial and that everyone is perceiving the same thing the same way. Perceptions are influenced by our values, attitudes, and beliefs. Perceptions can only be known significantly by the individual perceiver and cannot be measured or observed by others. Realizing this, we can take steps to "perception check." Paraphrasing and asking other group members for clarification and offering our own defuses potential conflict situations.

Creativity means that meaning is created by the individual and influenced by society. *Meaning is not created by the object or thing.* There is no intrinsic quality in objects or events that dictates that we must perceive them in a certain way or assign them a specific meaning.

Uniqueness can be illustrated by pointing out that no two perceptions of an event are *exactly* alike. Each person will perceive the same set of circumstances in slightly or vastly different ways.

Perception is the basis for human communication. We create reality in our minds, and this perception then governs every communication situation. Communicators can influence but not control others' perceptions of them. By increasing awareness of messages we are intentionally or unintentionally sending, we can affect (but never fully predict) the perceptions others will have. Being aware allows us to make responsible decisions to maximize opportunities for effective group interaction.

There is no one right or accurate perception. However, each person tends to assume that his or her perception is the only accurate one in spite of the fact that there are few universal truths. Group members may have an illusion of unanimity because people often voice the same perception even when they don't have the same reaction. The pressure to conform, to be one of the crowd, as well as the usual tendency to have self-doubts, will lead many people to imply agreement when it's not really there. This practice reinforces the false notion that everyone agrees and encourages groups to develop groupthink.

The way we view the world is tremendously influenced by how we view ourselves. **Self-concept** involves an internalized set of perceptions that each of us has about ourselves. The treatment that we receive from other group members plays a role in determining how we will feel about ourselves and our place in the group. For example, if others ignore or ridicule us, our self-concept is likely to reflect their attitudes. This process is known as **reflected appraisal**.

Groups can further influence group members' behavior through **self-fulfilling prophecies**. When others expect us to behave in a certain way and treat us accordingly, we often assume the assigned role and fulfill the prophecy.

Verbal Communication in Small Groups

Verbal communication is the creation of meaning between individuals through the use of words. Words, spoken or written, give us the tools we need for communication.

Words affect group climate because the very words that empower people to create meaning can also build barriers between them. The use of words gives group members a means for sharing ideas, influencing attitudes, and expressing emotion; but words can also serve as a source of conflict. Words can intentionally or unintentionally be used as roadblocks to effective communication.

One reason for these barriers is that *meaning is not in words*. Instead, communicators give meaning to the words they use or encounter. Words are symbols that represent a concept. Because concepts differ and because people assign symbols to concepts in an unpredictable manner, misunderstandings occur. Each sender and receiver creates the meaning for each word he or she perceives.

Another reason for misinterpretation is that words are **culturally influenced**. The meanings assigned to words and the way in which language is used are closely tied to the cultural segment to which an individual belongs. The acceptability of a word or phrase to a group will be determined by that group's norms. For example, a group of ministers may prohibit the use of certain words, but the members of a sports team might use those words regularly and consider them acceptable.

Saying that *verbal communication is content oriented* means that the main focus of verbal communication is what is said. The group we are in will influence the words we choose, and we will impact the group by our choice of words. Every communication situation involves both what is said and how it is said. Verbal communication deals with the **content** of the message, while nonverbal communication addresses the **context** or how the message is said.

Word choice and the meanings we assign to words can reveal our attitudes and the attitudes of our culture. Words can also reveal the sender's self-concept. People with positive self-concepts tend to use assertive, nonmanipulative languages; and they are capable of saying "I don't know," and "I was wrong."

The types of words we choose will contribute to or detract from communication effectiveness. *Concrete* words help clarify the message while *abstract* words tend to cloud meaning.

Abstract words are unclear because they are broad in scope. They tend to lump things together, ignoring uniqueness. Abstract terms describe things that cannot be sensed or are difficult to sense. Because these words are vague and nonspecific, they encourage generalizations and stereotyping. Ambiguous language can confuse others when we say things like "Dress casually," "I'd like a little off the top," and "Get there early."

Concrete words are words that are more specific. Concrete words frequently describe things that can be perceived by one of the five senses or that can be described in behavioral terms. They clarify the sender's meaning by narrowing the number of possibilities. Using concrete words tends to decrease the likelihood of misunderstanding.

Descriptive words are concrete words that stress observable, external, objective reality. These words focus the receiver's attention on the thing being described rather than on the sender's reaction to that thing. These words are nonjudgmental and neutral and describe the *facts* as the sender knows them. Statements of fact tend to bring people together, while statements of inference and judgment tend to cause problems.

Judgmental words, on the other hand, show evaluation and stress personal reactions. They are words that direct the receiver's attention to the sender's positive or negative reaction to a situation rather than to a description of the situation. This often engenders a defensive reaction in the receiver. Judgmental words tend to be vague and abstract.

"You" oriented speech tends to focus on the receiver and often implies a judgment or blame. Whether the evaluation is stated outright or merely implied, the receiver often reacts defensively. Conversely, "I" language shows ownership of emotions and reactions and reduces the likelihood that the hearer will react defensively.

Being aware of owned language is particularly important in a group situation because others often become embarrassed and defensive if they think we are trying to blame or belittle them in front of others.

Polarized words are abstract, judgmental words that tend to trigger an opposite reaction in the receiver because the words are extreme. Using hot or cold, good or bad, or right or wrong encourages others to polarize their speech, too, so that finding a common ground becomes more difficult. Also, since most of our ideas and opinions are not as radical as polarized words would imply, these words don't truly represent our points of view.

Individuals who use such words can intentionally or unintentionally encourage the polarization of attitudes among group members. This can lead to the formation of subgroups or alliances and can detract from overall group cohesion.

Paraphrasing, on the other hand, is a skill that can greatly improve the chances that communication will be effective. It is a descriptive restatement of another person's message *stated in our own words*. It is not simply repetition but is a sincere effort to improve understanding and to communicate empathy.

Paraphrasing is especially useful in conflict situations because it provides a mechanism for encouraging listening and for demonstrating what the receiver is trying to understand. Paraphrasing in a group setting encourages active listening and improves understanding among the group's members.

Paraphrasing will help clarify the ideas of the sender but pays attention to the speaker's words in only part of the process. Noticing the speaker's nonword cues will also help group members grasp each other's meaning.

Nonverbal Communication in Small Groups

Nonverbal communication is the process of creating meaning by using nonword symbols. These symbols are the first things we notice about people. They give information about gender, age, status, occupation, religion, personality, self-esteem, personal preferences, and group membership. Nonverbal communication can send messages even when no words are being exchanged.

The overwhelming majority of our communication takes place on a nonverbal level. About 60 percent of the meaning of personal messages will be related to nonverbal communication. Groups provide a rich source of nonverbal messages because so many behaviors occur simultaneously. Being aware of the impact of nonverbal communication helps group members realize the importance of paying attention to subtleties and of trying to use consistent verbal and nonverbal messages.

Any symbol that is not specifically a word is automatically defined as nonverbal communication. These symbols include gestures, objects, actions, and so on. Even the way in which a word is presented is defined as nonverbal communication. This means that communicating without the presence of at least some nonverbal symbols is virtually impossible.

There are not enough verbal symbols to represent the complex feelings we have for each other, so we rely on nonverbals to compensate partially for this inadequacy. Relying on nonverbal gestures helps us to show our feelings when we can't state them in words. Nonverbals are sometimes difficult to keep under control, so our true feelings often leak through whether we want them to or not.

One problem associated with nonverbal communication is that it is *not* a precise language. A receiver can easily assign more than one meaning to a single gesture. Nonverbals are often vague or unintended, and compared to verbal communication, nonverbal communication is highly prone to misinterpretation. Furthermore, nonverbal communication is **continuous**. *We cannot not communicate.*

Proxemics, kinesics, eye contact, facial expression, posture, tone of voice, and clothing are all aspects of nonverbal communication. There are a variety of explanations for the differences in nonverbal behavior. Physiological differences, socialization, status differences, and sex roles all affect our nonverbal communication.

Nonverbals are sometimes difficult to keep under control. As a result, our true emotions will often "leak" through in telltale hints of nervousness, anger, boredom, and other feelings. We are frequently unaware of what nonverbal messages we are sending.

Receivers often see nonverbal messages as more credible than verbal messages. When a contradiction occurs between the verbal and nonverbal messages, we tend to believe the nonverbals more. This can create misunderstandings, however, since nonverbals are so vague.

Nonverbal communication is culturally learned and dictated by cultural norms. In order to communicate effectively with another culture, we must not only learn and comprehend their verbal language systems, but we also need to understand their nonverbal language.

There are **eight major forms** of nonverbal communication that allow senders and receivers to share information. Unfortunately, because nonverbal communication is so imprecise, misinterpretations often occur.

Proxemics refers to the human use of space as symbolically significant behavior. There are two types: *personal space* and *territoriality*. Assumed roles, the status of those roles, the degree of intimacy in the communicators' relationships, and cultural norms all strongly influence proxemics. Violation of personal and/or territorial space often leads to defensive behaviors.

Personal space is the invisible bubble of space that surrounds a person. Individuals become more disturbed when others stand too close rather than when they stand too far away. Generally speaking, Americans are most comfortable when others are at least an arm's length (three to four feet) away. However, group members who sit closer to each other (two to three feet) often enjoy more effective communication.

Territoriality refers to our need to establish and maintain certain immovable spaces of our own. Women, in general, are allowed to have less territory than men. Few women have a particular, unviolated room in their homes; while many men have dens, studies, or garages that are off-limits to others. Groups and individuals use "markers" such as articles of clothing, purses, tilted chairs, and cups or glasses to indicate ownership of a space. Invading or violating another's turf can lead to conflict.

Kinesics refers to any body movement such as random motions, gestures, walking, and posture. Our faces give other people information about how we feel, but our bodies communicate the intensity of the particular emotion.

Group members will use these cues to determine if others are happy, sad, open, or credible. Also, group members will use turn-acquiring cues such as leaning forward to indicate a desire to speak. Similarly, speakers often change head and eye positions and shift positions to indicate the end of a point. People tend to imitate or "mirror" the posture and gestures of group leaders and of members with whom they want to be affiliated.

Sign language includes any type of gesture that is assigned specific denotative meaning by the sender. This means the sender can reasonably assume the receiver will give his or her gesture a meaning that is similar to the one intended. There is no certainty that the receiver will assign a meaning that is similar to the one intended because there is no meaning in the symbol or gesture. Some examples of sign language include nodding yes or no, waving hello or good-bye, shrugging the shoulders, and shaking a fist.

Facial expressions communicate judgments, interest, and intensity. Basic facial expressions are universal and can be associated with the same emotions throughout the world. We can increase our communication effectiveness by realizing that we are showing our emotions through our facial expressions.

People who smile are seen as having many positive characteristics including intelligence, good personality, and pleasantness. Men who smile receive higher evaluations on such characteristics than do women.

Smiling, usually viewed as a positive behavior, can also be a demonstration of submissiveness. Chimpanzees smile when they wish to avoid confrontation with a higher-status chimpanzee. Mothers smile so frequently that their mood cannot be determined by their smile alone. Men are often less expressive than women but are also less confusing.

Eye contact may express friendship, affection, and affiliation with another person. It encourages feedback by signaling that the communication channels are open. In a small group, looking at another group member signals your interest in him or her and invites interaction, especially when the group leader is involved. Eye contact may also indicate a wish to become more intimately involved with the other person. A look held longer than *three seconds* can show that there is sexual interest.

On the other hand, eye contact can be used to establish dominance and control. People use hard stares to signal danger to others. Eye contact may indicate status or dominance, serve to regulate the conversation, and transfer the floor from one speaker to another. Group members often interpret the lack of eye contact to be a display of disinterest, apathy, rudeness, or deceit. Several factors will affect a group's eye contact, such as distance between communicators, topics of discussion, appearance and personality of the communicators, cultural norms, and gender, since women engage in more eye contact than men do.

Physical presentation includes artifactual communication or object communication and refers to our intentional or unintentional display of material things, including perfume, hairstyles, clothing, jewelry, cosmetics, and other adornments. Before verbal communication is initiated, people in a small group begin to make judgments about others based on their physical appearances. We send statements about ourselves through our choice of objects. Accurately or inaccurately, others use artifactual communication to infer demographic data about us: income, status, political attitude, religion, age, and attitudes.

Awareness of the influence of object language can help us to make informed decisions about the messages that we send and about the ways that others might interpret our use of objects.

Tactile communication refers to touching behavior, which can be either positive or negative. Touch is positive when it is used appropriately to show affection or intimacy. If touch is used reciprocally, it indicates solidarity among the people in the group. Groups tend to develop their own norms about touching behavior. Gender, race, age, and background will all play a role in defining what kinds of touch are appropriate and in determining when touch will be viewed as supportive and affirming. The handshake is one of the few forms of touch that is universally acceptable in groups and in the workplace.

Some controversial studies suggest that in adult relationships, men touch more than women. This behavior has been interpreted as reflecting a higher status privilege for men. Without question, however, touch is culturally regulated.

Paralanguage or vocalics refers to how we speak, the nonverbal elements of the human voice. It includes all that accompanies language and consists of all of the vocal cues that individuals use to communicate: pitch, rate, inflection, volume, quality, enunciation, flatness, nasality, breathlessness, thinness, tenseness, throatiness, and fullness.

The use of a sarcastic tone can be particularly confusing in a group situation since not all individuals understand it or respond positively to it. Awareness of paralanguage can help the sender to show more interest and enthusiasm when the words are presented in a more animated fashion.

Chronemics is the study of how we perceive, structure, use, and react to time. It includes perceptions of when someone is "on time" and the significance of being "late." Our perception of time is culturally determined and differs greatly among different groups.

Group members within a given culture will also often vary in their use of group time. Certain individuals are slow in speaking and in responding. Others might enjoy deviating from the task for periods of time, a practice that some would view as "wasting time." Flexibility and sharing speaking time will contribute to the group's communication effectiveness.

Environment refers to all of the factors in the environment that influence the communication climate, such as the following: temperature, seating arrangement, elevation differences, and color. Seating arrangements that allow group members to see each other and to interact directly create an environment that is usually more conducive to problem solving, cooperation, and credibility. *Once again, appropriateness is culturally determined and regulated.*

All human interaction depends on communication. Without it we would have no way of building relationships, and group association would be pointless. When group members are able to practice effective message sending and receiving, they can build the trust and cohesion that will help them reach their goals. Respecting the interrelated and integrated parts of the communication process allows each person to exercise control over words and action and, therefore, to improve group participation.

Introduction to Readings

In recent years teachers and students of human communication have stressed the fact that we generate and send nonverbal as well as verbal messages. In group situations people often pay more attention to these nonverbal behaviors than they do to verbal messages. In the opening selection, Judee K. Burgoon reviews an important dimension of nonverbal communication—spatial relationships. Specifically, *informal space* (how we orient toward and distance ourselves from other members of the group), and *fixed feature* and *semi-fixed feature space* (the ways in which architecture, interior design, furniture arrangement, and the like influence spacing behavior). Burgoon is concerned with how these two factors relate to comfort, status, leadership, interaction patterns, relational communication, and spatial deviancy.

Our next essay not only looks at how we receive verbal and nonverbal messages, but also the ways in which we respond to those messages. This cycle of message—response—message is called **feedback**. Feedback represents the messages people send each other regarding what is happening at the moment. This important form of message exchange is investigated by Beth Haslett and John R. Ogilvie in a selection titled "Feedback Processes in Task Groups." While they begin by looking at feedback in general, their main focus is on feedback in the small group. They discuss the dimensions of feedback, feedback and group performance, and feedback as a communication process. Also, they examine some of the factors that influence feedback such as trustworthiness, power and status, and communication style. Because feedback is crucial to the productivity of any group, they conclude with a summary of the most effective ways to offer feedback to others. As you read this essay keep in mind that feedback represents one of the best ways participants have to keep their peers informed of what they think and feel about what is transpiring.

Throughout this book we have stressed the idea that communication is a two-way process in which all parties are both listeners and speakers. Although this axiom is widely acknowledged in the writings on communication, the literature reveals an uneven distribution in favor of the person who is sending the message. One possible reason for this one-sided approach might be that many people make the mistake of believing that *receiving* a message is the same as *listening* to a message. The acceptance of this false assumption leads to the corollary belief that reception, comprehension, and memory are all the same. It is our position that this is simply not true. Reception is physical process and only the first step of the listening cycle. We maintain that you must understand the entire cycle and all the variables that intervene if you are to become an effective listener.

Many of the important variables of listening are treated in an essay written especially for this book. Kittie W. Watson begins by reminding us of the importance of listening to the group setting. She underscores the obvious yet often overlooked premise that poor listening habits can waste valuable time and lead to countless misunderstandings. To help refine the manner in which people listen in a group, Watson discusses principles of listening, listener preferences, and also offers a number of specific skills that can easily be put into practice.

One of the points we have tried to stress throughout this book is that successful group discussion can be both profitable and enjoyable. We are now suggesting that it can also be fun. In our final selection, W. Jack Duncan, Larry P. Smeltzer, and Terry L. Leap treat the subject of humor as it applies to group situations. Although they are aware of the hazards of misusing humor (e.g., harassment, gender, racism, and "horseplay"), they nevertheless believe it can be very useful when people come together in an organizational setting. They maintain humor can combat boredom, contribute to group cohesiveness, diffuse and reduce organizational conflict, and help define the group roles.

Spatial Relationships in Small Groups

Judee K. Burgoon

An old German fable has it that one fall night, the porcupines came together in the forest for a little socializing. Finding the night air to be quite cold, they tried to move close together for warmth but found they kept pricking each other with their quills. So they moved farther apart but once again became cold. They continued moving back and forth until they finally arrived at a distance that afforded them both warmth and comfort. Henceforth, that distance became known as good manners.

Like the porcupines, we humans also seek optimal spacing arrangements when in groups. Our *proxemic* patterns—the ways in which we perceive, utilize, and arrange our spatial environment—seem to be governed by two competing needs. One is the *need for affiliation*. We are social creatures who desire to associate with other people and to form bonds of attachment with them. Close proximity both signals that desire and permits those social bonds to develop.

The other requirement is a *need for privacy*. There are times when we wish to distance ourselves from the group to achieve greater physical security, to escape stimulation and stress, to gain a greater sense of personal control, or to permit greater psychological freedom and self-reflection. Greater distance provides a form of insulation, a cushion against intrusions from others.

These two conflicting needs sometimes lead us to approach the group and sometimes to avoid it. Typically, group spacing behavior reflects an equilibrium state in which these approach-avoidance tendencies are brought into balance within individual members and among members of the group. Because our proxemic patterns relate to some of our most fundamental human needs, proxemic behaviors, and especially deviations from the equilibrium or expected spatial arrangement, can convey some very powerful albeit subtle messages.

The Organization of Space

There are two perspectives from which group spacing behavior can be examined. One is to consider the nature of the people involved and the purposes of the interaction factors that dictate how individuals choose to distance themselves from one another. This aspect of spacing is what the anthropologist Edward T. Hall has called *informal space*.[1] The second is to consider what constraints on spacing are imposed by the environment, or the arrangement of what Hall calls *fixed feature* and *semi-fixed feature space*.[2] At any point in time, the proxemic patterns of a group will be influenced by both considerations.

Permission to reprint must be obtained from the author. Judee K. Burgoon is affiliated with the Department of Speech Communication, University of Arizona, Tucson.

Informal Space

This facet of proxemic behavior concerns how we orient toward and distance ourselves from other members of the group. Whether that group be our family, a circle of friends at a social gathering, a committee working on a task, or a department within an organization, we will have characteristic distances that we adopt and characteristic means of insuring that those distances are maintained. These spacing patterns usually operate outside our conscious awareness but are of great importance. As Hall has said,

> ". . . informal spatial patterns have distinct bounds, and such deep, if unvoiced, significance that they form an essential part of the culture. To misunderstand this significance may invite disaster."[3]

There are three levels at which informal space can be analyzed. One is *territoriality*. A territory is a fixed, geographically identifiable space to which an individual or group has laid claim. An obvious example is one's home or neighborhood. These often have *territorial markers* such as fences, signs, or locks that clearly signal boundaries and degree of accessibility to "outsiders."

There are also other kinds of territories to which we lay claim, however, ones for which the right of possession may be more ambiguous. Have you ever noticed that in a classroom, many people gravitate to the same seat time after time? They come to feel it is "their" seat. If someone else then sits in it, they feel their territory has been violated. At public beaches, we claim a space for ourselves and attempt to ward off intrusions by spreading out towels and other personal possessions as territorial markers, even though the space actually belongs not to us but the public at large.

This territorial urge seems to be deep-seated and possibly innate. By demarcating a tangible geographic area under our personal control we apparently gain a greater sense of security and autonomy. In times past, the ability to secure and defend a territory undoubtedly had survival value. Today, one's physical survival may not be at stake (street gangs defending their turf being one exception), but the ability to maintain a territory provides greater protection and privacy for the individual and for the group. Consequently, when our territory is violated, even when the violation seems unintended or inconsequential, we react strongly. Archie Bunker's vitriolic reactions to people sitting in "his" chair are a prime example. Because territorial invasions provoke such strong emotional reactions and may lead to physical aggression, it is important to understand how individuals within groups express their territorial proclivities and how groups in turn operate on these territorial imperatives.

The instincts that give rise to territorial behavior also shape a second level of informal spacing behavior that has been identified: *personal space*. In contrast to the visible and fixed nature of territory, personal space is an invisible, flexible, and portable "bubble" of space that surrounds us. It expands and contracts according to our needs and the situation. It may be very large when we are interacting with a hostile stranger and may temporarily disappear entirely in an intimate situation. As with territorial invasions, personal space invasions arouse and distress us. We will therefore want to consider how groups can recognize these distress signals and can arrange themselves in ways to minimize such stress.

Our personal space needs in turn determine the third level of informal spacing: *conversational distance*. This is the distance at which we normally conduct face-to-face interactions. This may coincide with or exceed the personal space needs of the individual participants. It permits a measure of spatial insulation and comfort, and is largely governed by cultural norms. Hall attempted to identify four categories of interpersonal distance that correspond to different sensory experiences and different interaction purposes. His widely accepted categories are as follows:

1. *Intimate distance* (0–18 inches)—a distance reserved for physical contact or intimate encounters and entailing high sensory involvement.
2. *Personal distance* (1½–4 feet)—a distance used for close interpersonal relationships or more private discussion topics; it entails a high degree of kinesthetic involvement but doesn't have the same impact on cutaneous, visual, olfactory, auditory, and thermal receptors as does intimate distance.
3. *Social distance* (4–12 feet)—a range of distances used for informal social activity, business consultations, and other relatively impersonal encounters; this distance category is outside the range of touch and involves less sensory impact.
4. *Public distance* (12 feet and beyond)—a distance reserved for highly formal encounters, platform presentations, and interactions with public figures; this distance minimizes kinesthetic involvement and requires a louder speaking voice than normal.[4]

While these distance categories have proven useful in elevating awareness that people adjust distances according to the intimacy level of their interpersonal relationships and conversational topics, some social science research (to be discussed shortly) indicates that these categories fail to capture the complexity of the norms governing spacing behavior. For example, gender, age, degree of acquaintance, social status, and personality, among other factors, will all dictate the normative distance for a given interaction.[5] If groups are to maximize their effectiveness, they must recognize how these various factors influence the behaviors and desires of individual members.

Fixed Feature and Semi-Fixed Feature Space

This facet of proxemic behavior encompasses the ways in which architecture, interior design, furniture arrangement, and the like influence spacing behavior. Fixed feature space, as the name implies, concerns the spacing patterns resulting from permanent structures such as walls, doorways, and the configuration or use of those spaces. For example, in this culture we divide homes into a number of smaller compartments, some of which become individual bedrooms, some of which are designated for private and personal hygiene activities (bathrooms), and some of which are available for multiple functions (e.g., family rooms).

Fixed features of the environment may dictate what proxemic patterns people establish among themselves. The volume of space available is one major influence. Take the case of a committee assembling to plan campaign strategy. If they meet in a large hall, they may adopt rather close seating positions in the center of the room but distribute themselves evenly within the space. This permits an audible conversation while giving everyone a "share" of the space around the perimeter of the group. If, instead, the committee meets in a small conference room, members may distribute themselves unevenly and closer to the walls to maximize their spatial freedom.

The normal functions of the environment may also constrain behavior. If the committee meets in the family room of someone's home, the informality associated with the room may encourage more informal seating arrangements. On the other hand, if the committee is forced to meet in the sanctuary of a church, the normal reverent behavior elicited in this environment, coupled with the large volume of space, may cause people to cluster close together so that they can speak in hushed tones.

Semi-fixed feature space refers to the proxemic arrangements resulting from movable environmental structures such as partitions and furniture. As with fixed feature space, the configuration of these elements at a given point in time will affect how people distance themselves from one another. A formal conference table, for example, specifies one kind of spacing pattern; sofas in a lounge necessitate another.

Environmental psychologists have identified two different arrangements of semi-fixed feature space that produce very different kinds of interaction. One is a *sociopetal* arrangement. This pattern, as exemplified in Figure 1, brings people together. Well-designed restaurants, bars, or living rooms use a sociopetal spatial pattern to facilitate interaction among people. By contrast, *sociofugal* patterns turn people away from one another and discourage interaction. These types of arrangements, as illustrated in Figure 1, are commonly found in public places such as hotel lobbies or airports, where social interaction and loitering are intentionally discouraged. Psychologist Robert Sommer also found this pattern in state institutions such as hospitals. Often chairs lined the walls of lounges so as to ease the work of custodians and orderlies. Sommer found

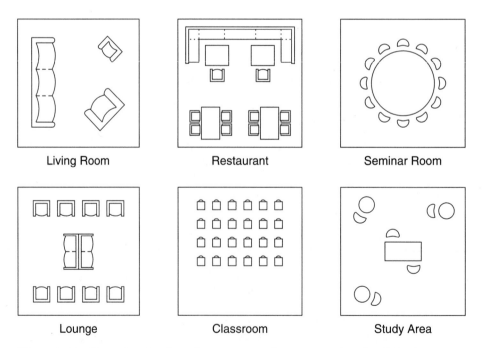

Living Room   Restaurant   Seminar Room

Lounge   Classroom   Study Area

Figure 1. *Top*, Examples of sociopetal arrangements; *bottom*, examples of sociofugal arrangements.

that after he rearranged the chairs to create a sociopetal space, previously depressed and noncommunicative patients showed significant improvement in their mental health and their ability to relate to others.[6] His observations confirmed the profound effects that environmentally imposed spacing can have on our emotional states, our behavior, and our relationships with other people.

Having identified the various perspectives from which the organization of space can be analyzed, we are now ready to consider in greater specificity how proxemic patterns relate to small-group communication. Of interest will be how proxemics regulate our interactions and what messages are implied by various spatial behaviors.

Comfort

Underlying all of the effects of proxemics on human behavior is how comfortable people are with the amount of space provided them. If we were to trust Hall's distance categories as a guide, we would assume that anything closer than eighteen inches would typically be an uncomfortable interaction distance because it is an intimate distance and therefore reserved for only the most personal and arousing interchanges. In fact, a classmate of mine and I set out to demonstrate this in a study we conducted as graduate students. However, we got some unexpected results.[7]

Our primary interest was in discovering what kinds of classroom seating arrangements are most conducive to comfort, attention, learning, and participation. We hypothesized that students, given the opportunity to voluntarily arrange their classroom, would select distances apart that exceeded eighteen inches. (We also had some expectations about what pattern they would choose in which to arrange the chairs.) We selected some classrooms that had movable chairs and prior to the students arriving for class, pushed all of the chairs into a jumble in the center of the room. After the students had arrived and created their own arrangement, we entered the room, measured the distances between chairs, recorded the arrangement, and gave students a grid on which to record their preferred classroom arrangement.

The unexpected result from the study was that students voluntarily placed themselves an average of seventeen inches apart. This was greater than the average distance of thirteen inches that we found in comparable, undisturbed classrooms, but still less than we had anticipated. We concluded that people are able to tolerate relatively close distances without becoming uncomfortable and in fact may prefer some degree of closeness. The results also made us aware that the four distance categories alone do not give us enough information; a number of other factors need to be taken into account in ascertaining at what distances people are most likely to be comfortable.

Research suggests that there are three kinds of considerations that will determine what the normative, and presumably most comfortable, distance is for a given interaction. These considerations include the nature of the people in the group, the nature of the interaction itself, and the environmental constraints. Regarding people characteristics, the following have all been identified as important:[8]

1. *Gender:* Females sit and stand closer to other females than do males interacting with one another. The research is mixed on whether opposite-sex pairs adopt closer distances than female-female pairs. Specifically, in a group setting females

tolerate crowding far better than males and may respond in a more intimate, pleasant way to close proximity, while males may respond with aggressive, unpleasant reactions.

2. *Cultural background:* Some cultures interact at closer distances than others. Those who are accustomed to close proximity during face-to-face encounters are called contact cultures. Those that display more distant interaction patterns are called noncontact cultures. The United States in general is considered a noncontact culture, although many subcultural groups (such as those from southern Europe, the Middle East or Central America) would qualify as contact groups.

3. *Race:* The research here is very mixed but there is some evidence that black males in the United States adopt the greatest distances and black females adopt the closest, compared to white males and females. Blacks also appear to have a more fluid approach to distancing, as compared to the more static (fixed) pattern exhibited by whites.

4. *Age:* People maintain closer distances with people who are the same age than with those who are younger or older than they are, even if the older person is a parent.

5. *Status:* Like age, the greater the differential between interactants, the greater the distance.

6. *Degree of acquaintance:* Not surprisingly, people adopt the closest distances with close friends, adopt intermediate distances with acquaintances, and maintain the greatest distance from strangers.

7. *Personality:* Different personality types have characteristic distances they adopt from others. For example, introverts and highly anxious individuals require more space than their extroverted or less anxious counterparts. Some research with violent prisoners has documented that they require as much as twice the space that nonviolent prisoners need, suggesting that the discomfort they experience in close proximity to others may be a factor in their aggressive tendencies.

Other people factors no doubt also play a role. In addition, the nature of the interaction itself influences how comfortable people are likely to feel. For example, if the group is gathering for a social purpose, people will expect and be comfortable at closer distances. If the purpose is a formal meeting or a task-oriented discussion, they may be more comfortable at greater distances.

The environment plays a role by setting limits on the options available to people. In a living room situation, if people have a choice they will usually opt for across seating. This is particularly true if the available side-by-side seating is one to three feet. However, if the across seating exceeds three and one-half feet, and especially if it is farther away than an alternative side-by-side seat that is at a reasonable distance, people will choose to sit alongside another. This implies that the "arc for comfortable conversation" is about a five and one-half foot distance nose-to-nose.

If the available seating arrangement forces people into close proximity, such as in an auditorium, a classroom, or a small meeting room, people may adapt temporarily, recognizing that the proximity between themselves and their neighbors has been imposed upon them rather than being a matter of choice. One way that people adapt is to develop a *nonperson orientation*. This means essentially acting as if the other person were not present or were merely an object. This is exactly how people adjust to being confined in an elevator with a group of strangers. They look straight ahead, avoid contact with the other riders, and pretend that they are unbothered by the closeness of the others.

Collectively, all research on proxemic norms indicates that the process of arriving at a comfortable distance is a rather complex one. It is governed by a large number of factors that must all be brought into balance. This becomes particularly complicated in a group situation, where there is a mix of individual characteristics and preferences that must be accommodated. Fortunately, the research also reveals that we are adaptable creatures who can tolerate deviations from our preferred spacing for short periods of time.

Nevertheless, we have strong physiological reactions to inappropriate spacing and over a period of time will display evidence of our discomfort. Studies have shown that, compared to being in close physical proximity to a paper figure or an object (such as a hat rack), people manifest much greater physical arousal (as measured by galvanic skin response) when their personal space is invaded by another person.[9] Other reactions to spatial invasions that have been documented include: (1) displaying anxiety through such behaviors as restless leg and foot movements, fidgeting with objects, scratching the head, and touching oneself; (2) sometimes staring hostilely at the intruder but more often avoiding eye contact; (3) erecting barriers with personal possessions such as books or coats; (4) erecting "body blocks"—shading the eyes or putting arms and elbows between oneself and the intruder; (5) increasing distance by leaning away, moving farther apart, or reorienting the body away from the intruder; and (6) if the invasion is prolonged, taking flight (i.e., actually leaving the situation altogether). It is interesting to note that people rarely respond to an invasion or experience of crowding verbally. Rather, they rely on nonverbal signals to reveal their discomfort and to ward off continued intrusion.

If it can be assumed that discomfort reduces a group member's satisfaction and the quality of his or her contributions to group process, then groups would be wise to watch for these symptoms of spatial inadequacy and attempt to compensate for them. As a minimum it might mean making adjustments between members within a location. As a maximum it might mean finding a different location in which to interact.

Status and Leadership

As noted earlier, status confers the privilege of greater spatial insularity. Politicians, celebrities, and corporate presidents are always accorded greater distances from those of lesser status. The story is told that when John F. Kennedy became president, friends with whom he had formerly socialized suddenly began observing an invisible threshold some thirty feet from him that they would not cross until he first breached the distance. It served as eloquent recognition of the significant change in status he had achieved.

People in positions of status and power enjoy other proxemic privileges. They are permitted to initiate whatever seating arrangement or distance is going to be observed, they are free to violate spatial norms, they have access to more and better territory, and they are accorded more privacy.[10]

In the context of small-group communication, individuals of power and status often emerge as group leaders, or the person designated as leader takes on status and power by virtue of his or her position. Therefore, these proxemic power relations should and do have analogues in the group setting.

The high-status individual and/or group leader typically occupies the best position in the group. Selecting the best position, in turn, confers status on its occupant and the expectation that the individual will demonstrate leadership. Research has shown that leaders, high-status members, and dominant individuals gravitate toward the end positions of a rectangular table; that is, they take the head of the table, or they choose to sit opposite the most other people. In unacquainted groups, the people who select these positions will more often be perceived as the leader, and people placed in these positions will be induced to become more dominant in the ensuing interactions.[11]

For those wishing to have influence in a group, the implications are clear: Choose a spot that places you at the symbolic head of the group or across from the most other people. If your goal is to elicit more leadership from a particular member, place him or her in one of those positions. If your goal is merely to identify who in a group is most likely serving as its leader, look for the individual around whom the spatial arrangement revolves, who is accorded more space, and who occupies a central position within the group.

Interaction Patterns

Just as group proxemics affect leadership emergence and vice versa, so do proxemic patterns influence the ways in which the group communicates. Proximity in itself encourages interaction. The act of bringing people together usually impels them to speak to one another. Even a group of strangers will often strike up a conversation if placed in close proximity long enough. In a classroom, unacquainted individuals seated next to one another will often develop a friendship before the term is over. There is even a high rate of marriages among people who live within six blocks of each other!

Physical closeness alone is a powerful force determining to whom we will talk. The "who" and "how" of small-group communication also depend on the existing furniture arrangement and the purposes of interaction.

One type of group context that has been frequently studied is the classroom. It will be recalled that in my study with Pat Garner, we observed what spatial arrangements students adopted and asked them what arrangement they would prefer so as to maximize participation, learning, and attention. Overwhelmingly, students expressed a preference for a U-shaped or circular arrangement and tended to approximate such an arrangement when they placed their own chairs in the room. This preference seems to be based on two considerations: the proximity and visual access to one another and to the instructor that this arrangement affords to students.

Other classroom research supports the importance of the twin elements of proximity and eye contact. Classrooms with straight-row seating tend to produce the greatest interaction from the front and center seats, creating almost a "triangle of participation." It should be obvious that such seats, by virtue of their spatial and visual access to the instructor, make it easier to see the teacher and gain his or her attention. Similarly, classrooms with laboratory seating (i.e., everyone seated around small lab tables) produce the greatest amount of total participation, presumably because students are close to one another and can maintain a high degree of eye contact with one another. Proximity alone, however, apparently is not sufficient to induce equal participation. In seminar seating arrangements (i.e., everyone seated around one large table), the most participation comes from those opposite the instructor and the least comes from those seated at the instructor's side. So long as the instructor takes an active role in leading the group, most interaction comes from those who can maintain eye contact with the instructor.[12]

In small-group discussions, the same principle holds: Whoever is in the most central position or has visual access to the most other people is likely to participate the most. This conclusion must be tempered somewhat by the nature of the interaction and the presence or absence of a strong leader. There is some evidence that task discussions produce more "across" interaction, while social discussions produce more "alongside" interaction. However, the presence of a directive leader may also encourage more conversation among people seated next to one another.[13]

The nature of the task also affects people's preferences for a seating arrangement. A number of studies have demonstrated that people prefer corner-to-corner or side-by-side seating for cooperative and conversational activities. They prefer opposite seating for competitive activities. One study even suggests that competitors prefer some degree of distance which permits surveillance of one's opponent. When people are engaged in coaction (i.e., they are engaged in simultaneous, noninteracting activities) they prefer greater separation and less opportunity for direct eye contact.[14] These preferences suggest that when planning seating arrangements for group activities, one could facilitate cooperative and social interchange by placing people close together but with some ability to make eye contact with one another (as in a circular or "catty-corner" arrangement). If the activities require competition, somewhat greater distance is desirable with a concomitant increase in the ability to make direct eye contact with one's competitors.

Relational Communication

An aspect of proxemic behavior that is gaining recognition is the relational messages that are conveyed by distance and seating selection. Relational messages are statements that help define the nature of a relationship: whether people like each other, how involved they are in the relationship, who is controlling the relationship, and so forth. Usually such messages are expressed nonverbally, and one of the chief nonverbal channels through which they are communicated is proxemics.

One of the more obvious relational messages signalled proxemically is liking and attraction. Musical lyrics speak of being "close to you," of "getting together," and "the nearness of you." We show our attraction and favorable regard for others by moving closer to them physically and we show our dislike by distancing ourselves. If people choose to sit near us in a group meeting, we take that as a sign of their affection or positive regard for us. Conversely, if they elect to sit at the opposite end of the room, we may interpret that as a message that we are being rejected.

In a similar vein, we interpret distance as a message of involvement. If someone sits very close, orients himself or herself so as to face us directly and/or leans forward, we take that as an indication that this person is very interested in what we have to say, that he or she is involved in our relationship. Certainly that kind of closeness insures high-sensory involvement. If, on the other hand, someone takes a more distal position, orients himself or herself more indirectly (that is, faces away to some degree), or leans away from us, we are likely to read detachment into such behavior. We think that the individual is disinterested in us personally, in our conversation, or in our total relationship; however, the person may simply be expressing a desire for greater privacy.

Another kind of message we may read into a person's distancing behavior is how aroused and uncomfortable, or relaxed and composed, that person is in our presence. Because people in a rage or a high state of emotional arousal often move extremely close to others, sometimes even putting their noses in others' faces, we tend to equate extreme proximity with more arousal and less self-control. By contrast, someone who is very relaxed may lean sideways or backward (if in a chair), thereby increasing the distance to some degree. This creates some difficulty for us in the interpretation of proxemic relational messages because we could interpret backward leaning as having either the negative connotations of disinterest and disregard or the positive connotation of relaxation. We could likewise construe close proximity as a sign of affection and attraction, or as a sign of hostile emotional activation. In other words, the meaning of the proxemic message may be ambiguous by itself. In practice, we rely on other nonverbal cues and the verbal content to decide which interpretation to select.

One final set of meanings associated with spatial behavior further compounds our interpretation task; these concern dominance and control. We have already noted that high-status individuals and group leaders maintain greater distances between themselves and others, and in group meetings tend to occupy the most central, controlling position. The selection of distance or seating position by such individuals not only is instrumental in their gaining control of the group, it also conveys the relational message that they are dominant. By contrast, those adopting subordinate or submissive roles wait for more dominant individuals to dictate the pattern to be observed and may find their personal space violated by the more powerful individuals.

The knowledge that proxemic choices carry relational meaning can be used to your advantage. If you wish to make a group member feel better liked and accepted, you can place him or her in closer proximity to others. If you instead want to communicate rejection and exclusion, you can symbolically convey that message by placing the person at the periphery of the group. If you wish to elicit greater participation on someone's part, you can convey your own interest in what this person has to say by moving closer, facing him or her more directly, and leaning forward. Finally, you can assert power and dominance by violating another's territory or distancing yourself (both of which are ploys that have been recommended for people seriously engaged in power games). If you wish to communicate submissiveness or deference, you may do so by waiting for another's proxemic initiative and then conforming to the pattern that person establishes.[15]

Effects of Spatial Deviancy

Some of the recommendations in the last section may have struck you as unorthodox because most writers in the area of nonverbal communication tell you to conform to the norms if you want to be successful. At least that is the dictum in most popular literature. For some time I have felt that conformity to the norms may not always be the best strategy. Therefore, my colleagues, students, and I undertook a series of experiments to test this thesis.

The initial research began with the premise that deviations from the normative or expected distance may have positive or negative communication consequences, depending on who engages in the distance violation. After some false starts, my cohorts and I arrived at the following predictions: People who are "rewarding," that is, who are high status, attractive, givers of positive feedback, controllers of tangible rewards, or favorably regarded for some other reason, have the freedom to violate distancing expectations with impunity. In small-group language, they have idiosyncratic credits; they are allowed to be deviants at no or little cost. Moreover, when they engage in a violation, they arouse the "victim," making him or her more attentive to the relationship between violator and victim. In the process of searching out explanations for the arousal, they become more conscious of the violator's rewarding characteristics and therefore choose to select positive connotations for the violator's proxemic behavior. The final result is that the violator gains even better communication outcomes than if he or she had conformed to the norm.

In the case of a less rewarding person, for example, someone who is unattractive, who is unpleasant to be around, who is always criticizing, or who is of low status, exactly the opposite predictions are made. Violations of the expected distance—moving closer or farther away—has negative consequences because the aroused victim is more sensitized to the violator's negative characteristics and ascribes more unfavorable meanings to the violator's proxemic behavior. For example, a "close" violation is seen as pushy or threatening; a "far" violation is seen as dislike or disinterest. People who enter a situation with few rewards to offer the recipients, then, are better off conforming to the norms.

A series of experiments has largely supported these predictions. What is of special interest here is one study we conducted using small groups. We wanted to see whether violations would still be effective for a "high-reward" person when in the presence of another rewarding individual who did not deviate. We wanted to see how it would affect ability to influence others and how it would affect the individual's credibility and attraction. At the same time, we were interested in whether the negative consequences for a "low-reward" person would become even worse if that individual engaged in deviant behavior in the presence of another nonrewarding individual who did not deviate.

In brief, this is how we designed the experiment: We told subjects that they were going to participate in a small-group activity intended to test the effects of different sizes of juries on decision making. They were told they had been assigned to a three-person group. Unknown to them, the other two members of the group were our confederates who were dressed to be physically attractive and given more prestigious background in their introductions (high-reward condition) or were made to look unattractive and given less prestigious background (low-reward). One confederate presented defense arguments from an actual murder trial and one presented prosecution arguments. The subject was asked to serve as an undecided member. In the process of presenting their arguments, the confederates either maintained their initial distance (normative condition) or one of them engaged in a violation, moving eighteen inches closer (close violation) or eighteen inches farther (far violation) than the initial distance.

The results were intriguing and have real implications for actual group processes. In the high-reward discussions, the deviating confederate was more persuasive and rated as more attractive, competent, and of good character when he or she engaged in a distance violation—particularly a far violation. This was true both when compared to his or her own results in the normative condition and when compared to the other, nondeviating confederate. In other words, deviant behavior improved the person's influence and interpersonal evaluations relative to conforming to the norm *and* relative to another rewarding group member. In the low-reward discussions, distance violations lowered the confederate's perceived persuasiveness and caused him or her to lose ground on persuasiveness, sociability, and attraction, as compared to the other nondeviating confederate. In other words, the nonrewarding person's deviant behavior tended to confer greater credibility and persuasiveness on his or her opponent. These results thus strongly suggest that deviant proxemic behavior may pay off for people who are well regarded by the rest of the group. For those who are less well regarded, the main beneficiaries of their deviant behavior are their opponents.[16]

Summary

It should be clear from this brief review that proxemic patterns play a subtle but powerful role in human interactions. People's proxemic behavior reflects competing needs between desires for affiliation and desires for privacy. Usually, the distance or seating position they adopt will indicate at what distance they feel comfortable in that context with those participants. The voluntarily selected or environmentally imposed spatial relationships may signal or influence who exercises leadership, may affect who talks to whom on what kinds of topics, and may convey messages about the interpersonal relationships among group members. Finally, contrary to popular opinion, spatial deviancy may sometimes prove profitable in gaining greater control over the group and/or improving others' evaluations of one's credibility and attractiveness.

Notes

1. Edward T. Hall, "The Anthropology of Space: An Organizing Model," in H.M. Proshansky, W.H. Ittelson, and L.G. Rivlin (eds.), *Environmental Psychology: Man and His Physical Setting* (New York: Holt, Rinehart & Winston, 1970), 16–27.
2. *Ibid.*
3. *Ibid.*, 20.
4. Edward T. Hall, *The Silent Language* (Garden City, NY: Doubleday, 1959).
5. Judee K. Burgoon and Stephen B. Jones, "Toward a Theory of Personal Space Expectations and Their Violations," *Human Communication Research*, (1976), 131–146.
6. Robert Sommer, *Personal Space: The Behavioral Basis of Design* (Englewood Cliffs, NJ: Prentice-Hall, 1969).
7. Judee K. Heston and Patrick Garner, "A Study of Personal Spacing and Desk Arrangement in the Learning Environment," Paper presented to the International Communication Association convention, Atlanta, April 1972.
8. For a review of research on norms, see Burgoon and Jones, *op. cit.*, and Judee K. Burgoon and Thomas Saine, *The Unspoken Dialogue: An Introduction to Nonverbal Communication* (Boston: Houghton Mifflin, 1978), 93–96.
9. *Ibid.* Also see Judee K. Heston, "Effects of Anomia and Personal Space Invasion on Anxiety, Nonperson Orientation and Source Credibility," *Central States Speech Journal* 25 (1974), 19–27.

10. For a comprehensive summary of proxemic correlates of status and power, see Nancy M. Henley, *Body Politics* (Englewood Cliffs, NJ: Prentice-Hall, 1977).

11. For some of the classic research in this area, see A. Paul Hare and Robert F. Bales, "Seating Pattern and Small Group Interaction," *Sociometry* 26 (1963), 480–486; L.T. Howells and S.W. Becker, "Seating Arrangement and Leadership Emergence," *Journal of Abnormal and Social Psychology* 64 (1962), 148–150; D.F. Lott and Robert Sommer, "Seating Arrangements and Status," *Journal of Personality and Social Psychology* 7 (1967), 90–95; F.L. Strodtbeck and L.H. Hook, "The Social Dimensions of a Twelve Man Jury Table," *Sociometry* 24 (1961), 397–415; Robert Sommer, "Leadership and Group Geography," *Sociometry* 24 (1961), 499–510; Charles D. Ward, "Seating Arrangement and Leadership Emergence in Small Discussion Groups," *Journal of Social Psychology* 74 (1968), 83–90. See also Marvin E. Shaw, *Group Dynamics: The Psychology of Small Group Behavior* (New York: McGraw-Hill, 1971), 117–154.

12. For a review of this literature, see Heston and Garner; Sommer, 1969.

13. Some of the original research in this area includes Hare and Bales; G. Hearn, "Leadership and the Spatial Factor in Small Groups," *Journal of Abnormal and Social Psychology* 54 (1957), 269–272; Bernard Steinzor, "The Spatial Factor in Face to Face Discussion Groups," *Journal of Abnormal and Social Psychology* 45 (1950), 552–555; Strodtbeck and Hook.

14. M. Cook, "Experiments on Orientation and Proxemics," *Human Relations* 23 (1970), 61–76; Gary A. Norum, Nancy Jo Russo, and Robert Sommer, "Seating Patterns and Group Task," *Psychology of the Schools* 4 (1967), 276-280; Robert Sommer, "Studies of Small Group Ecology" in R.S. Cathcart and L.A. Samovar (eds.), *Small Group Communication: A Reader* 2d ed. (Dubuque, IA: Wm. C. Brown, 1974), 283–293.

15. For reviews of relevant literature and a report of one experiment on relational communication, see Judee K. Burgoon, "Privacy and Communication," in M. Burgoon (ed.), *Communication Yearbook 6* (Beverly Hills, CA: Sage Publications, 1982), 206–249; Judee K. Burgoon, David B. Buller, Jerold L. Hale, and Mark deTurck, "Relational Messages Associated with Immediacy Behaviors," paper presented to the International Communication Association convention, Boston, May 1982.

16. For the details of this particular study, see Judee K. Burgoon, Don W. Stacks, and Steven A. Burch, "The Role of Interpersonal Rewards and Violations of Distancing Expectations in Achieving Influence in Small Groups," *Communication: Journal of the Association of the Pacific* 11 (1982), 114–128. For a review of research on proxemic violations of expectations, see Judee K. Burgoon, "Nonverbal Violations of Expectations," in J. Wiemann and R. Harrison (eds.), *Nonverbal Interaction* 11, Sage Annual Reviews of Communication, (Beverly Hills, CA: Sage, 1983).

Feedback Processes in Task Groups

Beth Haslett and John R. Ogilvie

Human communication involves dialogue between at least two people. An essential part of this dialogue is **feedback**, the response listeners give to others about their behavior. Both communicators give feedback—they respond to each other's behavior. Feedback from others enables us to understand how our behavior affects them, and allows us to modify our behavior to achieve desired goals. Finally, feedback is essential for personal growth and development since others' responses to our behavior help us define our identities.

The setting in which feedback occurs is also important. Task groups, like any work context, are rich in information (Hanser & Muchinsky 1978). Considerable research suggests that individuals actively seek information about themselves and their role in the group (Ashford & Cummings 1983; Larson 1984). A key motivator for this search is uncertainty. It is this uncertainty that gives feedback its value (Ashford & Cummings 1983). When uncertain, individuals feel a tension or uneasiness and seek to reduce those feelings through feedback from others. Early stages of group development are fraught with uncertainty; members are tentative and reluctant to take action. Thus, in task-oriented groups, feedback is a primary means of reducing uncertainty and moving the group along to productive ends.

The function of feedback in systems and cybernetics has long been recognized. Negative feedback acts to correct deviations in the performance of a system that serves to stabilize and maintain it. An example will help to clarify this point. A thermostat in a house controls the furnace by giving the furnace feedback. When the temperature in the house falls below a certain point, say 60 degrees for the brave and energy conscious, the thermostat signals this drop to the furnace, which then starts up. When the temperature rises to a certain level, the thermostat signals a shutdown and the furnace no longer runs. This is an example of a closed loop system, using negative feedback. The thermostat uses only one type of information, which serves to maintain a relatively steady state of room temperature.

Positive feedback in systems terminology is not "good news." It is the amplification of deviations that act to destabilize a system. A manager may at times amplify a disagreement for constructive ends. The disagreement serves as a basis for making changes, which are temporarily destabilizing but beneficial in the long run. Humans, however, do not function as *closed systems* restricted to only limited forms of information. Interpersonal feedback occurs in an open system setting, using negative and positive feedback features. As such, it is varied, flexible, and gathered from a variety of sources.

This article will focus on feedback processes in small task groups. Task groups are a collection of individuals who work interdependently on a task to accomplish a goal.

Permission to reprint must be obtained from the authors. Beth Haslett is affiliated with the Department of Speech Communication, University of Delaware. John R. Ogilvie is affiliated with the Department of Management, University of Delaware.

They are different from informal or friendship groups in that they have a specific purpose to achieve or accomplish. Task groups could include a group of four students required to make a presentation on the dangers of acid rain or a task force in a corporation deciding on which configuration of computer technology to acquire. We all belong to task groups, whether they are in work organizations or social clubs. Groups interact over time to reach goals and satisfy needs (Palazzolo 1981). They also evolve a structure for individual roles and norms to guide behavior. For the group, feedback provides important information on group interaction and group performance. Feedback can improve the effectiveness of group performance since it provides information about how successful the group has been and gives specific suggestions for improvement.

Our research has tried to understand what makes some feedback work more effectively than others. In this paper we will draw on the results of a recently completed study (Ogilvie & Haslett 1985), in which we videotaped a group of students who had to complete several tasks. They were also required to meet and exchange feedback with one another. We then played the videotape of the feedback session to other students several semesters later and asked them to evaluate the way in which feedback was exchanged. Thus, our conclusions are based on our research of task groups, and our suggestions for giving feedback effectively are based on our own personal experiences with groups. In what follows, we will present a discussion of the nature of the feedback process, and the factors influencing the feedback process, and we will offer suggestions for giving feedback effectively.

The Nature of Feedback

Given the important functions of feedback for group performance, it seems crucial that a clear understanding of feedback be developed. However, feedback as a concept and as a process is poorly understood. Scholars analyzing feedback have attempted to conceptualize the underlying dimensions of feedback in order to better understand how feedback works.

Dimensions of Feedback

Dimensions reflect the distinct underlying features of feedback that are evaluated by people. A number of studies have detailed different aspects of feedback. Falcione (1974) had workers fill out a questionnaire on the feedback that they received from their supervisors. He found that workers were sensitive to the reciprocity, perceptiveness, responsiveness, and permissiveness of the feedback. O'Reilley and Anderson (1980) found that managers rated three dimensions of feedback as important: its perceived accuracy and relevance, its developmental nature, and the quantity of feedback. They judged the relevance and accuracy of the feedback as more important than the amount of feedback. Herold and Greller (1977) asked people in a variety of settings how often they received feedback on many different topics. From analysis of these responses, they identified five dimensions of feedback: negative feedback, positive feedback from persons higher in authority, positive feedback from peers, internal (or self-determined) criteria, and work flow

Table 1
Composite Dimensions of Feedback

Dimensions
Message:
Sign (+ or −)
Clarity/Accuracy/Relevance
Source:
Multiple locations
Forceful
Trustworthy
Responsive

feedback. Since each study asked people to evaluate different aspects of feedback in different contexts, these underlying dimensions appear quite diverse.

To address this diversity, we (Ogilvie & Haslett 1985) had students observe and assess feedback with a set of descriptive adjectives compiled from other studies. In our study, the critical dimensions in the feedback process were its dynamism, trust-worthiness, clarity, mood or general tone, and critical nature. This study identified some of the same feedback features as previous studies, establishing the critical nature of feedback.

Several conclusions can be drawn from these studies. (See Table 1 for a set of general underlying dimensions.) The positiveness or critical nature of the feedback appears to be very important. This feature reflects the valence (positive or negative) of the feedback. Another important feature is the clarity, accuracy, or relevance of the message. Other important dimensions of feedback involve the *source* of the feedback. Feedback comes from multiple sources, and those sources are judged on the basis of their trustworthiness, forcefulness, and responsiveness.

Feedback and Group Performance

Since we have defined task groups in terms of accomplishing goals, we will present a model that discusses group productivity and performance. Hackman and Morris (1975) developed a model of group performance, emphasizing the interaction processes among group members. Across groups, performance can vary widely; some groups perform well with little apparent difficulty. Others struggle constantly and still barely reach mediocrity. According to Hackman and Morris,

> The challenge is to identify, measure and change those aspects of group interaction process that contribute to such obvious differences in group effectiveness (1975, 46).

To this end, they identified three determinants of performance. First, group members need relevant skills and knowledge. If those skills are absent, group performance will be hurt, and goals cannot be attained. Second, sufficient motivation must be present to coordinate activities with fellow group members and complete tasks. The third

Feedback Functions	Process Determinants	Outcomes

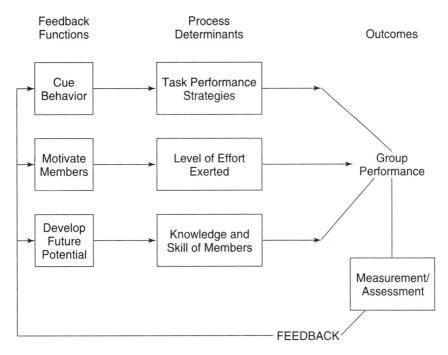

Figure 1. Feedback and group performance. (Adapted from Nadler 1979.)

determinant is the selection of appropriate task performance strategies. Groups can have the necessary knowledge and effort, but may not be effective because of inappropriate approaches to completing the task. (See Figure 1 for a model of this process.)

This model can also be used to understand the functions of feedback, its influence on performance, and its influence on the attitudes of group members (Nadler 1979). One important function of feedback is to correct inappropriate behavior of members. This corrective effect is often called *cueing*. It signals that the task behavior is not desired and has the effect of correcting inappropriate strategies. Feedback can also function to set goals and *motivate* members, addressing the effort determinant. Individuals may receive feedback judging their efforts to be below the group's standard (i.e., norms) or that more cooperation is needed to accomplish goals. Supervisory appraisals often establish specific goals to motivate future performance. These appraisals may also suggest areas for skill improvement or enhancement. Similarly, other group members may suggest specific areas of knowledge or skill development through feedback, which can improve performance. This type of feedback functions to develop members' *potential* for future activities. By developing new skills and acquiring knowledge, feedback functions to help individuals to acquire some degree of mastery over their environment (Ashford & Cummings 1983). Thus, feedback appears relevant for all aspects of group performance. To be effective, performance must be measured or assessed and feedback sought from multiple sources. In short, groups cannot be effective without feedback.

Feedback as a Communicative Process

While the underlying dimensions of feedback are useful in revealing the complexity of feedback, additional insight into feedback can be gained when feedback is viewed as a communicative process (Ilgen, Fisher & Taylor 1979). That is, while feedback is an essential component of any communication model, feedback itself can be studied as communication. As suggested by dimensional studies and other research, we can assess feedback by examining the *source* of the feedback, the feedback *message* itself (e.g., is the feedback positive or negative, is it task-oriented or process-oriented, etc.?), and the *receiver* of the feedback (e.g., an individual, group, or organization).

Ilgen, Fisher, and Taylor (1979) attempted to understand how and why individuals respond to feedback. They identified four important processes in feedback. First, individuals must *perceive* the feedback. Second, they must *accept* it. Third, they must then develop the *intentions to respond*, and finally must set specific, moderately difficult *goals for improvement*.

They concluded that the perception of feedback is a function of the source, message, and recipient. In addition, they suggested that the perception and acceptance of feedback are critical elements in determining the receiver's response to feedback. Generally, the source of the feedback has the greatest impact on its acceptance, although other research has indicated that the influence of the source and message interact with one another (Ilgen, Mitchell & Fredrickson 1981; Ogilvie & Haslett 1985).

Viewing feedback as a communicative process allows us to look more specifically at the different aspects of feedback. We now turn to an examination of factors influencing the giving and receiving of feedback. These factors will be examined as source characteristics, message characteristics, and recipient characteristics.

Factors Influencing Feedback

A. Source Characteristics

We receive feedback from a variety of sources. In task groups and in work organizations, there are generally five sources of feedback: self (intrinsic), the task, peers, supervisors, and the organization itself. Task and self-generated sources are psychologically closer to the individual and are seen as more valuable (Greller & Herold 1975). More external, distant sources of feedback require more scrutiny because they cannot be trusted as automatically as intrinsic sources. If feedback from some of these sources is blocked, other problems arise. Obstruction of task and supervisory sources of feedback results in higher levels of anxiety among workers. Blockage of supervisory sources is also strongly related to job satisfaction and intention to leave the company (Walsh, Ashford & Hill 1985).

A number of other characteristics of these sources have been found to influence the feedback process. Among the influential variables are the trustworthiness of the source, the power and status of the source, the relationship between the source and recipient, and the communicative style of the source.

1. *Trustworthiness.* A source's trustworthiness and credibility (believability) are major influences on the acceptance of feedback (O'Reilly & Anderson 1980).

These two issues—trustworthiness and credibility—cannot be discussed separately since we tend to believe those we trust, and trust those whom we believe. Feedback from credible, trustworthy sources receives more attention as well as acceptance from recipients. Those giving positive feedback to others are also perceived as being more trustworthy and credible. Leaders' feedback is also perceived as being more accurate, trustworthy, and credible than that of peers, although peers and leaders show high agreement on their feedback of others.

In our study, trust was an important dimension of giving feedback. Trusted feedback was also viewed as being credible and fair. When comparing the trustworthiness of feedback to other variables, we found that it was associated with perceptions of how effectively the feedback was given. Feedback that was communicated in a responsive and relaxed manner was also more trusted. Trust seems linked to reciprocity. If the person believes that you are fair in giving feedback, you should be relaxed and responsive to them. If you are defensive and nervous, then the feedback will not be trusted. Clearly, trust is an important feature; it may be the "golden rule" of feedback. If you trust the feedback, you assume that the motives and intentions of the source are fair.

2. *Power and Status of the Source.* In general, the more powerful the source, the more attention and acceptance the recipients give the feedback. Power can be measured in a number of ways. A supervisor who has direct control over his or her employees will exert a powerful influence over the people she or he supervises. This influence may also explain the strong effect that the obstruction of supervisory feedback has on employees. The absence of information causes anxiety and uncertainty. Thus, leaders generally are perceived as giving more accurate, credible feedback.

Power could also be measured in terms of expertise. We are not likely to accept feedback from a source we consider inexperienced or unknowledgeable about a particular area. Generally, it appears that for feedback to be readily accepted the source of the feedback must have some competency with respect to the type of feedback being given.

Our research suggests that in many groups where there is no formally designated leader, the manner in which feedback is given can also have much influence on the receiver. In our research, dynamism (a combination of activity and strength) accounted for much of the variation in perceptions of feedback. Dynamism was most strongly related to the overall impression group members leave and accounted for most of the individual differences in the way that feedback was given. Similarly, a communication style that was verbally assertive was strongly related to dynamism and to perceptions of the effectiveness with which the feedback was given.

3. *Communicator Style.* Communicator style refers to the *manner* in which feedback is given. The more consideration and influence a leader has, the greater perceived relevance for that leader's feedback. Ogilvie and Haslett (1985) found significant communicative differences across group members in their styles of giving feedback. Group members varied in the dynamism, clarity, mood, and criticalness of their feedback. Effectiveness of feedback was significantly related to the source's verbally assertive style, dynamism, responsiveness, and being relaxed. Dynamism

and clarity of feedback were also positively related to the impression group members made. Feedback style has been positively related to a recipient's job satisfaction and acceptance of feedback as well.

B. Message Characteristics

1. *Content.* A message can contain several types of information. One type of information refers to behaviors which help to attain a desired goal. This type of information is referred to as *referent* information and is similar to the cueing function described above. Thus, a feedback message containing referent information should improve group productivity. Another type of information is more subjective—it tells a person how their behavior is perceived and evaluated. This type of message contains *appraisal* information and is actually more useful to the individual in reducing their uncertainty about their role in the group.
2. *Timing.* A number of studies have demonstrated that effective feedback is more effective when closer in time to the occurrence. That is, feedback should be given relatively close to the behaviors or job being done. Delays may reduce the impact and relevance of the feedback.
3. *Channel.* Feedback can be given across a number of different modes or channels: feedback can be written or oral, verbal or nonverbal. Zajonc (1980) found that important affective/evaluative information is given nonverbally, while cognitive information is presented verbally. The evaluative content delivered through nonverbal channels is similar to the appraisal content mentioned above. Thus, some channels may be used more for some types of content than others. Both effect and cognitions are important aspects of giving feedback (Larson 1984).

   Furnham (1982) investigated the effect of message content and channel on giving messages. He found that people preferred to give messages face-to-face, rather than by writing or the telephone. In general, "the nature of the communication to be made determines the choice of situation in which to communicate." Subjects preferred to communicate most messages in a one-on-one situation, especially for messages that were situation-specific (e.g., giving bad news or disclosing some personal information).

   Daft and Lengel (1984) have noted that the channels or media used to communicate vary in terms of their information richness. Face-to-face communication is the most rich while data on a computer printout are relatively low in richness. Very rich media, like oral communication, allow for more rapid, timely feedback and are more useful in solving complex problems in which more feedback is needed.
4. *Message Valence.* Perhaps the most important message characteristic influencing feedback is whether it is positive or negative (i.e., its sign or valence). In general, positive messages are more accepted than negative, while negative messages seem to be rejected unless they are from high-status sources. Positive messages produce higher trust among individuals as well as enhance group cohesion. Generally, individuals also find positive messages more believable and acceptable. Gordon (1985) also found a significant correlation between individuals giving positive information and receiving positive comments. The more a group member was perceived as giving conducive feedback, the more she or he received in turn.

In contrast, negative messages are often not transmitted to the intended recipient. People are reluctant to give negative information to others, even while they acknowledge that the intended recipients have a right to know, and a greater desire and interest to know than others. This generalization has been documented in a wide variety of situations, across different communicators and recipients, and across different channels. Tesser and Rosen (1975) found that pleasantness of a message was significantly correlated with the likelihood of its being transmitted (r = 0.73). If there is a negative message to be transmitted, frequently a subordinate is asked to do it. They suggest that people are reluctant to transmit negative messages because they fear being negatively evaluated themselves; they are concerned about the mood created for the intended recipient, and they experience guilt and anxiety over transmitting the message. Tesser and Rosen also suggest that negative messages are threatening to the self-image of the intended recipient and thus would negatively influence the relationship between the source and intended recipient. However, negative messages have the greatest potential for improving performance. The manner in which these messages are delivered is most critical so that one avoids eliciting defensive reactions and/or damaging the relationship. (See the last section of this article for more suggestions on giving feedback.)

C. Recipient Characteristics

The characteristics of the intended recipient also influence the feedback process. People send messages to accomplish specific goals that are designed for a specific target audience. It seems reasonable to assume that individuals design their feedback with specific purposes and specific recipients in mind. Since feedback is designed to give an individual information about his or her behavior, obviously those messages will vary as a function of the particular intended recipient. While some studies have explored the recipient's characteristics and their impact on the feedback process, more research needs to be done in this area.

1. *Recipient's Mind-Set.* One of the most influential factors in determining the recipient's response to feedback is his or her mind-set or frame-of-reference when feedback is received. This temporary frame-of-reference influences the recipient's perception, acceptance, and response to feedback. If an employee has just had a difficult time with a customer, he or she will not be receptive to a co-worker providing critical feedback about her or his work habits. Expectations can also influence a recipient's mind-set and be a major factor in his or her perception of feedback (Ilgen et al. 1979). We tend to see and hear what we expect, distorting the feedback received.

2. *Personal Qualities.* Several more stable enduring characteristics of the recipient also influence the feedback process. Self-esteem and social anxiety were two personality variables that have been studied in this context (Ilgen et al. 1979). People who have varying degrees of self-esteem interpret feedback differently. Individuals with high *self-esteem* interpret negative feedback in an ambiguous way and thus do not respond as strongly to it. In contrast, people with high *social*

Table 2
Summary of Communication Features in Feedback

Source Characteristics	Message Characteristics	Recipient Characteristics
Trustworthiness	Content	Mind-Set
	Referent	
Power and Status	Appraisal	Expectations
Communication Style	Timing	Personality
Assertive		Repressors/
Dynamic	Channel	Self-Esteem
Relaxed		Sensitizers/
Responsive	Sign or Valence	Social Anxiety

anxiety anticipate receiving more negative feedback than those having less social anxiousness and consequently tend to interpret feedback as being more negative.

Varca and Levy (1984) examined several related variables in the way that people respond to feedback. They noted that critical feedback represents a threat to an individual's self-esteem. However, people may cope differently with these threats. Some choose to ignore or deny the threat posed by critical feedback. These people are *repressors*. Repressors tend to have high self-esteem since the feedback is not seen as relevant. An alternative means of coping is to amplify the threat and its consequences by an excessive expression of anxious feelings. These individuals are *sensitizers*. The exaggeration by sensitizers helps them cope by reducing the possibility of consequences from negative events. Such exaggerated expectations of consequences are rarely met and the sensitizer is much relieved. Again, sensitizers are similar to those with high social anxiety in that they interpret feedback more negatively.

Source, message, and recipient characteristics are summarized in Table 2.

How to Give Feedback

Giving and receiving feedback is an integral part of interpersonal communication. Many interactions will occur in a small-group setting, whether it be a sorority or a task force recommending changes in organization structure. Within organizations, feedback is critical because employees need to perform their tasks adequately so the organization continues to survive. For every organizational member, then, understanding feedback is important. However, we also need to know how to give feedback effectively in order to maximize our performance and the performance of others. Giving feedback effectively is, of course, particularly important for those in managerial positions. In what follows, we suggest some general strategies for giving feedback effectively and deal particularly with the problems of giving negative feedback.

General Communicative Strategies

The best general suggestions for effective communication in small groups has been succinctly expressed by Gouran and Fisher (1984).

In general, those communicative behaviors that are task oriented, that serve to keep energy focused on the group's goals, and that show a concern with maintaining workable interpersonal relations have correspondingly positive effects on the quality of interaction, the ease with which a task is completed, members' acceptance of group positions, and the satisfaction of the participants (630).

Generally, then, maintaining good working relationships with others requires that we communicate as constructively as possible.

Some communicative strategies for giving feedback (and receiving it as well) that facilitate a constructive working environment are outlined below. First, in order for feedback to be effective, it needs to be fairly *direct* and *specific*. A general remark such as "That's the wrong way to do that" is so vague and general as to be of no value in changing how the task is done. In contrast, a specific, direct message such as "The water pressure must always be maintained at 100 pounds by adjusting this valve" details the necessary activities for successful task completion. An example from the small group that was videotaped in our study makes this point quite succinctly:

C: I put __ as a dominator because he—asserts authority and especially I think over __ umm—I think that the group impact I think—you know, I also put you as task and socially oriented but—I think it's a little annoying sometimes how—I don't know—it seems—like you ummmmmmm/

D: /Say it.

In this situation, C is struggling for words, and D, who is receiving this feedback, quite clearly wants C to spit it out! Contrast this with the following example of specific, direct feedback:

A: I put __ as a harmonizer, um, when we have a lot of tension in the group she tends to try and break it down. . . .

Second, effective feedback needs to be *supported by evidence*. Generally people are much more responsive and accepting of comments when some rationale has been given. This can be seen in the following comment made in the small-group feedback session.

B: I see you in a very dominant role because of your personality. You're aggressive, you're assertive, and you have your own ideas and you display them. Impact on the group as far as that's concerned I find very good for one thing because you provide direction and you also push the group to achieve. . . .

In this example, a judgment was made, but B gave reasons for his judgment and the effect of these behaviors. In addition, providing reasons for actions may forestall or defuse critical reactions, as well as giving the appearance of thoughtful deliberation behind the recommendations.

Finally, feedback should clearly *separate the issue under discussion from the personalities* involved. That is, as Gouran and Fisher suggest, messages should be focused on the task to be accomplished. Both sources and targets of feedback messages should maintain a careful distinction between task and personality.

While these general strategies are useful in giving feedback to others, negative messages represent a situation that deserves special consideration. It deserves separate

Table 3
Summary of Suggestions for Giving Feedback

1. Be specific and direct.
2. Support comments with evidence.
3. Separate the issue from the person.
4. "Sandwich" negative messages between positive ones.
5. Pose the situation as a mutual problem.
6. Mitigate or soften negative messages to avoid overload.
7. Timing: Deliver feedback close to occurrence.
8. Manner of delivery:
   a. Assertive, dynamic;
   b. Trustworthy, fair and credible;
   c. Relaxed and responsive;
   d. Preserve public image of recipient.

discussion because of people's general tendency to avoid sending negative messages, and the guilt and anxiety produced by giving negative messages. However, there are situations in which negative assessments must be given and our concern here is how they might be conveyed most effectively. (See Table 3 for a summary of suggestions for giving feedback.)

Giving Feedback Containing Negative Messages

While a voluminous literature on feedback has noted the reluctance to transmit negative messages, very little research has addressed the issue of how such negative information can be transmitted. One study (Davies & Jacobs 1985) looked at the effect of combining negative (N) and positive (P) messages and assessing the effectiveness of various combinations. Specifically, chains of feedback (PNP, PPN, NPN, and NNP) were examined. It was found that the PNP chain (positive message, negative message, and a final positive comment) was the most effective format for giving feedback. PNP sequences were rated as significantly more accurate, credible, desirable, and had the most positive emotional responses. In addition, PNP sequences contributed most to group cohesiveness and a positive group experience. Interestingly, NPN sequences were viewed most negatively and PPN sequences were not superior to NNP sequences except in desirability. This study suggests that when it is necessary to give negative information, it is most effective to "sandwich" the negative message between two positive comments. For example, "Our engineering division has been doing exceptionally well. Although your group has had the lowest performance, the latest figures show some improvement." The negative comment about low performance has been surrounded by positive comments.

Beyond "sandwiching" the negative feedback, another communicative strategy is to approach the problem area from a collective or collaborative perspective. That is, rather than saying what the problem with the target's group or behavior is, it is more effective to approach the situation as a *problem* that affects both of us. For example, instead of saying "Your group is really performing poorly," a supervisor might say, "We seem to have a problem with the group's decreasing productivity. What do you think might be done about it?" The latter comments invite the subordinate to think constructively about an issue that admittedly affects both of them, rather than blaming the subordinate and creating resentment and hostility.

Another strategy might be to *mitigate* or *soften* the force of the negative message through the use of disclaimers or qualifications. Phrases of uncertainty, such as "I'm really not sure about this but I think that . . . ," or the use of tag questions such as "don't you think so, too?" soften the force of a negative comment. In the videotape data collected by Ogilvie and Haslett (1985), group members frequently used disclaimers or tag questions to soften the force of their remarks and thus preserve all participants' positive public image. Below are some examples of this from our data.

> A: I also put, um, gatekeeper down for myself because I feel that I encourage others and facilitate participation, and I'm always interested in what other people have to say within the group.
> *And I guess that's, I don't know,* a positive impact. I'm sure there are negative things about what I do *but I'm not quite sure* what they are.

In this example, the italicized portion reflects A's qualifications about what the effects of her actions are and thus weakens her self-criticism. Another member of the group, a male, uses the same qualifying strategy in giving feedback to other group members on their performances.

> B: *I think, I find that I don't know,* I see us struggling to be dominating, a dominant role, we seem like we're trying to compete with one another at times for either attention or even impact and input into the group.

The uncertainty projected through these comments softens the impact of the negative comment and lessens the likelihood of a negative response to the initial negative comments. Such qualifiers help preserve good working relationships when difficult evaluative comments must be made—and all groups will experience moments when negative comments must be made.

Finally, the *language* used in giving feedback is important. Generally, group members should be descriptive in their language, rather than being evaluative. The American Management Association, in its pamphlet on supervisory management, suggests that supervisors focus on describing the problem, rather than blaming employees for the problem. For example, instead of stating "Bill, you are arrogant and domineering," rephrase that and say, "Bill, many colleagues perceive your attitude as being arrogant and domineering." With that rephrasing, attention is focused on the behavior rather than the person: this lessens the likelihood of a negative, defensive response on the part of Bill.

Generally, then, although negative messages are difficult to give and receive, it can be done when attention is given to *how* such feedback can be constructively given. We suggest that the most important consideration is to maintain everyone's positive public image. By maintaining all participants' public images, the group, as a whole, preserves good working relationships among its members. This, in turn, enables the group to be productive, efficient, and cohesive. When negative feedback must be given, members can: (1) sandwich the negative comment with positive comments;

(2) frame the problem or issue as one that involves both of you; (3) use qualifiers to soften the force of the negative feedback; (4) give reasons for the negative feedback; and (5) use descriptive rather than evaluative language.

Conclusions and Implications

Throughout this article, we have suggested that feedback is a central component of human communication. Feedback is a complex, multifaceted process that is critical to interpersonal and group effectiveness since it enables communicators to understand the effects of their behavior.

Feedback itself, as a process, may also be analyzed as a separate communicative activity. We have analyzed feedback as a communicative process and assessed the impact of source, message, and recipient on the feedback process. The most influential source characteristics are the source's power and status, trustworthiness, credibility, forcefulness, and responsiveness. It is also important to keep in mind that feedback comes from many different sources, and that each source may be valued for a different type of feedback. The feedback message, to be effective, should be clear, accurate, relevant, and positive. Negative feedback is generally avoided by both source and recipient, and anxiety and guilt are associated with negative feedback. Finally, recipients of feedback perceive feedback differently as a function of self-esteem and other personal characteristics. While these general findings provide insight into the feedback process, feedback processes are still in need of further study. We have little understanding, for example, of the complex interactions among the various dimensions of feedback: What occurs when a trusted source gives very negative feedback? What are the effects of that negative feedback on the source's perceived trustworthiness and his or her subsequent relationship with the recipient?

Given the complexity of feedback and its importance, we have suggested some strategies to follow in order to enhance the effectiveness of feedback offered to others. Generally, sources need to be constructive, clear, direct, and specific. In addition, a source's remarks should clearly separate the issue from the recipient's personality: critique the behavior at issue rather than the person.

Negative feedback, as already pointed out, creates special difficulties because of the general avoidance of negative messages. However, at times, negative feedback must be given, and we suggested a number of strategies by which this could be done to maximize the feedback's effectiveness. In particular, we suggested trying to "sandwich" the negative comments among positive comments; to use descriptive rather than evaluative language; and to maintain all participants' positive public images.

To effectively communicate, we believe it is particularly important to communicate in such a way that all participants have positive attitudes about themselves and others in that group. Even very difficult, negative comments can be given *if sufficient attention has been paid to how to express those comments as constructively as possible*. This, we submit, is especially important in giving feedback to others and the most challenging part of the communicative process. With the information provided in this article, hopefully both sources and recipients will have a better understanding of the feedback process and how to give/receive feedback with maximum effectiveness.

References

Ashford, S.J., and Cummings, L.L. (1983). "Feedback as an Individual Resource: Personal Strategies of Creating Information." *Organizational Behavior and Human Performance* 32, 370–398.

Daft, R.L., and Lengel, R.H. (1984). "Information Richness: A New Approach Managing Information Processing and Organizational Design." In B. Staw and L.L. Cummings (eds.), *Research in Organizational Behavior* 6, 118–133.

Davies, D., and Jacobs, A. (1985). "'Sandwiching' Complex Interpersonal Feedback." *Small Group Behavior* 16, 387–396.

Falcione, R. (1974). "Communication Climate and Satisfaction with Immediate Supervision." *Journal of Applied Communication Research* 2, 13–20.

Furnham, A. (1982). "The Message, the Context and the Medium." *Language and Communication* 2, 33–47.

Gordon R. (1985). "Self-Disclosure of Interpersonal Feedback." *Small Group Behavior* 16, 411–413.

Gouran, D., and Fisher, B.A. (1984). "The Function of Human Communication in the Formation, Maintenance, and Performance of Small Groups." In G. Miller and M. Knapp, (eds.), *The Handbook of Interpersonal Communication.* Sage: Beverly Hills, CA.

Greller, M.M., and Herold, D.M. (1975). "Sources of Feedback: A Preliminary Investigation." *Organizational Behavior and Human Performance* 13, 244–256.

Hackman, J.R., and Morris, C.G. (1975). "Group Tasks, Group Interaction Process and Group Performance Effectiveness: A Review and Proposed Integration." In L. Berkowitz (ed.), *Advances in Experimental Social Psychology* 8. New York: Academic Press.

Hanser, L. and Muchinsky, D. (1978). "Work as an Information Environment." *Organizational Behavior and Human Performance* 21, 47–60.

Herold, D.M., and Greller, M.M. (1977). "Feedback: The Definition of a Construct." *Academy of Management* 20 (1), 142–147.

Ilgen, D.R., Fisher, C.D., and Taylor, M.S. (1979). "Consequences of Individual Feedback on Behavior in Organizations." *Journal of Applied Psychology* 64 (4), 349–371.

Ilgen, D.R., Mitchell, T.R., and Frederickson, J.W. (1981). "Poor Performers: Supervisors and Subordinates Responses." *Organizational Behavior and Human Performance* 27, 386–410.

Larson, J.M., Jr. (1984). "Performance Feedback Processes: A Preliminary Model." *Organizational Behavior and Human Performance* 34, 42–76.

Nadler, D.A. (1979). "The Effects of Feedback on Task Group Behavior: A Review of Experimental Research." *Organizational Behavior and Human Performance* 23, 309–338.

Ogilvie, J.R., and Haslett, B. (1985). "Communicating Peer Feedback in a Task Group." *Human Communication Research* 12 (1), 79–98.

O'Reilly, C., and Anderson, J. (1980). "Trust and Communication of Performance Appraisal Information: The Effect of Feedback on Performance and Job Satisfaction." *Human Communication Research* 6, 290–298.

Palazzolo, C.S. (1981). *Small Groups, an Introduction.* Belmont, CA: Wadsworth Publishing.

Tesser, A., and Rosen, S. (1975). "Reluctance to Transmit Bad News." In L. Berkowitz (ed.), *Advances in Experimental Social Psychology* 8, 193–232. New York: Academic Press.

Varca, P.E., and Levy, J.C. (1984). "Individual Differences in Response to Unfavorable Group Feedback." *Organizational Behavior and Human Performance* 33, 100–111.

Walsh, J.P., Ashford, S.J., and Hill, T.E. (1985). "Feedback Obstruction: The Influence of the Information Environment on Employee Turnover Intentions." *Human Relations* 38 (1), 23–46.

Zajonc, R. (1980). "Feeling and Thinking: Preferences Need No Inferences." *American Psychologist* 35 (2), 151–175.

Listener Preferences: The Paradox of Small-Group Interactions

Kittie W. Watson

Group interaction is essential for achieving goals in families, schools, civic organizations, and businesses. In fact, the number of meetings used to address issues and solve problems is on the rise. Take a look at newspaper listings for groups meetings. You'll find self-help, therapy, civic, business, and focus groups. Especially when problems arise, most people think of the positive benefits of a united front and seek group affiliation rather than tackling problems alone. The power behind neighbor watch, union, family, and business groups encourages people to get involved with others.

Group Membership: To Be or Not to Be

Most people enter groups with a positive frame of mind and anticipate personal, professional, or economical rewards from participation. At the same time, people look forward to influencing group members and outcomes. Unfortunately, as we participate in groups, we are quickly reminded of the difficulty of working with others. Group decisions take time, require cooperation, and usually benefit the majority rather than the individual.

When group outcomes are different from those that individual members would like, some people find groups oppressive. Think about the groups to which you have belonged. Teenagers feel frustrated with parents who are unwilling to listen to views about curfews. College students may enjoy the social association of a fraternity or sorority but dislike decisions made concerning functions and dues. Employees may like a job but become irritated with demanding supervisors or uncooperative coworkers who fail to listen to suggestions. In some instances the negative associations become so strong that teenagers, college students, and employees strike out on their own and vow to live or work independently. Still, the need for affiliation seldom entirely disappears.

Smith and Berg (1987), in *The Paradox of Group Life*, suggest that individuals tend "to forget or ignore the problems created by groups while attending to the problems we hope will be alleviated by them. In a way, we find ourselves caught in a paradox, for remembering what we know about groups is both enabling and disabling. Attention to the difficult and problematic aspects of life in groups makes it possible to manage them more effectively, but the memories generated by this attention may dissuade us altogether from connecting with groups (4)." Group communication provides many opportunities and challenges. This essay is designed to help you examine one particular challenge in groups: *listening*. It will explore principles of listening and listener preferences, and will suggest ways for improving listening in small groups.

This essay was written especially for this edition. All rights reserved. The discussion of listener preferences is adapted from *Listeners, Lemmings, and Black Widow Spiders: Understanding the Listening Paradox* copyrighted by Larry Barker and Kittie Watson. Kittie Watson is affiliated with Tulane University.

The Powerful Role of Listening in Small Groups

As individuals mature and seek professional positions, the time they spend in meetings and groups increases dramatically. The substance that connects group members and allows group functioning is listening. Even though we are a society of talkers, nothing gets accomplished without listeners. Much too often group members concentrate on getting their ideas heard rather than on listening to what others have to say. Listening in a group involves more than just hearing. Listening is hard work and requires effort to do well. In the most successful groups, everyone takes mutual responsibility for communication and listening. Our role as a listener is to plan strategies to help us listen better and as speakers it is to plan strategies to help others listen more effectively.

What Group Members Gain from Listening

When group members listen to each other, group member relations improve. Members feel as though they are valued and tend to contribute more frequently during interactions. Along with the likelihood of improving relationships, effective listening can also reduce meeting time. With an estimated fifteen million meetings taking place each morning in the United States, think about the time wasted due to ineffective listening. When information has to be repeated because one person doesn't listen, the time of all group members is wasted. In a six-person group, repeating five minutes of information wastes thirty minutes of time. When group members listen effectively they decrease time waste and may even limit the number of meetings necessary.

The Power of the Listener: To Listen or Not

Because speakers initiate communication, more emphasis is placed on the role of speakers during meetings than on the role of listeners. Small-group classes give speakers advice about how to conduct problem-solving sessions and usually grade group members on verbal contributions they make to group processes. Few courses emphasize the role of listeners. Too often we forget that listeners are the ones who choose to listen or not. No matter how skilled, charismatic, or engaging a speaker is, the listener determines when, to whom, and how he or she listens. In actuality, listeners hold the power during small-group interactions. Therefore, it is critical to understand the process of listening and to discover what encourages us to listen.

Listening Energy: Keep an Eye on Your Gauge

Group members attend meetings with varying degrees of listening energy (Barker & Watson 1994). Some people attend enthusiastically; however, many attend because they have to. Especially when group members have little or no incentive to attend meetings, their energy may be low and listening errors may occur. Factors such as listener fatigue, disinterest, or personal bias increase the likelihood of listening mistakes. Unfortunately, unlike other communication skills that can be observed directly, most listening errors go unnoticed until it is too late.

We, as listeners, enter meetings with a supply of listening energy. The energy we have influences how well we listen. At the beginning of meetings, most people may have a full tank of listening energy. As meetings progress, listening tanks empty and listening ability diminishes. Listening energy is zapped by boring speakers, competing outside noises, low lighting, hunger pangs, or thoughts about other responsibilities. During routine and pleasant interactions, little energy is used. If, however, an argument or conflict occurs, listeners begin to empty their tanks. Thus, by the time the most important issues are discussed, many group members have lost the ability to concentrate.

Think about how difficult it is to listen when you feel tired, sick, rushed, or hungry. In most of these instances, energy reserves are used to maintain body functioning rather than for listening. Listeners with low energy usually prefer to avoid difficult or challenging listening situations that require concentration. Instead of engaging in heated conversations, for example, group members with low listening energy probably daydream, fake attention, or agree with others just to avoid further discussion.

Why Listening Mistakes Occur in Groups

Group members often fail to listen effectively during group interactions because of diffusion of responsibility (Barker, Johnson, & Watson 1991). With diffusion of responsibility, accountability for the success of the group is shared among group members. In small groups, members usually spend far more time listening than speaking. In a three-person group in which all members participate equally, for example, each person listens approximately two-thirds of the time. In a ten-person group, each person listens 90 percent of the time. The social pressure to listen is not as strong in a group as it is in a dyad. During one-on-one conversations, poor listening can be detected easily. During meetings it is difficult to attend to all group members at once and ineffective listening goes unnoticed.

One way to help ensure more accurate communication is to examine the challenges and difficulties listeners face during meetings (Watson & Barker 1994). When attention is high, people make conscious efforts to listen to others through attending behaviors such as eye contact, forward lean, facial expressions, and concentration on the message. Unfortunately, many listeners start out with focused attention but become distracted, unconsciously allowing objects, speakers, or events to divert their attention.

It is common to miss information when trying to listen to more than one conversation, thinking about what we want to say next, or daydreaming. In addition, since group members differ in their experiences, knowledge, and attitudes, we often interpret messages differently. For example, consider a team meeting with five people present. One group member says, "We need to discuss male and female compatibility issues." A person with a computer background might think cable compatibility. Another person, not listening carefully, may hear "mail compatibility issues" and assume the discussion is about the new e-mail system. Others may know that gender diversity topics will be discussed. To ensure accurate communication we must be sure that messages are interpreted correctly.

After ideas are shared, listeners judge what they've heard and determine whether or not to believe the message, agree with the speaker, and/or retain the information. Listeners often evaluate the relative importance of the individual parts of a message and the message as a whole differently. These assessments are based on the listener's perceptions of what the speaker believes is important as well as on the listener's values. When the group leader says, "Please get your comments to me as soon as possible," individuals react variously. Some respond immediately, others in a few days, and some may never respond.

Without prior training, most people make hasty evaluations. Probably one of the most dramatic assessing errors that has received national attention occurred before the space shuttle *Challenger* disaster. Engineers warned officials that the O-rings were defective and needed further inspection. Tragically, the information was evaluated as not critical enough to stop the launch. It was not until later that a full investigation discovered that the disaster could have been avoided if someone had made a different evaluation. Today NASA employees receive training in listening.

Listening errors occur because of a lack of or unclear feedback. Many of us have been trained to mask or minimize our responses to avoid giving our feelings or thoughts away. During meetings, however, it is critical to give feedback about the message to speakers. When others get feedback, they can check for understanding and test the accuracy of their interpretations. Even if we don't speak, we send nonverbal responses. In fact, a nonverbal response such as the "silent treatment" can actually be a clearer message than words.

If listeners fail to attend to messages, there is little or no chance that listeners can make accurate interpretations, evaluations, or responses. Remember, however, that speakers often don't find that errors have occurred until it is too late. Therefore, if we want to guarantee accurate communication, we need to know where listening errors are likely to occur and take steps to minimize them.

As you've read about how and why listening errors occur, you've become aware of one of the listening paradoxes. Groups can be used to help insure better decision making, but at the same time they can cause decision making to get bogged down. In addition, the nature of group processes both encourages and discourages mistakes. When energy is high and group members work to insure quality decisions, groups are very helpful. However, when listening energy is depleted, many groups make poor decisions without being aware of the possible outcomes. Finally, different characteristics among listeners can serve both destructive or productive purposes. The next section examines differences among listeners.

How People Listen in Groups: Listener Preferences

Most of us find it easier to listen to some people than to others. Based on our preferences, we unknowingly make judgments and decisions that affect communication in groups. Some people prefer to hear from only credible sources, others want to be entertained, some focus on the others' needs, and still others want a speaker to get to the point as quickly as possible. The following discussion provides general descriptions of four listener preferences: *people-oriented, action-oriented, content-oriented, and time-oriented* (Watson & Barker 1992; Watson, Barker & Weaver 1992; Weaver, Watson & Barker 1993; Watson, Barker & Weaver 1994).

Our listening preferences develop over a lifetime as a function of socialization and reinforcement. Before trying to determine your preferences, consider the following (Watson, Barker & Weaver 1993; 1994).[1]

There is No One Best Way to Listen

Try not to label listener preferences as good or bad. Each preference has characteristics that can be either positive or negative. However, listeners need to learn to adapt to the demands of the group. The best listeners go beyond their preferences so their behaviors match group needs. Understanding listener preference patterns in the general population can help us identify people's preference traits. Based on research results using the *Listener Preference Profile* (Watson, Barker & Weaver 1992; Weaver, Watson & Barker 1993), approximately 40 percent of the general population uses a single-listener preference. Of this percentage, *people- and action-oriented preferences are the most prevalent*. About 25 percent of the general population has two listening preferences, and about 15 percent of the general population has three or four preferences. About 20 percent of the general population failed to indicate any listening preference.

Effective Communicators Adapt to Different Situations

Because of our preferences, we get in the habit of listening in only one way in most listening situations. While we don't usually think about changing the way we listen, listening would be more efficient and enjoyable if we did. Wouldn't it be more appropriate to *modify* our listening rather than expect others to adapt to us? Think of different listening needs when serving as a juror, chatting with a group of friends, planning a family vacation, or participating in a natural work team. Some require critical- and others social-listening skills. We need to learn to adjust our preferences to meet the needs of unique listening situations.

Listener Behaviors are Influenced by Time Pressures and Relationships

The way we choose to listen to others is influenced by how much time we have to listen as well as the relationship we have with group members. For example, because of time pressures during midterm exams, one group member may interrupt others and work to abbreviate discussion of agenda items. At less stressful times, the same person may encourage side conversations, give their undivided attention, or ask questions. Even when under pressure, we usually listen differently to people we value or who have influence over us. During family conferences, for example, children usually listen more closely to their parents' comments than they do to their brothers or sisters. At work, professionals may rush conversations with their subordinates and give undivided attention to their bosses.

Listener Preferences: Pros and Cons

As you read the following descriptions, keep in mind the reminders we previously described and remember that there is no "best" listener preference. Each preference is described using both positive and negative characteristics to help provide a balanced perspective. As you read about characteristics for each preference, check the ones that remind you of yourself.

People-Oriented. People-oriented listeners are most concerned with how listening influences their relationships with others. They listen to understand the emotional states of others, giving their undivided attention. While listening, they usually remain nonjudgmental. In addition, when confronted with personal problems or crises, others seek out people-oriented listeners. Open to most types of people, people-oriented listeners can get overly involved with others and waste a lot of time. At times, people-oriented listeners lose their objectivity when listening.

Positive:	Caring and concerned about others
	Nonjudgmental
	Provide clear verbal and nonverbal feedback signals
	Identify emotional states and moods in others quickly
	Interested in building relationships
Negative:	Over-involved with feelings of others
	Avoid seeing faults in others
	Internalize/adopt emotional states of others
	Intrusive to others
	Overly expressive when giving feedback

Action-Oriented. Action-oriented listeners concentrate intensely on the task at hand. They often prefer to listen in outline form and find it difficult to listen to people who are disorganized. The action-oriented listener is an appreciated member of most meetings because he or she encourages others to stay on task and to present information in a logical, organized way. At times, because they appear to be task-driven, action-oriented listeners come across as impatient and not very interested in building relationships with others.

Positive:	Get to the heart of the matter quickly
	Give clear feedback concerning expectations
	Concentrate energy on understanding task at hand
	Help others focus on what is important
	Encourage others to be organized and concise
Negative:	Tend to be impatient with rambling speakers
	Jump ahead and move to conclusions quickly
	Get distracted easily by unorganized speakers
	Ask blunt questions of others
	Appear overly critical

Content-Oriented. Content-oriented listeners tend to carefully evaluate everything they hear. At times it appears that they are looking under a microscope to dissect information. They prefer to listen to experts and highly credible sources. Content-oriented listeners have the ability to see all sides of issues and enjoy listening to challenging or complex information. At times, this listening style may hinder spontaneous discussions and creative exchanges of ideas. Content-oriented listening is often preferred by people with technical degrees or interests.

Positive:	Value technical information
	Test for clarity and understanding

Encourage others to provide support for their ideas
Welcome complex and challenging information
Look at all sides of an issue
Negative: Overly detail-oriented
May intimidate others by asking pointed questions
Minimize the value of nontechnical information
Discount information from unknowns
Take a long time to make decisions

Time-Oriented. Time-oriented listeners are clock-watchers and encourage others to be the same. They are direct in how they value time and often are impatient with others who waste it. While they encourage efficiency and time management, their self-imposed time constraints stifle discussion. Time-oriented listeners must be careful not to interrupt or discount relationships with others. Time-oriented listening is usually valued during meetings. However, these same traits may be troublesome at home or with friends.

Positive: Manage and save time effectively
Let others know listening time requirements
Set time guidelines for meetings and conversations
Discourage wordy speakers from wasting time
Give cues to others when time is being wasted
Negative: Tend to be impatient with time wasters
Interrupt others, putting a strain on relationships
Let time affect their ability to concentrate
Rush speakers by frequently looking at watches/clocks
Limit others' contributions by imposing time pressure

Now that you have learned about the four listening preferences and their positive and negative traits, decide what you consider to be your strongest preference. During meetings it is best to work to keep positive listener characteristics in the forefront. By understanding when and what factors are likely to call out certain preferences, you are in a better position to have a choice.

Suggestions for Working with People with Differing Preferences

You're speaking, but who's listening? The best listeners are aware of their own preferences as well as the preferences of others in their group. Since good listeners know how to read listener preferences, it is important to adapt messages to the preferences of group members. Those who adapt how they listen to other people's preferences gain the advantage of being heard. Just as we tend to get in the habit of listening in only one way, we also tend to speak with others in habitual ways. To make the most of interactions, think of the best ways to package information so others will listen.

Adapting to others' preferences in different listening situations takes practice. Our listening preference habits in particular environments can be deeply entrenched. For example, Albert, an action-oriented listener, has been working on developing his people-oriented listener preference traits. He decided to demonstrate more of the people-oriented traits in a meeting with his peers. At the beginning of the meeting, he made sure to be more relational by asking more personal questions, showing interest in other people's ideas, and attending to nonverbal cues such as vocal inflections and facial expressions. Toward the middle of the meeting, Sarah, an advertising competitor, mentioned her success in getting two new clients, one of which was Albert's. Discovering this information created stress in Albert. Immediately his body orientation and way of relating with the group went back to his action-oriented preference. Forgetting his people-oriented goals, he started interrupting others and began ignoring group member contributions and nonverbal cues.

New Acquaintances and Strangers

Individuals who are most difficult to assess are ones we don't know well. During initial meetings, group members provide information about how we can best adapt our messages to fit their listener preferences. By attending to personal cues, we can determine the best ways to communicate with each person. Keep in mind that our own listening habits are likely to interfere when meeting someone for the first time. For instance, during a first meeting, some people are so busy talking and trying to make a good impression that they fail to notice behaviors such as the other person's speaking rate, time consciousness, presentation of ideas, use of descriptive or factual images, and/or relational cues. Assessing these cues can help you determine what type of listener preference the person has and tell you how to make the best impression. Remember, the more time we spend with others, the better we are at making educated guesses about their listening preferences.

Since preferences are habits, they don't represent your only option for listening. You do have a choice about which preference to use. Think about it for a moment: If your habits include a strong preference for action-oriented listening, then these habits influence how you listen. If you use action-oriented listening when people-oriented listening is more appropriate, then you are less effective and waste listening energy for later meetings. It is unrealistic, for example, to expect conversations during a first group meeting to be logical or to be structured in an outline form. To impose your preferred listening style or habits on the situation would be frustrating to you and your colleagues.

Listener Avoiders

People who have no clear listening preference may tend to avoid listening. Listening avoidance is not necessarily a negative trait but can cause problems if taken to the extreme. Avoiding listening, regardless of the situation, context, topic, or person involved should be examined carefully. Group members who are physically and mentally exhausted often do not have energy to listen well to complex information or topics of little interest to their areas of expertise. At the same time, group members may be willing to and even enjoy listening to topics that are entertaining or that take minimal effort. In this case, listening avoidance is situational rather than a consistent preferred condition.

Many individuals prefer to receive information in ways other than through listening in groups. When communicating about group assignments, listener avoiders may avoid face-to-face contact and use electronic mail, faxes, or written documents and request that others do the same. Because of bad experiences in previous groups, some people will do anything to avoid the situation.

Adapting to Listener Preferences in Groups

When three or more people gather they are likely to have multiple and/or different listener preferences. To work effectively, try to get a feel for other group members. If possible, think about the make-up of your listeners in advance. Your goal is to decide how you can best help your listeners "stay tuned" to what you have to say. You may have to make group assessments on the spot. Consider getting to meetings early. Mingle with others to get an impression about what listening strategies will work best. Based on the reactions, you can determine whether to use a more people-, action-, content-, or time-oriented delivery.

You might assume your goal should be to keep each person listening to you all of the time. While this might be ideal, it is unrealistic to expect to make every listener happy throughout a meeting. As a speaker, often the best you can do is to decide who your target listeners are.

While preparing a presentation for a club meeting, for example, Freida analyzed her listeners carefully. She knew seven people would attend. The president and primary decision maker, Tom, is a content- and time-oriented listener. Two committee chairs and voting members, Carmen and Ralph, are almost exclusively action-oriented listeners. Gina, a people-oriented listener, is the secretary and frequently influences Tom's decisions. The other two members often avoid listening situations but are required to attend and vote. Delivering a generic presentation would hurt Freida's cause. In this case, she decides to focus on Tom and Gina as her listeners. She has fifteen minutes, but plans to give a ten-minute talk with handouts and visuals aids. For Tom, she organizes her thoughts carefully, quotes credible sources, and supports each point with facts. For Gina, she uses the names of group members, personal examples Gina is familiar with, and nonverbally gives her special attention by smiling and looking in her direction frequently. She is energetic and asks for involvement whenever possible.

Adapting to Listener Preferences when Speaking

Before opening your mouth, determine a strategy for the best way to communicate with others in your group. Some people may not prefer to listen, and you may have to think of ways to keep them involved. Others may need a highly structured presentation. Consider using the following strategies in your next meeting.

People-Oriented Strategies:
—Use stories and illustrations that contain human-interest value
—Use "We" rather than "I" in conversation
—Use emotional examples and appeals
—Show some vulnerability when you can afford to do so

Action-Oriented Strategies:
—Keep main points to three or fewer (short and to the point)
—Have a step-by-step plan and label each step
—Watch for cues of uninterest and pick up vocal pace at those points or change the subject
—Speak at a rapid but controlled rate
Content-Oriented Strategies:
—Use two-sided arguments when possible
—Provide hard data when available
—Quote credible experts
—Use charts and graphs
Time-Oriented Strategies:
—Ask how much time the person has to listen; get to the point quickly
—Try to go under time limits when possible
—Be ready to cut out unnecessary examples and information
—Be sensitive to nonverbal cues indicating impatience or desire to leave

Remember, making faulty or incorrect assessments is common. A person may have multiple preferences or may demonstrate some cues and clues that are confusing or contradictory. Continue to look for feedback when adapting to others to see if your strategy is working. If it isn't, as a contingency, be prepared to adjust on the spot.

Tuning in: Listener Involvement Cues

Speakers should strive to keep each audience member involved but must keep their targets in mind. With any audience, keep your ideas concise. Stop talking before your audience is ready for you to stop. These guidelines should help you to keep listeners with you until you finish a presentation.

We need to constantly be on the lookout for signs listeners are tiring or are becoming uninterested. Verbal and nonverbal behaviors that indicate people are not listening effectively involve the face, eyes, body posture, or body movements. Pay particular attention to listeners when they:

—Avoid or lessen eye contact
—Use hostile or angry sounding vocal tones
—Display closed body postures (e.g., crossing arms in front, leaning back)
—Cut conversations short or end interactions abruptly
—Attempt to leave early (e.g., standing up, closing briefcase, shuffling papers on desk, looking at watch)
—Play with objects such as pencils or paper clips
—Nervously tap fingers, swing feet, or shift from side to side when standing
—Frown or show tense facial expressions
—Sigh heavily or often
—Interrupt more frequently as the conversation progresses
—Make remarks unrelated to the conversation

By paying attention to these cues, we can gauge when listeners may be tiring or running low on listening energy. Depending on how important it is to finish the discussion, take one or more of several actions:

—Suggest a stretch break
—Add extra examples
—Use visual illustrations
—Ask questions to involve listeners
—Say that energy is running low and ask if they would like to continue the discussion later

When attempting to identify and adapt to other people's listening preferences, you will make mistakes. You may identify the wrong preference or ignore the presence of multiple preferences. At times you may lack energy to make assessments. Even so, if you persist, you will discover the value of understanding your own and others' preferences. We have examined what you can do as a speaker to help group members listen to what you have to say. Now, we will examine what you can do as a listener.

Listening for Disruptive and Productive Purposes

Some listener preferences may cause group members to behave destructively in groups. Time- and action-oriented listeners may interrupt others when they become impatient or think the topic is getting off track. People-oriented listeners get distracted by other people's moods. They tend to have side conversations and take breaks to avoid conflict. People-oriented listeners may begin daydreaming and tuning in and out when they don't feel a part of discussions. Content-oriented listeners may become overly critical and ask pointed questions that cause defensiveness in others. They also may rehearse a response or plan the great comeback to ideas that are presented without satisfactory evidence or support. When listener preferences get in the way, they limit creativity, cause discussions to come to a close too soon, or derail agendas.

Some preferences focus more on time than on fulfilling objectives or focus on relationships rather than the task at hand. In these situations, discussion can be too long or short and people may be afraid to interject new ideas or contradict others. For example, during a company retreat a group discovered that all but one person had strong people-oriented preferences. Understanding this helped group members understand why most disagreements were discussed after meetings rather than one-on-one or in front of the whole group. Unfortunately, talking behind others' backs tore down group morale. Paradoxically, they were concerned with feelings and group members dealt indirectly with each other and created what they wanted to avoid: conflict.

While the negative characteristics of certain listening preferences can be destructive, the positive characteristics can improve small-group interactions. The following behaviors are ones that maximize listening effectiveness (Watson 1993).

Effective Listening Skills

Listeners demonstrate specific observable behaviors and mannerisms. If you are aware of these clues, you can determine the mood, role, or energy of your listeners and can make accurate predictions about how effectively or ineffectively others are listening to you each moment. The skills most useful for improving listening are: *focusing, tracking, reflecting, digging, and redirecting.*

Focusing. If we want to get the most from a listening situation, we must plan for meetings in advance. Effective listeners make sure they have an adequate energy supply and use the energy to concentrate on what others are saying. Paying attention to others requires effort and most listeners have not practiced the skills necessary to stay involved when others are talking. It does little good to attend to others as listeners if the message doesn't have a chance of getting through to them. The following suggestions provide a basic foundation for taking responsibility for the success of communication and for getting ourselves ready to listen.

—Remove or reduce distractions by shutting doors or closing blinds
—Sit or move closer to the speaker
—Minimize interruptions by unplugging the phone and putting do-not-disturb signs on the door
—Ask the speaker to talk louder
—Focus attention and concentrate
—Prepare for the meeting in advance

Tracking. Most of us have been guilty of interrupting or discouraging others from talking. The tracking strategy encourages others to keep talking and you to keep listening. Especially when we listen to people with different points of view, it is easy to begin evaluating their messages before they finish talking. We all have been guilty of planning the great comeback or rehearsing a response. Rather than jumping to conclusions, it would be best to mentally note or write down points you'd like to clarify, and then keep listening. Good listeners know when to be silent and when to speak. They avoid interrupting a speaker in the middle of an emotional idea or important thought, but need to ask questions to ensure accurate understanding. During meetings effective listeners should:

—Avoid interrupting
—Withhold or defer judgment
—Remain objective with minimum bias
—Be aware of the speaker's biases
—Show nonverbal encouragement through head nods, eye contact, etc.
—Ask about priorities of requested actions
—Demonstrate they are following the speaker's message by saying such things as: "Go on. . . ." "What happened next?" or "I see. . . ."
—Tell others how much time they have to listen
—Tell others when their listening energy is low

Reflecting. Listeners may need to test their understanding. Listeners can clarify messages by using such questions as, "So are you suggesting that we wait until next week to go to the mountains?" or "Do you want me to come to the meeting at 9:00 or 9:30?" Remember that listeners are put at a disadvantage if they fail to get involved with the speaker throughout the communication interaction. There are times that listeners need to ask questions or take control of the communication situation to ensure that they have interpreted messages correctly. The skill of listening is often demonstrated in how well you repeat or summarize what you have heard. When listening:

—Summarize key points accurately
—Describe the emotional state of the speaker
—Repeat ideas or paraphrase the speaker
—Identify words with multiple meanings
—Analyze and adapt to the speaker's point of view
—Check for understanding by asking for clarification

Digging. Identify a time when you have tried to hide what you were thinking or feeling from someone else. Perhaps you didn't want to hurt someone's feelings or were afraid of what the other person would think of you. Keeping thoughts and feelings hidden interferes with accurate communication. Digging helps listeners discover underlying issues and concerns. Digging clarifies verbal and nonverbal messages by gathering more data about the emotions and thoughts of speakers. Think carefully before asking too many questions, though. Be sure questions are pertinent to the discussion and not merely for curiosity. To get additional information:

—Ask clarification questions
—Use open-ended questions that require more than a yes or no answer
—Ask for examples
—Use preliminary closes ("You mean that . . ."; "We have finished the discussion, so we can now . . .") to check for feelings
—Ask for additional evidence or supporting material

Redirecting. It is not unusual for speakers to be side-tracked during meetings. While digressions can be appropriate, many are not and as a listener you may need to move the speaker back to the topic or task at hand. When people digress, redirecting helps get them back on track. Use comments such as: "Now that we've discussed . . . how can we use the information to . . . ?" or "Since this topic wasn't on the agenda, why don't we table this until our next meeting?" To get a person back on the subject:

—Restate the original topic or issue
—Make statements that clarify the message
—Ask questions to get the person back on track
—Summarize what has been said to provide feedback
—Explain how the topic changed direction
—Ask clarification questions

This section has given a number of suggestions for improving your listening skills. Keep in mind that listening is a skill that requires practice and effort to do well. Rather than trying to apply all the skills at once, take one at a time. Work the one that is most important to you right now. After you have successfully applied the new skill in groups to which you belong, then begin work on another one.

Balancing Strengths and Weaknesses of Differing Listener Preferences

At times, you may have the opportunity to form a group of your own. If you do, what ratio of people who have listener preferences should you include? Most leaders unknowingly choose people with listener preferences similar to their own. Unfortunately, when group members listen in the same ways, problems occur.

Having various listener preference types in a group can be frustrating, but can also serve to enhance creativity and group decision making. In fact, groups with heterogeneous listener-preference and personality compositions are likely to perform most effectively (Barker, Whalers, Watson & Kibler 1991; Shaw 1981). When you're asked to form a group, then, consider your goals and objectives; these, along with an understanding of listener preferences, should help you design a group to maximize your efforts.

Conclusion: The Paradox of Group Member Listener Preferences

This chapter has described listening, listener preferences, and suggestions for improving listening in groups. When we leave college, we have more associations with groups. In business, groups or teams are the fundamental unit of work. Schools insist on individual effort much of the time. Businesses by contrast, require team effort and the ability to read, shape, and listen in group environments. Paradoxically, just as we may seek to join or avoid participating in groups and teams, at different times, we may seek to listen or avoid listening. Even so, group decisions benefit from an awareness of listener preferences and use of effective listening skills.

Notes

1. The Listener Preference Profile instrument (developed by Watson, Barker, and Weaver 1992) is designed to identify preferences. A self-administered instrument, copies are available from Pfieffer & Company or SPECTRA, Inc.

References

Barker, L.L., Johnson, P.M., and Watson, K.W. (1991). "The Role of Listening in Managing Interpersonal and Group Conflict." In D. Borisoff and M. Purdy, (eds), *Listening in Everyday Life*. New York: University Press of America, 139–162.

Barker, L.L., and Watson, K.W. (1994). *Listeners, Lemmings, and Black Widow Spiders: Understanding the Listening Paradox.* (In publication.)

Barker, L.L., Wahlers, K., Watson, K.W., and Kibler, R. (1991). *Groups in process* 4th ed. Englewood Cliffs, NJ: Prentice-Hall.

Shaw, M.E. (1981). *Group Dynamics* 3d ed. New York: McGraw-Hill.

Smith, K.K., and Berg, D.N. (1987). *Paradoxes of Group Life: Understanding Conflict, Paralysis, and Movement in Group Dynamics.* San Francisco: Jossey-Bass Publishers.

Watson, K.W. (1993). "Listening and Feedback." In L. Barker, and D. Barker (eds.) *Communication*, 6th ed. Englewood Cliffs, NJ: Prentice-Hall, 49–77.

Watson, K.W., and Barker, L.L. (1992). "All Listeners Are Not Created Equal: Listener Preference Assessment and Validation." Paper presented at the annual meeting of the International Listening Association, Seattle, WA.

Watson, K.W., Barker, L.L., and Weaver, J.B. (1992). "Development and Validation of the Listener Preference Profile." Paper presented at the annual meeting of the International Listening Association, Seattle, WA.

Watson, K.W., Barker, L.L., and Weaver, J.B. (1993). *Listening Preference Profile*. New Orleans: SPECTRA, Inc.

Watson, K.W., Barker, L.L., and Weaver, J.B. (1994). *Listening Preference Profile*. San Diego: Pfeiffer & Company.

Weaver, J.B., Watson, K.W., and Barker, L.L. (1993). "Personality and Listening Preferences: Do You Hear What I Hear? Paper presented at the annual meeting of the International Listening Association, Memphis.

Humor and Work

W. Jack Duncan, Larry R. Smeltzer, and Terry L. Leap

Humor and work are frequently thought of as mutually exclusive activities. In spite of this perceived exclusiveness, most would admit that a characteristic of all work groups is joking behavior. People joke with others at work for many reasons: It makes work bearable; it overcomes the monotony associated with "earning our daily bread"; it reduces tension and adds a sense of belonging.

We believe that humor and joking on the job are much more, and this view is shared by others as shown by the periodic attempts to study work group humor. Vinton (1989) illustrates, for example, that humor provides important insights into a group's cultural characteristics as well as a basis for understanding organizational phenomena like socialization. However, as we reviewed the literature, it became clear that the interest was sporadic. If, as Cheatwood (1983) argued, the sociology of humor has reached a dead end among sociologists, we have to conclude that the study of humor in management has never really gotten started.

Even though the study of humor and work has a long tradition, the longevity can be deceiving (Klapp 1949). Serious studies of the subject have been erratic, as illustrated by the fact that there were several important studies of humor and work in the 1960s, only a very few in the entire decade of the 1970s, and only slightly more in the 1980s. If one is interested in work group humor it takes time and patience to analyze the diverse literature on the subject.

Fortunately, the significance of a research issue in any field is a function of neither the number of people professing interest in a topic nor the volume of papers published each year. Instead, the significance relates to the potential the subject has for helping us understand the behavior of people in organizations. On this criterion we believe humor rates relatively high.

The literature on humor and work is diverse. Articles and books on the subject range from highly comprehensive reviews like that of Zijderveld (1983), to pioneering books like Chapman and Foot (1976). The reader who wishes to gain an insight to the general subject of humor should refer to Volume 26 of the *Journal of Communication,* an entire issue devoted to the subject (Chapman & Badfield 1976). Articles in this special issue dealt with a variety of topics, including the anatomy of a joke, joking at work, and ethnic humor.

Conceptual Framework

This discussion of humor and work will not follow the format of many literature reviews. Because studies of humor and work have involved scholars from a multitude

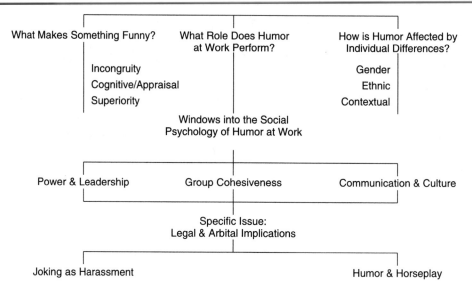

What Makes Something Funny?   What Role Does Humor   How is Humor Affected by
                                    at Work Perform?   Individual Differences?

Incongruity   Gender
Cognitive/Appraisal   Ethnic
Superiority   Contextual

Windows into the Social
Psychology of Humor at Work

Power & Leadership   Group Cohesiveness   Communication & Culture

Specific Issue:
Legal & Arbital Implications

Joking as Harassment   Humor & Horseplay

Figure 1. Conceptual framework for the Review

of disciplines, there has been no common framework for inferring general conclusions and future directions for research.

The conceptual framework of this review is presented in Figure 1. As the figure illustrates, the review will begin with an examination of more general issues regarding the theory of humor and work. It then moves to a review of related literature and concludes with a specific example of how humor is a relevant issue for management.

The first section of the review discusses the role of humor in organizations and the impact that humor has as a result of gender and ethnic differences. Also discussed are what makes a job or incident funny, along with the different theories of humor.

The next major section deals with small-group research as it relates to joking behavior in organizations. Topics include the function of humor in defining leadership, power, and status relationships; humor as a facilitator of group cohesiveness; the value of humor as a communication device; and the importance of humor in building and maintaining organizational cultures. Throughout this section, attention is directed specifically to the empirical studies of work group humor and the methodologies employed in gathering relevant data.

Finally, this review looks at one specific area where humor has presented special problems for managers—the legal implications of humor as a form of harassment. The review concludes with some arguments about the importance of humor for managers and suggestions for using it to accomplish organizational goals.

An attempt will be made throughout to familiarize the reader with current directions of research and practice as they relate to work group humor and management. Humor in management is far from a mature topic of organizational research. There have been important findings, but there have been few attempts to follow up and refute or verify speculations. For this reason we should look at humor research as a developing field in search of both a theory and appropriate methods for examining this complex phenomenon.

. . . . .

Individual differences in humor may be difficult to understand at times because all humor occurs within a social context. Nevo and Nevo (1983) state that in the last decade researchers have referred more to the complex, multifaceted nature of humor. Humor is a complex phenomenon to understand because it can ultimately only be understood in relation to the context within which it appears (Rossel 1981).

Winick (1976) maintains that any attempt to interpret the relative significance of jokes in American life must be done in terms of large social contexts. Early in this century, Bergson (1912, 6) maintained "the natural environment of humor is society . . . laughing needs other people . . . it is always in a group." It cannot be ignored that the potentially disruptive or constructive effects of humor are felt more in some contexts than others. Also, individuals have greater or lesser tolerance or acceptance for humorous interjection at different times. As a result, a focus of much of the recent research is the use and effects of humor in various settings (Goldstein 1976).

Research on Humor and Work

The remainder of this review presents an analysis of humor in a specific setting: management. It will indicate that humor has both potentially positive and negative consequences within the context of organizations.

Humor is not a subject that has been seriously researched for long periods of time in the study of work and management. In fact, some believe that management is such serious business that there is little room for humor. One reviewer of an article on humor in management cited in this review made the comment that his "thirty years in business had convinced him that by and large business was not a place for fun." In spite of this harsh judgment of humor, and perhaps of business if it were true, one of the most frequently observed phenomena in work groups is joking behavior. When a group of people is assembled to accomplish a task, there is always some form of joking behavior and work group humor.

The writings on humor, management, and work group humor fall into two primary categories. The first, and by far the largest, contains all the applied, nonempirical, trade-oriented literature. Examples of these writings are found in practice-oriented media like the *Wall Street Journal* (April 30, 1989), *Computer Decisions* (1985), and *Nonprofit World* (1985).

The second category of articles includes the theoretical, sometimes empirical, scholarly studies of humor at work. These will be the focus of this review, although an attempt will be made to summarize what the more systematic literature says in a way that will be meaningful to practicing managers. There is also a subcategory of articles that does not fit neatly into either of the categories previously noted. These articles, which are relatively few in number, are primarily directed toward practicing managers but present theoretical perspectives, collect reasonably good data, and/or formulate historical arguments in a way that defies precise classification.

For example, Cullather (1983) presented an analysis of the *New Yorker's* view of business ethics by tracing the image of business people presented in the magazine's cartoons over a period of years. The author concluded that in the magazine's cartoons, humorists had taken liberty with sins in the business sector more than with other occupations. The humor evidenced in the cartoons had, by and large, reinforced the stereotype of the business person as a greedy and uncaring individual.

In another example, Duncan and Feisal (1989) collected data from a number of small task-oriented groups in business, health care, and human services. The data were summarized in a way that made it possible to speculate about four stereotypical types of managers and the outcomes each might expect from the use of work group humor.

Early Research in Work Groups

The potential importance of humor in the work place has been recognized for more than three decades. Bradney (1957), in one of the very early studies, specifically addressed humor in the industrial setting, adopting a psychological perspective in an effort to understand what joking, humor, and laughter meant to and for the individual worker. Roy (1960) illustrated how joking was used by workers to alleviate the boredom of work. Cosier (1960) studied joking among the staff in a hospital for the mentally ill and found joking patterns to be related to formal status.

Sykes (1966) also used industry as his focus in extending some of the anthropological findings presented by Radcliffe-Brown (1940). Specifically, joking between male and female workers was analyzed and revealed that its function was to identify potential sexual partners while protecting others. With the exception of Sykes (1966), most of the early humor research in industrial settings was psychological. That is, the emphasis was on the individual and the role humor played in understanding individual behavior.

Humor in the Context of Groups

Although the psychological aspects of humor at work are important, Lundberg (1969) raised important questions about the sociological dimension. In fact, after the publication of Lundberg's article, three important things happened to the study of work group humor. In addition to adopting a sociological perspective, Lundberg provided a convenient and efficient way of diagramming joking relationships. Several additional empirical studies resulted that were designed to test propositions suggested in his study of an electric motor repair shop. All of these influences can be found to a greater or lesser extent in later studies.

Unfortunately, with regard to the first point, the interest in the sociological aspects of humor has been erratic at best. Extensive works like the "trend report" by Zijderveld (1983) build enthusiasm and maintain interest in the subject. Even though these reviews cite all the studies in industrial and other work-related settings, they devote relatively little attention to specific issues of humor and work.

In fact, Cheatwood (1983) laments, as we noted in the introduction, that there has been a lack of a serious search for the true sociological meaning of humor in any context. He contends that the general failure to take into account humor in the understanding of social behavior in organizations not only results in the loss of an appreciation of the role it performs but deprives us of "an important lens for examining the very

Table 1
Examples of Selected Studies on Humor in Work Groups

Author(s)	Date	Publication	Sample	Method
Duncan	1983	*Small Group Behavior*	Six small, task-oriented groups.	Self-administered questionnaires
Duncan	1984	*Human Relations*	Nine work groups.	Self-administered questionnaires
Linstead	1985	*Sociological Review*	Workers on ten large production lines in a confectionary bakery.	Participant observation
Lundberg	1969	*Human Organization*	Employees in an electric motor repair shop.	Participant observation
Traylor	1973	*Human Relations*	Six permanent members of petroleum party in Alaska.	Participant observation
Vinton	1989	*Small Group Behavior*	Thirteen members of a small business.	Participant observation

structure of that behavior" (326). Reluctantly, he cites another source as stating about the only valid generalization sociologists can make with confidence about humor is "that it is fun" (325).

Relative to a convenient and efficient way of diagramming joking behavior, Lundberg (1969) identified four "analytical categories" of individuals involved in joking behavior.

1. *Initiator*. The person who tells the joke or starts the humorous episode.
2. *Target*. The person(s) to whom the joke is directed. In most cases the target is the person to whom the joke is told.
3. *Focus*. Commonly called the "butt" of the joke. This is the individual at whom the humor is directed.
4. *Public(s)*. The individuals or group beyond the initiator, target, and focus who observe or hear the joke.

In discussing various points throughout the remainder of this review, we will use these terms as a common vocabulary. It is important to note that although these terms (i.e., initiator, target, focus, public) are used in a variety of ways in the humor literature, we will use them as suggested by Lundberg for purposes of analytical convenience.

Finally, and perhaps most important, even though management research on humor at work has been limited, there have been a few studies that have attempted to look specifically at the issue. Table 1 provides a brief summary of selected studies.

Methodological Approaches in Empirical Studies of Humor at Work

Until the mid-1980s, almost all studies of humor at work employed qualitative applied anthropological methods. Lundberg (1969) used participant observation in his study of an electric motor repair shop. Specifically, he used a series of actual incidents to illustrate the analytical categories assumed by the different employees and supervisors in the shop.

Traylor (1973) joined the six permanent members of a petroleum exploration party on the North Slope of Alaska over a 5½-week period. He lived in the tent camp with the team and recorded joking behavior that took place at meal times. This period was selected because it was the time when all members of the team assembled in the cook tent.

Unlike prior studies, Duncan (1984) employed self-administered questionnaires in small, task-oriented groups in business, health care, and human service organizations to generate data about work group humor. These studies consequently reported perceptions of group members about humor instead of the interpretations of observers. The actual instruments used consisted of modified sociometric items because of the author's desire to understand humor within the total context of social choice (Ziv 1979).

Additional Studies of Humor and Management

Other attempts have been made to examine issues relating to humor and management that have not been published in the mainstream literature. For example, Vinton (1989) spent seven weeks in a small, family-owned business in the Midwest where she collected incidents of joke telling, bantering, and teasing on the job. Decker (1984a) used a sample of business students as the research sample and collected self-administered questionnaires as a means of analyzing sex differences in reactions to aggressive humor by managers. Decker (1984b) used another sample of evening management students to investigate the effects of self-disparaging joking on the part of managers.

Results of Research on Humor and Management

Malone (1980) presented management researchers with an agenda for investigating the role of humor in management. He raised five questions management researchers should consider:

1. Can humor, properly used, serve as a tool to enhance the managerial process?
2. Can humor be used effectively by most managers or should the use of humor be reserved for those who are naturally funny?
3. Under what conditions can humor be used most effectively? Under what conditions is humor appropriate?
4. What types of people respond most readily to humor? What types of people are most likely to react negatively?
5. What types of humor are most effective? What types are most likely to produce negative reactions?

Duncan (1982) attempted to answer some of these questions in a review of the research in the area of management and related fields.

Issues Addressed in Humor and Management

A review of the management-oriented scholarly literature on humor demonstrates that most of the focus has been on four major issues. These are: leadership, power, and status relationships; group cohesiveness; the effects of humor on communication in group settings; and the role of humor in organizational cultures.

Leadership, Power, and Status. Lundberg (1969) and Traylor's (1973) extension took as their inspiration the work of Radcliffe-Brown's (1940) pioneering work in primitive cultures. Of particular interest was the anthropological view that joking was a "peculiar combination of friendliness and antagonism" (196). This perspective suggested the importance of joking behavior in defining and reinforcing power and status relationships in groups.

Of the five major findings of Lundberg (1969), three related specifically to power and status within the group. He found, for example, that peers have more fun than higher-status leaders, a low-status butt of a joke did not joke back to a higher-status initiator, and if the peers of the butt of a joke were present or if the initiator was of lower rank than the butt, then the joke was not considered funny. Traylor (1973), similarly, found that the status of a person and the frequency with which he or she was the focus of intragroup joking was inversely related. Cosier (1960) found in his study of a mental hospital that junior staff members joked less than senior staff. Moreover, the senior staff rarely used self-disparaging humor in the presence of junior staff. These findings led to the suggestion that managers and other high-status group members enjoy a "joking monopoly" that allows them to joke about others but does not allow reciprocity.

Attempts to verify the existence of a joking monopoly have been generally unsuccessful. Duncan (1983) found no support for the idea in the numerous small, task-oriented groups surveyed in his research. Aggregated data from a series of group studies indicated that one's formal status in a group is less a determinant of one's position in the joking pattern than the individual's role in the larger social network. If, for example, high-status members are considered friends more than bosses they may be carefully integrated into the humor network (Duncan & Feisal 1989).

Group Cohesiveness. Although work group humor can be cruel and divisive it may also be used to make members know they belong. LaFave and Mennell (1976) believe ethnic humor, when done in an environment of trust and mutual respect, could actually "provide the heat for the melting pot" of interpersonal relations (117). However, as will be noted in a forthcoming section, ethnic and sexual humor when not conducted in an environment of trust can be more than disrespectful; it can be discriminatory and illegal.

Communicating with Humor. The work group is frequently characterized by uncertainty and ambiguity. False messages invite risky behavior that can often be made less risky with the use of humor. For example, rather than openly oppose a higher-level organizational official, an employee might use a joke to "test the water." In other words, as Ullian (1976) observes, humor is often used to transfer information that is socially risky to the initiator.

To illustrate, a South American executive tells a story about how employees joked with bosses rather than openly challenge a manager's decision. The common practice in this particular organization was that anytime top management announced a decision that lower-level managers regarded as ill-advised, the standard practice was for the lower-level manager to say "I'll bet you lunch." In this manner, and everyone knew it, lower-level managers were able to let bosses know they disagreed without experiencing unnecessarily large risks. If the boss was offended by the statement, the employee could easily say "I was only joking; you know I am behind the company all the way."

This particular custom was taken even further. If the decision proved to be a bad one, the employees who cautioned against it were permitted to tell the boss "You owe me lunch." Everyone knew that this was an acceptable, low-risk way of telling the boss "I told you so!"

Humor and Organizational Culture. Increasingly, researchers in the area of organizational culture suggest the importance of humor and the need to understand joking patterns in order to fully appreciate an organization's culture (Fine 1977). This idea should not be surprising because early anthropological researchers recognized the same thing about modern day and primitive cultures.

Ott (1989) includes jokes along with stories, metaphors, and myths as important artifacts of organizational cultures. Linstead (1985) found in his examination of the ELS Amalgamated Bakeries that humor played an important role in both changing organizational cultures and reinforcing existing cultures.

Dandridge (1986) illustrates the dysfunctional affects of the creation and fostering of the work/play distinction in task-oriented settings. The result is a paradox whereby work is looked at as something one does for material gain devoid of fun; meanwhile, play is looked at as a freely chosen activity devoid of any form of productivity. In fact, there is increasing evidence that work and play are quite complementary activities. Mergen (1978, 200) stated that play "forms the flow between the rhythms of work and the rhythms of family and individual life."

In an effort to illustrate the importance of the ceremony as an integration of work and play, Dandridge (1986) uses examples of familiar "ritualized events." These events are preplanned and occur at designated times to show how these ceremonies combine work and play in the task-oriented context. Work-related examples include company picnics, parties, retirement dinners, and so on. In all these cases, according to the author, work goals are combined with play processes and provide functional outcomes (164).

Joking Behavior and Harassment

When does humor deteriorate into harassment? In recent years. increasing attention has been paid by both the courts and labor arbitrators to the issue of harassment in the workplace. A question that is central to this discussion is the extent to which jokes and pranks might constitute harassment that is violative of equal employment opportunity (EEO) law. Title VII of the Civil Rights Act of 1964 forbids certain types of discrimination in employment when such discrimination is based on a person's race, sex, religion, color, or national origin. Similarly, the Age Discrimination in Employment Act of 1967 (ADEA) proscribes age-related discrimination against persons age forty and above. In 1987, the Equal Employment Opportunity Commission (EEOC) issued a set of age harassment guidelines that, among other things, suggested that derogatory remarks and joking about a person's age might violate the ADEA (*Equal Employment Opportunity Commission* 1987).

Harassment that is based on a person's sex, race, or age may also be illegal under state EEO legislation.

The courts and arbitrators continue to wrestle with the question of what constitutes illegal harassment. Furthermore, it is difficult to draw the line between joking behavior that is a natural part of workday life and behavior that constitutes sex, race, or age discrimination. To what extent are racist, sexist, and age-related jokes likely to create a hostile work environment? When does humor or joking behavior become vicious and insulting? What types of conduct between the initiators, targets, focus, and publics are apt to create legal liabilities for an employer?

For example, Priest's (1985) proposed theory of Moderate Intergroup Conflict Humor (MICH) claims that hostile joking will occur only if there is a *moderate* level of conflict between two or more groups (e.g., male and female, black and white employees). Hostile jokes, according to the theory, are less likely when the two groups are either closely allied or, at the other extreme, bitter enemies. An examination of court and arbitration decisions also indicates that legal problems are more likely when racist or sexist jokes are shrouded in moderate hostility.

In *Meritor Savings Bank v. Vinson* (1986), the U.S. Supreme Court held that Title VII could be violated if a member of a protected group was forced to work in a hostile environment. Although *Vinson* involved sexual advances and activities, other forms of employee conduct such as offensive and unwanted touching and a pattern of lewd, obscene, and suggestive comments may also constitute sexual harassment. The Supreme Court unanimously held that harassment suits based on a hostile environment theory are actionable under Title VII, even if the plaintiff suffers no loss of job or benefits. The Court observed that, along with economic or tangible discrimination, Title VII guarantees employees "the right to work in an environment free from discriminatory intimidation, ridicule, and insult." In a survey of 13,000 federal employees, it was discovered that the most prevalent form of sexual harassment was "unwanted sexual teasing" (*The Bureau of National Affairs, Inc.* 1988).

Based on two 1988 "hostile environment" cases, sexual harassment claims appear to be legitimate in situations where a plaintiff is not the direct recipient of sexual advances (*Broderick v. Ruder* 1988; and *Hall v. Gus Construction Co.* 1988). Rather, working in an atmosphere of excessive sexual overtones—of which sexual remarks and joking are a part—poisons the environment and demonstrates that women have little opportunity for advancement and are not taken seriously as professionals (May 1988). This point is illustrated by the fact that a California court awarded a female sales representative $62,000 after she was victimized by the frequent use of profanity, sexual comments, and jokes by a company manager (*Department of Fair Employment and Housing v. Sigma Circuits* 1988).

Race and ethnic discrimination cases have also increased in recent years. Cases of this nature are often precipitated by jokes, derogatory and insulting remarks, and pranks of a racial or ethnic nature. Leap and Smeltzer (1984) analyzed this subset of racial discrimination cases and categorized them as follows: (a) cases that are flagrant violations of Title VII of the Civil Rights Act; (b) gray-area cases; and (c) isolated incidents that are not normally violative of federal or state law.

. . . . .

How Offensive is Joking Behavior?

Most joking behavior that has racial, sexist, or other overtones does not result in civil litigation. When civil litigation arises, the plaintiff must generally be able to (a) demonstrate pervasive and offensive joking behavior or (b) link joking behavior to well-documented incidents of racial or sexual harassment. Preliminary research indicates that the focus or target of a joke may not always be offended by joking behavior. Smeltzer and Leap (1988) analyzed the acceptability of joking behavior among blacks, whites, men, women, and experienced versus inexperienced employees. Subjects were asked to evaluate the appropriateness of three types of jokes (racist, sexist, and neutral) in work settings. Inexperienced employees rated neutral jokes as less appropriate than experienced employees. Women regarded sexist jokes (that were disparaging to females) as being less appropriate than did men. In addition, women were more offended by racist jokes than sexist jokes. Perhaps most surprising was the finding that blacks were less offended by racist jokes than whites. There are several possible explanations for this result.

First, jokes that disparage a group seem more acceptable when told by a member of that group. As mentioned when discussing self-disparagement earlier, there seems to be a certain degree of delight in ridiculing ourselves. Second, it is commonly said that people who can poke fun at themselves are blessed with a sense of humor and, as noted earlier, a sense of humor is valued in organizational life. A third possibility is that the black subjects in this study were conditioned to show that they had a sense of humor and accepted racist jokes. However, the more serious question remains as to whether these jokes are "accepted" but not appreciated by minority group members.

Humor and Horseplay: One Final Thought

Horseplay in the workplace is frequently the result of employee attempts to be humorous—sometimes with disastrous results. Although horseplay among employees does not usually attract public attention or result in civil litigation, there are a number of arbitration cases involving horseplay in which the employees have been disciplined or discharged. Sticking lighted cigarettes in an unsuspecting employee's pocket, bringing a live snake into the workplace and confronting an employee who is known to be deathly afraid of snakes, and pulling chairs from beneath employees are extreme examples of horseplay whose primary intent is humor and amusement.

Arbitrators generally support disciplinary actions taken against the perpetrators of horseplay when it causes a disruption in the workplace, damages property. poses a safety hazard, or represents malicious intent by the employee. In the above example, the lighted cigarettes were placed in the pockets of an employee who worked in a spray paint booth (*Decar Plastics Corp.* 1965); the employee who was afraid of snakes also had a heart condition (*J.R. Simplot Co.* 1976); and the chair-pulling incident posed a safety hazard but did not represent malicious intent by the prankster, according to the arbitrator (*Fisher Electronics, Inc.* 1964).

Summary

The analysis of the research and literature on humor presented here indicates that the study of humor has followed a somewhat disjointed and irregular path. Unlike other academic specialties within the field of management, research on humor has evolved from a number of academic disciplines that range from psychology to anthropology. The conceptual framework presented here could mark the beginning of a greater unification of the body of knowledge surrounding humor as it pertains to organizations.

Our discussion of humor in organizations may also suggest additional avenues of research that, to date, have remained unexplored. Humor research may lead to useful managerial applications above and beyond those discussed here. For example, humor has already been found useful by clinical psychologists in psychotherapy and may perhaps be used by employee assistance program counselors to alleviate employee stress. The literature discussed here suggests that humor is used to combat boredom in the workplace. Of course, when the humor is in the form of horseplay, the consequences can lead to bodily injury or property damage. However, humor that is properly channeled may also relieve the monotony and boredom that create safety hazards and accidents. Humor may also be useful in diffusing and reducing organizational conflict. For example, the use of humor by labor mediators may provide a fruitful area for research. Such research might focus on the role, timing, and appropriateness of humor during labor-management conflicts. Humor may also have a pervasive effect on organizational cultures and serve to define the roles of employees at different levels within an organization. Thus, humor may serve as a potentially important tool for organizational development.

The study of humor is clearly a serious business. Humor also provides a number of untapped research opportunities, some of which have been briefly mentioned above. We anticipate that research on humor within organizations will increase in the future. Not only is humor research novel and intrinsically interesting, but many of the organizational barriers that have plagued management research (e.g., management's fear of revealing proprietary information, concerns that longitudinal studies will cause disruptions in the workplace) may not pose major problems for those interested in humor.

References

Bergson, H. (1912). *Laughter: An Essay on the Meaning of the Comic.* New York: Macmillan.

Bradney, Pamela (1957). "The Joking Relationship in Industry." *Human Relations* 10, 179–189.

Broderick v. Ruder. (1988). 46 FEP Cases 1272.

Bureau of National Affairs Inc. (1988). "Sexual Harrassment Among Civil Servants." *Fair Employment Practices,* July 7, 82.

Chapman, A.J., and Foot, H.C. (eds.), (1976). *Humor and Laughter: Theory, Research, and Applications.* London: Wiley.

Chapman, A., and Gadfield, N.J. (1976). "Is Sexual Humor Sexist?" *Journal of Communication* 26, 37–48.

Cheatwood, D. (1983). "Sociability and the Sociology of Humor." *Sociology and Social Research* 67, 324–338.

Cosier, R.L. (1960). "Laughter Among Colleagues: A Study of the Social Functions of Humor Among the Staff of a Mental Hospital." *Psychiatry* 23, 81–95.

Cullather, J.L. (1983). "Has the Laughter Died? Musings on *The New Yorker's* Business Cartoons." *Business Horizons* 26 (2), 30–33.

Dandridge, T.C. (1986). "Ceremony as an Integration of Work and Play." *Organizational Studies* 7 (2), 159–170.

Decar Plastics Corp. (1965). 44 LA 921.

Decker, W.H. (1984a). "Sex Differences in Reactions to Manager's Aggressive Humor." In R.G. Flood (ed.), *Proceedings of the 14th Annual Meeting of the Southeast American Institute for Decision Sciences,* 157–159.

Decker, W.H. (1984b). "Perceptions of Managers Using Self-Disparaging Humor." Unpublished manuscript.

Degrace v. Rumsfeld. (1980). 21 FEP Cases 1444.

Department of Fair Employment and Housing v. Sigma Circuits. (1988). Calif. FEHC, No. 88–114.

Duncan, W.J. (1984). "Perceived Humor and Social Network Patterns in a Sample of Task-Oriented Groups: A Re-examination of Prior Research." *Human Relations* 11, 895–907.

Duncan, W.J., and Feisal, J.P. (1989). "No Laughing Matter: Patterns of Humor in the Work Place." *Organizational Dynamics* 17 (4), 18–30.

Duncan, W.J. (1983). "The Superiority Theory of Humor at Work: Joking Relationships as Indicators of Formal and Informal Status Patterns in Small, Task-Oriented Groups." *Small Group Behavior* 16, 556–564.

Equal Employment Opportunity Commission. (1987). *Directive on Age Harassment.* March 2. Washington, DC: U.S. Government Printing Office.

Equal Employment Opportunity Commission. (1980). *Guidelines on Discrimination Because of Sex.* Washington, DC: U.S. Government Printing Office.

Equal Employment Opportunity Commission, (1970). Decision No. 71–909, 3 FEP Cases 269.

Fairchild Industries. 75 LA 288, 1980.

Fine, G.A. (1977). "Humor in Situ: The Role of Humor in Small Group Culture." In A.J. Chapman and H.C. Foot, (eds.), *It's a Funny Thing, Humor,* 315–318. New York: Pergamon.

Fisher Electronics, Inc. (1964). 44 LA 343.

Goldstein, J.H. (1976). "Theoretical Notes on Humor." *Journal of Communication* 26, 104–107.

Hall v. Gus Construction Co. (1988). 46 FEP Cases 573.

J.R. Simplot Co. (1976). 67, LA 645.

Klapp, O.E. (1949). "The Fool as a Social Type." *American Journal of Sociology* 60, 157–162.

LaFave, L., and Mennell, R. (1976). "Does Ethnic Humor Serve Prejudice?" *Journal of Communication* 26, 116–123.

Leap, T.L. and Smeltzer, L.R. (1984). "Racial Remarks in the Work Place: Humor or Harassment." *Harvard Business Review,* November–December, 74–78.

Lukens, J. (1985). "Humor in the Nonprofit Organization." *Nonprofit World* 3 (4), 16–17.

Lundberg, C.C. (1969). "Person-Focused Joking: Pattern and Function." *Human Organization* 28, 22–28.

Malone, P.B., III. (1980). "Humor: A Double-Edged Tool for Today's Managers." *Academy of Management Review* 5, 357–360.

Mergen, B. (1978). "Work and Play in an Occupational Subculture." In M.A. Salter (ed.), *Play: Anthropological Perspectives,* 106–134. West Point, NY: Leisure Press.

Meritor Savings Bank v. Vinson. (1986). 40 FEP Cases 1822.

Nevo, O., and Nevo B. (1983). "What Do You Do When Asked to Answer Humorously?" *Journal of Personality and Social Psychology* 44, 188–194.

Ott, J.S. (1989). *The Organizational Culture Perspective.* Chicago, IL: Dorsey Press.

Priest, R.F. (1985). "The Future of Sexist Humor in the Work Place." In D.L.F. Neilsen and A.P. Neilson (eds.), *Western Humor and Irony Membership Serial Yearbook.* Proceedings of the 1984 WHIM Conference. Tempe, AZ: Arizona State University.

Radcliffe-Brown, A.R. (1940). "On Joking Relationships." *Africa* 13, 195–210.

Rossel, R.D. (1981). "Chaos and Control: An Attempt to Regulate the Use of Humor in Self-Analytic and Therapy Groups." *Small Groups Behavior* 12 (2), 195–219.

Roy, D.F. (1960). "Banana Time: Job Satisfaction and Informal Interaction." *Human Organization* 18, 158–168.

Sykes, A.J.M. (1966). "Joking Relationships in an Industrial Setting." *American Anthropologist* 68, 188–193.

Traylor, G. (1973). "Joking in a Bush Camp." *Human Relations* 26, 479–486.

Ullian, J.A. (1976). "Joking at Work." *Journal of Communication* 26, 129–133.

Vinton, K.E. (1989). "Humor in the Work Place: It's More Than Telling Jokes." *Small Group Behavior* 20 (2), 151–166.

Winick, C. (1976). "The Social Contexts of Humor." *Journal of Communication* 26, 124–128.

Zijderveld, A.C. (1983). "The Sociology of Humour and Laughter." *Current Sociology* 31 (3), 103.

Ziv, A. (1979). "Sociometry of Humor: Objectifying the Subjective." *Perceptual and Motor Skills* 49, 97–98.

ACTIVITIES

Activity 1

Purpose: The purpose of this activity is to point out that perceptions influence words, and words in turn influence perceptions.

Procedure: The class is divided into groups of three to five people. After reading the explanation, each group will decide what pantyhose should be called. All of the groups' suggestions can then be put on the board so that the class can vote on the best option.

What's in a Name? That Which We Call Pantyhose. . . .

The Washington Institute of Military Pursuits (WIMPS), located in Washington DC (where else?) has determined that the wearing of pantyhose by military personnel in combat situations will have several positive effects:

—Pantyhose provide warmth without adding bulk or weight. This is particularly significant because the findings suggest that avoiding additional weight would be beneficial to both aviators and ground troops.
—Control-top versions of the hose have been found to reduce the number of hernia-related injuries. Additionally, minimizing **V**isible **P**anty **L**ines (VPLs) gives the uniform a sleeker look and a more flattering fit.
—Pantyhose add support to the legs, an important consideration in reducing fatigue during long marches.
—Support hose augment the desired effects of the "G Suits" worn by air crews.
—The user-friendly male version of the hose will feature **F**ront **L**ine **I**mmediate **E**vacuation **S**ystems (FLIES) and will be available in a variety of colors to match the uniform of the day.
—In the case of a fire, pantyhose made of flame retardant Nomex™ fibers provide protection by insulating the skin from burning outer clothing.

In spite of these impressive findings, the president's advisors fear that military men will resist wearing government issue pantyhose because of the obvious link to women's clothing. Controlled studies have concluded that monumental morale problems can be expected.

Obviously, men can be ordered to wear the hose, but at what cost to esprit de corps? Your group has been assigned the task of renaming the pantyhose so that men will be less likely to resist wearing them.

Activity 2

Purpose: The purpose of this assignment is to demonstrate how many nonverbal communication behaviors are culture-bound.

Procedure: In small groups give the dominant North American interpretation for the following nonverbal actions:

—Two people are speaking loudly, waving their arms, and using a great deal of gestures.

—A customer in a restaurant waves her hand over her head and snaps her fingers loudly.

—A woman is dressed entirely in black.

—An adult pats a child's head.

—Two men kiss in public.

—Someone is twenty minutes late for a meeting.

—Someone makes the zero sign with their thumb and forefinger.

Activity 3

Purpose: The purpose of this activity is to show the importance of nonverbal communication to effective group process.

Procedure: The class is divided into groups of three to five students to complete the following assignment. After about 20 minutes, the groups share their conclusions with the rest of the class.

Nonverbal Rules

An alien has just landed from outer space and wishes to learn about life in America. The alien has learned the language with the help of sophisticated technology, but since the rules that govern nonverbal behavior are usually not spoken, the alien has no way of knowing how to behave. The U. S. government has decided to cooperate with the aliens since everyone wants a peaceful relationship with our new neighbors in the universe and every attempt must be made to avoid national hysteria. Therefore, the alien must be schooled in the ways of fitting in.

This is a top secret assignment, and your group's advice is needed to protect national security. What "rules" does this alien, who knows nothing of human interaction, need to learn about appropriate nonverbal behavior?

For each of the eight categories, list two important rules that you would like to share with our visitor from another galaxy. For example, you might state: "Never wear a bikini to a wedding—at least not to an after-five wedding," as a rule for physical presentation. Think of different situations and then write a helpful hint for the alien.

1. Proxemics
2. Movement
3. Facial Expressions
4. Eye Contact
5. Physical Presentation
6. Touch
7. Paralanguage
8. Chronemics

Activity 4

Purpose: The purpose of this exercise is to show that humor is one of the most wonderful and yet dangerous forms of communication, especially in groups.

Procedure: In groups of three to five people, the class explores the telling of culture-bound jokes and jokes about cultural groups to determine: What is humor in this culture? For this group? Answer the following to help you find the answers to the above questions.

1. Find a nonoffensive joke that you have heard that people from another culture might not understand. What makes this joke funny for you and this group but not funny for someone from another culture?

2. Are there any situations when telling cultural, racist, or sexist jokes would be appropriate or acceptable?

3. How are group dynamics impacted when people tell jokes like this? How are the individuals perceived?

Activity 5

Purpose: The purpose of this exercise is to introduce the members of the class to the concept of "shared participation."

Procedure: Divide the students into small groups for a problem-solving discussion. Give each person ten poker chips. Each chip is worth thirty seconds of speaking time. The students must buy time in thirty-second increments when they wish to talk. At the close of the discussion, point out that some students have used up all their time, others a portion of their allotment, and others hardly any. As a follow-up with the class, discuss the differences in participation rates that occur in group discussions.

6
Diversity in Groups

When Confucius said "Human beings draw close to one another by their common nature, but habits and customs keep them apart," he might well have been addressing a problem that small groups face today. Diversity, or differences—the very things that can cause groups to be a wealth of talent, knowledge, insight, and wisdom—can also be the reason that the individuals fail to work well together.

Problems with accepting people's differences are not new to this age. Wandering nomads, religious missionaries, and conquering soldiers have been encountering people different from themselves since the beginning of time. Those early meetings, like those of today, were often confusing and hostile. In the 1990s intercultural contacts are more common and in many ways more significant than those earlier meetings, but being aware of some of the hurdles that groups face when dealing with differences can make members better able to see obstacles, to overcome them, and to use the group's diversity to its advantage.

International Concerns

The last thirty years might well be characterized as that period when, in a figurative sense, Marshall Mcluhan's **global village** prophecy became a reality. The world has indeed been shrinking. We appear to live in a common "village," and we can no longer avoid each other. Trips once measured in days are now counted in hours. Supersonic transports place the tourist, business executive, and diplomat anywhere in the world within hours. This ease of mobility has allowed many of us to travel overseas and other world residents to visit North America. When they can't leave home, people of different nations are linked through communication satellites and digital switched networks. We can now form work groups with people whom we have never met who live on the other side of the world!

All is not positive about this new freedom to associate with peoples of other cultures, however. When we leave the boundaries of our own culture, we often find that conflicting perceptions go far beyond differences in eating utensils and modes of travel. We observe cultural idiosyncrasies in the use of time and space, the treatment of women and the elderly, and even in the meaning of truth. Even after the barrier of different languages is overcome, our inability to respect and accept one another stands in the way of our forming cohesive groups that can tackle global issues or even less complicated business problems.

Domestic Concerns

While this global phenomenon involving transportation and communication is taking place, there is a kind of cultural revolution within our own boundaries. People from Asia, Central and South America, Cuba, Haiti, and Mexico have entered the United States and become part of the new society. As these people adjust their lives to this culture, we will have many opportunities for group association with them. Business, church, school, civic, and social situations place us in groups with people about whom we may know very little. Contacts with cultures that previously appeared strange are now a normal part of our daily lives. All of this means that, like it or not, we are no longer grouped only with persons of similar ethnic backgrounds the way we once were.

As changes throughout the world have caused the demographics of our nation to change, a revolution within the United States has been taking place, too. Even within the dominant mainstream culture, we are unable to accept diversity; for example, we find ourselves deeply divided over such issues as abortion. When we must further cope with the diversity of customs, values, views, and behaviors inherent in a multicultural society, we find ourselves in a state of frustration and peril. Groups that previously remained in the shadow of the dominant culture are now becoming more visible and vocal. Co-cultures and groups such as Native Americans, Blacks, homosexuals, the disabled, the elderly, women, the homeless, and countless other groups are crying out for recognition and their place in the new global village.

This attention to co-cultures makes us realize that although intercultural contact is inevitable, it is often not successful. Frequently, the communicative behavior of the co-cultures disturbs many of us. Others' behaviors seem strange—at times even bizarre—and they frequently fail to meet our expectations. We discover, in short, that intercultural communication is difficult. We encounter people who still say: "I do not want to be part of the global village. I want to communicate and associate only with people who resemble me."

This reaction is contrary to effective group process. The negative behavior cripples the holder of the prejudice, the target of the narrowness, and the group itself. Group polarization is often the result. Sometimes individuals feel forced to support the bias of a friend in the group, to give him or her support, even when they don't feel the same prejudice. Members align themselves with others and form subgroups that are at odds with one another and at cross purposes with the group's goal.

Even if the challenges of accepting one another are met and the natural barrier of a foreign language is overcome, we can still fail to understand and be understood. This is an ongoing problem for individuals who are trying to work together or socialize with one another. These challenges become more pronounced when several people form a group and bring with them all of their prejudices, limitations, and frustrations.

Even when we have the best intentions and the strongest desire to communicate, we are faced with the difficulties imposed on us by cultural diversity and the impact that diversity has on the communication process. As Chapter 5 points out, there are numerous opportunities for communication to fail when groups try to process information and reach decisions. The opportunities for problems multiply as the intercultural component is added.

To help understand what is involved in intercultural communication, we offer a fundamental definition: *Intercultural communication occurs whenever a message produced in one culture must be processed in another culture.* In all respects, everything said about communication in Chapter 5 applies to intercultural communication. The functions and relationships between the components of communication obviously apply, but what especially characterizes intercultural communication is that sources and responders come from different cultures. This fact alone is sufficient to identify a unique form of communicative interaction that must take into account the role and function of culture in the communication process.

A member of one culture producing a message for receipt by a member of another culture is problematic because culture forges and shapes the individual communicator. Culture is largely responsible for the construction of our individual social realities and our individual repertoires of communicative behaviors and meanings. The communication repertories people possess can vary significantly from culture to culture, which can lead to all sorts of difficulties.

Social Perception

Social perception is the process by which we construct our unique social realities by attributing meaning to the social objects and events we encounter in the environment. Culture impacts us by influencing our perceptual processes so that we develop culturally inspired perceptual sets. To understand others' worlds and actions, we must try to understand their perceptual frames of reference; we must learn to understand how they perceive the world. Often when we strive to understand the how and why of other group members, we find that we have many overlapping experiences and commonality of perceptions. Finding these similarities may not be easy at first because we are easily distracted by all of the varied and frequently strange and unfamiliar perceptions that the other members have. Usually, however, we have many important things in common, not the least of which is the group's purpose. Keeping this purpose in mind can often help to magnify the important issues and to minimize the less important ones.

The chief problem associated with intercultural communication in groups is error in social perception brought about by cultural diversity that affects the perceptual process. For example, the comfortable physical distance between people differs from culture to culture. One group member might consider sitting close to another a friendly gesture, but some might find the closeness invasive. This happens because the attribution of meaning to messages is in many respects influenced by the culture of the person responding to the message. When the message being received has been encoded in one cultural frame of reference and is then decoded in an entirely different frame of reference, breakdowns are likely. Consequently, unintended errors in meaning may arise because group members with different cultural backgrounds are unable to understand one another accurately.

The prevailing direction in the United States today seems to be toward a pluralistic, multicultural society. This means that with increasing frequency we will find ourselves in groups with people who don't look like us, but who may be like us in significant ways. An underlying assumption of this position, one that is seldom expressed or perhaps often realized, is that this perspective requires us to understand and accept the views, values, and behaviors of other cultures. Some people do not seem able or willing to do this, however, nor are they sure that it is proper to do so in all circumstances. However, if we are to get along with one another in general and in groups in particular and meet the demands of an emerging global village, we must develop tolerance for others' culturally diverse customs and behaviors—a task that will be difficult but rewarding.

Introduction to Readings

The central theme of this chapter is that gender and culture greatly influence the manner in which we behave in small groups. The first essay by Richard E. Porter and Larry A. Samovar canvasses this topic in an essay titled "Communication in the Multicultural Group." The authors' purpose is to isolate various dimensions of culture that condition how we send and receive messages. The selection begins by explaining what culture is and how it impacts both perception and interaction. Once the power of culture is analyzed, Porter and Samovar offer specific examples that demonstrate how culture modifies and influences our messages, displays of emotion, use of time, negotiation styles, and pace of communication. The authors also discuss problems related to racial, ethnic, and gender prejudice by looking at differences in cultural perceptions and values.

In an essay by Myron W. Lustig and Laura L. Cassotta, we can see the effect of culture on three small-group variables: leadership styles, conformity, and discussion procedures. It is the hypothesis of the authors that these three variables, and how they are acted out in groups, will differ from culture to culture. For example, in cultures such as the United States, Sweden, and France, where the individual is highly valued, people are less likely to conform to group standards. However, in Latin American and Asian cultures, where collectivism and group loyalty are paramount, people tend to acquiesce to the wishes of the group. Lustig and Cassotta offer many other instances that demonstrate the strong influence of culture on how people participate in groups.

In recent years researchers have come to realize what women have known for a long time: that one's gender, much like culture, affects group communication. In our next essay, Susan B. Shimanoff and Mercilee M. Jenkins discuss the place of gender in group leadership. Their essay, "Leadership and Gender: Challenging Assumptions and Recognizing Resources," presents an exhaustive review of research devoted to the differences and similarities of women and men in group roles. The authors' summary of the research refutes many of the myths about women as leaders—for example, that they are more emotional and less task oriented than men—and points out how gender alone (sex biases) can limit women's leadership opportunities and effectiveness. The authors conclude the essay with practical suggestions for identifying and overcoming barriers to women becoming leaders.

Our final selection continues with the basic assumption underlying this entire chapter: simply put, that culture influences the manner in which people behave in small groups. This time two very specific cultures become the focus of the investigation conducted by Robert and Dolores Cathcart. They examine how Japanese and Americans might interact differently when thrust into a group setting. The authors maintain that early life experiences with "permanent and nonpermanent groups" is at the heart of these differences. The Japanese culture teaches people to perceive group affiliations, whether the family or the corporation, as enduring long-term relationships. Americans, on the other hand, see group contacts as impermanent and short-lived. These perceptions, according to Cathcart and Cathcart, transfer into the small-group communication setting. To clarify this key point they construct a hypothetical small group and isolate a number of communication variables that will be altered by culture. For example, they compare and contrast differences with regard to group harmony and consensus, directness and indirectness, verbal and nonverbal language, and patience and impatience. While these communication discrepancies are significant, the authors conclude with the optimistic view that cross-cultural groups are not doomed to failure. Rather, Cathcart and Cathcart propose that if we have a fund of knowledge about a particular culture we can adapt and adjust to many of the cultural differences. This essay offers just such a fund of knowledge about Americans and Japanese.

Communication in the Multicultural Group

Richard E. Porter and Larry A. Samovar

Today, in the United States, we find numerous cultures and co-cultures. Indeed, the United States is emerging rapidly as a diverse multicultural society. Some cultures are based on race: Black, Hispanic, Oriental, and the Native American. Others are based on ethnic differences: Jew, Italian, German, Cambodian, Mexican, are but a few of the many ethnic cultures we find in the United States. There are also cultures based on socioeconomic differences. The culture of a Rockefeller or a Kennedy is vastly different from that of a third-generation welfare family living in Detroit. The magnitude of cultural diversity in the United States can be seen in New York City where 185 different countries are represented with substantial populations. It is also seen in the California public schools where there is no longer a majority segment of the population. Whites account for 49 percent of the student population while people of color account for 51 percent. Of that 51 percent, 31 percent are Hispanic, 9 percent are Black, and 11 percent Asian.[1] These statistics strongly suggest that intercultural contact is inevitable.

Furthermore, court decisions and legislative actions have forced increased intercultural contact. Equal opportunity and affirmative action employment practices, desegregation and integration of public schools, and the establishment of minority quotas for admission to unions, colleges, universities, and graduate and professional schools have increased intercultural contact.

Changes in immigration patterns have shifted segments of the world population. People from Vietnam, Cambodia, Laos, Cuba, Haiti, Colombia, Nicaragua, El Salvador, and Ecuador, among others, have entered the United States and become our neighbors. As these people try to adjust their lives to this culture, there are many opportunities for intercultural contacts in our daily lives.

Almost every facet of our lives finds us increasingly in the presence of and having greater awareness of others who are culturally different. Contacts with cultures that often appear unfamiliar, alien, and at times mysterious may now be a part of our day-to-day routine. We are no longer isolated from one another in time and space. Instead, we face each other on a daily basis.

With this momentum toward multiculturalism comes a cultural diversity that in the past has not received adequate recognition. If our society is to be one of peace where all people are accorded respect and dignity, we must learn to interact successfully with culturally diverse people.

Successful interaction within culturally diverse settings requires that we develop a facility for intercultural communication and learn to use it in a wide variety of communication situations. One of these situations, and the one we will examine, is the

This essay was written expressly for the seventh edition. Permission to reprint must be obtained from the authors. Richard E. Porter is affiliated with the Department of Speech Communication at California State University, Long Beach. Larry A. Samovar is affiliated with the Department of Speech Communication at San Diego State University.

small group. Before considering this, however, brief attention will be given to the relationships between culture and communication.

Culture and Communication

The link between culture and communication is crucial to understanding intercultural communication because it is through the influence of culture that people learn to communicate. A Japanese, an Austrian, or an American learns to communicate like other Japanese, Austrians, or Americans. Their behavior conveys meaning because it is learned and shared; it is cultural. People perceive their world through categories, concepts, and labels that are products of their culture.

Culture

Culture is an all-encompassing form or pattern for living that is acquired through the process of being born into and raised in a particular society. Culture is complex, abstract, and pervasive. It impacts on many aspects of human social and communicative activity.

Cultures develop around ways of life and value systems. Religious, philosophical, political, economic, and social role views may differ greatly from our own, as may communities, modes of life, forms of work, degrees of industrialization, and social organization. In these cases, we find people are noticeably different from ourselves in their ways of life, customs, and traditions. Even within dominant cultures we find diversity among co-cultures. Members of the drug culture, for instance, share values and perceptions of the world that are quite different than those shared by members of the white supremacy movement, gay community, or feminist movement.

Perception

One of culture's most significant effects is on the perceptual process. In its simplest sense, *perception is the internal process by which we select, evaluate, and organize the external environment.* In other words, perception is the conversion of the physical energies of our environment into meaningful experience. A number of corollary issues arise out of this definition that help explain the relationship between perception and culture. It is believed generally that people behave as they do because of the ways in which they perceive the world, and that these behaviors are learned as part of their cultural experiences. Whether in judging beauty or describing snow, we respond to stimuli as we do primarily because our culture has taught us to do so. We tend to notice, reflect on, and respond to those elements in our environment that are important to us. In the United States we might respond principally to a thing's size and cost while to the Japanese, color might be the important criterion. Culture tends to determine which are the important criteria of perception.

Cultural similarity in perception makes the sharing of meaning possible. The ways in which we communicate, the circumstances of our communication, the language and language style we use, and our nonverbal behaviors are primarily all responses to and functions of our culture. As cultures differ from one another, the communication practices and behaviors of individuals reared in those cultures will also be different.

Social Perception

Social perception is the process by which we construct our unique social realities by attributing meaning to the social objects and events we encounter in our environments. It is an extremely important aspect of communication. Culture conditions and structures our perceptual processes so that we develop culturally inspired perceptual sets. These sets not only help determine which external stimuli reach our awareness, but more importantly, they significantly influence the social aspect of perception—the social construction of reality by the attribution of meaning to these stimuli. The difficulties in communication caused by this perceptual variability can best be lowered by knowing about and understanding the cultural factors that are subject to variation and honestly and sincerely desiring to communicate successfully across cultural boundaries.

Intercultural Communication

The difficulties that cultural diversity poses for effective communication have given rise to the marriage of culture and communication and to the recognition of intercultural communication. Inherent in this fusion is the idea that intercultural communication entails the investigation of culture and the difficulties of communicating across cultural boundaries.

To help us understand what is involved in intercultural communication, we begin with a fundamental definition. *Intercultural communication is defined as a communication situation in which a message produced in one culture must be processed in another culture.* In other words, whenever a person who is a member of one culture sends a message—whether verbal or nonverbal, spoken or written—to someone who is a member of another culture, both are engaged in intercultural communication.

Intercultural communication can best be understood as cultural diversity in the perception of social objects and events. A central tenet of this position is that minor communication problems are often exaggerated by perceptual diversity. To understand the worlds and actions of others, we must try to understand their perceptual frames of reference. We must learn to understand how they perceive the world. In the ideal intercultural encounter we would hope for many overlapping experiences and a commonality of perceptions. Cultural diversity, however, tends to introduce us to dissimilar experiences, and hence, to varied and frequently strange and unfamiliar perceptions of the external world.

Communication Context

Any communicative interaction takes place within some social and physical context. When people are communicating within their culture they are usually aware of the context and it does little to hinder the communication. When people are engaged in intercultural communication, however, the context in which that communication takes place can have a strong impact. Unless both parties to intercultural communication are aware of how their culture affects the contextual element of communication, they can be in for some surprising communication difficulty.

We begin with the assumption that communicative behavior is governed by rules. By a rule, we mean a principle or regulation that governs conduct and procedure. In communication, rules act as a system of expected behavior patterns that organize interaction between individuals. Communication rules are both culturally and contextually bound. Although the social setting and situation may determine the type of rules that are appropriate, the culture determines the rules. In Iraq, for instance, a contextual rule prohibits females from having unfamiliar males visit them at home. In the United States, however, it is not considered socially inappropriate for unknown males to visit females at home. Rules dictate behavior by establishing appropriate responses to stimuli for a particular communication context.

Communication rules include both verbal and nonverbal components. The rules determine not only what should be said but how it should be said. Nonverbal rules apply to proper gestures, facial expressions, eye contact, proxemics, vocal tone, and body movements.

Unless one is prepared to function in the contextual environment of another culture, he or she may be in for an unpleasant experience. The intercultural situation can be one of high stress both physically and mentally. The effects of this stress may result in culture shock. In order to avoid culture shock, it is necessary to have a full understanding of communication context and how it varies culturally. We must remember that cultural contexts are neither right nor wrong, nor better nor worse; they are just different.

Intercultural Communication Within Multicultural Groups

Small-group communication settings involve intercultural communication when a group is composed of people from diverse cultural backgrounds. This quite naturally occurs in international settings when people from various countries and cultures meet to discuss international politics, economics, and business. We may also find it in domestic areas when civic bodies attempt to solve problems within the community or when students representing various ethnic and racial backgrounds meet to recommend school policies and actions.

Small-group communication is a complex process involving highly complicated interrelationships between many dynamic elements. The sharing of common goals or purposes, a social organization, the establishment of communication channels, and the sharing of relevant beliefs and values are all recognized necessary ingredients for the emergence of a group and the development of an atmosphere suitable for small-group communication. In general, a certain similarity between people is necessary for the creation of this atmosphere and the development of what Fisher calls *groupness*.[2] Successful small-group formation and communication are difficult enough when group members are culturally similar, but when members are culturally diverse, the task may become formidable.

Intercultural small-group communication occurs in both international and domestic settings. In either setting, however, successful intercultural communication is dependent on both a desire to communicate successfully and a recognition of cultural influences on communication processes.

A further aspect of culture that can have a significant effect on multicultural small-group communication is what anthropologist Edward T. Hall has identified as the context dimension of culture.[3] According to this view, cultures vary along a context dimension that ranges from low to high. What this refers to as far as communication is concerned is the amount of shared cultural knowledge and background the communicators possess. Hall states:

> Any transaction can be characterized as high-, low-, or middle-context. HC transactions feature preprogrammed information that is in the receiver and in the setting, with only minimal information in the transmitted message. LC transactions are the reverse. Most of the information must be in the transmitted message in order to make up for what is missing in the context.[4]

An example of where various cultures lie along the context dimension can be seen in Table 1.

In high-context cultures most of the information is either in the physical context or is internalized in the people who are a part of the interaction. In low-context cultures, however, most of the information is contained in the verbal message and very little is embedded in the context or within the participants. High-context cultures such as Japan, Korea, and Taiwan tend to be more aware of their surroundings and their environment and do not rely on verbal communication as their main information source. The Korean language contains a word *nunchi* that literally means being able to communicate through your eyes. In high-context cultures, so much information is available in the environment that it is unnecessary to state verbally that which is obvious. Oral statements of affection, for instance, are very rare because it is not necessary to restate what is communicated nonverbally. When the context says "You are welcome here," it is not necessary to state it orally.

This notion of context poses problems when members of a small group are from cultures that differ in context level. When we meet with members of high-context

Table 1
High- and Low-Context Cultures in Order

High-Context Cultures[5]	
	Japanese
	Arab
	Greek
	Spanish
	Italian
	English
	French
	American
	Scandinavian
	German
	German-Swiss

Low-Context Cultures

cultures, unless we have the requisite contextual programming, we are liable to have difficulty in communicating because the high-context messages do not contain sufficient information for us to gain true or complete meaning. What is worse, we may interpret a high-context message according to our low-context disposition and reach entirely the wrong meaning.

There are four aspects of cultural context that can affect multicultural small-group discussion. First, verbal messages are extremely important in low-context cultures. It is in the verbal message that the information to be shared is coded. It is not readily available from the environment because people in low-context cultures do not tend to learn how to perceive the environment for information. Second, low-context people who rely primarily on verbal messages for information are perceived as less attractive and less credible by people from high-context cultures. Third, people in high-context cultures are more adept at reading nonverbal behavior and the environment. Fourth, people in high-context cultures have an expectation that others are also able to understand the unarticulated communication; hence, they do not speak as much as people from low-context cultures.

A consequence of cultural context can be seen by comparing Asian and American communication patterns. Asians usually assess the feelings and state of mind of those present. The harmony of the group is paramount, and they do not want to do anything that would lessen that harmony. Thus, they tend to give their opinions in an indirect manner.[6] Asiatic modes of communication can be labeled as defensive and situational. Their conversation often stops abruptly, or the subject is changed without obvious reason, as soon as a speaker feels that the listener does not agree totally with the expressed point of view or that feelings may have been hurt.[7]

On the other hand, Americans tend to be task oriented, direct, and businesslike. They want to get immediately to the heart of the matter. They depreciate what are considered to be irrelevant concerns such as individual feelings and urge immediate action to get the job done.

Cultural diversity in the concept of time can also affect multicultural small-group communication. In American, Australian, German, English, Israeli, Swiss, and Scandinavian cultures, for example, time is treated as a valuable, tangible, and limited resource. Like money, time is saved, wasted, given, taken, made, spent, run out of, and budgeted. Because time is so valuable, it is used productively, and is compartmentalized into efficient intervals of activity.[8] In Oriental countries, such as Japan, China, and Korea, as well as Middle Eastern countries such as Saudi Arabia and Latin American countries such as Mexico, Brazil, and Chile, the cultural rules specify that people take their time before becoming engaged in activity. In many of these countries, meetings begin with extended social acquaintance and the establishment of social rapport over many cups of coffee or tea. The development of an extended social acquaintance does not mean five or ten minutes. It may take hours or perhaps even several meetings during which the group task may not even be mentioned in order to establish an appropriate social climate.

This diversity in the use of time can be frustrating to the American who is culturally biased toward rapid activity and being engaged. Americans work by deadlines, and once given a deadline, they race to meet or beat it. Giving a task a deadline heightens its importance and creates a sense of urgency. Deadlines elsewhere, however, may produce opposite results. An Arab may take a deadline as an insult. Arabs consider the drinking of coffee and chatting as doing something whereas the American sees it as doing nothing. Ethiopians attach prestige to things that take a long time.[9]

Culture also governs the process by which negotiation takes place. Perceptions of both the concept and the process differ culturally. For instance, in the Persian language the word for compromise does not mean a midway solution that both sides can accept as it does in English; instead, it means surrendering one's principles. Also, a mediator is seen as a meddler, someone who is bargaining uninvited. In India and the Middle East the process of negotiation is enjoyed. Negotiation is seen as an act of bargaining in which there is give and take. Each person sets out to obtain the best deal he or she can, and most enjoy the process of striking a bargain. The influence of Islam gives the Saudi businessman a strong sense of honor and of personal dignity. Although Saudis are often tough and skilled negotiators, an agreement will be honored to the letter. The same, of course, is expected in return.

The pace of conversation is another culturally influenced communication variable that can affect multicultural group communication. Asians prefer a reflective or slow pace. They often let other group members begin so that they can respond to arguments and set the pace once the other side has had its say. The Chinese are prone to seem passive and ask a lot of questions. They probe for information and conceal any eagerness they may feel. They listen carefully and give subtle hints about their requirements for reaching group consensus. The French and Koreans prefer to give their arguments first and then their conclusions. Americans begin with their position and then develop the evidence to support it. Chinese and Japanese tend to be very detail oriented, while Americans like to develop the big picture. Americans often are not trusted by members of other cultures because they omit perceived essential details.

Cultural diversity in rhetorical practices also influences the multicultural group. In Mexico and many Middle Eastern countries, people are selected to participate in multicultural groups because of their rhetorical skills. Among Arabs, "strong manhood is co-extensive with strong rhetoric."[10] Educated and illiterate alike have extraordinary mastery of their language expressed through a rich vocabulary and well-rounded, complex phrases. In Western countries, gender is no longer much of a factor, but in Middle Eastern and Asian countries where women have little status, participants are nearly always men.

Another problem we may face in intercultural small-group communication is the actual communication process itself. This is readily seen if we examine the differences in approach between Americans and Japanese. We Americans want to talk to the one in authority who can make tough decisions. We want to get down to business and drive a hard bargain, and we want answers now. We are busy; time is money, and we cannot fool around. The Japanese, however, are quite different in their approach. "If we were to place Japanese concepts of self and group at one end of a continuum it would be possible to produce an almost perfect paradigm by placing American concepts at the other."[11] In other words, Japanese concepts of self and group are essentially the opposite of our own. Some distinctions between American and Japanese concepts will be discussed in order to see how different approaches to group interaction influence communication.

Americans tend to view groups as being composed of individuals, in which the role of the individual is paramount. This concern with the individual is reflected in the

American culture through admiration of "rugged individualism" and the desire to interact with the responsible party. The Japanese, on the other hand, have a selfless view of groups. The group is the social entity; individual identity is submerged for group identity.

This distinction between the concept of self in relation to groups is important in terms of decision making and the outcomes of intercultural negotiation. The American concept of individual importance leads to a notion of individual responsibility. A single, unique person is ultimately responsible for decisions and their consequences. This individual is also expected to accept blame for decisions that lead to bad consequences. In a sense, Americans want to know whom to "hang" when things go wrong. The Japanese, however, operate in a group sense rather than an individual sense. Decisions result from group interaction and group consensus; the group, not the individual, is responsible for the consequences of its action, and when something goes wrong the group, not the individual, is held responsible. The extremes of this position are aptly described by Cathcart and Cathcart:

> This embodiment of group can be carried to the point where, in the extreme circumstances, those persons at the top of the group hierarchy feel constrained to answer for the misdeed of individual group members by committing *harikiri* (suicide) in order to erase the blot on the group's honor. The act of *harikiri* reflects a total denial of self and a complete loyalty to the group.[12]

Contrast this in your imagination, if you will. Can you imagine the president of a top U.S. corporation committing suicide because a machine shop supervisor made a poor decision that adversely affected profits and angered stockholders and customers?

In discussing the international dimension of intercultural communication, we have reviewed several cultural differences that might be found among participants in multicultural group interaction. The point here is to emphasize how culture affects our participation in small-group communication and how it may influence our behaviors and the meanings—both social and literal—that we attribute to other people and to their messages. Much of what we have viewed may seem trivial; to others, however, these matters are very important. If we are to be successful intercultural communicators, we must realize how seemingly insignificant matters can affect the dynamics of our intercultural groups.

When we shift our interest to the domestic dimension of intercultural communication, we are still faced with the problems of cultural diversity but in a way that frequently manifests itself in terms of trust, values, and expectations.

Inherent in a culturally diverse community are problems of racial, ethnic, and gender prejudice. There are many members of the community who have grown up with negative beliefs about other races and ethnic backgrounds as well as the role and place of women. This is not a perception peculiar only to white Anglos; it is common across races and ethnic groups. This diversity in experience can lead to differences in ideas about who can be trusted. In an ideal group situation, everyone trusts each other; they do not feel that someone will try to do them harm. In many multicultural settings, though, the situation is different. Some people, because of their previous experiences and current expectations, may sense that others cannot be trusted, that they will ultimately harm or cheat them.

Frequently, culturally diversified groups are found when civic bodies or panels are formed. In this case the first effort is often to empanel as members a priest, a minister, a rabbi, a Black, an Oriental, and a Hispanic as well as women and representatives of other diverse groups within the community such as gays, civil libertarians, youth, welfare recipients, and senior citizens. However admirable this effort may be in terms of democratic institutions, it can result in artificially created groups whose compositions defy the formation of an atmosphere conducive to the cohesiveness and member satisfaction that are necessary for the feeling of "groupness" mentioned earlier. This is especially the case when there are culturally diverse values, beliefs, and attitudes. Whereas a natural group—one formed through the ongoing process of group dynamics—is composed of members who share similar relevant values, beliefs, and attitudes. Artificial groups—those we form by administrative action—may be composed of persons who have diverse value systems and who distrust or even dislike the cultural systems of each other. Toleration may be practiced, but it may not overcome differences in basic beliefs and values that influence the outcome of group interaction.

The value systems of people engaged in small-group communication get in the way of their achieving consensus or agreement on an issue at times. When group members are from different cultures, this variance often amplifies the problem because of the influence culture has on the development of values. As cultural diversity increases, the chance of value conflict also increases. This aspect is especially a problem in final phases of discussions when decisions are being made. An example from a group-discussion class illustrates this point. A group had been formed at the beginning of the semester to discuss the common interest problem of divorce in the United States. For several weeks everything went well. During the initial phases of the discussion, agreement was easily reached on the nature of the problem, its extent, its effects, and even its causes. When the solution phase of the discussion began, however, difficulty soon developed. One member of the group of South American origin was a deeply devout Catholic. To him, the only possible solution was to make divorce illegal because it was an immoral act that should not be permitted. This alternative was his only answer; he was adamantly opposed to any other possible solution. The result was an initial attempt by other members of the group to communicate with him and attempt to have him modify his position or at least listen to alternatives that could be available to non-Catholics. This effort met with no success, and when it became evident that he would neither alter his position nor listen to other views, he was in effect banished from the group. He became a mere observer where he had once been an active participant; after a short time, he began to miss the discussions altogether. Here was a case where the prevailing belief-value system of the group was too different from his, and it soon became more rewarding for him not to be a member of the group than to continue his group membership. Consequently, he dropped out of the group.

Granted, this is an extreme example, but it does illustrate vividly the situation in which the value system of an individual derived from his cultural heritage was of sufficient strength to prevent him from interacting with his fellow students and to even consider their positions. We also must realize that although Catholicism transcends culture, it is mediated by various cultures. This was one case where the cultural tradition of this man's origin maximized Catholic dogma and made it a very strong part of his value system.

Similar situations can easily arise when we form groups that represent all views and interests within a community. Perhaps it will not always be so severe as to disrupt the group or lead to its disintegration, but it can lead to problems that must be understood and resolved before a group can form its identity and reach consensus. We must remember that some views are not compatible with others, just as some interests are not compatible with others. When diverse views and interests are forced to interact, the outcome may not be what is expected or desired, and may ultimately frustrate attempts to obtain representative views in the formulation of community policies.

In a multicultural community there are also problems of language differences. Because many people are new to the United States, they may have difficulty with the English language; they may not speak English or may not speak it sufficiently. Their command of the language may be inadequate, which can result in misunderstandings. Suspicion and feelings of uneasiness can develop when some members of the community speak a language that cannot be understood by others. The presence of diverse languages can create feelings of resentment among those who do not understand the languages being spoken.

Cultural differences in nonverbal behavior can also lead to difficulty in the multicultural group. It might be in the form of dress and appearance: A Black wearing a cornrow hairstyle or a Hindu wearing a turban can cause people to feel strange because they do not understand the self-significance of a person's appearance. Diverse nonverbal behavior may also be expressed in forms of greeting that employ special handshakes or embraces. Again, that which is different is viewed suspiciously.

Summary

Here we have emphasized the view that the chief problem in intercultural communication lies in social perception. We have suggested that culture strongly influences social perception, which leads to errors in the interpretation of messages. If there is to be successful intercultural communication within small groups in both domestic and international arenas, we must be aware of the cultural factors that affect communication in both our own cultures and the cultures of others. We must understand both cultural differences and cultural similarities. Understanding differences can help us recognize problems, and understanding similarities can help us become closer.

Notes

1. N.S. Mehta, S. Monroe, and D. Winbush, "Beyond the Melting Pot." *Time,* April 9, 1990, 28–31.
2. B.A. Fisher, *Small Group Decision Making Communication and the Group Process* (New York: McGraw-Hill, 1976).
3. Edward T. Hall, *Beyond Culture* (Garden City, NY: Doubleday, 1976).
4. Hall, 101.
5. L. Copeland and L. Griggs, *Going International: How to Make Friends and Deal Effectively in the Global Marketplace* (New York: Random House, 1985).
6. Jan Servaes, "Cultural Identity in East and West." *Howard Journal of Communications* 1 (1988), 68.
7. Servaes, 68.
8. Copeland and Griggs, 8.
9.. Copeland and Griggs, 9.
10. R. Patai, *The Arab Mind,* rev. ed. (New York: Scribner's, 1983), 49.
11. D. Cathcart and R. Cathcart, "Japanese Social Experience and Concepts of Group." In L. Samovar and R. Porter (eds.), *Intercultural Communication: A Reader* 2d ed. (Belmont, CA: Wadsworth, 1976), 58.
12. Cathcart and Cathcart, 59–60.

Comparing Group Communication Across Cultures: Leadership, Conformity, and Discussion Processes

Myron W. Lustig and Laura L. Cassotta

Few studies of small-group processes have been concerned specifically with cross-cultural comparisons. For instance, all of the small-group research published in communication journals in the 1970s (Cragan & Wright 1980) was based on subjects from the United States, as were nearly all such studies published in the 1980s (Cragan & Wright 1988). Unfortunately, one cannot assume that U.S. subjects will necessarily react like group members from other cultures.

Despite the lack of solid cross-cultural research comparing group communication across cultures, the work of Geerte Hofstede can be used to understand cultural differences in group-communication processes. Hofstede (1980, 1984) has assembled some impressive information concerning cultural differences in work-related value orientations. Hofstede's theory is based on the assertion that people carry "mental programs" that are developed during childhood and reinforced by society. These mental programs contain aspects of one's culture and are expressed through the dominant values of that culture. In order to identify the principal values of different cultures, Hofstede surveyed over 116,000 employees of a large multinational business organization in forty countries. Through theoretical reasoning and statistical analyses, Hofstede identified four dimensions along which dominant value systems of a culture can be ordered: power distance, uncertainty avoidance, individualism-collectivism, and masculinity-femininity. Recent evidence suggests that Hofstede's dimensions are applicable not only to work-related values but to cultural values generally (Forgas & Bond 1985; Hofstede & Bond 1984). Table 1 provides a ranking of the forty countries on each of the four dimensions. In order to provide a better understanding of Hofstede's theory, each of the dimensions will be briefly outlined.

Power distance indicates the degree to which the culture believes that institutional and organizational power should be distributed unequally. Cultures with a small power distance, such as Austria, Denmark, Israel, and New Zealand, believe in minimizing social or class inequalities, reducing hierarchical organizational structures, and using power only for legitimate purposes. Cultures with a large power distance, such as Mexico, the Philippines, Venezuela, and India, believe in a social order in which each person has a rightful and protected place, hierarchy presumes existential inequality, and the legitimacy of the purposes desired by the power holder is irrelevant.

Uncertainty avoidance refers to the extent to which the culture feels threatened by ambiguous situations and tries to avoid uncertainty by establishing more structure. Cultures with weak uncertainty avoidance, including Great Britain, Hong Kong, Ireland, and Sweden, believe in the reduction of rules, the acceptance of dissent, a willingness to take risks in life, and tolerance for deviation from expected behaviors.

This essay appeared in print for the first time in the sixth edition. Permission to reprint must be obtained from the authors. Myron Lustig is affiliated with the School of Communication at San Diego State University.

Table 1
Ranking of Forty Countries on Hofstede's Four Dimensions of Cultural Differences

	Power Distance	Uncertainty Avoidance	Individualism- Collectivism	Masculinity- Femininity
Argentina	25	10	23	18
Australia	29	27	2	14
Austria	40	19	18	2
Belgium	12	3	8	20
Brazil	7	16	25	23
Canada	27	31	4	21
Chile	15	8	33	34
Colombia	10	14	39	11
Denmark	38	39	9	37
Finland	33	24	17	35
France	9	7	11	29
Germany	30	21	15	9
Great Britain	31	35	3	8
Greece	17	1	27	16
Hong Kong	8	37	32	17
India	4	34	21	19
Iran	18	23	24	28
Ireland	36	36	12	7
Israel	39	13	19	25
Italy	23	17	7	4
Japan	22	4	22	1
Mexico	2	12	29	6
Netherlands	28	26	5	38
New Zealand	37	30	6	15
Norway	34	28	13	39
Pakistan	21	18	38	22
Peru	13	7	37	31
Philippines	1	33	28	10
Portugal	16	2	30	33
Singapore	6	40	34	24
South Africa	24	29	16	12
Spain	20	9	20	30
Sweden	35	38	10	40
Switzerland	32	25	14	5
Taiwan	19	20	36	27
Thailand	14	22	35	32
Turkey	11	11	26	26
U.S.	26	32	1	13
Venezuela	3	15	40	3
Yugoslavia	5	5	31	36

Note: A low ranking (e.g., 3) indicates a high rating on that dimension.

Adapted from Hofstede (1980), 315.

Cultures with strong uncertainty avoidance, including Greece, Belgium, Japan, and Portugal, have high levels of anxiety and aggressiveness that create a strong inner urge to work hard, the need for extensive rules and regulations, a desire for consensus about goals, and a craving for certainty and security.

Individualism-collectivism describes the degree to which a culture relies on and has allegiance to the self or the group. Cultures with an individualist orientation, such as the United States, Australia, Netherlands, and Belgium, believe that people are only supposed to take care of themselves and, perhaps, their immediate families, such that autonomy, independence, privacy, and an "I" consciousness are the ideal. Cultures with a collectivist orientation, such as Venezuela, Thailand, Pakistan, and Peru, expect their in-groups to take care of them, in exchange for which they feel an absolute loyalty to the group. Consequently, collectivist cultures believe in obligations to the group, dependence of the individual on organizations and institutions, a "we" consciousness, and an emphasis on belongingness.

Masculinity-femininity indicates the degree to which a culture values "masculine" behaviors such as assertiveness and the acquisition of wealth or "feminine" behaviors such as caring for others and the quality of life. Cultures with a masculine orientation, including Japan, Italy, and Mexico, believe in performance, achievement, ambition, the acquisition of material goods, and ostentatious manliness. Cultures with a feminine orientation, including Norway and Portugal, believe in the quality of life, service to others, equality between the sexes, nurturing roles, and sympathy for the unfortunate.

Each of Hofstede's four dimensions provides insights into the influence of culture on the communication process. Based on an analysis of existing literature and the ideas of Hofstede's value dimensions of international cultures, we will now discuss cross-cultural effects in three areas of small-group communication: leadership styles, conformity, and discussion procedures.

Leadership Styles

Differences in leadership style often affect group communication (Shaw 1976). Leadership differences are based, in part, on a culture's values (Hofstede 1980) and the group members' responsiveness to a particular leadership style. "Leadership style" means the dominant set of behaviors that typically characterize a leader's activities (Fiedler 1967). Though various leadership styles have been proposed, most concern behavioral patterns that focus on either an autocratic (directive, authoritarian) style of leadership or a democratic (nondirective, consultative) style of leadership (Shaw 1976).

Autocratic leadership is primarily characterized by decisiveness, control, and strict enforcement of rules. An autocratic leader usually makes decisions promptly and communicates them to subordinates clearly and firmly. Such a leader expects others to carry out decisions loyally and without raising difficulties. An autocratic leader typically utilizes coercive or referent power (Hofstede 1980, 1984).

Democratic leadership typically meets with subordinates when there is a decision to be made. A democratic leader puts problems before the group, invites discussion, and accepts the majority viewpoint. Such a leader exercises limited control and promotes self-initiative and cooperation. Democratic leadership is commonly associated with the use of legitimate or expert power (Hofstede 1980, 1984).

Leadership Styles and Power Distance

A culture's power distance and preferred leadership style are closely related. A culture's power distance index (PDI) can be used to predict the leadership style preferred.

Hofstede (1980) operationally defined high-PDI countries as those in which decisions were usually made in an autocratic, persuasive, or paternalistic style, rather than in a consultative or democratic style. Cultures with a high PDI value inequality between group members, hierarchical order, and directive behavior (Hofstede 1984). Members of a culture with a high PDI, such as Mexico and India, should react positively to autocratic leadership because they have been socialized to defer to the authority of those with power.

Cultures with a low PDI value equality, independence, and the use of power for legitimate purposes (Hofstede 1984). These characteristics are indicative of a democratic style of leadership. Members of low-PDI cultures, such as the United States and Austria, are socialized to value cooperative work, deferring to power only for legitimate purposes. Consequently, group efficacy and satisfaction in low-PDI cultures will be much higher under democratic rather than authoritarian leadership.

In an interesting study based on U.S. subjects, Remland (1984) found that behaviors that functioned to reduce status differences in superior-subordinate interactions were judged very favorably. However, Remland's (1984) findings would apply for low-PDI cultures but not for high-PDI cultures, as only low-PDI cultures believe in minimizing institutional and organizational power by distributing power equally.

Leadership Styles and Uncertainty Reduction

The manner in which members of a culture respond to a leader is somewhat contingent on the uncertainty of the situation and how that culture typically copes with uncertainty. One strategy used to cope with uncertainty is to adhere to rules (Hofstede 1984). Commonly, a leader's primary responsibility is making and enforcing the group's rules. Therefore, a culture's uncertainty-avoidance index (UAI) should predict the leadership style preferred.

Cultures with a high UAI rely on the enforcement of rules, hierarchical structure, and the competence of those with authority to reduce uncertainty (Hofstede 1984). A leader exercising autocratic behaviors, thus functioning to reduce uncertainty, will be more effective in high-UAI cultures such as Greece and Portugal. Conversely, low-UAI cultures are characterized by a greater tolerance for uncertainty and less dependence on rules, established order, or authority. Consequently, group members from low-UAI cultures such as Sweden and Denmark should be more satisfied under a democratic style of leadership.

Leadership Styles and Individualism

Hofstede (1984) found that a culture's power distance and individualism (IND) indexes have a strong negative correlation. Thus, as a culture's PDI (which includes the culture's dependency on powerful individuals such as group leaders) increases, IND (including the culture's dependency on the group) decreases. Because cultures with a low PDI prefer a democratic style of leadership and PDI is negatively correlated with IND, it can be predicted that group members from high-IND cultures will be most satisfied under a leader who promotes self-initiative and exercises influence only when legitimate. Examples of such cultures include Denmark and New Zealand. Conversely, group members from low-IND cultures will be more satisfied under an autocratic leader who promotes traditional points of view. Examples of such cultures include Venezuela and Chile.

Leadership Styles and Masculinity

Cultural conditioning, particularly sex-role socialization, is manifested through behaviors such as leadership style. A culture's preferred leadership style can be predicted based on values toward sex-role patterns.

Commonly, masculinity is associated with objectivity, assertiveness, discipline, and control (Berryman-Fink 1985). These attributes are consistent with an autocratic style of leadership. Group members in high-masculinity index (MAS) cultures such as Japan and Germany will be more satisfied under an autocratic leader who exercises strong influence. Conversely, low masculinity or high femininity is typically associated with subjectivity, an emphasis on interpersonal relations, and openness (Baird & Bradley 1979; Berryman-Fink 1985). These characteristics are indicative of a democratic style of leadership. Therefore, group members in low-masculine cultures such as Norway and Sweden should function more effectively under a democratic leader.

Conformity

The cultural environment influences the level of conformity in groups (Berry 1976; Milgram 1961; Shuter 1977). Hofstede's value dimensions help to determine the effects of cultural values on group members' susceptibility to conform.

The everyday conception of conformity as agreement with the majority only for the sake of agreement is incomplete (Shaw 1976). Two types of conformity can be differentiated: conformity based on informational social influence and conformity based on normative social influence. Informational social influence is the result of the value that conformity may have for the individual. Normative social influence results from a desire to conform to the expectations of the group (Shaw 1976). As the primary concern of this paper is with group processes, the explanations proposed will focus on conformity resulting from normative social influence.

Certain personality traits, stimulus factors, situational factors, and intragroup relations predispose an individual to conform (Shaw 1976). Individuals susceptible to conform to group norms typically are authoritative, traditional, loyal to the group, compliant to status and rules, and dependent on social approval (Frager 1970; Milgram 1961; Shaw 1976). In contrast, individuals less likely to conform are nonauthoritative, independent, individualistic, and self-reliant. These characteristics are consistent with Hofstede's (1980) value dimensions of cultures.

Research indicates that Americans are responsive to group pressure (Asch 1952; Milgram 1964), but social conformity is not exclusively an American phenomenon

(Milgram 1961). However, just because conformity studies have demonstrated that American behaviors are influenced by the group, one cannot safely generalize that characteristic to all cultures (Shuter 1977). The cultural environment can be an influential factor in determining individuals' sensitivity to conform. Cross-cultural research has indicated that members of other cultures, including the Japanese, Norwegians, and Germans (Frager 1970; Milgram 1961) conform to social pressures. A review of pertinent cross-cultural literature and the application of Hofstede's value dimensions in the formulation of hypotheses should provide a better understanding of the relationship between culture and conformity.

Conformity and Power Distance

Power distance is a measure of the influence one individual has over another or others (Hofstede 1980, 1984). A key concept of the power-distance dimension is the strength of an individual's authority. Cultures with a high PDI prefer a hierarchical order in which few individuals hold the power and the less powerful are expected to conform to the authority of the powerful (Hofstede 1980, 1984). Authoritarians conform to the majority opinion more than nonauthoritarians (Shaw 1976). Consequently, cultures with a high PDI, valuing obedience, an autocratic decision-making style, and status (Hofstede 1980, 1984), should also demonstrate a strong predisposition toward conformity. One way a high power distance is maintained is by the conforming behaviors of the powerless.

Group members from a culture with a small power-distance index (PDI) would be less likely to conform to the majority. Cultures with a small PDI value independence, a consultative decision-making style, and the use of power only for legitimate reasons (Hofstede 1980, 1984). Such a culture does not rely on the authority of the powerful imposed by the hierarchical structure as much as a high-PDI culture. Therefore, one can assume that a culture with a low PDI would be less likely to demonstrate conforming behaviors than a culture with a high PDI.

Based on the previous line of reasoning and a culture's location on Hofstede's PDI, one can predict cultural differences in conforming behavior. For example, countries with high-PDI scores, such as Mexico, Venezuela, and Brazil, should also exhibit a sensitivity toward social pressures. In contrast, cultures with a low PDI, such as Sweden, would demonstrate less conformity.

Conformity and Uncertainty Avoidance

Ambiguous stimuli produce greater conformity than unambiguous stimuli (Asch 1951; Shaw 1976; Sherif & Sherif 1956). Likewise, individuals in a high-uncertainty-avoidance (UAI) culture, who feel threatened by ambiguous situations (Hofstede 1980, 1984), will be more conforming than individuals in a low-UAI culture. Typically, individual characteristics of cultures with a high UAI include high anxiety and stress levels, fear of the future, and a need for security and predictability of behaviors. Group members of such cultures are conditioned to value rules, rituals, the opinions of others, and consensus as defenses against uncertainty (Hofstede 1980, 1984). Conformity introduces order and coordination of individual behaviors and expectations from group members (Shaw 1976), thus functioning as an effective way to cope with uncertainty.

Based on research on conformity and the dominant values of Hofstede's UAI, one can predict cultures that would exhibit a high level of conformity. For instance, one can predict that the Japanese, a culture that values collectivity and group cohesiveness (Frager 1970) and has a high-UAI score (Hofstede 1980, 1984), is likely to be sensitive to group pressures for conformity. Although this prediction is theoretically logical, it deserves further investigation. Studies (e.g., Frager 1970) have demonstrated that the common stereotype of the Japanese as conformist may be exaggerated. One may also predict that the Spanish culture, which values group cohesiveness and is moderately high on Hofstede's UAI (Hofstede 1980, 1984), would expect conforming behaviors of its members.

Cultures that have a high tolerance for ambiguity should be less conforming. Characteristics typical of a low-UAI culture include a low anxiety level, readiness to live day by day, and little resistance to change. Group members from a culture with a low UAI are conditioned to value broad guidelines and risk taking. Rules and rituals are not strongly upheld in order to cope with uncertainty (Hofstede 1980, 1984).

From the relationship of low-UAI cultures and typical nonconforming individuals, one may predict that cultures with a low UAI would also exhibit low conformist behavioral patterns. For instance, Sweden, a typically individualistic culture and one that scores low on Hofstede's UAI, would likely demonstrate less conforming behaviors than a high-UAI culture such as France.

Conformity and Individualism

The cultural value of individualism is conceptually consistent with the display of conformity by cultural members. Individualism-collectivism is a measurement of allegiance to self or the group. Similarly, conformity is a measurement of the degree to which an individual yields to or resists group pressures toward uniformity of behaviors. As conformity and individualism-collectivism are parallel constructs, Hofstede's individualism (IND) dimension can be conveniently utilized to draw conclusions regarding the effects of cultural values on tendencies to conform.

Members from a high-IND culture value independence, individual initiative, and self-reliance (Hofstede 1980, 1984). Such people do not strongly identify with the group. The dominant characteristics of a high-IND culture strongly parallel nonconformity behavioral patterns; consequently, one can predict that group members from a high-IND culture would not be as sensitive to pressures toward conformity as group members from a low-IND culture. For instance, one may assume that group members from France, which is high on the IND dimension, would also exhibit nonconforming behaviors. The French, a culture characterized by diversity of opinions and dissent, have been found to be individualistic and nonconforming (Milgram 1961).

Members from a low-IND (collectivist) culture are strongly devoted to the group. Dominant values include group decision making, traditional points of view, and a "we" consciousness (Hofstede 1980, 1984). These values indicate a cultural predisposition toward conformity. Thus, collectivist cultures such as Venezuela and Colombia should exhibit conformist behavioral patterns. Germany, a culture that scores low on the IND dimension, has also demonstrated conformist behaviors.

Conformity and Masculinity

Sex-role socialization is very much a function of culture. Consequently, the relationship between a culture's gender orientation and conformity is revealing. Hofstede's MAS dimension, indicating the degree to which a culture values typically "masculine" or "feminine" behaviors, reflects a culture's sex-role system. Likewise, gender differences in conformity may reflect cultural gender differences in sex roles (Shaw 1976).

Cultures scoring high on the masculine (MAS) dimension value achievement, motivation, assertiveness, and decisiveness. Such values connote a nonconforming culture. Most likely, in a culture where assertiveness is valued, predispositions toward conformity would be weak. One can also assume that males, who usually function in the dominant roles in society, would be less conforming than females. Evidence exists supporting this conclusion (see Shaw 1976).

Cultures with a feminine orientation, believing in cooperation, intuition, and group decisions, would be likely to demonstrate conforming behaviors. In low-MAS cultures, in which promoting a friendly atmosphere is regarded as very important (Hofstede 1980, 1984), conformity may be one way to maintain the preferred group environment. Thus, low-MAS countries such as Sweden or Norway would be more conforming than a high-MAS country such as Italy.

Discussion Processes

The patterns that group members use in order to accomplish their tasks have long been a subject of interest and inquiry in the communication discipline. Yet, cross-cultural differences in discussion patterns have received little attention. In order to provide insight into this area, we will apply the tenets of Hofstede's cultural value dimensions.

Discussion Processes and Power Distance

Power distance (PDI) refers to the degree of status inequality desired by the members of a culture. In high-PDI countries, group members would likely seek group norms that maintain their preferred level of social inequality. There is also a greater likelihood in high-PDI countries that status hierarchies among group members will be favored and maintained. Because status is ascribed rather than achieved in high-PDI countries, status characteristics such as age and title are perceived to be very important.

The value of equality in low-PDI countries would lead group members to encourage consultative decision-making procedures. This decision-making style would encourage the less powerful group members to express their ideas and opinions, thereby counterbalancing the tendency for high-status group members to dominate. Conversely, subordinates' dependence on the established power hierarchy in high-PDI countries would lead group members to expect and solicit talk only from the more powerful, high-status members.

Discussion Processes and Uncertainty Avoidance

For group discussions to be sustained over time, members must be willing and able to endure the task-related tensions and ambiguities that inevitably arise. High-uncertainty avoidance (UAI) countries, which are characterized by an elevated level of social stress and anxiety, have a powerful need to diminish these social tensions. One way to reduce both the level and the duration of social tensions within group discussions is to solve the problem quickly. Additionally, members from high-UAI countries are less likely than members from low-UAI countries to take risks, engage in conflict, compromise, or seek change from the status quo (Hofstede 1980).

Hirokawa, Ice, and Cook (1988) found that group members who had a strong preference for procedural order functioned most effectively in groups that followed a structured and organized discussion format, whereas group members without a strong need for procedural order tended to make higher-quality decisions when the discussion format was relatively unstructured. Preference for procedural order can be thought of as the individual-level equivalent of the cultural-level need to reduce uncertainty. Consequently, cultures high in uncertainty avoidance would most likely use and benefit from structured discussion formats. Hofstede's cultural-level correlations can be interpreted to mean that high-UAI countries are more likely to produce task-oriented group members, while low-UAI countries are more likely to produce relationship-oriented group members.

Discussion Processes and Individualism

The need for individual prominence is a characteristic of members of individualistic cultures. Within the context of discussion groups, individual prominence is usually achieved by those who talk somewhat more than their fair share. In collectivist cultures, where group harmony is regarded as more important than individual prominence, one would expect a devaluation of verbose behaviors and a greater preference for silence. In a study comparing the United States to Korea, Elliott, Scott, Jensen, and McDonough (1982) found that highly verbal individuals were favorably regarded in the United States, whereas less verbal individuals were favorably regarded in Korea. Though Hofstede's research doesn't include data from Korea, it is likely that Korea is similar to other Pacific Rim countries in degree of cultural collectivity.

An orientation toward collectivity is a prerequisite for group members to make a group decision; that is, group decisions can only be made if the group members value collective action. Collectivist cultures, with their emphasis on belonging to the group and their belief in group decisions (Hofstede 1980), would therefore be more likely both to enter into and to remain engaged in group discussions. Further, consensus is more likely in group discussions within collectivist cultures because emphasis on agreement with the group is greater there.

Discussion Processes and Masculinity

Hofstede (1980) has reported that in high-masculine cultures, cultural members have a very high level of achievement motivation. Since task-related roles are typically given more status by group members than relational or socioemotional group roles, one would expect that males within groups in high-MAS cultures would seek task-related roles, whereas females in high-MAS cultures would either be excluded from the decision-making process or would fulfill the group's socioemotional roles. Hofstede

(1980) reported greater occupational segregation by gender within high-MAS cultures. Similarly, in high-MAS cultures, fewer women were found in jobs with mixed-sex composition (Hofstede 1980). Alderton and Jurma (1980) found that group members in U.S. groups were equally satisfied with males and females who attempted to exhibit task-related control. Bunyi and Andrews (1985), also in a study of U.S. decision-making groups, found that task competence related to leadership emergence regardless of gender. However, the United States is near the middle of Hofstede's (1980) masculinity dimension. For high-MAS countries, one would expect gender to be more salient in predicting participation in group roles. In this regard, Buck, Newton, and Muramatsu (1984) found that the Japanese (a high-masculine culture) valued "being independent" over "being obedient" only for men, whereas Americans valued independence over obedience for both men and women.

Concluding Remarks

Group-communication phenomena can be found in the families, organizations, and institutions of virtually every culture, yet their common and unique processes and structural characteristics remain relatively unexplored. We believe that an examination of these communication phenomena can be used both to extend theories of cross-cultural differences and to test propositions about the underlying structure of communicative acts.

References

Alderton, S.M., and Jurma, W.E. (1980). "Genderless, Gender Related Task Leader Communication and Group Satisfaction: A Test of Two Hypotheses." *Southern Speech Communication Journal* 46, 48–60.

Asch, S.E. (1951). "Effects of Group Pressure Upon the Modification and Distortion of Judgements." In H. Guetzkow (ed.), *Groups, Leadership, and Men.* Pittsburgh, PA: Carnegie Press.

Asch, S.E. (1952). *Social Psychology.* Englewood Cliffs, NJ: Prentice-Hall.

Baird, J.E., and Bradley, P.H. (1979). "Styles of Management and Communication: A Comparative Study of Men and Women." *Communication Monographs* 46, 101–111.

Berry, J. (1976). "Independence and Conformity in Subsistence Level Societies." *Journal of Personality and Social Psychology* 7, 415–418.

Berryman-Fink, C. (1985). "Male and Female Managers' Views of the Communication Skills and Training Needs of Women in Management." *Public Personnel Management* 14, 307–313.

Buck, E., Newton, B., and Muramatsu, Y. (1984). "Independence and Obedience in the United States and Japan." *International Journal of Intercultural Relations* 8, 279–300.

Bunyi, J.M., and Andrews, P.H. (1985). "Gender and Leadership Emergence: An Experimental Study." *Southern Speech Communication Journal* 50, 246–260.

Cragan, J.F., and Wright, D.W. (1980). "Small Group Communication Research of the 1970s: A Synthesis and Critique." *Central States Speech Journal* 31, 197–213.

Cragan, J.F., and Wright, D.W. (1988, November). *Small Group Communication Research of the 1980s: A Synthesis and Critique.* Paper presented at the annual meeting of the Speech Communication Association, New Orleans.

Elliot, S., Scott, M.D., Jensen, A.D., and McDonough M. (1982). "Perceptions of Reticence: A Cross-Cultural Investigation." In M. Burgoon (ed.), *Communication Yearbook* 5, 591–602. New Brunswick, NJ: Transaction.

Fiedler, F.E. (1967). *A Theory of Leadership Effectiveness.* New York: McGraw-Hill.

Forgas, J., and Bond, M. (1985). "Cultural Influences on the Perception of Interaction Episodes." *Personality and Social Psychology Bulletin* 11, 75–88.

Frager, R. (1970). "Conformity and Anticonformity in Japan." *Journal of Personality and Social Psychology* 15, 203–210.

Hirokawa, R. Y., Ice, R., and Cook, J. (1988). "Preference for Procedural Order, Discussion Structure, and Group Decision Performance." *Communication Quarterly* 36, 217–226.

Hofstede, G. (1980). *Culture's Consequences: International Differences in Work-Related Values.* Beverly Hills, CA: Sage.

Hofstede, G. (1984). *Culture's Consequences: International Differences in Work-Related Values.* (abridged ed.). Beverly Hills, CA: Sage.

Hofstede, G., and Bond, M. H. (1984). "Hofstede's Culture Dimensions: An Independent Validation Using Rokeach's Value Survey." *Journal of Cross-Cultural Psychology* 15, 417–433.

Milgram, S. (1961). "Nationality and Conformity." *Scientific American* 205, 845–851.

Milgram, S. (1964). "Group Pressure and Action Against a Person." *Journal of Social Psychology* 69, 127–134.

Remland, M. S. (1984). "Leadership Impressions and Nonverbal Communication in a Superior-Subordinate Interaction." *Communication Quarterly* 32, 41–48.

Shaw, M. E. (1976). *Group Dynamics: The Psychology of Small Group Behavior.* New York: McGraw-Hill.

Sherif, M., and Sherif, C. W. (1956). *An Outline of Social Psychology* (rev. ed.). New York: Harper & Row.

Shuter, R. (1977). "Cross-Cultural Small Group Research: A Review, an Analysis, and a Theory." *International Journal of Intercultural Relations* 1, 90–104.

Leadership and Gender: Challenging Assumptions and Recognizing Resources

Susan B. Shimanoff and Mercilee M. Jenkins

Among the many roles group members can perform, the role of leader has received more attention from researchers than any other. What is a leader? In the studies we reviewed for this article we identified four major approaches to defining "leader": (1) the person named by the group as the leader, (2) the person who group members *perceive* to be performing leaderlike behaviors, (3) the person who has the greatest influence on the group's final decision, and (4) the *actual performance* of leadership behaviors. It is our position that the fourth approach is the best one.

Who a group names as leader or who members perceive as being the leader may be influenced by stereotypes or selective perception. This is particularly important when comparing females and males. Research has shown that even when they perform the same behaviors, males are often given more leadership credit than females (Brown & Geis 1984; Geis, Boston, & Hoffman 1985; Butler 1984). Further, when women with inclinations to lead were not named the leader, they still performed leaderlike behaviors (Nyquist & Spence 1986).

Leadership behaviors may lead to a greater say in a group's decision, but a group member can get what he or she wants in other ways as well. For example, a group may acquiesce to a member's desires because it feels manipulated, apathetic, generous, exhausted, or frustrated. Stake (1981) argued that getting one's way should be perceived as dominance instead of necessarily leadership, and we agree.

Leadership, it seems to us, is best understood as the behaviors that help a group to achieve its goals. Previous researchers have associated the following behaviors with leadership: appropriate procedural suggestions, sound opinions, relevant information, frequent participation, active listening, supporting group members, and asking for the opinions of other group members. When one focuses on *who* is called the leader, leadership is seen as belonging to one person, but when one concentrates on *behaviors*, leadership can be performed by multiple members and can be the responsibility of the group as a whole rather than a single person.

However, most of the previous research has taken a single-person approach to leadership, and when we reviewed this literature we were struck by the prejudice against women. Research has demonstrated that there are far more similarities than differences in the leadership behaviors of women and men, and that they are equally effective. Still, women are less likely to be preselected as leaders, and the same leadership behavior is often evaluated more positively when attributed to a male than a female. In exploring gender and leadership, we would like to address five topics: (1) the behaviors of male and female leaders, (2) the effectiveness of female and male leaders,

(3) the effects of sex-role stereotypes, (4) the role of group dynamics, and (5) practical suggestions for challenging false assumptions and for recognizing the resources that both women and men bring to group interactions.

Leadership Behaviors of Females and Males

The most common claim in regard to stylistic differences has been that women are more concerned with the social-emotional dimensions of group process and men are more concerned with getting the job done (Anderson & Blanchard 1982; Denmark 1977; Hollander & Yoder 1980). However, researchers have found either no differences or minimal ones (about 4 percent) regarding these two types of behaviors by female and male leaders (Anderson & Blanchard 1982; Dobbins & Platz 1986).

Task Behaviors

In problem-solving groups, the talk of both men and women is predominately task related and this intensifies when one is the leader: "approximately 91 percent of a male leader's behavior is devoted to active task behavior (giving answers) and approximately 88 percent of a female leader's behavior is active task behavior" (Anderson & Blanchard 1982, 135). Women emphasize production, whether they are classified as task or relational leader types, and they continue their strong contributions to task endeavors even when the group is doing well; men tend to reduce their task contributions under similar circumstances (Millard & Smith 1985).

Further, one study of actual leadership behavior in student problem-solving groups found that female leaders devoted a greater proportion of their total communication to task issues than male leaders (Wood 1981), and in other studies males have been shown to make more off-task comments than females (Gigliotti 1988; Winther & Green 1987). Fortunately, group members have indicated that they were equally satisfied with male and female leaders who exhibited equal frequencies of task-oriented behaviors (Alderton & Jurma 1980).

Leaders are more likely than other members to make procedural suggestions for how a group should conduct its business; this is true for both males and females (Bunyi & Andrews 1985; Andrews 1984). In addition, Hirokawa (1980) found that constructive procedural discussions were more typical of effective groups than ineffective ones. Making procedural suggestions seems to be one of women's strengths. In resolving conflicts, Carrocci (1985) found that women generated twice as many procedural suggestions as men did.

Two other task-related behaviors that may be particularly important for women are (1) demonstrated expertise and (2) the use of evidence. When expertise is low or members do not use evidence, males in the group are evaluated more positively than females. When women and men are equal in expertise and their use of evidence, however, they tend to be evaluated similarly (Bradley 1980, 1981; Wentworth, Keyser, & Anderson 1984).

Owen (1986) maintained that when women emerge as leaders in mixed-sex groups it is largely because they have worked substantially harder than any other member. In addition, the women he observed were most likely to be the ones who provided organizational skills, suggested procedures, set the agenda, and took the notes. We find it interesting that a traditionally female task—taking the minutes—was one of the behaviors that contributed to a woman becoming a leader. This task provided her useful information that she could then use to guide the group's interaction.

One factor that has been shown to influence task behaviors is performance self-esteem. Persons with high performance self-esteem see themselves as productive, assertive, responsible, competent, articulate, powerful, persuasive, willing to take a stand, and forceful (Stake 1979), and they are more likely to be selected as leaders than those with low performance self-esteem (Andrews 1984). Group members with high performance self-esteem are more likely to provide relevant information, sound opinions, appropriate procedural suggestions, and counter arguments, and to get the group to embrace their perspective (Andrews 1984; Stake & Stake 1979). The performance of these behaviors leads group members to view them as leaders.

Females, however, typically have lower performance self-esteem than males (Stake 1979), and performance self-esteem is more related to their leadership behaviors than it is for men (Stake & Stake 1979). On the other hand, efforts to increase a woman's performance self-esteem increase her leadership behaviors and her influence on group decisions (Stake 1983), especially if group members are given time to assimilate positive information about her abilities (Stake 1981). Further, when females are thought to be superior on a task, they have as much influence as males, and this boost in self-confidence and influence carry over to subsequent dyads (Pugh & Wahrman 1983).

Social-Emotional Behaviors

When the behaviors of male and female leaders differ, women are likely to meet the social-emotional needs of group members slightly more (Anderson & Blanchard 1982). Women leaders were rated as more interpersonally warm during initial interactions than male leaders (Goktepe & Schneier 1989; Spillman, Spillman, & Reinking 1981). Interestingly, positive social-emotional behaviors frequently contribute more to group satisfaction than task-related behaviors (Schriesheim 1982). Further, group members think that they are just as likely as leaders to perform task behaviors and negative social-emotional behaviors, but that leaders are much more likely to perform positive social-emotional behaviors than nonleaders (Schneier & Bartol 1980).

If the degree to which women meet the social-emotional needs of group members was more often acknowledged, we might come to associate women with leadership more frequently. Instead, group members tend to expect even more from women, and when they are not *more* responsive than males to the needs of others, group members tend to evaluate women more harshly (Faranda 1981; Helgesen 1990; Russell, Rush, & Herd 1988; Wright 1976). Similarly, three separate studies have shown that females using an authoritarian style of leadership were perceived less favorably than males using the same style (Faranda 1981; Haccoun, Haccoun, & Sallay 1978; Jago & Vroom 1982). It is not surprising, then, that sometimes women use a more democratic or participative style than men (Baird & Bradley 1979; Helgesen 1990; Jago & Vroom 1982; Ragins & Sundstrom 1989; Rosenfeld & Fowler 1976).

Men were particularly satisfied with the leadership of women when they led by providing orientation, information, and clarification; by asking for the men's opinions;

by not giving more suggestions or disagreements than their male partners; and by having equal influence on the groups' decisions (Stake 1981). Likewise, Alderton and Jurma (1980) reported that female leaders agreed more with followers than male leaders did, but in spite of this, group members were more likely to disagree with female leaders than male leaders. These studies suggest that women support group members more, but receive less support in return.

To provide effective social-emotional messages, one must be a good listener. Listening has also been strongly linked to effective leadership. When listening skills, speaking ability, and traditional management behaviors like organizing work, setting goals, and influencing others were compared, listening was the most related to group satisfaction and effectiveness (Willer & Henderson 1988). Several scholars have noted that listening skills are especially important to women (Belenky, Clichy, Goldberger & Tarule 1986; Gilligan 1982; Helgesen 1990). In her analysis of women executives, Helgesen (1990) observed that the women valued "listening as a way of making others feel comfortable and important, and as a means of encouraging others to find their own voices and grow" (244–245).

Combined Task and Social-Emotional Leadership

In combination, the studies on the task and social-emotional behaviors of leaders show that while women may show more concern with interpersonal relationships, they also devote considerable energy to the group's task. Further, group members expect women leaders to perform well in both task and social-emotional dimensions (Cirincione-Coles 1975; Jenkins 1980). Similar research has also been reported dealing with black versus white business students. Thomas and Littig (1985) found that black students have a tendency to self-report a more highly structured management style, coupled most often with high consideration.

While this approach may have advantages for group members, Dumas's (1980) study of black women managers indicated the possible negative consequences for leaders trying to do it all. Black women managers report that they are often expected to fulfill the "Black Mammy" role (to take care of everyone's needs at the expense of her own) or risk being seen as the "Terrible Mother" (selfish, punitive, and frightening). These overwhelming expectations often force the women to choose between burning out in an effort to fulfill them or incurring the anger of their subordinates. What might prove more constructive is a shared understanding that fulfilling the social-emotional and task needs of a group is the collective responsibility of all members.

Women's Ways of Interacting[1]

Many studies indicate that girls and women interact differently than men in same-sex groups (Maltz & Borker 1982). Research on all-female groups suggests that girls and women have an equalitarian ideology among themselves (Goodwin 1980; Helgesen 1990; Maltz & Borker 1982) and that they sanction members who directly confront each other (Jenkins 1984; Wilensky 1988). Similarly, females report greater dissatisfaction than males in autocratically led groups (Kushell & Newton 1986).

Some writers of popular self-help books have asserted that women do not do as well as men in business because their relative inexperience with competitive team sports makes it more difficult for them to be good team players (Harragan 1977; Hennig & Jardim 1976). In contrast to these assumptions, though, women have been found to be more cooperative and supportive (Jenkins 1984), while men are described as more self-assertive and competitive (Maltz & Borker 1982). Given their greater efforts at cooperation, it would seem that women may be the "real team players" (Nelson 1988). For example, both women and men on predominately female research teams noted the differences in the way group members worked together when compared to mixed or male-dominated groups. They described the group as an open, cooperative but challenging, and supportive context where learning and growth were promoted (Nelson 1988).

If women interact differently in groups, it seems likely that they would also lead differently. Although men and women agree on many ideal traits for leaders, women are more likely to desire leaders who are "cooperative, empathetic, supportive, democratic, and calm," while men are more likely to desire leaders who are "demanding, active, aggressive, rational, and decision-oriented" (Graves & Powell 1982, 690). Men are more prone to hierarchical leadership, and women are more likely to rotate leadership (Aries 1976; Helgesen 1990; Wyatt 1988). In keeping with this approach women may see leadership more in terms of facilitation and organization rather than power and dominance (Owen 1986; Wyatt 1988).

In Owen's groups of college students and in Wyatt's group of women weavers, members were reluctant to call themselves leaders and instead described their roles in the group in terms of organizing and facilitating the group to reach its goal. Nelson (1988) further suggests that this facilitative style of leadership allows leaders to model the behavior they want to see in group members. Thus, when women lead differently than men, we should not assume they need to change their behavior.

These studies indicate that female leadership styles may have some advantages not previously recognized in studies of mixed-sex groups. Helgesen (1990) details four case studies of successful female leaders in organizations and outlines why she believes these women are effective: (1) they create a web of associations through which they communicate with all levels of the organization; (2) they are able to be spontaneous as leaders and respond to situations with flexibility; (3) they tend to break down barriers between employees; and (4) they are effective transmitters of information and ideas throughout the organization.

The women see themselves as "being in the middle of things. Not at the top, but in the center; not reaching down, but reaching out" (Helgesen 1990, 45–46). Using the metaphor of a web, Helgesen (1990) describes this type of leadership as more connected and inclusive: "You can't break a web into single lines or individual components without tearing the fabric, injuring the whole" (49).

Women's metaphors for leadership reflect less traditional ways of thinking about this process. A woman in a class on small-group communication said a leader is like a sponge. A leader should absorb all that the group produces and then be prepared to give it back whenever the group requests it. Helgesen (1990) furnishes similarly enlightening metaphors from women executives. A leader is a teacher, a magician (making changes while serving others and maintaining one's personal identity), a gardener ("watering the flowers, helping them to flourish and grow" [xiv]), and a transmitter ("picking up signals from everywhere, then beeping them out to where they need to go" [27]). These metaphors reflect a much more participative view of leadership than the more traditional concepts of power and dominance.

Summary

Across the studies on leadership behavior, it can be said that in problem-solving groups both female and male leaders concentrate on task-related behaviors, but that females are slightly more responsive to the social-emotional needs of group members and tend to be more attentive listeners. Males are inclined to talk more, which may increase their power, but women can be equally effective in using evidence and making procedural suggestions, two key behaviors for leaders. Further, features more typically associated with women, such as inclusion, spontaneity, equalitarianism, and dissemination of information, have been shown to be important leadership skills.

The evidence on leadership style indicates that members generally seem to prefer both male and female leaders to be task oriented, but prefer females to be more responsive to social-emotional needs than males; women leaders seem to comply with these demands. Still, as Baird and Bradley (1979) noted, it is possible that because of sex-role biases, a female leader may need to be superior to a male leader to be rated equally.

Effectiveness and Group Satisfaction

Anderson and Blanchard (1982) reviewed seventy-one reported findings regarding group members' satisfaction with and the effectiveness of leaders. They found that in 77 percent of the cases male and female leaders were rated equally; 14 percent favored male leaders and 8 percent favored female leaders. Clearly there is not a consistent preference for male or female leaders. This same pattern was observed in naturally occurring groups, experimental/laboratory groups, case studies, and simulated groups. They also found no consistent preference for a stereotypical feminine (social-emotional) or masculine (task) style of leadership for either males or females. Additional evidence for the lack of difference in effectiveness of male and female leaders is provided by two sets of extensive field research projects dealing with military groups and sensitive or encounter groups.

Rice and his colleagues have conducted research focusing on the integration of women at West Point since the first coeducational class. In a group that met only for a short time, males with conservative views toward women rated female leaders lower than male leaders on initiating structure, but males with liberal views toward women rated female leaders higher than male leaders (Rice, Bender, & Vitters 1980).

In later studies, male cadets were rated slightly higher (about 8 percent) on overall leadership ability than female cadets by their peers and superiors (Rice, Yoder, Adams, Priest, & Prince 1984), but male and female leaders were rated equally successful and skillful by their followers (Rice, Instone, & Adams 1984). Similarly, another study found that male and female squad leaders were rated equally positive by their followers (Adams, Rice, & Instone 1984). Collectively these studies suggest that if people are asked to rate females and males when they have had only limited contact, they will sometimes resort to their preconceived attitudes, but after extended interactions, group members rate male and female leaders as equally effective.

Another type of group that has been studied extensively in the field is self-reflective groups from the Tavistock Institute in England. The groups are composed of psychology undergraduate and graduate students who are themselves studying group processes. These groups are typically assigned one of two types of leaders: those who are supposed to be emotionally responsive and those who are supposed to remain emotionally detached and merely comment on the group process.

The research on the effects of gender on leadership in these groups is not consistent. In some cases emotionally responsive women were rated as the most effective (Wright 1976), and at other times they were considered the least effective (Morrison & Stein 1985). In one study, emotionally detached males and females were rated equally as leaders (Morrison & Stein 1985), but in another study this detachment resulted in female leaders being perceived as more potent and active and male leaders receiving more positive messages (Wright 1976). In still another study, male co-leaders were perceived as more potent, active, instrumental, and insightful than female co-leaders, but female and male co-leaders were rated equally on skills and emotional responsiveness. Further, group members behaved similarly regardless of whether the female or male was the first or second in command (Greene, Morrison, & Tischler 1981; Tischler, Morrison, Greene, & Stewart 1986). Across these studies, there is no consistent evidence that Tavistock groups are more effective or satisfied if a female or male assumes the position of leader.

Summary

Collectively the studies on effectiveness and satisfaction demonstrate that groups are equally satisfied with effective leaders of either gender and that generally women and men lead equally well. If males and females exhibit the same behaviors as leaders and they are equally effective one would expect them to emerge as leaders equally. Yet, more men than women are in positions of power. What will account for this discrepancy? One possibility is the biasing effects of sex-role stereotypes.

Sex-Role Stereotypes

Porter and Geis (1981) remind us that in our culture becoming a leader is tied to the perceptions of others:

Leadership is a social phenomenon. Becoming a leader depends on acting like a leader, but even more crucially, it depends on being seen by others as a leader. In our society people do not become leaders by their own individual fiat. They become leaders by being appointed to the position, being elected to it, or by emerging over time as the group member to whom others look for guidance. In every case leadership depends on recognition by others, by fellow group members or by those doing the voting or appointing (39).

Evaluations of Identical Messages

Given that leadership depends on the *recognition* of others, it is important that we ascertain how observers evaluate the same behaviors when they are performed by a female or a male. Across several studies there tends to be a pro-male bias; that is, males are more often rated more positively than females for the same behavior (Butler & Geis 1990; Nieva & Gutek 1980). Still, this is not always the case. Four factors would appear to help to reduce sex-role biases: (1) additional, unambiguous, and relevant information, (2) sex-role-neutral tasks, (3) positive evaluations by others, and (4) actual interaction with the person (Brown & Geis 1984; Butler 1984; Butterfield & Powell 1981; Heilman & Martell 1986; Nieva & Gutek 1980; Seifert & Miller 1988).

When group members were neither praised nor blamed by others, Brown and Geis (1984) found that observers rated males as: (a) showing significantly more leadership, (b) having higher-quality contributions, (c) being more desirable for hiring, (d) meriting a higher salary, and (e) meriting a more responsible job than females. The actual behavior of males and females in this case did not differ. The same behavior was evaluated differently merely on the basis of whether a male or a female performed that behavior.

Recent research has also noted that sex-role biases may have become more subtle. In three studies where males and females were rated equally as leaders for performing the same behaviors, males were nonetheless rated more positively than females in other ways. For example, two different studies found that for the same behaviors, female leaders were rated as bossier, more dominating, more emotional, less warm, less sensitive, and less attractive than male leaders (Brown & Geis 1984; Butler 1984). In addition, group members expressed greater disapproval of identical ideas when they were presented by a woman and more approval when the suggestions were expressed by a man (Butler & Geis 1990). In Seifert and Miller's (1988) study the very same message was rated as clearer when attributed to a male leader rather than a female leader. Further, in several studies, even people who firmly believed they held equalitarian or feminist attitudes nonetheless discriminated against female leaders in more subtle, unconscious ways (Butler 1984; Butler & Geis 1990; Porter & Geis 1981; Porter, Geis, Cooper, & Newman 1985).

Effects of Sex-Role Attitudes on Behavior

Reinforcing or challenging sex-role attitudes also has an effect on group dynamics. Group size and shared attitudes affect the leadership emergence of females and males, and the behaviors of group members (Porter et al. 1985). Males with traditional sex-role attitudes were more likely to dominate the group interaction if the group was comprised of four members sharing their attitudes than if there were only two such members. On the other hand, groups comprised of four androgynous members interacted in a more equalitarian manner than groups of two. That is, the more other group members share one's attitudes about sex-roles the more likely one is to behave in accordance with those attitudes; the shared attitudes serve to reinforce each other.

Further, *reminding* people of their own attitudes toward sex-role stereotypes affected group interactions and leadership emergence. Groups who held equalitarian attitudes behaved in a more equalitarian manner when they were reminded of those attitudes than when they were not, while groups who held more traditional sex-role attitudes had more male dominance when they were reminded of their attitudes than when they were not. Porter et al. (1985) argued that sex-role "scripts" for males and females may be so ingrained in our habitual, subconscious behavior that the scripts will override equalitarian attitudes unless such attitudes are reinforced by reminders and interaction with others who value equality.

Designating a Leader

Another type of sex-role bias has been demonstrated in studies in which groups are given little or no time to interact before selecting their leaders. A series of studies has examined the role of viewing oneself as possessing "dominant" qualities (e.g., self-confident, articulate, forceful, persistent, logical, and responsible) and being designated the leader (Carbonell 1984; Fleischer & Chertkoff 1986; Megargee 1969; Nyquist & Spence 1986). In same-sex groups in which gender differences are not an issue, the dominant person is named the leader 70 percent of the time. However, for mixed-sex dyads the pattern is quite different. When the more dominant person is male, he is named the leader 84 percent of the time, but when the more dominant person is a female she is named the leader only 41 percent of the time on the average and sometimes only 20 percent. Further, when both partners are high in dispositional dominance, the male rather than the female was named the leader 71 percent of the time (Davis & Gilbert 1989).[2]

A similar kind of bias occurred in Porter and Geis's (1981) study of the effects of seating arrangements on perceived leadership. When observers looked at photographs of same-sex groups, they thought the person at the head of the table was the most likely to lead, contribute, talk, and dominate. When the same males and females were shown in mixed-sex groups, the males at the heads of the tables were again designated the leaders, but females at the heads of the tables were not perceived as leaders.

Summary

It is disturbing that a person's gender *alone* could change how the very same message or person is evaluated. These sex-role biases may have serious consequences for hiring and promoting women into leadership positions, especially when group members have had little opportunity to interact. Still, it can be useful to acknowledge this bias. Women, who have become discouraged because their words and ideas seem to carry less weight than the same ones expressed by their male colleagues, can stop wondering if the situation would be better if they had only behaved differently.

These studies, as well as those on leadership style, cast doubt on the appropriateness of special training programs for women *per se* to enhance their leadership skills, but the findings indicate the need to make groups aware of their biases and means for reducing them. Research has demonstrated that concrete and specific information is more effective and less ambiguous than global discussions in reducing sex-role-biased attitudes (Auerbach, Kilmann, Gackenbach, & Julian 1980; Heilman & Martell 1986).

Reinforcing equalitarian attitudes has also been shown to be effective in reducing male dominance.

Group Dynamics

Several studies have indicated that if groups are allowed to interact before choosing a leader they are more likely to make their decision on the basis of performance rather than gender. For example, Schneier and Bartol (1980) found that after fifteen weeks of working on various projects fifty different groups were equally likely to name a female or a male as their leader, as were the twenty-eight groups who met for six to fifteen weeks in Goktepe and Schneier's (1989) study. Similarly, a high-dominant woman was named as the leader over a low-dominant male only 36 percent of the time when they did not interact, but when they worked on a project before selecting the leader, her ascendancy rose to 71 percent (Davis & Gilbert 1989). Even in a male-defined domain, such as the military, males and females were evaluated equally on actual performance over time (Rice, Instone, & Adams 1984). Thus, simply allowing group members to witness the strengths of individual men and women helps to reduce sex-role biases.

In addition, how people behave toward each other and how others interact with leaders have been shown to have a profound effect on their behavior. For example, leaders produced more task and less negative social-emotional behaviors when followers asked them for direction than when group members tried to control the leader's behavior (Beckhouse, Tanur, Weiler, & Weinstein 1975). If group members treat each other on the basis of mutual respect rather than sex-role biases, potential leaders are more likely to act like leaders. In the sections that follow we will discuss various aspects of group dynamics that affect leadership.

Patterns of Interaction

Numerous studies have indicated that the amount of participation is positively correlated with leadership. People who talk more frequently are named as leaders more often than less talkative members of a group (Fisher 1985). Wentworth, Keyser, and Anderson (1984) report that this relationship is almost two times stronger for women than men. Being one of the first group members to speak may also influence who is perceived as a leader. In Fleischer and Chertkoff's (1986) study of dyads, the person who spoke first was selected as the leader 60 percent of the time. Lamb (1981) found that the earlier a woman spoke in a group the more she participated, and Kimble, Yoshikawa, and Zehr (1981) reported that the first woman to speak in a group was viewed as the most assertive, while the assertiveness scores of males were unrelated to the order in which they spoke. These studies suggest a stronger relationship for women than for men regarding initiation, amount of speech, and influence in groups.

The overall greater verbosity of men may be due to various aspects of small-group interaction. For example, when presenting the same information and arguments, women received more negative feedback than males (Butler & Geis 1990). This kind of reaction could easily discourage the participation of women. In addition, there is some evidence that men and women may have different rules for taking turns speaking. Some studies have indicated that females are more likely to call on other members or invite them to speak while males are more likely to allow whoever speaks first to have the floor (Aries 1976; Jenkins 1984). An invitation to speak rather than having to fight for the floor might increase the participation of women.

Shimanoff (1984) also discusses how group members could manipulate the turn-taking rules to influence who emerges as the leader. Consistently returning the floor to a particular person or to coalition members can shape who is the most active participant and who is perceived as the most competent, and thus who leads the group. Groups seeking equalitarian participation may wish to guard against such manipulation. On the other hand, it may be a useful tool if others are unfairly discriminating against particular members.

Groups may also influence the participation of women by the degree to which women are interrupted. Zimmerman and West (1975) demonstrated that interruptions lead to the original speaker falling silent, and many studies have found that women are more likely to get interrupted than men (e.g., Brooks 1982; Kennedy & Camden 1983; Octigan & Niederman 1979; West & Zimmerman 1983; Willis & Williams 1976; Zimmerman & West 1975). It is also worth noting that although Dindia (1987) found no gender differences for many types of interruptions, she discovered that males were more likely to interrupt women to change the subject than the reverse. Davis and Gilbert (1989) also reported equal levels of interruptions by males and females, but that high-dominant persons were more likely to interrupt than low-dominant persons.

Acknowledging that interruptive patterns may be gender related could be useful. When males and females were told that "research has shown that male speakers are more likely than female speakers to interrupt partners in conversation," the interruptive behavior of both males and females dramatically decreased (for males from 88 interruptions to 29 [decrease of 67 percent] for females from 34 interruptions to 7 [decrease of 79 percent]) (Octigan & Niederman 1979).

Members may also wish to monitor their own verbosity in an effort to equalize participation. This awareness may be particularly relevant for men who tend to talk more than women in groups (Thorne, Kramarae, & Henley 1983). If women participate equally in discussions, groups may then need to watch their attitudes. Edelsky's (1981) research on group participation demonstrated that when women merely speak as much as men they are often thought of as being overly talkative. At the end of her study when she recognized this perceptual bias even in herself, Edelsky wrote: "Perhaps our subjective impression of a talkative woman is simply one who talks as much as the average man" (1981, 415).

Group Composition

Group composition can also influence leadership emergence. In one study of triads, when males were in the majority they emerged as the leader 100 percent of the time. When females were in the majority they were more likely to serve as leaders, but this increase was not statistically significant (Bunyi & Andrews 1985). Similarly, Schneier and Bartol (1980) reported that as the number of women in a group increased the likelihood that a female would emerge as the leader increased. Other studies have indicated that women have more trouble getting group members to treat them equally if they are the solo representative of their sex or in a small minority than when a man is the only male or a token (Craig & Sherif 1986; Fairhurst & Snavely 1983; Ott 1989; Wolman & Frank 1975).

Expertise and Validation

Assumed or attributed expertise increases the likelihood that one will emerge as the leader or be evaluated more positively (Bunyi & Andrews 1985; Dobbins, Stuart, Pence, & Sgro 1985; Fleischer & Chertkoff 1986; Offermann 1986). Sometimes group members assume expertise on the basis of sex-role stereotypes. For example, males were most likely to be named as the leader if the task required stereotypically masculine or neutral expertise (e.g., investment or entertainment), while females and males were equally likely to emerge as leaders if stereotypically feminine expertise was required (e.g., a wedding) (Wentworth & Anderson 1984).

External validation of women leaders is also important. It increases the possibility that her work will be valued by herself and others (Brown & Geis 1984; Butler 1984; Dobbins, Stuart, Pence, & Sgro 1985; Fleischer & Chertkoff 1986; Pheterson, Kiesler, & Goldberg 1971; Peck 1978; Stake 1983). This validation is especially important because the credibility of women is often challenged. Further, validation can yield more leadership. Females who were told they were selected as leaders because of their skills performed more leadership behaviors than women who thought the position had come to them by chance, even though their actual abilities were identical (Eskilson & Wiley 1976).

The mere presence of a female authority figure has been shown to increase the credibility of other women (Butler 1984; Etaugh, Houtler, & Ptasnik 1988; Geis, Boston, & Hoffman 1985). Similarly, a woman's abilities will be rated more favorably if one is exposed to success stories about other women in similar circumstances (Heilman & Martell 1986). Positive validation can lead to increases in performance self-esteem and consequently more leadership behaviors (Stake 1983). More should be done to increase women's levels of performance self-esteem because as Stake and Stake (1979) write: "When females have confidence in their abilities, they do assert themselves" (82). The achievements of women should be acclaimed by authority figures, group members, and women themselves.

Summary

The studies on group dynamics lead us to conclude that an individual group member cannot by himself or herself orchestrate who will become a leader. Groups are systems; that is, the behavior of one group member influences the behavior of others. Interacting before designating a leader, striving for more equalitarian interactions and balanced groups, and validating the accomplishments of women are all ways of increasing the probability that the most effective persons will lead.

Practical Suggestions

This essay has identified several barriers to women becoming leaders. Since groups are typically more productive and satisfied when the most qualified persons lead and since those persons are as likely to be women as men, we would now like to highlight ways for reducing these barriers.

Before we do, we need to note still another kind of bias. Most of the research on leadership has been limited to groups comprised of persons who are white and middle-class. This limitation in the research has affected what we have been able to write about in this chapter, and we want to acknowledge that shortcoming. Just as new studies that include women where they were previously neglected have altered conceptions of effective leadership (Helgesen 1990), we suspect that the investigations of more diverse groups, cultures, and leadership styles will bring further modifications in how leadership ought to be viewed.

Based on the studies we have reviewed in this chapter, we make the following recommendations for groups who wish to maximize effective leadership. Group members should:

1. Acknowledge and challenge sex-role biases.
2. Affirm equalitarian attitudes and remind group members of their value.
3. Celebrate the "traditional" strengths of women.
4. Increase the visibility and support of female role models.
5. Validate the performance and self-confidence of women.
6. Designate leaders only after interacting, if at all.
7. Listen attentively.
8. Support group members and treat them with respect.
9. Ask others for their opinions; invite others to participate.
10. Draw upon the strengths of all group members; recognize the contributions of each as a valuable resource.
11. Make procedural suggestions.
12. Offer relevant information.
13. Provide evidence for claims.
14. Be an active participant, but monitor your own verbosity.
15. Discourage unequal interruptions; especially those that change the subject.
16. Learn from diverse groups and individuals.

Conclusion

At the beginning of this chapter we recommended that groups view *leadership* as the responsibility of all members rather than concentrate on one person fulfilling the role of lone *leader*. Leadership is the performance of behaviors that help a group reach its goals. It includes behaviors like making procedural suggestions, offering sound opinions, providing relevant information, and presenting counter arguments. Both men and women do these behaviors well and often with equal frequency. Leadership also involves listening attentively, supporting group members, and asking for the opinions of others; women are expected to perform these behaviors—and they do so with slightly more frequency than men.

Groups have many needs. A group-centered approach to leadership taps into the talents and energies of all its members. Consequently, it is likely to be healthier and more effective than if it had tried to rely on a single individual. So far, women seem more willing to embrace the ideal of shared leadership than men. Ideally, each group member would match her or his strengths to the group's needs. If different members serve as facilitator, organizer, note taker, attentive listener, sponge, teacher, gardener, transmitter, magician, or whatever else the group needs, then a lone leader would not have to be the "Black Mammy" or "Iron Maiden," and the entire group could be empowered to fulfill its goal.

Notes

1. Scholars who have identified "women's ways" of leading or interacting in groups have noted that not all women behave in this manner and that many men utilize the same skills and values (Helgesen 1990; Nelson 1988). Still, they have been called women's ways because they were more typical of women than men. In a similar vein we want to acknowledge that the research shows considerable variability; that is, one cannot claim that all males or all females lead in a particular way. Both women and men lead effectively and poorly; some members of both sexes are autocratic, democratic, sensitive, demanding, responsive, detached, and so forth.

2. We found comparing the results for the dispositional dominance literature with those for performance self-esteem interesting. The scales used in both studies (i.e., dispositional dominance and performance self-esteem) seemed very similar and yet for the most part the results were very different. Again we think whether the groups chose their leaders before or after interacting is the best explanation for this difference. When groups interacted, males and females were equally likely to emerge as the leader in both types of studies. It was only when they did not interact that males emerged more often. It just happens that most of the studies using dispositional dominance did not involve interaction, while group members did interact in the performance self-esteem study.

References

Adams, J., Rice, R.W., and Instone, D. (1984). "Follower Attitudes Toward Women and Judgments Concerning Performance by Female and Male Leaders." *Academy of Management Journal* 27, 639–643.

Alderton, S.M., and Jurma, W.E. (1980). "Genderless/Gender Related Task Leader Communication and Group Satisfaction: A Test of Two Hypotheses." *Southern Speech Communication Journal* 46, 48–60.

Anderson, L.R., and Blanchard, P.N. (1982). "Sex Differences in Task and Social-Emotional Behavior." *Basic and Applied Social Psychology* 3, 109–139.

Andrews, P.H. (1984). "Performance-Self-Esteem and Perception of Leadership Emergence: A Comparative Study of Men and Women." *Western Journal of Speech Communication* 48, 1–13.

Aries, E. (1976). "Interaction Patterns and Themes of Male, Female, and Mixed Groups." *Small Group Behavior* 7, 7–18.

Auerbach, S.M., Kilmann, P.R., Gackenbach, J.I., and Julian, A., III. (1980). "Profeminist Group Experience: Effects of Group Composition on Males' Attitudinal and Affect Response." *Small Group Behavior* 11, 50–65.

Baird, J.E., and Bradley, P.H. (1979). "Styles of Management and Communication: A Comparative Study of Men and Women." *Communication Monographs* 46, 101–111.

Beckhouse, L., Tanur, J., Weiler, J., and Weinstein, E. (1975). ". . . And Some Men Have Leadership Thrust Upon Them." *Journal of Personality and Social Psychology* 31, 557–566.

Belenky, M.F., Clinchy, B.M., Goldberger, N.R., and Tarule, J.M. (1986). *Women's Ways of Knowing: The Development of Self, Voice, and Mind.* New York: Basic Books.

Bradley, P.H. (1980). "Sex, Competence and Opinion Deviation: An Expectation States Approach." *Communication Monographs* 47, 105–110.

Bradley, P.H. (1981). "The Folklinguistics of Women's Speech: An Empirical Examination." *Communication Monographs* 48, 73–90.

Brooks, V.R. (1982). "Sex Differences in Student Dominance Behavior in Female and Male Professors' Classrooms." *Sex Roles* 8, 683–690.

Brown, V., and Geis, F.L. (1984). "Turning Lead into Gold: Evaluations of Men and Women Leaders and the Alchemy of Social Consensus." *Journal of Personality and Social Psychology* 46, 811–824.

Bunyi, J.A., and Andrews, P.H. (1985). "Gender and Leadership Emergence: An Experimental Study." *Southern Speech Communication Journal* 50, 246–260.

Butler, D. (1984). "Can Social Consensus Bias Evaluations of Emergent Leaders?" Unpublished master's thesis, University of Delaware.

Butler, D., and Geis, F.L. (1990). "Nonverbal Affect Responses to Male and Female Leaders: Implications for Leadership Evaluations." *Journal of Personality and Social Psychology* 58, 48–59.

Butterfield, D.A., and Powell, G.N. (1981). "Effect of Group Performance, Leader Sex, and Rater Sex on Ratings of Leader Behavior." *Organizational Behavior and Human Performance* 28,129–141.

Carbonell, J.L. (1984). "Sex Roles and Leadership Revisited." *Journal of Applied Psychology* 65, 44–49.

Carrocci, N.M. (1985). "Perceiving and Responding to Interpersonal Conflict." *Central States Speech Journal* 36, 215–228.

Cirincione-Coles, K. (1975). "The Administrator: Male and Female?" *Journal of Teacher Education* 26, 326–328.

Craig, J.M., and Sherif, C.W. (1986). "The Effectiveness of Men and Women in Problem-Solving Groups as a Function of Group Gender Composition." *Sex Roles* 14, 435–466.

Davis, B.M., and Gilbert, L.A. (1989). "Effect of Dispositional and Situational Influences on Women's Dominance Expression in Mixed-Sex Dyads." *Journal of Personality and Social Psychology* 57, 294–300.

Denmark, F.L. (1977). "Styles of Leadership." *Psychology of Women Quarterly* 2, 99–113.

Dindia, K. (1987). "The Effects of Sex of Subject and Sex of Partner on Interruptions." *Human Communication Research* 13, 345–371.

Dobbins, G.H., and Platz, S. (1986). "Sex Differences in Leadership: How Real Are They?" *Academy of Management Review* 11, 118–127.

Dobbins, G.H., Stuart, C., Pence, E.C., and Sgro, J.A. (1985). "Cognitive Mechanisms Mediating the Biasing Effects of Leader Sex on Ratings of Leader Behavior." *Sex Roles* 12, 549–560.

Dumas, R.G. (1980). "Dilemmas of Black Females in Leadership." In Rose LaFrances-Rodgers (ed.), *The Black Women.* Beverly Hills, CA: Sage, 203–215.

Edelsky, C. (1981). "Who's Got the Floor?" *Language in Society* 10, 383–421.

Eskilson, A., and Wiley, M.G. (1976). "Sex Composition and Leadership in Small Groups." *Sociometry* 39, 194–200.

Etaugh, C., Houtler, B.D., and Ptasnik, P. (1988). "Evaluating Competence of Women and Men: Effects of Experimenter Gender and Group Gender Composition." *Psychology of Women Quarterly* 12, 191–200.

Fairhurst, G.T., and Snavely, B.K. (1983). "A Test of Social Isolation of Male Tokens." *Academy of Management Journal* 26, 353–361.

Faranda, J.A. (1981). "The Influence of Sex-Role Stereotypes on the Evaluations of Male and Female Leaders." *Dissertation Abstracts* 42 (5B), 21–28.

Fisher, B.A. (1985). "Leadership as Medium: Treating Complexity in Group Communication Research." *Small Group Behavior* 16, 167–196.

Fleischer, R.A., and Chertkoff, J.M. (1986). "Effects of Dominance and Sex on Leader Selection in Dyadic Work Groups." *Journal of Personality and Social Psychology* 50, 94–99.

Geis, F.L., Boston, M.B., and Hoffman, N. (1985). "Sex of Authority Role Models and Achievement by Men and Women: Leadership Performance and Recognition." *Journal of Personality and Social Psychology* 49, 636–653.

Gigliotti, R.J. (1988). "Sex Differences in Children's Task-Group Performance: Status/Norm or Ability?" *Small Group Behavior* 19, 273–293.

Gilligan, C. (1982). *In a Difference Voice: Psychological Theory and Women's Development.* Cambridge, MA: Harvard University Press.

Goktepe, J.R., and Schneier, C.E. (1989). "Role of Sex and Gender Roles, and Attraction in Predicting Emergent Leaders." *Journal of Applied Psychology* 74, 165–167.

Goodwin, M.H. (1980). "Directive-Response Speech Sequences in Girls' and Boys' Task Activities." In Sally McConnell-Ginet, Ruth Borker, and Nelly Furman (eds.), *Women and Language in Literature and Society.* New York: Praeger, 157–173.

Graves, L.M., and Powell, G.N. (1982). "Sex Differences in Implicit Theories of Leadership: An Initial Investigation." *Psychological Reports* 50, 689–690.

Greene, L.R., Morrison, T.L., and Tischler, N.G. (1981). "Gender and Authority: Effects on Perceptions of Small Group Co-Leaders." *Small Group Behavior* 12, 401–413.

Haccoun, D.M., Haccoun, R.R., and Sallay, G. (1978). "Sex Differences in the Appropriateness of Supervisory Styles: A Nonmanagement View." *Journal of Applied Psychology* 63, 124–127.

Harragan, B.L. (1977). *Games Mother Never Taught You.* New York: Warner.

Heilman, M.E., and Martell, R.E. (1986). "Exposure to Successful Women: Antidote to Sex Discrimination in Applicant Screening Decisions?" *Organizational Behavior and Human Decision Processes* 37, 376–390.

Helgesen, S. (1990). *The Female Advantage: Women's Ways of Leadership.* New York: Doubleday.

Hennig, M., and Jardim, A. (1976). *The Managerial Women.* New York: Pocket Books.

Hirokawa, R.Y. (1980). "A Comparative Analysis of Communication Patterns Within Effective and Ineffective Decision-Making Groups." *Communication Monographs* 47, 312–321.

Hollander, E.P., and Yoder, J. (1980). "Some Issues in Comparing Women and Men Leaders." *Basic and Applied Social Psychology* 1, 267–280.

Jago, A.G., and Vroom, V.H. (1982). "Sex Differences in the Incidence and Evaluation of Participative Leader Behavior." *Journal of Applied Psychology* 67, 776–783.

Jenkins, M.M. (1984). "The Story Is in the Telling: A Cooperative Style of Conversation Among Women." In S. Tromel-Plotz (ed.), *Gewalt durch Sprache: die Vergewaltigung van Frauen in Gesprachen.* Frankfurt an Main: Fischer Taschenbuch Verlag.

Jenkins, M. (1980). "Toward a Model of Human Leadership." In Cynthia Berryman and Virginia A. Eman (eds.), *Communication, Language, and Sex.* Rowley, Mass.: Newbury House, 149–158.

Kennedy, C.W., and Camden, C.T. (1983). "A New Look at Interruptions." *Western Journal of Speech Communication* 47, 45–58.

Kimble, C.E., Yoshikawa, J.C., and Zehr, H.D. (1981). "Vocal and Verbal Assertiveness in Same-Sex and Mixed-Sex Groups." *Journal of Personality and Social Psychology* 40, 1047–1054.

Kushell, E., and Newton, R. (1986). "Gender, Leadership Style, and Subordinate Satisfaction: An Experiment." *Sex Roles* 14, 203–210.

Lamb, T.A. (1981). "Nonverbal and Paraverbal Control in Dyads and Triads: Sex or Power Differences." *Social Psychology Quarterly* 44, 49–53.

Maltz, D.N., and Borker, R.A. (1982). "A Cultural Approach to Male-Female Communication." In John J. Gumperz (ed.), *Language and Social Identity.* New York: Cambridge, 196–216.

Megargee, E.I. (1969). "Influence of Sex Roles on the Manifestation of Leadership." *Journal of Applied Psychology* 53, 377–382.

Millard, R.J., and Smith, K.H. (1985). "Moderating Effects of Leader Sex on the Relation Between Leader Style and Perceived Behavior Patterns." *Genetic, Social, and General Psychology Monographs* 111, 305–316.

Morrison, T.L., and Stein, D.D. (1985). "Member Reaction to Male and Female Leaders in Two Types of Group Experiences." *Journal of Social Psychology* 125, 7–16.

Nelson, M.W. (1988). "Women's Ways: Interactive Patterns in Predominantly Female Research Teams." In Barbara Bate and Anita Taylor (eds.), *Women Communicating: Studies of Women's Talk.* Ablex Publishing, 199–232.

Nieva, V.F., and Gutek, B.A. (1980). "Sex Effects on Evaluation." *Academy of Management Review* 5, 267–276.

Nyquist, L.V., and Spence, J.T. (1986). "Effects of Dispositional Dominance and Sex Role Expectations on Leadership Behaviors." *Journal of Personality and Social Psychology* 50, 87–93.

Octigan, M., and Niederman, S. (1979). "Male Dominance in Conversations." *Frontiers* 4, 50–54.

Offermann, L.R. (1986). "Visibility and Evaluation of Female and Male Leaders." *Sex Roles* 14, 533–544.

Ott, E.M. (1989). "Effects of the Male-Female Ratio at Work." *Psychology of Women Quarterly* 13, 41–57.

Owen, W.F. (1986). "Rhetorical Themes of Emergent Female Leaders." *Small Group Behavior* 17, 475–486.

Peck, T. (1978). "When Women Evaluate Women, Nothing Succeeds like Success: The Differential Effects of Status Upon Evaluations of Male and Female Professional Ability." *Sex Roles* 4, 205–213.

Pheterson, G., Kiesler, S., and Goldberg, P. (1971). "Evaluation of the Performance of Women as a Function of Their Sex, Achievement, and Personal History." *Journal of Personality and Social Psychology* 19, 114–118.

Porter, N., and Geis, F. (1981). "Women and Nonverbal Leadership Cues: When Seeing is Not Believing." In Clara Mayo and Nancy M. Henley (eds.), *Gender and Nonverbal Behavior.* New York: Springer-Verlag, 39–61.

Porter, N., Geis, F., Cooper, E., and Newman, E. (1985). "Androgyny and Leadership in Mixed-Sex Groups." *Journal of Personality and Social Psychology* 49, 808–823.

Pugh, M.D., and Wahrman, R. (1983). "Neutralizing Sexism in Mixed-Sex Groups: Do Women Have to Be Better than Men?" *American Journal of Sociology* 88, 746–762.

Ragins, B.R., and Sundstrom, E. (1989). "Gender and Power in Organizations: A Longitudinal Perspective." *Psychological Bulletin* 105, 51–88.

Rice, R.W., Bender, L.R., and Vitters, A.G. (1980). "Leader Sex, Follower Attitudes Toward Women, and Leadership Effectiveness: A Laboratory Experiment." *Organizational Behavior and Human Performance* 25, 46–78.

Rice, R.W., Instone, D., and Adams, J. (1984). "Leader Sex, Leader Success, and Leadership Process: Two Field Studies." *Journal of Applied Psychology* 69, 12–31.

Rice, R.W., Yoder, J.D., Adams, J., Priest, R.F., and Prince H.T., II. (1984). "Leadership Rating for Male and Female Military Cadets." *Sex Roles* 10, 885–902.

Rosenfeld, L.R., and Fowler, G.D. (1976). "Personality, Sex, and Leadership Style." *Communication Monographs* 43, 320–324.

Russell, J.E.A., Rush, M.C., and Herd, A.M. (1988). "An Exploration of Women's Expectations of Effective Male and Female Leadership." *Sex Roles* 18, 279–287.

Schneier, C., and Bartol, K.M. (1980). "Sex Effects in Emergent Leadership." *Journal of Applied Psychology* 65, 341–345.

Schriesheim, C.A. (1982). "The Great High Consideration-High Initiating Structure Leadership Myth: Evidence on Its Generalizability." *Journal of Social Psychology* 116, 221–228.

Seifert, C., and Miller, C.E. (1988). "Subordinates' Perceptions of Leaders in Task-Performing Dyads: Effects on Sex of Leader and Subordinate, Method of Leader Selection, and Performance Feedback." *Sex Roles* 19, 13–28.

Shimanoff, S.B. (1984). "Coordinating Group Interaction Via Communication Rules." In Robert S. Cathcart and Larry A. Samovar (eds.), *Small Group Communication: A Reader.* Dubuque, IA: Wm. C. Brown, 31–44.

Spillman, B., Spillman, R., and Reinking, K. (1981). "Leadership Emergence: Dynamic Analysis of the Effects of Sex and Androgyny." *Small Group Behavior* 12, 139–157.

Stake, J.E. (1979). "The Ability/Performance Dimension of Self-esteem: Implications for Women's Achievement Behavior." *Psychology of Women Quarterly* 3, 365–377.

Stake, J.E. (1981). "Promoting Leadership Behaviors in Low Performance-Self-Esteem Women in Task-Oriented Mixed-Sex Dyads." *Journal of Personality* 49, 401–414.

Stake, J.E. (1983). "Situation and Person-Centered Approaches to Promoting Leadership in Low Performance-Self-Esteem Women." *Journal of Personality* 51, 62–77.

Stake, J.E., and Stake, M.N. (1979). "Performance-Self-Esteem and Dominance Behavior in Mixed-Sex Dyads." *Journal of Personality* 47, 71–84.

Thomas, V.G., and Littig, L.A. (1985). "Typology of Leadership Style: Examining Gender and Race Effects." *Bulletin of the Psychonomic Society* 23, 132–134.

Thorne, B., Kramarae, C., and Henley, N. (1983). *Language, Gender and Society.* Rowley, Mass: Newbury House.

Tischler, N., Morrison, T., Greene, L.R., and Stewart, M.S. (1986). "Work and Defensive Processes in Small Groups: Effects of Leader Gender and Authority Position." *Psychiatry* 49, 241–252.

Wentworth, D.K., and Anderson, L.R. (1984). "Emergent Leadership as a Function of Sex and Task Type." *Sex Roles* 11, 513–524.

West, C., and Zimmerman, D.H. (1983). "Small Insults: A Study of Interruptions in Cross-Sex Conversations Between Unacquainted Persons." In Barrie Throne, Cheris Kramarae, and Nancy Henley (eds.), *Language, Gender, and Society.* Rowley, MA: Newbury House, 103–118.

Wilensky, J. (1988). "Women and Conflict." Paper presented at the Fifteenth Annual Student Conference in Communication.

Willer, L.R., and Henderson, L.S. (1988). "Employees Perceptions of Manager's Communication Competence versus Traditional Management Behaviors." Paper presented at the Academy of Management Conference, Anaheim, CA.

Willis, F.N., and Williams, S.J. (1976). "Simultaneous Talking in Conversation and Sex of Speakers." *Perceptual and Motor Skills* 43,1067–1070.

Winther, D.A., and Green, S.B. (1987). "Another Look at Gender-Related Differences in Leadership." *Sex Roles* 16, 41–58.

Wolman, C., and Frank, H. (1975). "The Solo Woman in a Professional Peer Group." *American Journal of Orthopsychiatry* 45, 164–171.

Wood, J.T. (1981). "Sex Differences in Group Communication: Directions for Research in Speech Communication." *Journal of Group Psychotherapy, Psychodrama, and Sociometry* 34, 24–31.

Wright, F. (1976). "The Effects of Style and Sex of Consultants and Sex of Members in Self-Study Groups." *Small Group Behavior* 7, 433–456.

Wyatt, N. (1988). "Shared Leadership in the Weavers Guild." In Barbara Bate and Anita Taylor (eds.), *Women Communicating: Studies of Women's Talk*. Norwood, NJ: Ablex Publishing, 147–176.

Zimmerman, D.H., and West, C. (1975). "Sex Roles, Interruptions and Silences in Conversations." In Barrie Throne and Nancy Henley (eds.), *Language and Sex: Difference and Dominance*. Rowley, MA: Newbury House, 105–129.

Group Lifetimes: Japanese and American Versions

Robert Cathcart and Dolores Cathcart

It is our purpose in this chapter to explore some of the cultural concepts and practices in Japan and America that demonstrate how cultural imperatives can and do determine the way people behave in small groups. We will particularly focus on the importance of viewing groups as either permanent or temporary for its effect on attitudes and behaviors in small groups. We will demonstrate how this underlying concept of the lifetime of a group can create barriers to communication and understanding when Japanese and Americans participate together in group discussion. We recognize, of course, that many persons of Japanese descent are American citizens and have families who have lived in the United States long enough to be entirely assimilated into American culture. For our purposes here, however, we want to distinguish between those who are "American" in their cultural behavior and those who are "Japanese" in their cultural behavior. Thus, we hope that readers will understand that we are not being ethnocentric or racist when we use the terms "Japanese" and "American" to distinguish between persons with these two different cultural backgrounds.

Permanent and Nonpermanent Groups

Americans frequently experience difficulties in dealing with permanent groups, while Japanese are often at a great loss when confronted with impermanent or short-term groups. The image of the big burly American charging into a Japanese business group and demanding that decisions be made immediately while the Japanese smile and bow, apparently saying yes while they mean no or perhaps has now been well established on our film and TV screens. Even President Clinton furthered this stereotype when he tried to warn American business people doing business with the Japanese not to be fooled when the Japanese seemed to be saying yes but actually meant no. The American belief that an outsider can immediately become a member of a group simply because she or he is in the same business or faces a similar problem is entirely strange to the Japanese. Just as strange to an American is the idea that she or he would never leave a group, even at the expense of personal advancement and satisfaction. Put in simple terms, most Japanese expect to be members of a select few groups all their lives; most Americans expect that in their lifetimes they will participate in hundreds of groups and are free to join or leave groups at will.

When Americans think of participating in small groups they usually envision working with two or three other people on some task that can be accomplished in a relatively short period of time. Americans seldom place small groups in the same category

Permission to reprint must be obtained from the authors. Dolores Cathcart is a freelance writer. Robert Cathcart is Professor Emeritus at Queens College of the City of New York.

as the more permanent groups they are part of such as family, clan, fraternal, or religious group. Committees and other short-term groups are usually put together "on the spot" by superiors, whereas permanent groups are formed through family, community, and life work—groups with which members are associated most of their lives. These permanent small groups are characterized by concern for the integrity of the group and the welfare of its members rather than the accomplishment of an assigned task or set goal. They tend to be hierarchically organized by age or length of membership and a great deal of time is devoted to relationships within the group rather than on task achievement. There are, of course, decisions to be made and tasks to be accomplished in permanent groups, but these often are secondary to emotional and relational struggles. All of these factors produce quite different challenges for participants in permanent groups than those associated with membership in an impermanent or short-term group.

In modern industrial cultures the business or institutional groups take on a role similar to the family group since people often spend more years in active participation in the institution where they are employed than they do in their family or religious group. This is particularly true in a country such as Japan where lifetime employment has become a feature of its postwar society (Reischauer 1981, 179–95). It is less likely to be the case in highly individualistic cultures such as the United States where individuals see each place of employment as a temporary source of personal economic gain and self-satisfaction. Though Americans may remain in the employment of a company or institution for many years, neither the company nor the individual considers it a lifetime commitment. For most Americans, the concept of lifetime employment with a single company is contrary to free-enterprise capitalism and belief in freedom of opportunity. For Japanese, on the other hand, a lifetime commitment to company and to family is a cultural given. In America, even devotion to the family as a lifelong group is tempered by a cultural dedication to the principle that each person should, at some point, leave the family unit and establish her or his own independent family or at least maintain a separate household. While the Japanese also marry and form new families, the cultural concept of an ongoing permanent family group remains.

Cultural Practices and Concepts of Group

Child Raising

These divergent outlooks on group lifetimes are founded in two important cultural imperatives: child rearing and social context. Pursuing these two avenues, we will examine first, in a general way, the effects of Japanese and American child raising on group culture. We will then review some aspects of Japanese culture and American culture for their effects on group life.

Attitudes towards groups and one's place in them are formed early in the lives of children and are maintained by the rituals, taboos, and rewards the culture upholds. A Japanese baby, for example, is kept in close physical contact with the mother, carried on her back during the day, and allowed to sleep with her until several years old. Babies in Japan are nursed over a long period, fed at will, fondled constantly, and seldom handed over to others for care (see Doi 1973). This mother/child bond begins a lifetime of dependence on others, producing *amae*—the desire to constantly maintain the warm, harmonious relationship first experienced physically with the mother and then psychologically with other members of the family. Japanese psychiatrist Takeo Doi explains *amae* (derived from the verb *amaeru,* meaning "sweetness") as a state of mind encompassing the warmth and good feeling that comes when one depends entirely on others for affection and protection. Doi holds that it is the most significant factor in determining why Japanese are group rather than individualistic in orientation. He believes it is an essential part of *nihonjin-ron*—"the Japanese way."

The Japanese pay more than just lip service to the importance of the family. Family is perceived as the *basis of all social order* (Kizaemon 1954). It is commonly accepted that at the moment a child is born it is "individual" and then it is the job of the mother, the father, and all other family members to make the child part of a family group. It is within the family group that a child learns the intricate rituals and linguistic nuances that shape the Japanese personality and that are operative in all relationships inside and outside the family. That is, the Japanese *replicate* the family group structure and process throughout their society.

The warmth and support for the Japanese child continues well beyond infancy. Young children are seldom admonished, rarely punished, and are allowed behavior that would be deemed extremely permissive by American standards. The child develops an expectation of understanding indulgence but at the same time is persuaded to accept the authority of the parent and older siblings, carefully conforming to their patient acceptance and their expectations of group harmony. Throughout early life the child is protected—overly pampered in American eyes—and completely enfolded in the family without pressures toward self-sufficiency. In other words, the Japanese child is expected to be childlike and completely dependent on others, not a miniature adult who can exert independence and autonomy (Reischauer 1981, 140–41).

When a child enters school this dependence is carried over to the classroom. Children depend on the teachers and the school to prepare them for adult group life. Each school class is treated as a group and rewarded as a group. The training is rigorous and uncompromising. Intricate Japanese *kanji* (written characters) must be mastered along with the intricacies of spoken and written honorifics. Cultural mores allow no choice and no deviation in these matters because they are the essence of what it means to be Japanese In all schools the same things are taught in the same way and at the same time.[1]

Once in school, Japanese children have little free time. They spend long hours at school (schools operate six days a week) and devote after-school time to further study. Thus, children have little opportunity to form friendships or neighborhood groups. They are expected to devote all of their time, both at school and home, in preparation for "exam hell week"; those few days at the end of high school that will determine their future education, their lifetime work, and their lifetime groups. Until they reach college or vocational school, Japanese children are expected to be pliant, obedient, and diligent. They are not encouraged to become independent, to decide how to spend their time, or to freely choose their friends, nor are they rewarded for the rebellious behaviors that are often unwittingly nurtured in American culture.

In college or technical school, Japanese children experience another period of *amae*—"sweetness." After years of grueling competition for placement in higher education, students are permitted a time to throw off restraints, to date, to drink, to protest or act out against the older established order. It is at this point that new permanent (nonfamily) groups are established. Peer groups are formed around those who entered school at the same time and are the same age. Students form their own *nakamas* (small groups), most often around special-interest clubs such as poetry, photography, hiking, golf, etc. They drink together, confide in one another, and come to know each other intimately. This is not only practice for joining a company group, it also forms links that help connect company groups. This has special importance because the groups formed and the connections made while in college or vocational school will continue throughout each person's life

Finally, at graduation, Japanese students join company, bureau, or trade groups; these become permanent groups in which members will participate for most of the remainders of their lives. Graduation ceremonies are often accompanied by rituals that "adopt" the individual into the company "family." The company or trade group affords the same protection and *amae* as did the birth family and each participant is expected to give complete devotion and dedication in return (Cleaver 1976).

It is not difficult to contrast American ideas of child raising and group commitment with this description of Japanese society. In America there is an almost frantic urge to make each child an independent unit as quickly as possible, able "to stand on his or her own two feet," to be a "rugged individual," capable of fending for herself or himself at the earliest possible age. American children are literally "pushed out of the nest." They are placed in cribs and playpens away from their parents, and if possible, they are given their own rooms separate from siblings and parents. Americans resist "coddling" their children for fear they will become too dependent, unable to face the hardships of ordinary life. Americans take pride in showing off children's ability to take responsibility and make decisions by themselves, free from the influence of peers and adults.

At school, each American child learns that she or he is in competition with all other students. Being rewarded as a good team member is usually a consolation prize. American children are taught to be competitive, to move out ahead of the crowd, and to be suspicious of those who place the needs of the group ahead of the interests of the individual. This mindset makes American children wary of joining groups unless they afford opportunities to develop and display individual talents. Sports teams are places to develop and practice individual skills. Children are taught to continually seek out new teams or groups that will better serve and reward their individual talents. Though some students join fraternal organizations because they offer a lifetime commitment to a select group and some families are honored because they remain close knit over many decades, most American children are raised to believe they must make their own decisions, maintain their freedom to choose their own associates, and never sacrifice their individuality to the tyranny of the group.

American children first learn the formalities of small-group participation in their schools. Though they may have experience with neighborhood and "pick-up" groups, it is in school that most children learn about organized groups as useful means to accomplish tasks that are too difficult or arduous for an individual to take on or as situations in which several persons have to be considered before making a decision. They learn that groups can be formed at almost any time and be made up of persons with very little in common as long as the task is clear and the time constraints are realistic.

Beginning early in school and continuing throughout their working careers, Americans are accustomed to being assigned to small groups at the direction of some higher authority (teacher or boss) and given a superior-assigned task to accomplish. This lack of participation in the formulation of groups and the little regard expressed for interpersonal relationships within the group lead many Americans to feel that a group is something to be endured while an assigned task is completed. Americans often express ambiguity towards groups in general and in particular to their own involvement with groups. This is due in part to the fact that students (and adults, too) are usually assigned to small groups with little or no preparation and no experience with the others assigned to the group. In such cases members may become hostile toward others, the group, and those who assigned them. This hostility is usually kept beneath the surface but frequently results in defensive behavior (Allcorn 1989). Despite the fact that participation in small groups can be both emotionally and materially rewarding, most American school children learn to view assigned groups as a potential imposition or a limitation on their individual freedom.

By the time the average American student has reached college age, she or he has participated in dozens of small groups, athletic teams, academic teams, church and school clubs, dance and cheerleading groups, school and classroom committees, neighborhood groups, and even personal therapy groups. Participation in these groups probably lasts no more than two or three years at the most, and a few hours at the least. Members do not see themselves as committed to any one of these groups for the rest of their lives. What they learn from all of this group participation is how to join groups, how to leave groups, ways to avoid groups, how to adapt quickly to widely varying group contexts, and how to protect their individuality within groups. By adulthood most Americans have developed an attitude toward group involvement that stresses the temporality rather than the permanence of small groups.

Cultural Rituals

In addition to the attitudes that are formed through child-rearing practices, individuals are influenced regarding group participation by the rituals and taboos that each culture creates around group life. We have already noted the Japanese rituals for life transitions that call for the individual to be "adopted" into a new "family" in which she or he will maintain the same kind of filial piety that existed in the birth family. In America we tend to emphasize group-ending rituals more than entering rituals. We stress graduation rituals that mark the end of involvement with a group and signal the individual's embarkation on a new path. We are more likely to throw a party for a colleague who is leaving the company and going on to a new, higher position than a party for a new person joining the company. We look forward to the end of a small group, feeling good when a group has finished its task and is about to dissolve. We are likely to be apprehensive when we join a new group that will involve long and intimate involvement with colleagues. These differing cultural rules, particularly as they cluster around the concept of permanent versus temporary groups, are reflected in the widely varying behaviors of Japanese and Americans in small groups. These behaviors cannot easily be changed, even if one understands the differences between the two cultures.

Group Behaviors: Japanese and American

Let us consider a hypothetical small group of Japanese and American college students or business people who all speak either Japanese or English and who are brought together to deal with some problem or task; in doing so we might better understand how deep seated some of these differences are as well as the challenges they offer. The first thing a Japanese would want to understand on entering a new group would be its hierarchical order (Taylor 1983); that is, who is the oldest, next oldest, etc., who has been with the organization the longest time, next longest, etc. The purpose of this questioning would not be to determine who the leaders are, but rather to determine exactly where the new member fits into the group order.[2] Having found their position, the Japanese would then know where to sit, when to speak, what language (honorifics) to use when addressing others, how low to bow, and so forth. Without knowing these things the Japanese would probably be reluctant, even unable, to discuss the group topic or to make other contributions to the group.

The American, on the other hand, when first entering a group, is most likely (if male) to "size up" the group to see what he could gain (points with the boss or colleagues, personal satisfaction, material reward, etc.). To put it another way, the American would want to figure out the work-reward ratio; that is, how much effort to put forth to gain possible personal and material rewards. He might quickly speak up in the group, asking questions, joking around, or pontificating to "test the water" and to learn what this group has to offer. Even before the group first meets he might button-hole other members individually to learn how they perceive the group and its potential. Almost simultaneously, the American male would be deciding what role to play in this particular group. Should he try to be one of the leaders, the leader's "yes man," the "doubting Thomas," or the group comedian? His early contributions might very well test some of these roles to see which one would be most rewarding but he would not necessarily have to stay with one role.

If the participant is an American female, however, her first concern is likely to be the power structure: Who has control and who gives out the rewards and punishments? Her next concern will be about existing factions or networks: Who goes with whom, who can be trusted, and who can she count on for support? At the same time, she will probably look for clues about what is expected in terms of female participation: Can she be outspoken, will anyone take her comments seriously, or must she play the role of reticent female?

Understandably, the idea of roles in the group will be quite different for the Japanese and for the American. The Japanese, having learned his or her place in the group hierarchy, would expect to remain in that position throughout the life of the group, and even beyond if in contact with any of the group members. There would be no jockeying for position or shifting of roles unless it was clearly agreed upon by all members of the group that she or he should take on an organizational role such as secretary or liaison with another group. The American will feel free to try out various roles, even alternating among roles, if she or he feels these shifts will be more satisfying and perhaps better suited to the group and the roles played by others.

After determining her or his place in the group hierarchy, the Japanese group member would set about establishing an *on* relationship with other group members

(Hall & Beardsley 1965). *On* functions as a means of linking all persons in the group in an unending chain of obligation.[3] The *on* relationship is the opposite of in-group competition. A Japanese group member will seek out ways to prove loyalty and respect for members higher in the group hierarchy while at the same time acting to assist and protect those lower in the group order.

This Japanese way of viewing relationships creates a distinctive style of group decision making known as *consensus* decision (Terasawa 1974). The process of consensus building in order to make decisions is a time-consuming one. Not only must everyone be considered, but the Japanese also avoid verbalizing objections or doubts in order to preserve group harmony. Japanese group participants look at group decisions either enhancing or diminishing the group's harmony and status rather than determining who is right or wrong. One of the consequences of Japanese decision making through consensus is that it makes the group and not the individual responsible for the decisions made. Once an opinion or solution is accepted, it becomes the group's and is no longer associated with its originator. This keeps group unity and harmony intact by not singling out any one individual as being responsible for the initiative (Golden 1982, 137).

In a system that operates on *on* relationships, nothing is decided without concern for how the outcome will affect all members of the group. This reactive process is not so much one of exerting pressure to force acquiescence but of making certain that all matters affecting the group and each member are taken into consideration. For this reason, group decisions cannot be rushed without chancing a slight or oversight that will cause future problems.

Americans often view Japanese devotion to consensus building with suspicion because they view it as a form of groupthink. They believe it is more important to maintain one's integrity and hold out against other members of the group if they think they are in the right. This behavior, they feel, will lead to a more "honest" or practical decision instead of one based on agreement for agreement's sake. In contrast to the American style of confronting issues head-on and arguing openly so that points of difference can be quickly recognized and dealt with, Japanese prefer a nonconfrontational approach to group communication.

Japanese participants utilize indirectness, placing a premium on avoidance of open conflict and the preservation of group harmony (Barnlund 1989, 112–20). If a Japanese participant disagrees with another over a claim or a preference, she or he is more likely to use an indirect approach to indicate lack of agreement. This variance might take the form of diverting the discussion to a point on which all can agree or pointing out her or his own inadequacies in understanding what has been said in hopes that the contributor will recognize there is some point of difference. A Japanese who felt insecure about her or his place in the group would probably smile and nod but say nothing, meaning that she or he had heard but not agreed with the contribution. As a result, Americans dealing with Japanese often mistakenly believe that there is agreement when actually they are far from it. The advice in American small-group literature—that group communication should be characterized by frank, open, and candid statements expressing individual personal feelings, wishes, and dislikes—is the antithesis of the Japanese belief that indirectness and sensitivity lead to cooperation, consensus, and group harmony.

Though Americans are more open and frank, not all American group members take on confrontational roles. American groups usually have one or more members who are quiet participants, sometimes referred to as "silent agreers." It is assumed that if these members say little or nothing it is because they are essentially in agreement with what is being presented in the group, and that if they had some objection they would speak. More active members may ask them if they have any objections, and if they don't voice their opinions the others feel that they should not raise objections later. Sometimes even outgoing and argumentative participants will be quiet if they feel the group is a waste of their time and they have little to gain from putting forth effort. The latter form of participation is possible when members feel their involvement with the group is short term but would be almost impossible if the group were to go on for many years.

Another form of indirectness can be observed in the Japanese reluctance to say no to a question or a conclusion presented in the group. They do, of course, disagree with or reject proposals but usually seek some indirect way of stating disagreement without using the direct and abrupt "no." Japanese employ indirect ways that can mean no without using the word (Satoshi & Klopf 1975). The reason for this avoidance of the negative is to refrain from pitting one group member against another or appearing to put down a group member by directly rejecting a contribution. This response sometimes presents problems for American participants who equate such indirect negativity with being "wishy-washy" or unable to make up one's mind. Americans often feel obligated to force people to make a simple yes-or-no decision. This type of directness lets the group know where everyone stands and can be helpful in identifying where there is real disagreement—but it can also lead to the hardening of positions and stifling of group progress.

In general, American participants find verbal indirectness time consuming and confusing. Some feel that it is hypocritical to pretend to agree with others when there are doubts or objections. They are often impatient and uncomfortable with discussions that talk around the issues and do not hold individuals directly responsible for what they say. American are much more comfortable with the Western tradition of argument and debate in which the best solutions are arrived at in the give and take of freely expressed opinions no matter how members may feel about them personally. There are, of course, many examples of corporate groups that are populated with people who agree with whatever the boss says. This characteristic is, however, usually viewed as a shortcoming that is likely to produce bad solutions.

It has been claimed that Japanese culture is primarily visual, rather than verbal in orientation (Barthes 1982). Social decorum holds that silence and nonverbal acts communicate the most significant meanings. Japanese believe it is not the voice alone that communicates, but the whole body (eyes, smile, hair, gestures, clothing, etc.). Japanese indirectness and reluctance to speak continually is related to the high value they place on nonverbal communication and their skills at interpreting it. For Japanese, it is important that group participants continually search for nonverbal cues revealing whether other participants are happy, comfortable, uneasy, doubtful, eager, etc. Japanese tend to place a higher value on these indicators than on what is spoken. Americans, though aware that a smile or gesture can greatly alter what is said, are more likely to listen for cues in the tone of voice indicating anger, impatience, excitement, and so forth. American group participants will often look only at one or two other members of the group (usually leaders or friends), ignoring the nonverbal responses given by other group members. For Americans, silence is usually interpreted as negative—a void that should be quickly filled with verbiage—whereas Japanese participants are more likely to welcome silence as an opportunity to observe others and to interpret their moods and feelings. This silence, too, accounts for some of the slowness of pace in Japanese group proceedings. It also makes Americans uneasy because they view silence as a breakdown in communication. On the other hand, Japanese group participants are often confused and confounded by the rapid barrage of spoken discussion (frequently with more than one or two persons talking at the same time) that typifies many American group discussions.

Our hypothetical Japanese-American group could find itself in difficulty if there were marked disparity in the abilities of various group members to handle the group task. It is not uncommon for Americans to feel unfairly burdened if their group has members who lack the mental ability and social acuity to keep up with the most competent group members. They are also known to complain bitterly to each other and to superiors if the group has shirkers or members who do not do the work necessary for the group to succeed. They might even demand that such members be ejected and/or replaced. This would seem strange and unnecessary behavior to the Japanese members of the group. Their acceptance of lifetime groups carries with it the unquestioning acceptance of all members who formed the original group. They do not expect that each member will be equal in talent or want to perform with similar zeal. They do, however, expect all members will be completely loyal to the group and no member will be shunned or left out of the group. In each Japanese group there exists a subtle form of hierarchy in which each member is expected to perform in areas where she or he has the most talent and skill and no members will be given tasks they are not capable of performing. Thus, each group makes up for or carries and supports those members who have lesser abilities. Japanese see the group as a totality and all members must be included and considered—even those who are not very helpful. It is the *on* relationship, again, where participants are responsible *to* those above and *for* those below.

Even more strange to a Japanese is the form of American pragmatism that allows people to ignore a group that fails to complete its task (e.g., never finishes its study, never gets around to a conclusion, fails to give its report); or leave the group in limbo until it fades away or exists only on paper. Americans can more readily accept that some small groups simply do not have the ability or the desire to perform their tasks and the easiest thing to do is ignore the group and find another way to solve the problem. Japanese groups, because they are more permanent, will always find something to do and will work at it diligently, even though what they accomplish may not be worth much to the larger organization.

Conclusion

We hope that these few examples will provide the reader with some understanding of how cultural imperatives influence people's perceptions of small groups and their place in them. Small groups exist in all cultures, but they do not exist in the same ways nor do their participants engage in the same behaviors. In other words, small groups are not culture-free, just as their individual members are not free of the cultural mores that dictate their attitudes toward small groups and their performance within them. As we have pointed out, the way that children are raised, the existence of societal rituals for entering and leaving groups, and cultural emphasis on groupness or individuality all play a part in determining how persons will feel and what expectations they will have about small groups. When people from different cultures are placed together in small groups—though they speak the same language and know something of each other's culture—they will still be bound by the cultural imperatives they have learned since birth. Neither Japanese or Americans can be expected to completely overcome the attitudes resulting from their differing ideas about groups as permanent or temporary. Japanese unquestioning belief in group harmony and consensus will come into conflict with American individualism and majority rule. Japanese preference for indirectness, suspicion of verbal facility, and reliance on nonverbal communication will create barriers when confronting American beliefs in frankness and confrontation, respect for verbal acuity and quick response, and impatience with nonverbal communication.

Though such cultural differences are deeply and permanently ingrained, it does not mean that successful communication cannot take place or that group work is impossible; rather, it means we should not expect to achieve the same outcomes with cross-cultural groups as with in-culture groups. We have to accept that mixed-culture task groups will take longer to reach agreements, perhaps even meeting again and again to go back over discussions in which different cultural assumptions have been overlooked. Most of the time we will have to accept a certain amount of frustration and something less than group satisfaction.

It is not easy to be aware constantly of the underlying concepts that members of other cultures bring to a small group. Even when group members are versed in the ways of each other's culture, every person works out of a framework of her or his own cultural background and cannot completely escape those dictates. We have to learn to accept that cultural imperatives are deeply embedded and not all differences can be smoothed over, no matter how good our intentions. We can, however, offer understanding and extend an open hand, and hope that we receive the same in return.

Notes

1. No changes can be made in any school's curriculum without the express approval of the Japanese Minister of Education.
2. Taylor (1983) points out that hierarchy is the context for all relationships in Japan:
   > All societies establish hierarchies. In few societies, however, are they so widespread or important as in Japan. For the Japanese, rank is so finely determined that equality is rare—everyone and everything are at least slightly above or below the nearest apparent equal. Family members, work mates, schools, companies, even nations and races all have their places. Hierarchy is inseparable from orderliness; a group is not properly organized unless its members are ranked (42).
3. *On* is based on a system known as the *oyabun-kobun* relationship (Hall & Beardsley 1965). Traditionally, the *oyabun* is a father, boss, or patron who protects and provides for a *kobun*—a son, employee, or student—in return for his or her service and loyalty. Each group member expects the person above in the group hierarchy to act as an *oyabun* and each below to function as a *kobun*. This dependency is not one-way. Each boss or group leader recognizes his or her own dependency on those below. Without their undivided loyalty, he or she could not function successfully.

References

Allcorn, S. (1989). "Understanding Groups at Work." *Personnel,* August, 29.

Barnlund, D. (1989). *Communicative Styles of Japanese and Americans.* Belmont, CA: Wadsworth.

Barthes, R. (1982). *Empire of Signs.* (Translated by Richard Howard). New York: Hill & Wang.

Cleaver, C. (1976). *Japanese and Americans: Cultural Parallels and Paradoxes.* Minneapolis: Minneapolis University Press.

Doi, Takeo (1973). *The Anatomy of Dependence.* (Translated by John Bester). Tokyo: Kodansha.

Golden, A. (1982). "Group Think in Japan, Inc." *The New York Times Magazine.* December 5, 133–140.

Hall, J., and Beardsley, R. (1965). *Twelve Doors to Japan.* New York: McGraw-Hill.

Kizaemon, A. (1954). "The Family in Japan." *Marriage and Family Living.* 16 (4), 362.

Reischauer, E. (1981). *The Japanese.* Cambridge: Harvard University Press.

Satoshi, I., and Klopf, D. (1975). "A Comparison of Communication Activities of Japanese and American Adults." Paper presented at the Communication Association of the Pacific, Tokyo, 1975.

Taylor, J. (1983). *Shadows of the Rising Sun.* New York: Harcourt Brace Jovanovich.

Terasawa, Y. (1974). "Japanese Style in Decision-Making." *The New York Times.* May 12, D3.

ACTIVITIES

Activity 1

Purpose: The purpose of this activity is to demonstrate how words are culturally based and can therefore cause confusion within a small group.

Procedure: In small groups, play a word-association game. Your instructor will compose a list of potentially culture-bound words such as democracy, AIDS, freedom, affirmative action, and sexual harassment. Write down the first definition that comes to your mind. Then, compare your responses to other members of your group and discuss them. Finally, compare your group's answers with those of the entire class. If your group or class has members from different cultures it will be interesting to note cultural differences and similarities.

Activity 2

Purpose: The purpose of this activity is to point out the differences among people, their perceptions, and their preferences.

Procedure: In small groups prepare the lists that follow the explanation.

We have been raised with the golden rule, "Do unto others as you would have them do unto you." This rule is intended to make us aware of how our behavior impacts others and to raise our sensitivity to the feelings of others. However, do you always want the same things that others want? If we all liked the same thing, cars would be made in only one color, and restaurants would serve only one type of food.

Obviously we all differ in our attitudes. Perhaps we need a rule that is *better* than a golden rule. The *Platinum Rule* could be "Do unto others as *they* would have you do unto them."

Identifying behaviors you like that are different from what others like might help to clarify some of the kinds of things people view differently.

1. List some of the behaviors that you like that others sometimes don't:

2. List some of the behaviors that others seem to find acceptable that you object to:

Activity 3

Purpose: The purpose of this activity is to introduce the members of the class to the cultural composition of their classmates.

Procedure: In small groups, identify your culture or co-culture. After identifying yourself, discuss the following questions:

1. How many in the group identify with the dominant culture of North America?

2. How many in the group identify with cultures or co-cultures in addition to the dominant culture?

3. In what setting do you most often interact with people from cultures other than your own?

4. What problems do you most often encounter when you interact with people from different cultures?

Activity 4

Purpose: The purpose of this activity is to demonstrate the role of sexual stereotyping on perception and communication.

Procedure: In small groups identify the following list of traits as being either (a) male, (b) female, or (c) neutral.

TRAIT	MALE	FEMALE	NEUTRAL
leader			
ambitious			
secretive			
independent			
analytical			
complex			
passive			
controlled			
impulsive			
intuitive			
insensitive			
manipulative			
objective			
neurotic			
rational			
tough			
caring			

Each group should share its findings with the entire class.

Activity 5

Purpose: The purpose of this activity is to illustrate the great diversity in values and world views found in different cultures.

Procedure: In small groups, consider what a group of people (culture) would be like if collectively they had believed

1. in reincarnation and karma.

2. that all people are infidels.

3. that all events in the world are determined by fate.

4. that a person's worth is determined solely by his or her birth.

5. in a passive approach to life instead of an active approach.

6. that old people were to be revered, honored, and deferred to in all instances.

7. that a spiritual life was more important than a material life.

8. that rights of the group were more important than rights of the individual.

9. that women are superior to men.

The class can also discuss how some of these views would be translated into small-group interaction.

Source: This exercise is adapted from L. Robert Kohls, *Developing Intercultural Awareness* (Washington, DC: SEITAR, 1981), 64.

Activity 6

Purpose: The purpose of this activity is to explore differences in male and female communication patterns.

Procedure: Have the class divide into four groups. Group One will be composed of all males. Group Two will be all females. Groups Three and Four will be composed of males and females. Have groups One and Two discuss the following topic: What communication behaviors are most conducive to successful small-group communication? Group Three will observe Group One. Group Four will observe Group Two. Groups Three and Four should try to identify some of the following communication characteristics: (The list is only intended to offer examples. Additional items should be included.)

1. Eye contact.

2. Volume.

3. Enthusiasm.

4. Shared participation.

5. Interruptions.

6. Affiliation.

7. Posture.

8. Pace of deliberations.

9. Facial expressions.

10. Cooperation.

7
Leading Groups

One of the most intriguing expressions of human behavior is the leader-follower phenomenon. Since the beginning of civilization people have sought answers to the questions of who becomes a leader and why. Philosophers, political scientists, and psychologists have produced extensive literature on leaders and leadership, but despite this, we are still not certain why and under what circumstances some people become leaders and others remain followers. There is no universal theory of leadership and no precise formula for producing leaders, and yet we continue to seek answers. Perhaps one of the best ways to answer some of these questions is to describe some of the views about leadership. This provides a beginning for defining leadership, for explaining the power associated with it, and for discussing the various current theories about it.

Plato believed that only a select few with superior wisdom should be leaders. Aristotle contended that "From the moment of their birth, some are marked for subjugation and others for command." Machiavelli felt that those princes who had the cunning and the ability to organize power and knowledge in the defense of the state should be followed. He believed that people are weak, fallible, gullible, and dishonest; therefore, manipulation is acceptable to achieve one's goals when the end justifies the means. St. Paul said only those deemed worthy through divine blessing could truly lead.

The "nature/nurture" controversy continues today. Whether leaders are born with talents and traits that allow and even cause them to be successful leaders, or whether effective leadership behaviors can be learned through experience, is a difficult question. There is not even consensus about **universal traits** that cause leaders to be effective. Often leaders are intelligent, knowledgeable, attractive, sociable, and persistent; but there are exceptions. We can probably call to mind effective leaders that did not embody one or more of these traits. The **behaviors** associated with great leadership are not consistent either. Some would describe effective leaders as being initiating, organizing, encouraging, mediating, and coordinating. But again, exceptions exist.

Some of the confusion and disagreement concerning this topic can be traced to a failure to distinguish between "the leader" and "leadership." If nothing else, twentieth century social science research has established that leadership is a **function** of group process, rather than a series of traits residing in a particular individual. Clearly, there is no such thing as a "leader" apart from some particular group or organization.

Individuals form groups to satisfy needs that cannot otherwise be satisfied, and they accept direction for the same reason. A particular leader or shared leadership represents a means of fulfilling the group's needs better than could be done without direction. Leaders lead because groups demand direction and rely on leaders to satisfy needs. In this frame of reference, describing the "universal" leader or the "ideal" leader is impossible.

We can, however, describe leadership **functions** and **roles** and then discover which members perform accordingly. In this way, distinguishing between "leadership" as a group function and "the leader" as the person who is performing this function in a particular context is possible. Functioning in a leadership role involves exerting **influence** and **power**. One person can play this role, or it can be shared among the group members. In most successful groups, there is one recognized leader, but the leadership responsibilities are shared among the members.

Power in Groups

One of the ways that group members exert influence is through the use of **power**. Power is the control that the group gives to one or more of its members. It affects goal accomplishment and interpersonal relationships because it governs behavior and regulates resources. The group members' **perception** of power is significant to this discussion because the members determine the variables that will influence their unique group. This power can be based on a variety of forces: legitimate power, coercive power, reward power, expert power, referent power, and informational power.

Legitimate power is sometimes referred to as position power because it is the power that the leader has based on an official role that he or she is performing in the group. This type of leader is appointed, elected, designated, or emergent; but the members all recognize this person as the one who is officially in charge of the group. Often, but not always, this type of leader will have some of the other kinds of power that will augment the leadership role.

One of these kinds of power may be **coercive power**, or the authority either to negate positive consequences or deliver negative consequences. Using this type of control in a group usually does not work well since people seldom perform at optimum levels when they feel threatened. Fear of punishment might stimulate the group members to work hard to finish a project if they fear that their vacations will be canceled if they don't, but usually other kinds of pressure work better.

Using **reward power**, for instance, can have a more positive impact on group performance. Often tangible rewards such as monetary bonuses and vacation time will be the source of the power, but more often the rewards will be intangible. Delivering goodwill, offering recognition, and giving compliments are all ways that any member of the group can exercise reward power. Using this intangible reward power is one way for individuals to share the leadership role; failing to use it is one way to miss a valuable opportunity to build group cohesion.

Expert power exists when group members consider a person to be qualified in a specific area. Often the nature of the expertise will be special knowledge, talent, or skill that the others recognize as superior. With regard to expert power, the interesting phenomenon that takes place is that being an expert is not enough; the others in the group must also recognize the person as an expert and treat him or her accordingly.

Sometimes the nature of the power is not that the person is an authority in a certain field but that the individual possesses certain information. If a person has access to information or knowledge that other group members don't have, that person has some control over how and when to use the knowledge.

Another type of power that can be linked to expert power is **referent power.** Frequently group members will respect a person who is competent and trustworthy. This person can acquire referent power by being an expert in a given field, but sometimes this is not the case. At times an individual will acquire referent power by being likable, admirable, honorable, or charismatic. This type of power, unlike some of the other kinds, is available to all group members. Power is not something that a person can demand from the group; it must be given by the group. Even a legitimate leader who has been assigned the role of leader may find exercising controlling prerogatives to be challenging if the group resists. The way that a person will choose to use power will depend on the situation and the individual's style.

Styles of Leadership

Leadership style, more than leadership traits determines how effective a leader will be. The leader's **style** or manner of dealing with the group members and communicating with them will contribute to or detract from the group's overall functioning. There are three general approaches to these interactions: **authoritarian** leadership style, **democratic** leadership style, and **laissez-faire** leadership style.

Authoritarian, or autocratic, leadership relies on legitimate, coercive, and reward power to influence others. Sometimes these leaders are aggressive, parental, and dictatorial in their dealings with the group. However, while these approaches often work well in crisis situations, a constant use of this style can cause the group members to be apathetic and unproductive when the leader's back is turned. In other words, when a leader constantly uses authoritarian leadership, the group members fail to develop a sense of ownership of the group's work. They will work if they are watched, but since they don't feel a part of the decision-making process, they are not motivated to do more than absolutely necessary.

Democratic leaders, on the other hand, share the decision-making process. Members tend to be more satisfied and less frustrated when they play a part in the group's functioning. Sometimes the designated leader will still make the final decision, but the group members feel more validated if their ideas are considered, and they are usually more motivated to implement the decision.

Laissez-faire leaders exert little or no influence on the group. In essence, these groups are a collection of equals. Since no one dominates the group, the members rely on each other for direction. This can work if the individuals are capable and driven; however, it can fail if the group is unmotivated or immature in the task.

Democratic leadership has been hailed as the best of the three styles, but no one style is indicated all of the time. Democratic leadership works well when nonstressful, moderate conditions prevail, but autocratic leadership is more suitable during a crisis or high-stress situation. Even the laissez-faire style can work well if the group is self-directed and motivated.

Leadership Theories

Not only is there no agreement about a theory of leadership, there are those who question the very notion of leadership. They believe our present emphasis on individualism and freedom of choice is at odds with the traditional reliance on strong, effective leaders. Some people would purposefully avoid leadership because they believe it requires the manipulation of other persons and limits people's freedom of choice. These individuals tend to associate leadership with elitism and the kind of power seeking which sometimes leads to corruption of group goals and unnecessary intergroup conflict.

Some would go so far as to say that modern education and mass communication make leaders unnecessary. As yet, however, there has been no noticeable change in leaders or leadership, and apparently there are no successful groups without leadership. Even when some members of a group consciously avoid leader roles, others arise to fill the void. The question, then, is not whether there should or should not be leaders, but what constitutes the most effective and desirable leadership for a given group.

The **situational theories** or contingency theories began in the 1960s. The basis of these theories is that individuals' characteristics make them suitable leaders only in certain situations. Since each situation requires a leader to vary behavior to fit the prevailing circumstances, groups do well to match the leader to the present state of affairs. In other words, there is no right or wrong way to lead all of the time. Matching leaders and groups who meet each other's needs and skills is advised.

The situational theorist addresses the need to consider both the task and social-emotional needs of the group. In 1967 **Fred Fiedler** proposed his theory to determine when a task-oriented approach would be most effective and when a relationship-oriented style would be more productive. He concluded that **task-oriented** *leaders are effective when conditions are either good or bad.* When conditions are favorable, member relations are strong; there is a positive relationship between the group and the leader; and the task is clear and structured. The group members are ready and willing to work, and their energies can be focused on the goal.

The same type of task-oriented leader is called for if the situation is bad. When conditions are unfavorable, when there are poor relations among the group, or when the task is ambiguous or undesirable, the group will need to stay goal oriented in order to achieve any success, so the task-oriented leader is once again indicated.

According to Fiedler, when **moderate** terms exist, the relationship-oriented or social-emotional leader will be a more effective leader. When an intermediate situation is present in a group, the leader can help to build confidence and cohesion by focusing on the personal needs of the individuals. Democratic leadership tends to trigger group involvement, and that, in turn, tends to engender individual satisfaction.

Another situational theory that deals with task behaviors and relationship behaviors is the **Hersey/Blanchard Theory.** This theory was introduced about ten years after Fiedler's theory, and while similar in its focus on task and relationship, it differs in significant areas. First, Paul Hersey and Kenneth Blanchard assume that leaders are more flexible than Fiedler does. They maintain that the leader should change behavior as the group's maturity increases.

A new, immature group needs direction and goal-oriented behavior that they call **telling.** As the group matures, it will be ready to build relationship behavior, and then the leader's **selling** ideas is appropriate. As the experience level, motivation, and willingness to take responsibility increases, the leader's involvement should decrease. The encouragement of the groups **participating,** and the leader's eventual **delegating** of responsibility are the next two steps in the process. As the group shows its readiness to be more autonomous, the leader should allow shared leadership and responsibility.

One of the most popular explanations of leadership behavior is the **Blake/Mouton Managerial Grid.** Once again, this approach describes the relationship between the leader's concern for task and the concern for people, but this theory differs in its perspective. Robert Blake and Jane Mouton offer a model that is more concrete in depicting the variations that can take place in a leader's behavior. The leader's concern for goal achievement and people's feelings are each assigned a 1–9 numerical equivalent, with 1 showing very little concern and 9 showing high concern. Charting these numbers on a horizontal axis that measures a leader's concern for production and comparing it to a vertical axis that measures the leader's concern for people gives a clearer picture of the balance that exists between the two behaviors. A leader who adopts a 9–9 style will, according to Blake and Mouton, be the most successful because of the high concern for both task and people.

Each of the theories differs slightly, indicating that there is no one best, all-purpose style of leadership. The successful leader is the one who can adapt to the unique demands of an ever-changing group. An effective leader needs to diagnose the needs and wants of the group and then react accordingly, remembering all the while that the group is becoming more experienced and less dependent on direction. Recognizing the power that the leader has and the power that the group members share helps leaders and group members more effectively share the leadership functions and contribute to overall group productivity.

Introduction to Readings

We begin with an essay on leadership by Martin M. Chemers. Chemers reviews more than seventy years of scientific study on this topic. By understanding the conclusions of these studies, and what they reveal about leadership, we can better interpret our role when we are either a leader or a participant. Chemers suggests that leadership studies can be divided into three interrelated periods: the trait period, approximately 1910 until World War II; the behavior period, from the onset of World War II through the late 1960s; and the contingency period, from the late 1960s to the present. After a discussion of these three periods and an analysis of what they reveal about leadership, Chemers advances some specific conclusions that may help us predict the directions leadership studies will take in the future.

The next essay in this chapter, "The Leader–Trainer–Facilitator," by John (Sam) Keltner, examines the topic of laboratory training in group process. Keltner reaches the conclusion, after his review of the facilitating process, that all group leaders are heavily involved in facilitative behavior whether in training or task groups. He explains that facilitators are "group process trainers" and points out that all group leaders are involved, to some degree, in group training. He then describes the role of group facilitator, explains the facilitative process, and considers some of the questions that arise when group leaders function as group facilitators.

Philosophers from Buddha to Bob Dylan have tried to call our attention to the simple truth that nothing remains the same. Over two thousand years ago the Greek essayist Plutarch stated this notion rather clearly when he noted that "All things are daily changing." With or without our blessing, change is inevitable—including the changes that take place within a group. Hence, it seems only fitting that we include an essay that focuses on the kinds of changes that are common in organizations and groups. More specifically, in an article titled "Developing Leadership for Change," Steven C. Schoonover and Murray M. Dalziel look at how leaders must prepare for, cope with, and utilize change to their advantage. The basic assumption behind their essay is a simple one, and one all leaders must learn to accept—"A leader's choice is not whether to change, but how." By reading this selection you should be able to better adapt to and even stimulate change when you are in a small group.

Our next essay, by Beatrice Schultz and Sandra M. Ketrow, takes a somewhat idiosyncratic approach to the question of leadership. Based on a series of research studies, the authors conclude that the quality of decision making in a small group can be improved by designating a single person to take on the role of the "reminder." The authors maintain that groups produce better results if they (1) follow a logical sequential pattern, (2) generate alternatives for solutions, and (3) thoroughly evaluate those solutions. They further suggest that the "reminder" can greatly aid the group if he or she continuously asks the other members of the group, in a nonaggressive manner, to consider questions regarding evidence, possible solutions, consequences of the solutions, and premature judgments. This constant effort to remind the participants to refocus on key issues can help any group accomplish their main objective.

The final selection in this chapter also advances a somewhat unique perspective on the topic of leadership. This time the call is for leadership in "bossless" groups. In an essay titled "The Bossless Team," David Barry maintains that if self-managed teams and groups are to be effective it is imperative for the members of these groups to understand the role of the leader. Barry begins by discussing all of the forces in the workplace (for example, technology, expensive equipment, and global competition) that have contributed to the need for groups to function as teams. He then tells us that traditional styles of leadership may not be compatible with the team approach to problem solving. As a means of adapting to the team setting Barry advances four "broad clusters" of leadership roles and behaviors: (1) envisioning, (2) organizing, (3) spanning, and (4) social. To help us when we are in a team environment he takes these four general categories and offers specific advice that can be easily translated into action.

The Social, Organizational, and Cultural Context of Effective Leadership

Martin M. Chemers

The Nature of Leadership

Organizational Functions

A first principle in the study of group effectiveness is that a group is relatively inefficient. A group, as opposed to an individual working alone, must coordinate the knowledge, abilities, and actions of its members.[1] The time, effort, and resources devoted to coordination represent potential decrements in performance. However, there are many tasks which cannot be accomplished by a single individual. Such tasks necessitate the creation of groups. Many tasks further require the coordination of several groups into larger organizations. The dictionary defines the word *organize* as "to make into a whole with unified and coherent relationships." Thus, a primary function of any organization is to create this unified set of groups in coherent relationships. All organizations must attend to two major functions in accomplishing this goal.

One function, which can be called *internal maintenance,* refers to the efforts of the organization to maintain the integrity of its various subsystems. An apt analogy is to the internal maintenance activities of the human body. Any living organism must coordinate its various parts to maintain a steady state or equilibrium that permits life to proceed. A human being must maintain a relatively constant body temperature, blood saline level, neuronal activity level, and so forth. The organism accomplishes this function through the activities of preprogrammed systems that respond to stimulation from sensing devices within the system. Task-directed organizations have a similar function. Day-to-day activities within the organization must be reliable and predictable. Job descriptions, standard operating procedures, and chains of command are examples of preprogrammed organizational systems designed to maintain equilibrium. Payroll forms, monthly reports, and inventory statements are sensing devices that establish and maintain the accountability of subsystems. Thus, the modern organization is built around a pervasive set of rules, regulations, and functions that ease the performance of standard duties and routine activities. The maintenance of these internal regularities is so essential to organizational functioning that it is possible to lose sight of another essential responsibility of organizations, *external adaptability.* An organization that overemphasizes internal maintenance turns inward, losing touch with the demands of its environment.

External adaptability requires that an organization be sensitive to its environment and internally flexible enough to respond to change. An effective organization is one that balances the functions of internal maintenance and external adaptability. Control and order coexist with responsiveness and change. The requisite amount of emphasis on each function is influenced by the larger environment of which the organization is a part. An adaptive human being changes his or her wardrobe as the seasons change. Likewise, an effective organization attends and responds to changes in the supply of resources, the demand for a product, the availability of capital, or other critical aspects of its environment.

Small-Group Functions

Organizational functions have their analogues at the level of the small group or unit. Here the function of internal maintenance is translated into the *motivation* and *control* of group members. The leader must direct the activities of subordinates and motivate them to carry out those activities efficiently. The rules, regulations, and systems of the larger organization, or general context, guide the leader in the direction of subordinates. A well-defined and structured task specifies the group's goal and procedures for reaching the goal. However, just as an organization's environment presents new challenges requiring response, so also a work unit or small group will be confronted with tasks for which no standard operating procedures exist. The leader and the group must then engage in the functions of *information processing* and *decision making*. Goals are defined, problems are solved, and procedures for attaining objectives are developed.

An extensive body of leadership research has demonstrated that the styles, behaviors, and activities of leadership that can accomplish these disparate organizational and small-group functions are quite different. Current organizational and leadership theory adopts the notion of "contingency." This notion argues that the organizational structure or leadership style that will be most effective depends or is contingent upon the nature of the task environment. Contemporary research attempts to identify and categorize the most critical features of the leadership situation and relate them to the most important aspects of leadership style and behavior.

Contemporary Leadership Theory

A Brief History

The scientific study of leadership can be roughly divided into three periods: the trait period, from around 1910 to World War II, the behavior period, from the onset of World War II to the late 1960s, and the contingency period, from the late 1960s to the present.

Traits. The early research on leadership emergence and leadership effectiveness proceeded from the premise that, somehow, those who became leaders were different from those who remained followers. The objective of the research was to identify specifically what unique feature of the individual was associated with leadership. The success of the mental testing movement in the early part of the century encouraged researchers to employ the recently developed "personality tests" in their search for the leadership trait. Many studies were done in which leaders and followers were compared on various measures hypothesized to be related to leadership status or effectiveness.

Measures of dominance, social sensitivity, moodiness, masculinity, physical appearance, and many others were used. The typical research design involved the administration of one or more individual difference measures to members of an organization that had leaders and followers (for example, a military unit, industrial organization, or university student bodies). The scores of leaders and followers on the measures were compared for significant differences.

In 1948 Ralph Stogdill[2] reviewed over 120 such trait studies in an attempt to discern a reliable and coherent pattern. His conclusion was that no such pattern existed. The mass of inconsistent and contradictory results of the trait studies led Stogdill to conclude that traits alone do not identify leadership. He pointed out that leadership situations vary dramatically in the demands that they place upon the leader. For example, compare the desirable traits and abilities for a combat military officer with those for a senior scientist on a research team. Stogdill predicted that leadership theorizing would be inadequate until personal and situational characteristics were integrated.

Behaviors. The failure of the trait approach and the growing emphasis on behaviorism in psychology moved leadership researchers in the direction of the study of leadership behavior. A classic study of leadership styles was conducted by Kurt Lewin and his associates.[3] These researchers trained graduate research assistants in behaviors indicative of three leadership styles: autocratic, democratic, and laissez-faire. The autocratic style was characterized by the tight control of group activities and decisions made by the leader. The democratic style emphasized group participation and majority rule, while the laissez-faire leadership pattern involved very low levels of any kind of activity by the leader. Groups of preadolescent boys were exposed to each leadership style and the effects measured. Results indicated that the democratic style had somewhat more beneficial results on group process than the other styles. The importance of this study is not so much in its results but in its definition of leadership in terms of behavioral style. Also, the emphasis on autocratic, directive styles versus democratic and participative styles had a profound impact on later research and theory.

In the 1950s the research focus turned even more basic and behavioral. A number of independent researchers using rating scales,[4] interviews,[5] and observations[6] attempted to identify the specific, concrete behaviors in which leaders engaged. Here the emphasis was to move away from the focus on the internal states of leaders (that is, their values or personalities, as well as any preconceived leadership styles) to the more basic question of what it is that leaders actually do.

The most comprehensive study of leader behavior employed a rating scale labeled the Leader Behavior Description Questionnaire (LBDQ).[7] After extensive observation and rating of large numbers of military and industrial leaders, it was found that most of the variation in leader behavior could be described by two major clusters or factors of behavior. One factor that included items relating to interpersonal warmth, concern for the feelings of subordinates, and the use of participative two-way communication was labeled *consideration* behavior. A second factor whose items stressed directiveness, goal facilitation, and task-related feedback was labeled *initiation of structure*. A number of other research projects confirmed the existence of these two general behavioral configurations, although they might be labeled *employee oriented* versus *production oriented*[8] or *task* versus *socioemotional*.[9]

The identification of two reliable dimensions of leader behavior was a major step forward for the field of leadership. Optimism was high that research had finally cracked open the complexity of leadership affects. Unfortunately, attempts to relate the behavioral factors to group and organizational outcomes proved quite difficult. Although the leader's consideration behavior was generally associated with subordinate satisfaction, this was not always the case. Furthermore, the relationship between leader-structuring behavior and group productivity revealed very few consistent patterns.[10]

During both the trait and behavior eras, researchers were seeking to identify the "best" style of leadership. They had not yet recognized that no single style of leadership is universally best across all situations and environments. For this reason, leadership theorists were quite disappointed when the behavior patterns that they had identified were not consistently related to important organizational outcomes such as group productivity and follower satisfaction.

Current Theory

Contingency Approaches. The reliable prediction of the effects of leadership style on organizational outcomes awaited the development of the modern contingency theories. The first of these was developed by Fred Fiedler.[11,12] Fiedler's approach centered on a personality measure called the "esteem for the least-preferred co-worker," or LPC scale, which he found to be related to group performance. The person who fills out the scale is asked to rate an individual with whom the rater had difficulty accomplishing an assigned task. The most widely accepted interpretation of the meaning of this measure is that a person who gives a *very negative* rating to a poor co-worker is the kind of person for whom task success is very important. Such a person might be labeled "task motivated." A leader who gives a least-preferred co-worker a relatively positive rating would appear to be more concerned with the interpersonal than the task aspects of the situation, and is called "relationship motivated."[13,14,15]

A considerable body of research[16] indicates that the task-motivated leader is more attentive to task-related aspects of the leadership situation, more concerned with task success, and under most circumstances, more inclined to behave in a structuring, directive, and somewhat autocratic style. The relationship-motivated leader, on the other hand, is more attentive and responsive to interpersonal dynamics, more concerned with avoiding conflict and maintaining high morale, and more likely to behave in a participative and considerate leadership style.

After a very extensive series of studies covering some fifteen years, Fiedler determined that leadership style alone was not sufficient to explain leader effectiveness.[17] He set about to develop a model that integrated situational parameters into the leadership equation. He saw the most important dimension of the situation to be the degree of certainty, predictability, and control that the leader possessed. Fiedler developed a scale of *situational control* based on three features of the situation. These were: (1) leader-member relations, that is, the degree of trust and support that followers give the leader; (2) task structure, that is, the degree to which the goals and procedures for accomplishing the group's task are clearly specified; and (3) position power, that is, the degree to which the leader has formal authority to reward and punish followers. The research results indicate that neither style is effective in all situations. In *high control* situations, where predictability is assured by a clear task and a cooperative group, the task-motivated leader is calm and relaxed but maintains a strong emphasis on successful task accomplishment, which is very effective. However, under conditions of *moderate control,* caused by an ambiguous task or an uncooperative group, the task-motivated leader becomes anxious, over-concerned with a quick solution, and sometimes overly critical and punitive. The more open, considerate, and participative style of the relationship-motivated leader can address the problems of low morale or can create an environment conducive to successful problem solving and decision making, making the relationship-motivated leader more effective under these conditions. The crisis nature of the *low control* situation calls for a firm and directive leadership style, which is supplied by the task-motivated leader. Such a situation is too far gone to be quickly solved via a participative or considerate style, although such styles may be effective in the long run.

The Contingency Model, as Fiedler's theory is called, has been the subject of considerable controversy.[18,19,20] Arguments have raged over the meaning of the LPC scale, the appropriateness of situational variables, and the general predictive validity of the theory. However, a recent extensive review indicated that the predictions of the theory are strongly supported by data from both laboratory and organizational studies.[21]

Research on the Contingency Model has been quite extensive and broad. The person/situation perspective has provided insights into leadership phenomena that were obscured by "one best way" approaches. One example is in the area of leadership training. Reviews of research on leadership training had concluded that such training had few consistent effects on group performance or subordinate satisfaction.[22] However, Contingency Model research on the effects of leadership training has shown that training has its most powerful effects on the leader's situational control.[23,24] Training provides the leader with knowledge, procedures, and techniques that increase his or her sense of control over the group's task activities. Since the relationship of leadership style to group performance varies across different levels of situational control, the increased control provided by training can either improve or lower a particular leader's performance. For example, if a situation was of moderate control for untrained leaders, the relationship-motivated leaders would perform most effectively. Leadership training that clarified and structured the task would change the situation into one of high control. Under these conditions, the task-motivated leaders would perform better than the relationship-motivated leaders. With the task-motivated leaders getting better and the relationship-motivated leaders getting worse, the net effect of training would appear to be null. However, when both leadership style and situational control are analyzed, the effects of training become clear. These findings helped to explain why leadership training has not been found to be a consistent positive factor in leadership effectiveness. More importantly, the utility of the situational-control dimension as a mediator of leadership effectiveness gained further support, suggesting that aspects of certainty, predictability, and control could well be the most critical factors in the leadership equation.

A number of other contingency-oriented leadership theories have also addressed the relationship of leadership decision-making style to group performance and morale. The best known of these approaches is the Normative Decision Theory presented by Vroom and Yetton.[25] These authors have identified a range of decision-making styles.

These include *autocratic* styles, in which the leader makes a decision alone without consulting subordinates; *consultative* styles, in which the leader makes the decision, but after consulting with subordinates; and a *group* style, in which the leader allows subordinates to share in the decision-making responsibility. The dimension that underlies the range of decision styles is the degree to which the leader allows the followers to participate in the process of decision making. As the word *normative* in the name of the theory implies, the model specifies which of the styles is most likely to yield effective decisions under varying situations. Like Fiedler's Contingency Model, and other contingency theories, it is assumed that there is no one best way to make decisions, and that the most effective style will depend on the characteristics of the situation.

The situational characteristics that are considered most important in this model are (1) the expected support, acceptance, and commitment to the decision by subordinates; and (2) the amount of structured, clear, decision-relevant information available to the leader. Three general rules determine which styles or sets of styles will be most effective. The first rule is that, other things being equal, autocratic decisions are less time consuming and, therefore, more efficient. However, the second rule specifies that if the leader does not have sufficient structure and information to make a high-quality decision, he or she must consult with subordinates to gain the necessary information and enlist their aid and advice. The third general rule specifies that if the leader does not have sufficient support from subordinates to be assured that they will accept the decision, the leader must gain subordinate acceptance and commitment through participation in decision making.

Research support for the Normative Decision Theory is somewhat sparse.[26,27] Managers who are asked to recall and describe the characteristics of good and poor decisions that they have made in the past have been shown to usually describe situations and styles that would be predicted by the theory. Such recollective analyses are clearly open to distortion and bias. However, a comparison of Normative Decision Theory with the Contingency Model, described earlier, helps to strengthen and clarify both theories.

The two most important features of Fiedler's situational-control dimension are leader-member relations and task structure, which are extremely similar to Vroom and Yetton's characteristics of follower acceptance and structured information availability. Thus, the various situations presented in Vroom and Yetton's analysis would fit closely into Fiedler's situational-control dimension. Further, Fiedler's task-motivated and relationship-motivated leaders are typically described as using decision styles that fall toward the two poles of Vroom and Yetton's dimension of style. Task-motivated leaders are more likely to tend toward autocratic or minimally consultative styles while relationship-motivated leaders more often use group-oriented and participative styles.[28,29,30] The two theories make very similar predictions. Autocratic decisions are likely to be efficient and effective when the leader has a clear task and the support of followers. Relatively more participative decisions will fare better when either support or clarity are absent.

Despite the similarity of the two theories, they diverge sharply on the question of the ability of people to modify and change their decision styles. The normative model assumes that leaders can quickly and easily change their behavior to fit the demands of the situation, while Fiedler sees leadership style arising out of stable, enduring, well-learned personality attributes which are quite difficult to change. Some research by Bass and his associates[31] on decision styles is relevant to this question. Bass and others identified five decision styles that are quite close to those already discussed. These are called directive, negotiative, consultative, participative, and delegative. In a large survey conducted in several organizations, Bass asked managers to rate a number of features of the leadership situation that affect or are affected by these decision styles. The results indicate that the effects of decision style on group performance and subordinate satisfaction depend on the situation, although the pattern of results in these studies is not yet clear and consistent. However, of great interest was Bass's finding that the various leadership styles were not independent of one another. The directive and negotiative styles seemed to form one related set, while consultative, participative, and delegative formed another. This suggests that some leaders across many situations tend to use more directive, task-oriented, autocratic styles while another type of leader is more likely to employ the participative, open, relationship-oriented styles. The possibility, then, that leadership decision and behavioral style are stable and enduring aspects of the individual leaders seems reasonable.

Another prominent contingency theory of leadership is the Path-Goal Theory.[32,33] This is a more restricted theory that deals primarily with the effects of specific leader behavior on subordinate motivation and satisfaction, rather than the more general issues of decision making and performance. The Path-Goal research has studied the effects of the LBDQ categories of considerate and structuring behavior. The theory predicts that leader-structuring behavior will have the most positive effects on subordinate psychological states when the subordinate's task is unclear and/or difficult, that is, unstructured. The structure provided by the leader helps to clarify the *path* to the *goal* for the subordinates. On the other hand, consideration behavior will have its most positive effects when subordinates have a boring or distasteful job to perform. Subordinates then appreciate the "strokes" provided by their boss, more than they would if their job were intrinsically satisfying.

It is difficult to integrate Path-Goal Theory with the more general theories of leadership discussed earlier. It is not concerned with participative decision styles. In fact, it is not concerned with decisions at all, and might more properly be thought of as a theory of supervision under conditions where the supervisor has high clarity and follower support. However, even with this model, the dimension of clarity, predictability, and certainty of the situation is a variable of critical importance. Research support for the Path-Goal Theory is variable. The most clear and consistent results show up on studies of follower satisfaction rather than group performance. However, a most interesting recent finding by Griffin indicates that in addition to job characteristics, the needs, attitudes, and expectations of the follower have an important effect on the follower's reaction to leader behavior.[34] Griffin found that managers who scored high on a measure of the need for personal growth preferred not to receive structuring supervision, even under conditions of ambiguity. These subordinates would rather work the problem out for themselves. Conversely, subordinates low in growth need were not upset by a boring, routine job. The supervisor's considerate behavior had little effect since the subordinates were not really suffering. This result is especially important because the theoretical orientations of the three theories described so far tend to largely ignore the characteristics of subordinates.

Transactional Approaches. The theories discussed above might all be regarded as "leader-oriented" approaches. They tend to focus most of their attention on the leader's actions and attitudes. Although followers make their appearance in features related to leader-subordinate relationships, the leader is clearly the central figure and prime actor. However, some transactional or exchange theories of leadership addressing the relationship between leader and followers have had considerable impact.

One of the most important bodies of research in leadership are the studies of leader legitimation by Hollander.[35,36] Hollander developed the notion of "idiosyncrasy credit" to refer to the freedom that valued group members are given to deviate somewhat from group norms, that is, to act idiosyncratically. Idiosyncrasy credits are earned through the demonstration of competence and shared values, which serve to make the group member more indispensable to the group. The individual's achieved value, which is the same as status, allows him or her to introduce new ideas and new ways of doing things into the group or society, thus creating adaptability and change. Hollander's work shows us that the legitimation of leadership is a process of social exchange. Members of groups exchange their competence and loyalty for group-mediated rewards which range from physical rewards such as income or protection to the less tangible rewards of honor, status, and influence.

The work of George Graen and his associates has shown that the nature of exchange processes between leaders and subordinates can have far-reaching effects on group performance and morale.[37,38,39] Research with the Vertical Dyad Linkage Model has shown that a leader or manager develops a specific and unique exchange with each of his or her subordinates. These exchanges might range from a true partnership in which the subordinate is given considerable freedom and autonomy in defining and developing a work-related role to exchanges in which the subordinate is restrained, controlled, and little more than a "hired hand." As might be expected, the more positive exchanges are associated with higher subordinate satisfaction, reduced turnover, and greater identification with the organization.[40]

On the one hand, these findings are not surprising. Good interpersonal relationships in dyads make people feel better about each other, themselves, and their work. The importance of this research is that it redirects our attention to the relationship between leader, follower, and situation, and encourages a broader and more dynamic approach to the study of the leadership phenomenon. However, the Vertical Dyad Linkage Model does not elucidate the causes of good and poor exchanges.

Over the years, a number of studies have examined follower effects on the leadership process. Although not organized into a comprehensive theory, the research makes some interesting and important points. For example, a number of studies[41,42,43] have shown that leader activity, specifically the leader's willingness to engage in attempts to move the group toward its goals, is dramatically affected by followers' responses to the influence attempts. Leaders lead more with follower acceptance.

Individual differences in follower attitude or personality traits have long been associated with leadership effects. Early studies by Haythorn and others[44] and Sanford[45] showed that differences in authoritarian versus egalitarian attitudes of followers determined reactions to a leader's style. A recent study by Weed and others[46] updates the same effect. They found that followers who are high in dogmatism respond better to leaders who engage in high levels of structuring behavior. Low-dogmatism followers perform better with considerate leader behavior.

A number of other characteristics, including need for achievement,[47] work values,[48,49] and locus of control[50,51] have been shown to impact on leader behavior and follower attitudes. At this point, the literature on follower characteristics is not well integrated. However, the results occur frequently enough to suggest that leadership theorizing will benefit from attention to leader *and* follower characteristics and to the resultant relationship.

Cognitive Approaches. Perception and cognition have played a major role in leadership research. Many dependent measures such as leader-behavior ratings, satisfaction, and role ambiguity, are judgmental or memory processes. Social psychology has been strongly influenced by attribution theory,[52,53,54] which is concerned with the cognitive processes which underlie interpersonal judgments. Recently, leadership theorists have begun to apply attribution-theory-based propositions to judgments involved in the process of leadership.

One of the key features of interpersonal judgments is the strong tendency for an observer to develop causal explanations for another person's behavior. Explanations of a person's behavior often center on the question of whether the behavior was determined by factors internal to the actor, such as ability or motivation, or factors external to the actor, such as situational forces, role demands, or luck. Reliable findings indicate that observers have a strong bias to attribute an actor's behavior to internal causes.[55] This tendency may result from the observer's desire for a sense of certainty and predictability about the actor's future behavior. Further, if the observer might be considered responsible for the actor's behavior, internal attributions to the actor remove that responsibility. For example, a teacher might be inclined to attribute a student's poor academic performance to a lack of ability, thereby relieving the teacher of responsibility for that performance.

Recent work by Green and Mitchell has adapted some of the propositions of attribution theory to the processes that leaders use to make judgments about subordinate performance.[56] They have shown that these processes are affected by factors that are not directly related to the subordinate's actual behavior. Studies indicate that supervisors make more negative and more internal attributions when the negative outcomes of a subordinate's behavior are more severe.[57,58] This happens even when the behavior in the two situations is identical. For example, nursing supervisors asked to judge a hypothetical subordinate's performance made more negative judgments of a nurse who left a railing down on a patient's bed if the patient fell out of bed than if the patient did not. These judgments have important implications for later actions the supervisor might take with respect to promotion, termination, or salary. The role-making processes which are discussed in the Vertical Dyad Linkage Model might benefit from an analysis of the ways in which supervisory judgments affect leader-follower exchanges.

Calder's attribution theory of leadership argues that leadership processes and effects exist primarily as perceptual processes in the minds of followers and observers.[59] In fact, most of the measuring instruments used in leadership research ask the respondent for perceptions of the leadership process. These perceptions, judgments, and attributions are distorted by the biases that the perceiver brings to the situation. Each individual holds an implicit personal theory of leadership that serves as a cognitive filter to determine what the observer will notice, remember, and report about the leadership process.

A number of recent studies indicate that such implicit theories are especially problematic in ratings of leader behavior.[60,61,62] Raters who are led to believe that a group has performed well or poorly will modify their ratings of leader behavior to conform to the performance feedback. In other words, if I think that good leaders are very considerate of their followers, I am more likely to notice and report the consideration behavior of leaders whom I believe have performed well.

Ayman and Chemers have found that the structure of leader-behavior ratings depends more on the culture of the raters than on the behavior of the leader.[63] These researchers factor analyzed leader-behavior ratings made by Iranian subjects. They found that the structure of the behavior ratings was very different from the structure normally found in studies in the United States and Europe. In most leadership studies done in Western Europe and the United States, analyses of leader-behavior ratings yield two distinct and independent behavior clusters. These are the familiar structuring, task-directed behaviors and the considerate, relationship-directed behaviors. However, the Ayman and Chemers analysis of ratings made by Iranian followers resulted in a single category of behavior that included both structuring and considerate items. This global factor depicting a directive but warm supervisor was labeled "benevolent paternalism." Furthermore, the factor was found to be strongly related to group performance as assessed by superiors and to satisfaction with supervision expressed by subordinates. Interestingly, this unique pattern of behavior ratings was found when the leaders being rated were Iranian or American. This led Ayman and Chemers to conclude that leader-behavior ratings are more a function of the implicit theories which guide the "eye of the beholder" than they are of what the leader actually does.

On the one hand, these distortions in the observation of leadership effects are very problematic. This is especially true for research with certain theories (for example, Path-Goal Theory, the Normative Decision Theory, and the Vertical Dyad Linkage Model) because in many tests of these theories subjects are asked to rate several aspects of the leadership situation, for example, their leader's behavior and their own satisfaction. The relationships observed among these measures may reflect the implicit theories held by the subjects rather than accurate reflections of the constructs studied. However, it is also true that perception, judgments, and expectations form the core of interpersonal relationships. The desire and expectations of a subordinate for some type of leader behavior (for example, consideration) may elicit or compel that behavior. This represents an interesting and necessary area for future research.

Cross-Cultural Approaches. Berry has argued that American psychology is "culture bound" and "culture blind."[64] The generalizability of our findings are bound by the fact that most of our research is done with European or American samples. Furthermore, because we rarely compare cultures, we are blind to the potential effects of cultural differences. Chemers points out that this problem becomes more salient when we attempt to export our theories and training programs to cultures which are different from those in which the theories were developed.[65] Cross-cultural research can benefit leadership theory in two ways. Comparative studies can show us the generalizability of Euro-American theories, helping us to recognize the inherent limitations in their transfer to other cultures. More importantly, comparative research gives us a much broader range of variables that may highlight relationships previously ignored. For example, since most studies done in the developed countries are done on subjects who are relatively well educated and technologically sophisticated, educational level becomes a background variable to which we pay little attention. However, in a broader context, the socialization or educational background of workers may be an important determinant of work-related attitudes and responses.

Leadership researchers have not totally ignored culture, but the results of the research leave much to be desired. Reviews by Roberts,[66] Nath,[67] Barrett and Bass,[68] and Tannenbaum[69] all concluded that the cross-cultural research on leadership has been characterized by weak methodologies and by a paucity of theory, both of which make the interpretation of the scattered findings very difficult. However, a few cross-cultural models do exist. Negandhi presented a model of cultural effects on organizational structure in which cultural or national differences act indirectly on management practices by affecting the organizational environment.[70] He argues that organizational structure and managerial policy are more important than cultural factors in determining behavior. This view contrasts with earlier views, which saw culture as directly determining managerial values, attitudes, and behavior.[71]

The actual role of culture probably lies somewhere between these two views. Neither culture nor organizational structure are static forces. Rather, they interact in dynamic process influencing one another, and both contribute to managerial attitudes and behavior. For example, studies that have compared the attitudes or behaviors of managers have found national differences somewhat moderated by organizational policy.[72] Unfortunately, after we have dealt with the broad question of whether culture is important, we are still left with few theories that make any specific predictions about the role of culture in shaping leadership process.

A potentially useful theoretical framework relating values to managerial and organizational process has been offered by Hofstede.[73,74,75] Comparing responses to a value survey of managers from forty countries, Hofstede found that the pattern of results could be described by four factors. These are: (1) power distance, that is, the relative importance of status; (2) tolerance for uncertainty; (3) individualism versus collectivism; and (4) masculinity. Hofstede argues that a culture's standing on these four value dimensions determines the kind of organizational structure and managerial policies that will be most likely to develop.[76] For example, he argues that cultures which have a low tolerance for uncertainty combined with a low emphasis on status are likely to develop highly bureaucratic organizational structures to reduce ambiguity. Cultures which are also low in tolerance for uncertainty but high in power distance will develop autocratic organizational structures in which the high-status persons resolve ambiguity by fiat.

The validity of much of the cross-cultural research has been questioned by Ayman and Chemers.[77] In a study of the leadership behavior of Iranian managers, these researchers found that traditional measures of leadership behavior and subordinate satisfaction resulted in very different factor structures in their Iranian sample than did those measures when used with European or American samples. Ayman and Chemers[78] and Chemers[79] argue that the imposition of Euro-American theories, measures, and research designs on other cultures may lead to very inaccurate conclusions.

Summary and Conclusions

We can now look back on over seventy years of scientific research on leadership in small groups. For much of that time, the literature has been characterized by false starts, dead ends, and bitter controversies. Even today, the student of leadership is consistently confronted with acrimonious debates among theorists, giving the field an appearance of chaotic disarray. In fact, much of the controversy resembles a "tempest in a teapot." Various theories say much the same thing in slightly different ways, and advocates engage in quibbling over relatively minor differences. The current crop of theories has more that unites than separates them. The last twenty years of research have reinforced and clarified certain common threads, and the study of leadership stands poised for a thrust into a new era of growth. Let us examine these commonalities and the directions toward which they point.

At the broadest level, most contemporary theories adopt a contingency perspective. One would be hard put to find an empirical theory of leadership which holds that one style of leadership is appropriate for all situations. At a somewhat deeper level, the similarities continue. The most frequent dimensions on which leader behavior, style, or decision processes are differentiated are (1) the relative focus of the leader on goal-directed task functions versus morale-oriented interpersonal functions, and (2) the relative use of autocratic, directive styles versus democratic, participative styles. These related dichotomies have been part and parcel of the leadership equation since the first behavioral studies of the late 1940s and early 1950s.

Turning to the situational parameters embodied in most current theories, another area of commonality is revealed. Almost all of the contemporary approaches are concerned with the degree of predictability, certainty, and control which the environment affords to the leader. At an even more specific level most approaches integrate interpersonal and task features into the specification of the situation. Indeed, in retrospect, it is hard to imagine how it could be otherwise. Leadership involves a job to do and people to do it with. The likelihood of successful goal accomplishment must, then, depend upon the degree to which the support of the people and the control of the task are facilitative.

Finally, a careful examination of these leadership theories results in a common set of predictions as well. Autocratic decisions and directive styles in which the leader tells followers what to do are most likely to work when the leader knows exactly what to tell the subordinates (that is, a structured task) and when the subordinates are inclined to do what they are told (that is, good follower acceptance and loyalty). When the leader is not so sure what to do or not so sure that followers will go along, considerate and participative styles have the double benefit of encouraging follower acceptance and increasing follower input into the problem-solving process.

The presence of common themes in the research literature does not mean that we have answered all the questions and solved all the problems in leadership. The contingency approaches do provide us with a stable platform from which to step into the next set of issues. However, these issues are quite complex and will require a more integrated, multifaceted, and systemic view of leadership process.

A major gap in most current leadership theories is the lack of attention to the leaders and followers as people. We focus on behavior or decision style with very little understanding of the values, needs, and motives that give rise to the observed behaviors. It is assumed that any leader can engage in any behavior, and that leaders and followers can easily identify the correct or ideal set of behaviors in a situation. When the possibility arises, as it has recently, that our observation of behavior may be flawed, we are left with nowhere to turn.

The differences in the factor structure of leader behavior across cultures highlights the role of personal values in the social process of leadership. In the research done in the Western industrialized nations, for example, leader behaviors that are directive and task oriented are usually differentiated from those that are more considerate and interpersonally oriented. The two sets of behaviors load on separate and distinct factors. However, Ayman and Chemers's research in developing nations such as Iran and Mexico reveals a different pattern.[80] The leaders who have the highest group performance and the most satisfied subordinates are those who combine directive task styles with interpersonal warmth and consideration. The factor structure of leader-behavior ratings in these cultures indicates that both structuring and considerate behavior correlate within a single global cluster.

In order to understand why leader-behavior factors differ across cultures, it is necessary to have some theory about the manner in which culture affects behavior. The culture, through the processes of socialization, helps to shape the needs, values, and personality of leaders and followers. The personality of the leader will affect the kinds of behaviors most often used. Further, cultural norms create expectations and judgments about the appropriate behavior of leaders and their group members. The cultural expectations of the society's members then influence the patterns of leadership exhibited.

Thus, one interpretation of the differences in leader-behavior patterns across cultures relates to the very strong emphasis on individualism in the Western democracies and on collective, group-oriented values in much of the rest of the world. When individual responsibility and individual autonomy are stressed, considerate supervisory behavior is that which reinforces the autonomy of subordinates; in other words, egalitarian, participative leadership. Thus, considerate behavior is generally likely to be somewhat incompatible with high levels of directive and structuring behavior. However, in more collective and authoritarian cultures, in which group members subordinate individuals' goals to group needs, a leader can maintain control over subordinates *and* satisfy them by being directive and structuring in a warm, supportive, "fatherly" manner. Cultural values are reinforced by social norms that prescribe elaborate codes of politeness and make the exercise of a "benevolent paternalism" the most acceptable mode of behavior.

The role of culture in leadership is much broader and more complex than the abbreviated explanation given here. But this analysis does turn our attention to the role of the leader's and the follower's personalities as an influence on behavior and the perception of behavior. The research on follower characteristics makes it very plain that the way in which one individual reacts to the behavior of another is dependent upon individual differences in styles and needs as well as variations in situational characteristics.

The transactional and exchange theories have shown that the relationship between leaders and followers is a dynamic one extending longitudinally in time. Roles are defined, negotiated, and redefined. People move toward or away from one another with effects on motivation, satisfaction, and individual and group performance.

Observations and judgments are made that facilitate and enhance positive or negative relationships. Admittedly, such dynamic relationships are difficult to study. It is also true, however, that leadership theory will make major strides forward when we can begin to tie together the ways in which personal characteristics influence judgments which, in turn, influence role perception and performance, which, subsequently, determine group behavior and effectiveness.

These simplistic trait approaches were superseded by the behavioral studies that were replaced by the contingency theories. The next major era of leadership research will begin with the recognition that group and organizational performance are dependent upon the interplay of social systems. A social-systems approach will recognize that the leadership process is a complex, multifaceted network of forces. Personal characteristics of leaders and followers interact in the perception of and reaction to task demands and to each other. The small group is further embedded in an organizational and societal context that influences personal characteristics, social roles, and situational contingencies. If general leadership theory can begin to span the gaps between the various levels of analysis (that is, individual, group, organization, society), the resultant theories will provide us with a much stronger base, not only for understanding leadership but also for improving its quality.

Notes

1. Ivan D. Steiner, *Group Process and Productivity* (New York: Academic Press, 1972).
2. Ralph M. Stogdill, "Personal Factors Associated with Leadership: A Survey of the Literature," *Journal of Psychology* 25 (1948), 35–71.
3. Kurt Lewin, Ronald Lippitt, and Ralph K. White, "Patterns of Aggressive Behavior in Experimentally Created Social Climates," *Journal of Social Psychology* 10 (1939), 271–299.
4. Ralph M. Stogdill, Carroll L. Shartle, Willis L. Scott, Alvin E. Coons, and William E. Jaynes, *A Predictive Study of Administrative Work Patterns* (Columbus: Ohio State University, Bureau of Business Research, 1956).
5. Robert L. Kahn and Daniel Katz, "Leadership Practices in Relation to Productivity and Morale," in Dorwin Cartwright and Alvin Zander (eds.), *Group Dynamics* (New York: Harper & Row, 1953).
6. Robert F. Bales and Paul E. Slater, "Role Differentiation in Small Decision Making Groups," in Talcott Parsons and Robert F. Bales (eds.), *Family, Localization, and Interaction Processes* (New York: Free Press, 1945).
7. Ralph M. Stogdill and Alvin E. Coons, (eds.), *Leader Behavior: Its Description and Measurement* (Columbus: Ohio State University, Bureau of Business Research, 1957).
8. Kahn and Katz, *Group Dynamics*.
9. Bales and Slater, *Family, Localization, and Interaction Processes*.
10. Abraham Korman, "Consideration, Initiating Structure, and Organizational Criteria—A Review," *Personnel Psychology* 19 (1966), 349–362.
11. Fred E. Fiedler, "A Contingency Model of Leadership Effectiveness," in Leonard Berkowitz (ed.), *Advances in Experimental Social Psychology* vol. 1 (New York: Academic Press, 1964).
12. ———, *A Theory of Leadership Effectiveness* (New York: McGraw-Hill, 1967).
13. ———, "The Contingency Model and the Dynamics of the Leadership Process," in Leonard Berkowitz (ed.), *Advances in Experimental Social Psychology*.
14. Fred E. Fiedler and Martin M. Chemers, *Leadership and Effective Management* (New York: Scott, Foresman, 1974).
15. Robert W. Rice, "Construct Validity of the Least Preferred Co-worker Score," *Psychological Bulletin* 85 (1978), 1199–1237.
16. Ibid.
17. Fiedler, *A Theory of Leadership Effectiveness*.

18. Ahmed S. Ashour, "Further Discussion of Fiedler's Contingency Model of Leadership Effectiveness: An Evaluation," *Organizational Behavior and Human Performance* 9 (1973), 339–55.

19. George Graen, Kenneth M. Alveres, James B. Orris, and John A. Martella, "Contingency Model of Leadership Effectiveness: Antecedent and Evidential Results," *Psychological Bulletin* 74 (1970), 285–296.

20. Terrence R. Mitchell, Anthony Biglan, Gerald R. Oncken, and Fred E. Fiedler, "The Contingency Model: Criticism and Suggestions," *Academy of Management Journal* 13 (1970), 253–267.

21. Michael J. Strube and Joseph E. Garcia, "A Meta-analytical Investigation of Fiedler's Contingency Model of Leadership Effectiveness," *Psychological Bulletin* 90 (1981), 307–321.

22. Robert J. House, "T-Group Education and Leadership Effectiveness: A Review of the Empirical Literature and a Critical Evaluation," *Personnel Psychology* 20 (1967), 1–32.

23. Martin M. Chemers, Robert W. Rice, Eric Sundstrom, and William M. Butler, "Leader LPC, Training and Effectiveness: An Experimental Examination," *Journal of Personality and Social Psychology* 31 (1975), 401–409.

24. Fred E. Fiedler, "The Effects of Leadership Training and Experience: A Contingency Model Interpretation," *Administrative Science Quarterly* 17 (1972), 453–470.

25. Victor H. Vroom and Paul W. Yetton, *Leadership and Decision-Making* (Pittsburgh: University of Pittsburgh Press, 1973).

26. Arthur G. Jago and Victor H. Vroom, "An Evaluation of Two Alternatives to the Vroom/Yetton Normative Model," *Academy of Management Journal* 23 (1980), 347–355.

27. Victor H. Vroom and Arthur G. Jago, "On the Validity of the Vroom-Yetton Model," *Journal of Applied Psychology* 63 (1978), 151–162.

28. Martin M. Chemers, Barbara K. Goza, and Sheldon I. Plumer, "Leadership Style and Communication Process: An Experiment Using the Psychological Isotope Technique," *Resources in Education* (September 1979).

29. Martin M. Chemers and George J. Skrzypek, "An Experimental Test of the Contingency Model of Leadership Effectiveness," *Journal of Personality and Social Psychology* 24 (1972), 172–177.

30. Rice, "Construct Validity of the Least Preferred Co-worker Score."

31. Bernard M. Bass, Enzo R. Valenzi, Dana L. Farrow, and Robert J. Solomon, "Management Styles Associated With Organizational, Task, Personal, and Interpersonal Contingencies," *Journal of Applied Psychology* 60 (1975), 720–729.

32. Robert J. House, "A Path-Goal Theory of Leadership," *Administrative Science Quarterly* 16 (1971), 321–338.

33. Robert J. House and Gary Dessler, "The Path-Goal Theory of Leadership: Some Post Hoc and A Priori Tests," in James G. Junt and Lars L. Larsen (eds.), *Contingency Approaches to Leadership* (Carbondale, IL: Southern Illinois University Press, 1974).

34. Ricky N. Griffin, "Relationships Among Individual, Task Design, and Leader Behavior Variables," *Academy of Management Journal* 23, (1980), 665–683.

35. Edwin P. Hollander, "Conformity, Status, and Idiosyncrasy Credit," *Psychological Review* 65, 117–127.

36. Edwin P. Hollander and James W. Julian, "Studies in Leader Legitimacy, Influence, and Innovation," in Leonard Berkowitz (ed.), *Advances in Experimental Social Psychology* vol. 5 (New York: Academic Press, 1970).

37. Fred Dansereau, Jr., George Graen, and William J. Haga, "Vertical Dyad Linkage Approach to Leadership Within Formal Organizations: A Longitudinal Investigation of the Role Making Process," *Organizational Behavior and Human Performance* 13 (1975), 46–78.

38. George Graen and James F. Cashman, "A Role-Making Model of Leadership in Formal Organizations: A Developmental Approach," in J. G. Hunt and L. L. Larsen (eds.), *Leadership Frontiers* (Kent, Ohio: Kent State University Press, 1975).

39. George Graen, James F. Cashman, Steven Ginsburgh, and William Schiemann, "Effects of Linking-Pin Quality of Work Life of Lower Participants," *Administrative Science Quarterly* 22 (1977), 491–504.

40. George Graen and Steven Ginsburgh, "Job Resignation as a Function of Role Orientation and Leader Acceptance: A Longitudinal Investigation of Organizational Assimilation," *Organizational Behavior and Human Performance* 19 (1977), 1–17.

41. Alex Bavelas, Albert H. Hastorf, Alan E. Gross, and W. Richard Kite, "Experiments on the Alteration of Group Structure," *Journal of Experimental Social Psychology* 1 (1965), 55–70.

42. Lawrence Beckhouse, Judith Tanur, John Weiler, and Eugene Weinstein, "And Some Men Have Leadership Thrust Upon Them," *Journal of Personality and Social Psychology* 31 (1975), 557–566.

43. Leopold W. Gruenfeld, David E. Rance, and Peter Weissenbert, "The Behavior of Task-Oriented (Low LPC) and Socially-Oriented (High LPC) Leaders Under Several Conditions of Social Support," *Journal of Social Psychology* 79 (1969), 99–107.

44. William Haythorn, Arthur Couch, Don Haefner, Peter Langham, and Launor F. Carter, "The Effects of Varying Combinations of Authoritarian and Egalitarian Leader and Follower," *Journal of Abnormal and Social Psychology* 53 (1956), 210–219.

45. Frederick Sanford, "Research on Military Leadership," in John Flanagan (ed.), *Psychology in the World Emergency* (Pittsburgh: University of Pittsburgh Press, 1952).

46. Stanley E. Weed, Terrence R. Mitchell, and William Moffitt, "Leadership Style, Subordinate Personality, and Task Type as Predictors of Performance and Satisfaction With Supervision," *Journal of Applied Psychology* 61 (1976), 58–66.

47. Richard M. Steers, "Task-goal Attributes, N Achievement, and Supervisory Performance," *Organizational Behavior and Human Performance* 13 (1975), 392–403.

48. Milton R. Blood, "Work Values and Job Satisfaction," *Journal of Applied Psychology* 53 (1969), 456–459.

49. Ramon J. Aldage and Arthur P. Brief, "Some Correlates of Work Values," *Journal of Applied Psychology* 60 (1975), 757–760.

50. Thomas L. Ruble, "Effects of One's Locus of Control and the Opportunity to Participate in Planning," *Organizational Behavior and Human Performance* 16 (1976), 63–73.

51. Douglas E. Durand and Walter R. Nord, "Perceived Leader Behavior as a Function of Personality Characteristics of Supervisors and Subordinates," *Academy of Management Journal* 19 (1976), 427–431.

52. Fritz Heider, *The Psychology of Interpersonal Relations* (New York: John Wiley, 1958).

53. Edward E. Jones and Keith E. Davis, "From Acts to Dispositions," in Leonard Berkowitz (ed.), *Advances in Experimental Social Psychology* vol. 2. (New York: Academic Press, 1965).

54. Harold H. Kelley, "The Processes of Causal Attribution," *American Psychologists,* 28 (1973), 107–128.

55. Jones and Davies, "From Acts to Dispositions."

56. Stephen G. Green and Terrence R. Mitchell, "Attributional Processes of Leaders in Leader-Member Interactions," *Organizational Behavior and Human Performance* 23 (1979), 429–458.

57. Terrence R. Mitchell and Laura S. Kalb, "Effects of Outcome Knowledge and Outcome Valence in Supervisors' Evaluations," *Journal of Applied Psychology* 66 (1981), 604–612.

58. Terrence R. Mitchell and Robert E. Wood, "Supervisors' Responses to Subordinate Poor Performance: A Test of an Attributional Model," *Organizational Behavior and Human Performance* 25 (1980), 123–138.

59. Billy J. Calder, "An Attribution Theory of Leadership," in Barry M. Staw and Gerald R. Slancik (eds.), *New Directions in Organizational Behavior* (Chicago: St. Clair, 1977).

60. Dov Eden and Uri Leviatan, "Implicit Leadership Theory as a Determinant of the Factor Structure Underlying Supervisory Behavior Scales," *Journal of Applied Psychology* 60 (1975), 736–741.

61. Robert G. Lord, John F. Binning, Michael C. Rush, and Jay C. Thomas, "The Effect of Performance Cues and Leader Behavior in Questionnaire Rating of Leadership Behavior," *Organizational Behavior and Human Performance* 21 (1978), 27–39.

62. H. Kirk Downey, Thomas I. Chacko, and James C. McElroy "Attribution of the 'Causes' of Performance: A Constructive, Quasi-Longitudinal Replication of the Staw (1975) Study" *Organizational Behavior and Human Performance* 24 (1979), 287–289.

63. Roya Ayman and Martin M. Chemers, "The Relationship of Leader Behavior of Managerial Effectiveness and Satisfaction in Iran," *Journal of Applied Psychology* 68 (1983), 338–341.

64. John W. Berry "On Cross-Cultural Comparability" *International Journal of Psychology* 4 (1969), 119–128 .

65. Martin M. Chemers, "Leadership and Social Organization in Cross-Cultural Psychology" paper presented to the Meetings of the American Psychological Association, Los Angeles, 1981.

66. Karlene H. Roberts, "On Looking at an Elephant: An Evaluation of Cross-Cultural Research Related to Organizations," *Psychological Bulletin* 74 (1970), 327–350.

67. Robert A. Nath, "A Methodological Review of Cross-Cultural Management Research," in Jean Boddewyn (ed.), *Comparative Management and Marketing* (Glenview, IL.: Scott, Foresman, 1969).

68. Gerald V. Barrett and Bernard M. Bass, "Cross-Cultural Issues in Industrial and Organizational Psychology," in M. D. Dunnette (ed.), *Handbook of Industrial and Organizational Psychology* (Chicago: Rand McNally, 1975).

69. Arnold S. Tannenbaum, "Organizational Psychology," in Harry C. Triandis and Richard W. Brislin (eds.), *Handbook of Cross-Cultural Psychology, Social Psychology* vol. 5 (Boston: Allyn & Bacon, 1980).

70. Anant R. Negandhi, "Comparative Management and Organizational Theory: A Marriage Needed," *Academy of Management Journal* 18 (1975), 334–344.

71. Richard N. Farmer and Barry M. Richman, *Comparative Management and Economic Progress* (Homewood, IL.: Richard D. Irwin, 1965).

72. Tannenbaum, "Organizational Psychology."

73. Geert Hofstede, "Nationality and Espoused Values of Managers," *Journal of Applied Psychology* 61 (1976), 148–155.

74. ———, "Motivation, Leadership, and Organization: Do American Theories Apply Abroad?" *Organizational Dynamics* (Summer 1980).

75. ———, *Culture's Consequences: International Differences in Work-Related Values* (London: Sage, 1981).

76. Ibid.

77. Ayman and Chemers, "The Relationship of Leader Behavior to Managerial Effectiveness and Satisfaction in Iran."

78. Ibid.

79. Chemers, "Leadership and Social Organization in Cross-Cultural Psychology."

80. Ayman and Chemers, "The Relationship of Leader Behavior to Managerial Effectiveness and Satisfaction in Iran."

The Leader-Trainer-Facilitator

John (Sam) Keltner

The facilitation process is inherent in the role of trainer. Facilitation is also one form or characteristic of the training process. Group leaders who are not primarily involved in training (such as a task group leader) are still heavily involved in facilitative behaviors that are aimed at helping their group meet its needs and accomplish its goals. Although the role of facilitator is, in part, a function of the personality of the facilitator, there are a number of group constants that exist in every situation. Peter Smith (1980, 75) observed that "effective trainer behavior is seen as a pattern of responses to a group culture which trainers themselves cannot unilaterally create."

Who Facilitates?

Facilitators, no matter what the context, are group *process trainers*. Theirs is a special and unique function that requires that they understand group processes and that they be able to help a group diagnose and solve process problems. Regardless of a group's nature, then, facilitators assume a training posture. Peter Smith (1980, 74) notes also that "trainers differ from others in the group in that they are influential and trusted."

The facilitator-trainer, described by Blumberg and Golembiewski (1976, 78–86) and others, engages in several sets of activities, some more useful and important than others, as follows:

> creates situations conducive to learning
> establishes a model of behavior
> provides new values in process
> facilitates the flow of information
> participates as an expert
> protects participants from unnecessary stress and attack
> confronts the group regarding its processes.

All of these functions are behaviors that can operate in a task group, a training group, a sensitivity group, or a T-Group.

Facilitative behavior emerges from at least three levels.

The Group Member as Facilitator

In many groups a member, particularly sensitive to and aware of group processes, may intervene in content discussion to comment on process matters. This can be a very effective role when such people are perceptive, skilled, and trusted by the group. There

From John Keltner, *Management Communication Quarterly,* Vol. 3 (1), August 1989, pp. 8–32, copyright © 1989. Reprinted by permission of Sage Publications, Inc.

is, however, the danger that because they are also involved in the content of the discussion, a member/facilitator's interventions will be perceived as controlling discussion content and influencing the nature of the decision. On the other hand, if all group members are sensitive to the processes and are able to monitor and accommodate to them, the group may be a very effective team.

The Group "Leader" as Facilitator

It is often assumed that a group leader is responsible for seeing that the group adopts and maintains an adequate process for carrying out its task. The leader's role, however, can be quite unclear. Within a given group it is likely that several different leadership functions will be performed by different people. There are informal leaders who influence group process and content direction, and there are elected or assigned leaders who have titular influence and power. Informal leaders, as members, often run into the problems inherent in balancing both roles. Their power in managing group behavior, while significant, is transient. Anderson (1985, 271) points out that "The most effective leaders are those who help the group develop to the point at which members themselves are the primary source of help."

Formal leaders may be able to facilitate the group process without unduly manipulating the content. However, many formal group leaders (elected, appointed, or assumed), such as chairholders, have their position because they expect, and are expected, to have a more persistent influence on content and decision making than other group members. They can, then, easily influence the process to bring content decisions in favor of their personal goals rather than the goals of the group.

The Facilitator Specialist

The third and least understood facilitative role is that of the facilitator specialist. The specialist does not deal with group content, but functions either as a nongroup member or as a member with a very special and restricted role. Some task groups assign members to this capacity on a rotating basis. This often creates problems because the member has difficulty separating content roles from process roles. Other groups bring in an outside specialist to serve as the facilitator.

Controversy exists over who should serve as a facilitator. One view holds that the facilitator specialist is a trainer and therefore operates within an implied contract with group members. In this view, the facilitator-trainer is seen as "an effective member." That is, he (or she) "is concerned about his own learning in the group, his own gratification, and his standing with other members" (Kingsbury 1972, 110).

Another view sees the facilitator specialist as a nongroup member, aloof from internal content and personal group struggles. The facilitator's interventions are, in this case, separate from the flow of group discussion themes. With this concept the facilitator is perceived as a kind of benign, superior being who watches the group from outside the circle but, from time to time, fires in a thunderbolt of process information that seems to be unrelated to what is being discussed. Tannenbaum found that a facilitator of this type is viewed as a target for hostility; as a perceived source of advice, support, and reassurance; as being in a role heavy with therapeutic connotations; and as an object of transference or displacement of feelings (Tannenbaum, Weschler & Massarik 1977, 135).

The true process facilitator is more than an effective member, but not an aloof figurehead or arbiter of power. The facilitative function makes the perspective of regular membership impossible. The facilitator can no longer be *just* a member. There is a significant power focus on the role. For example, the acknowledged facilitator, psychologically, has more than one "vote" in any group decision. He or she performs a function that transcends the usual membership role and thus is in a powerful position to influence group decisions.

A number of issues are related to this controversy. Culbert points to the facilitator (trainer) as a model with special functions to perform: keeping participants aware of what is happening, developing group norms consistent with his or her learning theory, providing perspective on the participants' information, keeping group tension at an optimum level, lending vitality to the group, and acting as referee. These functions illustrate the facilitator's significantly different role from that of a regular member (Culbert 1972, 116ff.). All of these functions, however, can be assumed by the group members at one time or another.

Culbert also points out that facilitators should not expect or require participants to accept their own assumptions about learning. Rather, group members should be presented with the facilitator's guiding rationale. Further, Culbert argues, the facilitator may influence the climate of the group for learning or task purposes so long as there is sufficient latitude for the group to use variations suited to itself. In addition, the facilitator must not interfere with the democratic processes necessary for the participants to learn. At the same time the facilitator is required to give some direction through explicit objectives and reasons for action. Culbert points out that the authentic self of the facilitator is an important instrument in instructing others. There are risks that the facilitator must take at every stage of the process. Alternative choices are always present for the skilled facilitator. The more personally involved the facilitator becomes in the emotions of the situation, the more serious the dilemma of intervention (Culbert 1972, 116–146).

The group situation is no place for a facilitator to deal with his or her own problems, particularly those not based on the relationships within the particular group. The facilitator need not come off as a cold and unfeeling person by refusing to deal with personal problems in a group, but the effective facilitator cannot become as fully involved as other members without decreasing the impact and effectiveness of the process interventions. Many groups try to engage the facilitator in personal problems as a ploy to manipulate the facilitator from an inherent position of power to a less powerful member "of the crowd." As cohesion develops in a group its desire to include surrounding persons in its orbit becomes very strong. The effective facilitator resists this but maintains a friendly and accepting relationship with the group.

Power and the Facilitator

Yaro Starak (1988) writes:

The bigger our myth of omnipotence, the more we lose our humanity. A false guru is one who has lost his or her humanity—who has no friends, only followers. In other words, the antidote to the superhelper lies in peers, friends, and intimate contacts and in a place where being human, having close relationships, and having secrets serve us as a reminder that a giant is only another human being. (108)

In group process work a great deal of power resides in the facilitator's role. As indicated here, the professional facilitator specialist is not a member of the group as are the other participants. His or her role is functionally and objectively different from the group member or trainee. The role and function of the facilitator are unique and should not be performed casually. It has its most significant and apparent influence in groups trying to learn about their own process with the help of a facilitator. The professional facilitator brings to the group an expertise, a point of view, an observational status, an objective awareness of process, and a set of skills not assumed to be present in the group itself. Whether this professional is used in training groups, growth groups, task groups, quality circles, and so on, the inherent power of that person is usually great because the group looks to the facilitator for special services and is willing to accept what the "expert" provides. However, we must recognize clearly the significance of the underlying principle that "the fate of the group leader is potentially self-destructive" (Starak 1988, 105).

Even nonprofessional "member" facilitators, who emerge from a task group because they are skilled in group process and intervention, operate differently from the usual group member. It is not likely that task groups could operate very effectively if all the members were primarily concerned with the process and no one seemed to have interest in the task.

The role of the professional facilitator specialist contains a great deal of power. Some use this power to benefit their group. Others, enamored of the power they feel, force their power needs to become issues with which the group must deal. When this happens the function of the facilitator is seriously impaired. He or she may need to be replaced.

Effective facilitators will have dealt with their power issues in another context so such issues do not become a matter of group concern. When the facilitator's personal power issues have not been resolved there can be a serious mix-up between group issues and the facilitator's personal concerns. Any group has ample power issues of its own with which it must deal. These are a constant in group life. Adding to them the power and control needs of a basically nongroup member seriously interferes with the group's development and growth toward process independence.

The Intervention Paradox

The Facilitator as Intervenor

Facilitators aid groups by influencing group structure and behavior, thereby enhancing normal operations. Facilitation intrudes into the existing flow of group behavior, interrupting that flow in order to insert additional process data and to help the group accomplish its goals. Left alone, the group would probably continue its own process, no matter how inept, until crisis or failure.

The intervention function of the facilitator is a very delicate one. Argyris (1970, 15) says, "To intervene is to enter into an ongoing system of relationships, to come between or among persons, groups, or objects for the purpose of helping them . . . the system exists independently of the intervenor." He identifies the essential conditions of the facilitation process as the generation of valid information; maintenance of a discrete and autonomous client system through free, informed choice; and the existence of the client's internal commitment to the choices made.

The nature of the role or relationship between the facilitator and the group (intervenor and client) is a unique role not comparable to most of the other roles in human relationships. Benne, Bradford, Gibb, and Lippitt (1975, 253) suggest that it is *not* equivalent to leader-follower, manager-subordinate, colleague-colleague, or friend-to-friend relationships.

The Paradox of Facilitation

The role of the facilitator is to assist the group in performing more effectively. To perform that role the facilitator must intervene and interrupt a process in order to initiate changes. Benne et al. (1975) suggest that the ultimate success of intervention is the *termination of the relationship between the intervenor and the client.* The success of such a relationship, therefore, hinges on the degree to which the group (the client) becomes able to function *independently.*

Golembiewski and Blumberg (1977, 123) described three paradoxical functions that any trainer-facilitator must perform: to function as an expert rather than to project one's personal self, to function both as an "outsider but also as an insider" in order to participate meaningfully and helpfully in group life, and to maintain a central role while also helping the group to trust and rely on its own resources. The manner in which these polarities are resolved determines the style and quality of the facilitator.

There are some key behaviors commonly ascribed to facilitators who have *not* been adequately trained, are *not* skilled in the process of facilitation and intervention, and who unconsciously allow these issues to control their in-group behavior. According to Reisel (1962, 93–108), this type of trainer intervenes in terms of his or her own control needs, acceptance or inclusion needs, and desire to succeed.

Facilitator intervention has to be examined in light of the effects and the conditions of the intrusion on the process of the subject group. The nature of the group and its goals, the nature of the facilitator-intervenor's goals, and the conditions under which they all come together are important dimensions to consider. Dealing with such considerations implies an understanding of the assumptions of facilitation, the paradoxes present, and the necessary development of an intervention strategy.

Facilitator Intervention Strategy

Facilitator intervention strategy is usually determined by resolving such questions as When? How often? What focus? How much control? What is my relationship? What are my assumptions? What do I select to identify? and What data should be discarded?

These questions are a guide for the facilitator in determining basic intervention strategy in the ongoing group process. Dyer points out that we really don't know which strategy is best for which group. It depends on the intervenor(s) and the group.

At this point group training is still more an art than a science. Any strategy must be dynamic and subject to change. The effective facilitator must have access to many strategies (Dyer 1972, 184–185).

In determining the strategy to be used in a particular situation a number of *guidelines* should be considered. These guidelines involve issues such as purposes, supporting behavior, facilitator feelings, process focus, intervention frequency, individuals versus groups, feedback, group tolerance for intervention, timing, authenticity, nonevaluation, availability of alternatives, language style, statements versus questions, objectivity, and termination.

At any given time during the group process a number of things may be brought into *focus*. One of the facilitator's most critical tasks is selecting those processes on which to focus. The criteria for selection of these foci relate to the purposes of the group, the group's status at the specific instant of observation, the focus's significance to the total group process behavior, and finally, to the group's ability to deal with that particular information and focus. It is critical to the whole process that the facilitator not deal with the content of the discussion.

The many dimensions on which a facilitator may focus involve process, structure, feelings, process rationale, role functions, diagnosis, and protection, among others.

Interventions occur in some form or *mode*. Modes are the structural types of behavior in which the content of the intervention is contained and through which it is communicated. Some modes are more facilitative than others. Characteristic modes are message feedback (for a special description of the use of message feedback, see Keltner, 1988), nonadvocacy, corrective, directive, interpretive, helping, being a member, and support.

Whichever modes are selected by the facilitator, *the essential function of the facilitator-intervenor is to create and protect the environment in which group process learning can take place. Along with that comes the necessity of maintaining an external boundary within which the group and members may experiment with their own processes.*

Conclusions

The art of facilitation in small task groups is, for the most part, still developing. A clear understanding of the facilitator's role is clouded by the fact that many practitioners see their own rationale and style as more justifiable than others. Even so, there appears to be some agreement on the areas of expertise that the facilitator must have in order to function effectively. There is no agreement on the nature of the facilitator's role in a task group when he or she is not a regular part of that group's function. Styles range from the therapeutic at one end to the strictly procedural at the other.

Likewise, there is considerable variation in the understanding of the member-facilitator's role. That is, the function of member as facilitator has not been studied, nor have the unique problems of membership under those conditions been adequately examined.

We know that task group members can and do facilitate problem solving and decision making. We believe that the more training in process a group and its members have had, the more likely it is to provide its own built-in facilitative behavior. The paradox of the facilitation role is an important factor in both training facilitators and in their actual function. The role of the specialist is particularly paradoxical. The effective specialist teaches the group how to facilitate itself, thus eliminating the need for the specialist function. However, occasionally the same focus, styles, and forms of process intervention exist in groups that do not have the presence of a facilitator specialist but that get process help from members who are particularly sensitive to process and have facilitative skills at hand. This is an important area for study.

More than anything else, however, it is clear that there are too many persons who assume the facilitative role who are quite unprepared for the complexity of the functions. There are also many trainers who are attempting to train facilitators but who focus on one or two aspects of the function and leave many vital areas unexamined. They are the ones who become excited with a particular image, model, or theme and who then become evangelists for that system. For example, there are many counselor-type trainers who advocate the use of Rogerian intervention styles. Such training fails to address the infinite variety of styles available and the particular values of the various methods. It also avoids the fact that different groups have different goals and contexts and that the same facilitative model does not work equally well in all of them. We should try to build facilitator training on the process model as a base, but a base supported and enhanced by exploration of as many models as possible, given the time and facilities available. Finally, we need to mount some major research efforts on the factors of facilitation that many of us, over the years, have developed from our experience. It is time to put these to the test.

Notes

The type of group with which facilitators are involved significantly determines their broad approach toward facilitative behavior. *Task groups*, the most frequently experienced type of group, can carry out several functions. *Production groups* perform assigned tasks and have little or no problem-solving or decision-making responsibility. Special *problem-solving groups*, such as management teams, deal with mutual problems. The same group may make decisions during the problem-solving process, though decision-making responsibility may fall to a policy-making group, such as a board of directors. Facilitators also function within *therapy or growth groups,* which are person-centered in their content, and within *training groups.* which focus on problem-solving process, on performance training, and on enhanced understanding of particular subjects.

References

Anderson, J.D. (1985). "Working with Groups: Little-Known Facts that Challenge Well-Known Myths." *Small Group Behavior,* 16(3), 276ff.

Argyris, C. (1970). *Intervention Theory and Method: A Behavioral Science View.* Menlo Park, CA: Addison-Wesley.

Benne, K.D., Bradford, L.P., Gibb, J.R., and Lippitt, R.O. (eds.). (1975). *The Laboratory Method of Changing and Learning: Theory and Application.* Palo Alto, CA: Science & Behavior Books.

Blumberg, A., and Golembiewski, R.T. (1976). *Learning and Change in Groups.* Baltimore, MD: Penguin.

Culbert, S.A. (1972). "Accelerating Participant Learning." In W.G. Dyer (ed.), *Modern Theory and Method in Group Training.* New York: Van Nostrand Reinhold.

Dyer, W.G. (ed.). (1972). *Modern Theory and Method in Group Training.* New York: Van Nostrand Reinhold.

Golembiewski, R.T., and Blumberg, A. (eds.). (1977). *Sensitivity Training and the Laboratory Approach: Readings About Concepts and Applications* (3d ed.). Itasca, IL: F.E. Peacock.

Keltner, J.W. (1988). "When We Make Decisions: Commitment and Problem Solving." In K.A. McCartney (ed.), *Reading and Resource Book: Powerful Communication* (361ff.). Corvallis, OR: SAIC .

Kingsbury, S. (1972). "Dilemmas for the Trainer." In W. G. Dyer (ed.), *Modern Theory and Method in Group Training.* New York: Van Nostrand Reinhold.

Reisel, J. (1962). *Leadership and Organization: A Behavioral Approach.* New York: McGraw-Hill.

Smith, P.B. (1980). "The T-Group Trainer: Group Facilitator or Prisoner of Circumstances?" *Journal of Applied Behavioral Science* 16(1).

Starak, Y. (1988). "Confessions of a Group Leader." *Small Group Behavior* 19(1), 103ff.

Tannenbaum, R., Weschler, I.R., and Massarik, F. (1977). "Observations, on the Training Role: A Case Study." In R.T. Golembiewski and A. Blumberg (eds.). *Sensitivity Training and the Laboratory Approach* (3d ed.). Itasca, IL: Peacock.

Developing Leadership for Change

Stephen C. Schoonover and Murray M. Dalziel

"Change takes place no matter what deters it. . . . There must be measured, laborious preparation for change to avoid chaos."

—Plato

Ancient and modern pundits alike have been preoccupied with change. In all human endeavors change is inevitable. In its most raw and destructive form, change is truly "chaos"—a loss of control. When people in business initiate change or respond to it with adaptations that increase productivity, we call it innovation. But, how can change be harnessed to competitive advantage? And how can "chaos" be avoided?

In a drive to cut costs, a major old-line manufacturing company with a conservative workforce decided to institute a new manufacturing process based on the "just in time" principle. Inventories would be slashed; workers would be much more dependent on one another. Rumors about radical "Japanese-style" management spread rapidly. Japanese graffiti and sketches of top management in kimonos appeared in washrooms; unions held emergency meetings decrying the undermining of worker integrity and the "American Way."

Unfortunately, management had guaranteed a morale problem. They resisted making public knowledge the significant recent corporate losses and the vital savings on inventory. And they failed to publicize their sincere belief that corporate survival was at stake and that increased teamwork and tapping the energy and ingenuity of workers was a critical step in becoming competitive.

Many organizations have been victims of a poorly planned, wrenching change experience that has caused unexpected problems. A conservative view is to "leave things as they are," but history reminds us that change is inevitable. The innovative leader *expects* it, *fosters* it, *plans* it, *directs* it, and *uses* it for competitive advantage.

Why Change?

Successful businesses must provide a stable environment for productive work. They also must adapt constantly to: new market pressures; the changing composition and values of consumers; new information and technologies; and shifting practices and processes within.

In a very real sense change often is a prerequisite for organizational survival. It also helps people grow: New ways of exercising and creating power are discovered; new skills are developed; new ways of sharing and teaming are made possible. In short, both individuals and organizations can profit from a spirit of exploration and growth.

Changes can rejuvenate organizations, but only when channeled to:

☐ Improve productivity or quality of products and services;
☐ Confront dissatisfaction; and
☐ Create new opportunities.

The leadership of a large, heavy manufacturing corporation decided to introduce handheld microprocessors for inventory control. Anticipating significant resistance, the company publicized its plans up front and then debugged the new practice with a small, highly visible group of independent workers with little stake in the change process—"crane drivers" on the loading dock. Soon after introducing the new devices, the drivers became steadfast advocates of the change. Their group even developed a slogan—"The Best Is At Hand." As word spread about the ease of use and efficiency of the hand-held microprocessors, other workers actually requested them.

The Best Change Practices

Change leadership is a key role in any modern organization. It requires a range of skills that few possess naturally. Typically, simple oversights, lack of persistence, and human barriers underlie failed change efforts.

To determine the best change practices, we conducted and analyzed a series of interviews with change leaders in a variety of leading-edge companies. We have found that three groups of factors decide success (see Figures 1–4). They represent the critical assets or barriers in all change processes, and therefore should be the primary focus of any leader's efforts. Besides defining a framework for diagnosing vulnerabilities, we also specified effective strategies or "best practices" for overcoming barriers in each of the major dimensions of change (see Figures 5–7).

Change leaders can take the chance out of change by focusing on the critical areas of modification and the best practices to guide the process. To be effective, leaders must ensure enough flexibility for creative problem solving, enough protection to

---

History of Change: The prior experience of the organization in accepting change.

Clarity of Expectations: The degree to which the expected results of change are shared across various levels of the organization.

Origin of the Problem: The degree to which those most affected by the change initiated the idea or problem the change solves.

Support of Top Management: The degree to which top management sponsors the change.

Compatibility with Organizational Goals: The degree to which the proposed change corresponds to past and present organizational practices and plans.

Figure 1. Five dimensions of organizational readiness.

Inventor: Integrates trends and data into concepts, models, and plans; envisions the "big picture" first; adapts plans.

Entrepreneur: Instinctively focuses on organizational efficiency and effectiveness; identifies critical issues and new possibilities; actively seeks advantages and opportunities.

Integrator: Forges alliances; gains acceptance of himself, his team, and their program; relates practical plans to strategic plans and organizational issues.

Expert: Takes responsibility for the technical knowledge and skills required for the change; uses information skillfully and explains it in a logical way.

Manager: Simplifies, delegates, assigns priorities; develops others; gets the job done at all costs.

Figure 2. Five change-team roles.

Clarifying Plans is the process in which implementors define, document, and specify the change.

Integrating New Practices is the process in which an organization incorporates change into its operations.

Providing Education refers to those programs in which end-users learn about and use new processes and procedures.

Fostering Ownership is the process through which end-users come to identify new processes and procedures as their own, rather than regarding them as changes imposed upon them.

Giving Feedback is the process in which a detailed objective is monitored and used to judge the effectiveness of the implementation plan.

Figure 3. Five dimensions of the implementation process.

Comprehensive
Implementation Plan

Figure 4. Effective planned change.

1. **History of Change**

Inform end-users fully; avoid surprises.

Make a reasonable case for change in end-users' terms.

Spend more time talking.

Involve end-users in diagnosing vulnerabilities.

Start implementation with receptive workers.

Start implementation with a small part of the change for quick, visible payoff.

Publicize successes.

2. **Clarity of Expectations**

Emphasize the benefits of change—to the organization, the unit, and end-users.

Avoid surprises; specify possible impact, outcomes, and problems.

Make change plans public.

Solicit formal and informal feedback.

3. **Origin of the Problem**

Specify who wants the change and why.

Clarify end-users' concerns about the change.

Specify the effects of the change on day-to-day operations and work routines.

Present potential problems clearly and completely.

Set goals that confront end-user problems first.

Use feedback as a barometer of how fast to proceed with implementation plans.

4. **Support of Top Management**

Define top-management concerns.

Develop an influence network—top management allies, informal coalitions.

Implement a small part of the change for quick results and good publicity.

Develop a formal management review from top management's perspective.

5. **Compatibility of the Change**

Frame the change in terms of present organizational values and goals.

Integrate the change into ongoing procedures when possible.

Make change plans overt, common knowledge.

Start the change in an accepting environment.

Don't oversell the change.

Figure 5. Organizational readiness problem-solving strategies.

maintain work group *esprit*, and enough control to complete specific critical tasks. In practice, four simple principles support the best change efforts:

1. Focusing on the proven critical barriers to change in organizations.
2. Choosing and enacting those selective "best practices" that fit the organizational setting.
3. Thinking about and completing any planned innovation in small, unintimidating steps.
4. Following a proven management framework that promotes understanding the change, refining appropriate implementation strategies, setting appropriate goals,

1. Inventor

Make a wide search for change suggestions.

Review the common organizational and social sources of innovation.

Talk about potential future problems.

Discuss the "What if" implications of new technologies, market changes, etc.

Use your team to review products and services periodically.

2. Entrepreneur

Work on tolerating partial answers, interim solutions, mistakes.

Practice framing ideas so that they "sell".

Develop change resources and influence networks.

Develop planning and goal-setting skills.

3. Integrator

Develop interpersonal skills.

Develop informal alliances and coalitions, as well as a formal team.

Protect the change project from the usual organizational pressures.

Confront conflicts and clarify distortions.

Inform and update key personnel.

4. Expert

Acquire knowledge and skills, or be responsible for finding experts.

Develop skills of working with "outside" consultant(s).

Develop presentation skills.

Update team members and end-users.

Monitor change plans.

5. Manager

Develop coaching skills.

Set goals skillfully.

Specify, review, and revise change plans.

Delegate responsibility freely.

Take responsibility for outcomes.

Keep morale high with frequent face-to-face feedback.

Figure 6. Change-team roles: improvement strategies.

formulating clear plans, and completing critical action steps (see Figure 8, page 400).

Change often is a reaction to pressures or a response to innovation. However, organizations sometimes make the wrong change for the wrong reasons, or the wrong change for the right reasons, or the right change in an inefficient and stressful way. Therefore, the first organizing step in planned change is to *test and specify your ideas*. By specifying change plans, a leader not only maps an initial direction, but also increases commitment.

Information Gathering

Information gathering is a process that operates from the beginning to the end of the change implementation.

Leaders direct the change process as much by example as by management skills. Therefore, the first prerequisite for discovering assets and barriers to change is open-mindedness and self-questioning that results in a personal inventory of organizational practices and available people and resources.

1. Clarifying Plans

Make one person responsible for implementation plans.

Formulate clear, simple, time-bound goals.

Make specific plans with milestones and outcomes.

Make plans public.

Give and solicit frequent face-to-face feedback.

2. Integrating New Practices

Limit the amount of change introduced at any one time.

Slow the change process.

Introduce the change to receptive users first.

Ensure that the rationale and procedure for change are well known.

3. Providing Education

Involve the end-users and incorporate their experience.

Provide "hands-on" training whenever possible.

Design training from end-users' perspective.

Train motivated or key end-users first.

Evaluate the effects of training or work practices and end-users' attitudes.

4. Fostering Ownership

Ensure that the change improves end-users' ability to accomplish work.

Provide incentives for end-users applying the change.

Specify milestones for getting end-user feedback.

Incorporate end-user suggestions in the implementation plans.

Publicize end-user suggestions.

5. Giving Feedback

Document and communicate the expected outcomes of the change.

Ensure frequent face-to-face feedback.

Identify clear milestones.

Make sure feedback includes the large organization.

Acknowledge key successes.

Figure 7. Implementation process problem-solving strategies.

After self-inquiry, effective change agents form wider visions of organizational vulnerabilities by assessing employee and management attitudes and practices. They gather a variety of opinions from colleagues and end-users of the change, managers from other sections of the business, and even those outside the organization who use its products or services. Short, efficient, focused discussions can yield the vital information in the normal course of a few days without disrupting the work routine.

A spirit of inquiry also fosters effective group involvement and dialogue, both among system implementors and selected groups of end-users. In fact, information-gathering is in itself an intervention—a method of comparing perceptions and confronting discrepancies among various organizational groups.

Defining Barriers to Change

Often skilled leaders instinctively focus on critical barriers to change, and then foster it by directing the attention of decision-makers and end-users to a selective group

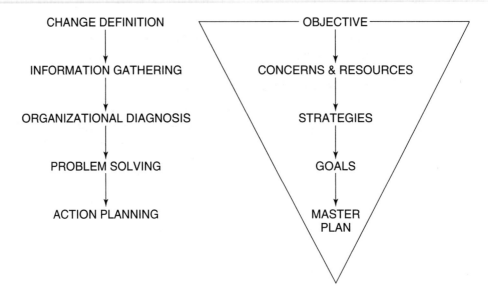

Figure 8. Effective leadership steps.

of factors. All too often, vital vulnerabilities are left unattended. The five attributes of *organizational readiness,* the five roles of the effective *change team* and the five aspects of an effective *implementation process* provide a focus for discovering and confronting the critical vulnerabilities that interfere with planned change (see Figures 1–4, pages 395–396).

Hidden issues and personality conflicts inevitably influence all planned change. Leaders must confront these aspects of their organizations, but in a very special way. By making step-by-step plans the priority, while respecting the feelings and contributions of individuals, leaders can map a creative course that avoids personal issues and individual and group regression.

Setting priorities, however, requires more than determining selected vulnerabilities and avoiding emotional pitfalls. All barriers to change are not equally important to confront. Moreover, barriers to change are often deeply imbedded in stubborn, long-standing attitudes and practices. Trying to resolve too many problems in the context of a planned change can prove impossible, if not destructive. Therefore, a leader must focus on problems that would have very significant costs to the organization if ignored, and on factors that have the most positive leverage on productivity, quality, or worker satisfaction. Most often, these priorities are clarified in discussions that try "what if" simulations for the various vulnerabilities defined as problems.

To fullfill these mandates:

☐ Focus on the most common barriers to change;
☐ Discuss behaviors, not personalities;
☐ Confront only a few problems that have the highest potential cost to the organization if not addressed.

In addition, remember that although the major goal may be planned change, organizational development is a frequent salutory by-product.

Confronting Barriers

Problem-solving is a process that requires openness, creativity, and flexibility. It starts when you decide which organizational barriers to confront, and is applied during each subsequent step in the change process. Goal-setting, planning, feedback, and plan revision, although defined as separate tasks, each rely on effective problem-solving techniques.

Vulnerabilities defined by the three major dimensions of change must be translated into workable problems that are *clearly defined, small and specific in scale,* and *easily understood and accepted by implementors and end-users alike.* This requires wisdom, effort, and collaboration—and prompt action.

Once the process of discovering obstacles has begun, timely interventions are a prerequisite for building or maintaining momentum. In part, the problem-solving strategies ("best practices") speed the process of confronting obstacles. By encouraging the consideration of a variety of solutions, particularly suggestions from end-users, leaders can tailor solutions to the workplace. This means visible plans, in clear terms, framed in a manner that makes sense to those who must live with them.

Beyond defining the problem in an acceptable manner, the skilled leader also provides appropriate, timely resources, such as information or education about new procedures and processes. In addition, the good leader must increase the support of employees by:

- ☐ Increasing interpersonal, group, and written communications;
- ☐ Increasing opportunities for management feedback;
- ☐ Reporting frequently on the status of the problem-solving process; and
- ☐ Rewarding each step in confronting barriers to change.

Planning and Implementing

How can a leader make and complete plans most effectively? Often projects fail because they lack focus, or because steps are ill-defined or too difficult to implement. The first key to avoiding these pitfalls is effective goal setting. Goals, whether implicit or explicit, drive productive actions in a business setting. Moreover, evidence shows that just the act of setting goals increases the probability for goal completion and overall productivity.

In the initial planning phases of purposeful change, leaders must strike a careful balance. Specific goals are necessary for good work, but may produce opposition from anxious participants in the change process. Therefore, creative goal setting is necessary. (See Figure 9.) Leaders must:

1. Set broad performance goals in early phases of change with a great deal of dialogue to involve participants.
2. Set specific goals with short timelines covering only the initial phase of the change. This also gives immediate and probably positive feedback about the process of change.
3. Set preliminary goals focused on outcomes that are immediate concerns of end-users.

Use the following checklist to rate the quality of the goals you set.

____ Easy to understand.
____ Simply expressed.
____ Results-oriented, not activity-oriented.
____ Limited in number and scope.
____ Challenging.
____ Specific in their description of the following:
    ____ Qualities
    ____ Quantities
    ____ Responsible people
    ____ Constraints
    ____ Costs
____ Time-bound with specific deadlines and milestones.
____ Subject to measurement and feedback.

Figure 9. Have you set change goals that will work?

Most often, the best way to begin the goal-setting process is by asking, "What results do I want?" After defining a best outcome, then ask, "What objective measures or accomplishments represent an *excellent* result?" Make sure you allow adequate dialogue about these questions within your management team and with coworkers, and that you take the time to improve goals by simplifying, objectifying, and testing them.

Well-defined goals are a prerequisite for productive actions. However, they provide only one aspect of a plan—clear outcomes in the change process. They must be incorporated into a comprehensive framework—an action plan—to be truly effective. An *excellent* implementation plan:

☐ Assigns priorities to tasks;
☐ Simplifies and organizes the change process;
☐ Specifies responsibilities; and
☐ Outlines methods for measuring progress and making necessary revisions.

The plan represents a road map that expresses ideas and concerns in discrete, workable terms. It makes sure that you assess the critical factors that enhance or impede innovation and translate them into practical strategies and reachable goals.

Maintaining and Promoting Change

A leader's role in planned change extends well beyond the phase of implementation. By debriefing the experience, he or she refines plans and supports change as both a cultural value and a means of personal growth. In addition, the communication feedback and networking so vital for a specific project can become part of a leader's management repertoire through techniques such as:

☐ Periodic team meetings to discuss possible change plans;
☐ Larger organizational meetings with top management or other segments of the business to discuss vulnerabilities and opportunities;

☐ Organizational performance appraisals; or
☐ Consultant feedback about possible changes and barriers to change.

Change in any business system is inevitable. Competition, evolution, creativity, and even individual rebelliousness, inexorably alter the landscape of all organizations over time. Because of this inevitability *a leader's choice is not whether to change, but how.* Particularly in these turbulent times, when social, attitudinal, and technological changes are pervasive, managers must either embrace change as a normal, healthy process in the service of growth and adaptation, or perish because of their investment in the status quo. When values and knowledge undergo rapid change, people—their ideas, tolerances, skills, and idiosyncrasies—become the primary adaptive resource of organizations. In the new workplace, change must be acknowledged—even embraced—as a constant companion to be nurtured and exploited to competitive advantage.

Improving Decision Quality in the Small Group: The Role of the Reminder

Beatrice Schultz and Sandra M. Ketrow

One of the more exciting areas of research over the last two decades has been the search for methods that would have a positive influence on group decision making. Much of the focus has been on examining procedures leading to higher quality decisions. Researchers have concentrated in particular on a rational problem-solving approach developed by John Dewey in his book, *How We Think* (1910) as a method for increasing decision-making effectiveness.

The proposition that knowledge about rational problem solving and decision making would lead to better solutions has been tested in a variety of circumstances. Studies evaluating the effect of "rational models" have found that while no specific method was better than any other, all methods allowing a group to analyze a problem systematically, to generate options for solution, and to evaluate solution proposals seemed to encourage more effective problem-solving discussions than groups which use unstructured discussions.

Current research affirms that using certain problem-solving functions such as (1) intensely analyzing a problem, (2) generating alternatives for solution, and (3) evaluating the consequences of alternatives before coming to decision increases a group's decision quality. Poole (1983), for example, found that evaluations of opinions and of alternative solutions are related to decision quality. Jarboe (1988) found that the more alternatives a group considers, the more likely they are to reach a higher quality solution.

On the other hand, the Nobel Laureate Herbert Simon, among other decision-making experts, contends that a "rational-actor" model is inadequate either as descriptive or as prescriptive theory (1957; 1976). According to Simon, an unstructured approach better explains what a group actually does. He bases his conclusion on two factors: (1) that individuals are limited by how much information they can absorb; and, (2) since no individual has the wherewithal to predict the future or to assess every alternative course of action, human beings cannot meet the requirements of a normative, rational model.

Although the data that rational problem solving directly aids decision quality are not conclusive, indirect support tends to favor rational approaches (Hirokawa 1985; Gouran & Hirokawa 1986; Hirokawa & Pace 1983). While many studies examining functions leading to quality decisions can be criticized for shortcomings such as short-term, zero-history groups, limited involvement of group members, and poor choice of task—even with these limitations, the data generally support the premise that group members mindful of decision procedures are more apt to make high quality decisions (Cragan & Wright 1990).

This essay was written expressly for this edition. All rights reserved. Permission to reprint must be obtained from the publisher and the authors. Beatrice Schultz and Sandra M. Ketrow are affiliated with the University of Rhode Island. The authors would like to thank Randall R. Robey, University of Virginia, for his assistance with the statistical analysis, and Daphne R. Urban, University of Hartford, for her assistance with data collection.

Irving Janis's work (1972; 1982), confirms the functions that effective groups must perform if they are to avoid defective decision making. He provides a strong case for rational problem solving, a process he labeled as "vigilant" problem solving. In addition, Janis (1982) identified seven defective decision-making processes which groups should avoid if they are to be vigilant:

1. Not considering a number of alternatives.
2. Not discussing objectives or discussing them so briefly that the major values for the choices made are not taken into account.
3. Not examining the consequences of the preferred solution.
4. Not obtaining necessary information for critically evaluating the pros and cons of the preferred course of action.
5. Not confronting nonsupporting information nor examining group biases for a particular solution.
6. Not reconsidering the costs and benefits of previously rejected alternatives.
7. Not developing implementation or contingency plans.

Vigilant problem solving assumes that a group will be able to counteract group tendencies toward defective decision making; but, as Janis and Mann (1977) have observed, those who take rational approaches to decision tasks may be a minority. The dilemma for improving decision quality is two-fold: First, decision makers need to possess the relevant knowledge and skills for the tasks they will have to perform. Second, they will also need to employ them. Without effort, the conditions for rational choice do not simply emerge; and as Gouran explains (1991), the odds of having a climate in which rational choice is possible are increased by those who deliberately make an effort to create it.

We know that groups perform better when they employ "vigilant problem solving," but we also know that groups do not necessarily apply appropriate vigilance to their decision processes. The question becomes, what can be done to create the conditions conducive to high-quality decisions? The issue for the study presented in this essay was how to assure that groups would apply the appropriate procedures to optimize their decision-making discussions.

An Intervention Process: A Role for a Reminder

One deficiency identified in decision-making groups is the tendency of members to succumb to group pressures for conformity and unanimity. Group members under the influence of a majority position differing from their own sometimes feel compelled to sacrifice independence of judgment even when they know that the majority is in error or that the agreed upon decision is not defensible (Gouran 1982). On the other hand, there is evidence that although groups may be resentful of those members who do not adhere to group norms, they will sometimes be thankful that one of their members "held out" in the interest of assisting the group to make the right choice. Despite the potential for severe sanctions being applied to a deviant member, there is good reason to believe that an individual willing to take the risk of questioning a majority position can aid the group's process and decision outcome.

A major purpose of our study, therefore, was to examine whether imposing a "reminder," a process function carried out by a group member, would encourage members to adopt rational problem-solving methods to find a solution. We were also interested in using an intervention that fit naturally into a group's deliberations. There have been many types of interventions recommended for helping a group improve the quality of their decisions such as using trained discussion leaders to generate the creation of alternative solutions (Maier & Hoffman 1960a), Devil's Advocate or Dialectical Inquiry to stimulate critiques of solutions (Schweiger, Sanberg, & Ragan 1986), and Nominal and Delphi group techniques (Delbecq 1975) to aid in brainstorming. However, none of these interventions focus directly on processes leading to effective decision making, for example, the quality of evidence, the reasoning process, or the criteria for selecting alternatives for solution.

The reminder function was conceptualized as a way to impose a rational structure, but one that would not interfere with ongoing group interaction. Several factors influenced the decision to use a reminder function. One was Janis's prescription that "The most effective performers . . . are likely to be those who can be truly devilish by raising new issues in a conventional, low-key style, asking such questions as, "Haven't we perhaps overlooked . . . ?" "Shouldn't we give some thought to . . . ?" " (1982, 268). A second influence was Cragan and Wright's (1986) depiction of the "Central Negative," and a third factor was Janis and Mann's (1977) concept of "Vigilance." The central negative challenges the leader or the group whenever either has moved too quickly over the data or when uninformed opinion seems to be swaying the group. Vigilance implies that the reminder continuously attends to group process and, when needed, asks critical questions pertaining to dimensions of effective decision behavior.

A basic assumption of our study was that groups with reminders will be judged to have made higher-quality decisions than groups without reminders. An unanswered question, however, was which participant in a group can best serve as a reminder. An extensive literature indicates that leaders are usually the most influential members (Schultz 1982). Both emergent and established leaders participate more often in group activity than other members and use a greater variety of communication functions than nonleaders. Thus it was expected that emergent leaders would probably be more effective than nonleaders for carrying out the obligations of the reminder role. On the other hand, as Geier (1967) has pointed out, potential leaders are dropped from contention when they are perceived to be either overly talkative or overly directive. Further, although leaders tend to attempt more direct influence, such efforts are not necessarily effective. Indeed, as Fisher (1986) has stated, direct attempts to influence may be associated with ineffective leadership. Therefore, to obviate a possible confounding issue, both emergent leaders and nonleaders were trained to carry out reminder functions.

Method

This study explored whether groups trained in small-group processes with the addition of either a leader reminder or a nonleader reminder would produce higher-quality decisions than either groups trained in rational problem solving, but without a reminder or control groups which had neither training nor a reminder. Using 262 subjects in 45 groups, groups were randomly assigned to one of four conditions: (1) a control condition, with no training in problem solving and no reminder; (2) training in problem solving but no reminder; (3) training in problem solving and emergent leader members performing the reminder functions; (4) training in problem solving and nonleader members performing the reminder functions.

Participants in the experimental conditions were instructed in problem solving and decision making informed by Dewey's Reflective Thinking Model and a variation of this method, Force Field Analysis, developed by Lewin (1947). The assumption of this study was that strengthening the decision process through methodological decision-making procedures would enhance decision quality. Thus the training emphasized procedures that would help depersonalize group debate and ensure a thorough information search and a discussion of alternative solutions. In addition, to simulate bona fide groups as much as possible, all groups met frequently and independently over a one-month period to analyze a case addressing the complex problem of teenage pregnancy and to generate a policy recommendation detailing a course of action for solution of the problem.

To determine whether leaders or nonleaders would be the more influential reminder, all group members evaluated each other, self included, using the Behavioral Description Questionnaire leadership scale (Morris & Hackman 1969). The statement, "He/she is the true leader of the group" was found in previous research to be highly predictive of emergent leaders. Participants with the highest scores on this statement were chosen and trained as leader reminders. Randomly selected subjects rated in the middle range of scores on the leadership statement were trained for their role as non-leader reminders.

Training the Reminder

Participants trained as reminders were provided with a model for overcoming obstacles to effective decision making in one-hour sessions apart from their groups. The groups did not know there was a reminder among them until the experiment was completed. Reminders were to enact their functions such that their interventions were couched in their own language style, but in a friendly yet serious manner.

The training of reminders included the major components of vigilant problem solving along with suggested statements reminders could use to counteract inappropriate processes. For example, to counteract a tendency for groups to be swayed by majority opinion, reminders could ask, "Why do you think this proposal will work?" To counteract a group's premature decision, a reminder could say, "Maybe we shouldn't decide on our choices until we have spent a little more time analyzing other choices." Additionally, a checklist of questions was provided to help reminders perform the reminder functions, such as:

1. Does the group have enough evidence to support our choice for solution?
2. Have we looked at a sufficient number of alternatives?
3. Have we re-examined alternatives we rejected previously?
4. Have we avoided stereotypical thinking or premature judgment?

Reminders were asked to intervene whenever symptoms of defective decision making prevailed. They were not to be aggressive; rather, by their questioning, they were to assist the group in choosing an appropriate course of action.

Did Reminders Perform Their Functions?

Several procedures ascertained that the reminders performed their functions. Group members were asked to respond to questions about procedures in their group, roles people played, and any special problem-solving functions that were carried out. Members of groups which had reminders typically responded with such statements as "He pushed us to examine other alternatives," or "I knew something was going on when she kept insisting that we not make a decision until we had considered more alternatives." Additionally, trained raters evaluated the quality of decisions produced in the policy recommendations of each group. The criteria for judging reflected theories about decision effectiveness. Judges found that effective groups could be distinguished from ineffective groups on the basis of a careful definition of the problem, an examination of options for solution, and an appraisal of how well the suggested remedies met the needs of the problem.

What Did We Find?

Statistical analyses tested the hypotheses: (1) that groups with training in problem-solving processes will produce higher-quality decisions than groups without training; and (2) that groups with training in problem-solving processes and a reminder will produce higher-quality decisions than trained groups without a reminder. Although it was assumed that leaders would be more able reminders than nonleaders, a research question asked which member would most influence a group's decision quality. Hypothesis one was confirmed by the results. Hypothesis two was only partially confirmed, as results demonstrated that only groups with nonleader reminders produced significantly higher-quality decisions than did either of the other experimental groups or the control groups. The answer to the research question is that reminders who are not leaders are the better choice for influencing decision quality.

What Does It Mean?

The results of our study confirm that groups trained in rational problem solving will be judged to have made higher-quality decisions than untrained groups. These results support prior research indicating that groups which use rational problem-solving methods tend to make better decisions. The results also indicate that a reminder function significantly influences the quality of a group's decision.

The research question as to which participant, a leader or nonleader, would be better able to perform the reminder function, can now be assessed. Groups with nonleader reminders produced policy recommendations that were judged to be of significantly higher quality than recommendations produced by leader reminder groups. One question these results raise is why were leader reminders not as influential as nonleader reminders.

One possible explanation is that leaders could not carry out the dual function of leadership and remindership. The leaders employed in this study were not trained to be leaders; nor were they asked to be leaders. Rather, they were emergent leaders according to followers' perceptions, assigned to undertake the reminder function. According to Maier (1960), untrained leaders tend to play a dominant role in influencing the outcome of a group; yet they are more resistant to changing views compared to other participants. Groups in these circumstances also seem to produce lower-quality solutions; and, as Fisher (1986) pointed out, direct influence attempts by leaders are apt to be associated with ineffective leadership. Thus, if emergent leaders had opted to maintain their apparent leadership status, they may have been less willing to engage in reminder functions.

A study by Ketrow (1991) found that group members who are analytical are less likely to be identified as leaders than members who perform procedural functions. Data from the "Behavioral Description Questionnaire" at Time 2 indicate that some leader reminders held relatively high rankings on the leadership question. Nonleader reminders, on the other hand, were rated relatively consistently at a midpoint ranking on leadership. Without the need to compete to achieve leadership, nonleader reminders may be viewed as having been more able to perform reminder functions. Without the need to maintain a leadership position, nonleaders were apparently able to exert a more positive influence on the decision-making processes than were leader reminders.

One reasonable conclusion from this study is that a reliance on rational problem-solving methods produces desirable results, but these methods may not be employed unless they are imposed. To the extent that the results of this study demonstrate empirical support for imposing reminder functions, it seems clear that to optimize group effectiveness, a group could incorporate reminder functions carried out by a nonleader member as part of their decision process. Conversely, if the leader is also the reminder, the reminder functions may not be employed. Perhaps what the reminder offers is a way to increase the competence level of group members. By raising questions in a nonaggressive style, the reminder helps a group counteract such dysfunctional patterns as faulty information processing, faulty assumptions, faulty evaluation of alternatives, and the undue influence of particular group members.

The intervention by a reminder has the potential to help a group institute procedures known to produce choices having desired consequences. Clearly group members who have some knowledge of rational problem-solving methods perform to a higher criterion than members who do not have this knowledge. Employing nonleader reminders instead of leader reminders appears to be a more effective way to enhance decision making. But if a reminder role for a nonleader cannot be imposed, then providing group members with the knowledge and practice in problem solving is an effective alternative. Groups with problem-solving training performed better than controls and somewhat better than groups with a leader attempting to perform reminder functions. Because so many factors can undermine group decision making and because groups may not utilize processes that can improve their performance, the task for researchers is to discover the conditions conducive to effective decision making. The imposition of a reminder function appears to be one such intervention for facilitating effective group performance or for counteracting ineffective decision processes.

References

Cragan, J. F., and Wright, D. W. (1986). *Communication in Small Group Discussion: An Integrated Approach* 2d ed. St. Paul, MN: West.

Cragan, J. F., & Wright, D. W. (1990). "Small Group Communication Research of the 1980s: A Synthesis and Critique." *Communication Studies* 41, 212–236.

Delbecq, A.K., Van de Ven, A.H., and Gustafson, D.H. (1975). *Group Techniques for Program Planning.* Glenview, IL: Scott, Foresman.

Dewey, J. (1910). *How We Think.* Boston: Heath.

Fisher, B.A. (1986). "Leadership: When Does the Difference Make a Difference?" In R. Y. Hirokawa and M.A. Poole (eds.). *Communication and Group Decision Making* (197–215). Beverly Hills, CA: Sage.

Geier, J. (1967). "A Trait Approach to the Study of Leadership in Small Groups." *Journal of Communication* 17, 316–323.

Gouran, D.S. (1982). *Making Decisions in Groups: Choices and Consequences.* Glenview, IL: Scott, Foresman.

Gouran, D.S. (1991). "Rational Approaches to Decision-Making and Problem-Solving Discussion." *Quarterly Journal of Speech* 77, 343–358.

Gouran, D.S. and Hirokawa, R.Y. (1986). "Counteractive Functions of Communication in Effective Group Decision Making." In R.Y. Hirokawa and Poole, M.S. (eds.). *Communication and Group Decision Making* (81–90). Beverly Hills, CA: Sage.

Hirokawa, R.Y. (1985). "Discussion Procedures and Decision-Making Performance: A Test of a Functional Perspective." *Human Communication Research* 12, 203–224.

Hirokawa, R.Y., and Pace, R.C. (1983). "A Descriptive Investigation of the Possible Communication-Based Reasons for Effective and Ineffective Group Decision Making." *Communication Monographs* 50, 363–379.

Janis, I.L. (1972). *Victims of Groupthink.* Boston: Houghton Mifflin.

Janis, I.L. (1982). *Groupthink: Psychological Studies of Policy Decision and Fiascoes* 2d ed. Boston: Houghton Mifflin.

Janis, I.L., and Mann, L. (1977). *Decision-Making: A Psychological Analysis of Conflict, Choice, and Commitment.* New York: Free Press.

Jarboe, S. (1988). "A Comparison of Input-Output, Process-Output, and Input-Process-Output Models of Small Group Problem-Solving Effectiveness." *Communication Monographs* 55, 121–142.

Ketrow, S.M. (1991). "Valued Leadership Behaviors and Perceptions of Contribution: The Unsung Hero." *Proceedings of the Seventh SCA/AFA Conference on Argumentation.* Annandale, VA: Speech Communication Association.

Lewin, K. (1947). "Frontiers in Group Dynamics." *Human Relations* 1, 1–20.

Maier, N.R.F., and Hoffman, L.R. (1960). "Using Trained `Developmental' Discussion Leaders to Improve Further the Quality of Group Dynamics." *Journal of Applied Psychology* 44, 247–251.

Maier, N.R.F., & Hoffman, L.R. (1960a). "Quality of First and Second Solutions in Group Dynamics." *Journal of Applied Psychology* 44, 278–283.

Morris, C.G., and Hackman, J.R. (1969). "Behavioral Correlates of Perceived Leadership." *Journal of Personality and Social Psychology* 13, 350–369.

Poole, M.S. (1983). "Decision Development in Small Groups II: A Study of Multiple Sequences in Decision Making. *Communication Monographs* 50, 206–232.

Schultz, B. (1982). "Argumentativeness: Its Effect in Group Decision Making and Its Role in Leadership Perception." *Communication Quarterly* 30, 368–375.

Schweiger, D.M., Sandberg, W.R., and Ragan, J.W. (1986). "Group Approaches for Improving Strategic Decision Making: A Comparative Analysis of Dialectical Inquiry, Devil's Advocacy, and Consensus." *Academy of Management Journal* 28, 51–71.

Simon, H.A. (1957). *Administrative Behavior: A Study of Decision Making Processes in Administration Organizations* 2d ed. New York: Free Press.

Simon, H.A. (1976). *Administrative Behavior* 3d ed. New York: Macmillan.

The Bossless Team

David Barry

The use of self-managed teams (SMTs) in work settings not only has gained momentum but appears to be at a record high. These teams appear in many forms, such as quality circles, task forces, communication teams, new venture teams, and business brand teams. They are widely used among such companies as Digital, FMC, Frito-Lay, GE, General Foods, GM, Hewlett-Packard, Honeywell, and Pepsi-Cola, as well as among many smaller firms. SMTs have been credited with saving hundreds of millions of dollars, achieving conceptual breakthroughs, and introducing unparalleled numbers of new products. Increasingly, these "bossless teams" seem the key to solving complex problems, increasing productivity, and heightening creativity.

Although their proliferation has not been problem-free (especially in the case of quality circles), there are several basic forces that will continue to make teams an increasingly popular organizational device in the 1990s.

One driver is the technological information explosion. The logarithmic growth of technologically based information has resulted in unprecedented numbers of highly educated, self-motivated, self-directed specialists; most of these workers come to know far more about their given work area than their managers. For such specialists to work efficiently and effectively, highly participative and flexible work structures such as SMTs are necessary. This trend is gradually eclipsing the need for close, directive leadership in many settings.

Another force is the increased use of extremely expensive equipment and technology in all industries, ranging from laser-based cutting systems in heavy manufacturing settings to high-priced delivery and information systems in the service sector. The expense of interrupting such systems mandates that groups of operators be able to make real-time decisions and interventions on their own rather than relaying problems up to a supervisor.

Lastly, many companies, faced with growing levels of both domestic and global competition, are turning to SMTs as a means of reducing middle management costs and fostering more rapid product innovation.

Despite the growing popularity of SMTs, a significant question has gone unanswered: How should leadership be exercised in these leaderless settings—that is, in settings where differences in formal authority either do not exist or are downplayed? The demand for leadership does not simply disappear once the boss is gone. In many ways, actually, the opposite holds true; SMTs require even more leadership than conventional organizational units. In addition to needing task-based leadership (such as project definition, scheduling, and resource-gathering), they require leadership around group development processes (developing cohesiveness, establishing effective communication patterns, and so forth). Without the presence of formal authority, power struggles and conflict around both task and process issues surface more often, adding to the overall leadership burden that must be handled by the group. Because many members of SMTs never receive formal training in group process skills, these groups are frequently unstable, tending toward fission rather than fusion.

An added problem is that most of the existing leadership theories are inadequate for guiding SMT efforts. Currently, most leadership theories adopt a person-centered approach, in which leadership is a quality that exists in one person—the leader. In this category are universal trait theories (that interpret characteristics that all leaders must have), universal behavior theories that describe behavioral leadership styles (that apply across all situations), situational trait theories (that suggest that a leader needs different traits in different situations), situational behavior theories (that advocate the use of distinct, learned leader behaviors depending on the type of subordinates being supervised), and functionalist theories (that suggest that leader behavior should vary with the function being performed). Although certainly useful in classic supervisory settings, these theories tend to ignore leadership dynamics within a group context where the development of the group almost always requires frequent shifts in leadership behavior.

Leadership theories that are more group-centered include the Robert Tannenbaum-Warren Schmidt leadership model and Ken Blanchard's situational leadership theory for group development. The Tannenbaum-Schmidt model focuses on the extent to which decision making is centralized in a group. On one end of their scale is the leader who dominates decision-making activity, on the other is the leader who permits a group to make decisions within prescribed limits. Their model highlights the importance of focusing on a group's decisional process, particularly in managerial groups, where decisions are the main outputs. Only marginal mention is made, however, of how leadership should change as a group evolves; further, these decisional tasks form only part of the group leadership picture. Another dimension consists of social leadership roles that are acted out in a group, such as the management of participation and conflict. Current leadership research suggests that such roles are critical for effective group functioning.

More applicable to SMTs is Blanchard's extension (developed with Paul Hersey) of situational leadership theory to stages of group development. This framework demonstrates how both directive and socially centered support functions might vary as a group matures. Thus, in the first stages of a group's life, commitment is likely to be high and task competence to be low. Here, leadership that is high in directiveness and low in supportiveness would probably work best. Conversely, a style high in supportiveness and low in directiveness is probably most effective during the third stage of a group's life when both morale and competence are high.

Though these two approaches are better fitted to group processes than most, both tend to ignore situations in which a formal, legitimate leader is absent, thus making their application to SMTs somewhat difficult. Indeed, application of any of these person-centered approaches to an SMT can spell disaster as they tend to intensify power struggles among those believing that someone needs to "take charge."

There is a third class of leadership theory, the leadership substitutes school of thought, which has relevance for some aspects of SMT functioning. First popularized over a decade ago, this school suggests that certain individual, task, and organizational variables can reduce a group's need for leadership. In particular, it argues that the need for formal leadership decreases when team members are able, experienced, trained, and knowledgeable; when tasks are routine, intrinsically satisfying, and results driven; and when the organization possesses high levels of formality, inflexibility, cohesiveness, staff support, managerially independent reward structures, and spatial distance between workers and managers. My experience suggests, however, that at most this theory predicts when SMTs will require less formal task leadership; it virtually ignores the needs that most SMTs have for other leadership forms, such as social and boundary-spanning leadership.

In sum, it is evident that each existing approach to leadership has certain drawbacks when applied to the SMT. In the paragraphs below, I offer a different model of leadership that is uniquely suited to SMTs—a distributed leadership model (see Table 1). At its heart is the notion that leadership is a collection of roles and behaviors that can be split apart, shared, rotated, and used sequentially or concomantly. This in turn means that at any one time multiple leaders can exist in a team, with each leader assuming a complementary leadership role. It is this characteristic that truly differentiates this approach from the person-centered approaches described earlier. Also, unlike leadership substitute approaches, where attempts are made to reduce or eliminate the need for a leader, the distributed leadership model emphasizes the active cultivation and development of leadership abilities within all members of a team; it is assumed that each member has certain leadership qualities that will be needed by the group at some point.

The distributed leadership pattern that arises in an SMT is necessarily an emergent one. It normally begins with different members initiating directions in areas they are naturally predisposed toward and that are needed by the team. Thus, for example, someone having a strong organizing bent might suggest that the team develop an agenda for its meetings, or that a set of minutes be kept. If, over time, this person is able to get the group to regularly follow along with his or her suggestions, this person will gradually be accorded leader status in the area of organization. Similarly, someone who is quite innovative might come up with methods for enhancing overall group creativity. If these suggestions are consistently introduced in ways acceptable to other team members, this person will likely come to assume the status of an envisioning leader.

As different people seek—and are tacitly or openly granted—responsibility for different leadership functions, a dynamic pattern of distributed leadership gradually takes form. Over time, the predominance of various leadership types shifts as the team's needs shift. Thus, envisioning leadership is usually needed when project ideas are being developed; as the project takes form, this need diminishes and the envisioning leader is supplanted by team members exercising other leadership forms. Distributed leadership requires that attention be given not only to the type of leader behavior required at a given time but also to the interrelatedness and availability of leader behaviors. For example, SMTs frequently need social leadership early in their lives, especially in the area of conflict management. If no team members possess training in this area, several members having good networking skills might work together to fill this need, as skills needed to network frequently facilitate development of social abilities—that is, networking that requires the ability to quickly size up others and find a way to communicate with them; these same social leadership skills can be used to encourage dialogue between members having a conflict.

Table 1

Characteristics of SMTs Studied

Team	Type of Firm	Number of Team Members	Team Lifespan (in Years)	Overall Successes*	Type of SMT	Primary Operations Performed by SMT
1	Electronics	5	2	4	SBU	Projects, Some Policy Making
2	Electronics	5	.33	1	SBU	Projects, Some Policy Making
3	Electronics	7	3	3	Strategy Development Group	Policy Making
4	Electronics	6	3	4	SBU	Projects, Some Policy Making
5	Electronics	8	1.5	4	SBU	Projects, Some Policy Making
6	Electronics	4	1.5	2	Task Force	Problem Solving
7	Glass Mfr	5	5	3	Quality Team	Problem Solving
8	Machinery Mfr	7	1	1	Quality Team	Problem Solving, Some Project Work
9	Machinery Mfr	5	3	3	Quality Team	Problem Solving
10	Paper	8	1	4	SBU	Projects, Some Policy Making
11	Paper	6	1.5	2	Task Force	Problem Solving
12	Class Group	6	.5	2	Project Team	Projects
13	Class Group	6	.5	3	Project Team	Projects
14	Student Organization	4	.75	3	Task Force	Problem Solving
15	City Government	6	.5	1	Task Force	Problem Solving

*4=very successful, 3=strong performer, 2=problematic, 1=very problematic, early termination.

The distributed leadership model applies to three generic classes of SMTs: project teams, problem-solving teams, and policy-making teams. While functionally these classes can overlap (that is, a project team will move into a problem solving mode from time to time), experience has shown that collectively, these categories cover most situations in which SMTs are found. Further, numerous observations of successful and unsuccessful SMTs suggest that performance is maximized when certain basic leadership roles and behaviors are differentially enacted at specific times during the team's life. Thus, SMT performance is, in part, a function of having the right roles present at the right time.

Types of Leadership Needed in SMTs

The leadership roles and behaviors required for proper SMT functioning fall into four broad clusters: (1) envisioning, (2) organizing, (3) spanning, and (4) social. The clusters tend to be mutually exclusive; skills needed to master one area often interfere with mastery of the others. Further, each cluster serves a critical function in maintaining team dynamics; if any one is under or over-represented, the SMT's overall performance will usually suffer.

Envisioning Leadership. Envisioning revolves around creating new and compelling visions. Leading this process requires facilitating idea generation and innovation, defining and championing overall goals, finding conceptual links between systems, and fostering frame-breaking thinking. In terms of problem solving, people with strong envisioning abilities typically have many solutions—of which only a few may be acceptable to others. Because they usually march to a different drumbeat, these people can have trouble functioning in a group, preferring instead to invent and create independently.

As an example, an SMT set up as a strategic business unit within Unitron Electronics had two engineers who were highly envisioning, especially with product ideas. However, because they felt they could be more creative when working alone, they would frequently miss team meetings. Others on the team would become angry and would resort to a variety of retaliatory gestures, such as ignoring or denigrating the engineers' ideas. This created a spiraling conflict that ultimately ended in disbandment of the group.

The inexperienced envisioning leader is likely to do most of the envisioning alone and will continue to surface new ideas after the group has committed itself to specific actions. Conversely, the mature, more effective envisioning leader will help others in the group work through the envisioning process, thus fostering group ownership of central ideas. This person will also try to ground new ideas in what is currently known about a given problem or situation, link developing visions to previous ones, and ensure that everyone in the group clearly understands those visions that are agreed upon.

Organizing Leadership. This role brings order to the many disparate elements that exist within the group's tasks. Behavior and characteristics associated with the cluster include a focus on details, deadlines, time, efficiency, and structure. People successfully occupying this role often have an exacting nature and are usually concerned with making things predictable and clear, getting the task done, and not wasting time. They prefer well-structured situations. When solving problems, they favor working with a few, well-chosen solutions. A strong organizing leader can help an SMT forge ahead once a direction has been set and, then, can keep the group from straying off task. For instance, a product development SMT within a paper company floundered for a year, unable to launch any new products. Its members produced many ideas but could not agree on which ones would receive the most attention or on how product development efforts should be sequenced. Recognizing the problem, upper management added a highly goal-oriented woman who had established a good track record as a project manager. Within six months, due to her organizing leadership, the group had translated its ideas into three new product launches.

The organizing role is necessary, but it can become counterproductive when a completely new and innovative direction is needed. During such times, organizers may become impatient with what they perceive to be an impractical casting about for ideas and can consequently act to choke the search for alternatives. Going back to the team noted above, it accorded the leader considerable power. The result? She strengthened her inclination toward "safe," low-risk ideas. Responding to her guidance, the team gradually ceased to come up with any truly innovative products.

Spanning Leadership. Spanning leadership involves facilitating the activities needed to ridge and link the SMT's efforts with outside groups and individuals. Associated behaviors include networking, presentation management, developing and maintaining a strong team image with outsiders, intelligence gathering, locating and securing critical resources, bargaining, finding and forecasting areas of outside resistance, being sensitive to power distributions, and being politically astute. As with envisioners, people predisposed toward spanning can be self-centered, looking after their own needs first. In its extreme, this can be dangerous; it can quickly sabotage group efforts. That is why spanning leaders are most effective when they perceive that payoffs for the group are directly linked to their personal success. At the same time, these leaders must be well-informed and sensitive to the needs of other members, requiring they spend time with the group, even though the natural tendency is to circulate in the outside environment. Spanning leaders who maintain too wide an orbit will collect information and make deals that fit poorly with the team's needs.

Ideally, the spanning leader will provide the group with a constant source of reality checks, thus insuring that the group's outputs will be well received by others in the organization. An example of excellent spanning leadership was provided by a veteran salesman who was in an SMT responsible for a line of high-end audio products. He used his contacts with several industry trade associations to secure information about potential markets, competition, and regulatory information, all of which greatly shortened the time the team needed to create and launch products. He also set up team visits to trade shows and retail outlets, which provided members with firsthand information about how their products were being received.

Social Leadership. Social leadership focuses on developing and maintaining the team from a sociopsychological position. Related behaviors include surfacing different members' needs and concerns, assuring that everyone gets his or her views heard, interpreting and paraphrasing other views, being sensitive to the team's energy levels and emotional state, injecting humor and fun into the team's work, and being able to mediate conflicts. The effective social leader is adept at slowing the group down if it is working too hard, at talking about the emotional aspects of group work and development, at providing encouragement and reinforcement for individual efforts, at encouraging celebration of team accomplishments, and at fostering an environment where individual differences are respected and constructively used. This type of leadership is the most exhausting of the four. It demands constant vigilance and activity. If other types of leaders in the SMT are extreme in their orientation, the team will tend toward high levels of tension and conflict, making the social leader's job even more taxing. Because the social leader works in a fuzzy and ill-defined area, other members may question the level of his or her contributions or may simply discount the usefulness of the contributions altogether, labeling them as "touchy-feely" or "soft-hearted." Yet it is evident that when social leadership is absent, decisions are made prematurely, groupthink is common, and team life tends to be shortened. This was clearly the case with the team at Unitron Electronics, described earlier. Although this team possessed an abundance of envisioning and organizing leadership potential, a general absence of social leadership resulted in a great deal of unprocessed animosity among team members. The engineers in the group felt they were contributing by coming up with new product ideas. The other members, however, were so angry over the engineers' frequent absences that they tended to discount or even sabotage these ideas. An effective social leader would have persuaded these factions to talk through their differences, rather than letting the conflict escalate.

Application of Types Over Time

It is not enough for different types of leadership merely to be present; for optimal team performance, they must be differentially emphasized during the various phases of an SMT's life. Although some initial leadership activities are needed by all SMTs, different kinds of SMTs go through different phases, resulting in the emergence of varying leadership patterns. Table 2 summarizes these patterns, depicting the basic phases encountered in each class of SMT and the kinds of leadership required.

Although this framework is certainly not definitive, my observations suggest that when these leadership types are present at the designated times, an SMT is much more likely to succeed in its mission; the highest performing teams in my sample always had sizeable amounts of the needed leadership types during critical phases. In contrast, when one of the four types was missing, performance fell off, often dramatically. Among all failed SMTs (those that did not complete their assigned tasks), at least one of the leadership types was continuously absent or was diminished when a member enacting the role was transferred out of the team.

Within each phase, there exists a need for at least one primary form of leadership and usually one or more secondary, backup forms. Because the leadership types require such different skills, there are normally at least two people acting as leaders at any given time. Thus, in describing the different leadership types, reference is made to the kind of leadership required (for example, spanning leadership) and/or to a specific kind of leader (for instance, the spanner or the spanning leader). This is not to say that multiple leadership roles cannot be handled by the same person; it is just that in high-performing teams, they are frequently person-specific.

Table 2
Distributed Leadership Dynamics in Effective Self-Managed Teams

Team Phases	Project-Based Leadership Dynamics		Problem-Solving Leadership Dynamics		Policy-Making Leadership Dynamics	
	Team Activities	Leadership Requirements	Team Activities	Leadership Requirements	Team Activities	Leadership Requirements
Phase 1	• Getting Acquainted • Resource Discovery • Develop Goals & Vision • Assess Realism of Vision	• Social • Spanning • Envisioning • Organizing & Spanning	• Getting Acquainted • Resource Discovery • Finding & Assessing Problems • Locating Causes	• Social • Spanning • Organizing & Spanning • Spanning & Envisioning	• Getting Acquainted • Resource Discovery • Issue Finding	• Social • Spanning • Spanning & Organizing
Phase 2	• Surfacing of Differences; Conflict • Scheduling • Securing Outside Resources	• Social & Envisioning • Organizing • Spanning	• Finding Solutions • Getting Ideas from Everyone	• Envisioning & Spanning • Social	• Developing Policy & Strategy Alternatives • Idea Clarification	• Envisioning & Spanning • Social
Phase 3	• Enactment of Vision • Establishing Control Mechanisms • Presentations to Outsiders • Maintenance of Cohesion & Commitment	• Organizing • Organizing • Spanning • Social	• Assessing Costs & Benefits • Summarizing Positions	• Organizing & Spanning • Social	• Assessing Consequences • Tracking Team Progress • Interlinking Ideas	• Organizing & Social • Organizing • Envisioning & Spanning
Phase 4	• Project Completion • Presentations • Getting Closure, Looking at Total Effort • Team Disbanding	• Organizing • Spanning • Social & Envisioning • Social & Envisioning	• Solution Testing • Further Search for Causes & Solutions • Presentations • Disbanding	• Organizing • Envisioning & Spanning • Spanning • Social	• Presentations • Coping with Outside Resistance • Preparing Formal Reports • Disbanding	• Spanning & Organizing • Spanning • Organizing • Social

Leadership Dynamics Across All SMTs

Perhaps the most important initial step in all SMTs is the establishment of an acceptable leadership pattern. Since, by definition, no single designated leader is present to guide this process, progress is almost always difficult and occurs in a trial-and-error fashion. To establish an effective distributed leadership system, members must learn about the personal qualities of one another; a working knowledge of the different orientations, beliefs, and skills of the others is necessary so that those with leadership skills in a certain area can gain the team's consent to use those skills.

Unfortunately, we are often socialized in ways that prevent us from providing the kinds of questions and answers that would facilitate this process, questions such as "How do you like to work?" or "In what ways are you creative?" Consequently, the first few times together are usually awkward. Members end up trying to find out about one another in very roundabout ways—by talking about sports, outside company events, new hires, or practically anything that does not deal directly with the present reality of the group. In some SMTs, there is almost a taboo against talking about personal and social factors; the team norm is one of being "tough" or "staying cool." In such settings, leadership development can be painfully slow, with many subtle (and not-so-subtle) attempts for dominance taking place.

This was the case with a quality control SMT in a firm that manufactured industrial moving equipment. The team was made up of very rugged, competitive men who had a great deal of difficulty in handling their disagreements; either they would carefully avoid situations that they knew were likely to be conflicts or they would get into heated yelling matches filled with threats of physical violence. An unstated norm was that the "winner" of these bouts would set the team's direction, at least until another match occurred. One of the team members tried to minimize tensions through the use of humor, but, often as not, the effects were short-lived. In contrast, the company SMT that came up with the most quality improvements engaged in more open and even-handed interpersonal exploration early in its formation. This resulted in faster leadership development and, ultimately, more rapid team development.

Because so much of an SMT's success depends on effective distribution of leadership—and because this in turn is dependent on discovering and coordinating the team's untapped leadership resources—the early presence of someone with good interpersonal skills is critical. This person, who normally becomes the team's social leader, draws out other team members' values and needs and makes sure that everyone gets a chance to talk. She or he might simply suggest that some time be spent talking about each other's thoughts and about what things each person does best. In more effective teams, others concur with this kind of request by describing themselves in fairly comprehensive ways and by listening well to each other's comments. In less effective teams, either the request to talk about one another is never made or else is met with superficial responses. It is common for these latter teams to jump immediately to the task at hand, skirting the exploration phase altogether.

As the various qualities and skills of each member are brought out, the person exercising social leadership can begin identifying commonalties between members, which can in turn boost feelings of cohesiveness. This person can also point out how differences within the team can be complementary. This effort can be supplemented by team members having good networks. These people, who tend to emerge as spanning leaders, may have previous knowledge about others in the team and can help to surface where different skills lie. Since people with strong spanning skills tend to be self-assured, they can also impart a sense of confidence to the team. In one high-performing SMT, a spanner greatly boosted team confidence by providing assurance of needed outside resources. This freed the team from being overly anxious about resource issues and consequently allowed members to spend more time getting to know one another.

As different kinds of potential leaders emerge, the team gets to a point where it must learn to use these differences effectively. This entails developing genuine respect for the diverse styles and learning when and where different styles are needed. From here on, required kinds of leadership become specific to the task the SMT is working on.

Project-Based SMTs

In addition to needing good social leadership, project-based SMTs initially require development of overall team goals and a vision or grand plan that will accomplish these goals; this naturally falls into the province of the envisioning leader. Secondary activities center on making sure that the vision is realizable and providing various reality checks, which are roles occupied by the spanner and organizer. The spanner provides assurance that the vision will fit with the requirements of outsiders while the organizer detects logical stumbling blocks. Care must be taken, however, that these individuals do not overly criticize alternative visions, especially while they are being formed; this can result in plans that are stale or status quo. The social leader can often provide this check.

During the second phase, the team begins to experience differences among members, as various ideas on how to proceed come to the surface. Social leadership is needed to make sure that these differences are constructively handled and that an emphasis is placed on developing winning alternatives. The effective social leader, recognizing that constructive conflict is needed to make good decisions, tries to create a climate where differences are openly expressed and respected. The envisioner can assist by integrating the different opinions into the overall vision and showing how each view has its use. During this time, the tasks of scheduling and securing resources also become important. Leading scheduling efforts is most ably conducted by the organizer while finding outside resources requires spanning leadership.

During the third phase, the team is engaged in enacting the plans and schedules created earlier. This phase often lasts the longest and requires good organizing leadership throughout. From a task perspective, control procedures are primary. Feedback channels and ways of making corrections need to be developed and maintained. As the team begins formulating its products, the results will need to be presented to outsiders who will either use the products and/or provide additional resources. Consequently, spanning leadership is also required. From a group development perspective, social leadership is needed to maintain cohesion and commitment, especially from those having an envisioning bent; once the project is well under way, these people are likely to become bored and may unconsciously sabotage efforts by trying to impose new directions. The social leader can increase cohesion by making sure that the team has fun and that members do not overwork themselves.

In the final phase, the team completes its project and either disbands or goes on to a new effort. During this time, there are usually many details to be handled: reports to be filed, product transfer arrangements to be made, final presentations to be given. Strong organizing and spanning leadership are essential at this phase. The organizer ensures that all the details are covered while the spanner smoothes the path for the transfer of the product, and, should the team disband, transfer of individual members. The envisioner can help bring a sense of closure to the project by emphasizing the project's overall image and showing how past events contributed to that image. Lastly, the social leader can help members to cope with the feelings of loss or emptiness that usually accompany successful project completion by fostering times of celebration, by helping members to focus on future events and outside contacts, and by encouraging members to voice their emotions.

Problem-Solving SMTs

In problem-solving teams, early work usually focuses on finding problems, getting a sense for their impacts and urgency, and discussing their causes. Here, organizing and spanning leadership are most necessary. The organizer's function is to facilitate detection of what things are off track and the extent of the deviations. He or she can also lead a systematic probe through probable causes. The spanner helps to represent outsider's concerns and can facilitate more realistic prioritization of problems. The envisioner can sometimes aid in finding less obvious causes. Lastly, the social needs of the team are much the same as in project-based SMTs; consequently, social leadership is required to bring the team together as a social unit. The social leader can also facilitate a more comprehensive search for causes by making sure that everyone's input is heard.

In the second phase, different solutions are sought. Creative, frame-breaking solutions can result from envisioning leadership. Other possible solutions can be imported into the team with the help of the spanner. If true breakthroughs are going to be found, the social leader must work to minimize early criticism of alternatives. Where opposing solutions are developed, social leadership is needed to allow the differences to coexist at least temporarily.

During the third phase, choices are made around the existing alternatives. This requires determining and evaluating costs and benefits. Organizing leadership is most needed at this juncture, followed by spanning leadership. The organizer is typically adept at sorting, comparing, and passing judgement in an unemotional way; the spanner can help the team determine how outsiders may view different alternatives. Lastly, the social leader can facilitate a comprehensive review of alternatives by offering everyone a chance to participate and by paraphrasing and summarizing different conclusions.

In the last phase, the team tests out its solution, and, depending on whether it works, may move on to a new problem, return to an earlier phase, or disband. The organizer usually leads the first testing efforts. Should the solution not prove workable, the envisioner and/or the spanner may assume the search for new causes and solutions. Finally, the social leader can help ease the tenseness that may surround testing efforts; she or he can also help with transition efforts should the team need to break up.

Policy-Making SMTs

Policy-making SMTs are less likely to follow a clear sequence of team phases than project or problem-solving SMTs. They usually have multiple issues, events, and areas to consider simultaneously, and they tend to build up relevant policies and strategies in an incremental fashion. For example, one strategy-making SMT was comprised of three division managers, a manufacturing general manager, and a marketing vice president. For the first two months of its existence, the team's biggest problem was to figure out its focus—whether to upgrade and expand the distribution systems used by the product divisions, which of several related companies to purchase, what kind of image they wanted the company to portray, and so forth. In the course of talking about these things, different ideas would constantly come up. Some would get dropped immediately, but others would be modified and expanded. By the fourth month, a fairly cohesive strategy had emerged, and it was clear to team members where the strategy fit with current operations and where change would have to be effected. The team didn't seem to follow a clear progression of decision-making steps in developing this strategy, but there was evidence of some broad leadership shifts.

During the issue-finding period, an SMT needs to make sure that the right issues are being surfaced and that the ramifications of these issues are explored. Consequently, spanning and organizing leadership tends to be somewhat more dominant in the beginning. The spanning leader is normally sensitive to what issues are most important in a company and has the necessary contacts to get more information on a given issue. Similarly, good organizing leaders are aware of those things that are "off track" and usually have the skills needed to quickly and efficiently audit a given situation. Once the various issues have been identified, the SMT might engage in issue prioritization. Again, the spanning leader can help identify "how they're incredibly slow to see new things." Ken was older than the others and was very easy-going and philosophical. Chuck, in addition to his engineering training, had a background in cost accounting. He was neat, precise, and methodical in his approach. Lastly, Jeff was a natural extrovert, having a strong social bent and many friends within the company.

Distinct forms of leadership began to emerge during the first week of the team's life. For instance, Ken exhibited social leadership by starting off the first meeting with the suggestion that members give each other some background information about one another's experiences and expectations of the team. From then on, discussion became animated as each person opened up. Later that week, the team met for four hours at Jeff's house; again, Ken demonstrated social leadership by making sure that Henry and Chuck, who were the quieter members, got their ideas out and that Jeff, who was the most vocal member of the team, did not monopolize the conversation. At the conclusion of this meeting, Ann began to exert spanning leadership by volunteering to set up a number of site visits with companies that might be interested in the product ideas the team was considering.

Within a month, team members had visited the plants of seven different customers; three of these visits were made as a whole team. By this time, a distributed leadership system was clearly in effect. Ann made initial contacts at outside firms and introduced the other members, thus acting as an external spanner. Henry, exerting envisioning leadership, would come up with different ideas that he would then try out on those visited. His efforts would spark others to generate ideas as well. Chuck exercised organizing leadership by keeping track of all the travel arrangements and expenses. He also would query clients about where products and systems were inadequate, carefully recording all their responses. Jeff, acting as an internal spanner, talked up the team's progress to other managers in the company and kept the team atmosphere upbeat with his humor. Ken, who became the team's social leader, spent a lot of time getting the others to share their ideas and summarizing the team's progress.

As the team moved toward developing a prototype imaging device, the amount that various leadership styles were used shifted, though the type of leadership exercised still gravitated towards specific individuals. For instance, people began to rely heavily on Chuck's organizing leadership for direction about what to do next and for information about each other's progress. Jeff continued to provide internal spanning leadership by initiating efforts to commandeer needed parts and get the team additional funds. During the creation of the prototype, Ann spent a lot of time discussing the team's progress with the customer groups that were visited earlier, still working as an external spanner. Social leadership became less important at this stage, and consequently, Ken remained comparatively quiet. Largely as a result of the mix of skills and leadership styles present, the group quickly moved on to demonstrate their prototype and transfer the imager into initial production.

During interviews conducted at this time, it was evident that team members and management considered the overall effort to be an outstanding success. Management was pleased with the quality of the team's ideas and with the speed at which the team moved. Team members reported the work to be exciting and satisfying—all remarked that they really enjoyed coming to the plant on Mondays. All also mentioned feeling very confident; Henry echoed this with his comment, "Sometimes I feel we could make anything we set our minds to. This group is that strong."

As the team begins to center on certain issues, members begin coming up with alternative actions, futures, strategies, and the like. Here, strong envisioning leadership becomes helpful, especially where the issues being faced are complex and the future is uncertain. If current policies and strategies are not working well, intuition and an ability to see beyond the status quo are required if the team is to succeed. Thus the envisioner must be able to foster an atmosphere that allows new and creative views to emerge. Helping him or her in this can be the spanner who might know of alternatives that have worked well in other places. Good social leadership is also needed to help team members understand one another's ideas. As more and more ideas begin to develop, organizing leadership becomes increasingly essential. The organizer helps the team to think through the consequences of different alternatives and can help the group to keep track of its progress. In a similar fashion, the social leader can assist the team by pointing out how their decisions might make others feel and how the social fabric of the organization will be affected. In addition, different ideas need to be interlinked and cross-checked so that the implementation of one alternative does not negatively affect another. Therefore, the skills of both the envisioner (who focuses on the big picture) and the spanner (who can see how different alternatives connect to various parts of the organization) become necessary.

Gradually, policies and strategies are shaped, and a time comes when the team's deliberations must be communicated to outside stakeholders. Presentations, reports, and informal hallway talk all become possible channels; if the team is to have its efforts well received and implemented, it must exercise some control over what is said. Thus, spanning and organizing leaders are especially important during this time. The spanner is most likely to know how different groups might receive the team's outputs, the preferred ways in which these groups get and use information, and where different pockets of resistance might lie. Where others might be especially antagonistic, the spanner can also help in softening the conflict by approaching them informally. The organizer can help the team put its proposals and decisions into a more formalized form, such as a written report or memo. Finally, as with the other teams, the social leader can facilitate the disbanding process.

Overall, it is evident that implementing a distributed leadership system in an SMT can be time-consuming and difficult. Even having all the needed leadership resources does not assure success. In fact, distributed leadership presents something of a paradox. On the one hand, a team can benefit from increasingly heterogeneous leadership styles. Yet these differences heighten the potential for serious conflicts. The only way that the paradox can be resolved is if team members realize that different kinds of leadership can coexist if exercised at different times. When this happens, the team becomes positioned for breakthrough results. Envisioning leadership provides creative ideas, organizing leadership channels and implements these ideas, spanning leadership insures that the ideas fit with those of other stakeholders, and social leadership provides the interpersonal glue to keep the team together.

Because of the complexity and variation inherent in an SMT's leadership structure, an SMT's existence can be chaotic. Without conscious effort, they can easily degenerate into political battlegrounds; and when one member leaves or a new one is added, the team's balance can be thrown off. Hence, setting up SMTs should not be lightly undertaken. Team members should be carefully picked with an eye toward the varying leadership skills required. The team must also be given time to develop a viable system of distributed leadership. Management external to the group should encourage the use of multiple leaders and avoid jumping in and co-opting the team's leadership process. With the right leadership mix, enough time, and support from outside, an SMT can achieve remarkable results. Without these factors in place, an SMT can easily become one more fire to be extinguished.

ACTIVITIES

Activity 1

Purpose: The purpose of this exercise is to compare and contrast how groups respond to democratic and autocratic leadership.

Procedure: The instructor chooses a leader for each small group. The groups then examine the first list of controversial statements. Each member of the group assigns each statement a number between one and five, with one being the truest statement, and five being the least true statement. The group then discusses the statements and through an interactive method of decision making, that is, consensus, averaging, or voting, the group determines the best way to rank the statements. The leader then notes the group's decision.

The small groups then look at the second list of statements. Once again, each member of the group ranks the statements according to his or her own beliefs. The leader also ranks the statements. After the individuals have ordered the statements, the leader can choose to listen to their ideas, or can choose to present the group with his or her own ideas. Discussion is optional, and the leader need not adhere to the group's wishes.

After both lists are completed the class members can discuss how they felt in each decision-making event. What differences and similarities did they notice? How do they think that they respond to different types of leadership?

LIST 1

____ Motorcycle helmet laws should be mandatory in every state.

____ This country was founded on the right to personal freedom, so the government has no right to decide whether a person must wear a helmet.

____ If the government is going to pass helmet laws, helmets should be available at low costs.

____ If the taxpayer or fellow insurance holders will end up paying for victims of motorcycle accidents, then laws must mandate the wearing of helmets.

____ We're better off with no helmet laws because a motorcycle helmet will often save the life of the individual, but the person will be severely damaged for life. People are better off dead.

LIST 2

____ Parents have a right and duty to keep a firm hand on their minor children and should be legally responsible for their children's acts.

____ Children have rights that must not be violated. Parents owe their children the consideration of consulting them before moving or divorcing.

____ Direction and control stunt creative development; therefore, parents should give their children the freedom and encouragement to live their own lives.

_____ When underage minors have babies, the minors' parents should be held financially responsible. The rest of society should not have to pick up the tab for people who can't teach their children self-control or morals.

_____ The best thing parents can do for their teenagers is to give them responsibility and freedom as soon as they can handle it.

Activity 2

Purpose: The purpose of this exercise is to have members of the class evaluate and analyze their perception of leadership.

Procedure: Below are a number of statements concerning the topic of leadership. Have each person in the class indicate their position on each statement by using the following scale:

> 1 = strongly agree
> 2 = slightly agree
> 3 = slightly disagree
> 4 = strongly disagree

_____ 1. It is the leader's responsibility to see that a standard set of norms is established.

_____ 2. The best way for a leader to operate is by becoming a member of the group.

_____ 3. It is best for someone from a culture that stresses individualism to serve as the leader.

_____ 4. A leader's primary function is to serve as a resource person.

_____ 5. The exclusive duty of the leader is to have the group function in the "here and now."

_____ 6. The group leader should limit his or her self-disclosure.

_____ 7. The person with the most power should be the leader.

_____ 8. The leader should be as much like the other participants as possible.

_____ 9. The leader should be firm at the start of discussion and then reveal a kinder side.

_____ 10. Part of the role of the leader is to establish what specific behavior should be allowed in the group.

Follow-up activity. Have the entire class discuss the results of their questionnaire.

Activity 3

Purpose: The purpose of this activity is to determine the characteristics of great leaders.

Procedure: The class is divided into groups of three to five people. Each group is given the task of listing the five most important characteristics of great leaders. Since there are so many qualities to consider, the group will be forced to decide on only the *most* significant. After ten to fifteen minutes, each small group will share its decision with the rest of the class. The class can then vote to determine which of the qualities are the most essential for great leadership.

Activity 4

Purpose: The purpose of this activity is to analyze great leaders.

Procedure: The class is divided into groups of three to five people. Each group must then decide on the *five* greatest leaders of all time. The groups can all use the same criteria for making this decision, the criteria established in the previous activity; or the individual groups can use their own criteria. After about twenty minutes of discussion, each small group nominates its five candidates for the master list of greatest leaders of all time. The small groups then defend their nominees. After the large group discusses each of the candidates, the entire class votes to determine the overall winners.

Activity 5

Purpose: The purpose of this activity is to enable you to identify and evaluate your leadership behavior.

Procedure: Using the form provided below evaluate your leadership role after your next group discussion. (Scale: 0–1 poor, 2–3 fair, 4–5 average, 6–7 above average, 8–9 excellent.)

LEADERSHIP ROLE:	(Circle the Most Appropriate Number)								
Provide agenda	1	2	3	4	5	6	7	8	9
Start the discussion	1	2	3	4	5	6	7	8	9
Regulate participation	1	2	3	4	5	6	7	8	9
Encourage ideas	1	2	3	4	5	6	7	8	9
Encourage evaluation	1	2	3	4	5	6	7	8	9
Provide emotional support	1	2	3	4	5	6	7	8	9
Offer periodic reviews	1	2	3	4	5	6	7	8	9
Help resolve conflicts	1	2	3	4	5	6	7	8	9
End the discussion	1	2	3	4	5	6	7	8	9

Index

437